Incidental and Dance Music in the American Theatre from 1786 to 1923

Volume 2

Incidental and Dance Music in the American Theatre from 1786 to 1923

by John Franceschina

Volume 2

Biographical and Critical Commentary

Alphabetical Listings from Alfred E. Aarons to Joe Jordan

BearManor Media
2017

Incidental and Dance Music in the American Theatre from 1786 to 1923:
Volume 2, Biographical and Critical Commentary –
Alphabetical Listings from Alfred E. Aarons to Joe Jordan

© 2017 John Franceschina

All Rights Reserved.

No part of this book may be reproduced in any form or by any means, electronic, mechanical, digital, photocopying, or recording, except for in the inclusion of a review, without permission in writing from the publisher

For information, address:

BearManor Media
P. O. Box 71426
Albany, GA 31708

bearmanormedia.com

Typesetting and layout by John Teehan

Published in the USA by BearManor Media

ISBN—978-1-62933-169-0

Table of Contents

Preface vii

Biographical and Critical Commentary

    A – Aarons to Ayer 3

    B – Baker to Broschi 15

    C – Caldwell to Cutty 75

    D – Dabney to Dyring 127

    E – Edwards to Eysler 163

    F – Fehrmann to Furst 197

    G – Gabriel to Gress 227

    H – Hadley to Hydes 281

    I – Itzel 365

    J – Jacobi to Jordan 369

Endnotes 407

Bibliography 487

Index 513

Preface

VOLUMES 2 AND 3 of *Dance and Incidental Music in the American Musical Theatre 1786–1923* focus on the composers and arrangers who created the music discussed and chronicled in Volume 1. The second volume provides biographical and critical commentary for composers whose surnames range from A through J, while the third volume includes composers from K through Z. Both volumes include a great many musical examples that are both illustrative of the composer's compositional style and indicative of the theatrical dance music of the period. In addition, each entry is accompanied by notes that identify source material, and each volume contains an index and bibliography.

Although each record provides biographical data (date and place of birth, facts of education, immigration, marriage, and date and place of death, if known) the emphasis is understandably on each individual's musical theatre career. As a result, each commentary is crowded with the names of musicals, dates of performance, names of collaborators, and duties performed. For example, the dance arranger of two Broadway musicals may have been composer of the songs of four other musicals and the musical director of seven additional shows. Therefore, when known, a complete overview of the individual's career is given. Dates without comment always signal the opening nights in New York City. When out-of-town productions are significant, dates and places are so noted. Every dance and incidental music arranger and composer included in the chronology in Volume 1 can be located in the biographical and critical commentary of Volumes 2 and 3 and, while the chronology indicates the more notable efforts of each, the commentary attempts to offer a more complete survey of the composer-arranger's musical theatre career.

Biographical and Critical Commentary

A

AARONS, Alfred E.

Born in Philadelphia on 16 November 1865, Alfred E. Aarons began his theatrical career at the age of fifteen, working in the box office of Gilmore's Central Theatre in Philadelphia.[1] The following year, he established a vaudeville and dramatic agency at 809 Walnut Street, which he operated successfully until 1890, when he transferred his business office to the Gilsey Building in New York City. Shortly after his arrival, Aarons became house manager for J.M. Hill's Standard Theatre and, five years later, he began his association with Koster and Bial, booking all the European and American acts that performed at Koster and Bial's Music Hall. At the same time, Aarons presented international vaudeville at Harriman's Theatre and managed the Manhattan Opera House Roof Garden theatre for Oscar Hammerstein I. After Hammerstein built the Victoria Theatre in 1899, Aarons was sent to Europe to represent the impresario's interests abroad.

While acting as a theatrical manager, Aarons composed ragtime numbers and songs interpolated into Broadway productions. His first major successes were "Rag Time Liz" performed in Koster and Bial's *In Gotham* (1898) and "Honi Soit Qui Mal Y Pense," written (in collaboration with Richard Carle) for his wife Josephine Hall in *The Girl from Maxim's* (1899). Encouraged by his early successes as a song writer, Aarons inaugurated his career as composer *and* producer of musical comedy on 26 February 1900 with the production of *Mam'selle 'Awkins* at the Victoria Theatre. The "March" published from the score displays Aarons's ability to create easily assimilated dance music that is rhythmic, syncopated, and highly reminiscent of John Philip Sousa's popular marches. Later in 1900, Aarons leased Krause's Music Hall (renamed as the Savoy Theatre) to produce *The Military Maid*, an eight-performance flop that again featured songs composed by the producer. The Savoy Theatre venture proved unmanageable and by March 1901, Aarons was bankrupt, owing creditors (including restaurant proprietors, chorus girls, and lawyers) in excess of $34,000.[2] Undaunted, Aarons continued producing and composing musicals: *The Ladies Paradise* (16 September 1901), *My Antoinette* (13 January 1902), and *The Knickerbocker Girl* (15 June 1903). Aarons was slated to compose the score for Harry B. Smith's *The Girl from Dixie* (14 December 1903) but he withdrew from the project when he discovered that he would be working with Bob Cole, J. Rosamond Johnson, and James Weldon Johnson, African-American songwriters.[3]

Harry B. Smith convinced Aarons to compose the score for *A China Doll* (19 November 1904) a musical about a stolen mechanical doll belonging to a Mandarin's daughter who refuses to marry the son of the lo-

Example 1. Ländler in "What Will China Do?" from *A China Doll*

Example 2. Irish Reel in "What Will China Do?" from *A China Doll*

cal police chief until the doll is recovered.[4] Though the libretto was weak, Aarons's music was considered tuneful and interesting if lacking in individuality.[5] Especially interesting was the variety present in Aarons's dance music for the production. The opening incidental music evoked the faux pentatonic strains of Gilbert and Sullivan's *The Mikado* while the merry dance accompanying "I Never Took a Lesson in My Life" was simply a reiteration of the melody of the song. The schottische patter number "Hist! Hist! Hist!" was followed by a lively schottische dance that borrowed musical phrases from the vocal melody but was, in essence, an original tune.

Most interesting, perhaps, were the three dances imbedded in "What Will China Do?" a number imagining the takeover of China by some foreign nation. The first to assume imaginary control were the Germans who were represented by a Ländler, a popular three-beat folk dance that involved a fair amount of hopping and stomping (example 1). Note the changes in the dynamics and articulations of the dance music and the heavy "um-pah-pah" nature of the accompaniment.

If the Germans did not succeed in conquering the Chinese, the Irish most certainly would, if not with their brogue or shillelagh, with an Irish Reel, a four-beat soft shoe folk dance (example 2). Note the two-measure structure of the dance music and the droning bagpipe-like accompaniment.

Finally, if the Irish were not successful, the Scotchmen would come to the rescue singing "Annie Laurie" and dancing the Highland Fling. Example 3 continues the exhibition of Aarons's ability to simulate national folk dances with a Highland Schottische. Note the dotted rhythms and triplets in the melody over a steady "um-pah" accompaniment in the bass. Note also the accented 4th beat in measures 4 and 8 suggesting a particularly dynamic choreographic movement.

Aarons's facility for imitation proved to be an important asset in his dance music, immediately communicating to the audience a lively national spirit in familiar dance forms. Such a talent was less efficient for Aarons the composer of songs that were too often found to be lacking in individuality.

Following *A China Doll*, Aarons produced and composed (with Julian Edwards) *The Pink Hussars* which was later to become *His Honor the Mayor* (28 May 1906), at 104 performances, his greatest success to date. Also in 1906, Aarons became associated with the Klaw and Erlanger Syndicate and in subsequent years developed a system for the theatrical booking of road shows while taking time off to manage the Broadhurst, Vanderbilt, National, and New Amsterdam theatres on Broadway.

Example 3. Highland Schottische in "What Will China Do?" from *A China Doll*

Whatever free time Aarons had was spent composing new musicals: *(The Girl from) Yama* (4 November 1907), *The Hotel Clerk* (27 April 1908), *The Deacon and the Lady* (4 October 1910), though none were as successful as *His Honor the Mayor*.

In additional to his production responsibilities, Alfred E. Aarons organized the International Theatre Managers Association with branches throughout the United States and Canada. He served on the board of trustees of the Actors Fund of America and on the board of directors of the Lambs Club. He was also a member of the Episcopal Actors Guild and the Pacific Lodge of Masons. He was married twice: first to Josephine Hall who appeared in much of his earlier work and later to the musical comedy actress Leila Hughes. On 16 November 1936, his 71st birthday, Aarons died due to complications following surgery.

ACCOOE, Will

The son of a Methodist minister, Will Accooe was born in Winchester, Virginia in 1874 and educated at the Princess Anne Academy in Maryland. At an early age he taught himself to play the piano and organ and in 1890, when he had developed a facility on those instruments Accooe became the organist at the Zoar Methodist Episcopal Church in Philadelphia. He was granted a scholarship to study at Philadelphia's Walnut Street Conservatory of Music after which he had hopes of securing a position as organist in one or another of New York City's churches. When no offers came his way, Accooe decided to pursue a career in the theatre: first as a pianist with Puggsley's Tennessee Warblers, and, in 1896, as the musical director for John W. Isham's *Octoroons*, a touring minstrel show company based in New York City. In 1897 Accooe began advertising as a music teacher residing at 115 West 26th Street, and the following year he married Alice Mackey, a noted contralto. As of 1899, the entire Accooe family had moved from Philadelphia and established residence at 297 Bridge Street, Brooklyn.

In September 1899, Accooe was musical director for Cole and Johnson's *A Trip to Coontown*; the following month, his score for the 1899 edition of the *Octoroons* appeared on Broadway. In October 1900 Accooe contributed "The Phrenologist Coon" and "The Promoters"/"Ragtime Schottische" to Williams and Walker's *Sons of Ham*, and "Mabel Moore" to Cole and Johnson's *The Belle of Bridgeport*. In 1901, he composed "Society" and "Love Has Claimed Its Own" for Ludwig Englander's *The Casino Girl, "(I'd Like to Be) A Gunner in the Navy" for *The Liberty Belles*, and the entire score for *The Hottest Coon in Dixie*. In the same year, Accooe was also involved with *The Cannibal King*, a comic opera reworking of Will Marion Cook and Paul Laurence Dunbar's *Jes Lak White Fo'ks* that opened for a brief New York run in August 1901 before going on tour.[6] Eileen Southern notes that Accooe joined the Williams and Walker Company as musical director in 1902[7] but theatre programs and advertisements indicate that by 1903 he was replaced by James Vaughn. Late in 1903, Accooe became seriously ill and, feeling that the end was near, he wrote a eulogy to be delivered at his funeral. Barely thirty years old, Will Accooe died on 26 April 1904 and, two days later, his self-penned funeral oration was read by his father, the Reverend J. Harris Accooe.[8]

The online blog AfriClassical[9] dated 27 December 2012 quotes from a tribute to Will Accooe written by the respected African-American critic Sylvester Russell in the *Indianapolis Freeman*: "[I]n justice to his ability I may well say that as a composer he gave less service and more promise in his limited amount of work than any composer of his race.... If he had lived, he would have been greater than Will Marion Cook, J. Rosamond Johnson and others less known than they. He might have become the greatest colored composer in America." His published compositions include the "Black Patti Waltzes" (1896), "Tennessee Centennial March" (1897), "Chicken" (1899), "Ma Dandy Soldier Coon" (1900), "Lulu. I loves yer, Lulu" (1901), "Southern Blossoms Waltzes" (1901), "In a Birch Canoe: A Kickapoo Romance" (1904), and "We'll Raise the Roof To-night: Whoop 'er Up, Boys!" (1904).

ANDERSON, Hilding

Composer, orchestrator, and musical director Hilding Anderson was born on 18 June 1876 in Lund, Malmohus, Sweden. When he was thirteen, the Anderson family immigrated to Chicago where Hilding began his musical career as a clarinetist around the turn of the century. In addition to performing in the orchestras of Chicago's lively musical theatres, Anderson composed music in the current popular style and, in 1908, he was first represented on Broadway by "The Old Buck and Wing" composed for the Joseph E. Howard musical *The Girl Question* (3 August 1908). In 1910, Anderson interpolated his "Zig Zag Rag" into another Joe Howard show, *Lower Berth Thirteen* at the Whitney Opera House in Chicago (16 October 1910), and six months later, he composed the score for the Sophie Tucker vehicle *Merry Mary* that opened and closed in Chicago in April 1911. The following month, he was musical director and dance arranger for *The Heart Breakers* (30 May 1911) another Chicago musical that failed to make its way to Broadway. Undaunted, Anderson was again represented on the New York stage later in the year by the musical direction and orchestrations for *The Never Homes* (5 October 1911) and the original song, "Take a Little Shine to Me," interpolated into Lionel Monckton's score for *The Quaker Girl* (23 October 1911).

Beginning in 1912, Anderson became a fixed presence in the American musical theatre primarily as a musical director and orchestrator, and as his career progressed he was in demand by many of the leading figures of the New York stage, including J.J. Shubert and Florenz Ziegfeld. In addition to his Broadway endeavors, Anderson also worked as house arranger for Broadcast Music, Inc. (BMI) and for the principal publishers of theatre music, Harms and Chappell.[10] Most active on Broadway during the 1920s and 1930s, Anderson continued to compose and arrange until the early 1950s when illness forced him to retire at the age of seventy four. Ten years later, on 2 September 1961, he died at his home in New York City.

Although Anderson's greatest achievements in musical direction and orchestration lie beyond the scope of this book (i.e., *The Desert Song* [1926], *Rosalie* [1928], *Strike Up the Band* [1930]), his early work is well deserving of study. His original songs and dance music display unique harmonies and imaginative syncopations that raise them above the standard popular music of the early 20th century. It is, perhaps, Anderson's singular approach to popular music that rendered him so much in demand as an arranger for the musical theatre.

ARNOLD, Richard

Virtuoso violinist Richard Arnold was born in Eilenburg, Prussia on 10 January 1845. He went to the United States in 1853 and, three years later at the precocious age of eleven, he became the leader of the Columbus, Ohio, Theatre Orchestra. In 1864, Arnold returned to Europe to engage in a three-year study of violin technique with Ferdinand David at the Leipzig Conservatory, after which he left to establish a career in New York City. Not long after his arrival Arnold became the musical director for the Tammany Grand Theatre where he arranged dance music and led the orchestra for *The Queen of Hearts, or, Harlequin, the Knave of Hearts, who stole the Tarts, and the Old Woman that Lived in a Shoe* (16 August

1869), *Bad Dickey* (6 December 1869), and *The Glorious 7* (31 January 1870). Desirous of more serious musical employment, Arnold left the musical theatre and joined Theodore Thomas's orchestra as concert master. Eight years later, he became the concert master and solo violinist of the New York Philharmonic Society, a post he held until 1909.[11] In addition to his work with the Philharmonic Society, Arnold found himself in great demand as a violin teacher and commanded a large, wealthy, and fashionable clientele. After more than forty years spent in promoting serious music in New York City, Richard Arnold died on 21 June 1918.

ARONSON, Rudolph

Composer and theatrical manager Rudolph Aronson was born in New York City on 8 April 1856. He began playing the piano at the age of six and discovered his talent for musical composition at the age of sixteen. His musical studies in New York and Europe brought him into contact with Johann Strauss, Jr., Richard Wagner, Franz Liszt, and a variety of international musical artists, many of whom had a profound effect on Aronson's musical tastes. Returning from his studies in Paris, Aronson began his professional career in New York as the manager (and musical director) of the Metropolitan Concert Hall where popular concerts were offered by an orchestra of fifty musicians.[12] Although Aronson had conducted 150 successful concerts at the Metropolitan, it was the building and management of the Casino Theatre and its roof garden that brought him to the attention of the theatrical world as a producer of musical theatre entertainments. Under Aronson's management the Casino became known as the home of comic opera in New York City with the production of *Erminie* (1,256 performances) as its crowning achievement and performers such as Lillian Russell, Francis Wilson, De Wolf Hopper, and Jefferson de Angeles as its stars. After sixteen years at the Casino, Aronson moved on to manage the Bijou Theatre where he presented May Irwin in *The Widow Jones*. In his later years, Aronson revealed plans for developing land in Puerto Rico and constructing a Casino Theatre in Los Angeles but nothing came of those projects. Instead, he devoted his final years to composing and died quietly at the home of his sisters after a short illness on 4 February 1919.

A prolific composer of instrumental music that included "Sweet Sixteen," a waltz composed for the cornet virtuoso Jules Levy, and two marches named for presidents Roosevelt and Taft,[13] Aronson also ventured into the field of comic opera composing the music to Sydney Rosenfeld's libretto of *The Rainmaker of Syria, or, The Woman King*, a musical about an Egyptian who can predict the weather. The piece was mounted hurriedly at the Casino on 25 September 1893 and not a success even though the critic of the *New York Clipper* found the music tuneful, pleasing, and highly original.[14] Aronson's dance music assisted in creating an "Eastern" tonality for the musical while still appealing to the theatregoer more comfortable with traditional Western music. In example 4, "Syrian Dance," note the A natural minor scale used throughout the melody until the final measure where a suggestion of the Lydian mode adds an exotic flavor to the scale. Note also the sinewy, improvisatory nature of the melodic line that is both sensuous and mysterious.

The accompaniment to the "Syrian Dance" relies on a simple tonic, subdominant, dominant structure that is familiar to Western ears yet still sufficiently modal to suggest a non-Western ambiance.

Example 5, the "Military March" that signals the entrance of King Hatshepu (actually a beautiful woman in disguise) is more Sousa than Syrian, intentionally incongruous tonally to accompany the transvestite woman. There are certainly similarities between the "Syrian Dance" and the "March": melodically, both use grace notes and rely on an intervallic pattern of seconds followed by thirds; harmonically, both make use of a simple tonic-dominant pattern, though the presence of a secondary dominant in measures 13 and 15 of the "March" suggests a more sophisticated harmony than that of the "Syrian Dance." Of course the modal differentiation in the dances is highly significant: the "March" is in a major key

Example 4. "Syrian Dance" from *The Rainmaker of Syria*

Example 5. "Military March" from *The Rainmaker of Syria*

and sounds much more familiar to a Western audience than the "Syrian Dance" in a minor key modified by the Lydian mode.

Note that the melodic line of the "Military March" in measures 18–20, 22, and 24 emphasizes a non-chordal tone on the downbeat. Not only does this create forward movement propelling the melodic line to seek resolution, it provides an aural hint of the soon-to-be-revealed incongruity present in "King" Hatshepu. The published samples of Aronson's dance music demonstrate the composer's ability to create easily accessible music that is both dramatically evocative and eminently danceable. It is unfortunate that Aronson's responsibilities as a theatre manager prevented his composing more dance music for the theatre.

AYER, Nat[haniel] D[avis]

Typically credited as Nat D. Ayer, pianist-composer Nathaniel Davis Ayer was born in Boston on 30 September 1887.[15] Early in his career he began writing songs for Broadway musicals beginning with *The Newlyweds and Their Baby* (22 March 1909) a comic-book-based farce about a kidnapped baby being replaced with a midget. Ayer collaborated with John W. Bratton on the score (lyrics by Paul West and A. Seymour Brown), though individually, he composed the music for "Can't You See I Love You" (lyrics by Brown). Later in the year, Ayer and Brown composed the production number "Moving Day in Jungle Town" for the *Ziegfeld Follies of 1909* (14 June 1909) and contributed "I'm Not That Kind of Girl" to the return engagement of *Miss Innocence* (27 September 1909).[16] They wrote "Heigh Ho" and "You're Just the Girlie That I Adore" for *The Echo* (17 August 1910); "Mysterious Moon" for *The Red Rose* (22 June 1911); "Gee! But I Like Music with My Meals" for *The Million* (1911); "You're a Regular Girl" for *A Winsome Widow* (11 April 1912); and "(Gee!) I Should Have Been Born a Boy," "The Indian Rag" (including dance music), and "You're Some Girl," for *The Wall Street Girl* (15 April 1912). With lyricist Harry Williams, Ayer composed "Love Me to That Beautiful Tune for *The Siren* (21 August 1911), and with lyricist Paul West, Ayer composed the songs and dance music for *Let George Do It* (22 April 1912). In 1913, Nat Ayer and Harry Williams performed a duo-vaudeville act in London[17] and contributed songs to *A Ragtime Revel*, a revue scheduled to reopen the London Opera House.[18] Ayer's efforts were amply applauded by London audiences and critics; as a result, in 1914, the pianist-composer accepted a position as songwriter for an English publishing firm and remained in England for the rest of his life, returning only infrequently to New York to perform in vaudeville.

In London Ayer contributed songs to *Samples* (1915), *The Bing Boys Are Here* (1916), *Look Who's Here* (1916), *Houp-La!* (1916), *Oh! Caesar* (1916), *The Bing Girls Are There* (1917), *Yes, Uncle!* (1917), *The Hula Girl* (1917), *The Bing Boys on Broadway* (1918), *Baby Bunting* (1919), *After Dinner* (1921), *Come on Steve* (1921) *The Smith Family* (1922), and *Snap* (1922). By the end of 1922 Ayer was bankrupt[19] and reduced to taking whatever paying work he could find. He performed a string of solo vaudeville acts at the Victoria Palace (a success) and contributed songs to *School Belles*, a musical comedy that opened in Atlantic City in October 1923 (a failure).[20] In 1938, Ayer was bankrupt again and, even though he continued to perform, he was unable to repeat his earlier successes. He died on 19 September 1952 at his home in Bath.

Ayer's most famous song was "Oh, You Beautiful Doll" (1911) with lyrics by A. Seymour Brown. Twenty-five years after it was written, the still-popular song was interpolated into the *Casa Manana* revue (8 June 1936). Other significant compositions include the piano solo, "Rig-a-Jig Rag: A Slow Drag" (1912), "One on the Drum" (1915), "What Happened In the Summertime" (1916), and "If You Were the Only Girl in the World" (1916), written for *The Bing Boys Are Here* and interpolated into the *Ziegfeld Follies of 1916* (12 June 1916).

B

BAKER, Thomas

British-born composer, arranger, and musical director, Thomas Baker was a child prodigy displaying an exceptional musical talent on the violin from the age of seven. Not yet a teenager, he was granted admission to the Royal Academy of Music in London where he studied violin technique under François Cramer and piano, composition, and harmony under the tutelage of Thomas Attwood, a protégé of Wolfgang Amadeus Mozart. On 4 June 1832, Baker made his first public appearance as a violin virtuoso at the Theatre Royal, Covent Garden, performing between the acts of Shakespeare's *Romeo and Juliet*. So successful was Baker's performance that he immediately earned the patronage of the Royal family and, at the request of King William IV, performed several concerts before the royal court at Windsor Castle. When the renowned orchestral leader Louis Antoine Jullien arrived in England in 1840 he secured Baker's exclusive services as leader, solo violinist, and orchestral arranger with a lucrative seven-year contract. During his years with Jullien, Baker also arranged hundreds of orchestral selections for the piano and published *The Modern Pianoforte Tutor*, a new course of instruction skillfully arranged to suit the youngest student as well as the seasoned professional. Baker was still with Jullien's orchestra when it made a successful tour of the United States in 1853, and after the tour was over he decided to make New York City his home.[21]

Baker began his career in the New World by conducting and arranging English opera at Niblo's Garden. His abilities drew the attention of actress-manager Laura Keene, who contracted Baker as her exclusive composer, dance arranger, and musical director, beginning with the production of *Novelty* on 22 February 1856.[22] This was followed by a list of plays and musicals, including *Young Bacchus, or, Spirits and Water* (5 January 1857), *The Elves, or, The Statue Bride* (16 March 1857), *Variety, or, The Picture Gallery* (11 May 1857), *Our American Cousin* (18 October 1858), *Jeanie Deans* (9 January 1859), *Cinderella* (15 June 1859), *Massaniello, Hero and Martyr of Italian Liberty* (27 June 1859), *The Invisible Prince*

(11 July 1859; revival, 16 May 1860), *The Colleen Bawn* (29 March 1860), *Jenny Lind/Our Japanese Embassy* (4 June 1860), *The Tycoon, or, Young American in Japan* (2 July 1860), *The Seven Sisters* (26 November 1860), *The Seven Sons!* (23 September 1861), *Blondette, or, The Naughty Prince and the Pretty Peasant* (25 November 1862) *Jenny Lind/The Invincibles!* (10 January 1863), *The Pet of the Petticoats!* (26 January 1863), *The Fair One with the Golden Locks* (a collaboration with James Gaspard Maeder, 9 February 1963), and *Tib, or The Cat in Crinoline* (4 May 1863). [23]

Representative of the music Baker composed and arranged for Laura Keene is the "Military Galop" from *The Seven Sons!* (example 6). Note the

Example 6. "Military Galop" from *The Seven Sons!*

repeated usage of major and minor seconds and chromatic relationships that create a kind of nervous energy in the melody. Note also the deceptively simple "um-pah" figures that add forward movement to the "Galop" by means of scale patterns in the bass line and the use of inversions and chordal variety in the accompaniment. In addition, the vigorous spirit of the piece is amplified by the use of contrasting dynamics and articulations.

When Laura Keene closed her theatre in New York City, Thomas Baker moved on to assume the responsibilities of composer, dance arranger, and musical director at the Olympic Theatre beginning with *Brother and Sister* (8 October 1863), *Po-Ca-Hon-Tas, or, The Gentle Savage* (19 October 1863), *The Yankee Legacy* (30 November 1863), *Camilla's Husband* (9 January 1864), *Mazeppa, or, the Untamed Rocking Horse* (18 January 1864), *Ill Treated Il Trovatore!, or, The Mother, The Maiden and The Musicianer* (8 February 1864), *Loyalina, or, Brigadier-General Fortunio and His Seven Gifted Aides-de-Camp* (11 April 1864, *Aladdin, or, The Wonderful Lamp*[24] (2 June 1864), *The Comical Countess* (5 September 1864), *Martin Chuzzlewit* (25 September 1864), *The Rose of Castile* [25](2 November 1864), *Popping the Question* (3 November 1864), *The Sleeping Beauty in the Wood* (26 April 1865), *Monte Cristo, or The Lone Prisoner of the Chateau d'If* (4 December 1865), *Cinderella E La Comare, or, The Lover, The Lackey, and the Little Glass Slipper* (26 February 1866), *The Three Guardsmen, or, The Queen, the Cardinal, and the Adventurer* (2 April 1866), *Pages from the History of David Copperfield* (21 May 1866), *Our Mutual Friend* (4 June 1866), *The Ice Witch, or, The Frozen Hand* (23 July 1866), *Rip Van Winkle, or, The Sleep of Twenty Years* (in collaboration with M. Rivere, 3 September 1866), *The Huguenot Captain* (25 December 1866), and *Treasure Trove*, 20 May 1867.

On 4 February 1867 the spectacular religious drama, *The Christian Martyrs under Constantine and Maxentius* was produced at Barnum and Van Amburgh's Museum complete with a grand triumphal procession, featuring the entire Van Amburgh collection of wild animals, set to music, "The Emperor's March" (example 7), by Thomas Baker.[26] Note the vigorous trumpet fanfares that introduce the piece and the contrasting dynamics beginning in measures 5–13 that explore a variety of tonalities in preparation for the statement of the processional melody (measures 14–21). Note also the non-chordal tones on strong beats (measures 15–17, 19) that help drive the melody toward resolution. Even though the work is a majestic march it rarely settles; the triplets in the accompaniment as well as the melodic dissonances move the piece forward, mirroring musically the forward movement of the onstage procession.

Example 7. "The Emperor's March" from *The Christian Martyrs*

By 1868, Thomas Baker had become the musical director of Lester Wallack's Theatre composing incidental and dance music for a wide variety of plays that included *The Fire Fly, or, The Friend of the Flag* (10 August 1868), *Still Waters Run Deep* (1 November 1869), *Lost at Sea* (28 February 1870), *The Veteran* (24 February 1872), *The Shaughraun* (14 November 1874), *Marriage* (1 October 1877), *Diplomacy* (1 April 1878), *A Scrap of Paper* (10 March 1879), and *Rosedale* (2 February 1880). When Wallack and company moved into a new theatre in 1882, Baker found that the orchestra area, usually residing in front of the stage, had been sunk below the stage floor, evidently to dampen the sound and to allow for more audience seating. Refusing to be "stuck under the stage," Baker promptly re-

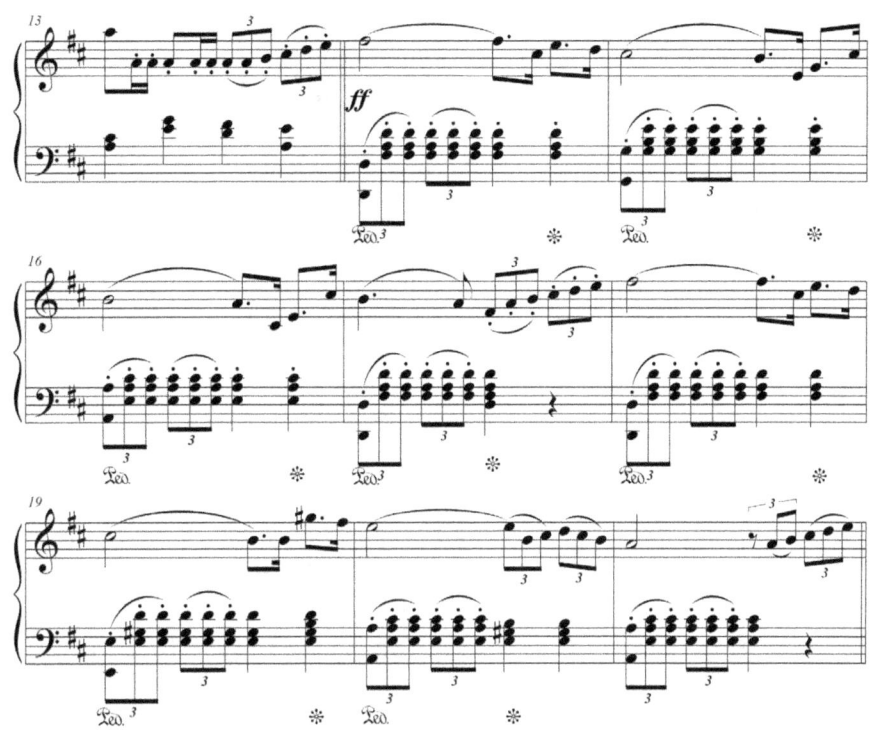

Example 7 (continued). "The Emperor's March" from *The Christian Martyrs*

tired from conducting.[27] He died on 10 December 1888 leaving Florence, a twelve-year-old daughter, his wife, Hannah F. Hogan, whom he married on 29 January 1875, having predeceased him.

Thomas Baker's most famous incidental and dance arrangements appeared at Niblo's Garden[28] on 12 September 1866 with the premiere of *The Black Crook*, Charles M. Barras's spectacular melodrama with songs, ballets, and incidental music cues (104 of them according to the promptbook at the Houghton Library, Harvard University). Conductor Benjamin J. Deane recollected:

> It is related of Tom Baker that Barras got him to arrange the music for "The Black Crook," and he went down to Niblo's to rehearse it, although Dodworth was then leader there. As the rehearsal progressed, the members of the orchestra maintained a muttered rumble of recognitions as each new passage was attacked. "Rossini!" "Meyerbeer!" "Men-

delssohn!" "Verdi!" broke forth here and there among them, until the incantation scene was reached when there was a choral burst of "Weber!" but the boldness of that portion of the musical Boucicaultization stunned them into comparative silence through the rest of the rehearsal. Baker only laughed good-naturedly. Admitted that he had appropriated his incantation music from "Der Freischütz" and other portions from other works, and added, "but none of the others were smart enough to do it, and you have to admit that it is good music.[29]

Example 8. "Transformation Polka" from *The Black Crook*

It is easy to accept the musicians' reaction to Baker's music when examining example 8, the "Transformation Polka" from the end of Act 4 of *The Black Crook*: "An elaborate mechanical and scenical construction of the realms of Stalacta [Queen of the Golden Realm], occupying the entire stage, This scene must be of gradually-developing and culminating beauty introducing during its various transformations Stalacta, the entire host of fairies, sprites, water nymphs, amphibes, gnomes, etc., bearing treasure."[30] The operatic arias of Verdi, Meyerbeer, and Rossini come to mind when studying the "Transformation Polka"; the simple tonic-subdominant-dominant harmony and effervescent, unlabored melodic line could find a place in the coloratura writing of any of those composers. But a lack of originality in the case of incidental and dance arrangements is of less significance than the ability of the music to convey the rhythm, tone, and spirit of the drama and/or terpsichorean event. Baker's composition was meant to be light and gossamer like the fairies it introduced, and as a result, if his music communicated the proper dramatic effect to the audience, Baker was unconcerned with where it came from. As Benjamin J. Deane concluded, "for the music of the theatre of the present day, familiarity with the music which has been written, a good knowledge of where to reach readily for what is wanted, and facility in working it in, are more important essentials to a leader than the divine inspiration for the construction of more music.... The leader's object must be to please the public, and so long as he does that, it doesn't make much odds where he gets the material."[31]

Thomas Baker is credited as being the first leader in the United States to use the baton in a theatre orchestra and also the first to introduce a more elegant style of entr'acte music which had hitherto been relegated to commonplace waltzes and German Ländlers incompetently played.[32] His vast body of work, even if not always original, was always theatrically successful and pleasing to the audience.

BARAVELLE, Victor

Also credited as Victor Baravalle, composer and musical director Victor Baravelle was born in Piedmont, Italy on 2 November 1885 and came to the United States at an early age. The son and grandson of musical directors and composers, Baravelle began his musical training with his father Vittorio and completed his studies at the Institute of Musical Art in New York City. He made his Broadway debut as musical director of Sigmund Romberg's *The Melting of Molly* (30 December 1918) and opportunities continued to fall his way for the next twenty years, particularly in musicals composed by Jerome Kern: *The Night Boat* (2 February 1920), *Good Morning Dearie* (1 November 1921), *The Bunch and Judy* (28 November 1922), *Stepping Stones* (6 November 1923), *The City Chap* (26 October 1925), *Criss Cross* (12 October 1926), *Show Boat* (27 December 1927), *The Cat and the Fiddle* (15 October 1931), *Music in the Air* (8 November 1932), and *Roberta* (18 November 1933). When movies began talking and singing, Baravelle established himself as a major presence in the industry with the musical direction for *Rio Rita* (1929), *Hit the Deck* (1929), *Dixiana* (1930), *Show Boat* (1936), *A Damsel in Distress* (1937), *Radio City Revels* (1938), *Carefree* (1938) and *The Story of Vernon and Irene Castle* (1939). He died on 11 March 1939 at his home in the Brentwood Heights neighborhood of Los Angeles, survived by his wife and three children.[33]

Few of Baravelle's original compositions survive except for the dance arrangements, incidental and continuity music he provided for Broadway and film. "A Garden at Versailles," a spectacular musical sketch he composed for the Lambs Gambol at the Manhattan Opera House (24 January 1926) and repeated for the benefit of the Actors' Equity Association at the Metropolitan Opera House (25 April 1926)[34] appears never to have been published.

BARRATT, [Walter] Augustus

Composer, dance arranger, and musical director Augustus Barratt was born in Scotland in 1874. Having displayed a talent for music from an early age, he won a scholarship for advanced musical studies in London and commenced a career there as a composer of light operatic music. He published the libretto and music for a dramatic cantata, *The Death of Cuthullin*, in 1897 and, along with Lionel Monckton, Howard Talbot, and Victor Rogers, contributed music to *Kitty Grey*, produced at the Prince's Theatre in Bristol on 27 August 1900. Barratt's name first appears in the theatre bills of New York City in December 1904 in the cast of *Lady Teazle*, a musical based on Sheridan's play *The School for Scandal*, and in September 1906, Barratt is next credited with the musical direction and incidental arrangements for the Astor Theatre's production of *A Midsummer Night's Dream*. In 1907, he served as musical director and composer of additional music ("The Mice Will Play") for *The Little Michus* (31 January); he collaborated on the score for *Miss Pocahontas* (28 October); and he conducted Franz Lehár's *The Merry Widow* as the inaugural production at the Lyric Theatre in Rome, New York (26 November). Barratt composed and arranged dance music for *The Love Cure* (1 September 1909), *My Best Girl* (12 September 1912), *Fancy Free* (11 April 1918), *Little Simplicity* (4 November 1918), *What's in a Name?* (19 March 1920), and *Jack and Jill* (22 March 1923).

Even after his first wife, Lizzie May, sued for divorce in 1914,[35] Augustus Barratt managed to enjoy a luxurious lifestyle with a country mansion and sizable yacht. Unpredictably, after his stint as musical director for the Viennese musical romance *The Silver Swan* (27 November 1929) ended,

Example 9. "Carril and the Bards disembark" from *The Death of Cuthullin*

Barratt found himself out of work. Whether it was due to his own personality (he could often be difficult to work with, especially since he fancied himself a lyricist) or the character of his music, Barratt did not find a place in the Broadway musicals of the 1930s. He was forced to sell his country home and yacht and take an apartment at 310 West 80th Street where he continued to compose and teach until his death in April 1947 at the age of 73.[36]

Barratt's musical tastes were resolutely Romantic as can be seen in an excerpt of incidental music from *The Death of Cuthullin* (example 9). The passage occurs in Act One scene three when Carril (a famous Bard) comes to tell Princess Bragéla, Cuthullin's betrothed, that Cuthullin has agreed to fight his rival, the Irish chief Torlath, for her hand. The music depicts Carril and his party leaving their ship and coming ashore.

The urgency of the arrival expressed in the tempo is juxtaposed with majestically-structured triads that remind us that Carril is seeking audience with a Princess. The lyrical and undulating motif that begins on measure 9 suggests the water surging against the shore and resolves in an impassioned phrase (measures 25–26) that repeats again and again over different harmonic structures, emphasizing the dramatic tension inherent in Carril's message. Note the presence of seventh chords throughout the excerpt helping to create a lushness of tone that characterized the Romantic period in music.

BARRETT, Oscar

Producer and musical theatre composer Oscar Barrett was born in 1846 in London. He was associated with Augustus Harris, the manager of Theatre Royal, Drury Lane, in the production of Christmas pantomimes[37] and spectacular drama including *Cinderella* (1884), *Aladdin* (1886) *Red Riding Hood* (1887), and *A Million of Money* (1890). Moving on to other theatres, Barrett typically produced two pantomimes a year, including *Dick Wittington* at the Olympic (1892); *Cinderella* (1893), *Santa Claus* (1894) and *Robinson Crusoe* (1895) at the Lyceum; *Jack and the Beanstalk* at the Crystal Palace (1893); and a revised *Dick Whittington* for the Adelphi (1898). Commenting on the production at the Adelphi, the *New York Clipper* described the musical aesthetic to which Barrett ascribed:

> Oscar Barrett at the Adelphi will, in his orchestra, combine fun with operatic illustration. There is to be no absence of up to date music in "Dick Whittington," for Mr. Barrett

has secured the rights of many songs which are popular in the music halls. In addition to these, in his score will be found many of those little touches and sly excerpts from well-known operas and classics which will lend point to the situations on the stage. By counter-pointing and other tricks of the musician's trade, the Adelphi audiences will hear the popular melody of today and the classical melody of all time, running side by side. The accompaniment of processions and ballets has had Mr. Barrett's especial care.[38]

An artistic success, *Dick Whittington* was a financial failure, losing between £5000 and £6000 and driving Barrett into bankruptcy at the age of fifty-three. After the turn of the century, Oscar Barrett continued to compose but produced little that achieved the success of his earlier work. He died in 1941 at the age of ninety five.

Two of Barrett's pantomimes were transferred to the New York stage: *The Grim Goblin* at Wallack's Theatre (5 August 1880), produced by the George Conquest Pantomime and Burlesque Company, and the fairy extravaganza *Cinderella* at Abbey's Theatre (23 April 1894), with the cast imported from the Lyceum Theatre production. The libretto of the production indicates the presence of a "Grand Autumn Ballet," a "grand *bal champêtre* illustrating the chronology of dance," and a "Grand Transformation Scene" in addition to individual songs, choruses, and dances. Hardly a page of text is found without the indication of a musical number. In his pantomimes, Barrett sought to integrate all the various musical events naturally into the story, especially the ballets. In this he anticipated by fifty years the "integrated musical" developed by Richard Rodgers and Oscar Hammerstein II in the 1940s.

BATCHELOR, W[illiam] H.

Musical director and composer W. H. Batchelor first appeared in theatre notices in December 1881 as a musician in Dockrill and Leon's Circus performing throughout Cuba.[39] After several seasons with Dockrill and company, Batchelor joined Heffron's Great Eastern Circus, which employment was terminated in the spring of 1890 when he was engaged as musical director by David Henderson's American Extravaganza Company in Chicago. His name first appears in Chicago's theatre listings on 19 June 1890 at the Chicago Opera House with the production of Harry B.

Smith's *The Crystal Slipper* for which he was credited as musical director and composer of the ballet, "La Carte D'Amour." A year later Batchelor was still in Chicago as composer of Smith's extravaganza, *Sinbad, or, The Maid of Balsora* (11 June 1891),[40] and the following year, he composed the score for Smith's *Ali Baba, or, Morgiana and the Forty Thieves* (3 June 1892) produced again at the Chicago Opera House by the American Extravaganza Company. Batchelor's next composition *Aladdin, Jr.*, a collaboration with J. Cheever Goodwin that opened at the Chicago Opera House on 7 June 1894,[41] was followed by an operatic burlesque, *Little Robinson Crusoe* (15 June 1895) produced again in Chicago, and composed in collaboration with Harry B. Smith and Gustav Luders.[42] On 15 August 1895, with the

Example 10. "March of the Forty Thieves" from *Ali Baba*

aim of pursuing a career in New York City, Batchelor resigned his position as composer and musical director with the American Extravaganza Company after four lucrative years of service.[43] A year later, Batchelor's early association with Harry B. Smith led to his being hired as musical director for the Broadway premiere and national tour of Smith's comic opera *Half a King* (14 September 1896), a position that sustained his employment through the end of October 1897. A short stint as composer and musical director for *Gayest Manhattan* (3 January 1898) led to the Broadway revivals of *Sinbad* (14 March 1898) and *Ali Baba*, revised and rechristened as *An Arabian Girl and 40 Thieves* (29 April 1899), and the musical directorship of a revival of Gustave Kerker's *The Belle of New York* (22 January 1900). Batchelor's final credited work in New York appears to have been the musical direction and orchestrations for *Foxy Grandpa* (17 February 1902), a cartoon strip musical that enjoyed a respectable run.

The character of Batchelor's dance music can be revealed by three excerpts from *Ali Baba, or, Morgiana and the Forty Thieves*. The first (example 10) is taken from the "March of the Forty Thieves," a nervously energetic piece that borrows liberally from the "Sequidilla" in Bizet's *Carmen* to express the itinerant spirit of the thieves. Like most of the galloping dance music at the turn of the century, Batchelor's harmony remains grounded in the tonic-subdominant-dominant tradition, with the occasional secondary dominant. His conspicuous use of the Neapolitan (measure 13) and augmented sixth chords (measures 17 and 19) amplifies the exoticism of the march, adding a startling tension that characterizes the erratic and unpredictable nature of the thieves.

Example 11 presents the brief dance that accompanies "The Original Bogie Man," a number that claims to explain the origin of the "Bogie Man" legend. Measures 1–3 are quite traditional: the harmony is simple and the melody clearly outlines the strong beats in each measure. With a missing downbeat and a lack of harmonization, measure four comes as a

Example 11. Dance in "The Original Bogie Man" from *Ali Baba*

Example 12. Hornpipe in "The Jolly Old Tar" from *Ali Baba*

complete surprise, and the chromatic phrase mirrored in treble and bass evokes a sense of mystery and danger that rings true even today.

Batchelor deliberately borrowed the hornpipe appended to "The Jolly Old Tar" (example 12) from "With Cat-like Tread," a production number in Gilbert and Sullivan's *The Pirates of Penzance* (1879) to evoke an atmosphere of sailors and swashbucklers. The dance itself subscribes to the traditional "Harvest Home" model in common time with a dotted note melody; measure 1 is especially interesting with its three strong beats that seem to tumble into measure 2, creating an artful dichotomy of tension and resolution at the beginning of the dance.

BAUER, Adolph

German-born pianist Adolph Bauer began his career in America in the 1880s, accompanying violinist Remenyi and soprano Jennie Dutton at the Mozart Hall in Richmond, Virginia and the National Theatre in Washington D.C. After several years of accompanying soloists on tour, in 1887, Bauer became musical director of the Fitzgerald Opera Company at Newmyer's Opera House in Connellsville, Pennsylvania.[44] In the summer of 1888, he accepted the position of musical director of Conried's Opera Company at Uhrig's Cave in St. Louis, Missouri, and the following year, as musical director for Nathaniel Roth's Company, he composed a "Love Duet" to be interpolated into the score of Francis Chassaigne's comic opera *Nadjy*, while it was on tour. On 3 August 1891, Bauer's opera *Aquilo* was produced at the Tivoli Theatre in San Francisco. Conveying the story of Silas Whipple who embarks on a voyage to the North Pole and discovers a continent with perpetual sunlight and warmth, the opera was a great success. In 1894 Bauer became musical director of William Furst's adaptation of Victor Roger's *The Little Trooper* at the Casino Theatre in

New York City and assisted Furst in the arrangement of dance music for the production. After *The Little Trooper* closed, Adolph Bauer suddenly disappeared from theatre listings. The name reappeared in 1902 as treasurer with Edison's Electric Theatre in Mobile, Alabama, but there is no certainty that Bauer the composer-musical director was the same person.

BEISENHERZ, Henry D.

German-born musical director and composer Henry Beisenherz (sometimes spelled Beissenherz) was the musical director at the Bowery and New Bowery Theatres in the 1850s and 1860s. There he selected and arranged ballet music for satirical burlesques and extravaganzas that included *Medea* (4 December 1858), *Harlequin Jack, the Giant Killer* (4 February 1861)[45] and *The Devil in the Bowery* (28 September 1863)[46] Earlier in 1863 Beisenherz became president of the "Musical Mutual Protective Association" that regulated musicians' salaries, places of performance, and hours of employment.[47] The present musicians' union (802) in New York City is the product of the "Protective Association." From the New Bowery Theatre Beisenherz moved to Wood's Theatre in the mid-1860s, becoming musical director, composer, and dance arranger for *The Elves, or The Statue Bride* (30 April 1866),[48] *The Invisible Prince, or, The Island of Tranquil Delights* (4 June 1866), *The Three Sisters!* (18 June 1866), and *Fra Diavolo* (2 July 1866), after which, he disappeared from theatre listings. In the 1870s, Beisenherz resurfaced in Indianapolis as a conductor of oratorios with the Choral Union, and there exists a Tamil-English Dictionary (1897) at the Library of Congress that was revised by a H. Beisenherz but it is doubtful that the author of the revision was also a musical director and dance arranger forty years earlier.

BENDIX, Max

Violinist, musical director, and composer Max Bendix was born in Detroit in 1865. A child prodigy, he made his debut as a violin soloist at the age of eight, and when he was eleven he joined an orchestra under the direction of Theodore Thomas. In 1891, when the orchestra moved to Chicago (to become the Chicago Symphony Orchestra), Bendix was named concertmaster and later became its conductor.[49] Five years later a dispute with Theodore Thomas caused Bendix to leave the Chicago orchestra though he remained in the city giving music lessons and occasional concerts[50] until after the turn of the century when he became concertmaster and frequent conductor at the Manhattan Opera House in New York City. After several seasons, Bendix moved on to the Metropolitan Opera House where he was transferred from the post of concertmaster to that of conductor in 1909.[51] In 1910, he began his career as musical director and composer of incidental music on Broadway with Heinrich Reinhardt's *The Spring Maid* (26 December). This was followed by *Miss Princess* (23 December 1912), *Her Little Highness* (13 October 1913), *Sari* (13 January 1914), *Experience* (27 October 1914), *Pom-Pom* (28 February 1916), *The Amber Empress* (19 September 1916), *The Chocolate Soldier* (12 December 1921), *Castles in the Air* (6 September 1926, and *Giroflé-Girofla* (22 November 1926. Throughout his Broadway career, Bendix continued to serve as a violin teacher at the National Academy of Musical Art in New York City. He returned to Chicago after 1930 to become the first conductor of the Illinois Symphony Orchestra and died of a stroke on 6 December 1945, survived by his daughter, Anya, his wife, Angelica, having divorced him in 1899.

BENDIX, Theodore

Max Bendix's older brother, Theodore, was born in Detroit in 1863.[52] At an early age he became an actor in local productions to support himself while he engaged in the study of music composition and violin performance. His first credit as a composer of musical theatre appeared on 27 August 1881 with the production of William Gill's *My Sweetheart* at Shattuck's Opera House in Hornellsville, New York.[53] In 1883, Bendix was the musical director of Salsbury's Troubadours, after which, in the same capacity, he joined Mr. and Mrs. George S Knight's touring company. He acted as composer and musical director for the revival of William Gill's *Mam'zelle* (20 September 1866)[54] and Barton Hill's English adaptation of Sardou's *Marita* (28 September 1886), both at the Union Square Theatre in New York City, and he contributed songs and dances to *Over the Garden Wall* (27 December 1886) at the Fourteenth Street Theatre. By 1888, Bendix was the musical director at the Globe Theatre in Boston[55] where he was arraigned in the Municipal Court on 26 May 1891 on the charge of non-support of his wife.[56]

Ten years later, Bendix was back in New York as musical director for *The Belle of New York* (24 October 1898), and *The Great Ruby* (1 September 1900) before touring with the Anna Held Company. In 1902 he sailed to London to become the musical director of the Theatre Royal, Drury Lane production of *Ben Hur* (31 March 1902) and, the following year, he conducted the summer run of *A Chinese Honeymoon* in Chicago before becoming musical director of the Hudson Theatre in New York City where he was contracted to compose all the incidental music for actor-producer James K. Hackett's plays.[57] In 1905, Bendix composed incidental music for Edwin Royle's *The Squaw Man* at Wallack's Theatre (23 October) and composed additional music for a cartoon musical extravaganza, *Simple Simon Simple*, at the West End Theatre (30 October). By 1909 Bendix's career as musical director and composer of incidental (and dance) music on Broadway was in full throttle with productions that included Mary Roberts Rinehart and Avery Hopwood's *Seven Days* (10 November 1909), William Harris, Jr.'s *A Skylark* (4 April 1910), James Forbes's *The Commuters* (15 August 1910), Clarence Harvey's *The Great Name* (4 October 1911), *The Rose of Panama* (22 January 1912), and *The Captive* (18 March 1912). In 1913, Bendix introduced the novelty of a string quartet (the Theodore Bendix Quartet) rather than an orchestra playing entr'acte music in the production of *The Love Leash* (20 October 1913)[58]

Bendix became musical director at the newly constructed Standard Theatre in 1914 where he arranged incidental and entr'acte music for *Kitty MacKay* and subsequent productions that changed on a weekly basis. In March 1919, he was sued for divorce by his wife, Sally, whom he abandoned more than thirty years previously. Mrs. Bendix demanded $100 weekly in alimony but was awarded only $13.[59] The following year, Bendix was the musical director for the Alcazar Theatre in San Francisco, and in 1923, he was back on the East Coast composing incidental music for the American National Theatre's production of *As You Like It* (16 April). Later in the year, Bendix and his orchestra was hired to provide incidental music for a new production of *Scaramouche* at the Morosco Theatre in New York City (24 October 1923), after which he planned to go to Hollywood to compose incidental music for films. During his tenure as musical director in New York City, Bendix kept a musical library which was subsequently sold to Tams-Witmark. In his later years he resided at the Percy Williams Actors Home at East Islip, Long Island where he died on 15 January 1935 from complications after surgery.

Fortunately for the student of musical theatre history, much of Bendix's incidental and dance music was published, permitting a primary source investigation of his work. Example 13 presents the schottische dance appended to the song, "I Am So Shy," from *My Sweetheart*, Bendix's

Example 13. Dance in "I Am So Shy" from *My Sweetheart*

Example 14. "A Suburban Scramble" from *The Commuters*

first musical theatre composition. Note the downward arpeggiated triplets that begin the antecedent and consequent phrases of the dance contrasted with the stepwise upwardly moving bass line (measures 1 and 5), both providing a forward thrust to the piece. The juxtaposition of bashfulness evoked by the triplets with the buoyancy of the bass line identifies the flirtatious irony of the song. Note also the descending stepwise construction of the chords in measure 3, a sophisticated use of chordal inversions, and the common-tone diminished seventh chord in measure 7 connecting the B minor chord with the D major tonic. The elegant sophistication of the harmony is also found in the specific articulation throughout, as well as

Example 15. "Nat-u-ritch, an Indian Idyll" from *The Squaw Man*

in the dynamics and expressive text, "*delicato*" (measure 7), all designed to illustrate and accent the dance steps.

Example 14, an excerpt from "A Suburban Scramble" a conventional march-galop composed for *The Commuters* is simpler harmonically than the previous example. The melodic material relies heavily on stepwise movement juxtaposed with leaps of thirds, fourths, and sixths, with the fourth being most prominent. The persistent chordal accompaniment evokes the jerky movement of a commuter train while the nursery-rhyme quality of the melody, with its ironic final chorus of "over the fence you go," playfully conjures up child-like images of going to grandmother's house.

"Nat-u-ritch, an Indian Idyll" (example 15), is an excerpt from the incidental music Bendix composed for *The Squaw Man*. Note the rhythmic drone of the Indian drum and the solo flute playing a plaintive hexachordal melody (measures 2–18). At measure 19, the melody shifts to the bass accompanied by an aggressive triad of unyielding eighth notes, and the character of the piece changes from softly introspective to loudly assertive. Note how the specific indications of dynamics, phrasing, and articulation in the example help build momentum as the composition moves forward.

BERNARD, G. P.

George P. Bernard was the musical director at the Columbia Opera House in New York City in the late 1870s and early 1880s. In 1882 he left his post to become musical director for Annie Pixley's touring company, which returned to New York to perform at the Grand Opera House early in 1883. For the pieces presented, *M'liss, Child of the Sierras* (29 January 1883) and *Zara!* (5 February 1883), Bernard created song medleys, arranged dance music, and provided orchestral arrangements, in addition to the responsibilities connected with leading the orchestra.

BING, George

English composer George Bing was the musical director at the Alhambra Theatre in London. There he arranged the music for the *Ballet of 1830* from the music of Lully, Couperin, Rameau, and other ancient French composers. The ballet, set in Paris of the 1830s, tells the story of a painter, Rudolfe, who is in love with Mariette, a peasant girl. He sells a painting to a rich Baron who steals Mariette away from him. On the rebound, Rudolphe becomes infatuated with the Vampire Girl and the two couples find themselves at a French restaurant crowded with dancers. Eventually Rudolphe and Mariette reconcile in the *Jardin des Amoureux* [*Garden of Lovers*] and the Baron finds solace with a pretty flower girl. After completing a profitable year's run at the Alhambra, the *Ballet of 1830*, complete with scenery, costumes, and dancers, crossed the Atlantic to appear at the Winter Garden Theatre as the opening act of the *Passing Show of 1912* (22 July 1912).[60] The music for the ballet was Bing's single contribution to the American musical theatre.

BLAKE, Eubie

Born to former slaves in Baltimore, Maryland, on 7 February 1887,[61] James Hubert Blake was a child prodigy, playing the organ from the age of five. When he was seven he began taking piano lessons from the organist from a local Methodist Church,; at the age of twelve, he composed the "Charleston Rag" (though he did not write it down until he learned to read music); and when he was fifteen, he played piano for $5 a week in Agnes Sheldon's sporting house, a Baltimore bordello. At the age of twenty he was hired to play piano at Joe Gans's Goldfield Hotel in Baltimore and for the next several years he alternated winter seasons at the Goldfield and summers in Atlantic City, performing at the Boathouse and the Bucket of Blood, popular nightclubs.[62] There he came into contact with ragtime pianists James P. Johnson, "Willie-the Lion" Smith, and "Willie" Gant each of whom had a tremendous effect on his playing. In 1910 Blake married Avis Lee, a friend from his Baltimore school days, and in 1915, he formed a vaudeville act, the "Dixie Duo," with Noble Sissle that toured throughout the United States and appeared with James Reese Europe's Society Orchestra intermittently from 1916 to 1919.[63] In 1920, Blake and Sissle joined forces with the vaudeville duo, Flournoy Miller and Aubrey Lyles to create *Shuffle Along* (23 May 1921), the Broadway show that legitimized the African-American musical and produced one of the most critically acclaimed scores of the 1920s.[64] Again collaborating with Noble Sissle, Blake composed songs for *Elsie* (2 April 1923), *Andre Charlot's Revue of 1924* (9 January 1924), and *The Chocolate Dandies* (1 September 1924). After the run of *The Chocolate Dandies*, Sissle and Blake performed on the vaudeville stage in England and contributed to Charles B. Cochran's London *Revue of 1926*.

When Blake returned to the United States he continued to compose music for new Broadway musicals: *Lew Leslie's Blackbirds* (22 October 1930), *Chamberlain Brown's Scrap Book* (1 August 1932), and *Swing It* (22 July 1937), in addition to supervising (and performing in) revivals and revisions of *Shuffle Along* in 1932 and 1952. During WWII, when Blake was touring with the USO as musical director (1941–1946), he married violinist Willy Tyler's widow, Marion Tyler (his first wife Avis having died of tuberculosis in 1938), and when the war was over, he announced his retirement and went back to school, studying the Schillinger System of Composition with Rudolph Schramm at New York University. In the 1950s Blake returned to public life as a concert ragtime pianist and lecturer, appearing in theatres, on college campuses, at jazz festivals, in concert halls, and on radio and television programs.[65] The many awards he received from theatrical, musical, professional, educational, and civic groups included honorary doctorates from Dartmouth (1974), Rutgers (1974) and the New England Conservatory of Music (1974), and the Presidential Medal of Freedom (1981). He died on 12 February 1983, a year after the death of his second wife.

In *The Music of Black Americans*, Eileen Southern identifies Blake as the "leading exponent of piano rag on the East coast,"[66] so it is not surprising that Bake's dance music in *Shuffle Along* exhibited the characteristics of his piano rags, especially since he played piano in the show. Southern suggests that the "most striking features of Blake's rags were the fast tempos and the powerful pulsating basses. The latter, consisting chiefly of 'um-pah' skips from low-octaves to mid-keyboard chords and octave passages are generally referred to as 'stride basses.' But Blake occasionally interrupted the straightforward patterns of his left hand to inject a few measures of stentorian broken octaves, his right hand continuing all the while in its flowing embellishing of the syncopated melody (he called the embellishments 'tricks')."[67]

BLAKE, Louis

Born in Ireland in June 1863, composer, dance arranger, and member of the New Orleans Press Club, Louis Blake immigrated with his family to the United States in 1870. His name first appeared in theatrical records on 27 April 1891 as the composer and dance arranger of *The Khedive*, an Egyptian comic opera with a libretto by Harry B. Edwards and Micah Blake, at the St. Charles Theatre, New Orleans. Four months later, the musical opened at Niblo's Garden in New York City (27 August 1891) to less than sterling reviews. The *New York Clipper*, for example, argued: "The best that can be said of *The Khedive* is that it is entertaining without being original. Its melodies are altogether reminiscent of half a dozen gifted composers, and its libretto is of the conventional order, not especially dull, yet never actually sprightly."[68] Undaunted, Louis Blake found employment in St. Louis, first at the Garden Theatre and later at Uhrig's Cave, where he produced a new comic opera, *Ollemus*, with a fellow New Orleanian Espy Williams.[69] By the turn of the century, Blake had composed the music for *The Military Maid* (1898) and *The Striped Petticoat* (1899), both with librettos by Henry Rightor, a fellow member of the New Orleans Press Club, as well as a number of successful songs including "Partners for Life" and "Why Do You Love Me So?"[70] Louis Blake is last credited as the composer of Espy Williams's burlesque Martian opera, *A Royal Joke*, produced at Athletic Park, New Orleans, on 18 August 1901, by the Metropolitan Opera Company.[71]

BÖTEFÜHR, W.D.C.

Composer W.D.C. Böteführ was musical director at the Varieties Theatre in St. Louis for a production of *The Black Crook* advertised in May 1867.[72] For that production, he composed a "Pas de Demons" (example 16) dedicated to the principal ballerina, Annetta Galetti. Note the melodramatic intensity of the opening chromatic passage (measures 1–8) signaling wildness and villainy, and the effective usage of the common-tone diminished seventh chord (measures 9–12) to emphasize the dangerous rowdiness of the event. Both devices are reminiscent of those used by Austrian composer Franz von Suppé in his celebrated overture to *Poet and Peasant* (1846). The chromaticism continues in the galop proper (beginning on measure 21) that playfully teases the listener with its repetitive phrases and placement of rests; and the evocation of the overture to *Poet and Peasant* returns at measure 37 with the descending stepwise melodic phrase, though without Suppé's syncopations. While the "Pas de Demons" does not sound especially demonic, it does evoke the melodramatic *sturm und drang* [storm and stress] that is typically associated with the underworld, and for that Böteführ (or Franz von Suppé) can be applauded.

Example 16. "Pas de Demons" from *The Black Crook*

BOULLAY, Louis

Violinist and composer Louis Boullay was one of the French musicians who fled to the United States from the West Indies in 1793, when the British attacked the islands during the French Revolutionary Wars. Immediately upon his arrival his name appears on concert programs as composer and violinist in Philadelphia and Boston and as a member of the Philadelphia Theatre and Federal Street Theatre orchestras.[73] On 26 June 1795, a ballet pantomime, *The Miraculous Mill; or, The Old Ground Young*, with music composed and selected by Boullay was performed in Philadelphia before moving to the Federal Street Theatre in Boston for its

Example 16 (continued). "Pas de Demons" from *The Black Crook*

1796–1797 season,[74] and on 4 July 1796, Boullay's "Bravura Song" with violin obligato was performed in concert in Philadelphia. By 1797 Boullay was in Worcester, Massachusetts, teaching music, and his name fades from theatre and concert listings.

BOWERS, Frederick V.

Composer, actor, and singer Frederick V. Bowers, the "P.T. Barnum of vaudeville," was born in Boston in 1875. At an early age he performed in vaudeville on the Orpheum circuit and at the Palace Theatre in New York

City[75] often appearing with Jennie Yeamans and Charles Horwitz, who wrote lyrics to many of Bowers's songs.[76] In 1900, Bowers and Horowitz collaborated with William Jerome on the hit, "When Sousa Leads the Band," interpolated into the score of the Broadway vaudeville farce, *Star and Garter* (26 November); and the following year, Bowers was sighted singing his hits, "When I Think of You," "Something that Money Can't Buy," and "When Sousa Leads the Band" on the Western vaudeville circuit.[77] By the summer of 1901, Bowers was back on the East coast performing at the Pines in Boston, the Grand Opera House in Philadelphia, and Proctor's Fifth Avenue Theatre in New York City. In 1902 Bowers composed the music for *The Major and the Judge*, a touring vaudeville act, and *King Highball*, a Martian musical comedy, both with librettos by Charles Horowitz. According to the reviews, Bowers and Horowitz produced two hit songs from the musical, "They Never Do That in Mars" and "Another High Ball," but it was Bowers's ballet music and the dancing that earned the critics' greatest approbation.[78] In 1904, Bowers toured with Imre Kiralfy's *Louisiana* and composed songs that were performed in the *Dockstader Minstrels* ("Everybody's Sleeping but the Bogie Man," "Every Day Is Sunshine When the Heart Beats True," "Give Me the Sunny South," "The Man We Will Always Love," "Moriarity," "Sadie, the Princess of Tenement Row," and "The Sun Flower Song"). By the summer of 1906 he had joined *The Ham Tree Company* in which he appeared with W.C. Fields at the New York Theatre (30 July) before going on a national tour. The following year, Bowers was on the road again performing in *College Days*, a vaudeville musical featuring his songs (with lyrics by Arthur Lamb and Harry Hoyt). Another musical for which he had contributed songs, *His Bridal Night*, closed before reaching Broadway but Bowers had better luck with *Too Many Wives* (2 November 1908), another collaboration with Horowitz that produced several hit songs ("He's Getting Like His Daddy Every Day," "When the Moon Shines on Broadway," "How'd You Like to Call Me Dearie?" and "Big Chief Oi, Oi"), as well as a Broadway run and tour. In 1909, Bowers signed a five-year contract with theatre manager John Cort to compose music for, and appear in, his productions. Bowers performed his sketch, *Here Comes a College Boy*, for six weeks in William Morris's music halls before leaving on tour with his first project with Cort, *Commencement Days* (again with lyricist Horowitz). *Commencement Days* was a critical and financial failure on tour and nothing more was heard of Bowers's connection with John Cort. Instead, he was listed in the Broadway cast of *The Young Turk* (31 January 1910), among the acts at William Morris's American Music Hall (April 1910), and in the Chicago production of *My Cinderella Girl* (1910), for which he and Horowitz composed the songs. Bowers continued to produce vaudeville acts into the 1920s when his name again became associated with the casts of touring productions, most notably *No, No, Nanette*.

Bowers was married twice: his first wife, Blanche, whom he married in 1898, deserted him in 1900 to live with George Pullman, Jr., son of the railroad magnate. After obtaining a divorce from Blanche and winning a lawsuit against Pullman to the tune of $50,000, Bowers married again. He died in Los Angeles on 29 April 1961, respected as a performer and composer and admired for his contributions to musical theatre dance music.

BOWERS, Robert Hood

Musical director and composer Robert Hood Bowers was born in Chambersburg, Pennsylvania, on 24 May 1877. He took his Masters of Arts degree from Franklin and Marshall College and studied music with composers and theorists Thomas Whitney Surette, Frederic Grant Gleason, and Constantin Von Sternberg. He left the musical directorship of the Rosedale Theatre in Chambersburg to accept a position with the Chicago office of Witmark and Sons, a large music publishing firm, and in 1904 he acted as composer and musical director for his first hit musical, *The Maid and the Mummy* (25 July), with a libretto by Richard Carle. The following year, Bowers was hired as musical director for *When We Are Forty-One* (12 June1905) at the New York Roof Theatre. Suddenly finding himself a man of means, he married Virginia Belvin on 16 September 1905 and the couple spent their honeymoon in Chicago while the groom began rehearsals for *The Pink Hussars*, composed by Alfred E. Aarons and Julian Edwards, and starring John Slavin. Bowers scored another Broadway hit with *The Vanderbilt Cup* (16 January 1906) for which he again provided music and musical direction. In the years that followed, he composed "Baby and Nursie" (lyrics by Richard Carle) for *The Spring Chicken* (8 October 1906), created the orchestrations for *The Hurdy Gurdy Girl* (23 September 1907), another Carle production, and provided the musical direction, incidental songs, choruses, and ballet music for *The Hoyden* (19 October 1907). He composed the songs for *The Silver Star* (1 November 1909), a vehicle for the internationally famous dancer, Adeline Genée, and provided vaudeville dancer Dazie with the music for what critic's called her most remarkable creation in her pantomime, *L'Amour de l'Artist* in December 1909. The *New York Clipper* noted that Bowers "understands this dancer's wants perfectly, and has written a most entrancing accompaniment, effectively arranged for vaudeville orchestras."⁷⁹

Bowers composed songs, incidental, and ballet music for *The Wife Tamers* (8 August 1910), *The Spring Maid* (26 December 1910), *A Certain Party* (24 April 1911), *Hell, a Profane Burlesque* (27 April 1911), *The Red Rose* (22 June 1911), and *California* (20 November 1911) and *The Antique Girl* (28 January 1912), two vaudeville musicals with libretti by Cecil DeMille. Bowers continued composing for vaudeville with *The Red Heads* (13 November 1913), and *The Beauties* (28 June 1914) both with libretti by William LeBaron. In addition to composing songs and dance music, Bowers was also a busy musical director on Broadway, leading the orchestras for *The Rose Maid* (22 April 1912), two of Victor Herbert's operettas, *The Madcap Duchess* (11 November 1913), and *The Only Girl* (2 November 1914), Irving Berlin's *Stop! Look! Listen!* (25 December 1915), Jerome Kern's *Miss 1917* (5 November 1917), and Gilbert and Sullivan's *Iolanthe* (19 April 1926). In 1919, Bowers collaborated with Malvin Franklin on the score for *A Lonely Romeo* (10 June) and, eight years later, he produced his last original Broadway score, the unsuccessful *Oh, Ernest!* (9 May 1927). One final effort to reach Broadway, *Listen In*, with music by Bowers and book and lyrics by Alonzo Price and Francis De Witt, opened in Springfield, Massachusetts in August 1929 and closed on the road.

In 1914, Bowers began writing incidental music for silent films including *Neptune's Daughter* (1914), *A Daughter of the Gods* (1916), *War Brides* (1916), and *Patria* (1917). In 1918, he composed the atmospheric incidental music for Samuel Shipman and John B. Hymer's play *East Is West* (9 December), producing arguably his most famous composition, "A Chinese Lullaby" which was uncredited when used in the film version of the play (1930).

Beginning in 1936, Bowers was the vocal coach and musical director of the School of Radio Technique and a conductor for the electrical transcription department of NBC; and in the summer of 1939, he conducted twelve weeks of opera at the Open Air Theatre in Memphis, Tennessee. He served as musical director for the Aeolian and Columbia record companies and conducted orchestras on radio stations WEAF, WOR, and WMCA. He died on 29 December 1941 after a brief illness.⁸⁰

Much of Robert Hood Bowers's legacy lies in the realm of theatrical dance music, the composition and arrangement of which he was an acknowledged master. The "Galop" from *The Vanderbilt Cup* (example

Example 17. "Galop" from *The Vanderbilt Cup*

17), and "Cute an' Cunnin'" from *A Lonely Romeo* (example 18) offer representative examples of his compositional style. The syncopations and sixteenth-note variations of the traditional "um-pah" accompaniment actively propel the "Galop," while the use of secondary dominants, suspended chords, augmented chords, and common-tone diminished sevenths create a varied and interesting harmonic fabric.

The slow foxtrot, "Cute an' Cunnin'" is a graceful schottische with a syncopated emphasis on the second beat throughout the first section of the dance. Note the sudden pauses following the accented bass note in mid-measure (measures 4, 10, and 12) that create an abrupt lurching

Example 18. "Cute an' Cunnin'" from *A Lonely Romeo*

Example 18 (continued). "Cute an' Cunnin'" from *A Lonely Romeo*

quality to the music, and the copious usage of secondary dominants that produce a series of climaxes beginning with measure 10. Note also the second section of the dance (starting with measure 18) in which the dotted rhythms of the schottische are contrasted with the ragtime rhythms of syncopated eighth notes (measures 23, 25), permitting a variety of choreographic movements.

BOWRON, George
BOWRON, William Lloyd

The musical Bowron brothers came to the United States from Liverpool in the 1860s. They first resided at Giesman's Boarding House in New York City where William and his British-born friends, teenage actor and singer Charles Algernon Sidney Vivian, and pianist Richard R. Steirly were instrumental in the establishment of the Benevolent and Protective Order of Elks in February 1868. George was the first to appear in theatre listings as a member of Buckley's Serenaders and Burlesque Opera Troupe about to commence a tour throughout the United States in September 1873.[81] On 26 February 1877, George joined the Berger Family Company during the New England leg of their tour and remained with them until the end of the 1879–1880 season, when he composed the mock-operatic song and chorus, "The Tourists in a Pullman Car" for the touring John P. Smith's Tourists Combination Company. For the 1880–1881 season, George composed incidental music and acted as musical director for the national tour of *Edgewood Folks*, a play with songs written by Boston playwright J.E. Brown and produced by the Sol Smith Russell Combination Company. The tour stopped in New York City for a four-week run beginning 23 August 1880, the same day that brother William, now musical director at Haverly's Fifth Avenue Theatre began conducting a four-week return engagement of *The Tourists in a Pullman Palace Car*. The following August, William was musical director for Frank Musgrave's musical comedy extravaganza, *Smiff* (22 August 1881), and in 1882, while George was still attached to *Edgewood Folks*, William composed and selected the incidental music for *Chipsa* (4 September 1882), a four-act drama about a "lazy, moody, monosyllabic, and thieving Indian"[82] produced at Haverly's Fourteenth-street Theatre.

The year 1886 found George Bowron in Chicago acting as musical director for a pirated production of Edward Jakobowski's *Erminie* (26 July) at the New Casino Theatre, after which he assumed the musical directorship of Chicago's Columbia Theatre. In 1889, George moved to Long Branch, New Jersey, where he became leader of the orchestra at the Ocean Hotel, and William, who had been the musical director at Haverly's Fourteenth-street Theatre, accepted a similar position at the Bijou Theatre where he continued to select and/or compose incidental and dance music for productions, such as Professor A. Herrmann's *Transatlantique Vaudevilles* (17 August 1889) and Charles H. Hoyt's *A Texas Steer, or, Money Makes the Mare Go* (10 November 1890.) In the summer of 1890, William was elected to the board of governors of the Actors' Amateur Athletic Association of America (commonly referred to as the "Five A's), and the following year, George Bowron appeared at the Bijou Theatre for a two-week engagement as musical director (and incidental composer and dance arranger) of *The Hustler* (23 November 1891), a musical farce comedy on a national tour. We hear no more about William Lloyd Bowron after 1890 and no more about George Bowron after *The Hustler* tour returned to New York to play a week's engagement at Niblo's Garden (29 February 1892).

BRAHAM, David

Violinist, composer, and musical director, David Braham was born in February 1834 in St. George's, Middlesex, a prosperous middle-class neighborhood in London's East End. Educated at Joseph Fletcher's British Union School, the young Braham developed a proficiency in the reading and writing of music at an early age and, when he was a teenager, he announced that he wanted to become a professional harpist. He soon, however, discovered the difficulties of transporting a harp to his various engagements using public transportation and, inspired by his older brother Joseph's performances on the violin, he decided to play that instrument instead. With violin in tow, Braham arrived in New York City on 28 April 1856, and soon after he accepted a position with Matt Peel's Campbell's Minstrels about to set out on an East Coast tour. He remained with the company until March 1859 when he left to become leader of the string section of Robinson's Military Band, one of the popular instrumental ensembles that concertized in and around New York City. During his tenure with the band, Braham continued to perform in pit orchestras, most notably at Niblo's Garden where he met the teenage acrobat Martin Hanley and his sister Annie, who soon became Braham's wife. After engagements as musical director at the Canterbury Music Hall, Wood's Minstrel Hall, a converted German opera house called "The New Idea," the American Theatre at 444 Broadway, the Mechanics' Hall, and the Eighth Avenue Opera House, "Dave" Braham (as he was then credited) was hired as musical director for the Theatre Comique at 514 Broadway.

During the 1867–1868 season, one of Braham's early compositions, "Adolphus Morning-Glory" became a staple of the repertoire of blackface singer and dancer Harry Bloodgood and performed with great regularity at the Eighth Avenue Opera House and wherever else Bloodgood appeared. The song was important since it characterized the style of composition in post-Civil War American music. An eight-bar introduction in a schottische style stated the tune, a simple triadic structure comprised of two four-measure phrases, accompanied by traditional tonic-subdominant-dominant harmonization. The sung portion of the piece, little more than an eight-measure ditty, reiterated the infectious and memorable melody previously heard in the instrumental introduction. Each verse of the lyric was followed by a repeated dance section that not only utilized the original melodic material but also interspersed it with rhythmically accented chords to add variety to the musical texture and emphasize the different dance steps employed in the choreography. Although the work was simple and typical of the period, it remained theatrically effective and demonstrated the technical prowess of a composer familiar with the needs of dancers.[83]

At the Theatre Comique, Braham composed overtures and incidental music designed to depict the spirit of the entertainment, intermingling familiar marches, jigs, polkas, and waltzes with his own compositions and arranging them to fulfill and challenge the expectations of the audience. So successful would Braham become in his choice of music that reviewers, typically unaccustomed to mentioning the incidental music in a performance, made special note of Braham's arrangements, praising their appropriateness, originality, and performance.[84] Among the productions Braham composed and arranged during his first years at the Theatre Comique, the most significant are: the burlesques, *Pluto, or The Young Man who Charmed the Rocks*, *The Maid and the Magpie, or, The Fatal Spoon*, *Arrah-Na-Brogue!*, *The Crook, or, The Hunchback of Not-er-dam*, and *Ixion, or, The Man at the Wheel*; the ballets, *Demonio*, *The Water Nymphs*, and *The Holiday Sports of Spain*; the holiday pantomime, *Tell-Tale-Tit*; and the spectacular extravaganza, *Warriors of the Sun*. While working at the Theatre Comique, Braham had the time to compose the music for the burlesques, *Aladdin the Second* (11 November 1872) and

Gabriel Grub, or, The Story of the Goblins who Stole the Sexton (23 December 1873) at the Olympic Theatre. In 1875, Braham became musical director of the Eagle Theatre creating music for *Robinson Crusoe, His Man Friday, Monkey, and the King of Caribee Islands* (18 October), *Kim-Ka!, or, The Adventures of an Aeronaut* (29 November), *The Dead Shot!/From St. Louis to New Orleans!* (6 December), *Harlequin! Demon Statue, The Enchanted Pills and Magic Apple Tree; or High Diddle Diddle, the Cat's in the Fiddle, the Cow Jumped over the Moon!* (27 December), and *Rosemi-Shell!, or, My Daughter! Oh, My Daughter!* (24 January 1876). In addition he conducted performances of Gilbert and Sullivan's *Trial by Jury* and Charles Lecocq's *Giroflé-Girofla*.

With the actor-writer Edward Harrigan, David Braham composed songs and dances for many of his greatest successes including: *The Donovans* (31 May 1874), *The Mulligan Guard* (8 September 1874), *Down Broadway* (25 September 1876), *Old Lavender* (3 September 1877), *The Rising Star* (22 October 1877), *Sullivan's Christmas* (31 December 1877), *Christmas Joys and Sorrows* (14 January 1878), *A Celebrated Hard Case* (18 March 1878), *The Mulligan Guard Picnic* (23 September 1878), *The Lorgaire* (25 November 1878), *The Mulligan Guard Ball* (13 January 1879), *The Mulligan Guard's Chowder* (11 August 1879), *The Mulligan Guards' Christmas* (17 November 1879), *The Mulligan Guards' Surprise* (16 February 1880), *The Mulligan Guards' Nominee* (22 November 1880), *The Mulligans' Silver Wedding* (21 February 1881), *The Major* (29 August 1881), *Squatter Sovereignty* (9 January 1882), *The Blackbird* (26 August 1882), *Mordecai Lyons* (26 October 1882), *McSorley's Inflation* (27 November 1882), *The Muddy Day* (2 April 1883), *Cordelia's Aspirations* (5 November 1883), *Dan's Tribulations* (7 April 1884), *McAllister's Legacy* (5 January 1885), *The Leather Patch* (15 February 1886), *Pete* (22 November 1887), *Waddy Googan* (3 September 1888), *McKenna's Flirtation* (2 September 1889), *Reilly and the Four Hundred* (29 December 1890), and *The Woolen Stocking* (9 October 1893). Braham's later efforts (*My Son Dan, Marty Malone,* and *The Finish of Mr. Fresh*) with and without Harrigan proved only marginally successful. In 1898, Braham became the musical director at Wallack's Theatre, occupying that position until his death from kidney disease on 11 April 1905. An inveterate family man whose favorite pastime was sitting on the front stoop, wearing a tennis cap, and smoking a cigar, Braham and his wife Annie had eight children: Annie-Theresa (who married Edward Harrigan), George, Adelaide, Alice ("Ida"), Henrietta ("Etta"), David Junior, Rose, and Edward ("Eddie").

Significant examples of Braham's dance music can be found in "The Golden Choir" (*The Muddy Day*), a schottische dance filled with mischievously teasing grace notes; the "Skidmore Masquerade" (*The Mulligan Guards' Nominee*), a spritely galop with the novel addition of a popgun; "Walking for Dat Cake," a moderately sprightly march that utilized melodic material from the song; a set of "Lancashire Songs and Dances," performed by John Williams, the famous "Lancashire Lad," that displayed a series of hornpipe-like dances in common time and with dotted rhythms, independent of the vocal melody; "Skidmore Fancy Ball" (*The Mulligan Guard Ball*), in which the 6/8 vocal melody was developed for use at the ball into an instrumental march and 3/4 waltz, much in the same way that "Goodnight, My Someone" and "Seventy-Six Trombones" shared the same melodic material in *The Music Man*; and "Jim Jam, Sailors Superfine" (*Reilly and the Four Hundred*) , an archetypal hornpipe, in which the first bar of each "A" section commenced with accented quarters on the beat; and the "B" section was made up almost entirely of triplets that accompanied the dance steps with a whirlwind of motion.

BRAHAM, George

Composer, dance arranger, violinist, and musical director George Braham was born in November 1865, at 283 Elizabeth Street in Manhattan, the son of composer David Braham and Annie Hanley Braham.[85] At an early age, George received violin lessons from his father and when he was a teenager he became a member of his father's orchestra at the Theatre Comique in New York City. In addition to his prowess on the violin, George was an expert walker and often demonstrated that fact to a gambler's advantage. Comedian Edward Harrigan, for example, would take the teenager to a bar and bet that the boy could beat anyone in the establishment in a heel-and-toe race to the nearest bar down the street. George would always win and Harrigan would collect a large amount of money, which he split with his confederate.[86] When he was eighteen, George became the musical director for a touring production of *McSorley's Inflation*, a musical play written by Edward Harrigan and composed by his father. Writing to his sister Annie (Edward Harrigan's wife) on 23 October 1883 from Rhode Island, George bragged about rehearsing his ramshackle three-piece orchestra comprised of cornet, bass, and second violin (George played the first violin part) until they performed his father's music perfectly.[87] During the 1884–1885 season George continued to tour as musical director for two more Harrigan-Braham shows, *Dan's Tribulations* and *Cordelia's Aspirations*, and on 13 April 1885, he provided music and musical direction for a revised version of Harrigan's 1878 sketch *Love vs. Insurance* called *Are You Insured?* which opened in Philadelphia to mostly positive reviews.[88] In the summer of 1889, George joined his father and a company of 50 performers on a fifty-two-week tour of Harrigan-Braham musicals starting with an eight-week engagement at the Alcazar Theatre in San Francisco on 1 July, followed by stops in Denver, Chicago, St. Louis, Buffalo, Washington, D.C., Philadelphia, and Boston. The tour ended on 28 June 1890 and, after a well-deserved vacation at Schroon Lake in Upstate New York, George found himself in his father's orchestra for *Reilly and the Four Hundred* (29 December 1890) and completely smitten with the actress Emma Pollock, a newcomer to Broadway. The affair began during rehearsals and proceeded smoothly until George pawned a ring Emma had given him so that he could bet on a horse that "couldn't lose." It was Pollock's practice to look down into the orchestra pit and smile at George during her number, and when George realized that she would notice the absence of the ring (his horse having lost), he doubled over and began to play with the violin in his lap so that she could not see his fingers.

Used to a well-disciplined pit, David Braham assumed that his son was inebriated. "What's wrong with you?" he whispered, not missing a beat. "Pain in my shoulder. Can't lift my arm," George replied. "Ridiculous," his father shot back. "Lift up that fiddle and play." George hesitated until the number was over, but miraculously recovered for the remainder of the show. The next day he and Harrigan resuscitated their walking race scam, going from bar to bar until George had earned enough money to buy back the ring, and that night, during Pollock's performance, George held his violin high and saw her smile at the ring on his finger.[89] After several years of serving as his father's assistant on tour, George became Edward Harrigan's official musical director at the beginning of the 1895–1896 season, and on 14 September 1903, he provided "catchy" music and musical direction for Harrigan's *Under Cover* at Manhattan's Murray Hill Theatre, which scored a "pronounced hit" with the public (if not all the New York critics).[90] The published selections from George Braham's score included an appealing dance in common time with an accompaniment pattern that resembled a French bourrée and an expansive lyrical melody that evoked the marches of Edward Elgar. Since the musical play centered on the possession of an African-American cemetery, the dance music would have well sufficed for an uplifting funeral procession.

In 1906 George provided incidental dance music as well as musical direction for the New York premiere of *Gallops* (12 February), a play by David Gray that also included songs from *George Washington, Jr.* by George M. Cohan. Braham's contributions included "Elysia. Valse Lente," "Sorilla," an intermezzo, "Hunting Scenes," a descriptive piece, and "Gallons," a march. In his later career, George Braham served as musical director for theatre manager, producer, playwright, and director David Belasco and shared a residence at 545 West 125th Street with his actress sister Rose who never left the house in the daylight. George never left the house at night, except to take the subway down to the Alvin Theatre where he enjoyed counting the attendees at performances of *Mister Roberts*, the long-running comedy co-written and directed by Joshua Logan, the husband of his niece Nedda Harrigan. At the age of eighty-seven, George Braham died peacefully at his home in 1952.

BRAHAM, Harry [Albert]

Like his uncle, David Braham, Harry Braham (born in London on 5 February 1855) was a violinist, composer, and musical director. A genial, fun-loving musician, Harry was often the butt of his cousin Annie, the soon-to-be Mrs. Edward Harrigan's criticism. In a letter dated 20 October 1875, Harrigan replied to one of her remarks about Harry:

> Harry Braham is a garlic eater? I never heard of that before. I have heard of opium eaters, laudanum takers… and bad Negro performers, but I have never heard of a garlic eater before. Oh, Annie, how could you speak of your cousin in that manner? Harry too, the darling! You wrong him. He's a nice boy, and should always try to be on hand for any lady. So forgive him.… I like Harry. He is so nice to the young ladies—always willing to let them get under his umbrella.

Helen Louise Leonard, one of the ladies under Harry's umbrella became his wife and brought him more notoriety than anything he did musically, if only because her stage name was Lillian Russell. The couple met in 1879 while Harry was conducting *H.M.S. Pinafore* for Rice's Opera Bouffe Extravaganza Combination.[91] During the run, Lillian found herself courted by two worthy admirers: Walter Senn, a rich and attractive young man, with a front-row seat to almost every performance, who sent flowers and love notes at nearly every intermission; and handsome Harry Braham, leading the orchestra and making sheeps' eyes at her whenever she was on stage. When Harry realized that he had a serious rival, he redoubled his efforts and, as Russell's biographer Parker Morell noted, swept Lillian quite off her feet, and blasted young Senn completely out of the picture.[92] By the time *Pinafore* completed its run at the Brooklyn Academy of Music, Harry and Lillian had secretly eloped and Mrs. Braham was soon to have a child.

After the baby was born, the couple resumed their separate careers. Harry continued his association with E.E. Rice, collaborating with him and others on the score for *Dreams, or, Fun in a Photograph Gallery* (30 August 1880), a feebly disguised vaudeville that toured with some success. In 1881, Harry was in St. Louis conducting at the Opera House before he joined the tour of *The Electric Spark* as musical director through the middle of 1883. He was offered the musical directorship of a production of Gilbert and Sullivan's *Iolanthe* in Cleveland, Ohio, but he turned it down in favor of an engagement at the Bijou Theatre in Boston, as violinist in his brother John's orchestra. Early in 1884, Harry Braham conducted the *Lights o' London* tour,[93] and later in the year, he became musical director and dance arranger for *A Rag Baby* (14 April 1884), touring extensively through the following year. On 6 May 1885, Braham was granted a divorce from Lillian Russell who had deserted him in favor of composer Edward Solomon.[94] Harry was quoted as saying, "I married her too soon. Money was the trouble. Lillian had a career to make, and gossips told her I stood in the way. They advised her to be single."[95] Following his divorce, Harry Braham faded from theatre news until the late 1880s when he became musical director at the Star Theatre, a position he kept well into the 1890s. He composed the score and dance music for William B. Gill's *Miss Blythe of Duluth*, a tour that began in New London, Connecticut (26 September 1992), and played New York's Grand Opera House (26 December 1892) without much success.[96] In May 1994, Braham composed, selected, and directed the music for *Henry VIII*, a burlesque of Henry Irving's production of Shakespeare's play, at Yale University, and in September, Harry composed, selected, and directed the music for Shakespeare's *The Merry Wives of Windsor* at the Star Theatre. In 1895, Braham left the Star Theatre to conduct the tour of Charles H. Hoyt's *A Runaway Colt*, in 1898–1899, he traveled with a revival of *The Old Homestead*, an earlier production at the Star Theatre for which he arranged music, and after the turn of the century he became musical director at Wallack's Theatre where he arranged the dances for Edward E. Kidder's play *Easy Dawson* (22 August 1905). Little more was heard of Harry until 1919 when *The Brooklyn Daily Eagle* reported that he was musical director of the Majestic Theatre in Brooklyn.[97] In 1938 he reappeared in the news when he and Fred Franklin, another musician, leased a store and basement at 900 Seventh Avenue with plans to open a Bohemian restaurant called *The Kabella*.[98] Harry's death in the same year put an end to the project.[99]

BRAHAM, John J[oseph]

Nephew of David Braham and brother of Harry Braham, John J. Braham was born in London in 1847. He came to the United States in 1859 and began a career as a virtuoso violinist in 1862 at the Canal Street Theatre in New York City, after which he toured extensively, performing in music halls and legitimate theatres. He first appeared in Boston in 1865 at the Morris Brothers' Opera House under the auspices of Tony Pastor,[100] an important engagement since Boston would become his home base for many years. After playing in a variety of theatre orchestras, Braham was hired as musical director at the New Pike's Opera House in Manhattan, and later he accepted the same position at the Griswold Opera House at Troy, New York, where he remained for two seasons. Braham then became musical director at the Adelphi Theatre in Boston and, by 1870, he was leader of a twelve-piece orchestra at the Howard Athenaeum where he arranged the dance music for Harrigan and Hart's sketch *The Little Frauds*. It was John who introduced his uncle David to Edward Harrigan, initiating a personal and professional collaboration that survived for more than thirty years.[101] Seven years later, John Braham was still musical director at the Athenaeum, but he composed music (with E.E. Rice) for the burlesque *Le Petit Corsair* (30 July 1877), libretto by J. Cheever Goodwin and Nathaniel Childs, produced at the prestigious Boston Museum. In the same year, he created the score for *Pippins* (24 December), again with words by J. Cheever Goodwin, at Boston's Globe Theatre.[102] In June 1878, Braham became musical director of the Boston Museum where, on 25 November, he conducted the American premiere of Gilbert and Sullivan's *H.M.S. Pinafore*, creating a flurry of interest among musicians and audiences. In June 1879, Braham leased a lot in Boston on which he planned to create a summer amusement enterprise called Braham's Park Garden in which light dramatic and musical entertainments would be performed in an arena built to accommodate 2,200–2,500 people. Refreshments, with the exception of beer and cigarettes, would be permitted in the auditorium.[103] By November, John, who had mortgaged his violin and published music to fund his dream, was bankrupt, with liabilities amounting to $5,000. Fortuitously, in February 1880, Braham and his orchestra (enlarged to twenty pieces) received an offer to furnish the summer entertainment at the Wentworth Hotel, Newcastle, New Hampshire, so his desire to provide summer work for his musicians and amusement for the public finally came to fruition.

In addition to his work as musical director, John Braham's career as a composer was in full swing. On 21 February 1880, the Standard Theatre in New York premiered his and E.E. Rice's *Hiawatha* to excellent reviews; in April, his and Nathaniel Childs's burlesque *Kafoozleum* was announced for production in New York; in June, he was at work on *Dreams*, again with E.E. Rice and Nathaniel Childs; and on 22 November, *Greek Fire*, another burlesque written by Goodwin and Braham was opening in Lawrence, Massachusetts. The following year, Braham orchestrated the scores of *Olivette*, *The Mascot*, and *Billee Taylor*, for their premiere performances in Boston and, before leaving for his summer engagement in New Hampshire, Braham composed the incidental music for *Coney Island, or, Little Ethel's Prayer*, playing in August at the Union Square Theatre in New York.

In 1882, John Braham was on tour conducting *Patience*, Gilbert and Sullivan's comic opera satirizing the Aesthetic Movement in art, produced by Braham and Scanlan's Boston Miniature Ideal Opera Company. When he returned to Boston, he became musical director of the new Boston Bijou Theatre, where, among other offerings, he conducted an authorized production of Gilbert and Sullivan's *Iolanthe*, and B.E. Woolf's operetta, *An Adamless Eden* (7 July 1884), an out-and-out flop that drove him into bankruptcy once again. Evidently undaunted by his financial losses, Braham continued to pump out musical scores: *Bottom's Dream* at the Park Theatre in Boston (25 May 1885), *Arcadia* at the Bijou Theatre in New York (26 April 1886), *Oxygen* at the Fourteenth Street Theatre (29 May 1886), *The Corsair* at the Bijou Theatre in New York (18 October 1887), *A Stuffed Dog* at the Hollis-Street Theatre in Boston (9 September 1889), *Oolah!*, which closed before reaching New York City (1889), and *Bluebeard, Jr., or, Fatima and the Fairy* at Niblo's Garden (13 January 1890). At the same time he continued to serve as musical director for a number of comic operas, including: an approved tour of Gilbert and Sullivan's *The Mikado* in repertory with *Princess Ida*, one of the team's lesser known works (1886); a New

England tour of Gilbert and Sullivan's *Ruddigore* (1887); a production of Paul Lacôme's *The Marquis* at the Casino Theatre in New York (19 September 1887); a production of Charles Lecocq's *Madelon* at the Casino Theatre (5 December 1887); an authorized tour of Gilbert and Sullivan's *The Yeomen of the Guard* (1888–1889); a revival of Edward Jakobowski's *Erminie* at Niblo's Garden (1 April 1889); the premiere of *The Seven Ages* (music by E.E. Rice; libretto by William Gill and Henry E. Dixey) at the Standard Theatre (7 October 1889); a sanctioned production of Gilbert and Sullivan's *The Gondoliers* at the Amphion Theatre, Williamsburg (Brooklyn)(3 February 1890); and an unsuccessful revival and revision of his burlesque *Pippins* at the Broadway Theatre (26 November).[104]

Braham returned to Boston as musical director at the Park Theatre, leaving his post in February 1894 to travel to London to rehearse and conduct the production of Gilbert and Sullivan's *Utopia, Limited* scheduled for a New York run at the Broadway Theatre beginning 26 March. After the production closed in May, Braham returned to the Park Theatre to begin rehearsals for *The Mascot*, and on New Year's Eve Braham conducted the premiere of B.E. Woolf's new opera, *Westward Ho!* at the Boston Museum. In the years that followed Braham conducted *Excelsior, Jr.*, the first production in Oscar Hammerstein's new Olympia Theatre (25 November 1895); a revival of *Evangeline* at Manhattan Beach (6 June 1896); *The Girl from Paris* at Wallack's Theatre in New York City (12 February 1898); *Rice's Summer Nights* at the Casino Roof Garden (18 June 1898);[105] *The Finish of Mr. Fresh*, a farce comedy composed by his uncle David, at the Star Theatre (7 November 1898); and *An Arabian Girl and Forty Thieves*, for which he composed additional music, at the Herald Square Theatre (29 April 1899).

In 1899, John Braham became the musical director for Koster and Bial's Music Hall in New York, composed the score and dance music for J. Cheever Goodwin's burlesque, *'Round New York in Eighty Minutes* (6 November 1899),[106] and collaborated with Romualdo Marenco on the ballet music for *The Regatta Girl* (14 March 1900). By March 1901, Braham had become the musical director at Daly's Theatre in New York; in August 1907 he was recruited by Jose Van Den Berg to conduct a season of opera at the West End Theatre; and, by the end of 1909, he was working for Lew Fields, conducting a production of *The Prince of Bohemia* at the Hackett Theatre (14 January 1910).

In 1913 Braham began composing incidental music for silent films, first for Frank E. Moore's *Hiawatha*, based on Longfellow's poem, "The Song of Hiawatha," and later for Edward S. Curtis's *In the Land of the Head

Hunters, a fictional documentary of the lives of the native peoples living on the central coast of British Columbia. Braham was supplied with wax cylinders of the native songs and dances but little, if any, of that material found its way into Braham's original score. The film premiered simultaneously at the Casino Theatre in New York and the Moore Theatre in Seattle on 7 December 1914 with Braham's score performed by a symphonic orchestra at each location. Both the music and the film earned the critics' praise[107] but the good reviews were unable to draw an audience and the film failed at the box office.

On 15 March 1901, Braham was arrested on a warrant sworn out by his wife of ten years, Sophia Broschart Braham, charging him with assault. The couple had separate residences: he lived in Prospect Park, Brooklyn, while she lived at Richmond Hill, Queens. She complained to a Queens magistrate that on the morning of 14 March, at five o'clock, Braham forced his way into her house and struck her with such force that her servants had to intercede to save her life. Braham was released on parole while the matter was under review.[108] No further incidents were reported and the couple continued living apart until Braham's death on 28 October 1919.

John J. Braham was a prolific composer of songs, incidental, and dance music for both theatrical use and private consumption. The dances in his published piano music include: "Margretta Polka," "The Mayflower Waltz," "Piccadilly Galop," "Pizzicato: Polka de Concert," "Killarney Quadrille," and the ragtime "The Hoo-Doo Dance." The extant incidental music that exists from his scores displays a serious musicianship and tasteful

Example 19. Dance from "Rowing on the Lake"

orchestration. Braham had a facility for capturing the spirit of the dramatic situation in just a few measures or phrases of music. The charming schottische dance (example 19) in "Rowing on the Lake" (1870), a song performed by Emily Wiseman of John L. Hall's Celebrated Comedy and Burlesque Company, used triplet phrases to depict the rippling effect of the water and evoke the romantic elation inherent in the lyrics of the song. Harmonically adventuresome, the accompaniment progressed seamlessly from the tonic (B flat) to its mediant (D minor) and back again (with the help of a common-tone diminished seventh chord in measure 7), suggesting the gentle undulations of the boat.

Braham employed similar devices in the dance from "Steady Company" (example 20), a song he composed with Edward Harrigan for the sketch, *The Little Frauds* (1872). Another song about romantic delight, "Steady Company" began with a schottische introduction, followed by a waltz verse, after which came a schottische chorus that concluded in waltz time (repeating the first sixteen measures of the first verse). Finally, the music for a schottische dance appeared, utilizing triplets and dotted notes to provide a fitting accompaniment to a sand dance or soft shoe and convey the lighthearted enjoyment expressed in the lyrics. Although the harmonization of the dance was less adventuresome than that of "Rowing on the Lake," another seamless chord progression was accomplished through the use of common-tone diminished seventh chords (measures 1, 3, 5, 7) and the subtle progression from tonic (D major) to submediant (B minor) (measures 1–2, 5–6), devices similar to those in the previous

Example 20. Dance in "Steady Company" from *The Little Frauds*

example. Dramatically, the repetition of measures 1–3 as measures 5–7 in the dance music intimated the steadfastness of the song's protagonist in his maintenance of steady company.

BRATTON, John W[alter]

Born in Delaware on 21 January 1867, singer and composer John W. Bratton was educated at the Harkness Academy in Wilmington and the Philadelphia College of Music. Upon graduation, he was cast in the chorus of *Ship Ahoy* (8 December 1890) and paid $18 a week during the modest run of 50 performances. When the show closed Bratton decided that he could make more money as a composer than as a singer and dashed off a tune, to which his friend Walter H. Ford set lyrics. After selling the song for the princely sum of $10, the pair agreed to write as a team. Their first effort to appear on Broadway was the musical farce called *Hodge, Podge and Co.* (23 October 1900) at the Madison Square Theatre. The reviews of Bratton's music were warm and two of the show's songs (i.e., "My Sunflower Sue" and "Dream Days of Seville") were singled out as above average and destined for popularity.[109] Next the team wrote the score for the vaudeville farce called *Star and Garter* (26 November 1900), after which Bratton began collaborating with lyricist Paul West. With West he wrote "She Reads the New York Papers Every Day" for *Fad and Folly* (27 November 1902), "I'm on the Water Wagon Now" for *The Office Boy* (2 November 1903), the entire score for *The Man from China* (3 May 1904), "In Black and White" for *The School Girl* (1 September 1904), "Can't You Guess" for *Mrs. Black Is Back* (7 November 1904), the entire score for *Buster Brown* (24 January 1905) based on the comic strip character,[110] "Sergeant Brue," "Skating," and "Line of Duty" for *Sergeant Brue* (24 April 1905), "Tricks (or, Put It in Your Repertoire)" for *The Rollicking Girl* (1 May 1905), the entire score for *The Pearl and the Pumpkin* (21 August 1905), "Somebody's Been 'Round Here (Since I've Been Gone)" for *The Gay White Way* (7 October 1907), "My Boy Bill" for *The Merry-Go-Round* (25 April 1908), and the songs for *The Newlyweds and Their Baby* (22 March 1909) in collaboration with Nat D. Ayer on the music and A. Seymour Brown on the lyrics.[111]

As a kind of side occupation, Bratton had been managing and producing shows since 1902 with his partner, John Leffler. Their productions included *Hodge, Podge and Co.*, *The Star and the Garter*, *The Man from China*, *The Pearl and the Pumpkin*, and several touring shows. In 1908,

Bratton joined the National Association of Theatrical Producing Managers and, after completing the score for *The Newlyweds and Their Baby*, he turned away from musical composition and devoted all his time to theatre management. During WWI he briefly returned to songwriting to produce the hit, "Then I'll Come Back to You," a catchy tune with a hopeful wartime message that literally stopped the show in vaudeville productions.[112] Bratton continued producing musical tours through the 1920s and 1930s and took up lyric writing for the compositions of Leo Edwards his collaborator since 1932. He died in his Brooklyn home on 7 February 1947 having just completed the lyrics for a song called "Time Brings Many Changes."[113]

Bratton's hit songs, the most famous of which was the instrumental "The Teddy Bears Picnic" (1907), tended to obscure the importance of the equally tuneful and well-crafted dance music he created for his Broadway musicals. Representative of his efforts are the two dance breaks in the flirtatious duet "Life Is Too Short to Be Wasting Your Time" from *The Man from China*. The first dance, a waltz (example 21) occurs after the initial chorus of the number when Cerise rebuffs Tommy's attempts to hug and kiss her.

Example 21. Waltz in "Life Is Too Short to Be Wasting Your Time" from *The Man from China*

The long, flowing legato melody line (not based on any song in the score) creates a highly romantic atmosphere and the chromatic and stepwise bass line evokes the nearness that Tommy desires. The common-tone diminished seventh chords help provide smooth and easily accessible chord progressions that accompany the melodic phrases with elegant simplicity.

Evidently the waltz gave Tommy the opportunity to sweep Cerise off her feet for, in the second verse, she agrees to accept him as her beau. The dance that follows is another schottische (example 22) full of dotted notes and triplets that appear to characterize the standard method for dance arrangements to express romantic elation and flirtatiousness. To the musi-

Example 22. Schottische in "Life Is Too Short to Be Wasting Your Time" from *The Man from China*

cal paradigm Bratton adds single and double grace notes, dynamic octave chordal leaps (most likely to accent the movement onstage), and specific articulations that alter the character of the music. It is noteworthy that, with the exception of measures 4–5 and 6–7, Bratton dispenses with the stepwise bass line in this dance, using skips to create an appropriately animated and bouncy accompaniment.

An interesting example of Bratton's ballet music is found in the "Prologue" of *The Pearl and the Pumpkin*, an instrumental work that accompanies dance and dialogue and assists in creating the fairy ambiance of

Example 23. "Prologue" from *The Pearl and the Pumpkin*

the production. The "Prologue" begins with majestic chordal structures that introduce the spectator to the Fairy Queen's domain. A ballet of fairies follows in which the sprites of the *dramatis personae* frolic onto the stage to music that is reminiscent of the ballet waltzes of Delibes or Tchaikovsky. The queen enters, the dancing comes to a halt, and the incidental music commences, underscoring the dialogue (example 23). Measures 1–8 underscore the queen's speech and display an appropriately majestic character; measures 9–16 underscore the fairy's lament and exhibit a tension that is commonly associated with melodrama and silent film music. The tonal structures of the first eight measures create an undisturbed consonance that emphasizes the relaxed and self-confidence of the queen; on the other hand, the staccato pedal tones of the bass clef in the final eight measures, create an edgy accompaniment to the often dissonant chordal structures of the treble clef and suggest the anxiety and diffidence of the speaking fairy.

BRAY, John

Actor, playwright, translator, and composer, John Bray was born in England in 1782 and associated with the Royal York Theatre before coming to America in 1805 to join the Chestnut Street Theatre Company in Philadelphia.[114] There he married an actress and the couple remained with the company until the 1813–1814 season [115] when they moved to Boston and joined the troupe at the Federal Street Theatre. Bray's final performance at that theatre occurred on 18 March 1822,[116] and five months later he died at the age of forty. John Bray's theatrical compositions included: *Of Age Tomorrow* (31 January 1806), *The Finger Post, or, Five Miles Off* (26 November 1806), *The Young Hussar, or, Love and Mercy* (26 March 1808), *The Indian Princess, or, La Belle Sauvage* (6 April 1808), *The School for Prodigals* (20 February 1809), *Whitsuntide Frolics, or Harlequin Hurry Scurry* (22 May 1809), *Alberto Albertini, or, The Robber King* (25 January 1811), *Hamlet Travestie* (7 March 1812), *The Boarding House, or, Five Hours at Brighton* (5 June 1812), *Marmion, or, The Battle of Flodden Field* (1 January 1813), *Freemen in Arms, or, A Tribute to the Memory of the Brave* (24 May 1813), and *The Miller and His Men* (4 July 1814).

The Indian Princess (libretto by James Nelson Barker) was Bray's only theatre score that was printed in its entirety, and as such, it offers fine examples of his dance and incidental music. At the end of the second act,

Example 24. "Dance and March" from *The Indian Princess*

for instance, in preparation for battle, Indian Warriors perform a war dance and march (example 24) accompanied by music that is frenzied and exotic sounding, but not the sort of thing audiences today might associate with Native Americans. Audiences (and composers) in the first decade of the nineteenth century, however, had little problem characterizing Indians musically with the use of the harmonic minor scale (with its exotic-sounding skip between the sixth and seventh steps) and chromatic passages such as those found in measures 3–4 of the example. Anything sounding modal or strange in the vocabulary of Western music would suffice because examples of true Native American music were unknown to theatre audiences, who might even find the real thing objectionable and too primitive for a theatrical performance. The fact that the libretto and score indicate that the Indians "march to battle" is an indication that the point of view was distinctly European.

Near the end of the drama, another frenzied piece of music (example 25) accompanies a thrilling melodramatic scene in the libretto:

The king's voice trembles; he stops, unable to proceed. The Indians' eyes are fixed on GRIMOSCO, waiting for the last signal. At this moment the PRINCESS rushes in.... At the same instant, drum and trumpets without. Music. The English seize the uplifted arms of the Indians, and form a tableau, as enter DELWAR and his party. After the music, the soldiers take charge of the Indians. POCAHONTAS flies into the arms of ROLFE.[117]

The music that underscores the action is stirring and hectic, though highly organized into six four-measure phrases. Measures 1–4, utilizing arpeggios

Example 25. "The Princess rushes in—Soldiers secure the Indians" from *The Indian Princess*

and agitated scale-like runs to move from tonic to dominant, are reflected in measures 5–8, employing the same musical devices to move from dominant to tonic. Measures 9–12, with a rousing tremolo effect and triplets in the treble, are echoed in measures 13–16, where the tremolo continues in the treble but the triplets move to the bass. The downward progressing stepwise melody in measures 17–20 outlines a traditional subdominant–tonic–dominant–tonic harmonization, leading to the cadence in measures 21–24, again using stepwise runs and arpeggios, followed by a two-measure coda that emphasizes the tonic and signals an end to the hostilities.

BREIL, Joseph Carl

Composer, arranger, conductor, and lyric tenor Joseph Carl Breil was born in Pittsburgh on 29 June 1870.[118] He was educated at the Pittsburgh Catholic College of the Holy Ghost (now Duquesne University),[119] St Fidelis College in Butler, Pennsylvania, and Curry Commercial College in Pittsburgh before traveling to Leipzig to study law. In Leipzig, Breil's academic interest moved from law to music and he entered the Leipzig Conservatory to study singing and music composition. Exhibiting a special talent as a vocalist, Breil continued his singing lessons in Milan and Philadelphia, where he became a protégé of Giuseppe del Puente, one of the most famous opera baritones in Europe in America. After touring as principal tenor with the Emma Juch Grand English Opera Company during the 1891–1892 season, Breil returned to Pittsburgh to become a singing teacher and choir director at St. Paul's Cathedral. In 1897, he left St. Paul's to become musical director for a variety of theatre companies touring out of Chicago and New York City, and beginning in 1903, he worked for Chappell, a major publisher of theatrical music, as a staff arranger and composer of instrumental music. In 1909, he composed the incidental music for *The Climax* (12 April, at Weber's Music Hall), a combination of music, drama, and comedy, with bohemian atmosphere, from which he achieved his first popular hit, "The Song of a Soul." On 3 June 1909, *The New York Times* reported that Joseph Weber commissioned Breil to compose an opera using the song as its theme, but instead, the composer replied the following year with the light opera, *Love Laughs at Locksmiths* (26 October 1910), produced by his own New Opera Company at Kingston, New York. In 1912, after several years of compiling cue sheets made from existing music for D.W. Griffith's Biograph short silent films, Breil composed and arranged the music for the American release of Sarah Bernhardt's *Les amours de la reine Elizabeth* (*Queen Elizabeth*), one of the earliest examples of a film score arranged specifically for a film.

In 1913, Breil composed two more light operas, *Professor Tattle* and *The Seventh Chord*, a musical about the struggles of a young composer who discovers a great singer and finds success, produced during the month of April at the Illinois Theatre in Chicago and conducted by the composer-arranger Gustave Kerker. In June 1914, Briel served as the musical director for a production of Gabriele D'Annunzio's *Cabiria* at the Illinois Theatre, and in 1915, Breil returned to film work, composing and arranging music for *The Birth of a Nation*, *Double Trouble*, *The Lamb*, *The Lily and the Rose*, *The Penitents*, *Martyrs of the Alamo*, and *The Sable Lorcha*. In 1916, he composed *Intolerance: Love's Struggle throughout the Ages*, and *The Wood Nymph*; in 1917 Breil supplied the music for the lyric tragedy in one act, *The Legend*; and in 1918, he selected and composed music for the films, *Carmen*, and *The Birth of a Race*. *The Legend* was produced by the Metropolitan Opera on 12 March 1919, as part of a triptych of American operas that also included John Hugo's *The Temple Dancer* and Charles Cadman's *Shanewis*. Breil's work did not receive favorable reviews: *The New York Times* called it "heavy as unleavened dough;... melodious and commonplace. It ambles along and chokes the action whenever it can."[120] Following the failure of his serious opera, Breil continued composing original scores for films that included *The White Rose* (1923), *The White Sister* (1923), *The Dramatic Life of Abraham Lincoln* (1924), *America* (1924), and the San Francisco world premiere of *The Phantom of the Opera*. On 24 Novemberr 1925, his last opera, *Der Asra*, opened at the Gamut Club Theatre in Los Angeles to bad reviews, and Breil died of a heart attack two months later, on 23 January 1926, survived by his wife Alta.

It is perhaps unfortunate that Breil was so driven to compose vocal music when his finest work appeared in the realm of incidental scores for film. Certainly the most interesting passages in his opera, *The Legend*, are the voiceless underscores that accompany onstage action. Especially effective are the sixty-nine measures that follow the love duet between Carmelita Stackareff and her soldier-lover, Stephen Pauloff, depicting a variety of moods and dramatic situations in the best tradition of melodramatic music. The scene depicted is described as follows in the score:

> They embrace, then sit before the fire and gaze dreamily into it. Meanwhile the storm outside grows in intensity. Holding hands they dream on oblivious of it. (*Lightning*.)

> (*Lightning and thunder.*) They are startled with the crash but soon regain their composure. (*Lightning and thunder.*) They are startled again. Stephen rises. Stephen goes to the window and looks out. Carmelita looks after him. (*Thunder and lightning.*) (*The winds shriek.*) Carmelita shows signs of alarm. Stephen returns to her and holds her protectingly in his arms. The storm abates. Stephen again goes to the window.[121]

The music that accompanies this romantic storm episode is hardly original; it emulates centuries of operatic storm music from Rossini to Wagner. But the purpose of underscore is to convey the spirit of the dramatic event and to do that, composers often rely on sounds and musical constructions that are familiar to an audience. Breil knew how to tap into an audience's understanding of musical associations and how to provide them with sounds that immediately connect them with the dramatic situation. In an article about film scoring, Breil noted: "It is no easy matter to score a motion picture. And the musician who is ambitious to do this type of work must have a comprehensive knowledge of the music that has been written, and a high degree of appreciation of the values necessary, for the scorer must fit his harmonies to the elusive emotions of the players on the screen."[122] Such was Breil's talent, both in film and on the stage.

BRINKWORTH, W[illiam] H.

English musical director, composer, and dance arranger W. H. Brinkworth was born in London in 1839. Before he came to America in 1869, he was musical director and composer at the Britannia Theatre in London, where he provided incidental music for the burlesques, *Old Daddy Longlegs and Sir Regent Circus, or, The Race for the Golden Apples* (January 1866), *The Dark King of the Black Mountains!, or, The Newly Married Man* (2 April 1866), *Faust, or, Marguerite's Mangle* (1 April 1867), *Cherry and Fair Star* (6 May 1867), and *Bhlutzherrhanbothrumh, or, The dwarf of the diamond dell!* (21 December 1868).[123] After arriving in New York City, Brinkworth accepted the post of musical director at Wood's Museum, where he first appeared in theatre listings as the musical arranger of *The Golden Butterfly* (5 September 1870), for which he supplied a variety of specialties, including "Delightful Concerted Music and Amazing Dance by the King," "The love of a Queen, which finds vent in a comic dance," "A splendid piece of concerted music and a stunning Dance," and a "Grand Transformation Scene." Brinkworth followed with *Humpty Dumpty Junior, or, The Fairy of the Diamond Mines and the Giant's Festival* (3 October 1870), for which he arranged a grand ballet, "Fleurs et Papillons"; *Rip Van Winkle, or, a 20 Year's Snooze* (3 October 1870), for which he again was credited as musical arranger as well as musical director; and *The Grand Duchess*, a revival of Offenbach's comic opera, for which he served as conductor beginning 14 November 1870. In the years that followed, the plays for which Brinkworth supplied musical direction included: the burlesque extravaganza, *Lucretia Borgia, or, The Cup of Cold Poison!* (13 February 1871); *Monte Cristo* (20 February 1871); *The Streets of New York* (24 April 1871); *Uncle Tom's Cabin* (1 May 1871); *Through by Daylight* (3 July 1871); *Les Misérables* (17 July 1871); *Lola* (21 August 1871); *The Octoroon* (16 October 1871); *Beauty and the Beast* (8 January 1872); *Little Red Riding-Hood* (15 January 1872); *Dick Whittington and His Cat* (5 February 1872), for which he also composed the score; *Poll and Partner Joe* (19 February 1872), for which he composed the music; *Luna, or, the Little Boy Who Cried for the Moon* (4 March 1872), for which he also provided the score; *Lurline, or, The Knight and the Naiads* (1 April 1872), for which he composed the music; *Ixion* (29 April 1872), a revival of the popular burlesque extravaganza; and *Red Mazeppa, or, the Madman of the Plains* (17 June 1872).

Brinkworth continued at his post at Wood's Museum for the next two seasons, composing and selecting overtures, incidental, and dance music for productions including *Chow, Chow, or A Tale of Pekin* (9 September 1872); *The Three Mus-Ke-Teers* (21 October 1872);*The Babes in the Wood* (16 December 1872); *Jack the Giant Killer* (30 December 1872); *Dick the Chevalier* (1 September 1873); *The Life and Death of Natty Bumpo* (13 October 1873); and *Davy Crockett* (30 October 1873). Brinkworth left Wood's Museum prior to the 1875–1876 season to become musical director at the Globe Theatre. His final appearance in theatre notices was associated with the abrupt closing of the theatre on 11 September 1875 caused by the management's failure to pay actors' and musicians' salaries.[124] The *New York Clipper* revealed that Brinkworth, "the leader of the orchestra, withdrew from the theatre on Thursday morning, and after the entertainments of that evening Manager [Robert W.] Butler, stage manager Mons. La Thorne, and ballet-master Blandowski withdrew from the concern.... The performers, learning that Mr. Butler had withdrawn from the management, became more clamorous for money than ever. On Friday several of the most prominent ones failed to appear, and on Saturday the theatre closed."[125] Unhappy with his prospects in New York, Brinkworth returned to London where he continued to compose and publish songs through 1890. In 1916 Brickworth died at his home in Kent, England.

A typical example of Brinkworth's American dance music is found at the end of "Happy Little Flip-Flaps" (example 26), a song composed for T. De Bonay and Charles Sturgis, African-American impersonators in the company at Wood's Museum.[126] The structure, chord progressions, and melodic contour of measures 1 through the second ending and 21 through the second ending are evocative of the "Rondeau des Métamorphoses" in

Example 26. Dance from "Happy Little Flip-Flaps"

Offenbach's *Orphée aux Enfers*, which was first performed in English in New York City on 22 April 1874, a year before Brinkworth's dance was published. Measures 13–14 (with grace notes and seconds in the melody) also imitate the introduction to the "Galop Infernal" from the same opera. It is not known if Brinkworth's dance was consciously composed to suggest the Offenbach melodies, but their presence certainly helped to create a lively schottische that was performed with great success.

BRISTOW, George F[rederick]

Composer, musical director, teacher, and performer, George F. Bristow was born in Brooklyn on 19 December 1825, the son of William Richard Bristow, a clarinetist and conductor who had emigrated from England. At an early age, Bristow studied the piano with his father; as he grew older, he studied the violin with Norwegian composer Ole Bull and took classes in harmony, counterpoint, and orchestration from German-born conductor Henry Christian Timm and English composer Sir George MacFarren, When he was thirteen, Bristow played violin (and, occasionally piano) in New York's Olympic Theatre orchestra, an able sextet that accompanied plays and musical theatre entertainments, and when he turned eighteen, he joined the New York Philharmonic Society Orchestra. In the mid-1850s he served as musical director for the summer season of the Pyne and Harrison Company at Niblo's Garden, conducting a series of operas in repertory, including Wallace's *Maritana* (25 May 1855), Balfe's *The Bohemian Girl* (2 June 1855), Fitzwilliam's *A Queen of a Day* (2 June 1855), Balfe's *The Daughter of St. Mark* (18 June 1855), and Pepusch's *The Beggar's Opera* (14 September 1855).

On 27 September, Bristow's original opera, *Rip Van Winkle* was produced by the company to generally favorable reviews. The work exhibited fine vocal writing as well as interesting incidental and dance music that demonstrated the proficiency of a classically-trained composer. Although Bristow relied heavily on traditional tonic-subdominant-dominant progressions in the "Morris Dance," the harmonies displayed unexpected chord changes that helped to create the rustic character of the work. The melody of the dance was composed in dotted rhythms in a kind of perpetual motion construction, reminiscent of Mendelssohn's incidental music to *A Midsummer Night's Dream*, with a sufficient number of syncopations and accented phrases to allow for attractive choreography. In addition to his theatre work, Bristow conducted various choral ensembles and served as choir director in New York's churches. He began teaching in the New York public school system in 1854 and in 1866 he founded the Westchester Philharmonic Society in Morrisania (South Bronx), New York. In addition he was conductor of the Union Harmonic Society in Morrisania in 1868 and the Harlem Mendelssohn Union in 1878.

A musical nationalist, Bristow was one of a group of nineteenth-century American composers who attempted to establish an "American" style in art music, even though his own compositions exhibit strong ties with the European music of his day.[127] Among his 135 compositions, Bristow left two incomplete operas, *Columbus* (1861) and *The King of the Mountains* (1894); an oratorio, *Daniel* (1867); cantatas, *The Pioneer* (1872), *The Great Republic,* and *Ode to the American Union* (1879); religious choral works, instrumental overtures, five symphonies, and various dance compositions for orchestra and solo piano. An interest in dance forms permeated his early work, beginning with "Zip Coon with Variations" (1840), and including "The Boatman's Dance with Variation" (1844), "Grand Waltz de Bravura" (1845), "Captain Raynor's Quickstep" (1849), and "Tripler Schottisch" (1850). Bristow's fascination with dance continued to be displayed in his later efforts, particularly in his evocation of the Italian hopping dance, "Saltarello" (1886). Bristow remained active in the musical life of New York and in the musical education of young New Yorkers up until his death on 13 December 1898.

BRODE, Herman

Composer, dance arranger, and musical director Herman Brode was born in Germany in 1849 where he received musical instruction from an early age. He came to America in the 1870s and is first registered in the theatre listings of New York City in June 1877 as the musical director of Wallack's Theatre.[128] Brode remained there for three successful seasons[129] before going on tour with the Kiralfy Brothers' production of *Sieba and the Seven Ravens*, which opened for an extended run at the Star Theatre on 18 August 1884. Brode was back at Wallack's Theatre (rechristened Palmer's Theatre) for the 1889–1890 season,[130] conducting, among other things, a revival of Gilbert and Sullivan's *Patience, or Bunthorne's Bride* (30 August 1892). Brode was still conducting at the newly refurbished theatre in 1897— two years after the name had been changed back to Wallack's. Shortly before the turn of the century, Brode became the musical director of the Grand Opera House, a post he held until his death on 16 May 1904, due to "a complication of diseases."[131] He was survived by his wife.

The Silver King, a melodrama by Henry Arthur Jones and one of the successes at Wallack's Theatre (28 January 1883), presents one of the few extant incidental scores composed by Herman Brode. The "March" (example 27) from the score is composed in a European march structure: Introduction–First Strain (A)–||:Second Strain (B) :||–Introduction to the Trio–Trio (C)–New Strain (D)–First Strain (A)–||:Second Strain (B) :||. The melody is fashioned from an interesting balance between stepwise motion and leaps and the accompaniment follows the traditional tonic–subdominant–dominant scheme with the occasional secondary

Example 27. "March" from The Silver King

dominant and common-tone diminished seventh chord added for color. Example 27 above presents the first and second strains of the march. Note the distinctive articulation marks clearly differentiating the character of each musical phrase.

Herman Brode may not have been innovative or especially original in his compositions and arrangements but he was a fine technician, able to create or judiciously select appropriate music for every play he accompanied.

BROSCHI, Karl

Little is known about the musical director and composer Karl Broschi, who arranged the ballet music for the historical dramatic pageant, *Claudius Nero*, at Niblo's Garden (21 October 1890). The spectacular production engaged a cast of five hundred people, including thirty actors and actresses, a large ballet corps, trained athletes, wrestlers, acrobats, performers of gladiatorial sports, charioteers, trumpeters, Roman musicians, an enlarged orchestra, and a sizeable and disciplined chorus.[132] The pageant featured a troupe of trained lions that "displayed considerable intelligence and docility"[133] in addition to a show-stopping castanet dance, a "Combat de Danse," a Grand Ballet, entitled "L'Amour Triomphant," a "Grand Ballet Divertissement," the dazzling burning of Rome (during which Nero watches from a balcony and plays a lyre), and a stunning "Apotheosis." *The New York Times* called *Claudius Nero* "a great spectacle, and as a perfect production easily occupies the foremost place in the records of old Niblo's many spectacular successes."[134] The *New York Clipper* suggested that "the Niblo's version may be at once credited with dignity, ingenuity and picturesqueness as a drama, while also possessing some excellent but not specially elaborate features as a spectacle."[135] Given the critical success of the presentation, it is unfortunate that nothing of Broschi's epic score has survived.

C

CALDWELL, Anne [Anna]

Librettist, lyricist, and composer Anne Caldwell was born in Boston on 30 August 1867 and educated at the Friends Academy in New Bedford, Massachusetts. At an early age, Anne learned to play the piano from her musician mother and started improvising words to the opera scores her mother played on the piano. She began her theatre career as a singer with the Juvenile Opera Company and became the leading lady with Farrar and Florence's Opera Company when she was seventeen.[136] The following year she made her debut in a dramatic role with Mann and Benoit's Company in Baltimore to outstanding reviews, but her career as a dramatic actress was cut short on 2 August 1885, when she married William Vinal. Caldwell retired from the stage and moved back to Boston to begin a family with her husband.[137] Four years later, when her daughter Molly (Marianna Sarah) was three years old, Anne returned to acting in a production of H. Grattan Donnelly's *Mamma* at the Harrisburg Opera House. In 1890, she toured with the *U and I* Company; on 1 August 1891, she joined the cast of *The Tar and the Tartar* in New York City; and in December, she was cast as the juvenile dancing lead in *The Spider and the Fly* tour. Over the next several years, both in plays and in vaudeville, Caldwell was listed as a performer in theatre playbills all over the country. Even, on 4 March 1897, when her husband was killed in a gas explosion at a subway stop in Boston, she was at the Hopkins' Grand Opera House in St. Louis doing her vaudeville act. In the summer of 1898, she was cast as the dashing ingénue in the tour of *A Sure Cure* that played the Star Theatre in New York in late September; and on 19 December, she and Charles Wayne made their first appearance as a team in New Haven, performing *To Boston on Business*, a vaudeville act written especially for them by George M. Cohan. The team continued playing the act until May 1902 when Caldwell retired from the stage again, and the partnership was dissolved.[138] Her motives for retirement were evidently unclear, for, a year later her name appears in vaudeville bills at theatres east of the Mississippi

River until 15 August 1904 when she married lyric-writer James J. O'Dea. In the year following their marriage, Caldwell and O'Day collaborated on the song, "Saturday Afternoon" featured in Liza Lehmann's musical farce *Sergeant Brue* (24 April 1905); and in 1906, the pair produced "Old Man Manhattan" for Gustave Kerker's *The Social Whirl* (9 April 1906). In the same year, Caldwell composed another melody to which her husband set lyrics. The result was "Young Antelope," a catchy and novel "Indianesque" song that the *New York Clipper* called "a happy inspiration" and "a sure-fire hit."[139] The following year, Anne collaborated with composer Manuel Klein on the music for *The Top o' Th' World* (lyrics by her husband), produced at the Majestic Theatre in New York City, beginning 19 October.[140]

The Christmas-themed musical inspired Caldwell to compose songs and dance music for a number of childlike situations. "Don't You Want to Be My Bow-wow-wow," a song and dance sung by six young girls and danced by them with six well-trained collies was the hit of the evening. Although Caldwell's dance music for the number was little more than an instrumental version of the sung melody, it was enough to allow the little girls and dogs to execute what the reviews called "the dancing novelty of the season." The *New York Clipper* provided a colorful account of the number: "In this number, after six small girls had executed several dancing steps, six beautiful collie dogs trotted on the stage and found their proper places, lying down, and allowing just enough space between each to permit the girls to dance around and jump over the dogs' bodies, and at the finish of the number each dog "sat up" on his haunches and received a kiss for his good behavior. During the dance each dog held his position rigidly and it was a fine example of animal training. This number received ringing applause."[141] "Hand Me Out a Laugh," sung by Aurora Borealis, Jack Frost, and Candy Kid, offered a more interesting dance arrangement developed from phrases of the song, rather than simply an instrumental duplication of the melody. The "Doll Song" included four distinctive dance arrangements: a syncopated ragtime cakewalk following the "Southern Doll" section of the song; a "Turkey in the Straw" buck-and-wing dance after the "Stumpy Soldier" section; a soft-shoe dance (with the indication "Very marked") in 6/8 and the minor mode following the Pierrot section; and a final galop (marked "furioso"), immediately after the soft shoe dance. Each of the dances was clearly based on the sung melody that preceded it; still, the development of each melody into a specific style of dance music required an arranger with a keen knowledge of the dance (Caldwell was, after all, a dancer) and an adroit musical technique. The dance music in Caldwell's other numbers—"Little Brown Hen" and "The One Girl"—was again based on instrumental versions of the songs, though the schottische transformation of the melody of "The One Girl" is of interest.

Anne Caldwell followed her success as a composer with writing plays and providing librettos and lyrics to many of the popular composer of the day:[142] Jerome Kern, Victor Herbert, Ivan Caryll, Hugo Felix, Raymond Hubbell, Vincent Youmans, and Dave Stamper. She moved out to Hollywood in 1929 to work in film at RKO Studios, where she contributed the story, dialogue, and lyrics for *Dixiana* (1930),[143] the dialogue and lyrics for *Half Shot at Sunrise* (1930), and the play on which *Flying Down to Rio* (1933) was based. She died quietly in the company of her children, Anthony Patrick O'Dea and Molly Vinal, at her home in Beverly Hills on 22 October 1936.[144]

CARR, Benjamin

Composer, dance arranger, performer, and teacher, Benjamin Carr was born in London on 12 September 1768. From an early age, Carr was educated in the business of music by his father, Joseph, who was a music publisher and retailer, and in the theory and art of music by noted Church musicians, Charles and Samuel Wesley, and Dr. Samuel Arnold, with whom Carr studied the organ and musical composition. When he was twenty-four, he composed a pastoral opera, *Philander and Silvia, or, Love Crown'd at Last*, produced at Sadler's Wells on 16 October 1892. The following year he immigrated to the United States and set up music publishing establishments in Philadelphia and New York.[145] While carrying on the daily business of engraving and publishing music, Carr continued to compose songs and dances for popular consumption as well as incidental and dance music for the theatre. According to Oscar Sonneck, "Carr tried his hand successfully at almost every branch of composition. He was a thoroughly trained composer of the [Carl] Philip Emmanuel Bach school and his works are distinguished by a pleasing softness of lines."[146] His early theatre compositions include: the ballet, *The Caledonian Frolic* (Boston) (2 November 1793); incidental music for *The Patriot, or, Liberty Asserted* (New York) (5 June 1794); musical arrangements for *The Spanish Barber, or, Fruitless Precaution* (Philadelphia) (7 July 1894); additional music for *The Children in the Wood* (Philadelphia) (24 November 1794); incidental music for *Macbeth* (New York) (14 January 1795); music for the pantomime, *Poor Jack , or, The Sailor's Return*; (AKA *The Sailor's Landlady; The Generous Sailor; The Shipwrecked Sailor*) (New York) (7 April 1795); incidental music for *School for Greybeards, or, The Mourning Bride* (New York) (20 April 1795); new accompaniments for *The Deserter* (New York) (19 May 1795); songs and incidental music for the opera, *The Archers* (New York) (18 April 1796);songs and incidental music for the comic opera, *Bourville Castle, or, The Gallic Orphan* (New York) (16 January 1897); music for the entertainment, *The American in London, or, Love at First Sight* [AKA *The American Merchant in London*] (Philadelphia) (28 March 1798); additional music for *The Red Cross Knights* (Philadelphia) (12July 1802); and new music for *The Wife of Two Husbands* (New York 4 April 1804).[147] Carr also performed as a ballad singer in the popular theatres and performed with the Old American Company in New York[148] during the 1794–1795 season; but as Oscar Sonneck has noted, it was as a pianist, organist, composer, teacher, publisher, and conductor, that he would exert the greatest influence on the musical life of Philadelphia.[149] Carr served as organist at St. Augustine's Catholic Church from 1801 until his death in 1831, and served in the same capacity at St. Peter's Episcopal Church for nearly as long. In 1820, he was one of the founders of the Musical Fund Society in Philadelphia whose prime object was to "reform the state of neglect into which the beautiful art of music had fallen."[150] In addition to his theatre compositions, Carr produced a great many secular songs and sacred works as well as three educational volumes: *Lessons and Exercises in Vocal Music* (1811), *The Analytical Instructor* (1826), and *Short Methods of Modulating from One Key to Another* (no date).

Carr's best-known composition, *Federal Overture*, which premiered at the Cedar Street Theatre in Philadelphia on 22 September 1894, includes a number of popular national tunes: the "Marseillaise," " Ça ira," "O, Dear, What Can the Matter Be?," "Rose Tree," "Carmagnole," "President's March," and "Yankee Doodle." The publication of a piano reduction of the *Federal Overture* in January 1795 marks the first time "Yankee Doodle" appeared in print in America. While the overture, popular in theatres in Philadelphia and New York, offers evidence of Carr's facility as an arranger and chooser of musical selections, it does not provide a complete depiction of Carr's own compositional style. For that we must turn to the extant instrumental and vocal fragments from *The Archers, or, Mountaineers of Switzerland*, Carr's ballad opera (libretto by William Dunlap), which was produced by the Old American Company at the John Street Theatre in New York City on 18 April 1796. Four excerpts from the opera are said to exist: The "Rondo" from the "Overture to *The Archers*" published as No. 7 of Carr's *Musical Miscellany* (1813), the song, "Why, Huntress, Why," printed in Carr's *Musical Journal* (1800), "A Fragment" ("There liv'd in Altdorf City fair"), appearing in Carr's second book of *Elegant Extracts* for the German flute or violin (1796), and the "March in *The Archers*" issued in Carr's *Military Amusement* (1796).[151] Each of these selections exhibit a style of composition called *empfindsamer Stil*, an aesthetic associated with northern Germany in the middle of the 18th century, designed to achieve an intimate, sensitive, and subjective expres-

Example 28. "Rondo" from the "Overture to *The Archers*"

sion, with gentle tears of melancholy the typically desired response.[152] In simple terms, music adhering to this style displayed a gracefulness without excessive ornamentation, a dramatic fluidity that permitted seamless transitions from one emotion to another, and straightforward homophonic constructions that accompanied an unpretentious melody, typically divided into eight-measure periods. The "Rondo" (example 28) presents a fine illustration of Carr's intimately sensitive and graceful style. Note how the melodic and harmonic structures in measures 1–6 are mirrored in measures 9–13, the melody almost exactly, the harmony, down an octave. Note also the conservative use of ornamentation (one *grupetto* or turn, two grace notes, and three trills) and harmony (tonic, dominant, subdominant, and secondary dominant constructions in a broken-chord, "Alberti bass" pattern), and the elegant extended cadence in measures 16–22, employing the simple up and down movement of a D major scale.

After Carr died in 1831, the Musical Fund Society erected a monument to his memory at St. Peter's Church in Philadelphia, with an inscription that read:

> Benjamin Carr
> a distinguished professor of music
> died May 24, 1831, aged 62 years.
>
> Charitable, without ostentation,
> faithful and true in his friendship,
> with the intelligence of a man
> he united the simplicity of a child.
>
> In testimony of the high esteem in which he
> was held, this monument is erected by
> his friends and associates of the
> Musical Fund Society of Philadelphia.[153]

CARR, F[rank] Osmond

Born in Yorkshire, England on 23 April 1858, composer F. Osmond Carr studied music at Cambridge and Oxford Universities before he began to compose music for burlesques on the London stage. His first effort (with lyricist Adrian Ross), *Faddimir, or, The Triumph of Orthodoxy*, was produced at the Vaudeville Theatre on 29 April 1889.[154] The work was sufficiently successful to earn the notice of London burlesque producer, George Edwardes, who immediately set the pair to work for him. With Ross, Carr composed the burlesque *Joan of Arc, or, The Merry Maid of Orleans* (17 January 1891); with Henry Pettitt and George Sims, he produced another burlesque, *Blue Eyed Susan* (6 February 1892); again with Ross, Carr composed the inchoate musical comedies, *In Town* (15 October 1892), *Morocco Bound* (13 April 1893), and *Go Bang* (10 March 1894). With W.S. Gilbert (no longer collaborating with Arthur Sullivan), Carr composed the comic opera *His Excellency* (27 October 1894) which proved to become an international success. Following his successful partnership with Gilbert, Carr worked with a number of wordsmiths, but without success. His later work was relegated to provincial productions,[155] with the exception of a ballet, *Sir Roger de Coverly*, produced at the Empire Theatre, London on 7 May 1907.[156]

In New York City, Carr's first production appeared on 2 May 1892 when the Columbia College Dramatic Club presented the burlesque *Blue Eyes Susan* at the Academy of Music.[157] Nearly three years later, "Di, Di, Di," a number from *Go Bang* was interpolated into the scores of *A Run on the Bank* (14 January 1895) at the Bijou Theatre and *Off the Earth* (21 January 1895) at the Harlem Opera House. A production of *His Excellency* followed at the Broadway Theatre on 14 October 1895, succeeded by *In Town* at the Knickerbocker Theatre on 6 September 1897. Carr's musicals produced in London all included a notable amount of dance and incidental music, and the three works that crossed the Atlantic remained relatively intact. Carr's dance music, often based on the vocal melody that preceded it, was invariably tuneful and rhythmic, with a dynamic and propelling accompaniment. Even in legato dance music, like that used in the "Ballet of Hussars" in *His Excellency*, there was a constant eighth note pulse in the accompaniment that maintained the momentum, never permitting the weight of chord structures or long-held notes to interrupt the thrust of the dance.

Carr died of a heart attack in Middlesex, England on 29 August 1816.

CARYLL, Ivan

Composer, musical director, and dance arranger Ivan Caryll was born Félix Marie Henri Tilkin on 12 May 1861 in Liège, Belgium. He studied music at the Liège Conservatoire then moved to France to study singing at the Conservatory in Paris. After completing his studies in Paris, Caryll moved to London in 1882, where he gave music lessons and produced a number of journeyman songs before getting his first "big break" in 1886, while working on Edward Jakobowski's hit musical, *Erminie*, at the Comedy Theatre. Violet Melnotte, the producer of *Erminie*, had been looking for a comic opera to follow her present hit, and she decided to produce Caryll's opéra-comique, *The Lily of Léoville*, a French composition dating from Caryll's days in Paris.[158] The London production was not a success, but the music was sufficiently lauded to earn Caryll currency with London's musical theatre producers who hired him to compose additional songs for their shows. Caryll was blessed with another golden opportunity when Henry J. Leslie hired him as musical director for his production of *Dorothy* at the Prince of Wales Theatre. He followed this position with the musical directorship of the Lyric Theatre where, after years of composing curtain raisers and revamping foreign musicals, Caryll composed his first full-length English musical, a burlesque entitled *Little Christopher Columbus* (10 October 1893), the success of which catapulted him to a fifteen-year residence at London's Gaiety Theatre as musical director and house composer. Caryll's triumphs at the Gaiety included: *The Shop Girl* (24 November 1894), *The Circus Girl* (5 December 1896), *A Runaway Girl* (21 May 1898), *The Messenger Boy* (3 February 1900), *The Toreador* (17 June 1901), *The Spring Chicken* (30 May 1905), *The New Aladdin* (29 September 1906), and *Our Miss Gibbs* (23 January 1909).[159] During his tenure at the Gaiety, Caryll's work was not limited to that theatre. His musical efforts that were produced at other theatres in London included: *The Gay Parisienne* (USA title: *The Girl from Paris*) (Duke of York Theatre, 4 April 1896), *The Girl from Kays* (Apollo Theatre, 15 November 1902), *The Duchess of Dantzig* (Lyric Theatre, 17 October 1903), *The Earl and the Girl* (Adelphi Theatre, 10 December 1903), and *The Little Cherub* (AKA *The Girl on the Stage*) (Prince of Wales Theatre (13 January 1906).

In 1910 Ivan Caryll turned his attention to the New York theatre scene and produced over a dozen musical comedies specifically for American audiences.[160] These included *The Pink Lady* (13 March 1911), *Oh! Oh! Delphine* (30 September 1912), *The Little Café* (10 November 1913), *Chin-Chin* (20 October 1914), *Papa's Darling* (2 November 1914), *Jack o'Lantern* (16 October 1917), *The Girl Behind the Gun* (AKA *Kissing Time*) (16 September 1918, and *The Canary* (4 November 1918). According to Kurt Gänzl, "Caryll's career encompasses three eras of musical theatre and he seemed equally happy in each of them. If his greatest successes were made in the light musical comedy area, epitomized by the

Gaiety Theatre shows in which he made his name, he proved with scores as divergent as the classic operetta *The Duchess of Dantzig*... on the one hand and the post-war *The Girl Behind the Gun*, with its modern fox-trot and one-step rhythms, on the other, that he was a theatre composer who ... could and would move with times and musical styles."[161] Harry B. Smith who collaborated with Caryll on *Papa's Darling* and *The Canary* recalled:

> Caryll was a clever business man as well as a successful composer. He occasionally bought the American rights to French farces and when he told the story of one of his purchases to a manager, Caryl would laugh so heartily that apoplexy seemed imminent. His laughter was infectious, and while he and the manager were in the throes of hilarity, a contract would be signed for the play. ...Caryll had related to [producers] Klaw and Erlanger the plot of his latest purchase in the Parisian farce line and the managers controlled their laughter long enough to make a contract with me to adapt this humorous masterpiece. Hence the invitation from Caryll to visit him in Normandy. When I arrived in Paris, I received a telegram from the composer, stating that the plumbing was out of order at the château.... Instead of going to Normandy, I was to be his guest at his villa at Cap Ferrat... on the Mediterranean shore near Monte Carlo.... He was very systematic in his work, starting in at daybreak and keeping busy at the piano till noon. In the afternoon we would drive over the mountain roads of the Alps Maritimes; sometimes dining at a little restaurant in the mountains where we could make the personal acquaintance of a trout in a brook and presently have him on a plate.[162]

Once he began to compose musicals for American audiences, it was Caryll's practice to commute from his castle in Normandy, or his homes in London and Paris, or his villa near Monte Carlo, to the Ambassador Hotel in Manhattan, or his country house in Ardsley, on the Hudson River. On 21 September 1921, he arrived with a new musical, *Little Miss Raffles*, ready to be produced by Charles Dillingham. On 20 November, he completed the final number of the show, and on the following day, in the middle of a rehearsal, Caryll suffered a severe hemorrhage that took his life on 29 November 1921, a week before *Little Miss Raffles* was scheduled to give its premiere performance in New Haven. Caryll's funeral was held three days later at St. Patrick's Cathedral. Ivan Caryll was married twice: first to the American musical comedy actress Geraldine Ulmar, and next to Maud Hill, an actress-singer who appeared in many of his works. He left an estate valued at £7,873.[163]

Ivan Caryll's dance music was, for the most part, conservative, relying mostly on instrumental arrangements of the vocal melody that preceded it, with an occasional flourish and orchestral embellishment. Certain of his shows, however, displayed period dance music, extended ballets, and incidental music that were not restricted to simple reiterations of vocal melodies. Notable examples include: the "Carnival Scene Ballet" in *A Runaway Girl*; the "Fricassée" dance and "Minuet" in *The Duchess of Dantzig*; "The Parisian Two-Step" in *The Pink Lady*; and the "Will O' the Wisp Ballet" in *Chin-Chin*.

The 186-measure "Carnival Scene Ballet"[164] was an energetic romp in 2/4 that adapted and elaborated melodic and harmonic phrases from the sung melody it followed ("Welcome to the Water Fête"). A jovial section in A major gave way to busier, more accented sections, in A minor, D minor, and A minor before relaxing in a buoyant D major segment that made effective dramatic use of opposing dynamics. The A minor theme returned, but before it can be developed, it modulated to the parallel major and propelled the ballet to an upbeat and confident conclusion. The work was organized throughout into four-measure units, though occasionally, shorter (or longer) transitional units occurred. A close reading of the score suggests that the work was composed in close consultation with a choreographer.

"Fricassée"[165] was an 84-measure, perpetual-motion rondo-galop, organized in four-measure units that combined into sixteen-measure groupings based on key signatures. The dance began in E major with the primary refrain (A); it moved to A major with secondary melodic material, or episode (B); and returned to E major repeating the original refrain (A). A second episode (C) emerged in the key of C major before the dance music returned to the original refrain to bring the dance to an end. The stately 83-measure "Minuet" was similarly constructed with a 16-measure refrain (A) in A major; a 16-measure episode (B) also in A major; and an 8-measure recapitulation of the refrain. A new episode in E major followed with five groupings of 4-measure phrases that were shaded through the juxtaposition of dynamics (evidently a favorite device); and finally the original A major refrain returned with an extended (though asymmetric) cadence.

"The Parisian Two Step"[166] was a dynamic 32-measure rag in 2/4 and D major that began with a highly syncopated 4-measure introduction preparing for the off-the-beat accents to follow. The rag itself was divided into two 16-measure units, the second of which reprised the melodic material in the first unit an octave higher. Every other measure of the rag accented the offbeat, establishing a systematic arrangement of syncopation throughout the piece. The use of heavy bass figures and traditional ragtime chord choices conveyed the spirit, if not the essence, of a ragtime two step. The dance music preceded and followed a 32-measure sung chorus in A major that employed similar musical devices.

The 303-measure "Ballet Divertissement: Will O' the Wisp"[167] began with tremolos and harp-like arpeggios that were grounded by a drone-like bass and the suggestion of the soaring rhapsodic melody of the curtain music that followed in 4/4 and A major (one of Caryll's favorite keys). The curtain rose and the music changed to triple meter, underscoring a voice calling: "Lanterns Fays, lanterns Fays, Through the shadows gather, As the moth of midnight seeks the ever-living flame, Weave your spells enchantly, 'Round the charming Bride-to-be, 'Tis the Goddess of the Lamp, Who bids me call your name Lantern Fays." A sensuous and lilting waltz, the "Dance of the Lantern Fays" began its 32-measure refrain (A) before a 7-measure transition modulated to the key of D major and another 32-measure waltz (B) filled with capering eighth note figures. A new section in F# minor (C) commenced its 40-measure passage, introducing clipped rhythms and sparse harmonies that softly led to a reprise of section (B). The original refrain (A) reappeared and the first three sections of the ballet (refrain [A], transition, waltz [B]) were played again before an extended musical apotheosis, weaving through a variety of harmonic constructions and tremolos, signaled the end of the ballet. Although none of the melodic units in the dance music was developed beyond its initial statement, that statement was often filled with interesting chord progressions and surprising melodic contours. Caryll sounded least original when he was aping a particular musical style, though, in such a case, familiarity might have been exactly the result he was seeking.

CATLIN, E[dward] N[oble].

Composer, dance arranger, orchestrator, and musical director E.N. Catlin was born in Clinton, New York, in 1836. When he was a teenager, Catlin took an interest in music and, after twelve lessons on the violin in Utica, New York, the young prodigy played in a theatre orchestra in that city. His name first appeared in theatre listings as musical director of the summer opera season at the Troy Theatre in upstate New York beginning 9 May 1860.[168] Three years later, the *New York Clipper*[169] indicated that Catlin's address was being sought, presumably by prospective employers and collaborators and, in 1864 Catlin went to Boston where he became musical director for [Robert Browne] Hall's Band. The following year, he was hired as musical director for Buckley's Serenaders, a Boston-based troupe that burlesqued famous operas and, after three years with Buckley's, Catlin crossed the Atlantic to organize and train the orchestra for the American Circus in Paris. Upon his return to Boston, Catlin became musical director at the Howard Athenaeum where he composed incidental and dance music for Harrigan and Hart's sketch, *The Little Frauds* (1 May 1871). In the 1871–1872 season, Catlin moved to the Boston Museum, where he conducted, composed, and arranged music until 1879, when he was hired as the musical director of the newly opened Park Theatre. At the Park, among other things, Catlin created a new orchestration for Gilbert and Sullivan's *H.M.S. Pinafore* (23 May 1879)[170] and composed new music for Sydney Rosenfeld's burlesque, *Those Bells* (14 January 1884).[171] He held his post at the Park for ten years before being transferred to the new Tremont Theatre where he began his tenure on 14 October 1889, selecting and composing incidental music for Charles Wyndham's production of *David Garrick*.[172] Catlin remained at the Tremont Theatre until his retirement in 1911.[173]

During his almost fifty-year career on Boston, Catlin composed, selected, and arranged incidental and dance music for forty-four plays. In addition, he composed the music for several well-known popular songs, including "Ring the Bell Softly," "Birdie Has Gone with the Angels," "Comrades, Lay Me Gently Down," "Write Me a Letter, Dear Mother," "The Happy Hottentot," "Darling Minnie Lee," "Love Among the Roses," and the perennial "Shoo, Fly, Don't Bother Me." He also composed dance music for piano, including "Annie Schottische," "Gavotte 'My Own,'" "Artist's Galop," "Anna Galop," as well as orchestral and band arrangements of his original dance music and overtures. *On the Track!*, a theatre score Catlin composed for Swaine Buckley, late of Buckley's Serenaders, was presented at the Bowery Theatre in New York beginning on 28 August 1871 as part of

Example 29. Dance in "Sweet Louisa" from *The Little Frauds*

Buckley's Northeastern tour. Although reviews were not kind to the work's literary merit, they did agree that there were a sufficient number of dances and songs to provide a constant flow of novelty to the proceedings.[174] Of greater interest is "Sweet Louisa," the German dialect song and dance that Catlin composed for Harrigan and Hart's *The Little Frauds*. The rhythmic structure of the dance (example 29) with the empty fourth beat in the accompaniment (measures 1, 2, 4, 5, 6) suggests a Bavarian folk dance called the *schühplattler* in which the body is hit percussively creating complex syncopated rhythms.[175] Note also how the half notes of the melody in the same measures accent the downbeat, allowing for the second and third beats in the accompaniment to be accentuated with hops, heavy footwork, or body slaps. Note also the dotted rhythms in the dance music suggesting a rhythmic pattern for both footwork and slaps.

An old-school musician who disliked jazz and ragtime calling them "musical nightmares," Catlin spent whatever free time he had making violins. He once joked that he "made the instruments for an orchestra, written the music, and conducted the playing."[176] During the summers, between seasons at the Boston theatres, Catlin retired to his farm on Otsego Lake in Springfield Center, New York, with his journalist wife and two daughters. At the age of ninety, E.N. Catlin died in May 1926 after only a few days' illness. His wife, Julia, having predeceased him in 1899,[177] he was survived by his two daughters, Lena and Gertrude.

CELLIER, Alfred

British organist, musical director, and composer, Alfred Cellier was born in London on 1 December 1844. As a child he attended Hackney Grammar School where his father was a professor of languages and when he was eleven years old, he became a choirboy at the Chapel Royal, St. James's Palace, in London. When he was eighteen, he became the organist at the Church of All Saints in southeast London and conductor of the Belfast Philharmonic Society. Six years later he was engaged as organist at St. Alban's Church in central London, and in 1871he became musical director at the Prince's Theatre in Manchester. During his tenure with the Prince's Theatre, Cellier composed a number of curtain raisers and comic operas that met with only limited success. The list includes: *Charity Begins at Home* (7 February 1972), *The Sultan of Mocha* (8 March 1874), *Topsyturveydom* (21 March 1874), *Tower of London* (4 October 1875), *Nell Gwynne* (17 October 1876), and *Two Foster Brothers* (12 March 1877). In December 1877, Cellier became the musical director at the Opera Comique in London where he conducted Gilbert and Sullivan's *The Sorcerer* and *H.M.S. Pinafore, or, The Lass That Loved a Sailor*, as well as three curtain raisers of his own composition, *Dora's Dream* (November 1877–February 1878), *The Spectre Knight* (February–March and May–August 1878), and *After All* (December 1878–March 1880).[178] In late November 1879, Cellier travelled to New York with producer D'Oyly Carte's First American Company to conduct *H.M.S. Pinafore* (1 December 1879) and *The Pirates of Penzance, or, The Slave of Duty* (31 December 1879) on tour. While Cellier was busy with the Gilbert and Sullivan tour, two of his curtain raisers, *Charity Begins at Home*, and *The Spectre Knight*, were produced at the Bijou Theatre in New York City, opening on 31 March 1880. In July, Cellier was back in London conducting *The Pirates of Penzance* and another of his curtain raisers, *In the Sulks* (April 1880–April 1881), but in September, he returned to New York to conduct his comic opera, *The Sultan of Mocha*, at the Union Square Theatre (14 September 1880), and on 10 January 1881, Cellier was in Boston, conducting the premiere of his *The Masque of Pandora*, adapted from the Henry Wadsworth Longfellow poem of the same name. A month later, Cellier began the musical direction for another of D'Oyly Carte's American tours from February 1881through February 1882[179] and in 1883 *Gray's Elegy*, the cantata he composed expressly for the Leeds Music Festival, was produced in West Yorkshire, England.

Back in New York, Cellier was represented by a "Mayday Chorus" and "Morris Dance" he composed for *Little Jack Sheppard* (13 September 1886) and "To Whit, To Whoo" (from *The Spectre Knight*) interpolated into the score for *Over the Garden Wall* (27 December 1886). On 5 November 1887, Cellier's enormously successful comic opera, *Dorothy*, opened in New York with the popular prima donna Lillian Russell in the title role.[180] *Dorothy* offered an abundance of Cellier's dance and incidental music, including a buoyantly vivacious "Country Dance" at the beginning of act two, a stately pavane-like "Graceful Dance" later in the act, and an extended "Ballet" that opened act three. The music was proficient and eminently danceable. That it often evoked the style and substance of Arthur Sullivan was, perhaps, more of a blessing than a curse, given an audience's predisposition for familiarity. After *Dorothy*, Cellier was again in the New York theatre listings as co-composer of *The Babes in the Wood, Robin Hood and His Merry, Merry Men*, and *Harlequin, Who Killed Cock Robin?* at Niblo's Garden, beginning on 30 December 1890, and *Cinderella* at the Academy of Music, opening on 23 November 1891. Cellier's final production in New York, *The Mountebanks* (for which he supplied the music to a text by W.S. Gilbert), was produced by the Lillian Russell Opera Comique Company at the Garden Theatre on 11 January 1893.[181] Cellier had always had delicate constitution that required constant care. Often he would take rest cures in Australia and the United States, expecting that the change of air would improve his health, and ignoring the fact that his travels were rarely restful. On 28 December 1891, Cellier finally succumbed to his infirmities at his home in Bloomsbury before the composition of *The Mountebanks* was finished. Ivan Caryll, the musical director at the Lyric Theatre where a production of the opera was underway, completed the score. Cellier's musical theatre works exhibited a melodic charm that was often dignified and refined, but taken as a whole, Cellier's music was lacking in dramatic intensity and was most successful in the handling of vocal ensembles and dance music.[182]

CHADWICK, George W[hitefield]

Composer, musical director, and educator, George W. Chadwick, often called the "dean of American composers"[183] was born in Lowell, Massachusetts, on 13 November 1854 to parents who were amateur musicians. His earliest musical studies were with his older brother, Fitz Henry, who gave him organ lessons. Chadwick continued his organ studies for a number of years with Eugene Thayer in Boston and attended the New England Conservatory as a special non-matriculating student.[184] In 1876, he was hired as an administrator and faculty member of Olivet College in Michigan where he produced two early compositions: a song, "Request" (words by B. Cornwall), and the "Canon for the Organ in E flat." A lost "String Trio" said to have been composed in 1877 may also have been composed during Chadwick's stay at Olivet. When the academic year concluded, Chadwick traveled to Leipzig and, after briefly studying with the renowned teacher and composer Salomon Jadassohn, he entered Leipzig's Royal Conservatory, where he enjoyed his first real successes as a composer.[185] His String Quartet No. 2 was warmly applauded by audiences and critics alike, and his graduation composition, the concert overture *Rip Van Winkle* won the Conservatory's award as the best composition of 1879. After studying with organist and composer Josef Rheinberger in Munich and sojourning with a group of American painters in Giverny, France, Chadwick returned to Boston in 1880, becoming the musical director of the music festivals in Springfield, Massachusetts (a post he held until 1899), and a private teacher of composition, music theory, and instrumental performance. In 1882, he began teaching at the New England Conservatory, and in 1883, he accepted the post of organist at the South Congregational Church in Boston, which he held until 1893, and for which he composed a series of choral works with organ, including "Dedication Ode" (1883), "Three Sacred Quartets" (1885), "Abide with Me," "O Cease, My Wandering Soul," "O Day of Rest," and "There Were Shepherds," (all 1888). In 1884, Chadwick composed his first musical theatre work, *The Peer and the Pauper*, a two-act comic opera (libretto by Robert Grant), highly indebted to Gilbert and Sullivan in its dramatic satire and musical style. The work surges with incidental music of varying lengths and character and, even though the melodies and harmonies of the various incidental passages are for the most part varied, the recurrent use of triple meter tends to suggest a similarity throughout. Particularly noteworthy, however, are the schottische interlude and dance (in a rare example of common time) in Lord Randolph's song, "And That's What's the Matter with me," and the extended "Introduction and Barcarolle" (in 9/8) at the beginning of act two.

In 1892, Chadwick was commissioned to compose an ode for the opening ceremonies of the World's Columbian Exposition in Chicago; he responded with *Ode to the Opening of the Chicago World's Fair* (text by H. Monroe), composed for solo soprano and tenor, a double SATB chorus, full orchestra (including harp), and two military bands (one to the north, the other to the south). In the same year, Chadwick created the incidental music for the Boston premiere of *Oedipus Rex* (30 January 1892) with the characters of Oedipus and Jocasta performed in the original Greek; in addition, he composed the score for *A Quiet Lodging* (libretto by A. Bates), a vaudeville in two parts performed in Boston on 1 April 1892. In October 1893, Chadwick signed a contract with Boston favorites E[dward] E[verett] Rice and R[obert] A[yres] Barnet by which Rice agreed to produce a new burlesque by Chadwick and Barnet by October 1894.[186] The object of the contract, a burlesque opera entitled *Tabasco* was first produced in Boston on 29 January 1894 by the Boston Cadets, and later throughout the United States by the Thomas Q. Seabrooke Company who

Example 30. "March of the Pasha's Guard" from *Tabasco*

Example 31. "Dance of the Harem" from *Tabasco*

brought the musical to the Broadway Theatre on 14 May, where "the ballet in the closing scene… proved an enjoyable feature of the performance" and "thunders of applause" greeted the final curtain.[187]

A musical about the Bey of Tangiers (Hot-Hed-Ham, Pasha) who beheads any chef who neglects to season his food with a sufficient amount of tabasco, *Tabasco* includes an ample amount of dance music of different lengths, meters, and styles. There is a Spanish bolero in triple meter; an Irish jig in 6/8 marked *molto vivace*; a French rigaudon, also in 6/8 and marked *vivace*; a "plantation" dance evocative of a minstrel-show banjo tune in duple meter with syncopations and dotted rhythms; the

"March of the Pasha's Guard" (example 30a), a basically traditional march in 6/8 reminiscent of the compositions of John Philip Sousa and Franz von Suppé, but without the exotic touches melodically or harmonically that might conjure up a Moroccan atmosphere; and the "Dance of the Harem"(example 30b) ballet music in triple meter that recalls the ballet music of French composer Léo Delibes.

In 1897, Chadwick was appointed the Director of the New England Conservatory, a position he held until 1930, and he became the musical director of the music festivals in Worcester, Massachusetts. In the same year Yale University conferred on him an honorary degree, on which occasion his "Ecce Jam Noctis" for male voices and orchestra was performed. In 1899, he contributed additional music to the musical comedy *Three Little Lambs* at the Fifth Avenue Theatre in New York, and on 25 September 1901, his lyric drama *Judith* (libretto by William Chauncy Langdon) was performed at the Worcester Festival.[188] The incidental music in *Judith* is modal, exotic, and highly atmospheric, capturing not only a sense a place and time but also illustrating tonally the dramatic action.[189] The same can be said of Chadwick's incidental score for Walter Browne's allegorical play *Everywoman*, produced at the Herald Square Theatre on 27 February 1911.[190] Producer Henry W. Savage had engaged Chadwick in the fall of 1910 to compose an incidental score for the play that would include a number of songs and choruses as well as entr'acte and introductory compositions.[191] The *New York Clipper* reviewer called Chadwick's music "ambitious and effective, raising the tone of the work by its operatic character."[192] Chadwick's next theatre work, a verismo opera, *The Padrone* (libretto by D[avid] Stevens), was composed in 1913 for the Metropolitan Opera but never performed there, and his final work for the theatre, *Love's Sacrifice* (libretto by D[avid] Stevens), described as a one-act Grecian Idyll[193] or pastoral opera, was composed in 1917 and performed in Chicago on 1 February 1923. Chadwick died at his home in Boston on 4 April 1931 after an illness of several months. He was survived by his wife of nearly forty years, Ida May, two sons, and four grandchildren. On 12 April 1931, *The New York Times* accessed Chadwick's long career as a composer and educator and concluded that "Chadwick's work, in its spirit if not in the letter of many pages, will live long. It is impossible to think of a more honest and accomplished musician, or one who, without pretense or megalomania, accomplished as much for the development of his native art."

CHANTRIER, Albert

French composer and dance arranger, Albert Chantrier, was born in Paris on 4 October 1874. Like most of the composers who studied music in Paris between 1850 and 1910, he was educated at the École Niedermeyer, a conservatory specializing in church music. Chantrier's earliest compositions met with little or no success, but between 1897 and WWI, he produced several works that achieved popularity, the first of which that resonated with the American musical theatre was the score for a pantomime called *La Chair* [*Flesh*] (libretto by Georges Wague) produced at the Manhattan Opera House on 4 December 1908.[194] Chantrier's score contained a succession of sprightly and evocative dance arrangements that seemed better suited to ballet rather than pantomime, a fact that the critic from *The New York Times*[195] did not fail to notice. "The story that is told is insignificant, with little point," wrote the reviewer, "and the music to which it is unfolded ... has very little to characterize the scene and the action, which is its only object." If Chantrier failed to find an enduring career in New York, he was still composing music for musical theatre in Paris. On 12 January 1910, his score for *Illusions!!!*, a one-act pantomime, was produced at the Théâtre Michel, and in the years leading up to WWI, he produced scores for a number of musical theatre works that included a three-act comédie burlesque *Le château des loufoques* [*The Nut House*] (1911); a comedy sketch in two scenes, *Le début de Chichine* [*Chichine's Debut*], produced in *The Revue of Revues* at the Winter Garden Theatre (27 September 1911); a one-act operetta, *Arsène, l'enfant de l'amour* [*Arsène, the Love Child*] (1912); and a three-act operetta, *Gräfin Fifi* [*Countess Fifi*], with a separately published dance duet (1913).

After the war, Chantrier continued to produce musical theatre works, often more than one a year with limited success. The list includes *Au béguin des dames* [*To Fancy the Ladies*] (1918); *Gros poupard modeste* [*Big Biddable Baby*] (1918); *La Bagatelle* [*The Knick-Knack*] (1919); *Les P'tites vertus* [*The Li'l Virtues*] (1919); *Gigoletto* [*Little Gigolo*] (1920); *Le Harem en folie* [*Harem Madness*] (1920); *Le Fruit défendu* [*The Forbidden Fruit*] (1920); *La Ceinture de chasteté* (*The Chastity Belt*] (1923); and *Bébel et Quinquin* [*Bebel and Quinquin*] (1923), the most successful of the series. It should be noted that the theatres where these works were performed were the bastions of minimalist musical theatre, with tiny auditoriums, and accompaniments often reduced to a single piano.[196] Chantrier's semi-breakout success came in 1925 when his *Elle ou moi* [*She or Me*] was produced at the Théâtre Daunou in Paris, after which he devoted himself to musical direction and arrangements and the composition of film scores. Chaintrier was an expert musician, a traditional theorist, and an outstanding composer of dance music in France. It is unfortunate that more of his dance arrangements did not cross the ocean for his scores display finely-honed melodic phrases with often surprising rhythms accompanied by easily assimilated harmonies. Chantrier was a loyal supporter of the *Société des Auteurs, Compositeurs, et Editeurs de Musique*, becoming secretary-general of the organization in 1945. His tenure in office was regrettably cut short by his death on 18 December 1946.

CHASSAIGNE, Francis

Born in Brussels on 30 October 1847, composer, and dance arranger Francis Chassaigne studied music at an early age and began his musical theatre career composing songs for popular chanteuses in Paris. By the time he was 30, Chassaigne had become a master of the one-act comic operas and short musical sketches that were flourishing at Parisian café-concerts and the Eldorado Music Hall. His contributions to the genre included *Un coq en jupons* [*A Rooster in Petticoats*] (4 July1872), *La bergère de Bougival* [*The Shepherdess of Bougival*] (20 July1872), *Les horreurs du carnival* [*The Horrors of the Carnival*] (27 February 1873), *Monsieur Auguste* [*Mr. Augustus*] (3 May 1873), *Le professeur de tyrolienne* [*The Yodeling Instructor*] (21 March 1874), *Un table de café* [*A Café Table*] (25 July 1874), *Deux mauvaises bonnes* [*Two Bad Maids*] (11 November 1876), *Les Enfants de la balle* [*The Children of the Theatre*] (24 March 1877), *La famille de Paméla* [*Pamela's Family*] (11 August 1877), *Actéon et le centaure Chiron* [*Acteon and Chiron, the Centaur*] (28 January 1878), *La tache de sang!* [*The Bloodstain*] (12 January1878), *Claude l'ivrogne* [*Claude, the Drunk*] (22 April 1879), and *Zizi* (1881). [197] Chassaigne's one-act musicals are rich in dance and incidental music. *Deux mauvaises bonnes*, for example, includes an extended "Boléro" with choreographic directions in the text;[198] *Les Enfants de la balle* contains an extended ballet that begins with incidental music underscoring Pomponette's entrance and dialogue and the subsequent arrival of the zephyr Durozeau. After more underscored dialogue, the couple dance an Adagio pas de deux followed by a Polka variation for Pomponette, a Bolero variation for Durozeau, and a vivacious Galop that concludes the ballet.

In 1882, Chassaigne was commissioned by Jules Brasseur, the artistic director of the Théâtre des Nouveautés, to compose a three-act opéra-comique for production at his theatre. Chassaigne responded with *Le droit d'ainesse* [*The Birthright*] (words by Eugène Leterrier and Albert Vanloo), a modestly successful musical that premiered at the Nouveautés on 27 January 1883, and an enduring hit in the English-speaking world via an English adaptation by H[enry] B. Farnie. Under the name *Falka*, Chassaigne's three-act opéra-comique opened at the Casino Theatre in New York on 14 April 1884 and, despite *The New York Times* review that pronounced the music unequal to the other offerings at the Casino, the musical ran for more than 100 performances and was revived on Broadway in 1886, 1887, and 1900.[199] With the exception of a brief march that reprises instrumentally the melody of the opening chorus, there is no set dance music in Chassaigne's score. There are entr'actes and extended orchestral introductions to various numbers, but the New York reviewer who complained that *Falka* "has none of those dashing, piquant galop and polka movements which sparkle through the works of the German comic opera composers,"[200] was correct in his appraisal.

Chassaigne's second full-length opéra-comique, *Les noces improvises* [*The Improvised Wedding*], appeared at the Théâtre des Bouffes-Parisiens in Paris on 13 February 1886 and, in an English adaptation by Alfred Murray, at the Casino Theatre in New York on 14 May 1888, under the title *Nadjy*. Again *The New York Times* (15 May 1888) objected to the musical, calling the efforts of designers and director, "not worth the trouble," and arguing that "As for the music of *Nadjy* it can only be said that there are a few airs which contain some dash and melody, but with the exception of two ineffective introductions of the familiar "Racoczy" [sic] march, no attempt has been made to utilize the characteristic rhythms of Hungary."[201] Nadjy does contain a traditional Hungarian "Czárdás," as well as the "Rakoczy March." Even if the music of the extended ballet sequence sounds more French than Hungarian or Viennese, Chassaigne made some attempt to provide an exotic flavor for his opéra-comique. As in the case of *Falka*, audiences again dismissed the opinions proffered by *The New York Times* and kept *Nadjy* running for 154 performnces.

Following the success of *Nadjy*, Rudolph Aronson, the artistic director of the Casino Theatre, commissioned a new comic opera from Chassaigne and H.B. Farnie to be called *La Mexicana*. Farnie died on 22 September 1889, leaving only an outline of the libretto; the task of completing the text for a production in Newcastle upon Tyne (19 April 1890) fell to Max Pemberton and William Lestocq, who renamed the musical *The Brazilian*; and Edgar Smith revised the British libretto for the New

York premiere at the Casino Theatre on 2 June 1890. Before the Casino production, rumors abounded that musical director Gustave Kerker had completely rearranged Chassaigne's music, which Aronson refuted as completely false: "Monsieur Chassaigne himself wrote thanking me for the sumptuous staging of his *Brazilian* and requesting me to convey to Mr. Kerker his thanks for the scrupulous care he had bestowed upon his score."[202] Aronson also noted a new comic opera that Chassaigne was planning for the Casino Theatre, a work dealing with the life of Louis XIV at Versailles. Unfortunately, that project was never completed. *The Brazilian* afforded Chassaigne many opportunities for dance music: a quick triple meter Castilian folk dance called "Sequidilla," a "Bolero," a traditional Spanish *Sevillanas* called "Castagnette Song," and an Andalusian-flavored ballet. Chassaigne composed all of the dance music for the British production but it is unknown how much of his music was revised or deleted by Kerker for the New York premiere. Chassaigne died at his home in Le Raincy, a suburb of Paris, on 21 December 1922. He was survived by his wife, Louise Roland, a popular operetta and vaudeville singer and dancer.

CHILVERS, Thomas H.

Thomas Chilvers, composer, dance arranger, and educator, was born in Detroit on 9 April 1872 to a British father (Captain Thomas R. Chilvers) and Irish mother (Margarett M. Mera). His younger brother, Hugh Chilvers, was an operatic baritone and leading man in musical comedies and operettas. Thomas displayed a precocious talent for music at an early age as well as the inclination to teach since he took responsibility for his younger brother's initial musical education.[203] Thomas Chilvers first appeared in musical theatre rosters in 1885 in connection with a Chicago production of *The Ivy Leaf*, a popular Irish melodrama, for which he composed incidental music. His "Maureen Mavourneen," a lovely Irish ballad in 6/8 meter, exhibited a dramatically expressive use of chromaticism that was quite unexpected from the pen of a thirteen-year-old composer;[204] and his "Beautiful Ivy Leaf," added for a later tour, was written in the finest tradition of Irish waltzes with a simple, yet haunting melody made poignant through artfully placed chromaticism. With composer William T. Francis, Chilvers composed the score for *The Little Host*, a musical comedy tour praised for its novelty, ingenuity, and delicacy,[205] and featuring his brother Hugh. In "I'm a Shy Little Innocent Thing," Chilvers composed a graceful (though melodically busy) waltz, underscoring a dialogue and pantomime in the middle of the song, as well as a jaunty schottische dance (based on the sung melody) at the end of the number. He followed *The Little Host* with *The Head Waiters* (28 April 1901), a plotless, farcical touring vehicle for the comedy team of Happy Ward and Harry Vokes that opened at the Great Northern Theatre in Chicago.[206] Without any real storyline, the musical relied on novel scenic effects, dazzling songs and dances, and up-to-date specialty numbers; and by the time it played the Grand Opera House in New York (20 January 1902), Herbert Dillea was added as co-composer to refresh the score. Chilvers had become supervisor of musical education for the Board of Education in Detroit, and he had little time, or opportunity, to provide the necessary changes in order to keep the production up to date. After *The Head Waiters*, Chilvers retired from the musical stage and devoted the rest of his life to the establishment of sustainable music programs in public schools. Chilvers died on 17 January 1936 at his home on La Salle Boulevard in Detroit.

CHIPMAN, J[ohn] S.

J.S. Chipman was a member of Harvard's Pi Eta Society, an organization that produced annual musical theatre productions. His name first appeared in connection with a quartet dance in the *Belles of Bellesly* (12 April 1899) in which he played a young lady dancer.[207] The next year, Chipman portrayed another female character in *The Campaigners* (10 April 1900), Pi Eta's musical about the Spanish-American War, and he also composed several musical numbers for the production.[208] After his graduation from Harvard in 1901, Chipman joined the First Corps of Cadets, a voluntary militia of young upper-class Bostonians who produced musicals in order to raise money to build an armory. During his tenure with the Cadets, Chipman published a piano solo, "The Sunbeam. The Shadow Dance" (1903) and appeared in another female role (Golden Hair) in *Cinderella and the Prince, or, the Castle of Heart's Desire* (1 February 1904).[209] For the production he also composed two songs, "Dottie's Dimples," and "Three Bears," a number about Goldilocks and the three bears followed by a dance. The "Three Bears" dance (example 31) is an ambling schottische that begins with the melody in the bass clef and accompaniment in the treble (measures 1–8) and ends with the melody an octave higher in the treble clef and accompaniment in the bass (measures 9–16). The inversion of the traditional melody-accompaniment arrangement in the

Example 32. Dance in "Three Bears" from Cinderella and the *Prince*

first 8 measures suggests the state of disorder created by the presence of Goldilocks in the bears' home (not to mention the commotion created by the fact that the bears are actually men who have been changed into bears), while the final eight measures reinstates the ordered arrangement of musical structures as the bears accept Goldilocks and, as the lyrics of the song suggests, "But when the bears caught sight of her they promptly fall in love,/And upon the spot chang'd right back into men."

In April 1904, Chipman portrayed another feminine role in the Pi Eta musical, *The Will-o'the-Whisp*, in which he performed a "charming solo dance,"[210] and on 5 February 1906, he appeared in the last Cadet musical, *Miss Pocahontas*, winning rave notices as Pocahontas.[211] After *Miss*

Pocahontas, J.S. Chipman disappeared from theatre listings. Approaching his later twenties, he began to lose the youthful look that rendered him in demand as a female impersonator, and he found himself replaced in the Pi Eta shows by younger Harvard undergraduates. As a composer of individual songs and dances, Chipman demonstrated a gentle wit and dramatic sense as well as fine musical craftsmanship; and as a performer, he was invariably singled out by critics for his finely-honed impersonations. Many great talents have emerged from amateur theatricals, and just as many have remained happily within their confines. John S. Chipman was one of the latter. The Boston City Directory of 1909 listed Chipman as a music teacher with rooms at 279 Dartmouth Street.

CHRISTIANI, Emil

Composer, dance arranger, and musical director, Emil Christiani was born in Denmark in 1851 and studied music at the Leipzig Conservatory. A musical prodigy, he began composing songs and piano pieces at an early age, and while he was still a teenager, his one-act operetta, *Mariner Liebchen* [*Sweetheart of the Sea*], was produced at the Concordia Theater in Hamburg. Two full-length musical theatre works followed: a romantic operetta, *Die letzie Nacht*[*The Last Night*], in 1887, and a comic operetta, *Zola*, in 1889. Following the production of Zola, Christiani traveled to the United States as the musical director of the Lilliputians, a company of German performers of diminutive size. He contributed musical and dance arrangements for the company's production of *Der Zauberlehrling* [*The Student of Magic*], performed in German and English at Niblo's Garden in New York City beginning 15 September 1890.[212] A year later he composed the music (along with Victor Holländer) for the Lilliputian bilingual production of *Die Zwergenhochzeit* [*The Dwarf's Wedding*], opening at the Thalia Theatre on 6 October 1891.[213] After an extended tour with the company throughout the United States, Christiani and the Lilliputians returned to Niblo's Garden on 1 January 1894 for a return engagement of *Der Zauberlehrling*. Before the turn of the century, Christiani gave up touring for a teaching post at the Washington College of Music, and by the end of WWI, he was involved with the War Camp Community Service in the inauguration of a national grand opera organization called "Community Opera" with headquarters in Washington, D.C. Christiani was responsible for organizing local musicians into an orchestra that would accompany the opera repertoire.[214] Three operas were produced during the 1918–1919 season, and six more were planned during the 1919–1920 season.[215] After a brief illness he died at his home in Washington in 1929. Christiani's music is cheerful, light, and tuneful, following in the best traditions of Viennese musical theatre in the nineteenth century, with stirring marches and lilting waltzes. For the Lilliputian Company he composed several ballets including "The Night Revels of the Automata" in *Der Zauberlehrling*, and "The March of the Amazons" in *Die Zwergenhochzeit*.

CHRISTRUP, Charles

Danish-born pianist, composer, dance arranger, and conductor, Charles Christrup first appeared in American theatre listings during the summer of 1874 as the musical director for the T. Charles Howard and Charles Carle tour of *The Black Crook*, which opened on 7 September 1874 at the Academy of Music in St. John, New Brunswick, Canada.[216] At the end of *The Black Crook* tour, Christrup joined Robinson's English Bouffe Company at Robinson Hall in New York, where he served as musical director for *Giroflé-Girofla* (19 May 1875), *Chilpéric* and *The Rose of Auvergne* (15 July 1875), and *The Princess of Trebizonde* (23 August 1875). Christrup subsequently moved on to Booth's Theatre, where he remained until October 1878, when he and his orchestra accepted an engagement at the Park Theatre during the run of *La Cigale*, an English adaptation of the play by Henri Meilhac and Ludovic Halévy, starring Lotta Crabtree. After several seasons at the Park Theatre, Christrup conducted tours of *Donna Juanita* and *Olivette*, which opened in New York during the fall 1882, before collaborating with brothers Imre and Bolossy Kiralfy on their revival of *The Black Venus*, for which he composed and arranged new dance and incidental music. Opening at Niblo's Garden on 5 February 1883, the spectacular production, "with its displays of wild beasts and its processions of symmetrical female limbs,"[217] featured a "Grand Nubian Ballet," a "Dance des Momboutous," a "Pas de huit des Cloches" ["Dance of Eight Bells"], and a "Grand Adagio," among other dances. The habitually unenthusiastic critic from *The New York Times* found that the "burning of the slave ship ... following the panorama of the Nile and a characteristic slave dance, were interesting features. The tableau of the second act, in which the Amazon warriors of Walinda run their fiery coursers up a rocky way, was made really 'thrilling,' according to the promise of the programme. ... The sand-storm and the caravan of animals and Nubian slaves were skillfully presented, but it was the multitudinous leg of the ballet that captured the fancy of the audience."[218] Following his work on *The Black Venus*, Christrup joined the faculty of the Grand Conservatory of Music of the City of New York[219] and devoted his time to teaching and concertizing.

CHUBB, T[homas] Youres

Born in England in 1803, violinist and composer T. Youres Chubb was the musical director and arranger at the Park Theatre in New York City during the 1830s and 1840s. He arranged the incidental music for *A Loan for a Lover* in September 1836 when British actress Mrs. Keely made her debut at the Park Theatre,[220] and he led the orchestra in a performance of *The Israelites in Egypt, or, The Passage of the Red Sea* on 18 November 1842, using music composed by Handel and Rossini.[221] He conducted Balfe's *The Bohemian Girl* beginning 25 November 1844 and arranged a series of quadrilles based on the popular melodies from the opera, under the titles : "L'Hymen de la Bohemiene," "L'Aveu," "L'Invitation," "Les Sybilles," and "La Rose."[222] On 2 December 1846, Chubb provided an overture for Charles Kean's production of Shakespeare's *King John* and composed, selected, and arranged the dramatic and entr'acte music for the presentation. In the same year, he also published his "Fifth Washington Greys" a majestic and heroic grand march filled with melodic flourishes.[223] Other than his small number of publications, there are few clues to the nature of Chubb's musical theatre arrangements and compositions. The accompaniments he devised for musical theatre songs were imitations of the early Romantic art-song accompaniments of Schubert, and his piano solos recalled the early piano compositions of Beethoven and Schumann, without the musical genius that guided their work. Similarities notwithstanding, Chubb had a talent for making theatre music sound effective, familiar, important, and immediately accessible to an audience of differing musical backgrounds and artistic tastes. At the age of forty-five, T. Youres Chubb died in Jersey City, New Jersey, on 16 November 1848.

CLARK[E], Cuthbert Edward

Musical director, composer, and dance arranger Cuthbert Clarke (or Clark) was born in January 1869 at Hampstead, in the London borough of Camden. He was educated at the North London Collegiate School in Camden Town and at the University in Boulogne-sur-Mer, France. In

October 1890, Clarke married Elizabeth Hoby in London's Saint Pancras parish. He was subsequently musical director for the Palace Theatre in Manchester and the Empire Theatre in Leicester Square, London, where he selected or composed music for several of the ballets designed for the prima ballerina, Adeline Genée. The list included *The Dancing Doll* (3 January 1905), for which Clarke contributed only a few numbers; *The Débutante* (15 November 1906), for which Clarke contributed light and spirited music for the first scene; *The Belle of the Ball* (30 September 1907), for which Clarke arranged a clever pastiche of popular melodies from the last half of the nineteenth century; and *The Pretty Prentice* (24 April 1916), for which Clarke added to the score familiar musical phrases that carried emotional or dramatic associations, in order to facilitate the audience's understanding of the pantomimic action of the ballet.[224] For American audiences, Clarke's greatest musical contribution to the dance occurred on 28 January 1908 when Adeline Genée appeared at the New York Theatre in the musical extravaganza, *The Soul Kiss*. Although composer Maurice Levi provided the music for the songs and dances that did not involve Genée, every step the ballerina took onstage was accompanied by music composed, selected, or arranged by Cuthbert Clarke. For Genée's first entrance, Clarke borrowed André Messager's music for the "Empire Dance" composed expressly for Genée when she joined the company of Messager's comic opera *The Little Michus* (19 August 1905). Clarke composed original music for the ballerina's second entrance, a "Money Ballet" in which Genée was pictured dancing in the Treasury of Monte Carlo, but he borrowed from Richard Eilenberg's score for the ballet, *Die Rose von Schiras* (15 July 1896) the music for Genée's whirling, encore eliciting variation. Genée's third appearance introduced a comic turn from the ballet, *The Milliner Duchess* (14 January 1903), for which Clarke adapted the existing score, a pastiche of musical theatre numbers; and for her final number, the famous "Return from the Hunt" dance from the ballet *High Jinks* (9 March 1904), Clarke rearranged the original music, a hunting song, "D'ye ken John Peel?" set to the Scottish tune, "Bonnie Annie."[225] In addition to his ballet scores, Clarke composed a number of musical monologues, for which he provided atmospheric incidental music to underscore a spoken narrative, and songs and dances for various London revues.[226]

Cuthbert Clarke died in London in 1953 at the age of 84.

CLIFTON, Arthur

Organist, pianist, teacher, singer, music publisher, composer, dance arranger, and dry-goods merchant, Arthur Clifton was born Philip Anthony Corri in Edinburgh, Scotland, in 1784. His father Domenico Corri, a famous opera composer, was a music publisher and teacher as well as the conductor of the Musical Society of Edinburgh.[227] When he was five years old, Philip Corri moved with his family to London, where he began his musical education under the tutelage of his father. By the time he was a teenager he was a published composer of songs, and as he grew older, Philip became skilled in all musical genres. He also developed a reputation in London as a piano teacher, and his instruction manual, *L'anima di musica* [*The Spirit of Music*] (1810), was considered the most extensive study of piano education of the period.[228] He was one of the original organizers of the London Philharmonic Society in 1813 and performed in the orchestra's first three concerts, the first of which was given on 8 March 1813. Evidently Corri's musical abilities were unmatched by his personality traits and scandal appeared to hound him in London. A letter addressed to him from piano manufacturers John Broadwood and Son, dated November 1809, drew attention to his bad behavior:

> We have received your letter containing the very prejudiced statements of the case you have thought proper to lay before several truly respectable gentlemen. It would ill become us to notice your most insulting and ungentlemanly insinuations. And the purpose of this is to recommend you not to subject yourself to the degrading treatment you might experience should you again enter our house.

That this was not an isolated example of Corri's behavior was demonstrated by the minutes of the London Philharmonic Society's meeting on 12 December 1816, in response to Corri's resigning from the organization:

> It was moved by Mr. Webbe and seconded by Mr. Neate that "This Society with feelings of the utmost indignation of the discovery that Mr. P.A. Corri has been guilty of atrocious conduct which [makes] him at once a disgrace to his profession, and to Society at large, anxiously hasten to express their horror of having associated with such a man, and do formally expel him from their body forever.

Whatever might have been Corri's offenses—many have speculated marital problems, perhaps an infidelity with an unwilling student—they created a scandal sufficiently significant to drive him from London to New York City in the early days of 1817. By the end of the year, Corri had made his way from New York to Baltimore (by way of a short stay in Philadelphia) and on New Year's Eve, the day before he married a Catholic Baltimore resident, Alphonsa Elizabeth Ringgold, Corri was christened Arthur Clifton in an Episcopal church.[229] Following his marriage, Clifton accepted the position of church organist at the First Presbyterian Church in Baltimore (and later at the First Independent Church); he gave music

Example 33. "Ballet" from *The Enterprise*

Example 33 (continued). "Ballet" from *The Enterprise*

lessons out of his home and appeared as a singer and pianist in local concerts and recitals.[230] By 1822, he had become the director of Baltimore's Anacreontic Society and the musical director for the Holliday Street Theatre, where his only known musical theatre work, an operatic drama called *The Enterprise, or, Love and Pleasure* (libretto by Colonel W.H. Hamilton) was produced in May 1822.[231] The score of *The Enterprise* contains bravura vocal displays, folk-like melodies, choruses, and glees that combine the intricacies of early nineteenth-century Italian opera with the unpretentious airs of English ballad opera. In addition, the score presents two exceptional dances: an "Entrée March," a majestic example of martial music designed to accompany the entrance of armies preparing for battle; and an extended "Ballet" (example 32) structured as a theme (measures 1–12) and variations (of which, measures 13–21 constituted variation 1, and measures 22–29, variation 2). A long variation in the parallel minor followed prior to a recapitulation of the first variation and an elaborate finale signaled the end of the ballet and brought the opera to a close. Reviews of the opera were lukewarm and the work received only one more performance (on 14 June 1822) before falling into obscurity.

On 17 June 1822, three days after the final performance of *The Enterprise*, an advertisement appeared in a London newspaper and was subsequently reprinted in the 14 September 1822 issue of Boston's *The Euterpiad, or, Music Intelligencer*:

> Whereas, Philip Anthony Corri, musical composer and teacher, left this country about five years ago for New York, and his personal abode is desired to be known to the advertiser, but not for any hostile purpose, this is to give notice whoever will, within six months from this date, furnish satisfaction to Mr. Harmer, solicitor, Hatton Garden, of the present residence of the said Mr. Corri, so that an interview may be obtained with him, shall be paid a reward of £100.
>
> N.B. It has been reported that the above-named P.A. Corri, after his arrival at New York, proceeded to Philadelphia, thence to Baltimore and there married a Quaker lady. It has also been asserted that he is returned to England. The said P.A. Corri has a sharp, Italian visage, sallow complexion, black curly hair, black eyes, and is bald on the crown of the head. He is forty years of age, five feet eight inches high, and has a soft voice and a gentlemanly manner.

The characteristics of "a soft voice and a gentlemanly manner" do not appear consistent with earlier documents emphasizing Clifton's insulting and ungentlemanly behavior, but, perhaps, Mr. Harmer wished to present a less aggressive depiction of the subject to potential informants. In any event, rumors about Clifton's past began to spread through music circles in Baltimore following the publication of the advertisement in *The Euterpiad*,[232] and while he continued to teach and compose until two years before his death in Baltimore on 10 February 1832,[233] he discovered that his public life was being scrutinized just as it had been in London before he escaped to New York. *Shadows on the Wall, or, Glimpses of the Past* (1877), the autobiography of composer John Hill Hewitt offered a doleful description of Clifton's final years in Baltimore: "He was a handsome man, but a man of care, always brooding over the miseries of life, looking on the dark side, never the bright. Nevertheless, when in company, he was full of wit and anecdote, and one of the pillars of the Anacreontic Society. He was found dead in bed, some averring that he died of a broken heart, his domestic misfortunes having been given to the public."[234]

COLON, Aberano

Born in Puerto Rico in 1852, composer and violinist Aberano Colon was a highly respected performer and teacher in Puerto Rico during the late nineteenth and early twentieth centuries. One of his many instrumental compositions, "Spanish Dance," was incorporated into the score of *1492, Up to Date or Very Near It*, produced by the First Corps of Cadets at the Tremont Theatre in Boston on 8 February 1892.[235] The production drew the attention of producer E.E. Rice who remounted it with a professional touring company that eventually made its way to New York City for a run of over 450 performances. Occurring just before the finale of act one, the "Spanish Dance" (example 34) is an *Aragonaise* in triple meter begin-

Example 34. "Spanish Dance" from *1492, Up to Date or Very Near It*

ning with a 16-measure introduction that features contrasting dynamics and articulations in a call-and-response structure. The formal melody in the key of E major (the "A" section) begins at measure 17 mirroring the melodic shapes of the introduction, and a "B" section follows at measure 27 in the relative minor. The dance music continues with a trio (or "C" section) in the key of A before returning to the original melody ("A") to conclude the dance. The *Aragonaise* formula is dramatically appropriate since the character of Ferdinand in the musical is the King of Aragon.

COLWELL, Victor

Born in Canada in 1878, composer, dance arranger, and musical director, Victor Colwell first appeared in New York City theatre listings in 1902 as musical director of the Third Avenue Theatre, where he selected incidental and entr'acte music for *The Outpost*, a play by Edwin Barbour and James W. Haskins, Jr. that premiered in New York City on 10 February.[236] In May 1902, Colwell joined Weber and Hennessey's *The Rounders* Company as orchestra leader of the national tour.[237] When he returned to New York, a year later, he was hired as musical director, composer, and dance arranger for *The Street Singer*, a new musical melodrama by Hal Reid that gave its first performance at the National Theatre in Rochester, New York, on 5 September 1904 and opened at the American Theatre in New York City a week later.[238] The street singer of the title, Violetta Vodray, was forced to marry Morgan Van Voort, a debauched millionaire (the father of Lawrence Winfield, her fiancé, an illegitimate son) in order to save her father, John Vodray, the millionaire's bookkeeper, from going to jail for an alleged embezzlement. During the course of the melodrama, Violetta successfully fought a sword duel, escaped from her husband's estate, evaded police by disguising herself as a street singer, and derailed the maneuverings of three villainous scoundrels so that virtue might triumph over evil.[239] Of course, four murky acts of mayhem required incidental music appropriate to the action, and Colwell composed and arranged chase music, dueling music, pathetic heroine music, hiss-the-villain music, and hero-saves-the-day music, as well as the songs and dances necessitated by the dramatic convention of the heroine disguised as a street singer. Following the national tour of *The Street Singer*, Colwell and his wife gradually retired from show business, and Colwell subsequently became manager of a movie theatre in Mount Holly, New Jersey.

COMER, Thomas

Composer, dance arranger, actor, singer, and musical director, Thomas Comer was born in Bath, England, on 19 December 1790. Although he demonstrated a musical talent at an early age and was classically trained as a singer, Comer believed that his vocation rested on the stage rather than in a concert hall. He debuted at the Bath Theatre at the age of twelve in the role of Don Cesar in *The Castle of Andalusia*. He remained with the Bath Theatre until 1816 when he was engaged as an actor and singer at the Theatre Royal, Covent Garden, where he made his first appearance as the Officer in Thomas Morton's play *The Slave* (12 November 1816). On 4 October 1819, Comer performed the Archbishop of Canterbury in William Charles Macready's revival of Shakespeare's *Henry V*, and a variety of character roles followed, including Procles in John Banim's play *Damon and Pythias*, beginning on 28 May 1821.Six years later, he made his debut on the New York stage in the role of Forage in the farce, *Turn Him Out*, at the Bowery Theatre (7 September 1827).[240] Through the 1827–1828 season Comer's parts at the Bowery included Ottavio in the opera *Don Giovanni* (19 October), Phelim O'Scud in the spectacle *Peter Wilkins, or, the Flying Indians* (22 October), Uberto in the opera *The Freebooters* (24 December), Gog in the melodrama *Alfred the Great, or, the Enchanted Standard* (5 January 1828), O'Slash in the musical farce *The Invincibles* (12 May) as well as roles in *John of Paris* and *The Poor Soldier*. After the Bowery Theatre was destroyed by fire on 26 May 1828, Comer and many of his fellow actors moved to the Tremont Theatre in Boston, where he first appeared as Looney McTwoiter in *The Review* (1 September 1828). After the Tremont Theatre season ended in May 1829, Comer returned to New York to spend the summer working at the American Opera House, Chatham Street, where he performed Compton in *The Agreeable Surprise* (20 May 1829), Robin in the musical afterpiece *No Song, No Supper* (1 June) and a variety of other roles to fill out the four-month season. Late in August, the American Opera House was closed and Comer moved back to Boston, where he remained for the rest of his career. In addition to his position as an actor, Comer was engaged as musical director, composer, and dance arranger for the Tremont Theatre, a position he held until 1847 when he became musical director for the Boston Museum. There he composed incidental and dance music for the "Grand Chinese Spectacle" *Aladdin, or, the Wonderful Lamp* (1847), Edwin Booth's production of *Richard III, or, The Battle of Bosworth Field* (1849), the "Magnificent Oriental Musical Romance" *The Forty Thieves* (1849), the "Musical Scenic Romance" *The Enchanted Beauty, or, the Dream of 100 Years* (1850), *Uncle Tom's Cabin* (1852), and *Valeria* (1852), to give just a few examples. In September 1854, Comer became the musical director of the new Boston Theatre, and on opening night, 11 September, he left the podium to act the role of Sir Lucius O'Trigger in Sheridan's comedy *The Rivals*. After several seasons at the Boston Theatre, Comer accepted the musical directorship of the Howard Athenaeum, a position he held until shortly before his death on 27 July 1862. Remembered as talented, affable and guileless, good humored, religious, and honest, Comer was buried on 30 July at Mount Auburn, on Mistletoe Path, beside his wife.[241]

Example 35. "Aladdin Quick Step" from *Aladdin, or, the Wonderful Lamp*

Example 35 (continued). "Aladdin Quick Step" from *Aladdin, or, the Wonderful Lamp*

Comer's published dance and incidental compositions include "The Boyleston Quadrilles" (1836), a set of five dances (of which, three were arrangements of operatic arias, two were original) composed for a dance recital at Highland Hall, Norfolk House, a popular assembly room in Roxbury, Massachusetts; "Medley Overture" (1842) composed for the Ethiopian opera *Bone Squash Diavolo, or Il Nicceretta* at the Tremont Theatre; "Yes Beda! Thus Beda!" (1847), composed for *Blue Beard* at the Boston Museum; "Aladdin Quick Step" (1847), and "Alone, Alone" (1847), composed for *Aladdin, or, the Wonderful Lamp* at the Boston Museum; "Quick Step" (1848), composed for *The Enchanted Horse, or the Peri of the*

Air at the Boston Museum; "The Grand Troubadour March" (1850), "Oh, Hope Is a Beautiful Warbling Bird" (1850), and "The Enchanted Quick Step" (1850), composed for *The Enchanted Beauty, or, the Dream of 100 Years* at the Boston Museum; "Our Homestead Is Surely the Sweetest on Earth" (1852), and "Early in De Morning" (1852), both included in Comer's incidental score for *Uncle Tom's Cabin* at the Boston Museum;[242] "It Is for Love" (1852), composed as part of the incidental music for the Boston Museum's production of *Valeria*; and "The Lucknow Quadrilles" (1858) composed for the production of *Jessie Brown* at the Boston Theatre.

The "Aladdin Quick Step" (example 35) provides a representative sample of Comer's dance music. Spirited, jovial, and easily assimilated by even the least discerning ear, the musical phrases are symmetrically grouped into four-measure units that employ the simplest of harmonic accompaniments. A ubiquitous repeated-note melodic motif propels and enlivens the dance music that grows in force with the addition of the sixteenth-note Alberti bass figure at measure 41. A variation of dynamics maintains interest throughout the repeated sections by suggesting different musical moods and textures. Particularly noteworthy are the quick changes from loud to soft (measures 8–9, 16–17, 32–33) or soft to loud (measure 16, 32), and the very loud (*fortissimo*) section from measure 41 to the end that adds power and passion to the dance by sustaining the dynamic intensity.

CONNELLY, Michael

Michael Connelly (AKA Michael Connolly) was born in Liverpool, England, in 1840 and became musical director of the Prince of Wales Theatre in Liverpool under the management of Alex Henderson in 1861. It was there that he began a long association with the "Queen of Burlesque," Lydia Thompson, and sailed with her and her core company to the United States on 11 August 1868 to commence a season of performances at Wood's Museum in New York City. Connelly first appeared in New York theatre listings on 28 September as musical director, composer, and arranger of the music in Lydia Thompson's production of *Ixion, or, the Man on the Wheel*.[243] Subsequent productions with Lydia Thompson for which he composed, arranged, and directed music included: *Ernani, or, The Horn of a Dilemma* (28 December 1868), *The Forty Thieves, or Striking Oil in Family Jars* (1 February 1869),[244] *Sindbad the Sailor, or, The Ungenial Gent and the Little Cabin Boy* (29 May 1869), *Pippin,* or, *The King of the Gold Mines* (4 April 1870), *Mosquito* (2 May 1870), *Lurline, or The Knight and the Naiads* (17 October 1870),[245] *Paris, or, The Apple of Discord* (14 November 1870), *St. George and the Dragon, or, The Seven Champions of Christendom* (9 January 1871), *Blue Beard, or, The Mormon, the Maiden and the Little Militaire* (16 August 1871),[246]*Robin Hood, or, The Maid That Was Arch, and the Youth That Was Archer* (22 July 1872), and *Kenilworth, or, Ye Queen, Ye Knight, and Ye Maiden* (21 September 1872). Connelly left the Lydia Thompson Company after the run of *Kenilworth* to become composer and musical director at Niblo's Garden, where he assembled the score for *Leo and Lotos* (30 November 1872) that included a ballet of jewels, a bird ballet, a military ballet, various specialties, and the obligatory transformation scene. Later productions at Niblo's Garden included: *Azreal, or, The Magic Charm* (28 April 1873), with a demon ballet, a harlequinade, a hornpipe, incidental music for Lulu, the "eighth wonder of the world," and another transformation scene; *The Black Crook* (18 August 1873), for which Connelly composed a new overture and incidental music;[247]and *The Children in the Wood* (8 December 1873), for which Connelly composed the overture and ballet music. For the 1874–1875 season, Connelly moved to Booth's Theatre, where he provided musical direction and incidental music for plays, such as Dion Boucicault's *Belle Lamar* (10 August 1874),[248] and *Macbeth* (7 November 1874). After the season at Booth's Theatre, Connelly returned to England to provide musical direction for the Lydia Thompson Company's tour of the provinces;[249]and in August 1877, Connelly, Thompson, and company returned to the United States for another American tour beginning at Wallack's Theatre in New York. There Connelly provided musical direction and incidental music for *Blue Beard* (18 August 1877), *Oxygen, or Gas in Burlesque Metre* (27 August 1877), and *Robinson Crusoe* (12 September 1877). Returning to New York after a six week tour, Connelly and the Lydia Thompson Company moved to the Eagle Theatre, where they performed *Robinson Crusoe* (12 November 1877), followed by *Piff-Paff, or The Magic Armory* (21 November 1877). On 15 December 1877, Michael Connelly joined Lydia Thompson and her core company on the steamship *City of Richmond* and sailed back to England[250]where he continued to compose and arrange music for Lydia Thompson's burlesques. In 1881 Connelly became associated with the actor-manager Wilson Barrett for whom he composed a great many incidental scores: *The Lights o' London* (September 1881), *The Silver King* (November 1882), *The Golden Ladder* (December 1887), *The Ben-My-Chree* (May 1888), *The Good Old*

Times (February 1889), *Now-a-Days, a Tale of the Turf* (February 1889), *The People's Idol* (December 1890), and *The Deemster* (November 1899), to name just a few. Connelly returned to New York in September 1883 to assume the musical directorship at Wallack's Theatre. Theatrical records of 1886 indicate that Connelly was the musical director of the Violet Cameron Opera Company performing at the Casino Theatre in October and November. Following the New York engagement, which turned out to be a financial disaster for the company, the British-based troupe sailed back to England, with Connelly in tow. He continued his association with Wilson Barrett through the turn of the century, but after Barrett's death in 1904, Connelly faded from public life and died late in August 1911.[251]

Example 36, the "Galop" Connelly composed for *The Forty Thieves* (1869) is representative of his style. Note that the dance music is built in four-measure phrases that connect to form eight-measure units. The first eight measures (not counting the anacrusis) are followed by a second-eight measure unit that begins as an exact replication of the first unit (measures 9–first part of 11 are exactly the same as measures 1–first part

Example 36. "Galop" from *The Forty Thieves*

of 3) but ends differently. The slyly conceived musical variation is certainly appropriate to evoke the crafty and devious nature of the forty thieves. The "um-pah" accompaniment employs the standard tonic-dominant progressions, but the addition of the common-tone diminished chord (measure 2, 10), a secondary dominant (measure 11) and the substitution of the ii chord for the IV chord (measure 6) create harmonic interest. In addition, the use of accented non-chordal tones in the melody (measures 3–6, 11–14, 19, 23) generates forward motion as the dissonance finds resolution in a chordal tone. The jovial atmosphere of the piece provides an interesting balance to the menace implied by the accented dissonances in the melody. The music seems to suggest that the thieves might be deceitful and underhanded, but their deviousness is fun to watch.

COOK, Will Marion

Composer, violinist, and musical director, Will Marion [Mercer] Cook was born in Washington D.C. on 27 January 1869 to upper middle-class college-educated parents. [252] After the sudden death of his father from tuberculosis in 1869, Will and his mother spent two years wandering around the United States, living for a time in Denver and Kansas City. Finally, in 1881, Will was sent to live with his grandparents in Chattanooga, Tennessee. It was there that Will heard African-American folk music for the first time and the experience had a profound effect on the rest of his life. It was also because of his grandfather that Cook developed an interest in playing the violin, and when he was fifteen, he was sent to Oberlin to study the instrument.[253] Encouraged by his violin instructor at Oberlin, Cook auditioned for the celebrated German violinist Joseph Joachim and was accepted at the Berlin Hochschule für Musik, where he studied harmony, counterpoint, piano, and violin from 1887 to 1889, thanks to the efforts of Frederick Douglas who organized a fundraiser to defray the cost of a European education. Upon his return to the United States in the fall of 1889, Cook pursued a career as a concert artist, beginning with a recital in Washington, D.C. in December. Further bookings as a soloist were rare so Cook accepted the position of musical director for a new orchestra organized by Christian A. Fleetwood and Frederick Douglas. The Cook Orchestra (as it was called) toured from 1891 to 1893 when it was scheduled to perform at the Chicago World's Fair. Cook composed *Scenes from the Opera of Uncle Tom's Cabin* for the occasion but the work was not performed. Cook left the orchestra to go to New York City where he studied with Antonin Dvořák at the National Conservatory of Music in 1894–1895, and during this time, Cook developed an interest in the popular music he heard in vaudeville. Gradually he came to the conclusion that ragtime, gospel, and theatre music were his true métier and he began composing songs.

Cook's first big success arrived on 5 July 1898 when his "Sensational African Singing and Dancing Novelty" *Clorindy, or, The Origin of the Cakewalk* (libretto by Paul Laurence Dunbar) was added to *Rice's Summer Nights* performing at the Roof Garden of the Casino Theatre.[254] The musical ran for over sixty sold-out performances and made Cook famous. For the African-American team of (Bert) Williams and (George) Walker, Cook reworked *Clorindy* into the *Senegambian Carnival*, a touring ragtime musical that opened at the Boston Theatre (5 September 1898). With R.C. McPherson he created the Gotham-Attucks Publishing Company to print his music and that of other African-American composers, and by the fall of 1899, when Cook appeared in theatrical listings as the musical director for the Williams and Walker production of *Policy Players*, he is referred to as "the famous composer Will Marion Cook."[255] Much of *Policy Players* was based on the Williams and Walker, Will Marion Cook musical, *A Lucky Coon*, a revised version of *Senegambian Carnival* which toured from December 1998 through the spring of 1899. During Christmas week 1899, the Boston Music Hall produced *Uncle Eph's Christmas*, a dialect sketch with a cakewalk finale composed by Cook and written by Dunbar. In 1900, Cook composed additional music for *The Casino Girl* (19 March); he created the book, music, and lyrics (with help from Dunbar) for *Jes Lak White Fo'ks* (26 June); and he composed music and appeared with his wife, Abbie Mitchell, in the Williams and Walker musical *Sons of Ham* (15 October). The following year, Cook and his wife reprised their roles in a revival of *Sons of Ham*; he provided additional music for *The New Yorkers* at the Herald Square Theatre (7 October 1901); and he composed *The Cannibal King* (August 1901), a vehicle for Bob Cole and Abbie Mitchell that went out on tour in November 1901.[256] In 1902, Cook composed three songs for *The Wild Rose* (5 May) and began work with Paul Laurence Dunbar on the Williams and Walker vehicle *In Dahomey*, opening at the New York Theatre on 18 February 1903.[257] Later in that year, Cook composed additional music for *The Girl from Dixie* (14 December) and began work on the score for *The Southerners* (23 May 1904), one of the first integrated musicals to play a Broadway theatre.[258] Cook composed an additional tune, "Bygone Days are Best," for *Mrs.*

Black Is Back at the Bijou Theatre (7November 1904); he toured with the Memphis Students,[259] a singing-dancing ensemble that had given popular "syncopated music" concerts at Hammerstein's Victoria Theatre (1905); he co-composed (with Bert Williams) the score for *Abyssinia* at the Majestic Theatre (20 February 1906); he arranged the music for *Dixie Ann* at the International Theatre in Chicago (January 1907); he composed songs for *My Friend from Georgia* (May 1907) and *In Zululand* (29 June 1907), both at the Pekin Theatre, Chicago;[260] he created the score (and acted as musical director, along with James J. Vaughn) for *Bandanna Land* at the Majestic Theatre, New York City (3 February 1908); and for *The Boys and Betty* at Wallack's Theatre (2 November 1908), he provided an additional number ("Whoop 'er Up with a Whoop La La"), which was also interpolated into Silvio Hein's score for *Judy Forgot* (6 October 1910). *A Blackville Corporation*, adapted by J. Leubrie Hill from Cook's *Bandanna Land*, began a national tour in Harlem (1910), and, the following year, Cook composed (with Alex Rogers) *In the Jungles* for the Black Patti Troubadours. Also in 1911, Cook and Rogers worked on the unproduced *Black Bohemia, or, Darkydom: an Act Depicting Life as Seen in the Negro Cafes and Rathskellers around New York City*. In 1913, Will Marion Cook (along with J. Rosamond Johnson, and James Reese Europe) produced the musical revue, *The Frog Families* in New York City; he composed music for the tabloid musical *The Traitor*, produced at the Lafayette Theatre in Harlem (17 March 1913); and 1914, *Darkydom*, co-composed and co-conducted by Will Marion Cook and James Reese Europe, began a tour that ended with a production at the Lafayette Theatre (23 October 1915).[261]

In 1915, tuberculosis abruptly put an end to Cook's whirlwind theatrical activities, and for almost three years, he rested and recovered. But in 1918, he organized the Southern Syncopated Orchestra (AKA the New York Syncopated Orchestra) that toured extensively throughout the United States and Great Britain, literally "playing the palace" at a command performance for King George V. In March 1919, Cook and the orchestra returned to New York and gave a concert at the Forty-fourth Street Theatre (6 March).[262] By 1922, Cook was the leader of the twelve-piece Clef Club Orchestra that toured in vaudeville on the Keith circuit,[263] and in 1923, Cook and his orchestra appeared in *Just for Fun*, a touring vaudeville review produced by Irvin Miller, a veteran African-American showman.[264] In 1929, Cook collaborated with Will Vodery to write and produce *Swing Along* at the Lafayette Theatre; he also directed the African-American choral group, the Jubilee Ensemble, for Vincent Youmans's *Great Day* (17

October 1929); and he composed an opera, *St. Louis 'ooman* (libretto by his son Mercer) that was never produced.²⁶⁵ Cook spent the final decades of his life teaching and mentoring African-American musicians. His student, Duke Ellington, for example, recalled that he and Cook used to ride around Central Park in a taxi and discuss music composition: "I'd sing a melody in its simplest form and he'd stop me and say, 'Reverse your figures.' He was a brief but strong influence. His language had to be pretty straight for me to know what he was talking about. Some of the things he used to tell me I never got a chance to use until years later, when I wrote the tone poem, *Black, Brown, and Beige*."²⁶⁶ He was not always liked by his collaborators or the musicians in his choruses and orchestras, but he was always respected for his musicianship and expertly crafted compositions. Cook died of cancer on 19 July 1944 at the Harlem Hospital.

COOKE, J[ohn] [P]

Musical director, violinist, and composer John Cooke was born in London in 1820.²⁶⁷ While he was still in his teens, he played in the orchestras of London theatres, including Drury Lane and Covent Garden, and in his twenties, he became musical director for the Adelphi Theatre. Before the 1852–1853 season, American theatre manager William E. Burton imported Cooke and his actress-wife to assume positions at his theatre in Manhattan. Consequently, Cooke's name first appeared in American theatrical records on 23 August 1852 as musical director for *The Gardiner's Wife* at Burton's Theatre.²⁶⁸ During subsequent seasons, the projects Cooke was involved with included the burlesque, *Shylock: A Jerusalem Hearty Joke* (9 October 1853), for which he was credited as musical director; the satirical *Apollo in New York* (11 December 1854), for which Cooke was credited as the musical arranger; and the fairy extravaganza, *King Charming, or, The Blue Bird of Paradise* (24 December 1855), for which he was listed as composer as well as musical director. By the 1857–1858 season, Cooke had moved to Wallack's Theatre, where he supplied the musical direction for burlesques (i.e., *Shylock, or The Merchant of Venice Preserved*), composed the incidental music for the Scottish military drama *Jessie Brown, or, the Relief of Lucknow* (22 February), and arranged the music for the historical spectacle *Deseret Deserted, or, the Last Days of Brigham Young* (25 May).²⁶⁹ In the season that followed, Cooke composed and arranged music for *The Merchant of Venice* (9 December 1858), *The Veteran* (17 January 1859), *As You Like It* (4 April 1859), *The Knight of*

Arva (22 June 1859), and *Lalla Rookh, or, The Fire Worshippers* (18 July 1859).[270] For the 1859–1860 season, Cooke was engaged as the musical director "for drama and ballet" at Niblo's Garden, a position he held until the fall of 1862 when he became musical director of the Winter Garden. There his compositions included incidental scores for *The Ticket of Leave Man* (30 November 1863), *The Sorceress* (26 April 1864), and *Fra Diavolo and Thrice Married* (23 May 1864). Cooke composed the incidental score for the grand spectacular drama *The Sea of Ice* (1 August 1864) at Niblo's Garden, and joined the staff at the Broadway Theatre as musical director for the summer season beginning on 12 June 1865.[271] Five months later, Cooke had contracted typhoid fever and died on 5 November 1865 at his home in New York City. He was survived by his wife and daughter.

In an interview with a correspondent from *The New York Times*, musical director Benjamin Deane recalled that "I hardly think I ever knew a more uniformly genial and witty man than Cooke. He was very ready with replies.... Cooke had a magnificent bass voice.... I was, on Sundays and other occasions, the principal tenor singer in Trinity Church, and afterward in Trinity Chapel during several years. Cooke used to sing bass with me at the chapel. Since he passed away, his pretty daughter, Rosa Cooke, made some reputation by her charming voice, singing in English opera."[272] Cooke's published songs and dance arrangements were representative of his personality: jovial, yet sensitive; witty, yet conservative; disciplined, yet surprising. Cooke made the most of traditional harmonic, melodic, and rhythmic structures, often with surprising and highly original results.

COOLMAN, DeWitt C[linton]

Musical director, and composer, DeWitt C. Coolman was born in Ravenna, Ohio, on 12 November 1881. Following his high school graduation, he joined the J.W. Carner Stock Company in Youngstown for the 1900–1901 season before becoming the musical director of the Corse Payton Stock Company, a position he held for several seasons.[273] During the 1908–1909 season he toured with the *Three Twins* company that played over two hundred performances at the Herald Square Theatre in New York (15 June 1908).[274] After he completed the tour, Coolman was hired as musical director by producer Charles Dillingham for his production of *The Echo* (opening at the Studebaker Theatre in Chicago on 25 April 1910), for which Coolman composed additional music as well as dance music.[275] His next project for Dillingham, *Over the River*, opened at Chicago's Studebaker Theatre on 1 October 1911 before going on tour. Three months later, the musical was produced at the Globe Theatre in New York (8 January 1912) to favorable reviews.[276] Producers Joseph Weber and Lew Fields borrowed Coolman to act as musical director for *Roly Poly*, a "double-Bill of a Vaudeville and a Travesty, Burlesque," that opened at Weber and Fields's Theatre in New York on 21 November 1912 to excellent reviews.[277] Coolman then provided the musical direction for *All Aboard*, a Lew Fields production at his 44th Street Roof Garden Theatre (3 June 1913); *The Red Canary*, a Mackay production that premiered at Ford's Theatre in Baltimore (29 September 1913);[278] and *Watch Your Step*, produced by Charles Dillingham at the New Amsterdam Theatre (9 December 1914), which opened to rave reviews.[279] Just before the end of the New York run (8 May 1915), Coolman contracted typhoid-pneumonia and was sent to Miss Alston's Sanitarium on West Sixty-first Street in Manhattan to receive treatment. None of the doctors' remedies were successful and Coolman died on 19 May 1915, at the age of thirty-three, survived by his wife, mother, sister, and two brothers.[280]

CORLISS, Edward W[arren]

Composer, and dance arranger, Edward W. Corliss was born on 11 March 1872 to a family of comfortable means in Providence, Rhode Island.[281] While a student at Brown University, he served as conductor (and official whistler) for the glee club and composed music for the banjo club, as well as several comic operas produced by the Hammer and Tongs society, including *Priscilla, or, a Maid of Brown* (1894), *Florida Water* (1896), and *The Game King* (1897). The latter drew the attention of playwright and producer Robert Ayres Barnet who engaged Corliss to compose music for *Queen of the Ballet* (7 February 1898), a comic opera designed for the First Corps of Cadets in Boston. As might be expected from the title, a significant amount of dance and incidental music was involved in the production, a sample of which is the "Pantomime and Dance" (example 37) in the "Three Little Lambs" number. The three little lambs are thieves delighting in their ability to rob and scam; in the pantomime (measures 1–11), they enact the various ploys they use in their profession; in the dance (measures 12–28), they pretend to be aristocratic and fashionable, upper-class and elegant in their movement. Note the dynamic marking, pianissimo, on the anacrusis to measure 1, and the repeated quarter-note chords in the treble clef that combine to suggest a skulking movement, covering the melody in the bass clef. The light and flowing melody of the dance music provides a bright contrast to the pantomime incidental, juxtaposing the earlier melodramatic tone with the more sophisticated ambiance of the ballet. The dance music is self-consciously modeled on traditional ballet music (Léo Delibes and Pyotr Ilyich Tchaikovsky immediately come to mind) and utilizes many of the musical devices associated with the ballet in a kind of pointed self-parody. The fermatas over the notes (measures 12, 20) followed by a bounding melodic phrase (measures 13, 21) is the stuff of musical caricature (even given musical tastes in 1898), especially considering the personalities of the three crooks who are dancing. Moreover, to accent the cadence in measure 20, Corliss em-

Example 37. Pantomime and Dance in "Three Little Lambs" from *Queen of the Ballet*

ployed grace notes, further agents of musical satire, to suggest a gracefulness of which the dancers are clearly incapable.

A revised version of *Queen of the Ballet* called *Three Little Lambs* opened at the Jefferson Theatre, Portland, Maine, on 16 October 1899 and appeared at the Fifth Avenue Theatre in New York on 25 December to generally positive reviews.[282] After composing *Queen of the Ballet* Corliss provided additional music for subsequent Robert A. Barnet productions: *My Lady* (11 February 1901), the Broadway production of *Miladi and the Musketeer*; *Miss Simplicity* (30 September 1901);[283] *Cap of Fortune and the Show Girl* (3 February 1902), revised for Broadway as *The Show Girl, or, The Cap of Fortune* (5 May 1902);[284] and *Cinderella and the Prince, or, The Castle of Heart's Desire* (1 February 1904). In August 1908, Corliss reappeared in theatrical records as the composer of *And What Happened Then*, a fantastic comic opera about the Pied Piper after he led all the children out of Hamelin and up into the mountain. Advertised as a vehicle for De Wolf Hopper, the piece was scheduled to open in Ottawa, Canada, on 14 September 1908, but it actually premiered at the Majestic Theatre in Montreal.[285] By the time the *And What Happened Then* tour made its way to the Majestic Theatre in New York (3 December 1908), the musical had undergone a change of name—*The Pied Piper*, a change of composer—Manuel Klein, and all of Corliss's original material had been discarded. Edward Corliss died on 20 September 1916 and was buried at Swan Point Cemetery in Providence. The inscription on his tombstone reads, "He hath put a new song in my mouth."

Considered by critics to be most successful when creating waltzes and marches,[286] Corliss composed several instrumental waltzes and marches, one of which, "Hats Off to the Flag," was regularly performed by the John Philip Sousa Band. Other popular compositions include "Gay Golf Rail" from *Queen of the Ballet*; "The Man behind the Gun" from *Three Little Lambs*; "One for All" from *Miladi and the Musketeer*; "Rosalie" from *Miss Simplicity*; "The One That He Loves Best" from *Cap of Fortune*; and "Send Me, Love, a Postal Card" from *Cinderella and the Prince*.

CRAWFORD, Clifton

In 1875, performer, composer, and dance arranger Clifton Crawford was born in Edinburgh to stage parents, with whom he traveled throughout Great Britain, Australia, and New Zealand on tour with the Crawford-Hunter Party. When, as a teenager, Clifton exhibited a talent for music, his father decided that he should become a church organist and placed him with a Presbyterian Church in Scotland, where he flourished until the pastor heard him improvising a selection of Scotch dance music on the organ. Since his career as a church musician appeared to be over, Crawford decided to try his luck on the vaudeville circuit and played two weeks at Keith's Theatre in Boston.[287] Not an immediate success in vaudeville, he tried his luck as a golf instructor to the wealthy members of New England society, who enjoyed Crawford's occasional solo song-and-monologue performances at the clubhouse after a long day on the course. Late in 1900, playwright and producer Robert Ayres Barnet was in attendance at Crawford's performance at the Providence Golf Club and, impressed with what he heard, Barnet invited him to compose additional music for *My Lady*, a revised version of *Miladi and the Musketeer*, a Boston Cadet musical that was scheduled to receive a professional production at Hammerstein's Victoria Theatre in New York City on 11 February 1901. In addition, Crawford was given the role of Arrah-Miss, his Broadway debut. Following *My Lady*, Crawford composed additional music for a number of shows that included *The Liberty Belles* (30 September 1901) for which he also composed dance music; *Miss Simplicity* (10 February 1902), also dance music; *The Wild Rose* (5 May 1902); *Mother Goose* (2 December 1903); *The Quaker Girl* (23 October 1911*)*; *My Best Girl* (12 September 1912); *The Peasant Girl* (2 March 1915); *The Passing Show of 1915* (22 June1915); *Her Soldier Boy* (6 December 1916); *The Passing Show of 1917* (26 April 1917); and *Fancy Free* (11 April 1918). Crawford, the composer, was often upstaged by Crawford, the performer, who appeared in many of the musicals for which he composed music, and several others, including *Foxy Grandpa* (17 February 1902), *The Jewel of Asia* (16 February 1903), *Seeing New York* (5 June 1906), *Three Twins* (15 June 1908), *A World of Pleasure* (14 October 1915), and *My Lady Friends* (3 December 1909). Best known for his performances of "Pack up Your Troubles in Your Old Kit Bag," Crawford died on 3 June 1920 from injuries sustained after falling 60 feet from his room at the Queens Hotel in Leicester Square, London.[288] Survived by his wife, Emma, Crawford, an only son, was buried beside his parents in Edinburgh.

CRUGER, Randolph ["Dox"]

Born in Oscawana, New York, in November 1861, composer, dance arranger, and musical director Randolph Cruger first appeared in American theatrical records as the musical director for New York's Minstrel Entertainers appearing at Dockstader's Theatre in December 1889.[289] After several seasons with the Minstrels, Cruger became the musical director for George Thatcher's Company of Comedians[290] for whom he composed *Africa* (libretto by J. Cheever Goodwin and Clay M. Greene), a spectacular comic opera, premiering at the California Theatre in San Francisco on 12 June 1893.[291] After San Francisco, the Thatcher Company toured with *Africa*, finally appearing at the Star Theatre in New York on 25 December 1893. For the opera, Cruger composed vocal solos, ensembles, and choruses, as well as the music for several ballets, including a "Feast Dance of the African Chiefs," various marches, and a "Grand Sacrificial Scene." A Boston reviewer called the score "tuneful" and noted that "Encores followed one another so continuously that several of the performers at different times were obliged to refuse to respond on account of sheer exhaustion."[292] New York reviewers were also positive. The critic from the *New York Clipper*, for example, exclaimed: "*Africa* is a musical comedy, and is one of the most if not the most entertaining of its class New Yorkers have seen. It is full of fun and sparkles with bright sayings. The company is excellent, the costumes pretty, and the settings would do credit to a much more pretentious work. The various specialties introduced were of the best order, and the vocal part of the performance was far above the average."[293] Following the remarkably successful tour of *Africa*, Cruger joined his brothers Bertram and Melvin in the creation of a music publishing firm that was highly active around the turn of the century. On 21 June 1937, Rudolph Cruger died at his home in Brooklyn, leaving Emma, his widow, and his son, Rudolph, Jr.

CUTTY, Thomas

Performer, and composer, Thomas Cutty was born to musicians William and Rebecca (Fisher) Cutty in Durham County, England, in 1869. With his two brothers, William, and John, and three sisters, Elizabeth, Eleanor, and Margaret, Thomas was a member of an instrumental and vocal sextet called "The Six Musical Cuttys." The boys played various brass instruments and the girls performed on the violin, viola, and cello, and, according to *The New York Times*, the six children played a total of thirty instruments.[294] After performing for Queen Victoria in 1880, the Cutty family moved to Baltimore where the parents resided while the children toured around the world, playing vaudeville engagements at the Empire Theatre in London, and the Wintergarten in Berlin, and performing with celebrities, such as De Wolf Hopper and John Philip Sousa, in the United States. In addition to fulfilling his vocal and instrumental responsibilities for the sextet, Thomas served as arranger and composer of incidental and dance music for Charles E. Blaney's musical comedy drama, *My Tom-boy Girl*, which opened in Baltimore on 10 April 1905. Following the Baltimore opening, the musical went on tour, stopping in Washington, D.C., Philadelphia, Jersey City, and New York City, where it played the Metropolis Theatre in Harlem (1 May 1905) and the Fourteenth Street Theatre in Manhattan (15 May 1905) to positive reviews.[295] While *My Tomboy Girl* was touring, "The Six Musical Cuttys" continued performing in vaudeville, with engagements at venues that included Keith's Maryland Theatre in Baltimore,[296] and in New York, the Harlem Opera House,[297] the New York Theatre,[298] and the Colonial.[299] After 1910, the sextet (now made up of forty-year-old adults) lost much of its earlier panache and performed only infrequently. As his brothers and sister began to pursue other careers, Thomas became a doctor and spent the remainder of his life in private practice in Baltimore. He died in that city's Lutheran Hospital on 4 April 1952.

D

DABNEY, Ford T[hompson]

Composer, musical director, dance arranger, and pianist Ford Dabney was born into a musical family in Washington, D.C. on 15 March 1883. His earliest musical training came from his father, James H. Dabney, and he would later sing in the choir at St. Mary's Chapel at St. John's Parish[300] and study privately with local music educators, Charles Donch, William Waldecker, and Samuel Fabian.[301] By the time he graduated from Washington High School (class of 1901), Dabney had become a well-known pianist in the district; and a year after graduation, he established a glee club at the Manual Training School (an African-American trade school he had attended as a youth) before going to New York City to study music theory and composition.[302] In 1904 Dabney began a series of four-month engagements as court pianist and composer to President Noro Alexis of Haiti at a salary of $5,000 per engagement[303] When he returned to Washington in 1906 he toured on the vaudeville circuit with an act called *Ford Dabney's Ginger Girls* featuring Lottie Gee (who would later find fame in the cast of *Shuffle Along*), and in 1908, he became co-proprietor of a vaudeville house in Washington, the Ford Dabney Theatre, advertised as the home of "first class and polite vaudeville—the theatre the people attend."[304] While he was managing the vaudeville venue, Dabney divided his time between Washington and New York where he began a long association with composer James Reese Europe and the Clef Club. In 1909 Dabney composed a musical entitled *The King's Quest*[305] and the following year, he and Will Marion Cook created the music and lyrics for "The Pensacola Mooch" in the Ziegfeld *Follies of 1910* (20 June 1910). Dabney's subsequent contributions to Broadway musicals included "That's Why They Call Me Shine" in *His Honor, the Barber* (8 May 1911); "The San Francisco Fair" (dance music) in *Nobody Home* (20 April 1915); and the entire score for *Rang Tang* (12 July 1927). Between the years 1913 and 1921, Dabney's orchestra became the first African-American orchestra to perform regularly at a Broadway theatre, on the New Amsterdam Theatre roof in

Ziegfeld's Midnight Frolics;[306] and between 1914 and 1917, Dabney and Europe's Tempo Club Orchestra toured with dancers Vernon and Irene Castle. Dabney collaborated with Europe on many of the Castles' dances, including "The Castle Walk," "Castle Innovation Tango," "Castle Maxixe," and "Castle's Half and Half," an early example of dance music composed in 5/4, a clever combination of waltz time (3/4) with ragtime (2/4). From 1917 to 1920, Dabney and his orchestra made a great number of recordings for the Aeolian Company, and in May 1920, his band was one of the many summer attractions at Luna Park at Coney Island.[307] Dabney and his orchestra spent much of the 1920s playing atop the New Amsterdam Theatre and at various venues in Atlantic City, New Jersey. He continued an active musical career until his retirement in the late 1940s. Following a long illness, Dabney died on 21 June 1958 at Sydenham Hospital in New York City, survived by his wife Martha and son, Ford Dabney, Jr.[308]

DALY, William [Merrigan]

Pianist, composer, orchestrator, and musical director William Daly was born on 1 September 1887 in Cincinnati, Ohio, and educated in Boston, after his theatrical parents moved there when he was a child. Daly was considered a piano prodigy in his teens, but his interest changed to literature when he attended Harvard, graduating in 1908 with a Bachelor of Arts degree. After college he worked in menial jobs until 1911 when he landed a position in New York City on the editorial staff of *Everybody's Magazine*, where he rubbed shoulders with the likes of Sinclair Lewis and Walter Lippmann. While in New York, Daly joined the Dutch Treat Club at Delmonico's Restaurant and composed the music for a number of satirical mini- operas produced by the club, including: *Everymagazine, an Immorality Play* (19 February 1913), *The Chicken, or, Biting the Hand that Feeds Us* (25 February 1913), and *Western Stuff: an Operetta in One Reel* (February 1917). In 1914, three years into his literary career, Daly conducted a choral composition at Carnegie Hall, in a recital at which the Polish pianist, Ignace Jan Paderewski, was present. Impressed by Daly's musicianship, Paderewski urged him to pursue a career in music, and Daly took his advice.

Almost immediately Daly found work on Broadway as the musical director and co-composer of *Hands Up*, opening at the Forty-fourth Street Theatre on 7 June 1915.[309] The following year, Daly was musical director of *Betty* (3 October 1916), a musical for which he composed interpolated dance music, a fox trot called "Spilling the Beans." In 1918, Daly was hired as the musical director at New York's largest theatre, the Hippodrome, for the three-act musical spectacle, *Everything*; in addition, he was also given the opportunity to co-compose the score with John Philip Sousa, Irving Berlin, Harry Tierney, and Raymond Hubbell. With George Gershwin and Vincent Youmans, Daly co-composed the score for *Piccadilly to Broadway*, a revue that opened in Atlantic City on 27 September 1920 but never made it to Broadway;[310] he provided additional music for *Kissing Time* (11 October 1920); and he was co-composer and dance arranger (with Paul Lannin) for the "bright and tuneful" musical, *For Goodness Sake* (21 February 1922) that featured Fred and Adele Astaire, and had additional music by George Gershwin.[311] Later in the year, Daly and Gershwin collaborated on the music for the musical melodrama *Hayseed*, arriving on Broadway with the title, *Our Nell* (4 December 1922), a "fresh and enjoyable entertainment" that closed after forty performances.[312] Daly worshipped Gershwin, and Gershwin called Daly his best friend and his favorite Broadway conductor.[313] Over the years Daly would conduct several of Gershwin's musicals, including: *For Goodness Sake, George White's Scandals* (1924), *Tip-Toes, George White's Scandals* (1926), *Oh, Kay!, Show Girl,* and *Let 'Em Eat Cake*. In addition, Daly provided orchestrations for Gershwin's *Lady Be Good, Rosalie, Treasure Girl, Of Thee I Sing,* and *Pardon my English*. Beyond Broadway, Daly and Gershwin often performed two-piano recitals, invariably playing Gershwin's compositions, at fund raisers and benefits;[314] Gershwin was so taken with Daly's pianistic abilities that he dedicated his *Three Preludes* (1927) to him.

After composing "Hello! Good-Bye" and "Pretty City Girl" for Augustus Barratt's *Jack and Jill* (22 March 1923) and "A Girl Is Like Sunshine" and "Laugh While You're Dancing Around" for *Earl Carrol's Vanities* (5 July 1923) Daly no longer appeared in theatrical notices as a composer; instead, the remainder of his career would be devoted to the musical direction and orchestration of other composers' music. In 1930, in addition to his Broadway responsibilities, Daly became the musical director of the NBC Orchestra, for which he arranged weekly Monday night broadcasts of orchestral and vocal music. Daly was described as "the Harvard gentleman: circumspect, leisurely in gait, spectacled and shy, tall and lanky, fair-complexioned with unruly hair, and… usually casually attired with clothes that bordered on the shabby."[315] On 4 December 1936, after a late night at his studio on 50 East 52nd Street, Daly returned to his home on Fifth Avenue around midnight and suffered a fatal heart attack as he was preparing for bed. He was survived by his wife, Elizabeth Harding Daly, and his daughter Eileen.[316] Daly's compositions were tuneful in the style of Jerome Kern and syncopated in the style of George Gershwin and Vincent Youmans. They displayed a great mastery of musical technique with interesting harmonic accompaniments and melodic contours, but they lacked an originality that would set them apart from their models. It was, perhaps, Daly's long association with Gershwin that led him to realize that his musical gift rested in skill rather than inspiration.

DANNENBERG, Louis

Born in Winsboro, South Carolina, on 23 December 1885, pianist and composer Louis Dannenberg studied the piano at New York City's National Conservatory of Music in 1896.[317] He composed dance music for the *Ziegfeld Follies of 1913* (15 June 1913), a novelette for the piano entitled "Cupid's Dart," published by Theodore Presser of Philadelphia in 1915. Other compositions for the piano included: "A Day's Frolic: Marche Populaire" (1905); "Jessamine" (1906), a mazurka; "Cabriola: a Tango" (1914); "The Angel's Story" (1915), and "Song to Spring" (1915). In the 1930s, Dannenberg had a regular radio program as a solo pianist on WPAP, as well as a career as an accompanist and nightclub performer.[318] Dannenberg's dance music was virtuosic in scope, exploring juxtapositions of dynamics, articulations, and rhythms within traditional meters and keys. Lyrical melodic fragments were surrounded by mountains of chordal harmonies that created a powerful ebb and flow in the musical development while maintaining rigorous sixteen-and-thirty-two-measure structures. Louis Dannenberg died at Lebanon Hospital in the Bronx on 22 May 1938. Three days later he was buried in Greenwood Cemetery in Brooklyn.

DARLEY, Francis T[homas] S[ully]

Millionaire composer, organist, conductor, and art collector, Francis T. S. Darley, the grandson of famed Philadelphia artist, Thomas Sully, was born in Philadelphia in 1833. His parents, William Henry Westray Darley, a music teacher, and Jane Cooper Sully, a painter, fostered the boy's interest in music from an early age. Darley received instruction from his father until he was a teenager,[319] after which he was sent to Europe to further his musical education. When he returned to Philadelphia, Darley became the organist and choir director at Holy Trinity Church for which he composed and arranged hymns and choral music, including the Christmas anthem, "Blessed Is He that Cometh" (1870), and "Te Deum Laudamus" (1873). In addition, he conducted concerts at the Handel and Haydn Society of Philadelphia[320] and was a founding member of the Philadelphia Musical Festival Association (i.e. the Philadelphia Orchestra) and its first vice-president.[321] In 1881, Darley told the press that he had chosen a drama called *The Memoirs of the Devil* as the subject for an opera he intended to compose entitled *The Demon's Record*.[322] The result of his efforts was a three-act romantic opera called *The Magic Bell*, which was published in

Example 38. "Matapa March" from *Fortunio and his Seven Gifted Servants*

1881 but never produced. Two years later, however, on 23 April 1883, the Cosmopolitan Theatre in New York produced Darley's next opera, *Fortunio and his Seven Gifted Servants,* based on the fairy extravaganza by James Robinson Planché. The review from *The New York Times* determined that "The music of this extravaganza, coyly announced as 'the great American opera,' and composed by Francis T.S. Darley, is not of such remarkable merit as to make Mr. [Arthur] Sullivan hide his diminished head, being in many parts of extremely light texture, but in several concerted passages there is considerable taking melody, which good singers last night made agreeable."[323] Irrespective of the reviews, Darley's score displayed a ma-

Example 39. "Transformation Music" from *Fortunio and his Seven Gifted Servants*

ture (if not necessarily original) handling of dance and incidental music throughout. The "Matapa March" (example 38), played at the end of scene three, accompanied the following stage action: "[Emperor] Matapa urges his troops against Fortunio and his servants. Boisterer [one of the Gifted Servants] takes position in front of his master and blows the soldiers back every time that they charge. At length Matapa, enraged, heads the charge. Boisterer blows so hard that Matapa, the Chamberlain and others fall flat, and the rest are blown off the stage."[324] The heroic tone of the upward-moving melody and the militaristic triplet rhythm in the accompaniment (consciously evocative of the marches of Franz von Suppé) provided an apt underscore for the mock heroic battle onstage.

The "Transformation Music" (example 39) occurred in scene four, immediately before the finale of the opera[325] and underscored the stage directions: "The pile of treasure gradually opens, and discovers a magnificent Fairy Chariot, drawn by twenty-four sheep with golden fleeces, in which is the FAIRY."[326] The bucolic lyricism of Darley's music (in the traditional pastoral key of F major) helped to establish a tone of tranquility at the end of opera, and the continuous motion of the accompaniment pattern reflected the systematic unveiling of the scene.

Francis Darley died on 22 August 1914 at his palatial residence on 520 South Broad Street in Philadelphia. He was buried in the Laurel Hill Cemetery beside his wife, Cecelia Baldwin Darley, the daughter of the millionaire locomotive builder Matthias Baldwin, who predeceased him.

DARLING, Frank N.

Composer, dance arranger, and musical director Frank Darling was born in the village of Clyde, New York, in 1868. The son of the director of the Lyons (New York) School of Music, Darling was a child prodigy, becoming the organist at the Lyons Presbyterian Church at the age of nine. In 1889, he joined the touring Deshon Opera Company as musical director[327] and by 1899 he held the same position with the touring Wilbur-Kirwin Opera Company.[328] The following year, he was engaged as musical director for a summer season with the Arnold Opera Company[329] and in the early years of the twentieth century Darling acted as musical director for *King Dodo* (12 May 1902) and *The Yankee Consul* (22 February 1904). After touring with *The Yankee Consul*, Darling joined the touring Henry W. Savage Opera Company, leaving them at the end of the 1907 season[330] to become the musical director of Richard Carle's production of

Mary's Lamb, which was produced at the New York Theatre from 25 May 1908 to 5 September 1908. Two weeks after the show closed, Darling began rehearsals for *Miss Innocence*, the musical composed by Ludwig Englander and starring Florenz Ziegfeld's wife, Anna Held, which enjoyed a successful production at the New York Theatre (30 November 1908) before going on tour for several years. Darling left the tour in May 1910 when Ziegfeld engaged him as the musical director for the *Follies of 1910* (20 June 1910).[331] Subsequently, Darling completed the musical direction for every edition of the *Follies* through 1919, often selecting and arranging dance music from the mass of melodies at his disposal. After leaving Ziegfeld, Darling went to Santa Monica, California, where he became involved with the Santa Monica Musical Association for some years before ill health forced him to return to his home in Lyons, New York. During his long career as a musical director, Darling was considered one of the most picturesque figures in show business. He sported a long, flowing mustache and conducted himself with the exalted demeanor usually associated with actors of an older generation.[332] He died on 9 November 1935 at his home, following a long illness.

DE KOVEN, [Henry Louis] Reginald

Composer Reginald De Koven was born in Middleton, Connecticut on 3 April 1859, the son of an Episcopalian minister who was descended from an old Colonial American family. In 1872, the family moved to England where Reginald De Koven completed a degree at St. John's College, Oxford, in 1879. Following his studies in England, De Koven studied piano with W. Spiedel in Stuttgart and musical theory with Tilo Pruckner in Stuttgart and Wilhelm Gottlieb Hauff in Frankfurt; he studied singing with Luigi Vannuccini in Florence; and studied musical theatre with Franz Friedrich Richard Genée and Franz von Suppé in Vienna, and with Léo Delibes in Paris. When he returned to the United States in 1882, he settled in Chicago where he took a job at a brokerage firm and married writer Anna Farwell, the daughter of United States Senator Charles Benjamin Farwell, after which he became a successful dry goods merchant and magazine writer.[333] In 1887, De Koven composed the music for his first comic opera, *The Begum* (21 November 1887) produced at the Fifth Avenue Theatre in New York. Although the reviewers generally complained about the lack of originality in the work, De Koven's music was considered of a sufficiently high quality to encourage him to pursue a career as a theatre composer.³³⁴ He followed *The Begum* with *Don Quixote* (18 November 1889) at the Boston Theatre; *Robin Hood* (9 June 1890) at the Chicago Opera House; *The Fencing Master* (14 November 1892) at the Casino Theatre; *The Knickerbockers* (29 May 1893) at the Garden Theatre; *The Algerian* (26 October 1893) at the Garden Theatre; *Rob Roy* (29 October 1894) at the Herald Square Theatre; *The Tzigane* (16 May 1895) at Abbey's Theatre; *The Mandarin* (2 November 1895) at the Herald Square Theatre; *The Paris Doll* (14 September 1897) at Parson's Theatre (Hartford, Connecticut); *The Highwayman* (13 December 1897) at the Broadway Theatre; *The Three Dragoons* (30 January 1899) at the Broadway Theatre; *Papa's Wife* (13 November 1899) at the Manhattan Theatre; *Foxy Quiller* (5 November 1900) at the Broadway Theatre; *The Little Duchess* (14 October 1901) at the Casino Theatre; *Maid Marian* (27 January 1902) at the Garden Theatre; *The Jersey Lily* (14 September 1903) at the Victoria Theatre; *Red Feather* (9 November 1903) at the Lyric Theatre; *Happyland, or The King of Elysia* (2 October 1905) at the Lyric Theatre; *The Student King* (25 December 1906) at the Garden Theatre; *The Girls of Holland* (14 November 1907) at the Lyric Theatre; *Nearly a Hero* (24 February 1908) at the Casino Theatre; *The Golden Butterfly* (12 October 1908) at the Broadway Theatre; *The Beauty Spot* (10 April 1909) at the Herald Square Theatre; *The Yankee Mandarin* (14 June 1909) at the Majestic Theatre; *The Wedding Trip* (25 December 1911) at the Broadway Theatre; *Her Little Highness* (13 October 1913) at the Liberty Theatre; and *Yesterday* (16 March 1919) at the Shubert-Belasco Theatre, Washington, D.C. In addition, De Koven contributed additional music to *The Man in the Moon* (24 April 1899) at the New York Theatre; *The Man in the Moon, Jr.* (23 December 1899) at the New York Theatre; *From Broadway to Tokio* [sic] (23 January 1900) at the New York Theatre; and *The Casino Girl* (19 March 1900) at the Casino Theatre. De Koven also composed two operas, *The Canterbury Pilgrims* (8 March 1917) produced by the Metropolitan Opera, and *Rip Van Winkle* (2 January 1920) produced by the Chicago Opera.³³⁵

Along with his career as a composer, De Koven enjoyed additional employment as music critic for the *Chicago Evening Post* (1889–1895), *Harper's Weekly* (1895–1897), the *New York Journal* (1898–1900), and the *New York World* (1892–1897; 1907–1912). At the turn of the century, during the residence of De Koven and his wife in Washington, D.C., he founded and conducted the Philharmonic Orchestra of Washington, D.C., and in 1902 De Koven entered into a partnership with the Shubert Brothers to build the Lyric Theatre for future productions of his comic operas and provide a home for his American School of Opera.[336] On 16 January 1920, De Koven and his wife hosted a party at their Chicago home, celebrating the success of De Koven's opera *Rip Van Winkle*, recently produced at the Chicago Opera. After taking part in the festivities and dancing, De Koven took a seat and began chatting amicably about his work. When the music started up again, he did not rise from his seat. A guest at the party, Dr. Ludwig Simon, rushed to his side and determined that the composer had suffered a stroke. Ten minutes later, De Koven was dead.[337] Funeral services were held at the Cathedral of St. John the Divine in New York City and the burial took place at Woodlawn Cemetery in the Bronx. He left an estate worth more than $200,000 in trust to his wife and daughter, Ethel.[338]

Example 41. "Japanese Ballet" from *From Broadway to Tokio*

Example 42. "Coconut Dance" from *The Beauty Spot*

De Koven was among the ranks of classically-trained composers who created all the music for their comic operas—songs, incidental and ballet music, arrangements, and orchestrations—and, like Victor Herbert, he also provided dance music (and orchestrations) for musical shows by other composers. For example, in *From Broadway to Tokio* [sic], De Koven composed a delightful "Japanese Ballet" (example 41) suggesting the pentatonic scale characteristically associated with Japanese music in both melody and accompaniment (measures 3–5, 7–10). The pentatonic scale is juxtaposed with Western tonalities especially in measures 27–33 to evoke the "Broadway" of the show's title, even in a Japanese setting.

In his own comic opera, *The Beauty Spot,* De Koven composed a lively "Coconut Dance" (example 42) to celebrate the arrival of a Dutch coffee planter from Borneo. Following a two-measure introduction, the "Coconut Dance" is organized into groups of six (measures 3–8, 19–24) and a structure of 4 + 2 + 4 (measures 9–18) instead of the eight-measure units typical in dance arrangements. Note the specific dynamics and articulations throughout the dance, the use of repeated chords as accompaniment in the six-measure groupings and the "um pah" style of accompaniment in measures 9–17, and the ubiquitous use of grace notes, all of which, added to the minor mode, create an exotic and folk-like dance arrangement.

Example 43. "Galop" from *The Man in the Moon*

For *The Man in the Moon* De Koven composed two full-length ballets, an "Orchid Ballet" and a "Grand March and Ballet of Expansion" that explored American imperialism under Teddy Roosevelt. Included in the ballet were numbered movements entitled "Cuba," "Hawaii," "Manilla," "Porto Rico," "Galop-Finale" (example 43), and a patriotic hymn, "Columbia," to end the piece. Note the patriotic reference to the American Colonial period (measures 17–32) with the musical allusion to "Yankee Doodle."

In the third act of *The Highwayman*, Rodney, a twenty-five-year-old naval officer who served with Admiral Nelson, sings a naval ballad about

Example 44. "Hornpipe" from *The Highwayman*

having a girl in every port. The number is followed by a "Hornpipe" (example 44), an indispensable appendage to songs about the navy, following the example set by Arthur Sullivan in the enormously popular *H.M.S. Pinafore*. De Koven's "Hornpipe" is of the "Sailor's Hornpipe" variety without dotted notes and an emphasis on three even eighth notes in the measure that signals the beginning of a phrase. De Koven caricatures the form somewhat by repeating that measure structure over and over again (measures 1–3, 5–6, 9–11, 13–14, 17–19, 21–22) in a traditional eight-measure unit. Note the simple tonic-dominant harmony, with the occasional secondary dominant to add variety, and the indication *pressando* in measure 25, a characteristic acceleration of the musical pulse at the end of a hornpipe.

DEANE, Benjamin J[ohn]

Composer, violinist, and musical director Benjamin J. Deane was born in England in the fall of 1822. When he was seventeen, he began his professional career, playing violin in second-tier theatre orchestras in London[339] and singing in church choirs. Eleven years later, in 1850, Deane traveled to New York and joined the orchestra at the Old Bowery Theatre, playing second violin to William T. Peterschen, the leader of the orchestra. Almost a decade later, he became the leader of the orchestra at the Bowery, and from there he became musical director at the Chatham Amphitheatre,[340] the New Bowery Theatre, the Theatre Comique,[341] and finally the refurbished Bowery Theatre.[342] At the New Bowery, Deane composed incidental music for plays, such as the *Cataract of the Ganges* (11 July 1864), and *Grant's Campaign, or, Incidents of the Great Rebellion* (11 December 1865). For the pantomime *Tom-Tom, the Piper's Son Stole a Pig and Way he Run* (3 December 1866) Deane composed and arranged a score that included ballet music for a transformation scene, several dances, and a shadow pantomime. During the first season of the refurbished Bowery Theatre (1868–1869), Deane provided music for melodramas and spectacle plays, including *Life on the Streets, or, the Vicissitudes of an Orange Girl* (31 August 1868), *The String of Pearls, or, the Barber Assassin and the Pie Woman of Bell Yard* (18 September 1868),[343] *The Crimson Shield, or, Nymphs of the Rainbow* (5 October 1868),[344] and *The Seven Dwarfs, or, Harlequin and the World of Wonders* (8 March 1869). In June 1869, Deane conducted a revival of the popular burlesque, *Ixion, or, the Man at the Wheel*, and in subsequent seasons, he provided musical direction for the trendy sensational drama *On the Track!* (28 August 1871); he arranged incidental music for *Life, its Morn and Sunset* (29 September1873); and he composed the original score for an unauthorized production of *Around the World in 80 Days* (29 March 1875). In the late 1870s, Deane was stricken with dropsy and confined to his home in New York City. After years of enduring swollen lower limbs, constant pain, weakness, and trembling of the upper limbs, Deane died on 3 April 1879.[345]

DEBILLEMONT, Jean-Jacques [Joseph]

Composer, violinist, musical director, and critic Jean-Jacques Debillemont was born in Dijon, France, on 12 December 1824. At the age of nine, he started playing the violin, and when he was fifteen he entered the Paris Conservatory where he was a pupil of violinist-composer Jean-Delphin Alard. He continued his training while playing in the orchestra of the Opéra-Comique, and later studied composition with opera composers Michele Carafa and Simon Leborne.[346] Debillemont premiered his earliest musical theatre compositions in Dijon before attempting to produce them in Paris. These early operas included *le Renégat* [*The Turncoat*] (1849), *le Bandolero* [*The Bandolero*] (1850), *Feu mon oncle* [*My Late Uncle*] (1851), and *le Joujou* [*The Toy*] (1852). Debillemont's successes in Paris included the operetta *C'était moi* [*It's Me*] (1860), the opera-comique *Astaroth* (1861), the operetta *la Vipérine* [*The Grass Snake*] (1866), the opera-bouffe *Grand Duc de Matapa* [*Grand Duke of Matapa*] (1868), and *Le Miroir magique* [*The Magic Mirror*] (18760).[347] While his music was being performed in Paris, Debillemont was also busy as a music critic, writing reviews for *L'élu du people* [*The People's Choice*] in Dijon and *la Revue et gazette des théâtres à Paris* [*The Review and Newspaper of the Theatres in Paris*]. In addition to his efforts as a composer and music critic, Debillemont was musical director for the Beaux-Arts Society, the Opéra-Comique, and the Porte-Saint-Martin Theatre. It was at the Porte-Saint-Martin that Debillemont began composing incidental and ballet music for melodramas, spectacle plays, and extravaganzas. He had, of course, composed melodramatic underscore in his operas but now he had the opportunity to create wordless, singer-less operas: theatrical tone poems that would communicate the mood, rhythm, action, and emotion of the drama. Of the spectacle plays at the Porte-Saint-Martin for which Debillemont created incidental tone poems, two of the most significant (if only because they were also produced in New York City) were *Le Tour du monde en 80 jours* [*Around the World in 80 Days*] (7 November 1874) and *Les Enfants du capitaine Grant* [*The Children of Captain Grant*] produced barely a month before Debillemont's death on 14 February 1879.

Under the auspices of producers Imre and Bolossy Kiralfy, *Around the World in 80Days* was produced at the Academy of Music in New York on 28 August 1875 and featured several ballets using Debillemont's original music: "Solemn March of the Rajahs" (a funeral pageant), "The Serpent Charmers' Festival," "Reptile Ballet," and "A Fete at the Excentric [sic] Club."[348] An excerpt from "The Solemn March of the Rajahs" (example 40) provides an effective view of Debillemont's work. The stage directions accompanying the march read, in part, as follows:

> A sound of instruments and of singing begins to be heard. At first are seen the Fakirs, a sort of Indian Shakers, half naked, who howl and gesticulate, and cry, "Kali! Kali! Goddess of Love and of Death," Then come the Priests, wearing mitres, and long embroidered robes. They are surrounded by men, women, and children, who utter a sort of Psalm, interrupted at regular intervals by blows of the tam-tam, and of cymbals. Torch-bearers light up the scene. They are followed by fanatics, tattooed with ochre, adorned with long tails, which are wound three or four times round their waist. They wear a monkey-faced mask and a mountaineer's cap, and hold in each hand a thick club. They dance, howl, and shriek. Then follow the musicians playing drums, cymbals, and long Hebrew trumpets, two yards long.[349]

The procession is leading Aouda, widow of the recently deceased Rajah, to the funeral pyre, since Brahman law requires that a wife must be buried with her husband. The dignified simplicity of Debillemont's music creates a dramatic contrast with what is happening on stage and emphasizes the solemnity of the action (particularly from the point of view of travelers Phineas Fogg and Passepartout). At the beginning of the procession, the dignified and impressive single-note melody is accompanied by octave bass notes on every beat that assist in propelling forward movement to the procession as well as evoking the inevitability of the dramatic situation. As more characters appear on stage, the music of the march develops in complexity, dynamically and rhythmically (measures 1–8). Triads replace the single-note melody and triplet patterns replace the quarter

Example 40. "Solemn March of the Rajahs" from *Around the World in 80 Days*

notes in the accompaniment. The section marked "Sostenuto cantabile" (measures 17–24) adds poignancy to the proceedings by means of a lyrical melody accompanied by harp-like arpeggios that provide a temporary relief from the martial cadence. By the end of the procession, however, the music becomes as frenzied as the action on stage and reaches a dramatic and fortissimo conclusion as Aouda is set on fire.

The Children of Captain Grant appeared in the United States as *Voyagers in Southern Seas*, first at the Boston Theatre on 26 October 1880, and later at Booth's Theatre in New York on 21 March 1881. Again Debilemont's score was used in the production and his music for the "Ballet of the Illuminated City of Valparaiso" was kept intact. Reviews for the Boston production were glowing[350] and the New York reviews were positive as well, with the *New York Clipper* notice even commenting on the excellence of the music.[351]

DEMARQUE, Charles

The name of French cellist and composer Charles Demarque[352] first appeared on theatre broadsides in New York City as the musical arranger for *The Elopement, or, Harlequin's Tour through the Continent of North America* (31May 1787).[353] He subsequently arranged the music of composer Egidio Romualdo Duni for the production of the pantomime ballet *Deux Chasseurs et la Laitière* [*Two Hunters and the Milkmaid*] (9 November 1790) at the City Tavern in New York; and he selected and arranged the music for *Harlequin Shipwrecked, or The Power of Enchantment* (13 June 1791) at the Southwark Theatre in Philadelphia. His name first appeared on a concert program in Baltimore on 25 November 1793 in connection with a cello solo that he composed and was scheduled to perform.[354] For the New Theatre [the Chestnut Street Theatre] in Philadelphia, Demarque composed and selected music for a number of pantomimes, including *Harlequin Shipwreck'd, or the Grateful Lion* (2 January 1795), a revised version of the Southwark Theatre production, with new music composed by Alexander Reinagle; *Rural Revels, or, the Easter Holiday* (10 April 1795); *Miraculous Mill, or, The Old Ground Young* (26 June 1795), a pantomime dance; *The Elopement, or Harlequin's Tour through the Continent of America* (29 June 1795), a new version of *The Elopement*, advertised as "entire new local pantomime"; *Deux Chasseurs et la Laitière* (22 August 1795) at the New Theatre, Baltimore, another production of the pantomime Demarque prepared for the City Tavern; *Miraculous Mill, or, The Old Ground Young* (21 November 1795) at the New Theatre, Baltimore, a revival of pantomime dance originally produced at the New Theatre, Philadelphia; and *Rural Merriment, or, The Humors of a Country Wake* (4 January 1796), at the New Theatre, Philadelphia. In addition to his duties as composer and arranger, Demarque was also a member of the orchestra at the New Theatre in Philadelphia from 1793 until 1797 when he moved to Charleston, South Carolina, and joined the orchestra of the City Theatre.[355] He died in Charleston in 1800.

DEVIN, William

Little is known about pianist and composer William Devin who created the ballet music for *The Casino Girl*, produced at the Casino Theatre in New York City on 19 March 1900. He received no credit in the theatre program but his name is clearly identified as composer in the published score.[356] Except for the four-measure introduction, the ballet music is devisable into eight-measure units, of which, the second, third, and fourth units are represented in example 45. Note the specific articulations throughout the excerpt that assist in defining the legato and staccato movements in the choreography. Note also the juxtaposition of the dynamics in measures 7–15, and 23–24 that also accents the subtleties of the dance.

Example 45. "Ballet" from *The Casino Girl*

Other published compositions by William Devin include "Valse Lente pour Piano" (1900), "Fleur de Jeaunesse. Caprice facile pour Piano" ["Flower of Youth. Simple Caprice for Piano"] (1900), "Danse des Sabots pour le Piano" ["Wooden Shoe Dance for the Piano"] (1902), "Passing Fancies. Valse de Ballet pour Piano" (1903), "Elaine: Intermezzo" (1912), and "A Happy Thought. Intermezzo for the Pianoforte" (1916).

DIET, Edmond-Marie

Pianist and composer Edmond-Marie Diet was born in Paris on 25 September 1854. At the Paris Conservatory he studied with pianist-and-opera-composer Ernest Guiraud and organist-composer César Franck. Diet's compositions for the theatre include the operas, *Stratonice* (1867), *Le cousin Placide* [*Cousin Placide*] (1887), *Fleur de vertu* [*Flower of Virtue*] (1894), *Madame Putiphar* (1897), *Gentil Crampon* [*Nice Clinging Bore*] (1897), *Madame la Présidente* [*Madame President*] (1902), and *La Revanche d'Isis* [*The Revenge of Isis*] (1906); and the ballets and panto-

Example 46a. "Opening of the First Scene" from *Temptations*

mimes, *Scientia* [*Science*] (1889), *La Grève* [*The Strike*] (1894), *Masque rose* [*Pink Mask*] (1894), *M. Ruy-Blas* (*Mr. Ruy-Blas*) (1894), *La Belle et la Bête* [*Beauty and the Beast*] (1895), *l'Araignée d'or* [*(The) Golden Spider*] (1896), and *Rêve de Noël* [*Christmas Dream*] (1896). In 1911, Diet composed the music to a scenario by Alfredo Curti for a pantomime ballet about a student (René) who resists the temptations of smoking, drinking, gambling, and women and secures the love of his fiancée (Lily). Entitled *Temptations*, the ballet was imported from Paris by producers Henry B. Harris and Jesse L. Lasky to be featured on the opening bill at the Folies Bergère Theatre (27 April 1911), a dinner-theatre establishment that ad-

Example 46b. "Love Theme" from *Temptations*

Example 46b (continued). "Love Theme" from *Temptations*

Example 47. "Virginia Tobacco" from *Temptations*

vertised a company of over two hundred performers, two separate orchestras, and a full dining room staff.[357] The pantomime ballet *Temptations* begins in René's library where he is discovered at his desk (example 46a). Note that the text used in the following examples is a translation of the French scenario printed throughout the score.

A brief pantomime scene marked *Allegretto grazioso* in the score follows Lily's entrance. Evidently she feels that René has been spending too much time in his laboratory and paying too little attention to her. René's reply (example 46b) introduces the expansive love theme that becomes a leitmotif in the ballet music. Unfortunately for René, this attempt at romance does not end well (measures 13–18).

Example 48. "Russian Cigarettes" from *Temptations*

Example 49. "Egyptian Cigarettes" from *Temptations*

After Lily's abrupt departure, René picks up the flowers she threw at him as she was leaving. He tries to go back to work, but he finds it impossible to concentrate. Suddenly the walls of his library split open, and an intermezzo, marked *Allegro con fuoco* in the score introduces the second scene, the Palace of Pleasure. Escorted by slaves who throw rose petals in his path, René makes an entrance. The Genius of Pleasure accompanies him, showing him around his magnificent palace. A bed of flowers is created, upon which René gently stretches out and sleeps. Cigarettes, the first temptations, enter, beginning with tobacco from Virginia (example 47), a cheerful galop, evoking the kind of music heard in the American musical theatre.

After the subtle temptations of Turkish tobacco, a pack of Russian cigarettes appears, breaking out into a dazzling Cossack dance (example 48).

A modal dance follows, representing Egyptian Cigarettes (example 49) before the Nicotine Fairy appears to dance a mazurka, and the scene changes to a Harem.

One of the nautch girls approaches René. A eunuch throws himself at her. Lady Nicotine intervenes and places her cigarette under the eunuch's nose, from which grows a handsome moustache. The eunuch lifts the nautch girl and disappears with her. The vision of the Harem disappears and an immense lighted cigar, upon which the nautch girl is reclining, rises up toward the curls of smoke. Different kinds of liquors enter and dance; Gambrinus, a sleeping monk is discovered, and the Spirit of Champagne appears (example 50).

A champagne dance, marked *Allegretto leggiero* in the score, follows, during which the Spirit of Champagne notices the sleeping monk. He goes to him and wakes him up by tickling him, but the drowsy monk slowly goes back to sleep. After another galop clears the stage, a trumpet fanfare signals the shuffling of playing cards. Cards march on stage and dance, constantly changing their position in the deck (example 51).

After the cards are shuffled, the Kings and Queens get in position to dance a minuet. A bright, *scherzando* "Joker's Dance" follows (example 52), before the appearance of a vision of Danaë and the golden rain.[358] The

Example 50. "Spirit of Champagne" from *Temptations*

Example 51. "March to Shuffle Cards" from *Temptations*

Daughters of Eve enter and dance before the appearance of Sensual Pleasures who perform a "Waltz of Desire" (example 53), more than slightly reminiscent of the sensuous waltz in *The Merry Widow*, before they galop off, leaving René alone onstage with Lily. The leitmotif of the "Love Theme" returns and the couple dance a final pas de deux as proof of their true love.

Although the ballet was cordially received by critics and audiences alike, producers Henry B. Harris and Jesse L. Lasky were unable to withstand the financial losses resulting from their over-ambitious venture, and after ninety-two performances, the Folies Bergère Theatre closed and reopened a few months later as the Fulton Theatre, without the tables, kitchen, and twin orchestras. Edmond-Marie Diet died in Paris on 30 October 1924.

Example 52. "Joker's Dance" from *Temptations*

Example 53. "Waltz of Desire" from *Temptations*

DODWORTH, Harvey B.

Composer, dance arranger, musical director, and bandmaster Harvey B. Dodworth was born in Sheffield, England, on 16 November 1822. The son of Thomas Dodworth, a well-known bandmaster, Harvey was given his earliest musical education by his father. In 1826, Harvey came to New York City with his father and two brothers, Allen and Charles, and the following year, the five-year-old prodigy made his first appearance as a flautist in New York. Harvey subsequently learned to play the trombone, the trumpet, and the violin. Almost as soon as the Dodworths arrived in America, father Thomas (who played trombone) joined a band, the Independent Band of New York, which had been organized in 1825 and soon became bandmaster; Harvey and his brother Allen, who was a virtuoso piccolo player, played with the band as well. Harvey Dodworth was also repeatedly engaged as a musician in the orchestras at the various theatres in New York City[359] until 1839, when he became bandmaster of the Dodworth Band (as his father's band became known in 1936). During the fifty-one years Harvey was leader, the Dodworth Band became associated with the 71st Regiment Band of New York with which he (and his younger brother Thomas) served in the first and second Battles of Bull Run during the Civil War. Harvey Dodworth supplied the Union armies with fifty bandmasters and 500 musicians; he introduced free park concerts in New York City and led the band in Central Park for twenty-four years. In addition, he supplied music for the inaugurations of Presidents Van Buren, Harrison, Polk, Tyler, Buchanan, Lincoln, Grant, Garfield, and Cleveland;[360] he was the first musician in America to arrange Richard Wagner's music for military bands and the first to introduce reed instruments in military bands.

In September 1862 Dodworth was engaged as musical director of Niblo's Garden, and members of his band were often hired to supplement the orchestra. Dodworth's production assignments included : *Hamlet* (15 September 1862); *Richard III* (10 October 1862); *Camille* (1November 1862); *Faust and Marguerite* (22 December 1862); *Leah, the Forsaken* (19 January 1863); *Satanella, or, the Power of Love* (23 February 1863);[361] *The Enchantress* (16 March 1863); *The Duke's Motto* (1 June 1863), for which Dodworth composed the incidental music;[362] Edwin Forrest's production of *King Lear* (28 September 1863), for which Harvey composed an original incidental score;[363] Edwin Forrest's production of *Coriolanus* (2 November 1863), for which Dodworth selected and arranged incidental music; *Adrienne, the Actress* (7 November 1863), for which he arranged incidental music; *Connie Soogah* (11 January 1864), for which he composed incidental music; *Fool's*

Revenge (28 March 1864); *Bel Demonio* (16 May 1864); *Sea of Ice* (1 August 1864);[364] *Shamrock* (2 January 1865); *Arrah-Na-Pogue, or, The Wicklow Wedding* (12 July 1865); and *The Black Crook* (12 September 1866).[365] In the autumn of 1973, Harvey Dodworth became the musical director of Augustin Daly's new Fifth Avenue Theatre,[366] where he selected, arranged, and composed incidental scores for plays, including *Connie Soogah* (13 April 1874); Edwin Booth's production of *King Richard II* (8 November 1875);[367] and Augustin Daly's "play of today," *Pique* (14 December 1875).[368] On 29 July 1876, Dodworth resigned from his position at the Fifth Avenue Theatre[369] having decided to spend the rest of his career working with and for the Dodworth Band.[370] He did, however, continue to compose music for the Daly organization and provided a new incidental score for a production of *Twelfth Night* performed at Booth's Theatre on 26 December 1877. In May 1879, after nearly two years of giving undivided attention to the administration of his band, Dodworth leased Gilmore's Garden (renamed Madison Square Garden) in order to present a summer season of concerts consisting of "popular melodies, with the introduction of occasional examples of high art" performed by a band numbering no less than "123 trained instrumentalists, under the personal leadership of Mr. Dodworth."[371] Eight years later, on 10 October 1887, Dodworth conducted his final incidental score, a band arrangement of Civil War melodies to underscore the *Grand Ulysseum*, a lecture and panorama of pictures at Chickering Hall, depicting the life and career of General Ulysses S. Grant. In 1890, the sixty-eight-year-old Harvey Dodworth turned over the musical direction and administration of the Dodworth Band to his son, Oleon; and, after only a few months of retirement, Dodworth died at his home in West Hoboken, New Jersey, on 24 January 1891, survived by his widow and three sons.

Harvey B. Dodworth's published compositions and instructional works include: "Santa Claus' Quadrilles" (1846); "Our Own Quadrilles" (1849); "Weird Polka" (1850); "Enchantress Quadrilles" (1851); "The Bell Polka" (1852); *Dodworth's Terpsichorian Repertoire*, including "Ami Polka," and "Albina Schottisch" (1853); "Belgian Gallery Polka" (1853); *Dodworth's Series of Gems from the Ball Room*, including "Varsoviana" (1854) and "Old College Sycamore Schottisch" (1856); "Tiger Polka" (1856);"Danish Dance" (1860); "Raw Recruit, Quadrilles" (1862); *The Rudimental Instructor for Valve Instruments* (1864); and "Will You Dance with Me Once Again: Galop" (1867).[372]

DRIGO, Riccardo [Eugenio]

Pianist, composer, dance arranger, and musical director Riccardo Drigo was born in Padua, Italy, on 30 June 1846. He began taking piano lessons when he was five years old and became something of a virtuoso on the instrument in his teens, when he entered the Venice Conservatory. Almost immediately, he exhibited a talent for musical composition and conducting. He became the musical director of the St. Petersburg (Russia) Imperial Italian Opera in 1878 and eight years later, he assumed the position of Director of Music for the Imperial Ballet, a designation that required him to compose ballet music, adapt the work of other composers, and fulfill the duties of musical director and conductor. Not long after he was made Director of Music, Drigo took up residence at the St. Petersburg Grand Hotel, where he remained until 1919, when he returned to Italy. During this period, Drigo developed a close friendship with Pyotr Ilyich Tchaikovsky and conducted his ballets, *The Sleeping Beauty* (3 January 1890) and *The Nutcracker* (12 December 1892). After Tchaikovsky's death

Example 54. "Serenade" from Miss *Information*

in 1893, Drigo revised the score of *Swan Lake* for a revival at the Imperial Ballet (27 January 1895), and in 1899 he composed an original score for *Les Millions d'Arlequin* (23 February 1900), of which the "Serenade" was interpolated into the score of Jerome Kern's *Miss Information* (5 October 1915) at the George M. Cohan Theatre in New York City.[373] Employed as ballet music for the star, Elsie Janis, the "Serenade" (example 54) is in triple meter and counterpoints a mandolin-like accompaniment with a lyrical folk-like melody. Once again, the characteristic eight-measure unit we continue to find in nineteenth-century dance music is employed, and, not untypically, each unit is divided into two four-measure phrases. The harmony is simple, with a touch of exoticism added through the use of an augmented triad in measures 2, 4, and 10; and, as the piece continues, the tone of romantic reverie is heightened by a tremolo mandolin effect on the melody.

After Drigo returned to Italy in 1919 he became musical director of the Teatro Garibaldi in Padua and continued to compose operas, religious works, and individual songs. He even added lyrics to his "Serenade" and called it "Notturno d'amour" ["Nocturne of Love"]. Drigo died at his home in Padua on 1 October 1930. Although Drigo never stepped foot in the United States, and his contribution to American theatrical dance music was limited to one composition, he deserves at least a mention in this book, if only because of his long career as ballet composer and dance arranger. There was little (if any) adaptation needed to ready Drigo's music for choreography since it had already been written for dance. It should be mentioned that not long after *Miss Information* opened, Drigo's "Serenade" was replaced by Chopin's "Waltz in A minor," a piece not originally composed as theatrical dance music.

DYRING, H[enry] T.

Composer and musical director H.T. Dyring was associated with showman Tony Pastor's Company throughout the 1870s and early 1880s, operating as musical director and incidental arranger for Pastor's tours as well as his theatre. Dyring's responsibilities typically involved the arrangement of an overture designed to set the tone for the evening's entertainment, and the creation of entr'acte and "continuity" music to introduce and play off the various sketches and entertainers. Tony Pastor's productions, for which Dyring selected and arranged the incidental music included the extravaganza *Dinklespeil's Blunders* (26 March 1877), the burlesque *Yeast*

Lynn! (2 April 1877), and the burlesque *The Emigrant Car, or, Go West* (26 January 1880). The bill for the week of 17 February 1879[374] at Tony Pastor's Music Hall is typical of the various entertainments for which Dyring would supply musical direction, dance, and incidental music:

> PROGRAMME.
> Overture .... H.T. Dyring and Full Band
> The performance will commence with the amusing sketch, entitled
>
> HARD CHEEK
> Charley Worley and Frank Dirard.
>
> MISS MAY VERNON
> In a new repertoire of Serio-Comic Songs.
>
> The DELANOS
> Jeppe & Fannie—In their beautiful Flirtation and Society Sketches
>
> MISS IDA SIDDONS
> Who will appear in her Skipping Rope Dance.
>
> TONY PASTOR'S SONGS
>
> NEIL BURGESS
> In his original creation
>
> THE COMING WOMAN
> Mrs. Barnaby Bibbs, the Coming Woman ... Neil Burgess
> Mr. Barnaby Bibbs .... C. Worley
> Mr. Benjamin Bibbs .... Frank Girard
> Mrs. Benjamin Bibbs .... Jennie Satterlee
>
> THE FRENCH TWIN SISTERS
> Minnie & Lena—in their Attractive and Popular Performance, introducing
> Songs, Dances, etc.

HARRY WOODSON
In his realistic representation of the Old Southern Darkey, with Songs, etc.

FIELDS AND HANSEN
In their Great Musical Sketch, entitled

WAITING FOR THE TRAIN
Performing upon numerous Musical instruments, Interspersed with Funny
Sayings and Doings

THE SPRINGERS
The Famed Hungarian Warblers, who will

Introduce the CAT DUETT.
To conclude with the Laughable Burlesque,
Written expressly for this Establishment, entitled T. P. S.

CANAL BOAT PINAFORE
RT. HON. SIR JOS LAGER (Ruler of the entire Navy) ...... Gus Williams
Capt. Corcoran, Commanding Canal Boat Pinafore ...... Frank Girard
Ralph Rackstraw, an able Seaman ...... Geo. Merritt
Dick Deadbeat ...... James Lamont
Billy Bobstay, a Boatswain ...... J.R. Morris
Bob Beckert, Carpenter's Mate .... Al. Welling
Tom Tucker, a Midshipman ...... Ed. Stanley
Tom Bowline ...... Chas. Merritt
Josephine, the Captain's Daughter ...... Alice Seidler
(Her first appearance here. Specially engaged for this part.)
Little Buttercup, a Canal Boat Cook ...... Neil Burgess
Hebe, a First Cousin to Sir Joseph Lager ...... Jennie Satterlee
Joseph Lager's Sisters, his Cousins, his Aunts,
Sailors, etc., by the Company.
During the Burlesque will be introduced
Tony Pastor's Sensation Phalanx
12 CLOG DANCERS

Dyring followed the burlesque of Gilbert and Sullivan's *H.M.S. Pianafore* at Tony Pastor's Music Hall with a burlesque of *The Pirates of Penzance* entitled *The Pie-Rats of Penn-Yann* (7 February 1881). For both productions Dyring rearranged Arthur Sullivan's music, altering the keys of the individual songs to accommodate the performers' vocal rangers, and adding incidental dances and musical jokes as directed. For the 1881–1882 season, Dyring moved with the Tony Pastor Company to the 14th Street Theatre where he supplied incidental music for the extravaganza, *Humpty-Dumpty* (22 October 1881) produced by the touring Nick Roberts' European Specialties and Clown Minstrels. Following the production of *Humpty-Dumpty*, however, Dyring's name is no longer associated with Tony Pastor's Theatre. It is unknown if he went on tour with the Nick Roberts Company or simply retired. He was certainly a popular musical director, and a favorite of vaudeville performers. On 26 October 1878, for example, Dyring was presented with a handsome gold-headed cane by Tony Pastor favorites Harry and John Kernell "as a token of their appreciation of his untiring efforts to please, and as a courteous and obliging gentleman at all times."[375]

E

EDWARDS, Julian

Composer and musical director Julian Edwards was born in Manchester, England, on 11 December 1855. He studied music at the University of Edinburgh with composer William Henry Oakley and in London at the Royal Academy of Music with composer and musicologist George Alexander Macfarren. By the time he emigrated to America in 1888 at the behest of producer James C Duff, Edwards had composed a symphony (1874); two operas, *Corinna* (1880) and *Victorian, the Spanish Student*, produced at the Theatre Royal, Sheffield (6 April 1883) and at the Theatre Royal, Covent Garden (19 January 1884); an overture to the unproduced opera *Elfinella* (8 August 1885); a cantata for treble voices, *De Montfort's Daughter* (1888); and a number of light comic operas. In addition, he toured Britain as musical director for the Carl Rosa Opera Company and for Horace Lingard's production of the comic opera *Pepita*.[376] In America, working as Duff's musical director, Edwards conducted Edward Jakobowsky's comic opera *Paola* (6 May 1889), Edward Solomon's *The Red Hussar* (3 August 1890), and Adam Itzel's *The Tar and the Tartar* (11 May 1891).[377] In 1892, while he was the musical director at Palmer's Theatre in New York, Edwards composed an unproduced one-act operetta, *Diana*, and the score for *Jupiter, or, The King and the Cobbler* (2 May) in which the king of the gods disguises himself as the drunken cobbler Spurius Cassius in order to make love to the cobbler's wife. Before he can carry out his plan, however, Jupiter is mistaken for the cobbler by the police and arrested, while the real Spurius Cassius is mistaken for the god in disguise and carried off to Olympus where he wreaks havoc among the gods.[378] The entrance of the inebriated cobbler was accompanied by incidental music (example 55) that suggested the wonky gait of a drunken man attempting to stay upright.

In 1893 Edwards began a long creative collaboration with librettist Stanislaus Stange with the production of *Friend Fritz* (26 January) by the Manola-Mason Opera Company for which he also was musical director.

Example 55. "Entrance of Spurius" from *Jupiter*

On 22 November 1893, Edwards's one-act opera *King René's Daughter* was produced in New York to mostly negative reviews, of which the notice in *The New York Times* (23 November 1893) was representative:

> It cannot be said that [Edwards] has a strong gift of melody, though there are some fluent and expressive passages in his little opera.... There is throughout, however, a lack of skill in the placing of the voice parts. The phrases are not always such as lend themselves readily to vocal treatment and some of the passages in the declamation are unnecessarily difficult. The orchestration is in many places overelaborate and heavy, while in others there are bits of bad instrumentation, notably in some of the trumpet measures.

Although the failure of his opera may have quashed Edwards's ambition to be accepted as a serious composer, he continued to produce scores for light comic operas, including *Madeleine, or The Magic Kiss* (25 February

1895), *The Goddess of Truth* (26 February 1896), *Brian Boru* (19 October 1896), *The Wedding Day* (8 April 1897), *The Jolly Musketeer* (14 November 1898), and *The Princess Chic* (12 February 1900). In 1900, Edwards also composed incidental and ballet music for Stange's dramatization of Henry Sienkiewicz's novel *Quo Vadis* (9 April),[379] for the double bill of Robert Browning's *In a Balcony* and William Butler Yeats's *The Land of Heart's Desire* (26 October), for Grace Livingstone Furniss's dramatization of Longfellow's poem, *King Robert of Sicily* (29 November), and for Lorimer Stoddard's play *In the Palace of the King* (31 December). The following year, he provided incidental music for the Boston production of Stange's play *Priscilla* (27 May)[380] and for Charles Klein's melodrama *The*

Example 56. Dance in "A Song of Expense" from *Dolly Varden*

Cipher Code (30 September); in addition, he composed the score for one of his most successful comic operas, *Dolly Varden*, produced at the Herald Square Theatre on 27 January 1902. Early in the musical, two ladies of fashion, Lucette and Alice, sing "A Song of Expense" about the cost of keeping a lady à la mode, after which is appended a twenty-measure dance (example 56) that depicts the flighty elegance and hauteur of these fashionable women. The tightly-clustered staccato chords with upper tones moving chromatically (measures 1–2, 5–6) and the descending stepwise thirds (measures 9, 11) are interrupted by glib, almost flippant legato passages (measures 3–4, 7–8, 10, 12). Those elements combine to create an aural image of the characters—sharp-witted, acerbic, frivolous, yet irresistible—that is reinforced by measures 14–20, quoting the final phrase of the song, "By the girls they love."

Later in the year, Edwards composed incidental music for Harriet Ford's dramatization of Stanley Weyman's novel, *A Gentleman of France*, and he completed another of his most enduring scores, the "Military

Example 57. "Melodrame" from *When Johnny Comes Marching Home*

Spectacular Comic Opera" *When Johnny Comes Marching Home* (26 December 1902).[381] Predictably, given the title, the musical was set during the American Civil War, and the popular ballad of the period, "When Johnny Comes marching Home" was integrated throughout the score. Example 57 is an excerpt from "Melodrame" (No. 4 in the program) in which the tune is used to underscore the entrance of the eponymous character, Union Colonel John Graham.

Edwards's subsequent compositions included the incidental music for *Gringoire the Street Singer* (17 November 1903); the comic opera, *Love's Lottery* (3 October 1904); incidental music for *The School for Husbands* (3 April 1905); the comic opera, *His Honor the Mayor*, co-composed with Alfred E. Aarons (28 May 1906); the sacred cantata, *The Redeemer* (September 1906); the comic opera, *The Girl and the Governor* (8 October 1906); the secular cantata, *The Mermaid* (1906); incidental music for *Barabbas* (1906);[382] the comic opera, *The Belle of London Town* (28 January 1907); the sacred cantata, *Lazarus* (1907; produced in concert at the Metropolitan Opera House in 1910);[383] the comic opera, *The Gay Musician* (18 May 1908); the one-act grand opera, *The Patriot* (23 November 1908);[384] the Easter cantata, *Lord of Light and Love* (1909); the comic opera, *The Girl and the Wizard* (27 September 1909); and the comic opera, *Molly May* (8 April 1910).

On 5 September Julian Edwards died at his home in Yonkers, New York, due to complications from heart disease following an illness of seven months. He was survived by his wife, the former *prima donna* Philippine Siedle.[385] Although Edwards had gained the respect of his Broadway colleagues because of his technical proficiency, he rarely earned their admiration. Even his best scores displayed labored melodies and often overwrought arrangements that seemed more the products of academic exercises than inspiration. Much of his most successful work, however, was in the composition of incidental and dance music, driven by character and dramatic situation rather than melody.

EDWARDS, Leo

Pianist, composer, and vaudevillian Leo Edwards was born Leo Simon on 2 February 1886 in Inowroclaw, Prussia. Shortly after he was born, his parents took him and his older brother Gus with them to a heavily German inhabited section of Brooklyn called Williamsburg. As a child, Edwards received piano lessons from his older brother Gus and the rudiments of musical theory from the Brooklyn public school system. By the time he was twelve, he was touring on the vaudeville circuit and when he was fourteen he appeared at the Third Avenue Theatre in New York in *The Katzenjammer Kids* (26 November 1900). On the strength of his published songs, "No. 1 Cupid Street," "When the Right Mr. Right Comes Along, " and "On a Spooney Mooney Night" (interpolated into the score of *Mr. Bluebeard* (21 January 1903), the 18-year-old Edwards was hired by the publisher M. Witmark and Sons in 1904 as a house composer and demonstrator (song-plugger) in their professional department.[386] The following year, Leo collaborated with his brother Gus on the music for *Breaking into Society*, a musical farce that opened at the National Theatre in Rochester, New York (4 September 1905), and toured, playing various theatres in New York City between October 1905 and May 1906.[387] Late in August 1906, Leo Edwards joined the Primrose Minstrels but, after three weeks on tour, he left the organization.[388] In the same year, he contributed "You're in Love" to the Broadway-bound *Too Near Home* and left the employ of M. Witmark and Sons and joined his brother's publishing establishment where he published "If You Must Make Eyes at Someone (Won't You Please Make Eyes at Me)" used on Broadway in *The Gay White Way* (7 October 1907). The musicals for which Edwards provided individual songs or nearly complete scores included *The Merry Whirl* (30 May 1910), Ziegfeld's *Follies of 1910* (20 June 1910), *The Winter Garden Revue* (summer 1911), *The Trained Nurses* (16 September 1912), *Ziegfeld Follies of 1912* (21 October 1912), *The Kissing Maid* (2 June 1913), *Ziegfeld Follies of 1913* (16 June 1913), and *Maid in America* (18 February 1915). On 22 May 1915, the day that *Maid in America* closed in New York, the *New York Clipper* announced that Edwards had split from Chas. K. Harris, the publishing house he had joined three years earlier, and was preparing to establish a new music publishing business to be financed by the Shubert Brothers, the producers of several of Edwards's shows, including *The Passing Show of 1915* (29 May 1915), for which he provided his most important nearly complete score. In addition to creating highly syncopated novelty dance numbers such as "Daddy Longlegs," "The Shakespearian Rag," "My Hula Maid," and "Panama Pacific Drag," Edwards arranged two dance breaks in a second-act chorus number about summer sports entitled "Fishing." The first dance episode, "Polo," transformed each measure of the chorus (written in 4/4) into two measures (with eighth-note backbeats) in 2/4, creating the illusion of a quicker tempo and a driving forward motion that supported the dancers' pantomime of a polo match. The second episode, marked "Baseball" was a variation of the chorus melody in waltz time, capitalizing on the popularity of "Take Me Out to the Ball Game" (1908) which was composed in 3/4.[389]

Later in the year Edwards contributed numbers (along with Sigmund Romberg) to Edmund Eysler's *The Blue Paradise* (5 August 1915) before returning to the vaudeville circuit, where he composed the score for *Copper at 64*[390] that included dance numbers such as "Yankee Doodle Rag," "I Want to Dance," and "Midnight Cakewalk Ball."[391] Edwards subsequently contributed songs to the *Ziegfeld Follies of 1916* (12 June 1916), *Hitchy-koo* (7 June 1917), the *Ziegfeld Follies of 1917* (12 June 1917), and the *Demitasse Revue* (21 October 1919).[392] On 7 April 1920, the *New York Clipper* announced that Edwards was no longer on the composing staff of music publishers McCarthy and Fisher, a firm he had joined along with Harry Tierney and others in September 1918.[393] The newly freelancing composer continued to contribute to Broadway revues, including the *Ziegfeld Follies of 1920* (22 June 1920), *The Midnight Rounders* (12 July 1920),[394] *The Whirl of New York* (13 June 1921),[395] the *Ziegfeld Follies of 1921* (21 June 1921), the *Ziegfeld Follies of 1923* (20 October 1923), *The City Chap* (26 October 1925), and *You'll See Stars* (31 December 1942), a revue commemorating the career of Gus Edwards, for which brother Leo assembled a score.

In 1921, Leo Edwards was elected a member of the American Society of Composers, Authors, and Publishers, and the following year he composed and musically directed the score for the film *Heroes of the Street*. He subsequently contributed music to a number of films, including *My Man* (1928), *Stopping the Show* (1932), *It Comes Up Love* (1943), and *The Merry Monahans* (1944). In 1949 he composed the official boy-scout song, "Tomorrow's America,"[396] and in his later years he became assistant dean of the Mannes College of Music in New York City. Edwards's private life may have been as theatrical as many of the revues to which he contributed songs. In 1916 he was caught *in flagrante* with Betty Randolph, a showgirl at the Winter Garden, by her husband Thomas Shryock Hauck and named as correspondent in the ensuing divorce case;[397] and in 1921 Edwards was sued for "breach of promise" by Sybil Schwartz, a stenographer, who claimed that the composer had won her heart and introduced her in society as his "future wife." However, Schwartz complained that Edwards would not set a date for the wedding, and when pressed to do so, he adamantly refused.[398] Roué, composer, dance arranger, vaudevillian, educator, and administrator, Leo Edwards died at his home in New York City on 12 July 1978, at the age of ninety-two.[399]

EICHBERG, Julius

Violinist, composer, conductor, and educator Julius Eichberg was born in Düsseldorf, Germany, on 13 June 1824. At an early age he studied the violin with his father who was a composer and violinist and, by the time he was seven years old, Eichberg had acquired such proficiency on the instrument that he was able to give public concerts and perform before the Emperor Nicholas of Austria.[400] In addition to his home schooling, young Eichberg attended the Musical Academy of Würzberg where he studied with F.W. Eichler and Julius Rietz, and at the recommendation of composer Felix Mendelssohn, in 1841 he entered the Brussels Conser-

Example 58. "Allegro Espagnola" from *The Doctor of Alcantara*

vatory where he studied the violin with Lambert Joseph Meerts, and composition with François-Joseph Fétis and Charles Auguste de Bériot. Two years later, Eichberg won first prize for composition and violin performance at the Conservatory, after which he went to Basel, Berne, and Geneva as musical director of an opera company. In the autumn of 1845 he accepted a position as professor of the violin at the Geneva Conservatory and was subsequently appointed director of church music by the Consistory of the Church of Geneva.[401] After eleven years in Geneva, Eichberg sailed for New York City where he planned to make his fortune as a violinist and musical director. After a two-year search, and still unable to find steady employment in the New York area, in 1859 Eichberg moved to Boston where he accepted the position of musical director at the Boston Museum. There he composed an opéra bouffe, *The Doctor of Alcantara* (7 April 1862), with a libretto by Benjamin Edward Woolf. Called "the most enduring musical of the season" (except for *The Black Crook*),[402] *The Doctor of Alcantara* (pronounced with an accent on the penultimate syllable) presented a farcical story of mistaken identity in which two young Spaniards in love, Isabella and Carlos are betrothed by their fathers to persons they have never seen. After two acts of misunderstandings, misinformation, and misjoinders, the loving couple realizes that each is betrothed to the other and the comic opera ends happily. Eichberg began the second act with an "Allegro Espagnola" (example 58), a spirited bolero that served as a curtain-raiser, emphasizing the Spanish setting and character of the musical.[403]

A year after *The Doctor of Alcantara* was produced Eichberg composed another opéra bouffe for the Boston Museum, *The Rose of Tyrol*, set in the Austrian Alps. In 1864 he provided dance and incidental music[404] for a production of Shakespeare's *Romeo and Juliet* (3 May) starring John Wilkes Booth, a year before he assassinated President Abraham Lincoln, and he composed *A Night in Rome*, another musical theatre piece that was produced on 26 November. In 1866, Eichberg left the Boston Museum and instituted the Eichberg Violin School; the following year he established the Boston Conservatory of Music and became director of music for the Boston public school system. Eichberg's final musical theatre composition, *The Two Cadis*, set in Iraq, gave its premiere performance on 4 March 1868 at Boston's Chickering Hall. With the exception of *The Rose of Tyrol*, all of Eichberg's musical theatre works were successful and helped establish the European opéra bouffe tradition in American theatre. In the words of Deane L. Root, "Of all the American popular stage-music composers of the 1860s, Eichberg was perhaps the most skilled. He was certainly one of the most knowledgeable, experienced, and familiar with contemporary European music."[405] In his later years, Eichberg spent his time as the director of the Boston Conservatory and co-director of the Harvard Concert Series, as well as the composer of chamber music and educational textbooks for students of the violin and music studies in the Boston public schools. He died at his home in Boston on 18 January 1893.

EINÖDSHOFER, Julius

Composer Julius Einödshofer was born in Vienna on 10 February 1863. He studied music at the Vienna Conservatory, and upon graduation he worked as musical director for theatres in the provinces of Austria. His activities in the provincial theatre circuit prepared him for the position of musical director and composer in residence at the Scala Theater in Berlin, a post he accepted in 1892. After a year at the Scala Einödshofer took a similar position at the Centraltheater, where he composed a series of musicals that included: *Berliner Voliblut* [*Full-blooded Berliner*] (31 August 1893); *O, diese Berliner* [*O, This Berlin*] (2 September 1894); *Unsere Rentiers* [*Our Landlords*] (16 February 1895; *Eine wilde Sache* [*A Wild Thing*] (20 September 1896); *Ein fideler Abend* [*A Jolly Evening*] (7 February 1897); and *Die Tugendfalle* [*The Virtue Case*] (20 January 1898).[406] In 1899, Einödshofer provided additional music ("Keep One Eye on Your Country") for the Casino Theatre's production of Offenbach's *La Belle Hélène* (12 January 1899), and in 1901 he became the musical director and resident composer at the Thalia-Theater where he continued to produce musical comedies in German. In 1903 he composed additional music ("Mr. Mosenstein") for *The Girl from Kay's* (2 November) at the Herald Square Theatre, and in 1907 his German musical *Die Gelbe Gefahr* [*The Yellow Peril*] was produced at the Irving Place Theatre in New York. In 1906 Einödshofer became the musical director of the Kurochester and in 1911 he became musical director and resident composer at the Admiralspalast in Berlin where he composed music for ice ballets and revues. In the 1912–1913 season, he created the score for the three-act ice ballet *Flirt in St. Moritz*, generally considered as the first ice ballet with an actual plot. It tells the story of Kitty Goldberg, the widow of an American millionaire, who travels to St. Moritz where she meets a Japanese nobleman and a Norwegian sportsman, both of whom fall in love with her. On 30 September 1915, the ballet (renamed *Flirting at St. Moritz*) premiered at the Hippodrome Theatre in New York

Example 59. "Flirt-Waltz" from *Flirting at St. Moritz*

as the third act of *Hip-Hip-Hooray*, the two-act musical that preceded it.[407] One of the principal features of Einödshofer's score was the "Flirt-Waltz" (example 59) that evoked the melody of the famous "Merry Widow Waltz" (1905)—hardly inappropriate given the similarities between the story of the ballet and that of *The Merry Widow*—as well as the simple, gliding spirit of Émile Waldteufel's "The Skaters' Waltz" (1882).

Another of Einödshofer's ice ballets, *The Merry Doll*, which originally premiered at the Admiralspalast on 27 October 1913, was also produced at the Hippodrome as the third act of *The Big Show* (31 August 1916) with additional music by Raymond Hubbell.[408] Einödshofer gave up writing and conducting for the theatre in 1921 to become musical director for recordings and radio broadcasts. He died on 17 October 1930 after suffering a heart attack during one of his broadcasts.[409] In addition to his theatre and ballet scores, Einödshofer composed incidental music for German silent films: *Eve* [AKA *When Honor Calls*] (1913), and *Verlorene Töchter* [*Lost Daughters*] (1918). One of the many German composers who were fascinated by American ragtime and syncopated music, Einödshofer also played and recorded cakewalks.

ELLIS, Melville M[orris]

Pianist, performer, composer, dance arranger, and costume designer Melville Ellis was born in San Francisco on 3 November 1875.[410] At an early age he displayed a prodigious talent as a pianist and vocalist, most often accompanying himself in solo performances that he called "pianologues," a monologue with piano. He joined the vaudeville circuit in his late teens and in 1899 he toured with Harry Woodruff and Mabel Dixey in the comedy sketch *Two Artists and a Model*[411] before accepting the piano-playing role of Willie Dew in the May Irwin vehicle, *Sister Mary*, a musical comedy opening on 14 September in New Haven.[412] In December 1899, Ellis contributed music to *The Lady from Chicago*, produced by the Strollers, an amateur theatre organization of which he was a member, and in December of the following year, he co-composed the score for the Strollers production, *The Cruise of the Summer Girl.*" In December 1901, Ellis was in rehearsal with the musical play, *The Toreador*,[413] scheduled to open in New York on 6 January 1902; and while he was touring with that show, he contributed music and dance arrangements to *The Wild Rose* (5 May 1902), *A Chinese Honeymoon* (2 June 1902), and *The Silver Slipper* (27 October 1902). He co-composed the music for the farce comedy *The Rogers Brothers In London* (7 September 1903), for which he also provided dance arrangements and performed the role of Lord Harry Hartford in New York and for almost two years on tour. When he returned to New York, Ellis played the part of millionaire Grant Bellyne in *Fritz in Tammany Hall* (16 October 1905) and composed dance music for the Casino Theatre production of *The Earl and the Girl* (4 November 1905). Published as "School Boy and Girl Dance," Ellis's dance arrangement is divided into four sections, each suggesting a different mood and style of dance. After a four-measure introduction, the piece begins with a jovial march in duple meter with phrases symmetrically organized into four-measure units. Next comes a hesitation waltz (example 60) with an emphasis on the second beat (measures 3–4, 7–8, 11–12, 15–16, 18), followed by a fairly square Schottische in 4/4 with the requisite dotted notes (measures 20, 24, 28, 30–33) and triplets (measures 22–23, 26–27, 34). A recapitulation of the original march tune concludes the dance.

In 1906 Ellis composed incidental music for Rida Johnson Young's play with music, *Brown of Harvard* (26 February) and he co-composed (with Raymond Hubbell) the score for the musical revue *About Town* (30 August). In addition, he provided the incidental score for Beulah Marie Dix's comedy, *The Road to Yesterday* (31 December) for which he com-

Example 60. "School Boy and Girl Dance" from *The Earl and the Girl*

Example 60 (continued). "School Boy and Girl Dance" from *The Earl and the Girl*

posed the exotic and evocative tango, *Malena* (example 61), named for the play's character Malena Leveson, acted by Helen Ware, to whom the music was dedicated.

Ellis returned to performing in 1907 with the characters of Dr. Ronald Fausset, a country practitioner, in *The Orchid* (8 April) and Van Cort-

Example 61. "Malena" from *The Road to Yesterday*

land Knickerbocker in *The Gay White Way* (7 October), but the following year he resumed his career as a dance arranger, creating the dance and vocal arrangement of "The Drawing Lesson" in *Nearly a Hero* (24 February 1908)[414] and the "Vision of Salome" for dancer Gertrude Hoffmann[415] in *The Mimic World* (9 July 1908).[416] In 1903, Ellis had contracted with the Shubert Brothers to act as artistic director for all their musical shows. The agreement put Ellis on call to perform, compose songs or incidental music, arrange dance music (and vocal music), and design costumes (and scenery) whenever necessary. It is no wonder that after a dozen years with the Shuberts, Melville Ellis suffered a nervous breakdown.

In 1908, Ellis designed costumes for the operettas *Mlle. Mischief* (28 September) and *Marcelle* (1 October). His subsequent assignments included: *Havana* (11 February 1909); *The Midnight Sons* (22 May 1909) for which he designed costumes, created dance music, and performed a pianologue specialty; *The Girl and the Wizard* (27 September 1909), costumes, and supervision of dance music; *Old Dutch* (22 November 1909), costumes only; *The Jolly Bachelors* (6 January 1910), costumes, musical direction, and the uncredited selection and arrangement of incidental and dance music; *The King of Cadonia* (10 January 1910), costumes and uncredited dance music; *The Prince of Bohemia* (14 January 1910), costumes and uncredited musical supervision; *Tillie's Nightmare* (5 May 1910), costumes, and uncredited dance music; *The Mikado* (30 May 1910), costumes only; *The Summer Widowers* (4 June 1910), costumes, and uncredited supervision of ballet music; *Up and Down Broadway* (18 July 1910), costumes, additional music, and uncredited dance arrangements; *He Came from Milwaukee* (21 September 1910), costumes and uncredited additional music and dance arrangements;[417] *The Girl and the Kaiser* (22 November 1910), costumes and uncredited dance arrangements; *La Belle Paree* (20 March 1911), costumes and uncredited dance arrangements; *The Revue of Revues* (27 September 1911), costumes and uncredited musical supervision;[418] *Vera Violetta* (20 November 1911),[419] costumes, performance (as Paul Voison), pianologue specialty, and uncredited additional music and dance arrangements; *Whirl of Society* (5 March 1912), costumes, pianologue, and uncredited supervision of incidental and dance music; *Patience, or, Bunthorne's Bride* (6 May 1912, costumes only; and *The Merry Countess* (20 August 1912), costumes, additional music, selection, composition, and arrangement of dance music, and production supervision. For the popular Dolly Sisters dancing with Martin Brown in *The Merry Countess*, Melville Ellis composed his most famous dance arrangement, "The Tango Dance." After a rather perfunctory four-measure introduction, the courtship dance begins with twenty-two measures of flirtatious staccato phrases before settling on the principal theme (example 62), an expansive legato melody juxtaposed with a pulsating and stimulating staccato accompaniment. The tango is both playful and sensual as each of the women entices the male through the titillating gestures and postures of the dance. Which of the two will conquer him is left to the audience's imagination for, instead of a dynamic ending, the music fades to a whisper, and the dancers disappear offstage.

Ellis followed *The Merry Countess* with a long line of costuming assignments[420] leading to *The Passing Show of 1914* (10 June 1914),[421] for which Ellis contributed costumes and selected, composed, and arranged ballet and dance music; *Pretty Mrs. Smith* (21 September 1914), costumes only; *Dancing Around* (10 October 1914),[422] costumes and dance music; *Experience* (27 October 1914), costumes only; *Maid in America* (18 February 1915),[423] costumes and additional dance and incidental music; and *The Peasant Girl* (2 March 1915), costumes only. On 22 May 1915, the *New York*

Example 62. "The Tango Dance" from *The Merry Countess*

Clipper announced that Melville Ellis had severed his relationship with the Shubert Brothers and planned to become associated with producer Charles B. Dillingham for the 1915–1916 season. The same article noted that Ellis was suffering a nervous breakdown and planned to spend the summer in California. Evidently Ellis recovered quickly because he was back in New York at the end of July designing costumes for the short-lived *Cousin Lucy* (27 August 1915). Before he left for the West Coast, Ellis signed with theatrical agent Elisabeth Marbury, the longtime partner of his friend, interior designer Elsie DeWolfe. Marbury represented many of the biggest names in the theatre (i.e., Oscar Wilde, George Bernard Shaw, Vernon and Irene

Castle) and Ellis was happy to put his career in the hands of a powerhouse negotiator. After *Cousin Lucy*, Ellis appeared in the second edition of *Ziegfeld's Midnight Frolic* (September 1915) performing a signature pianologue atop the roof of the New Amsterdam Theatre after midnight. In October, he appeared as Jules Bancourt, the pianist at Fychère's Midnight Restaurant, in *Miss Information* (5 October 1915),[424] Ellis's first collaboration with Dillingham, for which he also designed costumes, performed a pianologue, and composed dance music. In December, he and his friend Elsie DeWolfe designed the costumes and scenery for *Very Good Eddie* (23 December 1915), an Elisabeth Marbury-Ray Comstrock production at the Princess Theatre, and in January 1916, Ellis and the popular singing-actress Marie Tempest announced their plans to open a vaudeville act at the Palace Theatre.[425] After a successful turn at the Palace with Marie Tempest, Ellis designed the costumes and dance music for another Marbury production, *See America First* (28 March 1916), Cole Porter's first Broadway show, before joining up with singer Irene Bordoni as headliners on the vaudeville circuit. He designed the stage setting for the act as well as Bordoni's gowns, and he provided all the musical arrangements for the tour that played many of the best vaudeville houses—the Colonial, the Royal, and the Palace.[426] In early April 1917, Melville Ellis was suddenly stricken with typhoid fever while the act was playing the Palace Theatre. He was moved to New York Hospital and composer-pianist Anatole Friedland took his place beside Irene Bordoni to continue the vaudeville tour. On the morning of 4 April 1917 Melville Ellis died. He is buried in Maple Grove Cemetery, in Kew Gardens, Queens, in a plot owned by his friend Elsie DeWolfe.

Melville Ellis breathed the rarified air of the Broadway elite. His boyish good-looks and remarkable talents gained him entrance to the homes and hearts of most theatre professionals, and Ellis seemed to enjoy the same comfort in dealing with the Shubert Brothers as he did when vacationing with Al Jolson or working with Oscar Radin, the resident Shubert conductor. Virtually everything he did was lauded by the critics, though it is ironic that his best notices appeared after he became a costume designer, his "sideline" as he called it. Perhaps his most important contribution to the American musical theatre, his dance music, was routinely uncredited and invariably overlooked by critics and audiences alike. Still, Melville Ellis is arguably one of the most, if not *the* most significant dance arranger of the first two decades of the twentieth century and his work deserves notice and appreciation.

EMMET, J[oseph] K[line]

Comedian and composer J.K. Emmet was born in St. Louis on 12 March 1841, the eldest son of poor Irish immigrants. When he was very young he became the drummer in the band of the First Regiment of the St. Louis City Guard. He was quite talented as a percussionist and in much demand by local bands. After the death of his father in 1851, Emmet left Armstrong's military school in St. Louis to become the sole support of his mother and his four brothers and sisters. He became a sign painter, painting the lettering on the wheelhouses of Mississippi steamboats and billboards for traveling shows; he worked as a delivery boy and also found employment at a mill that paid him $1.50 a week[427] ($41.85 in 2016 dollars). At military school he exhibited an aptitude for music, and when he was not at one of his jobs, he entertained his siblings with original songs that invariably included a yodeling chorus and dances that permitted him to tap the rhythm with his feet or with his fingers on whatever object was close by. In his late teens, Emmet made his first public appearance as a snare drummer with Freeborthyser's Minstrels and Bellringers touring through the western half of the United States.[428] In 1860–61, he performed a similar role in the orchestra at Deagle's Old Bowery Theatre until the spring of 1863, when the orchestra leader Jacob Esher heard him sing one of his original songs and offered to pay him $20 a week to sing on stage. Calling himself "Joe Dutten, World's Greatest Warbler," Emmet made his debut as a singer,[429] performing the same kinds of songs and dances with which he used to entertain his family, and immediately became a hit with the audience. Four years later, he played the Palace Theatre in Cincinnati, advertised as "Joe Granfrau, the Great German Warbler—Just Over."[430] Subsequently, under his own name, Emmet joined Morris and Wilson's Minstrel Company, a St. Louis-based troupe, and by the time he appeared in New York City with Dan Bryant's Minstrels at Tammany Hall (July 1868) Emmet had perfected the character of the yodeling German immigrant who wore wooden shoes and spoke broken English. Billed as Joe Emmet "the great Western Dutchman"[431] he sang German songs in blackface.[432] By 1869, Emmet's German character was so popular with audiences that playwright Charles Gayler wrote *Fritz, Our Cousin German* as a vehicle for him. After a six-month tour that began in Buffalo, New York, *Fritz* appeared at Wallack's Theatre in New York City on 11 July 1870 and Emmet became "one of the most firmly established of stage favorites."[433] He subsequently appeared as the eponymous character in *Carl, the Fiddler* (18 September 1871) before making his debut with *Fritz, Our Cousin German* at London's Adelphi Theatre on 2 December 1872. Following a highly successful tour of British and Irish theatres,[434] Emmet returned to New York to perform the eponymous Fritz-like character in *Max! The Merry Swiss Boy* (6 October 1873) before going on another national tour. He traveled to Australia in 1876–1877, where he performed Fritz at Sydney's Victoria Theatre in June and July and premiered a new German dialect comedy, *Jan, the New German*, at the Melbourne Opera House in August. Returning to New York after a successful and lucrative tour of Australia,[435] Emmet continued to reprise the Fritz character in dialect comedies that included: *The New Fritz, Our Cousin German* (22 April 1878), *Fritz in Ireland, or, The Bell-ringer of the Rhine and the Love of the Shamrock* (3 November 1879), *Fritz among the Gypsies* (1 January 1883), *Fritz in England and Ireland* (12 March 1883), *Fritz the Bohemian* (5 November 1883), *The Strange Marriage of Fritz, or, The Love of an Irish Girl* (15 September 1884), and *Uncle Joe, or, Fritz in a Madhouse* (22 April 1889). In the years between 1883 and 1889, Emmet toured with revised versions of earlier Fritz shows and, starting in 1888, he performed with Pinlimmon, his prize-winning Saint Bernard who became known as the best canine actor on stage.[436] Saint Bernard dogs were one of Emmet's great hobbies. Another was his $150,000 home on the Hudson River near Albany, New York, a sixteen-acre estate with a Dutch windmill, and a Chinese junk and Venetian gondola on an artificial lake.[437] Emmet's greatest hobby, however, was the consumption of alcohol, a vice that caused him to perform while inebriated and often incapacitated him for weeks at a time.[438] In spite of Emmet's addiction, audiences continued to support him. Critics, on the other hand, did not. *The New York Times* succinctly revealed the general sentiment among reviewers:

> The secret of [Emmet's] popularity was never accurately determined. He was not an actor. The character he depicted in every play was not very much like any character ever seen in real life. His singing voice was neither remarkably strong nor remarkably sweet. He danced no better than many of his rivals. He never did anything new. His personality, however, pleased the great public. He always drew crowds.[439]

On 14 April 1890, Emmet began a week's engagement of *Fritz in Ireland* at Oscar Hammerstein's newly constructed Harlem Opera House. During the run, his wife accused him of having an affair with Maud White, the leading lady of the production, and sued for divorce.[440] A year later, Emmet an-

Example 63. Dance in "Emmet's Swell Song" from Fritz in Ireland and *Fritz among the Gypsies*

nounced that he planned to marry his new leading lady Helen Sedgwick. The couple (along with Emmet's usual entourage) spent the early days of June at the Storm King House in Cornwall, New York. Shortly after his arrival, Emmet complained of a slight cold but otherwise felt in perfect health. Within three days his condition displayed symptoms of pneumonia and by the end of the week the illness took complete control of him. On 15 June he lapsed into a state of unconsciousness and died peacefully at 11:15 A.M. in the arms of Miss Sedgwick.

J.K. Emmet selected and/or composed songs and dance music for all of the productions in which he was involved. Like many musical theatre composers that would follow in the twentieth century, he would sing and play his compositions on the piano and someone, such as a musical director or musical arranger, would create the piano-vocal or orchestral arrangement. In the 1870s, Emmet's musical amanuensis was musical director Ernest Nyer; in the 1880s the job fell to Frank Webb. A representative example of Emmet's dance music is found at the end of "Emmet's Swell Song" (example 63), used in both *Fritz in Ireland* and *Fritz among the Gypsies*. In the song, Fritz explains that, in spite of his tattered clothes, he saunters like a stylish, happy man because the girl he loves calls him a "swell." The dance music that follows, an eight-measure Schottische in common time, reinforces the elation expressed in the lyrics with a cheerful whistling tune divided into two almost identical four-measure phrases (measures 1–2 and 5–6 are exactly the same) that provide a delightful accompaniment to Emmet's characteristic soft-shoe dance.

ENGLÄNDER, Ludwig

Composer and musical director Ludwig Engländer was born in Vienna on 20 October 1853. In the late 1870s he moved to Paris where he studied briefly with opéra-comique composer Jacques Offenbach,[441] and in 1882 he immigrated to the United States where he became the musical director at the German-language Thalia Theater in New York City.[442] There Engländer's operetta *Der Prinz Gemahl* was produced in German on 11 April 1883, and in English (as *The Prince Consort*) at Wallack's Theatre on 4 June 1883. His second effort, *1776, or, Adjutant James* premiered in German at the Thalia Theater on 26 February1884, and in English (as *A Daughter of the Revolution*) at the Broadway Theatre on 27 May 1995. Since neither of his first two musical theatre compositions was successful in America, Engländer premiered his next comic opera, *Madeleine, or, Der Rose de Champagne* in Hamburg on 26 June 1888, but again success eluded him. Determined to triumph in the composition of English-speaking musicals, Engländer removed the umlaut from the spelling of his name and became the musical director at the Casino Theatre in New York, where he composed his first significant English work, *The Passing Show* (12 May 1894).[443] Englander's next musical endeavors[444] included: *Cleopatra*, a vehicle for musical theatre star Lillian Russell[445]that remained unproduced; *The 20th Century Girl* (25 January 1895); *The Caliph* (3 September 1896);[446] *Half a King* (14 September 1896); *In Gayest Manhattan, or, Around New York in Ninety Minutes* (22 March 1897); *A Round of Pleasure* (24 May 1897), revised as *One Round of Pleasure* (23 August 1897); *The Little Corporal* (1898); *La Belle Hélène* (12 January 1899), additional music only; *In Gay Paree* (20 March 1899) ; *The Man in the Moon* (24 April 1899), Englander's longest-running musical (192 performances), co-composed with Reginald De Koven and Gustave Kerker; *The Rounders* (12 July 1899); *The Casino Girl* (19 March 1900), co-composed with Harry T. MacConnell, Arthur Nevin, Will Marion Cook, and William Devin (uncredited); *The Cadet Girl* (25 July 1900), original music by Louis Varney, new music by Englander; *The Monks of Malabar* (14 September 1900);[447] *The Belle of Bohemia* (24 September 1900); *The Strollers* (24 June 1901); *The New Yorkers* (7 October 1901), with additional music by Arthur Weld, Will Marion Cook, et al.;[448] *The Wild Rose* (5 May 1902);[449] *Sally in Our Alley* (29 August 1902); *The Jewel of Asia* (16 February 1903); *The Office Boy* (2 November 1903); *The Girl from Dixie* (14 December 1903), additional music only; *A Madcap Princess* (5 September 1904); *The Two Roses* (21 Novmber1904), co-composed with Gustave

Kerker; *The White Cat* (2 November 1905), with additional music by Jean Schwartz, Philip Braham, and Edward Solomon; *A Modern Girl* (January 1906), unproduced;[450] *The Rich Mr. Hoggenheimer* (22 October 1906), with additional numbers composed by Jerome Kern and Jean Schwartz; *The Gay White Way* (7 October 1907); and *Miss Innocence* (30 November 1908), Engländer's second longest running show (176 performances). In 1910, Engländer reinstated his umlaut and returned to Vienna to produce *Vielliebchen [Philopena]* at the Theater an der Wein (3 May 1911) and *Kittys Ehemänner [Kitty's Husbands]* (1 November 1912). Neither was very successful and Englander, again minus the umlaut, returned to New York for one final attempt at a Broadway success, *Madame Moselle* (23 May 1914). The reviews were so bad that the musical closed after a week[451] and Englander, a broken man, retired to his home in Far Rockaway, Queens. A confirmed bachelor, he died of arteriosclerosis on 13 September 1914, survived by his two sisters. A final musical theatre work, *Seebaddrummel [At the Seaside Resort]* was produced posthumously in Vienna on 31 October 1914.

Although music-theatre historians tend to regard Englander as a hack[452] whose work was functional rather than memorable,[453] his dance arrangements for production numbers and ballets are certainly notable. In addition to the numbers noted for *The Passing Show*, Englander provided his musicals with a variety of dances that included: ballroom dances in *A Daughter of the Revolution*; dervish dances and a grotesque convict march in *The Caliph*; a dagger dance, a "Vanishing Ballet," a horse-show incidental, and a "Quadrille d'Honneur" in *A Round of Pleasure*; the "Animation of Diana," the "Bellamy Dance," and "Ballet of the Four Seasons" in *The Man in the Moon*; the "Entrance of marriageable daughters" incidental, the "Life Is a Toyshop" dance, "de Stories Uncle Remus Tells Us" dance, the "She Didn't Understand" dance, and "The Rounders' Song" dance in *The Rounders*; the "Melodrama" incidental, "The Bold Hussars" march, the Waltz, Irish jig, Schottische, and Chinese dance in "When the Orchestra Plays" in *The Strollers*; the "'Twas Better Late than Never" dance, the "Oh! What's the Use" march, the dance in "Love Is a Game," and the atmospheric "Wanted: a Fly (or, The Spider and the Fly)" dance in *The Jewel of Asia*; "The Ballet of Fruits" in *The White Cat*; and the "Le-Kic-King" dance in *The Gay White Way*. Much of Englander's dance music involves the simple recapitulation of the melody of the song that preceded it, but his ballet and incidental music is most often original or a highly developed variation of an appropriate phrase or tune from the show. Englander was not an especially effective melodist; it was in the development of his melodies where he was at his best, and that was in his creation of dance and incidental music.

EUROPE, James Reese

Composer, violinist, and band leader James Reese Europe was born into a musical family in Mobile, Alabama, on 22 February 1881. By the time he was ten years old, the family had moved to Washington, D.C. where he received private lessons on the violin from Enrico Hurlei and a rudimentary musical education in the public school system.[454] In his early twenties, Europe moved to New York City where he found employment playing piano in nightclubs and contributing songs to Broadway musicals, including *Mother Goose* (2 December 1903) and *A Little of Everything* (6 June 1904). Later in the year Europe was hired as musical director and composer for the "Jolly" John Larkins Company production of *A Trip to Africa* (17 October 1904),[455] and by May 1905, Europe had become a staff composer (along with Will Marion Cook) for the Gotham Music Publishing Company.[456] During the 1906–1907 season he functioned as composer and musical director for the touring John Larkins Company, after which he became musical director for Bob Cole and the Johnson Brothers'[457] *The Shoo-Fly Regiment* (3 June 1907) for which he composed the Spanish-flavored music and collaborated with J. Rosamond Johnson on the dance arrangement of "On the Gay Luneta." Three months later, Europe served as composer, dance arranger, and musical director for the Smart Set Company's production of *The Black Politician*, opening in Kingston, New York (14 September 1907) before moving to Montreal and other Canadian cities.[458] In the summer of 1908, Europe was one of the organizers of the Frogs, a theatrical club designed to promote "social intercourse between the representative members of the Negro theatrical profession and to those connected directly or indirectly with art, literature, music, scientific and liberal professions, and the patrons of the arts"; and "to elevate the race generally" by creating a repository relating to "the history of the Negro, and the record of all worthy achievements [in the arts and folklore] in which the Negro has participated."[459] As soon as the club was established, Europe was back at work with Bob Cole and J. Rosamond Johnson on a new native-American musical, *The Red Moon*, scheduled to premiere on 31 August 1908 in Wilmington, Delaware. Europe had been hired as musical director but he also composed the music to three numbers: the spirited production number, "Sambo," the lilting "I Ain't Had No Lovin' in a Long Time," and the show's hit, "Ada, My Sweet Potater."[460] At the end of November 1909, Europe left *The Red Moon* tour in Chicago and was immediately hired to replace musical director James Vaughn for the Bert Williams vehicle, *Mr. Load of Coal* (1 November 1909).

The following year, Europe was among the creators of the Clef Club, an organization with a symphony orchestra and chorus that also functioned as a union and contractor for African-American musicians. On 2 May 1912, Europe conducted the 125 members of the Clef Club Symphony Orchestra in a concert of African-American music at Carnegie Hall. The following year, he conducted another concert at the same venue to celebrate the fif-

Example 64. "The Castle Doggy Fox Trot"

tieth anniversary of the Emancipation Proclamation and produced—along with Will Marion Cook and J. Rosamond Johnson—a touring musical revue called *The Frog Follies* [AKA *Frolic of the Frogs*] opening at the Casino Theatre on 11 August 1913.[461] That same year Europe began his association with Vernon and Irene Castle with whom he is credited with the creation of the "Turkey-Trot" and the ever-popular "Fox Trot,"[462] of which "The Castle Doggy Fox Trot" (1913),[463] example 64, is a representative illustration. Europe was said to have been inspired by W.C. Handy's "Memphis Blues" (1913) in his creation of dance music for the fox trot[464] and Handy's influence is evident in Europe's syncopations (especially in measures 2, 4–6, 10, 12–14) and in the melodic contour of the piece (though Europe uses dotted rhythms and Handy does not). Note that after a pickup measure the music is structured in two-measure units, each comprising eight beats (a characteristic grouping for dancers and choreographers).

In early January 1914, Europe had resigned from the Clef Club and organized the Tempo Club, using its members to perform in his various orchestras, one of which—Europe's Society Orchestra—toured with the Castles at home and abroad.[465] In April 1915, Europe contributed dance music to "The San Francisco Fair" segment of the Princess Theatre musical, *Nobody Home*, and collaborated with Will Marion Cook on the composition and musical direction of *Darkydom* (AKA *Darkeydom*) another touring African-American revue that premiered at the Lafayette Theatre in Harlem (23 October 1915) and featured the comedy team of (Flournoy) Miller and (Aubrey) Lyles.[466]

When the United States entered WWI, Europe enlisted and was instructed to organize a band for the 15th Regiment. Called the Hell Fighters, Europe's band included musicians from across the United States as well as Puerto Rico and the Caribbean, and quickly became the most popular of all the army bands in Europe during the war.[467] After they returned to the United States, the Hell Fighters set out on a national tour that included stops in New York, Boston, Philadelphia, Buffalo, Cleveland, Indianapolis, Pittsburgh, St. Louis, and Chicago. On 9 May 1919 during the intermission at a matinee concert at Mechanic's Hall in Boston, James Reese Europe was killed by Herbert Wright, a delusional drummer in the band, who believed that Europe had been mistreating him. On 14 May Europe was buried with full military honors at the National Military Cemetery in Arlington, Virginia.[468]

EUSTIS, Fred J.

Composer, dance arranger, and musical director Fred J. Eustis was born in the Wakefield suburb of Boston in 1851. He first appeared in theatrical announcements as a member of the Blish Combination Company scheduled to perform a "musical and literary entertainment" at the Wakefield Town Hall on 4 October 1877.[469] On 25 November he appeared in concert with Brown's Brigade Band at Beethoven Hall in Boston, beginning a career as accompanist and soloist at that venue that extended to the spring of 1878 when he became associated with the Redpath Lyceum Bureau, the highly reputed Boston booking agency that supplied speakers and performers to public halls.[470] On 30 April 1878 he was a "well-liked" soloist and accompanist in a Redpath entertainment at Boston's Union Hall that featured an "acceptable" reading, "satisfactory" vocal performances, and the "marvelous" Drummer Boy of Shiloh.[471] The Bureau sent Eustis on tour until November when he joined Brown's Band in sacred concerts at Boston's Gaiety Theatre on 24 November and 1 December 1878. He sustained his concert career through the summer of 1879 when he served as composer, musical director, and stage director of his "American opera-bouffe" *Sancho Pedro* (libretto by Charles F. Pidgin), produced at the Gaiety Theatre on Monday 16 June. The musical earned poor reviews and closed at the end of the week.[472] Eustice returned to the fold at the Redpath Bureau and continued concertizing on tour until the summer of 1881 when he was hired as musical director for the "Warner and Stanley Combination" production of E.E. Rice's *Evangeline*.[473] Eustis remained with the *Evangeline* tour until the end of the 1882–1883 season when he became the musical director and dance arranger for the "Rice's Surprise Party" production of *Pop* (21 May 1883). At the beginning of the 1883–1884 season, he accepted the musical directorship of Mestayer's Tourist Specialty Company in their fifth annual tour of the popular musical and nonsensical play, *Tourists in a Pullman Palace Car*,[474] and by the end of the season, Eustis had composed the music and dance arrangements for another musical, the burlesque *Penny-Ante, or, The Last of the Fairies*, produced under his musical direction at the Fourteenth Street Theatre in New York (9 June 1884) before going on a summer tour.

When Eustis returned to New York, he was engaged as composer, dance arranger, and musical director for *We, Us and Company at Mud Springs*, and while he was preparing the show for a New York production on 29 December 1884, May Stembler was performing "The Electric Waltz Song," composed by Eustis explicitly for her, in the Broadway adaptation of Charles Lecocq's *Gandolfo* (18 December 1884). Subsequent to the New York production, *We, Us and Company at Mud Springs* went on tour and closed on 16 May 1885. Immediately Eustis entered into a partnership with former advance man Ben Tuthill to produce another tour of *Penny-Ante*, starting in Worcester, Massachusetts (22 June 1885) before moving to the Oakland Gardens in Boston (6 July1885). After Boston, the show made stops in Buffalo, Cleveland, Milwaukee, and Chicago (2 August) where it closed after two weeks of poor business.[475] Undaunted, Eustis co-composed (with Frank Howson) the original music for *Putting on Style*, an adaptation by John Howson of the French farce *La Poudre aux Yeux*, produced at the Opera House in Paterson, New Jersey on 10 September 1885.[476] Nine days later, Eustis was in Trenton serving as the musical director for the Alice Harrison Company touring with a production of Woolson Morse's musical comedy *Hot Water* (19 September 1885). When *Hot Water* ran dry, Eustis became the musical director of Rice's *Evangeline* Company opening the summer season at Hooley's Theatre in Chicago (30 May 1886). He followed *Evangeline* with a touring production of his new opera, *Mizpah*, opening at the Chestnut Street Theatre in Philadelphia on the afternoon of 21 December 1886 as a benefit performance for the Journalists' Club.[477] Typical of Eustis's original musicals, the critics were unkind, asserting that "There is certainly no originality in the *Mizpah* score, while the libretto [by Henry J.W. Dam] is patchy, and shows little continuity of style or effectiveness of execution."[478] Producer Colonel F.A. Burr was cautioned against taking such a poor offering on tour, but as he had a contract with Hooley's Theatre in Chicago, honor prevailed over sense and, a few days after the opening in Philadelphia, the tour left for Chicago where the show closed abruptly, stranding the company without salary or lodging.

Because his estranged wife, the actress Ida Bell, was a member of the *Adonis* Company at the Chestnut Street Theatre, Eustis made his way from Chicago to Philadelphia and took a room at the Continental Hotel, three blocks from the theatre. On 11 January 1887 he began to drink early in the day and in the evening while intoxicated he waited for his wife at the stage door of the theatre. When she arrived he tried to force her to accompany him to the hotel and, when she refused, he became abusive and threatened her with a gun he held in his pocket. The melodramatic scene was interrupted by the arrival of other performers enabling Ida Bell to run into the theatre. *The New York Times* published a lively account of what happened next:

> Mr. Eustis then went around to the Chestnut-street entrance and walked into the theatre. Henry J. Rice, a brother of E.E. Rice, recognized him and noticed his condition.
>
> "You can't come in," he said. "You have been drinking and you will create trouble."
>
> "I will behave like a gentleman," pleaded Eustis, striving to get past him.
>
> Rice remained obdurate, and finally asked: "What are you doing with a revolver in your pocket?"
>
> Mr. Eustis denied having the weapon, and Reserve Officer Nicholson, who was standing at the door, was called up to arrest him. A loaded revolver was found on him at the station. Upon being locked up he begged hard to be released, and said that he meant to do his wife no injury. At the hearing he made the same plea.[479]

On the following day, Eustis was charged with attempting to shoot his wife and carrying a concealed deadly weapon. Ida Bell testified that she did not believe that her husband intended to harm her. She also suggested that he came from the western United States (an obvious lie since she knew he had been born in Massachusetts) and was unaware of the law regarding the carrying of concealed weapons. As a result of her testimony, Eustis was released. He immediately arranged for a basket of flowers to be sent to her dressing room at the theatre, with a card requesting another meeting.[480]

Once the storm was over in Philadelphia, Eustis returned to New York to work on the score for *The Two Tramps*, opening on 11 March in Norwalk, Connecticut; and at the end of the month, he was on his way to London to take charge of the Weber Piano Exhibit at the American Exposition (featuring "Buffalo Bill's Wild West Show") scheduled to open at Earl's Court on 9 May. Back in New York in the fall of 1887, Eustis published a piano solo, *Juggins Polka*, in the Boston Daily Globe,[481] and married Kate Uart, an actress with E.E. Rice's *Corsair* Company, on 21 November in Jersey City, New Jersey.[482] After his marriage, Eustis joined David Henderson's Chicago-based Ideal Extravaganza Company and provided songs, dance arrangements, orchestrations, and musical direction for *The Crystal Slipper, or Prince Prettiwitz and Little Cinderella* (12 June 1888 at the Chicago Opera House; 26 November 1888 at the Star Theatre in New York) and *Bluebeard, Jr., or, Fatima and the Fairy* (11 June 1889 at the Chicago Opera House; 11 January 1990 at Niblo's Garden). Eustis remained with *Bluebeard, Jr.* until the end of the New York run (15 February), when he left to become musical director of comedian Frank Daniels's production of *Kleptomania*, scheduled for an early summer premiere in New York. Evidently that project failed to materialize because in April, Eustis was hired as musical director for a new farce comedy, *A Domestic Cyclone*, scheduled for a 5 May opening; and in August Eustis was advertised as the composer of the songs in *Honest Hearts and Willing Hands*, a play beginning a tour at Niblo's Garden on 8 September 1990. The following year Eustis was engaged as the musical director with the Lillian Russell Opera Company, a position he held until the end of 1892, when he advertised the production of *Columbiana, or 1992*, his new operatic extravaganza that investigated "matters and things as they may be one hundred years hence."[483] In the spring 1893, Eustis served as musical director and vocal and chorus director of the world premiere of Imre Kiralfy's "grand historical, allegorical and mimic spectacle," *America* (22 April). He toured with the production until the summer of 1894 when he became the musical director, musical arranger, and composer for *Off the Earth*, opening in Milwaukee, Wisconsin (9 September 1894)[484] before going on tour and playing the Harlem Opera House for a week beginning 21 January 1895.

Subsequent musical directing assignments included *Fleur-de-Lis* (29 August 1895); *The Caliph* (3 September 1896); *Very Little Faust and Much Marguerite* (23 August 1897), for which Eustis composed additional music; *A Dangerous Maid* (12 November 1898), for which Eustis composed additional music; *The Ameer* (4 December 1899), for which he also served as stage director; *Little Red Riding Hood* (8 January 1900), for which he composed music and arranged ballet music; *The Regatta Girl* (14 March 1900); *Miss Simplicity* (10 February 1902); and *The Tenderfoot* (22 February 1904). During his tenure as a musical director, Eustis also composed the songs and dance music of several musicals, most of which closed before Broadway: *Bo-Peep* opened at the Star Theatre in Buffalo on 6 September 1897 and closed on the road; *Mother Goose* (with co-composer Frederick Gagel) opened on Broadway on 1 May 1899; *Lolita* opened at Young's Pier in Atlantic City on 19August 1907 and closed there at the end of the week; and *The Campaigners* opened at the Auditorium in Los Angeles on 20 July 1908 and closed there three weeks later.[485] On 23 November 1908, Eustis was the musical director for *The Queen of the Moulin Rouge* when it opened at the New National Theatre in Washington, D.C., but when the show moved to New York two weeks later, he was no longer with the company. After two years of relative inactivity, Eustis joined forces with Joseph Van den Berg in 1911 to create the Van den Berg-Eustis Opera Company, opening a three-month engagement at Manhattan's Terrace Garden on 26 June with a production of Bizet's *Carmen*, and featuring a thirty-piece orchestra and a forty-voice chorus. According to advertisements in the New York newspapers, a $2.00 ticket paid for the opera, a dinner that began at 6:00 P.M., a vaudeville show after the opera, and taxi fare home.[486] *Carmen* was followed by Gilbert and Sullivan's perennial favorite, *H.M.S. Pinafore*, on 3 July but, typical of many of Eustis's enterprises, before the 4 July performance, the Van den Berg-Eustis Opera Company collapsed due to poor management.[487]

Even though his was a career filled with minor hits and major disasters, Eustis loved the theatre and needed to work; so when he was offered the musical directorship of the *Enchantress* Company, a northern touring unit of the Victor Herbert operetta with his wife in the cast, he welcomed the opportunity. However, in Rochester, New York, Eustis caught a cold, which, by the time the tour reached Toronto, Ontario, was diagnosed as pneumonia. Eustis was forced to give up his baton and his wife relinquished her role in the show to be able to nurse him back to health. Her efforts, unfortunately, were futile, since on 23 March 1912, Eustis died in her arms in their room at the Palmer House in Toronto. His body was shipped to Wakefield, Massachusetts, where private funeral services were held.[488]

Some composers rely on inspiration, others on their education; throughout his career, Fred Eustis relied on imitation. His gift for creating familiar-sounding melodies suited him better in his incidental and dance music than in the individual songs he composed. The same could be said of his harmonic and rhythmic accompaniments, which in the songs were characteristically sparse and designed to support the performer rather than draw the listener's attention. In this his early career as a singer's accompanist has had a marked influence. Melodic familiarity and harmonic simplicity is quite often necessary in incidental music to convey a specific mood or feeling and in dance music invariably structured in repeatable eight-beat units. Three dances from the original *Bluebeard, Jr.* score (published in 1889) provide representative examples of Eustis's compositional style. The duet, "If They Must Tear Me from Thy Heart" ends with the affirmation that "Our love will last forever, for day by day I love thee more, No love was half so deep." Such a positive and uplifting spirit is mirrored in the dance, marked *scherzando*, an eight-measure schottische divided into two-measure eight-beat units in which measures 1-2 are the same as measures 5–6, and measures 3–4 are similar to 7–8. The pattern is a familiar one and so is the buoyant melody comprised of triplets and dotted notes (though Eustis inserts a rest where the dot would normally occur, the effect is the same as a staccato dotted note). Similarly there are no surprises in the harmony which employs the traditional tonic-dominant-subdominant formula with a cadential use of a common-tone diminished chord. The lack of originality is not important. What matters is that the familiar elements create a dance arrangement that supports and enlivens the spirit of the song.

The dance at the end of the waltz duet, "What Do You Think," is designed to underscore pantomime business. The song ends with the characters singing "Papa must fondle his darling, Papa must kiss papa's pet," and what follows is an eight-measure appropriately structured common time dance with a melody that juxtaposes leaping staccato phrases with held-note places of rest. The playful game of courtship suggested by the dance is heightened in the final four measures in which the staccato melody continues until the final measure, withholding the outcome of the game until the very end. Additionally, the use of pickup notes is important in the dance, creating a sense of eagerness and impetuosity to the scene. The dramatic effect of Eustis's dance music is of much greater significance than the fact that its structure is reminiscent of that of Delibes's "Pizzicato" in the ballet *Sylvia*.

For the schottische patter number "Little Lord Fauntleroy" exploiting the foppish characteristics of the boy in Frances H. Barnet's book, Eustis produced another eight-measure dance in which measures 1–3 are repeated exactly in measures 5–7. Measures 1 and 5 are unusual because of the presence of rests on beats two and four, creating a kind of stop-time effect with quarter notes on beats one and three suggesting the sophisticated petulance of the dandy, stomping his feet when he fails to get his way. The absence of dotted notes in the familiar-sounding melody of the dance is also significant since the even eighth notes suggest precision and meticulousness, other features of the haughty foppish boy. As in the examples above, familiarity of melody and structure, as well as simplicity of harmony, are not defects in Eustis's dance arrangements, especially in burlesque extravaganzas that rely on familiarity for humorous effect. Eustis's art songs and solo piano compositions, however, demonstrate that he was capable of more original and complex melodies, harmonies, and rhythms than those often represented in his theatrical dance music.

EYSLER, Edmund [Samuel]

Composer Edmund Eysler [originally Eisler] was born in Vienna on 12 March 1874, the son of a marginally successful Jewish merchant. As a teenager, Eysler was being groomed by his parents for a career as an engineer, but since he displayed absolutely no aptitude for engineering, his school chum, Leo Fall, easily persuaded the family to allow Eysler to pursue a musical career instead. He spent six years at the Vienna Conservatory where he studied piano with Anton Door, harmony and counterpoint with Robert Fuchs, and musical composition with Robert's older brother, Johann Nepomuk Fuchs. After graduation, Eysler composed a ballet that was never performed and supported himself by giving private piano lessons. His second score, *Der Hexenspiegel* [*The Witches' Mirror*], an operetta with a text by the famous librettist Ignaz Schnitzer, won him the affection of the librettist, who subsidized him, and the attention of publisher Josef Weinberger who tried valiantly (but unsuccessfully) to get the work produced. Eysler subsequently found work at Venedig-in-Wien, a summer theatre where he composed dance music for Ivan Caryll's *Die Reise nach Cuba* [*The Trip to Cuba*] as well as incidental numbers for the after-performance cabarets by members of the theatre company.[489]

Eysler the composer finally became an overnight sensation with the production of the operetta *Bruder Straubinger* [*Brother Straubinger*] at the famous Theater an der Wien on 20 February 1903. The piece reused much of the music Eysler had written for *Der Hexenspiegel*, and featured Alexander Girardi, the headliner of the day in Viennese operetta. Eysler subsequently composed over 50 operettas in German, many of which reached Broadway in translation. *The Rollicking Girl* (1 May 1905) interpolated Eysler's hit song in *Bruder Straubinger*, the waltz "Küssen ist keine Sünd [Kissing Is Not a Sin]" translated as "Friends That Are Good and True." *The Florist Shop* (9 August 1909), Oliver Herford's adaptation of *Gluck bei Frauen* [*Luck with Women*] borrowed Eysler's song "The Love Cure," and *The Love Cure* (1 September 1909) was an English adaptation of Eysler's *Künstlerblut* [*Artists' Blood*] originally produced on 20 October 1906. Eysler's 1905 German hit, *Pufferl*, was produced at New York's Majestic Theatre in an Italian version called *Amor di Principe* [*Prince's Love*] (2 May 1911), and his *Vera Violetta* (30 November 1907) was given an American adaptation without a change in title on 20 November 1911. Eysler's *Johann der Zweite* [*John the Second*] (3 October 1908), adapted for Broadway as *The June Bride*, opened in Boston on 23 September 1912 but closed on the road; and his *Der Frauenfresser* [*The Woman-Eater*] (23 December 1911) came to Broadway under the slightly less offensive title *The Woman Haters* on 7 October 1912. Eysler's *Der lachende Ehemann* [*The Laughing Husband*] (19 March 1913) appeared in a Broadway adaptation on 2 February 1914, and his *Ein Tag im Paradies* [*A Day in Paradise*] (23 December 1913) began a year's run in New York City on 5 August 1915 in an adaptation called *The Blue Paradise*, with additional music by Sigmund Romberg and Cecil Lean. Although the German hostilities in WWI put an end to the importation of German musicals on Broadway (at least until the 1920s), Eysler maintained a seemingly inexhaustible creativity on the other side of the Atlantic Ocean, producing perhaps his greatest success at the Theater an der Wein on 13 September 1927 with the old-fashioned Viennese operetta, *Die gold'ne Meisterin* [*The Golden Champion*]. During the Nazi regime, the production of Eysler's operettas was prohibited because the composer was a Jew, though whether it was due to negligence or respect for his contribution to the German-speaking musical theatre, the Nazis made no attempt to deport Eysler or his family. When the war was over, he produced his final operetta, *Weiner Musik* [*Viennese Music*] on 22 December 1947 and scored another success. Eysler died in Vienna on 4 October 1949 and was interred at the Vienna Central Cemetery in a grave of honor.

Eysler's incidental and dance music was composed squarely in the neo-Romantic tradition of Viennese operetta, with little more than a nod toward ragtime or jazz. Rousing marches, effervescent waltzes, and highly melodic and chromatically harmonized underscoring (the kind of music one might expect to hear in a film) were characteristic of Eysler's work. Examples include the "Melodrama" (depicting an audience leaving a theatre at the end of a performance) at the beginning of act one of *The Love Cure*; the graceful "Flower Dance," the waggish "Drinking Scene" (that includes a jaunty two-beat underscore as well as a pizzicato waltz), and the "Finale" (that begins with the same jaunty underscore) in act two of *The Love Cure*; the stirring "Cupid Chorus" march, and the vivacious incidental music (as the guests seat themselves) at the beginning of the "Supper and Toast Scene" in act three of *The Love Cure*. The act three "Cupid Chorus" is particularly notable since it employs the same march tune that Eysler used in the "Tanz-Duett [Dance Duet]" from the original German score of *Vera Violetta*. When *Vera Violetta* came to Broadway the "Tanz-Duett" was replaced by the interpolated number, "Come and Dance," composed by Louis Hirsch.

F

FEHRMANN, Max

Actor, composer, and musical director Max Fehrmann was born in Berlin in March 1852 and immigrated to the United States when he was sixteen years old. He first appeared in theatrical records as an actor and musical director for the Milton Nobles Comedy Company in their 1879–1880 touring season.[490] In the fall of 1881 he made his debut at the Bush Street Theatre in San Francisco playing the eponymous character in Fred Maeder's play, *Uncle Isaac*, and became "the newest star in the theatrical firmament."[491] After touring for some years with *Uncle Isaac*, Fehrmann served as stage director, musical director, dance arranger, and composer for Milton Nobles's production of *Haunted Houses*, which premiered at the Opera House in Red Bank, New Jersey, on 4 June 1886 and closed there three days later. Fehrmann returned to playing Uncle Isaac on tour[492] until January 1892 when he assumed the musical direction for *Superba*, a three-act spectacular drama that had premiered in Albany, New York, on 1 October 1890[493] and was touring in preparation for an appearance at a Broadway theatre in December. When *Superba* opened at the 14th Street Theatre (26 December 1892), Fehrmann was credited with the composition, adaptation, and arrangement of all the music in the production, including a "Grotesque Dance," a Serpentine Dance," a "Fairy Ball," a "Bull Fight Tableau," and a grand "World's Fair" finale. Following the long tour of *Superba*, Fehrmann became the musical director for Bush's Victoria Burlesquers, a company that toured extensively from 1899 through the first decade of the twentieth century. When he retired from the stage around 1920, he and his family resided at the Percy Williams Home for aged and destitute actors until an illness forced him to move to the Brunswick Home for incurables in Amityville, Long Island. Fehrmann died there in November 1931, survived by his widow and son.[494]

FELIX, Hugo

Composer and dance arranger Hugo Felix was born in Vienna on 19 November 1866. He exhibited a talent for music at an early age, and although he matriculated from Vienna University with a Ph.D. in Science (for what artists often call a "fallback" or "safety" occupation), upon graduation he pursued a career in musical theatre with the composition of an operetta *Die Kätzchen[The Kittens]* produced on 23 January 1890. A number of operettas followed until he achieved his first major triumph with the score for *Madame Sherry* (1 November 1902), after which he moved to London where he was engaged by producer George Edwardes to compose a score for *Les Merveilleuses* [*The Dandy Ladies*] (27 October 1906) with a libretto by Basil Hood (from the play by Victorien Sardou).[495] On 30 August 1910, an English adaptation of *Madame Sherry* made its way to the New Amsterdam Theatre in New York with only three numbers retained from Felix's original score, the rest entirely recomposed by Karl Hoschna. Another sample of Felix's music was heard in New York in 1911 with the interpolation of "Or Thereabouts" into Lionel Monckton's score for *The Quaker Girl* (23 October).[496] Evidently concerned about the way his scores had been bowdlerized in various adaptations, Felix came to New York on 3 August 1912[497] to supervise the musical rehearsals for the American production of *Tantalizing Tommy*, opening in Chicago on 30 August and in New York on 2 October.[498] *The New York Times* review was particularly favorable regarding Felix's score:

> Dr. Hugo Felix ... knows how to write the lilting, soothing sort of thing that the public seems to like. He appears to have no hesitancy in making the humblest instruments in the orchestra do service to the cause. More than once in *Tantalizing Tommy* the rhythm and swing owe their agreeable effect to a liberal punctuating by the xylophone, while a miniature piano, with bell-like tones [celesta], does its share to give the music a popular tone. There is, for all this, some very good writing in the score of the piece, and were the book up to the standard of the music it might be possible to record another great success.[499]

The critic singled out an especially effective pantomime number in the first act called "Musical Clock" (example 65) in which the celesta and xylophone are prominent in the musical recreation of the whirling machinery of a clock.

Example 65. "Musical Clock" from *Tantalizing Tommy*

Although Felix's well-regarded score was unable to keep *Tantalizing Tommy* afloat in New York for more than a month, his next American effort, *Pom-Pom* (28 February 1916) with a libretto by Anne Caldwell fared better. Antecedent to its New York run, *Pom-Pom* premiered at Parson's Theatre in Hartford, Connecticut on 27 January 1916 before moving to the Colonial Theatre in Boston. Of the Boston production, the critic for the *Boston Daily Globe*[500] wrote: "Hugo Felix has contributed 18 musical numbers, and several of them are entitled to operatic distinction, especially the ensembles, which are spirited and splendidly effective. The score as a whole is removed from the commonplace, and, although it does not include many jingly tunes, it is music of the better sort, not lacking in gayety and grace of rhythm nor in charm of harmony." Of special note was an "Apache Dance Parody" (example 66) performed in the musical by a Gigolo and his mistress, Crevette ["Shrimp"] to music that consciously simulated the rhythms and melodic contours of the ballet waltz in Offenbach's *Le Roi Carotte*, the tune most frequently associated with the apache dance.

Example 66. "Apache Dance Parody" from *Pom-Pom*

Felix followed *Pom-Pom* with a score for *Prince Silverwings*, a spectacular musical fantasy[501] based on L. Frank Baum's 1903 unproduced play of the same name; and like the play, the musical was not produced. Subsequent projects included *Lassie* (6 April 1920), with a libretto by Catherine Chisholm Cushing based on her play *Kitty MacKay*;[502] *The Sweetheart Shop* (31 August 1920), with a libretto by Anne Caldwell;[503] *Marjolaine* (24 January 1922), libretto by Catherine Chisholm Cushing based on *Pomander Walk*, a play Louis N. Parker;[504] *Sancho Panza* (26 November 1923), based on episodes from *Don Quixote* by Miguel de Cervantes;[505] *Peg o' My Dreams* (5 May 1924), book by J. Hartley Manners based on his play, *Peg o' My Heart*, lyrics by Anne Caldwell; *Spring Magic* (October 1926), with a libretto by Rachel Crothers, based on her play *39 East*;[506] and *The Jealous Moon* (20 November 1928), incidental music for the play by Jane Cowl and Theodore Charles.[507] Following *The Jealous Moon*, Felix joined the many professional musicians who left New York for Los Angeles after the onset of talking pictures created a demand for composers, orchestrators, and musical directors in the film industry. In

1930, Felix was hired to orchestrate the score (that included three Vincent Youmans's songs) for *What a Widow*, an Allan Dwan film starring Gloria Swanson, and the only movie that the American Film Institute associates with Felix's name. Kurt Gänzl notes that in the seven months leading up to his death in August 1934, Felix earned only $15.00 from working in films.[508]

FÉVRIER, Henri

French composer Henri Février was born in Paris on 2 October 1875. Exhibiting a musical talent from an early age, he studied at the Paris Conservatoire with composers Gabriel Fauré, Jules Massenet, and André Messager who instilled in him a desire to compose music for the stage. His first opera, *Le roi aveugle* [*The Blind King*] was successfully produced in Paris in 1906 but it was *Monna Vanna* (libretto by Maurice Maeterlinck) that became an international success. Performed in Paris (10 January 1909), Boston (3 December 1913), and New York City (17 February 1914), *Monna Vanna* introduced Février's music to the Americas and secured for him the demand to continue to produce musical theatre works at the major theatres in Paris. Subsequent works included incidental music for *Agnès dame galante* [*Agnes the Courtesan*] (1912); the operettas, *La Princesse et le Porcher* [*The Princess and the Swineherd*] (1912), and *Carmosine* (1913); and operas, *Gismonda*, which premiered in Chicago (14 January 1919), *La Damnation de Blanchefleur* [*The Damnation of Blanchefleur*] (1920), *L'Ile désenchantée* [*The Disenchanted Island*] (1925), *Oletta* (1927), *La Femme nue* [*The Naked Woman*] (1929), and *Sylvette* (1932). His single contribution to the American musical theatre was the co-composition (with Anselm Goetzl) of the incidental music for *Aphrodite* (24 November 1919), a three-act spectacle drama with incidental music, songs, and ballets choreographed by Michel Fokine. Following several years of retirement Février died at his home in Saint-Germain-en-Laye on 6 July1957.

FINCK, Herman

Born in London on 4 November 1872, composer, musical director, violinist, and pianist Herman Finck (originally Hermann Van Der Vinck) was trained at the Guildhall School of Music and Drama where he studied music theory and harmony with British composer Henry Gadsby.[509]

He played the violin in theatre orchestras in Windsor and London before joining the Palace Theatre as violinist and pianist in 1892, leader and deputy conductor in 1896, and sole musical director from 1900 to 1921. The following year, Finck became the musical director of the Theatre Royal, Drury Lane, a position he held until 1931, after which he conducted Sunday evening concerts at Southport, a seaside town on the Irish Sea.[510] An inexhaustible composer of musical comedies, operettas, ballets, incidental music, songs, and instrumental works, Finck began his career as the composer of incidental and dance music for director-choreographer John Tiller's musical productions, as well as for the variety bills at the Palace Theatre.[511] In addition, he contributed songs and dance music to the American musical theatre, starting with "In the Shadows," a dance number (and, arguably, his most famous composition) interpolated into A. Baldwin Sloane's score for *The Hen-Pecks* (4 February 1911). Subsequent compositions for the theatre in the United States included "Oolie Girl of Panama" interpolated into Henrich Berté's score for *The Rose of Panama* (22 January 1912); "Gilbert the Filbert" and "Florrie the Flapper" in *The Girl from Utah* (24 August 1914); "Constant Lover" in *Miss Information* (5 October 1915); the score and original dance music for *Around the Map* (1 November 1915);[512] and "We Must Have a Ballet," a ballet arrangement for *Elsie Janis and Her Gang* (16 January 1922). Other examples of Finck's compositions for the British musical heater included *In Gay Paree* at the Palace of Varieties, Manchester (31 December 1900); *O-Mi-Iy* (co-composed with Frank Tours) at the London Hippodrome (25 March 1912); *The Slush Girl* at the Palace Theatre (14 September 1914); *Vivien* (co-composed with Howard Talbot) at the Prince of Wales Theatre, Birmingham (27 December 1915); *The Love Flower* at the Kensington Theatre, London (27 March 1920); *Kiki* at the Chiswick Empire Theatre, London (20 August 1921); *A Bunch of Keys* at the Ambassadors' Theatre, London (20 March 1922); and *Decameron Nights* at Drury Lane (17 April 1922).[513] Finck's dance music included the aforementioned "In the Shadows," a dance originally composed for the Palace Theatre; "Mystic Beauty," a veil dance (1912); "Processionelle et Danse Florale," "Valse des Adoratrices," and "Danse Barbare" from the revue *Hullo America* (1919); and the ballet *My Lady Dragon Fly* (1921). Rich in melodic invention and crowded with lush Romantic harmonies, Finck's dance compositions are firmly rooted in the late nineteenth-century European style, easily accessible, evocative, and exhibiting few of the ragtime syncopations found in American dance music of the same period. Whether accompanying a line of leggy chorus girls or solo dancers, Finck's music seemed to ennoble the experience, providing sufficient variety (through contrasting articulations, dynamics, melodic contours, and rhythms) to accompany the assorted dance steps, while maintaining the atmosphere that what was being done was significant. To discerning ears, the music may have sounded old-fashioned, but never trivial.

In addition to his efforts as a composer, Finck was a well-respected musical director who conducted the productions of *Rose Marie*, *The Desert Song*, and *Show Boat* at Drury Lane and on recordings as well. He composed scores for a number of a films (including incidental atmospheric music for silent movies) but he was best known as the composer and conductor for *The Old Curiosity Shop* (1934). His uncredited work on films included *The Black Hand Gang* (1930), *Cavalcade* (1933), *Letting in the Sunshine* (1933), *The Scotland Yard Mystery* (1934), *It's a Bet* (1935), *Sol över Sverige* [*Sun over Sweden*] (1938), and *Footsteps in the Sand* (1939). In 1937 he published a lighthearted memoir entitled *My Melodious Memories* recalling his work with theatre impresario Sir Alfred Butt at the Palace and Drury Lane Theatres. Two years later, on 21 April 1939, Finck died in London, following a long illness.[514]

FLETCHER, Percy E[astman]

Composer, violinist, and musical director Percy E. Fletcher was born in Derby, England, on 12 December 1879. Soon after graduating from the Conservatory where he studied violin, piano, organ, music theory, composition, and orchestration, Fletcher served as musical director for a number of London theatres, including the Prince of Wales, the Savoy (where, in 1906, he composed music for the curtain-raiser *An Exile from Home*), Daly's, and the Theatre Royal, Drury Lane. In 1915 he became musical director at His Majesty's Theatre, where he orchestrated and conducted the 2,235-performance initial run of Oscar Asche and Frederic Norton's *Chu Chin Chow* (31 August 1916). In addition, he composed the music for Asche's next eastern musical spectacle *Mecca*, produced at the Century Theatre in New York on 4 October 1920 (and as *Cairo* in London in 1921). The American production with a cast of four hundred was critically praised for its spectacle and choreography (by the Russian dancer and choreographer Michel Fokine), but roundly panned for its music. "There are some exceedingly striking things about Mecca," said one reviewer, "The music is not one of them. In fact, the value of the entire production might have been considerably enhanced if there had been one haunting refrain that stood out." The critic continued:

> The Bacchanale scene with which the second act ends contains a real artistic thrill. For Michel Fokine, who arranged its choreography, Leon Eakst, whose artistic functioning is evident in the costumes, and the Harkers, Joseph and Philip, who designed the majestic interior of the Egyptian palace, within whose walls the dancers do some mighty intimate rolling about, each and collectively furnished a definite eyeful. But Percy E. Fletcher's music for this number, though reminiscent, was wide of the mark.[515]

An excerpt from Fletcher's "Bacchanale" music (example 67) marked "Very quick, wild, and barbaric" looks and sounds like silent film chase music, particularly with the sixteenth-note runs in measures 1–8 and the repeated chords moving upwards melodramatically (and chromatically) in measures 9–16. The trappings of "wildness" may be present in the music but they are betrayed by the balanced division of the piece into four-measure units in which measures 1–4 are mirrored in measures 5–8; measures 9–12 and mirrored in measures 13–16; and measures 17–20 are repeated exactly. This kind of predictable musical architecture belies wildness and barbarism and it is not difficult to understand the point of view of the critic who, familiar with the furor caused by Stravinsky's 1913 feral ballet, *The Rite of Spring*, might find Fletcher's "Bacchanale" somewhat tame.

Other examples of Fletcher's incidental and ballet music in *Mecca* include a bombastic "Wrestling Scene"; a quasi-pentatonic "Introduction to Chinese Scene"; an interesting "Dance Poem," in which the music accompanies the recitation of a poem while women (dressed as desert dancers) dance; an effective eastern-flavored "Procession and Ballet" that displays many expansive and lyrical phrases; a dynamic descriptive musical scene called "The Slave Market" that underscores dialogue and characterizes each man on the block; a "Chinese Dance and Scene" which allows Fletcher a momentary escape from the rigid four-measure-unit structure; and the placid and beautiful "Returning from Mecca," which, again, underscores dialogue. If not especially innovative or original, Fletcher's incidental and dance music in *Mecca* is always efficient, employing familiar devices to tune the ears of the audience to the dramatic event. There is little subtlety in the music but the composer's bold strokes match and ac-

Example 67. "Bacchanale" from *Mecca*

centuate the pomp and pageantry inherent in the melodramatic *Arabian Nights* story.

Although Fletcher produced the score for only one additional British musical, *The Good Old Days* (7 October 1925), he was greatly active in the composition of art songs, ballads, sacred cantatas, solo piano pieces, orchestral marches, dances, suites, and military band music, very little of which has survived the test of time. He died in London on 10 December 1932.

FRANCIS, W[illiam] T.

Born in Mobile, Alabama, in December 1861, and raised in New Orleans, W.T. Francis was a young piano prodigy, prominent in concert programs from about the age of seven.[516] By the time he was in his early twenties, Francis was the published composer and arranger of "Chloé: Danza Mexicana" and "La Media Noche" performed at the World's Exposition in New Orleans by the Mexican National Band, of which he was the assistant manager during a United States tour that began in June 1885.[517] Upon his return to New Orleans in 1886, Francis became the musical director for the Children's Juvenile Opera Company, and after several years of touring with youngsters in the casts of Gilbert and Sullivan's *The Mikado* and Edmond Audran's *The Mascot*, Francis signed with the Slocum Opera Company in May 1890 to provide musical direction for a repertoire that included Johann Strauss, Jr.'s *Prince Methusalem*, and Offenbach's *La Perichole* on a twenty weeks' tour of the southern United States.[518] In 1891, Francis moved to New York where he found employment with the (Frederick) Hallen and (Joseph) Hart Company as composer and musical director for their production of *The Idea*, a comedy with music set in and around New Orleans. *The Idea* opened in St. Paul, Minnesota on 6 June 1892 and toured for two years before playing the Park Theatre in New York on 9 April 1894.[519] At the end of the 1894–1895 season, Francis joined the Garrick Burlesque Company as musical director for *Thrilby*, an operatic travesty of Paul Meredith Potter's dramatization of George du Maurier's famous novel, *Trilby*, that opened at the Garrick Theatre in

Example 68. Dance in the "Golf-Song" from *The Little Host*

New York on 3 June 1895 and toured through 1896. At the beginning of the 1896–1897 season, Francis's plantation song, "Louiser" was interpolated into the score of *The Gold Bug* (21 September 1896) at the Casino Theatre;[520] at the end of the season, he co-composed the music (with John Stromberg) for *Mr. New York, Esq.* (22 April 1897) at Weber and Fields Music Hall;[521] and in the middle of the 1897–1898 season, Francis's instrumental composition "Down Ole Tampa Bay" was introduced as a dance in *The Telephone Girl* (27 December 1897) at the Casino Theatre. After serving as musical director for John Philip Sousa's *The Charlatan* (5 September 1898) at the Knickerbocker Theatre, Francis provided the score (with Thomas Chilvers) and musical direction for the musical farce,

Example 69. "Priscilla" from *Twirly-Whirly*

Example 69 (continued). "Priscilla" from *Twirly-Whirly*

The Little Host (26 December 1898), at the Herald Square Theatre.[522] A schottische song proclaiming the advantages of playing golf ("Golf-Song") was followed by eight merry measures of dance music (example 68) filled with dotted notes, triplets, and simple diatonic harmonies (except for the cadential common-tone diminished seventh chords in measures 2, 6) that support the jovial soft-shoe dance on the stage.

Following *The Little Host*, Francis composed "Honey, You're My Turtle Dove," interpolated into the score of *An Arabian Girl and Forty Thieves* (29 April 1899); he provided the entire score (and musical direction) for *A Royal Rogue* (24 December 1900);[523] and he composed the music for "By-and-By" in *The Show Girl, or, The Cap of Fortune* (5 May 1892). On 10 July 1902, Francis was given a three-year contract by Weber and Fields to serve as composer and musical director at their Music Hall, replacing John Stromberg who had died a few days earlier.[524] Stromberg had written only seven songs for *Twirly-Whirly*, the new Weber and Fields burlesque scheduled to open the 1902–1903 season and Francis's first assignment was to complete the score.[525] Among the numbers Francis added to *Twirly-Whirly* was "Priscilla" a novelty dance performed in the show by Bessie Clayton. Example 69 displays an excerpt of the dance music beginning with the release (measures 1–12), marked "il basso ben marcato," and ending with the recapitulation of the principal theme (measures 13–28).

It was Weber and Fields practice to update their musicals during the run with new burlesques embellished by music from the house composer. As a result, following the opening of *Twirly-Whirly* on 11 September 1902 with the burlesque *I, Mary McPain*, Francis composed scores for the replacement burlesques *Humming Birds and Onions* (6 November 1902), *The Stickiness of Gelatine* (18 December 1902), and *The Big Little Princess* (26 February 1903).[526] For the next season at the Music Hall, Francis composed the songs and dance music for *Whoop-Dee-Doo* (24 September 1903) as well as the burlesque *Looney Park* and its replacement *Waffles* (10 December 1903). By the time the musical extravaganza returned from tour for a short run at the New Amsterdam Theatre (16 May 1904), *Waffles* had been replaced by the new burlesque *Catherine*.[527]

During the summer of 1904, Francis left Weber and Fields and accepted the position of "general musical director" for producer Charles Frohman's musical theatre companies.[528] Earlier on 21 May 1903, *The New York Times* had reported that Weber and Fields planned to produce *The Jolly Tar*, a musical comedy written by R.H. Burnside and Jefferson de Angelis with music by W.T. Francis. The show was not produced as promised, and conceivably the failure of Weber and Fields to mount one of Francis's more serious efforts led him to look elsewhere for employment. As Frohman's "general musical director," Francis's production assignments included musical direction and additional music for *The School Girl* (1 September 1904); songs and dance music for *The Rollicking Girl* (1 May 1905);[529] musical direction for *The Catch of the Season* (28 August 1905); musical direction for *The Little Cherub* (6 August 1906); musical direction and additional music ("It's Naughty to Be Kissed") for *The Dairymaids* (26 August 1907); musical direction for *Miss Hook of Holland* (31 December 1907); musical direction for *The Girls of Gottenberg* (2 September 1908); music for *Fluffy Ruffles* (7 September 1908); musical direction for *Kitty Grey* (25 January 1907); musical direction for *The Mascot* (12 April 1909); musical direction for *The Dollar Princess* (6 August 1909); and musical direction for *Our Miss Gibbs* (29 August 1910).

Earlier in 1910, *The Jolly Tar* was finally produced, giving its premiere performance at the Alvin Theatre in Pittsburgh on 1 April. Although the audience was large and enthusiastic, the critical reception was only kind: "While it may never become a burning success on the road, it is one that will have a call for roof gardens, etc. The music and words are pleasing."[530] On 19 September 1911, Jefferson de Angeles produced *The Jolly Tar* at the Illinois Theatre in Chicago under the title *The Ladies' Lion*, but even his appearance in the starring role (originally written for him) was insufficient to render the production a success. Following the failure of *The Ladies' Lion*, W.T. Francis faded from theatrical records. His name appeared in connection with the Weber and Fields reunion show *Hokey-Pokey* (8 February 1912) at the Broadway Theatre, but his contribution consisted entirely of numbers he had composed for the Music Hall from 1902 to 1904. Francis died on 4 September 1916 at his home in Manhattan, survived by his widow, Emily Seymour Francis, his daughters Annie and Mary, and his son, William T. Francis, Jr.

FRANKLIN, Malvin M.

Born in Atlanta, Georgia, on 24 August 1889, Malvin Franklin first appeared in the New York theatre scene in 1909 as the composer of "You're Getting Better Looking Every Day" (lyrics by Addison Burkhardt), a song interpolated into the score of *The Silver Star* (1 November 1909). The next year the same team created "The Osculation Bombashay," for *The Sweetest Girl in Paris*, a Joseph Howard musical that opened in Milwaukee on 21 August 1910 before moving to Chicago for a long run at the La Salle Theatre. Franklin's next project, *The Wife Hunters*, for which he co-composed the music (with Anatol Friedland) and arranged dance music, opened in Albany, New York, on 26 October 1911 prior to a New York City run.[531] Although the show was neither a critical nor financial success on Broadway, producer Lew Fields was sufficiently impressed by Franklin's work to hire the twenty-two-year-old composer to co-write the music (with lyricist E. Ray Goetz) for *All Aboard*, the show that would inaugurate Fields's Forty-Fourth Street Roof Garden Theatre (5 June 1913).[532] In 1914, Franklin began collaborating with lyricist L. Wolfe Gilbert (writer of "Waiting for the Robert E. Lee") to produce "The Sunny Riviera Bay," a "great big pretentious carnival number" for *The Lilac Domino* (28 October 1914) and all the syncopated specialty numbers for impresario Andreas Dippel's musical extravaganza, *Queen of the Roses*.[533] In 1914 Franklin also published the music for a series of dances in *Modern Dances: Society's Latest Dance Folio* that included instructions and illustrations for the "Tango," the "Hesitation Waltz and Boston," "Maxixe," "Trot and One Step," and "Half and Half."

Gilbert's vaudeville partner Anatol Friedland joined the songwriting team in 1916 and the trio produced two outstanding songs: the immensely popular "Shades of Night" (1916) and the wartime favorite, "Set Aside Your Tears" (1917). With lyricist Thomas J. Gray, Franklin composed "When All the Animals Are Gone" for *His Little Widows* (30 April 1917), and with composer Robert Hood Bowers, he co-composed the score for *A Lonely*

Romeo (10 June 1919), another musical produced by Lew Fields. Subsequent projects included the song, "World's Peace" (1919), played between acts at the Casino Theatre; the score for the musical, *The Lady Tiger* (1920), with a libretto by John P. Wilson; the score for *Dearie*, a musical adaptation by John P. Wilson of George Broadhurst and George V. Hobart's play *Wildfire* that opened in Detroit on 30 August 1920 and closed in Atlantic City at the end of October;[534] and dance music for *Snapshots of 1921* (2 June 1921), including the "Waltz Ballet" to accompany the burlesque of Sacha Guitry's play *Deburau*. In addition to his responsibilities as a composer, Franklin served as musical director and accompanist in vaudeville and on the cabaret circuit. He died in New York City in July 1981.

FREEBORN, Cassius [Marcelus Clay]

Born on 18 May 1877 in Providence, Rhode Island, performer, musical director, and composer Cassius ("Cass") Freeborn began his Broadway career as one of two gondoliers in the Frank L. Perley Opera Company's production of a brash and noisy comic opera called *A Venetian Romance* (2 May 1904).[535] Two months later, Freeborn appeared as J. Jeffries Fitzcorbett in *Paris by Night* at the Madison Square Roof Garden (2 July 1904) and on a long national tour.[536] While on the road, Freeborn produced a number of musical compositions that included "The Edna Waltzes," dedicated to Edna May, appearing in *The School Girl* (1 September 1904); a song ("Around the World") interpolated into the score of *The Catch of the Season* (28 August 1905); and the entire score for *Mam'zelle Champagne* (lyrics by Edgar Allan Woolf) produced at the Madison Square Roof Garden on 25 June 1906. On opening night the production was interrupted when, during a second-act production number, Henry K. Thaw, husband of showgirl Evelyn Nesbit, left his seat in the audience and murdered his wife's lover, architect Stanford White. Attempting to subdue the ensuing panic in the auditorium, stage director Lionel Lawrence instructed the musicians to play and chorus girls to continue dancing and, in spite of the number of fainting spells and heart attacks caused by the commotion, the audience gradually calmed down and left the theatre in an orderly fashion.[537] Regardless of the turmoil, critics found Freeborn's music "the most worthy portion of the entertainment."[538] Subsequent to *Mam'zelle Champagne*, Freeborn contributed "That Was Before They Were Married" to Reginald De Koven's score for *The Beauty Spot* (10 April 1909); he served as musical director for Julian Edwards's *The Girl and the Wizard*

(27 September 1909); and he composed incidental music and provided musical direction for Rida Johnson Young's play *Shameen Dhu* (2 February 1914).[539] In addition Freeborn composed incidental music for Augustus Pitou's production of *The Man from Wicklow* (26 August 1917); he served as musical director for Raymond Hitchcock's *Hitchy-Koo* revues in 1919 and 1920; and he participated as the "Singing Conductor" in Ned Wayburn's *Demi-tasse Revue* at the Capitol Theatre (17 October 1919). In August 1924, *The New York Times* reported that producers Lewis and Gordon had optioned a musical called *Primrose* composed by Freeborn with lyrics by Irving Caesar[540] but the work was never produced. In his later career, Freeborn served as musical director for the Manhattan Opera House and the Taylor Opera House in Trenton, New Jersey.[541] By 1944, Freeborn had retired to a farm in Bethel, Connecticut, where he died in May 1954, survived by his daughter, Barbara, and sons, Paul and Clay.

Arguably, the most interesting example of Freeborn's dance music is "The Stop-Trot Rag," subtitled "One-Step, Two-Step and Turkey Trot" (1914). The highly syncopated piece is unusual because, within the traditional 8-measure dance music structure, the melody stops playing at measures 5–6, but the metric pulse continues, allowing the melody to complete the phrase in measures 7–8. In the piano score, the "silent" sections are marked by small cued notes indicating what the melody would have sounded like had it been played. The dance is arranged in two 32-measure sections with the second section repeated after an 8-measure interlude. While the first section follows the pattern indicated above for each of its four 8-measure units, the second section does not stop during the third 8-measure unit, creating an unanticipated link to the final unit in which the "silent" measures again appear. The published sheet music gives no indication that the work was composed specifically for the musical theatre.

FREY, Hugo

Composer, dance arranger, musical director, and charter member of the American Society of Composers, Authors, and Publishers, Hugo Frey was born in Chicago on 26 August 1874. He studied music at the Chicago Conservatory and his proficiency on the violin, viola, piano, and organ enabled him to tour as violinist with the Listermann String Quartet (1896–1898) and as a pianist with the Red Path Grand Concert Company (1898–1899).[542] After two years of study in Vienna, Frey returned to the United States in 1901 and joined the French Opera Company in New Orleans as musical director before moving to New York City in 1902.[543] In New York, Frey composed dance music ("Dance of the Orchid") for Ivan Caryll and Lionel Monckton's *The Orchid* (8 April 1907) and provided orchestrations and incidental entr'acte music for the *Burlesque of the Merry Widow* (2 January 1908). In addition, Frey provided musical direction for Broadway shows, including *The Merry Widow and the Devil* (16 November 1908), *The Goddess of Liberty* (22 December 1909), *Alma, Where Do You Live?* (26 September 1910), and *Everywoman* (27 February 1911). In the summer of 1911 Frey composed the music for a musical comedy (libretto by John L. Shine) performed at the Indian Pow-wow on Bayshore, Long Island[544] and three years later he composed songs (with lyrics by Frederick Herendeen) and arranged dance music for *The Elopers*, a musical comedy produced in Chicago during the summer 1914.[545] Beginning in 1916 Frey arranged and conducted recording sessions for the Victor Phonograph label; in 1917 he composed "Sarah from Sahara" (lyrics by George Edwards) for Silvio Hein's *Flo-Flo* (20 December); and in 1919, Frey became a house composer for publisher T.B. Harms and Francis, Day and Hunter, and composed the score for the ill-fated *A Night Off* that opened at Ford's Theatre, Baltimore (7 April).[546] In the 1920s Frey was associated with Joe Raymond's Orchestra, the Manhattan Merrymakers, and Hugo Frey's Troubadours; and, beginning in 1929, he provided music (uncredited) for films, including *The Holy Terror* (1929), *All Quiet on the Western Front* (1930), *Sporting Blood* (1931), *Skyscraper Souls* (1932), *I'll Tell the World* (1945), *The Sea of Grass* (1947), and *Chain Gang* (1950). Frey died on 13 February 1952 at his home on West 171st Street in Manhattan, his wife Emily having predeceased him.

FRIEDLAND, Anatol[e]

Born in St. Petersburg, Russia, on 21 March 1884,[547] Anatol Friedland studied piano and musical composition at the Moscow Conservatory before coming to the United States after the turn of the century[548] and earning a degree in architecture at Columbia University, where in 1907 Friedland and librettist Allen Hopping created a student show called *The Ides of March*. Soon after graduation, Friedland began composing songs and incidental music for the Broadway stage, including "My Sist' Tetrazin'" (lyrics by Edward J. Madden) for *The Midnight Sons* at the Broadway Theatre (22 May 1909); "Every Fellow Wants Someone to Love" in *Just One of the Boys*, Chicago (7 March 1910); the songs (lyrics by David Kempner) for *Three Mil-*

lion Dollars at the New National Theatre, Washington, D.C. (19 September 1910); and the songs and dance music (with co-composer Malvin Franklin, lyrics by David Kempner) for *The Wife Hunters* at the Herald Square Theatre (2 November 1911). In 1912 Friedland composed the songs and dance music for *Countess Coquette* (lyrics by Melville Alexander and A.G. Delamater), which closed before Broadway; the songs and incidental music for *Freckles* (words by Seymour Brown and A.G. Delamater), a touring show; additional music for *(From) Broadway to Paris* at the Winter Garden Theatre (20 November); and the songs and incidental music for *A Persian Garden* (words by Edgar Allan Woolf), a vaudeville musical (9 December).

Subsequent musical theatre works included the songs in *First Love* (lyrics by Melville Alexander) a vaudeville act (1913); specialty numbers ('Love Is a Wonderful Thing" and "Lily of the Valley" both with lyrics by L. Wolfe Gilbert) performed in *Follow Me* at the Casino Theatre (29 November 1916); "I'm the Brother of the Lily of the Valley" (lyrics by L. Wolfe Gilbert and Henry Lewis) in *Doing Our Bit* at the Winter Garden Theatre (18 October 1917); the songs and dance music for *The Bride of the Nile* (lyrics by Edgar Allan Woolf), a vaudeville sketch (1917); "You're So Cute Soldier Boy" (lyrics by Edgar Allan Woolf) in *Toot-Toot* at the George M. Cohan Theatre (11 March 1918; and the score for *Musicland* (words by Herbert Stanwood), which closed on the road (1919).

During Prohibition, Friedland operated a speakeasy on 44th Street in New York City called the Club Anatole where he produced musical revues and specialty acts that toured the vaudeville circuit. In May 1926, one such revue played the Palace Theatre in New York and earned the notice of *The New York Times*:

> The Palace is again attempting to transfer the atmosphere of the night club to the vaudeville stage, with Anatole Friedland and his revue from the Club Anatole as the current attraction. The result is an elaborate and rather diverting act, which presents such familiar phases of night life entertainment as a pair of ballroom dancers, a number of highly sentimental songs, an oriental performer of some skill, and specialties by attractive dancing girls.[549]

In 1932 another of Friedland's acts, a *Show Boat Revue* also played the Palace Theatre,[550] and on 7 December 1932, *The New York Times* announced that producer Friedland had acquired the rights to the Herbert

Fields-Cole Porter musical *Fifty Million Frenchmen*, with plans to open a touring production in Albany, New York, the day after Christmas. A longtime vaudeville partner of L. Wolfe Gilbert, Friedland continued working the vaudeville circuit throughout the 1930s up until his death on 24 July 1938 in Atlantic City, New Jersey.

FRIML, Rudolf

Born in Prague on 7 December 1879, composer and concert pianist Rudolf Friml began composing when he was eight years old and became a published composer at the age of ten. Following his education at the Prague Conservatory where he studied piano with Josef Jiránek and composition with Antonin Dvořák, Friml worked as a rehearsal pianist for the ballet at the National Theatre[551] and toured as a concert artist with violinist Jan Kubelík, with whom he arrived in America in November 1901. Later, while Friml continued touring with Kubelík through Europe, his "Taz-Idyll" ["Dance Fantasy"] *Auf Japan* [*In Japan*] premiered at the Dresden Hoftheater (7 June 1903); and following a riot caused by Kubelík's concert in Ling, Austria, on 15 March 1904,[552] Friml gave up the tour and returned the United States. As the commencement of a series of recitals, on 17 November 1904 Friml performed his *Piano Concerto in B Major* at Carnegie Hall under the direction of Walter Damrosch to the delight of the audience and to the dismay of many reviewers.[553] The following year he produced his original ballet composition *O Mitake San* at the Dresden Hoftheater and in 1906 Friml was back in New York City where he composed entr'acte music for the Garden Theatre ("Garden Matinee") and began another recital tour, occasionally joining up with Kubelik who had returned to America. Friml's concertizing led him to Los Angeles in 1908 where he met Mathilda Baruch, the "attractive and accomplished" daughter of a wealthy wine merchant, and married her after a short courtship on 26 May 1909.[554] After the wedding Friml continued his recital career until he was invited by producer Arthur Hammerstein to compose the music for a comic opera specifically designed for prima donna Emma Trentini. Called *The Firefly* (libretto by Otto Hauerbach),[555] the light opera opened at the Lyric Theatre in New York on 2 December 1912 to excellent business and rave reviews.[556]

The jovial soft-shoe dance (example 70) following the third number in the score, "Call Me Uncle" offers a representative example of Friml's highly pianistic incidental and dance compositions in his comic operas. In the number, an older gentleman seeks to ingratiate himself with a group

Example 70. Dance in "Call Me Uncle" from *The Firefly*

of young ladies much to the displeasure and mistrust of the ladies' young men. The flirtatious dance that follows depicts the pantomime scene in which the older man attempts to press his attentions on the impressionable young ladies. In his comic operas, Friml created original compositions for national dances and extended dance sequences, but for comic pantomimes and dances that immediately related to, or completed the action of a song he typically arranged a variation of the melody of the antecedent vocal number. Such is the case with the dance in "Call Me Uncle" in which the instrumental version of the vocal melody is embellished with triplet figures (measures 1–2, 5–6) that reinforce the kittenish character of the scene.

Immediately following the dance is a perpetual-motion composition called "Incidental Music" (example 71) used at various points in the score to mark a change of scene. The anxious sixteen-measure piece creates a sense of anticipation and assists in establishing the dramatic rhythm of the production by means of unremitting sixteenth notes (except for the left hand in measure 8 and the eighth notes in measure 16) that evoke the movement of a firefly.

Friml followed *The Firefly* with the score for *High Jinks* (libretto by Leo Dietrichstein and Otto Hauerbach) (10 December 1913), which also

Example 71. "Incidental Music" from *The Firefly*

included a tango and ballet music[557] and *The Peasant Girl* (libretto by Leo Stein, adapted by Edgar Smith) (2 March 1915), an American version of Oscar Nedbal's Viennese operetta *Polenblut* featuring Emma Trentini, for which Friml composed the "Danse Poetique" as well as a "Gypsy Dance" and four additional songs.[558] On 6 May 1915, Mathilda Friml sued for divorce and named Emma Trentini as co-respondent claiming that she and her husband had been caught in flagrante during the pre-Broadway tour of *The Peasant Girl*.[559] Following his divorce, Friml composed the score for *Katinka* (libretto by Otto Hauerbach) (23 December 1915) that included an extended "Circassian Dance," a "Ballet Divertissement," and "Mignonnette," a piano piece (Opus 26 no.3) he had published in 1907, which was used as the finale of the ballet sequence. During rehearsals a chorus girl, Blanche Betters, caught the composer's eye and, after a short courtship, they were married. Subsequent dramatic compositions by Friml included *The Amber Empress* (libretto by Marc C. Connelly) (19 September 1916) for which he composed the popular "L'amour, Toujours, L'amour"; the scores for *You're in Love* (libretto by Otto Hauerbach) (6 February 1917), *Kitty Darlin'* (libretto by Otto Harbach) (7 November 1917), *Some Time* (libretto by Rida Johnson Young) (4 October 1918), which included an exciting "Argentine Dance," and *Glorianna* (libretto by Catherine Chisholm Cushing) (28 October 1918). During the production of *Glorianna*, Friml noticed the performance of Elsie Lawson as one of the chorus maids. Within the space of a few months he divorced Blanche Betters and married the maid.

Following his third wedding, Friml composed the scores for *Tumble In* (libretto by Otto Harbach) (24 March 1919), *The Little Whopper* (libretto by Otto Harbach) (13 October 1919), and *June Love* (libretto by Otto Harbach and W.H. Post) (25 April 1921). For the *Ziegfeld Follies of 1921* (21 June 1921), Friml composed "Bring Back My Blushing Rose" (lyrics by Gene Buck), "Four Little Girls with a Future and Four Little Girls with a Past" (lyrics by B.G. DeSylva), "Every Time I Hear a Band Play" (lyrics by Gene Buck), "Two Lovely Lying Eyes" (lyrics by Gene Buck), and "Roses in the Garden" (lyrics by Brian Hooker). Friml's subsequent musical theatre works included *The Blue Kitten* (libretto by Otto Harbach and William Cary Duncan) (13 January 1922); *Bibi of the Boulevards* (libretto by Catherine Chisholm Cushing) (6 February 1922); *Cinders* (libretto by Edward Clark) (3 April 1923); *Dew Drop Inn* (libretto by Walter DeLeon and Edward Delaney Dunn) (17 May 1923), for which Friml composed "Goodbye Forever" and "We Two" in collaboration with musical director

Alfred Newman and lyricist Cyrus Wood; *In Love with Love* (8 August 1923), a play by Vincent Laurence for which Friml composed the title song (lyrics by Dailey Paskman); and the *Ziegfeld Follies of 1923* (20 October 1923), for which Friml provided the music for "Lady Fair" and "Maid of Gold" (both with lyrics by Gene Buck).

Beyond the scope of the present book, Friml's compositions included the mega-hits, *Rose-Marie* (libretto by Otto Harbach and Oscar Hammerstein II) (2 September 1924), *The Vagabond King* (libretto by Brian Hooker and W.H. Post) (21 September 1925), and *The Three Musketeers* (libretto by William Anthony McGuire) (13 March 1928). Friml's the lesser known musicals and revues included *No Foolin'* (sketches by J.P. McEvoy and James Barton; lyrics by Gene Buck, Irving Caesar, and Ballard Macdonald) (24 June 1926), *The Wild Rose* (libretto by Otto Harbach and Oscar Hammerstein II) (20 October 1926), *The White Eagle* (libretto by Brian Hooker and W.H. Post) (26 December 1927), *Luana* (libretto by Howard Emmett Rogers) (17 September 1930), *Annina* (libretto by Rowland Leigh, George Roesner, and John Shubert) (10 March 1934), and *Music Hath Charms* (29 December 1934), a revised version of *Annina*.[560] In 1925 Friml began composing music for films, including *The Lost World* (1925), *Wings* (1927), *The Lottery Bride* (1930), *Min and Bill*, for which he composed "Dance of the Maidens" (1930), *The Vagabond King* (1930), *Private Lives* (1931), *Cain and Mabel* (1936), *Rose-Marie* (1936), *The Firefly* (1937), *Music for Madame* (1937), *Northwest Outpost* (1947), *Rose Marie* (1954) and *The Vagabond King* (1956). Of all of Friml's compositions, the three melodies most frequently used in motion pictures were "Indian Love Call," "L'amour, Toujours, L'amour," and "Chansonette," better known as "The Donkey Serenade."

In 1925, Friml divorced Elsie Lawson and became engaged to film actress Renée Adorée in February 1926,[561] but no date was set for the wedding and Adorée's attentions gradually moved on to other men. Friml might have been irascible and arrogant and difficult to work with—in 1936 a man was beaten by J.J. Shubert because the producer thought he was Rudolf Friml[562]—but he had a way with women that belied his homely face and idiosyncratic personality.[563] For example, *Time* magazine reported that Friml used a Ouija Board to communicate with operetta composer Victor Herbert; and later Friml announced to *The New York Times* that he derived many of his musical ideas from the same device.[564] Also when Friml moved into Ginger Rogers's former home on 8782 Appian Way in Los Angeles, he had a sprinkler system installed on the outside of the house to create the effect of rain on the windows because he believed that he was more creative in the rain.⁵⁶⁵ In 1952, the seventy-two-year-old composer married his thirty-nine-year-old secretary of fourteen years, Kay Ling, In the years that followed Friml continued to perform as soloist on concert programs in the United States and in Europe and as a musical director, conducting orchestras in performances of his music. In April 1963, the composer sent Jacqueline Kennedy the score for "Jacqueline," a piece he wrote to commemorate her 34th birthday, and on 7 December 1969, Friml's ninetieth birthday was celebrated at the Shubert Theatre in New York where the American Society of Composers, Authors and Publishers (of which Friml was a charter member) produced "The First 90 Years with Friml," a showcase of Friml's contributions to the American musical theatre. Never one to shun interviews, Friml announced the secret of his longevity: sensible diet, plenty of rest and sunshine, exercise, and massage. He began every day by standing on his head for ten minutes to get the blood flowing.⁵⁶⁶ On 12 November 1972, Friml died at Presbyterian Hospital in Hollywood. He was survived by his fourth wife, Kay, two sons, William and Rudolf, Jr., his daughter Lucille, and six grandchildren.

In 1963 Friml was quoted in an article for *The New York Times* about the state of music on Broadway:

> "You take the Broadway shows these days," he said recently. "They ain't even got one song. A lot of noise, but no music. What they do now in Broadway musicals is a lot of hokum. Now they have more talk than song. They write talking songs. Everything is in one octave. I don't understand how this happened.... You take *My Fair Lady*. A wonderful story. But songs? The most you can say for them is that they're appropriate. They have very little range, even Richard Rodgers. The secret of his recent songs is that he can get very charming melodies without going very high.... I hope musicals go back to the way they used to be.... You don't have to have good music in a musical any more. I don't understand it. It is a puzzle. I think people would like to hear good singing again on Broadway and a little less hokum."⁵⁶⁷

Friml's views on the state of Broadway musicals revealed much about the man. Even though his style of composition had been out of fashion for many years, he refused to embrace new musical forms and styles—he refused to give up the romantic and cultured Bohemian-Viennese genre of music that struck a chord of sentiment and nostalgia with theatre audiences.[568] Certainly poet Ogden Nash was insightful when he wrote: "I trust that your conclusion and mine are similar: 'Twould be a happier world if it were Friml-er."[569]

FURST, William W[allace]

William Furst was born in Baltimore, Maryland, on 25 March 1852. He received his musical education in Baltimore at an early age, and when he reached his teenage years, he was appointed organist at the Church of the Immaculate Conception and later at St. Ignatius Catholic Church.[570] In 1878, Furst began his career in the theatre as musical director of Ford's Opera House in Baltimore where, on 25 August 1879 he conducted his original comic opera *The Electric Light* (libretto by William B. Hazleton and Edward Spencer).[571] Spending the summers with Ford's Comic Opera Company at Uhrig's Cave Garden in St. Louis[572] and the autumn–spring theatrical season in Baltimore, Furst remained musical director at Ford's

Example 72. Hornpipe in "The North Pole" from *The Isle of Champagne*

Opera House until 1886[573] when he moved to San Francisco to assume the musical directorship of the Tivoli Opera House where he produced his only grand opera *Theodora* on 16 September 1889.[574] In 1887 also at the Tivoli, Furst composed and arranged incidental music for William Gillette's play *She* (4 July)[575] in a production that toured and eventually played Niblo's Garden in New York (29 November).[576] By the end of 1891, Furst had become the musical director at the Star Theatre in New York City where he conducted the first American production of Edmond Audran's *Miss Heylyett* (3 November 1891) under the direction of his friend David Belasco.[577] The following year Furst composed the songs and dance music for *The Isle of Champagne* (libretto by Charles A. Byrne and Louis Harrison) which opened at the Star Theatre in Buffalo, New York, on 16 May 1892 and at the Manhattan Opera House on 5 December 1892.[578] The hornpipe (example 72) following the sea shanty, "The North Pole," from *The Isle of Champagne* offers a fine illustration of Furst's jaunty and lively dance music.

In January 1893 Furst became the musical director of the new Empire Theatre with Charles Frohman's production of *The Girl I Left behind Me* (25 January 1893) for which he also composed incidental music.[579] On 23 October 1893, *The Honeymooners* (libretto by C.M.S. McLellan) opened at the Columbia Theatre, Boston, with songs and dance music by Furst, and on 25 October 1893, *Princess Nicotine* (libretto by Charles Alfred Byrne and Louis Harrison), for which Furst provided songs and ballet music opened at the Casino Theatre. On 30 August 1894, Furst's score for *The Little Trooper* (book by Clay M. Greene, lyrics by J. Cheever Goodwin) was first heard at the Casino Theatre[580] and a month later, on 24 September, Clyde Fitch's play, *His Grace de Grammont* opened in Chicago with dramatic music and a song by Furst.[581] In 1895, Furst's compositions included incidental music for C.T. Dazey's play *The War of Wealth* at the Chestnut Street Opera House in Philadelphia (25 February); songs and dance music for *Fleur-de-Lis* (libretto by J. Cheever Goodwin) at Palmer's Theatre in New York (29 August); incidental music for David Belasco's *The Heart of Maryland* at the Herald Square Theatre (22 October); and musical direction for *An Artist's Model* (book by Owen Hall, lyrics by Harry Greenbank, music by Sidney Jones) at the Broadway Theatre (23 December). Furst's compositions in 1917 included the score and dance music for *Papa Gou Gou* (libretto by J. Cheever Goodwin), opening on 30 August in Detroit, Michigan;[582] the incidental music for J.M. Barrie's comedy *The Little Minister* at the Empire Theatre on 27 September; and the incidental music for *Under the Red Robe*, Edward Rose's dramatization of Stanley Weyman's novel, at the Empire on 28 December. In 1898 Furst's musical projects included incidental music for *The Conquerors*, a play by Paul Potter, at the Empire Theatre (4 January);[583] songs and dance music for *A Normandy Wedding*, a revised version of *Papa Gou Gou* at the Herald Square Theatre (21 February);[584] incidental music for Charles H. Meltzer and A.E. Lancaster's farce *His Honor the Mayor*, at the Empire Theatre (25 April); incidental music for Hall Caine's play *The Christian*, at the Knickerbocker Theatre (10 October); entr-acte music for Henri Lavedon's comedy *Catherine*, at the Garrick Theatre (24 October);[585] and incidental music for *Phroso*, a dramatization by Edward Rose and H.V. Esmond of Anthony Hope's novel, at the Empire Theatre (26 December).[586] Furst's subsequent incidental music assignments included David Belasco's *Zaza* (9 January 1899); R.C. Carton's comedy *Lord and Lady Algy* (14 February 1899); Israel Zangwill's *Children of the Ghetto* (16 October 1899); William Gilette's *Sherlock Holmes* (8 November 1899); John Oliver Hobbes's *Osbern and Ursyne* (28 November 1899); Belasco's *Madame Butterfly* (5 March 1900); Basil Hood's *Ib and Little Christina* (8 September 1900); R. and M.W. Hitchcock's dramatization of Edward Noyes Westott's novel *David Harum* (1 October 1900);[587] Paul M. Potter's *Under Two Flags* (5 February 1901); Leo Trevor's *Brother Officers* (8 April 1901); J.M. Barrie's *Quality Street* (11 November 1901); Augustus Thomas's *Colorado* (18 November 1901); Belasco's *Du Barry* (25 December 1901); and Arthur Wing Pinero's *Iris* (23 September 1902).

On 17 October 1902 *The New York Times* issued the following notice, under the headline: Musical Director Furst Resigns.

> William Furst, for twelve years musical director of Charles Frohman's theatres and director of all music pertaining to the latter's productions, has resigned and will sever his relations with the Frohman interests a week from Saturday. He will at once begin the writing of musical compositions for David Belasco's productions, and on December 1 will assume the direction of all music pertaining thereto. He is to have a prominent part in the arrangements for the production of the new Japanese play, the cast of which will be headed by Miss Blanche Bates, and will be staged at Belasco's Theatre.

The work in question, *The Darling of the Gods*, written by Belasco and John Luther Long, opened at the New National Theatre in Washington D.C. on 20 November 1902 and at the Belasco Theatre in New York on 3 December 1902. Scored for thirty musicians including five Japanese playing native instruments (the biwa, samisen, koto, tsudzumi, and fuye),[588] Furst's incidental music was divided into the following sections: Geisha Dance: Hachisuba (Lotus Leaf), marked allegretto; Kara's Theme, andante; Geisha Dance: Hina Matsuri (Feast of Dolls), allegro con brio; Yo San's Theme, andante con espressivo; Zakkuri's Theme, andante misterioso; Taiko Hon Rei (Thunder Drummer), allegro moderato; Ragami Yama (Mirror Mountain), moderato; Parchment Theme, largo misterioso; Chidori's Entrance, allegro moderato; Serenade, moderato con moto; Geisha Dance: Ni Tomare (The Butterfly), allegro; Yoitomosé (The Cricket and the Beetle), moderato; and War March of the Samurai, marcia maestoso.[589] "Taiko Hon Rei (Thunder Drummer)" (example 73) provides an excellent sample of Furst's pseudo-Japanese music with its almost com-

Example 73. "Taiko Hon Rei (Thunder Drummer)" from *The Darling of the Gods*

plete reliance on the pentatonic scale G–A–C–D–E (the eighth note F in measures 7 and 11, and the grace note F in measures 34–14 are the only departures from the scale).[590]

Subsequent to *The Darling of the Gods* Theatre, Furst composed additional incidental scores for productions at the Belasco Theatre, including *Sweet Kitty Bellairs* (9 December 1903),[591] *The Music Master* (26 September 1904), *Adrea* (11 January 1905), *The Girl of the Golden West* (14 November 1905), *Pippa Passes* (12 November 1906), *The Rose of the Rancho* (27 November 1906), and *The Warrens of Virginia* (3 December 1907). Furst also composed the music for *The Christian Pilgrim*, James MacArthur's dramatization of John Bunyan's *Pilgrim's Progress* that premiered at the Garrick Theatre in Philadelphia on 8 October 1907 in preparation for a New York City opening at the Liberty Theatre on 11 November.[592]Other significant incidental compositions include *The World and His Wife* (2 November 1908), *The Winterfeast* (30 November 1908), *The White Sister* (27 September 1909), *As You Like It* (6 June 1910), *The Concert* (4 October 1910), *The Good Little Devil* (25 December 1910), *The Return of Peter Grimm* (17 October 1911), *The Yellow Jacket* (4 November 1912), *Electra* (September 1913), *Evangeline* (4 October 1913), *A Thousand Years Ago* (6January 1914), *The Song of Songs* (22 December 1914), *Marie-Odile* (26 January 1915), and *The Merry Wives of Windsor* (13 March 1916).

In September 1915, Furst composed and arranged the music that accompanied the silent films *The Iron Strain*, *The Lamb*, and *My Valet* at the Knickerbocker Theatre in New York[593]and the following year, he composed and arranged music for *The Green Swamp*, *Let Katie Do It*, and *Joan the Woman*, Cecil B. DeMille's rendering of the life of Joan of Arc. During the summer of 1917, as was his practice for many years, Furst moved to Freeport, Long Island, where he pursued his favorite avocation: gardening. About the middle of June, the sixty-six-year-old composer tripped over a flower pot and suffered an injury to his foot that became infected. Focusing more on the beautiful floral display that adorned his home than on the mishap, Furst unwisely left the wound untreated. What began as septicemia led to complications that resulted in a cerebra-embolism causing Furst's death on 11 July 1917. He was survived by his second wife, Charlotte, and his daughter, Lillian.

William Furst's distinctive personality was best described in an article in *The New York Times* dated 15 February 1903:

William Furst, musical director of the Belasco Theatre, besides being a very nervous man, has several idiosyncrasies which cause no end of amusement to the people about the theatre. One of Mr. Furst's pet abominations is the two eyrie boxes situated at the other end of the gallery in the Belasco house, so high up and so far in toward the stage that auditors who are forced to seek them as points of vantage to see the play must crane their necks at imminent danger of toppling over into the orchestra circle. Every night when Furst comes into the theatre his first glance is directed to the little upper boxes, and when they are occupied, which is usually the case, he seeks the first opportunity to berate the box office for selling the tickets.

One of Mr. Furst's trying moments comes in the scene in which Albert Bruning, the Tandi Tanji of *The Darling of the Gods* has to sing a little song. Mr. Bruning is not always in best voice, and his occasional lapses are the despair of the musical director. So, too, the slightest hitch on the stage sets all of his nerves a-quiver.

On Monday night last Mr. Furst, in company with David Belasco, was in Philadelphia attending the opening performance there of Mrs. Carter in *Du Barry*. In the course of the evening a messenger boy came into the house with a telegram for Furst. The musical director hastily tore it open, and this is what he read:

"Curtain stuck fourth act. Don't worry. Top boxes full. Bruning out of key. BENRIMO BRUNING."

Mr. Furst was for taking the first train back to New York, but his associate persuaded him that at that late hour the worst was probably over.

G

GABRIEL, Max

Born in Prussia in September 1861, composer Max Gabriel produced the three-act operetta *Steffen Langer* at Magdeburg in 1889, before becoming the resident musical director at the Theater Hanover in 1890. There he composed another three-act work *Der Freiwerber* [*The Suitor*] (1890) and two years later, at Breslau, he composed the score for the operetta *Der Garde-Ulan* [*The Guard Ulan*]. On 19 December 1892, Gabriel arrived in New York City with the German Opera Company of which he was musical director to begin an eight-week run of German light operas at the Amberg Theatre.[594] The company's first production was Carl Zeller's *Der Vogelhändler* [*The Bird Seller*] and subsequent productions included Carl Millöcker's *Gasparone* (24 March 1893), and Charles Lecocq's *La Fille de Mme. Angot* [*Mrs. Angot's Daughter*] (7 April 1893) sung in German. Beginning on 25 May, Gabriel conducted a summer season of opera in German at the Lexington Avenue Opera House[595] that included Daniel Auber's *Fra Diavolo* [*Brother Devil*], Jacques Offenbach's *Orphée aux Enfers* [*To Hell with Orpheus*], Millöcker's *Der Feldprediger* [*The Chaplain*, AKA *The Black Hussar*], and Richard Genée's *Nanon*. On 27 July Gabriel's three-act operetta *Der Garde Husar* [*The Hussar Guard*], a revised version of *Der Garde-Ulan*, was produced at the Lexington Avenue Opera House to favorable responses from audiences and critics who wrote that "the music is of the popular sort, and much of it is very catchy."[596] Following his summer activities, Gabriel became the musical director for the touring Marie Tavary Grand English Opera Company which began its season on 23 October 1893 in Syracuse, New York. After leaving the Grand English Opera Company in the summer 1894, Gabriel was represented on Broadway as the co-composer and arranger (with Charles B. Hoffmann) of the music in the Lilliputian production of *Humpty Dumpty Up to Date* (11 September 1894), for which he also arranged dance music, including "The Ballet of Drinks," "The Ballet of Flies," "The Ballet of Precious Stones and Metals," and a "Ballet of Pierrots." Subsequent to his work with the

Example 74. "Waltz" from *In Gotham*

Lilliputians, Gabriel became the musical director and composer at Koster and Bial's Music Hall where his original scores and dance music included *Le Rêve* [*The Dream*] (23 May 1898),[597] *Cook's Tour* (6 June 1898),[598] and *In Gotham* (19 September 1898),[599] for which Gabriel composed a ballet of wood nymphs in a rustic setting and a series of evocative waltzes, of which example 74 is a representative excerpt.

Following the production of *In Gotham*, Gabriel resigned his position at Koster and Bial's, effective 5 November 1898, explaining that he wanted to devote his time and attention to composing.[600] After a year of solitary creative activity, Gabriel returned to the podium at the New Columbia Theatre in Boston where he conducted the premiere performance of Herman Perlet and Richard Carle's musical comedy *Mam'selle 'Awkins* (12 February 1900). Following the tour of *Mam'selle 'Awkins* which included a month's run at Hammerstein's Victoria Theatre, Gabriel returned to Germany where he continued to produce musical theatre works with librettist Georg Okonkowski, including *Diana im Bade* [*Diana Bathing*] (1901), *Die schöne Cubanerin* [*The Beautiful Cuban Girl*] (1904), *Luxus-*

weibchen [*Women of Luxury*] (1911), *Stolze Thea!* [*Proud Thea!*] (1916), and *Der brave Fridolin* [*Brave Fridolin*] (1920). From 1904 to 1907, Gabriel was the director of the Rembrandt Theater in Amsterdam and lessee and manager of the Comedy Theatre in Antwerp; and in 1906 he toured Germany with his musical farce comedy company in a production of *The Man from Maxim's*.[601] In August 1902 Gabriel's orchestra faced public prosecution for performing in the Ausstellungspark in Berlin wearing American uniforms, a complaint raised by the German Musical Union because of the popularity of Gabriel's orchestra, whose advertisements were printed on posters representing the American flag.[602] On 9 August, the public prosecutor refused to pursue the case, arguing that the law did not forbid musicians to perform in costumes, unless the costume was that of the regular German military uniform, which was forbidden.[603]

GANNE, Louis-[Gaston]

Born in Buxières-les Mines, Allier, France, on 5 April 1862, composer Louis Ganne was a student of composers Théodore Dubois, Jules Massenet, and César Franck at the Paris Conservatory. When he was twenty years old, Ganne composed a ballet, *Les Sources du Nil* [*The Sources of the Nile*] that was produced at the Folies-Bergère and followed by a number of his dance compositions that included *Volapuk*, *Au Japon* [*In Japan*], *Le Reveil d'une Parisienne* [*The Awakening of a Parisian Woman*], and *L'Abeille et la fleur* [*The Bee and the Flower*].[604] While he was musical director of the Parisian Bals de l' Opéra, Ganne continued to compose dance music and achieved popular success with his marches, "Le Père la Victoire [Father Victory]" and "Marche Lorraine," and his Russian mazurka, "La Czarine [The Czarina]." He also found success composing light comic operas, notably *Les Saltimbanques* [*The Acrobats*] (30 December 1899), produced in Paris at the Théâtre de la Gaîté, and *Hans le joueur de flute* [*Hans the Flute Player*] (14 April 1906), produced in Monte Carlo where the composer had been installed as the musical director of "Concerts Louis Ganne" at the Casino in 1905. On 20 September 1910 *Hans the Flute Player* (libretto by Maurice Vaucaire and Georges Mitchell, English lyrics by A. St. John Brennan) opened at the Manhattan Opera House to excellent reviews:

> Ganne is a composer essentially French in manner, who turns out a succession of melodies which the ear finds grateful. To say that he has a good memory would not

detract from one's enjoyment. He has borrowed liberally, but usually well. There are fragments of *Parsifal* and *Madama Butterfly* in the score. Hans's farewell to his Flute reminds one of the "Berceuse [Lullaby]" in *Jocelyn*. The orchestral effects, too, are sometimes recognizable. For instance the descending figurations on the clarinet which accompany the waltz at its recapitulation are very much like Tchaikovsky.

However all this carping about sources is beyond the point. As a matter of fact the music is charming and of a sort which is almost entirely new to our stage, if one excepts *Les Contes d'Hoffmann* [*The Tales of Hoffmann*]. If for nothing more than the fact that the songs are not divided into verses and refrains the public ought to be grateful.[605]

Both of Ganne's comic operas made use of extensive incidental music that underscored dialogue and stage business or marked a change of scene. *Les Saltimbanques*, however, had an extensive "Défile du cirque [Circus parade]" in the second act with a procession of fiddlers (with music suggesting the violin's open strings played in fifths), followed by "Gitanes [Gypsies]" from Spain (with the music of a bright, rhythmic paso doble), "Zingaras [Gypsies]" from Hungary (with the quick music of the czárdás), "Gipsys" from Scotland (with music accompanied by a bagpipe-like drone), and "Tchingènés [Gypsies]" from the Orient (with music utilizing the heptatonic scale and suggesting Oriental folk rhythms). A lengthy ballet divertissement called "Les Bohémiennes" ensued beginning with a schottische dance, "Les Gipsys," then a Castilian jota , "Les Gitanes," another Hungarian czárdás, "Les Zingaras,"and a folk-like melody interrupted by an energetic perpetual motion episode, "Les Tchingènés."

Subsequent appearances of Louis Ganne's compositions on the New York stage included *The Paradise of Mahomet* (libretto by Harry B. Smith and Robert B. Smith) (4 February 1911), an adaptation of *Le Paradis de Mahomet*, Robert Planquette's comic opera completed by Ganne; *Il Saltimbanchi* [*The Acrobats*] (24 April 1911), an Italian adaptation of *Les Saltimbanques* (libretto by Maurice Ordonneau); *The Revue of Revues* (27 September 1911), in which the music of Ganne's ballet *Au Japon* [*In Japan*] is used in the "Novelties of Nations" segment; *The Captive* (24 March 1913), an Arabian pantomime on the vaudeville circuit with music by

Rimsky-Korsakov and Ganne; and "Marche Lorraine" choreographed by Isadora Duncan at Carnegie Hall (8 February 1918). On 16 January 1914 in Paris, Louis Ganne was named Chevalier of the Legion of Honor in commemoration of his efforts in promoting light classical French music through his compositions and with his Monte Carlo orchestra, which, according to *The New York Times* was still giving concerts at the Casino four times a week as of May 1923.[606] Two months later, on 13 July, Louis Ganne died at his home in Paris.

GAUNT, Percy

Born in Philadelphia in 1852, Percy Gaunt first appeared in theatrical records as a member of the Wilbur Comic Opera Company who replaced conductor Frederick Intropidi when he was absent on 17–19 March 1884 due to the death of one of his children.[607] In the summer of 1884, Gaunt was a member of Marlande Clake's Opera Company, playing the West-End Opera House in New Orleans. In late July he left the company and departed for New York City where he was engaged as musical director for the touring *Two Johns* Company during which time he completed the music for an opera, *Babille, the Little Coachman*.[608] In 1886 he became musical director for Pat Rooney's Comedy Company until he was discharged in February 1887 because of his participation (with Pat Rooney) in a public disturbance at the Walnut-Street Theatre in Cincinnati.[609] In 1888 Gaunt began his association with writer-producer Charles Hale Hoyt as musical director, composer, and arranger of plays with music that included the touring *A Tin Soldier* Company (24 December 1888); *A Midnight Bell* (5 March 1889), in which Gaunt also performed the role of Ezekiel Stover;[610] the touring *A Brass Monkey* (2 September 1889); the perennially popular *A Trip to Chinatown* (9 November 1891);[611] *Temperance Town* (18 September 1893); and *A Milk White Flag, and Its Battle-Scarred Followers on the Field of Mars and in the Court of Venus* (8 October 1894),[612] for which Gaunt composed a stirring military march for the Ransome Guards, "The Milk-White Flag March" (example 75).

In addition to his work with Hoyt, Percy Gaunt arranged the music for *Dreams*, a P.H. O'Connor production that opened in Buffalo on 22 April 1889; he served as musical director for the Actors' Amateur Athletic Association of America benefit at the Metropolitan Opera House on 31 May 1889; he composed the score and arranged dance music for *A Yenuine Yentleman* (27 May 1895), a play that capitalized on the audience's

Example 75. "The Milk-White Flag March" from *A Milk White Flag*

fondness for Irish songs, African-American songs, and Swedish dialect specialties. In addition, Gaunt composed the music for an extravaganza, *Princess Rosebud, or, The Magic Rose* that premiered on 12 August 1895 at Educational Hall in Asbury Park, New Jersey; and he composed an operetta for the touring Georgie Huntington Juvenile Vaudeville Company, in which all the characters appear on bicycles (18 November 1895). In May of the following year, Gaunt, who had become incapacitated by illness, was given a testimonial benefit at Hoyt's Theatre with the intention of using the receipts to send him to a health resort.[613] On 5 September 1896, in the company of his wife, Percy Gaunt died in a boarding house at Palenville in the Catskill Mountains of New York.[614]

GEBEST, Charles J[oseph]

Composer, musical director, violinist, and arranger Charles J. Gebest was born on 8 December 1872 in Madison, Indiana,[615] the son of Professor Gustave E. Gebest, a respected theatre orchestra leader and composer in the Midwest. A member of the "Gebest family of musicians," which included his sisters, Mary, Caroline, and Gertrude, and his brother Charles L., Charles J. Gebest was given a sound musical education by his father, and from an early age he embraced the thought of becoming a theatrical musical director and composer. In his early twenties, Gebest became the manager of the professional department of music publisher George L. Spaulding and in 1897, he published an early composition, a "polka characteristic" entitled "The Dawn of Love."[616] Two years later one of Gebest's compositions was included in the score of Gustav Luders's musical comedy *By the Sad Sea Waves* (28 February 1899), a fact that would have been insignificant had it not drawn the attention of the young George M.

Example 76. Dance in "Behold the Governor" from *The Governor's Son*

Cohan who hired Gebest as the musical director of his first Broadway show, *The Governor's Son*, opening in Hartford, Connecticut on 11 February 1901before moving to New York on 25 February.[617] Gebest was a perfect match for Cohan: he acted as his musical amanuensis, arranged incidental and dance music based on Cohan's tunes and musical ideas, provided vocal arrangements and musical direction for the singers, composed the orchestral parts, and conducted the orchestra. In short, Gebest functioned as Cohan's musical alter-ego and with few exceptions every show Gebest was connected with throughout his career was produced and/or written by George M. Cohan. In *The Governor's Son*, the Governor is introduced in "Behold the Governor," a patter-puff number evocative of Gilbert and Sullivan, followed by delightfully genteel dance music (example 76) arranged by Gebest to set the mood, and also to accompany the fancy footwork choreographed by the young Cohan. The break at the end of the dance was a special feature of Gebest's dance music with Cohan, creating a kind of built-in encore that displayed a final trick step before the dance was done.

During the tour of *The Governor's Son*, Gebest composed an instrumental march, "A Tip on the Derby" (1902), a novelty piece that suggested the bugle calls and galloping hooves typically associated with a horse race.

Gebest subsequent collaborations with Cohan included *Running for Office* (27 April 1903), *Little Johnny Jones* (7 November 1904),[618] *George Washington, Jr.* (12 February 1906), *The Governor's Son* (revival) (4 June 1906), *George Washington, Jr.* (return engagement) (11 February 1907), *Little Johnny Jones* (revival) (22 April 1907), *The Talk of New York* (3 December 1907),[619] *Fifty Miles from Boston* (3 February 1908), *The Yankee Prince* (20 April 1908), and *The American Idea* (5 October 1908), for which Gebest did not conduct the orchestra; instead, he provided musical arrangements and composed the instrumental "March Finale" (example 77). There are many stylistic similarities between the march in *The American Idea* and the dance in *The Governor's Son*: the use of triplets followed by repeated notes; the presence of an "um-pah-pah (rest)" accompaniment virtually throughout in the dance and in measures 2, 4, 6–8, 10, 12 of the march. Note that in the march, the "um-pah-pah" pattern is not always followed by a rest; rather, in measures 2, 4, 10, the pattern ends with an accented eighth note, creating an interesting syncopation that supports the onstage choreography.

In May 1909 the *New York Clipper* reported that producers Harris and Cohan had accepted for production a new musical comedy entitled

Example 77. "March Finale" from *The American Idea*

Constantinople, written by George Parsons and composed by Charles J. Gebest[620] but nothing came of the project. Instead Harris and Cohan produced *The Man Who Owns Broadway* (11 October 1909), another show for which Gebest provided all the musical arrangements but did not conduct the orchestra. In 1910 Gebest was hired as musical director for *Girlies* (13 June), a non-Cohan-Harris summer entertainment with a cast numbering 125 performers at the New Amsterdam Theatre.[621] After the show closed late in August 1910, Gebest was back with Cohan and Harris preparing for the production of *The Red Widow* (6 November 1911), a musical about a retired corset manufacturer, written by Channing Pollock and Rennold Wolf, with score, incidental and dance arrangements, and musical direction by Gebest.[622] The "Dinner (Quintet)" from the score is carefully constructed with incidental "Melodramatic Music" underscoring stage business between the sung portions of the number. After the first verse, for example, a romantic Viennese waltz (example 78) was used ironically to accompany the pantomime representing a husband and wife having dinner together; and, after the second verse, a march (example

Example 78. Melodramatic Music (Waltz) in "Dinner (Quintet)" from *The Red Widow*

Example 79. Melodramatic Music (March) in "Dinner (Quintet)" from *The Red Widow*

79) was employed comically to depict the uncomfortable passage of time when strangers at a dinner party have nothing whatsoever to say to one another.

While he was conducting *The Red Widow* Gebest composed an instrumental overture called "The Willies" using the melodies from the overture to *William Tell*, "Willie Off the Yacht," "Willie Knew Just What to Do," "Waltz Me Around Again, Willie," and "Billy." The work was dedicated to the actor William Collier who proposed to have it performed as a musical introduction to the first act of *Take My Advice* (27 November 1911) his starring vehicle at the Fulton Theatre.[623]

The creators of *The Red Widow*, Gebest, Pollock, and Wolf, repeated their tasks for another Cohan-Harris production, *The Beauty Shop* that opened in Chicago on 26 October 1913 before a New York City premiere on 13 April 1914.[624] Gebest's subsequent musical chores for Cohan and Harris included *Hello, Broadway!* (25December 1914), musical arrangements and musical direction; *The Cohan Revue of 1916* (9 February 1916), musical arrangements and musical direction; *The Cohan Revue of 1918* (31 December 1917), incidental and dance arrangements, and musical direction; *Going Up* (October 1918), musical direction for touring company; *Mary* (18 October 1920), musical direction; *The O'Brien Girl* (3 October 1921), musical direction; *Little Nellie Kelly* (13 November 1922), musical arrangements, and musical direction; *The Rise of Rosie O'Reilly* (25 December 1923), musical supervision; *The Merry Malones* (26 September 1927), incidental and dance arrangements, and musical direction; and *Billie* (1 October 1928), incidental and dance arrangements, and musical direction. Although this list does not include incidental music for Cohan's plays and melodramas, it is a reasonable assumption that Gebest had a hand in assembling much of that as well. Cohan may have earned the reputation of being difficult with many of his associates, but with Gebest he displayed a generosity born out of appreciation for all of the uncredited theatrical arrangements and published piano reductions Gebest had created for his music. An anecdote published in 1919 regarding Cohan's behavior toward the arranger and the William Jerome Music Publishing Company, the firm that launched Cohan's "Over There," was illustrative of his largesse:

> Gebest, according to the story, never was in the office of the publishing company, never wrote a number for it, in fact so far as anyone ever heard had no connection with the organization whatever, yet when the time of settling up the business arrived was given a check considerably in excess of $5,000. The gift came from George M. Cohan, who was the financial backer of the enterprise and when it was formed promised that Gebest with whom he had for years been friendly should have a share of the profits. When Leo Feist paid $25,000 for "Over There," the bank balance of the Jerome Company was in the most prosper-

ous condition of its entire career and Cohan who decided to wind up the business took his share of the profits and remembering his promise to Gebest sent him his check.[625]

Charles J. Gebest was married three times: first to Caroline Fredricks on 31 July 1898, divorced on 23 July 1909; next to Nell Stein on 9 November 1911, divorced on 20 August 1921; and finally to Katharine M. on 5 November 1921. In the early 1930s he settled in Miami, Florida, to care for his sister, Gertrude, who was badly burned in a gasoline fire. Following her death on 31 July 1934, Gebest returned to Manhattan where he died at the age of sixty-four on 11 January 1937.

GIDEON, Melville [Joseph]

Performer, pianist, dance arranger, and composer Melville Gideon was born in New York City on 21 May 1884. "I grew up and attended school here," he noted in an article he contributed to *The New York Times*. "Music—piano playing—was the chief interest of my life as far back as I can remember, and it was logical that I should eventually find my way to the song marts of Broadway."[626] Gideon began his musical theatre career as a composer of interpolated songs and dance music in Broadway shows, including "The Taxicab" for Ziegfeld's *Follies of 1908* (15 June 1908); "Take Plenty of Shoes" for *The Boys and Betty* (2 November 1908)' "Oh! That Yankiana Rag" for *Miss Innocence* (30 November 1908) and *The Florist Shop* (9 August 1909); "The Boulevard Glide" for *The Beauty Spot* (10 April 1909), "The Billiken Man" for *The Midnight Sons* (22 May 1909); and "When I Sang Toreador" for *The Girl and the Wizard* (27 September 1909). By June 1909 Gideon had become so popular a songwriter that he was chosen to direct the New York offices of the Chicago-based publisher, The Music House of Laemmle, and by the autumn of the same year he was co-composer (with Louis A. Hirsch and Jerome Kern) of *The Golden Widow*, a Shubert production that opened at the Belasco Theatre in Washington D.C. on 26 October. Among the numbers Gideon contributed was a song called "Ragtime Land" (lyrics by E. Ray Goetz) in which homesick American expatriates revealed that the sound of ragtime music evoked the feeling of home. The number concluded with a clever dance arrangement that transformed the melodies of "Old Kentucky Home," "Old Folks at Home," "Old Black Joe," and "Dixie (I Wish I Was in Dixie)" into slow ragtime. In 1910 Gideon co-composed (with Louis A. Hirsch) "When

Sist' Tetrazin' Met Cousin Carus'" for *Up and Down Broadway* (18 July 1910), and the following year he co-composed (with Harold Orlob) the score for *The Heartbreakers*, produced at the Princess Theatre in Chicago on 30 May 1911.[627] Again with Louis A. Hirsch, Gideon co-composed the score and ballet music for *The Revue of Revues* (27 September 1911), and on his own, Gideon composed the songs and dance music for Collins, La Belle, and Patton's vaudeville act.

In June 1912, Melville Gideon moved to London where he composed interpolated songs and performed ragtime dance music at the piano for fancy dress balls.[628] In the summer of 1913 he performed a solo music hall act at the London Pavilion, but by the end of the year he was bankrupt, due to heavy losses at gambling and horse racing. During his first year in London, he had earned $35,000 as a pianist but had accrued debts in the amount of $50,000.[629]To make matters worse, on 2 June 1914, Gideon was cited as co-respondent in a divorce case by millionaire David Wellesley Bell whose wife Enid, a Gaiety chorus girl, had met Gideon at a theatrical garden party and subsequently visited him frequently at his residence.[630] After the conditional discharge of his bankruptcy in July 1914,[631] Gideon and Louis A. Hirsch conducted the "All American" week" of music hall entertainment at the Finsbury Park Empire in London; Gideon and Muriel Hudson played the Empress Theatre in Brixton; and with Oscar Schwartz, Gideon appeared at the Oxford Music Hall in the fall of 1914. Six months after the outbreak of World War One, Gideon joined the Red Cross at Arras, France, about six miles from the front line of battle, and drove an ambulance that carried the wounded from the battlefield to the hospital.[632] Even during the war, however, he continued his musical performances in the revues *Quite So* and *Samples* at the Playhouse in London,[633]and after the war was over, Gideon was engaged to compose the music for a new revue at the Theatre Royal, Drury Lane.[634] Subsequent musical projects included librettist George V. Hobart's *Buddies* (1919);[635] co-composition (with Herman Darewski) of Charles B. Cochran's production of *The Eclipse* (1919);[636] Cochran's production of *Cherry*; the burlesque *Faust on Toast* (1921); the musical extravaganza *Thanks Very Much!* (1921); and a singing and dancing entertainment, *Fantasia* (1921).[637]

The shortage of fuel created by a coal strike in England in May 1921 forced the closing of several London theatres, putting a great many actors out of work. Gideon joined four other unemployed performers in the creation of a shareholding company called "The Co-Optimists," designed to produce intimate touring revues with limited production values but with "an all-star cast and with modern music and modern sketches."[638] A six-week engagement at the Royalty Theatre in June 1921 led to a year's run at the Palace Theatre and became an annual event in London for the next half-dozen years, followed by two years of touring throughout England and Scotland.[639] In January 1928, Gideon brought the "Co-Optimists" style of production to New York with *The Optimists*, opening on 30 January at the Century Roof Theatre (the Casino de Paris) to generally good reviews. Produced, composed, directed, designed, and performed by Melville Gideon, *The Optimists* was thus described by *The New York Times*:

> Happily set within the informal confines of the uptown roof theatre, *The Optimists* last night proved to be a reasonably diverting prank, compounded in about equal parts of amusement and artlessness. It is an unpretentious assemblage of songs, dances and quips, some of which you have heard before and not a few of which are blessed with sparks of wit and fun. By its very lack of ornateness it is a welcome change from its opulent and heavily upholstered contemporaries among the Broadway musical shows.... As supervised by Mr. Gideon, chief pianist and occasional songster, the program contains a half dozen or more numbers that are good—and sometimes better than that.... There is a novel ghost song and dance done by [Bobby] Watson and Fred Hildebrand.... A number staged by the male members of the ensemble under the title of "Optimistic Golf" has its moments, while several of the tunes are gentle, and even a bit persuasive, in their assault upon the ear drums.[640]

After *The Optimists* closed in New York, Gideon returned to London to prepare for the film version of the *Co-Optimists* released by the Gordon Craig Company on 21 February 1930. He also appeared in *Her First Affaire* produced by St. George's Pictures (7 December 1932) and contributed music to the musical comedy film *Boots! Boots!* released on 30 July 1934, nearly nine months after Gideon's death in London on 11 November 1933.

GILBERT, Jean

Born Max Winterfeld on 11 February 1879 in Hamburg, German composer and musical director Jean Gilbert took piano lessons at an early age and debuted as a concert pianist at the age of fifteen. From 1894–1897, he studied music in Kiel, Sonderhausen, Weimar, and at the Klindworth-Scharwenka Conservatory in Berlin. When he was eighteen years old, he began his musical theatre career as a conductor at the Stadttheater in Bremerhaven and, four years later, in 1901, he produced his first original operetta, *Das Jungfernstift* [*The Virgin Pin*] at the Centralhallen-Theater in Hamburg and assumed the pseudonym "Jean Gilbert." After years of working as the musical director of the touring Hagenbeck circus and various provincial theatres, Gilbert struck it rich with his score for *Die keutsche Susanne* [*Modest Suzanne*] produced at the Wilhelm-Theater in Magdeburg on 26 February 1910 and at the Liberty Theatre in New York City on 1 January 1912. Gilbert's score reveals a wealth of dance music including can-cans, polkas, marches, and waltzes, as well as a "melodrama" underscoring the stage action. Almost all the numbers have dance breaks of varying lengths and styles, though most of the pieces are bright and cheerful. Following the success of *Die keutsche Susanne* Gilbert became musical director and house composer at the Thalia-Theater in Berlin where he continued to produce popular operettas. Gilbert's music that crossed the sea to America (after *Modest Suzanne*) included the dance duet, "The Old Clarinet," inserted into Jerome Kern's score for *Oh, I Say!* (30 October 1913); the songs and dance music for *The Queen of the Movies* (12 January 1914) adapted from *Die Kino-Königin* (8 March 1913); the music for "My Lady of the Telephone" inserted into Sigmund Romberg and Harry Carroll's score for *Dancing Around* (10 October 1914); and a co-composed score (with Victor Hollander) for *A Modern Eve* (3 May 1915), an adaptation of *Die moderne Eva* (11 November 1911). The First World War put an end to German imports in America but almost four years after the armistice of 11 November 1918, Gilbert was back on the boards in New York with the score (adapted and co-composed by Alfred Goodman) for *The Lady in Ermine* (2 October 1922), an adaptation of *Die Frau im Hermelin* (23 August 1919). Additional Gilbert works included *Katja* (15 October 1926), adapted from *Katja, die Tänzerin* [*Katja, the Dancer*] (5 January 1922); *The Red Robe* (25 December 1928), derived from *Das weib im Purpur* [*The Woman in Purple*] (21 December 1923); and *Marching By* (3 March 1932), based on Gilbert's *Hotel Stadt Lemberg* [*Lemberg City Hotel*] (1 July 1929).

Jean Gilbert also composed incidental music for films including *Die Sylvesterwette* [*Sylvester's Bet*] (1919), *La fille et le garcon* [*The Girl and Boy*] (1931), *Two Hearts Beat as One* (1932), *One Week of Happiness* (1934), *World Crisis* (1937), *La chaste Suzanne* [*Modest Suzanne*] (1937), *The Girl in the Taxi* (1937), *Sweethearts for the Girls* (1941), and *Her First Ball* (1942). Fearing persecution from the Nazi regime, Gilbert left Germany and went to Vienna where his operetta *Die Dame mit dem Regenbogen* [*The Lady with the Rainbow*] was produced at the Theater an der Wein (25 August 1933). He subsequently traveled to Paris, London, Barcelona, and Madrid[641] before settling in Buenos Aires where he died on 20 December 1942.

GILFERT, Charles

Composer, dance arranger, and theatre manager Charles Gilfert was born in Hesse Cassel, Prussia, in 1787. Almost immediately after his birth, Gilfert's family moved to New York City, for late in 1787, George Gilfert (Charles's father, a music teacher, organist, and soon to be a member of the John Street Theatre orchestra) advertised a Musical Magazine (music store) at 14 Dey Street where music lessons were given and sheet music was purchased.[642] It was at the Musical Magazine where five-year-old Charles Gilfert learned the rudiments of music from his father; and, in 1793, it was at Mr. Gilfert's where tickets for Mrs. Pownall's benefit at the John Street Theatre on 22 May were advertised as available.[643] On 4 March 1800 Charles Gilfert, billed as "lately from Europe," first appeared in New York as a concert pianist,[644] an occupation he continued in the city and on tour until he became a member of the orchestra at the Park Theatre. In 1810 he moved to Charleston, South Carolina, where he joined the orchestra of the Charleston Theatre[645] before returning to New York in 1813 to become the musical director, composer, and arranger at the new Theatrical Commonwealth performing at the New Theatre, Broadway (formerly the Circus at Broadway and White Street).[646]On 23 February 1815, Gilfert married actress-singer Amelia (Agnes) Holman, with whom he toured for two years before assuming the management of the Charleston Theatre in 1817, a position he held until 1825. In 1823, Gilfert made a rare appearance in New York at City Hotel as accompanist for Louisa Gillingham in concert on 6 February, and a month later, he appeared at the Park Theatre in concert with his wife. Other programs arose in New York for which Gilfert served as musical director, and in 1825, following an especially disastrous season at the Charleston Theatre, he resigned his position and moved to Albany, New York, with his wife.[647] The next year, Gilfert became the general manager of the new Bowery Theatre that opened in New York City on 23 October 1826 and burnt to the ground on 26 May 1828. Three months later, a second Bowery Theatre was open for business featuring theatrical superstar Edwin Forrest as William Tell, Hamlet, and Virginius in addition to productions of English operas and ballet extravaganzas. Arguably the most interesting production during Gilfert's management, however, was *A Trip to Niagara, or, Travelers in America* (28 November 1828), which author William Dunlap called merely an excuse for the employment of dioramic scenery, with an incidental score composed by Gilfert.[648] The extravaganza did good business but not good enough to match expenses, and by the spring of 1829, it appeared that all of Gilfert's attempts to draw an audience had failed. On 30 July, overwhelmed by disaster and distress, he died. George C.D. Odell quotes from Gilfert's obituary in the *Morning Courier*:

> Charles Gilfert died on Thursday morning, a victim to keen sensibility and pecuniary misfortune. His death was instantaneous and awful—his frame broke down under the influence of mental agony.—Gilfert will long be remembered by those who were acquainted with his superior talents, his great musical genius, his wonderful conversational powers, and the warm and peculiar sensibility of his temperament.—He had his faults, faults arising from a warm, generous, and improvident disposition—but littleness and meanness were foreign to his nature. He was emphatically a man of genius—possessed all its high attributes, and an heir to its almost proverbial calamities. His life was a struggle of high-minded poverty against the oppression of wealth, and the envy of inferiors. His agitated existence is over,—peace to his memory.[649]

The theatrical productions for which Gilfert composed music and arranged dance and incidental music included *The Spanish Patriots, or, Royal Restoration* (4 January 1809), *Bee Hive, or, Industry Must Prosper* (23 October 1811), *Virgin of the Sun* (15 November 1813), *For Freedom Ho* (5 April 1815), and *A Trip to Niagara, or, Travelers in America* (28 November 1828). Gilfert's published songs and dances included "The

Bed of Roses" from *Virgin of the Sun*; "Dear Maid should I Never Return" from *For Freedom Ho*; "For Then I Had Not Learned to Love" from *The Spanish Patriots*; "The Grand Canal March" inscribed to DeWitt Clinton; "Hibernia's Tears" from the popular romance of *The Champions of Freedom*; "I Left Thee Where I Found Thee Love!" from the Oratorio given at the Park Theatre (1823); "Loud and Chill Was the Blast" from *For Freedom Ho*; "Grand March" dedicated to Commodore Decatur; "A Military Waltz"; "The Spanish Patriot's Grand March" from *The Spanish Patriot*; "Six Waltzes for the Piano forte"; and "Allen-A-Dale," his most successful song, published in 1813 and still in the catalog as late as 1870.[650]

GILLES, Napoleon

Composer, dance arranger, and musical director Napoleon Gilles was born in Lille, France, in 1809. As a young man he studied the violin and performed in concert orchestras in France before moving to New York City as an adult. There he was employed as violinist in various theatre orchestras before becoming the musical director at Wood's Theatre Comique, 514 Broadway, where he composed incidental and ballet music for *Oscar the Half-Blood* (25 March 1867). At the commencement of the 1867–1868 season, Gilles accepted the position of musical director (and the responsibilities of composer and dance arranger) at the new Fifth Avenue Theatre.[651] There he supervised the music for several burlesque extravaganzas, including *Cinderella, or, The Lover, the Lackey, and the Little Glass Slipper* (2 September 1867); *Fra Diavolo, or, The Beauty and the Brigands* (9 September 1867); *Aladdin, The Wonderful Scamp* (7 October 1867); *Shylock, or The Merchant of Venice Preserved* (28 October 1867); *Medea, or The Best of Mothers with a Brute of a Husband* (18 November 1867),[652] and *Ye Legend of Ye Grand Queen Bess* (9 December 1867). On 11 December 1867, in front of the Fifth Avenue Theatre, the comedy team of (Edwin) Kelly and (Francis) Leon became involved in an argument with actor Sam Sharpley and his brother Thomas Sharpe, in the course of which Kelly shot and killed Sharpe and was severely wounded by Sharpley.[653] The theatre did not withstand the bad publicity and closed its doors on 2 January 1868, ending the season abruptly and forcing Gilles to seek new employment. George C.D. Odell reported his participation at benefit performances at the Bowery Theatre on 8 May and 14 May 1868[654] but once the season ended his name disappeared from playbills. At the time of his death on 10 August 1880, his finances had been seriously depleted and his wife and daughter were left in poverty. Newspaper reports indicated that Gilles was owed a great deal of money from theatre managers for whom he had worked, and it was hoped that his family might receive at least some portion of the amounts due. To support herself and her daughter, Gilles's widow advertised the sale of his possessions: two violins, a viola, a box containing three or four flageolets, one box musette, and six trunks of orchestral music.[655] Napoleon Gilles, a well-respected musical director and composer, was also a member of the Musical Protective Union in whose plot he was buried at Cyprus Hills Cemetery.

GILLINGHAM, George

Violinist, composer, and musical director George Gillingham was born in Guddington, Bedford, England, in December 1768.[656] He mastered the violin at an early age, for when he was sixteen, he was among the first violins listed by Charles Burney as performing at the Handel Memorial Concerts at Westminster Abbey and the Pantheon in May and June 1784.[657] Also proficient on the viola, and cello, Gillingham played the principle second violin in the orchestra of the Theatre Royal, Covent Garden during the theatrical season; during the summer months, he was leader of the Birmingham Theatre orchestra. He was unanimously elected to the Royal Society of Musicians on 6 June 1790 and performed in Society-sponsored concerts in the spring of 1791, 1792, and 1793. At the behest of theatre managers Thomas Wignell and Alexander Reinagle, Gillingham moved to Philadelphia in 1793 where he became leader of the twenty-member orchestra at Wignell and Reinagle's New Theatre on Chestnut Street.[658] There he orchestrated and arranged dance music for productions that included *The Little Yankee Sailor* (27 May 1795) and *Harlequin's Invasion* (12 June 1795). In addition, beginning in 1794, he joined Raynor Taylor, Alexander Reinagle, and Benjamin Carr as one of the directors of the "Amateur and Professional Concerts" at Oeller's Hotel in Philadelphia.[659] Beginning with the 1797–1798 season Gillingham became leader of the orchestra of the Greenwich Street Theatre in New York City[660] and after the turn of the century, he was violinist and leader of the concerts of the Handel and Haydn Society at St. Paul's Church, and leader of the band at the City Hotel. In September 1821 Gillingham was the leader at the new Park Theatre, replacing James Hewitt.[661] British actor Joseph Cowell, who appeared to dislike everything American, spared no words when describing Gillingham and his orchestra:

> Gillingham was the leader.... This efficient conductor, with six or eight other *professors*, formed a very wretched orchestra, but then even so many, and of such a quality, could only be obtained at a very high price; they never came to rehearsal but on very particular occasions, and even then they were paid extra, and all the music in the performance was gone through, one piece after another, and an hour selected the least likely to interfere with their teaching, or other out-door avocations.... Robbins was the principal artist, and also played double bass; *he* always came to rehearsal, for he'd do anything rather than paint.[662]

The *Euterpeiad*, however, reported that Gillingham's "superiority of talent lies in leading a band, in which perhaps, he is inferior to no one living as well as to time, as to understanding every style of music,"[663] and *The Theatrical Censor* affirmed that "it would be unjust not to mention Mr. Gillingham, leader of the orchestra; the excellence of whose execution on the violin often compensates for the ear-rending discords occasioned particularly by the female singers. The importance of a good leader is easily conceived; and his services cannot be too highly appreciated."[664] In the summer 1821, Gillingham was the leader at the City Theatre, Warren Street, where he selected and arranged incidental and dance music for *The Belle's Stratagem* (2 July), *The Sultan* (4 July), *The Purse* (4 July), *The Review* (4 July), *The Honeymoon* (11 July), *The School for Scandal* (12 July), *The Curfew* (27 July), *She Stoops to Conquer* (31 July), *The Grecian Daughter* (7 August), *The Mountaineers* (19 August), *Harlequin's Gambols* (24 August), *The Day After the Wedding* (28 August), and *George Barnwell* (31 August). George Gillingham died on 16 September 1826 at his home in Philadelphia, survived by his second wife Ann Hazel Gillingham, and his daughters Emma, Julia, and Louisa. He was buried at St. George's Methodist Episcopal Burial Ground in Philadelphia.

GIORZA, Paolo

Composer and musical director Paolo Giorza was born in Milan, Italy, on 11 February 1837,[665] the son of a professional singer and organist who provided him with a musical education from the age of four. A few years later Giorza studied counterpoint and figured bass with Enrico La-Croix. When he was nine he composed a Mass as a composition exercise and when he was eleven, he won a scholarship to the Royal Conservatory of Music in Milan. Before he began his studies at the conservatory, however, the revolution of 1848 occurred and because of his father's political activities, the family was compelled to reside ten miles from Milan and forbidden to leave without permission. In exile, Giorza studied the works of Scarlatti, Clementi, Mozart, and Beethoven until 1852 when his father died leaving the family destitute. Fifteen-year-old Paolo supported the family by playing the organ at local churches for weddings and funerals, giving his mother the lion's share of his earnings, but keeping enough to enable him to walk ten miles to La Scala and buy a ticket to an opera.[666] At one of his opera excursions, Giorza happened to be standing by the stage door in the pouring rain when one of the sopranos emerged without an escort or umbrella. Giorza offered the singer his umbrella and proceeded to walk her home, revealing his life's story on the way. Impressed by the teenager's history, the singer introduced him to the ballet master at La Scala, Giuseppe Rota, who subsequently commissioned new ballets from him, including *Il Giucatore* [*The Player*], produced in 1853 at the Teatro alla Canobbiana in Milan and at La Scala on 14 January 1854, and *Bianci e negri* [*Whites and Blacks*] performed at La Scala on 10 November 1853 with great success.[667] Giorza became a staff composer at La Scala for a period of eight years, during which he composed the music for thirty ballets, including *Un fallo* [*A Foul*] (1853), *Ida Badoer* (Autumn 1854), *Shakespeare* (27January 1855), *Un ballo nuovo* [*A New Ballet*] (Autumn 1856), *La giocoliera* [*The Juggler*] (Lent 1857), *Rodolfo* (Carnival–Lent 1857–1858), *Fior di Maria* [*Mary's Flower*] (Carnival 1858), *La capanna di Tom* [*Uncle Tom's Cabin*] (autumn 1858), *Un'avventura di carnevale* [*A Carnival Adventure*] (19 March 1859), *I tre moschettieri o Ven'anni dopo* [*The Three Musketeers and Twenty Years After*] (Autumn 1859), *Il vampiro* [*The Vampire*] (26 December 1860), *La Contessa d'Egmont* [*The Countess of Egmont*] (2 March 1861), and *Nostradamus* (21 April 1862). Although Giorza's ballets were major successes, his attempt at composing an opera, *Corrado console di Milano* [*Corrado, Consul of Milan*], which was produced at La Scala during Lent1860, was a major fiasco.

In addition to his commitments in Italy, Giorza found the time to work in Vienna, where he produced his ballet *Die Gauklerin* [*The Juggler*] (May 1856); London (1863), where he composed the ballet *La farfalletta* [*The Little Butterfly*] for Queen Victoria's Jubilee; and Paris (1864) where his music was pointedly unappreciated.[668] Financial distress forced Giorza to tour North and Central America as the musical director of an opera company in 1867[669] and, when his promised appointment as director of the Mexican Opera was impeded by the execution of Emperor Maximilian on 19 June 1867, Giorza went to New York City to compose music for Adelaide Ristori's production of *Marie Antoinette* (7 October 1867), a play written especially for her by Paolo Giocometti.[670] He composed dance and operatic specialties for Rita Sangali whose opera company was touring with the burlesque extravaganza *Flick Flock* (18 October 1869) and in December Giorza was advertised as a member of the Brignoli Operatic Concert Troupe performing at the California Theatre in San Francisco.[671]

In 1870 Giorza's ballet *A fada nix* [*Nix to Fate*] was produced in Lisbon, and the following year he was in Australia providing the musical direction for the Agathe States Opera Company. He was later engaged by William Saurin Lyster at the Princess's Theatre in Melbourne; in 1874 Giorza worked for James Cassius Williamson's English Opera Company at the Theatre Royal, Melbourne; and in 1877, he was hired by Lazar's Royal Italian Opera Company also at the Theatre Royal, Melbourne. In his free time, Giorza served as composer and musical director for Catholic Churches in Melbourne and Sydney for which he composed Masses and other religious music. He collaborated with W.S. Lyster's brother Frederick on the songs and incidental music for a production of Jules Verne's *Around the World in 80 Days* (1877), and in 1879, he composed the music for the *Cantata written expressly for the Opening Ceremony of the Sydney International Exhibition* (words by Henry Kendall).

Giorza returned to Italy in 1883 and continued to compose, publish, and produce dance music, including *Souvenir d'Australia* (1884), his collection of polkas, waltzes, mazurkas, galops, and marches; and the ballets *Narenta* (Carnival–Lent 1886–1887) and *Rodope* (5 January 1892). In 1893 Giorza provided songs, ballet music, and musical direction for Bolossy Kiralfy's massive spectacular extravaganza, *Constantinople, or, The Revels of the East*, produced at the Olympia Theatre in London from 26 December 1893 until 31 November 1894. While he was in London, Giorza also contributed a gavotte called "Skirt Dance" (example 80), full of harmonic variety and melodic surprises, to Howard Talbot's score for *Monte Carlo* (27 August 1896 in London; 21 March 1898 in New York).

Giorza returned to America in the summer 1901 with *Constantinople* at the Teck Theatre in Buffalo, New York, and on 18 August he inaugurated a series of Sunday concerts entitled *The Musical Congress of the Pan-American Nations* at the same theatre.[672] In November 1901, Giorza moved to Philadelphia where *Constantinople* had been booked for an extended run

Example 80. "Skirt Dance" from *Monte Carlo*

at the Grand Opera House, and where in March 1902, one of his Catholic Masses was scheduled to be performed at the Cathedral of Saints Peter and Paul as a fundraiser for the building's renovation. For the next two years, Giorza remained in New York to collaborate with Imre Kiralfy on the development of Kiralfy's spectacle *The Louisiana Purchase* scheduled for the Louisiana Purchase Exposition (better known as the St. Louis World's Fair) and opening at the Odeon Theatre in New York on 28 May 1904.[673] The following year Giorza returned to San Francisco where, on 18 April 1906, he lost all of his possessions, including his musical scores, in the earthquake and fires that decimated the city. Destitute, he moved to Seattle where he offered music lessons for what little money his students could pay. Giorza maintained a meager existence in a boarding house in Seattle until 4 May 1914 when death relieved him of his suffering. A founder of the Italian Club of Seattle, Ambrose Chiappa, paid the cost of Giorza's funeral and interment. Although he died in anonymity, Paolo Giorza was considered by critics as an important voice in the history of dance music: "Giorza was considered by critics a reformer of the ballet because of his attempts to make his music, which is often pantomimic and sometimes melodramatic in character, fit the given subject by creating a sense of atmosphere, and he was one of the first composers to be listed along with the dancers and choreographers in reports of the ballet."[674]

GLASER, C.J.M.

Composer, dance arranger, and musical director C.J.M. Glaser began his association with prima ballerina Adeline Genée at the Empire Theatre in London as the rehearsal pianist for the ballet *Vineland* (26 September 1903) and the arranger of the music for Genée's famous "Champagne Dance." In 1906 Glaser provided additional music, dance arrangements, and musical direction for the 14 May production of Léo Delibes's ballet *Coppélia*,[675] and he co-composed (with Cuthbert Clarke) the score for *The Débutante* (15 November 1906), another ballet designed for Genée.[676] In the United States, Glaser composed and conducted the music for Adeline Genée's ballets in *The Silver Star* which opened at the Forrest Theatre in Philadelphia on 13 October 1909 prior to the New York City production at the New Amsterdam Theatre (1 November 1909) and a national tour.[677] The first act of *The Silver Star* ended with a scene called "The Living Christmas Tree," in which Genée appeared as the Christmas Fairy and performed a "Fairy Dance" (example 81) which she executed "with an ethereal lightness that savoured almost of the supernatural."[678] Glaser certainly assisted in the creation of the gossamer tone with a staccato melody that floated delicately above a simple chordal accompaniment and thirty-second notes (measure 15) that evoked the fluttering of wings.

The scene continued as the Christmas Fairy delivered presents to the children assembled around the tree, providing an acceptable rationale for a spirited military number, danced with the Stars and Stripes in hand, and a rollicking sailor's hornpipe (example 82).[679]

The ballet music for the end of the first act (example 83) was evocative of the "Christmas Tree" music and "Apotheosis" in Tchaikovsky's

Example 81. "Fairy Dance" from *The Silver Star*

The Nutcracker, with an expansive and majestic theme that soared above harp-like arpeggios and ended with a fanfare that evaporated into the silence of the children asleep beneath the darkened Christmas tree.

The second act of *The Silver Star* was set at a wine festival where Adeline Genée appeared as "The Spirit of Champagne." The ballet music commenced with a vivacious "Tarantella," the final measures of which are presented in example 84. Glaser made little attempt at originality in composing the dance music, preferring to adhere to the traditional rhythms and melodic contours that evoked an Italian tarantella in the minds of the audience. The lack of accompaniment on the downbeats of measures 1–2 and 9–10, designed to accompany a *jeté* in the choreography, also

Example 82. "Hornpipe" from *The Silver Star*

provided an interesting variation of the traditional pattern of accents in the tarantella.

After a seemingly obligatory but rather inconsequential waltz the divertissement continued with a beautifully crafted "Czardas" evocative of Brahms's "Hungarian Dance No. 5" and the "Lassan" movement of Listz's "Hungarian Rhapsody No. 2." Again, Glaser eschewed originality for familiarity since the music was designed to create a context and atmosphere for the choreography, not to draw attention to itself. Example 85 provides a sample of the *vivace* movement of Glaser's "Czardas."

The "Czardas" was followed by an extended "Variation" that included a movement reminiscent of the fairy music in act one, a lyrical adagio,

Example 83. "Finale Act One" from *The Silver Star*

a stately gavotte, and a *presto* finale recapitulating the music in example 85. Act three introduced a "Springtime" ballet in which Adeline Genée portrayed the "Queen of the Floral Fête" to the music of a waltz marked *con amore*, and a pizzicato gallop. As an encore, Genée performed "Rêverie," borrowed from Glaser's ballet music for *Robert le Diable*, entirely on *pointes*.[680]

After the national tour of *The Silver Star* that took Glaser to Boston, New Haven, Brooklyn, Newark, Baltimore, Washington, D.C., Pittsburg, Chicago, St. Louis, Louisville, Indianapolis, Columbus, Detroit, and Cleveland, he disappeared from musical theatre records in the United

Example 83 (continued). "Finale Act One" from *The Silver Star*

States. His music for *Coppélia* and *Robert le Diable* was used in Adeline Genée's Australian tour with the Imperial Russian Ballet in 1913, and his orchestral arrangement of Armand Vecsey's "The Charmers" was published by G. Schirmer in 1916.

Example 84. "Tarantella" from *The Silver Star*

Example 85. "Czardas" from *The Silver Star*

GLOVER, [William] Howard

Composer, arranger, musical director, and critic Howard Glover was born at Kilburn, London, on 6 June 1819.[681] When he was a teenager, Glover studied the violin with William Wagstaff, the musical director of the Lyceum Theatre orchestra, who invited him to become a member of the ensemble even though he was only fifteen years old. Glover later completed his musical studies on the Continent before returning to England where he was employed as accompanist and solo violinist in London and the provinces. With his mother, the actress Julia Glover, he created the Musical and Dramatic Academy in Soho Square where he gave lessons on the violin and taught singing and music theory. His success as a teacher inspired him to produce a season of opera in Manchester as a vehicle for his students and annual London concerts at St. James Hall and the Theatre Royal, Drury Lane, in which his better students, such as Emily Soldene, often participated. In 1850 Glover became music critic for the *Morning Post*, a position he held for fifteen years and through which he attempted to improve the musical tastes of his readers and introduce to the British public the works of contemporary Continental composers, such as Hector Berlioz, whose career Glover championed. On 4 July 1855 Berlioz conducted Glover's cantata for tenor solo, chorus, and symphony orchestra, *Tam o' Shanter* at the New Philharmonic, and the composition made such an impression that it was repeated at the Birmingham Festival the following August. The excerpt from the cantata's introductory music (example 86) offers a fine illustration of Glover's compositional style, rooted firmly in mid-nineteenth-century European Romanticism.

Glover's subsequent theatrical compositions included the comic opera *Aminta, the Coquette*, produced at the Haymarket (1857); the grand opera *Ruy Blas*, produced at Covent Garden (24 October 1861); and the comic opera *Once too Often*, produced at Drury Lane (20 January 1862);

In the 1860s, Glover led a comfortable life in London as a composer and educator, ably supporting his wife Catherine (McNamara), their nine children, and three servants. In late 1867, however, Glover was contacted by William Wheatley, the manager of Niblo's Garden in New York City, who offered him the position of composer and musical director at his theatre with the promise of a substantial rise in income and celebrity. With no misgivings, the Glover family moved to New York City early in 1868 where Glover began composing a new overture, songs, incidental music, and dance music for Wheatley's production of *The White Fawn* which had opened on 17 January 1868 with music and musical direction by Ed-

Example 86. "Introduction" from *Tam o' Shanter* (score notated in concert pitch)

ward Mollenhauer. Glover's version of the piece received its premiere on Easter Monday 13 April 1868 amid great fanfare[682] and continued under his musical direction until the middle of July when the theatre closed for the season. On 11 July, close to the end of the run, Glover took a benefit performance at which his comic opera *Once too Often* received its New York premiere. Evidently Wheatley and Glover did not get on well due to the "peculiarity of [Glover's] temperament,"[683] and the composer was not rehired for the subsequent season. Instead, Glover served as chorus master and dance arranger for *Undine* at the Academy of Music in Brooklyn (6 October 1868) and selected, composed, and arranged the music (vocal and ballet music) for *The Field of the Cloth of Gold* at Wood's Museum (1 February 1869). He also accepted the position of musical director at the Waverley Theatre where he conducted Elise Holt's Burlesque Troupe's production of *Ivanhoe* (31 March 1869) and arranged and orchestrated the music for the Troupe's production of *Paris, or, The Judgment* (28 April 1869). [684] Glover also provided new music and musical direction for the London Burlesque Combination's production of *Pygmalion, or, The Peerless and Beautiful Statue* (25 May 1869). By the end of the season, Glover had disappeared from theatre notices and sought employment as an accompanist, violinist, and educator in a city already crowded with musicians and music teachers. In December 1870, Glover was given a testimonial concert at Wallack's Theatre which was noted as "interesting in an artistic sense, but by no means remunerative"[685] and reports of benefits for the Glover family in 1874 indicate that it had fallen on hard times. [686] In 1875, in an attempt to raise money, Glover published his one-act operetta *Palomita, or, The Veiled Songstress*,[687] after failing for several years to get it produced in New York. The twelve numbers of the score are highly melodious and filled with bravura arias and lively dance rhythms, such as the bolero and cachucha. Unfortunately, because the work had not been produced, its publication escaped the notice of the public and raised little money for the Glovers.

Howard Glover's last recorded appearance in New York was as a violin soloist in L.F. Harrison's final concert at the Academy of Music in June 1875.[688] Four months later, on 28 October, Glover died, leaving his family completely destitute. The dire circumstances were related in an appeal for aid that appeared in the *New York Clipper* on 20 November 1875:

> [Irish-born playwright and theatre manager] John Brougham, to whose kindness the family of the late Howard W. Glover owe much, makes a strong appeal to the musical and dramatic professions for aid for the widow and children of the deceased, asking for employment for the older ones and relief for all. The friends and former associates of this artist, so well-known for his ability, but who unfortunately was latterly but little appreciated in a

pecuniary way, mainly on account of the peculiarity of his temperament, are asked to lend a generous hand to the assistance of the Glover family. The idea of a benefit has been almost abandoned, but there are other and more acceptable ways to substantially prove that the critic, musician and composer, Howard Glover has not been forgotten by the profession.

GLOVER, James ("Jimmy") M.

Jimmy Glover was born on 18 June 1861 in Dublin, Ireland, the son of Irish patriot James Mackay, and grandson of Irish composer and editor of *Moore's Irish Melodies*, John William Glover. Even though Glover displayed an aptitude for music at an early age and held the position of deputy-organist at two Churches, he was apprenticed for three years to druggist Cornelius Mannin for ten hours a day at four shillings a week. In his memoir, Glover described a typical day during this period: "I played the early service at the Pro-Cathedral [St. Patrick's Cathedral in Dublin] in the morning, sold senna and salts till 6 p.m. at Cornelius Mannin's, the Dublin druggist's, played another service in the evening at my mother's Church, St. Michael's, in Kingstown [now Dún Laoghaire], or at Mount Argus, which I left later on for the then greatest honor of all—in my view—to carry the red fire which, as a chemist, I had made in the daytime, to the property-man at the local Theatre Royal."[689] At his grandfather's insistence, Glover was sent to Caen and Paris to receive a musical education, after which, in 1880, he secured a job as solo pianist improvising incidental music for a female magician and mesmerist in Southampton, England. Dismissed from that job after two weeks, Glover found employment as musical director for a "Commonwealth" troupe of variety performers in Portsmouth and subsequently became musical director for the touring Charles Collette's Burlesque Company. On 14 January1882 Glover's musical sketch *Ten Minutes for Refreshment* (libretto by Richard Mansfield) was produced at the Olympic Theatre in London,[690] and on 7 April 1885 his burletta *The Fashionable Beauty* (libretto by George Moore) was produced at London's Avenue Theatre.[691] In the fall 1885, Glover became the musical director of the Empire Theatre in Leicester Square where he arranged music for the Guards' amateur theatricals and served as musical director, choral director, dance conductor, and emergency cast member for William Fullerton's *The Lady of the Locket* (libretto by Henry Hamilton).[692]

On 28 December 1885, Glover arrived in the United States to supervise the Carrie Swain Company's production of George R. Sims and Clement Scott's melodrama, *Jack-in-the-Box*, for which he composed incidental music, scheduled to open at the Chestnut-Street Theatre in Philadelphia on 25 January 1886.[693] Following his return to London in February 1886, Glover continued supplying musical direction at the Empire and later at London's Comedy Theatre and the Opera Comique. He composed the music for the burlesque *Mademoiselle Cleopatra* (libretto by Walter Sapte, Jr.) at the Avenue Theatre (2 March 1891) and the score for the ballet *The Prodigal's Return* (libretto by Cecil Raleigh) at the Criterion Theatre[694] before becoming accompanist, composer, and musical director at the Theatre Royal, Drury Lane in the fall 1892. There Glover created music for a great number of melodramas and Christmas pantomimes that included *A Life of Pleasure* (21 September 1893), *The Convict's Escape* (4 December 1893), *Robinson Crusoe* (26 December 1893), *The Derby Winner* (15 September 1894), *Dick Whittington* (26 December 1894), *Cheer, Boys, Cheer* (19 September 1895), and *Cinderella* (26 December 1895). In 1896 he co-composed the scores (with Eugen von Taund and Landon Ronald) for *The Little Genius* at the Shaftesbury Theatre on 9 July and *The Telephone Girl* (with Gaston Serpette) at the Grand Theatre, Wolverhampton, England, on 25 May.[695] Back at Drury Lane, Glover composed the scores for *The White Heather* (16 September 1897), *The Babes in the Wood* (27 December 1897), *The Great Ruby* (15 September 1898), *The Forty Thieves* (26 December 1898), *Hearts are Trumps* (16 September 1899), *Jack and the Beanstalk* (26 December 1899), and *The Sleeping Beauty and the Beast* (26 December 1900).

On 4 November 1901, *The Sleeping Beauty and the Beast* was produced at the Broadway Theatre in New York with the music credited to Glover and Frederick Solomon, with additional music composed by J. Rosamond Johnson, Jean Schwartz, Dave Reed, Jr. and Maurice Levi. The production was greeted warmly by the critics who were especially impressed by the many ballets, the music, and (of course) the spectacle:

> Two features of the production demand, however, special mention. The first of these was the grand ballet which closed the second act. It was called "Beauty's Awakening" (A Dream of the Year). This was certainly one of the most beautiful ballets ever seen upon our stage, The changing scenery represented landscapes under the influence of the

four seasons, and the accompanying ballet further illustrated by color and floral designs the varying beauties of Spring, Summer, Autumn, and Winter. Among the hundreds of brightly bedecked figures were introduced St. Valentine's Guards, Shamrocks, palm bearers, nest bearers, April fools, primroses, daisies… May Queen, pink roses, yellow harvest boys and girls… holly, snow, swallows, etc., and to the gorgeous result of this kaleidoscopic display was added the beautiful aerial ballet, the flight of swallows contributed by the Grigolatis troupe of aerialists.…The other noteworthy feature was, of course, the Palace of Crystal… the beauty of which far surpassed expectation. This palace, with its 30,000 pieces of glass and beautiful architecture, is a permanent structure which is raised to the level of the stage from a huge pit, formed especially for its reception, and with its hidden lights illumines the closing scene with a soft and charming radiance.[696]

In 1903 Glover composed the incidental music for Cecil Raleigh's melodrama, *The Flood Tide*, produced at Drury Lane (18 September)[697] and provided additional music and lyrics ("I Don't Want to be a Lady") to Frederick Solomon's score for *Mother Goose* at the New Amsterdam Theatre (2 December). In addition, he co-composed the score (with Frederick Solomon) for the Drury Lane Christmas pantomime *Humpty Dumpty* that was subsequently produced in New York on 14 November 1904 with additional music by Bob Cole, William H. Penn, and Jean Schwartz.[698] The last of Glover's Drury Lane pantomimes to appear in New York was *Hop o' My Thumb* (26 November 1913) for which Manuel Klein was credited with the music and Glover with the composition of the ballet music.[699] In London, however, Glover continued to create incidental music for pantomimes and melodramas through the first quarter of the twentieth century. In an article in the *New York Clipper*, analyzing the creation of Christmas pantomimes at Drury Lane, Glover's process for composing and compiling the music was explained:

> Early in the Autumn James M. Glover, who "composes and arranges" the music, casts an inquisitive eye, or eyeglass, on the popular songs of the hour. He is curiously expert

in subjugating the twaddle of the time to the masterpieces which his erudition recalls. The blatant vulgarities of the music hall are excused by a humorous application. The ewe lamb of the comedian—for instance, "Come where the booze is cheaper"—is ingeniously accommodated to the picture.

Three pianists are among the first engagements for the pantomime preparation—a *chef du chant* for chorus work; a pianist for the ballet; an accompanist for the principals. For five hours a day the chorus master hammers into his recruits—half of them musicians and an easy half of them mere beauties—a four part musical arrangement of every number in the pantomime. The music learned, the choristers are marshalled, the greatest care being taken to sort up the sizes, so that there shall be no comical contrasts in the fours, sixes and eights.[700]

When he was not composing music, Glover was writing musical reviews as the music critic for *The Sun, The Daily Mail, The London Telegraph*[701] and the *Era*. In addition, he was the founder and chief editor of *The Theatre Managers' Journal* until his death on 8 September 1931.

GODOWSKY, Leopold

Born in Soshly, near Vilnius in the Russian Empire (modern Lithuania) on 13 February 1870, Leopold Godowsky began composing music at any early age and quickly became proficient on the piano and violin. In 1879 he commenced a concert career that toured throughout Lithuania and parts of Prussia, and from 1881 to 1884, he studied with pianist-composers Ernst Rudorff and Woldemar Bargiel at the Königliche Hochschule für Musik [Royal Academy of Music] in Berlin. He toured the United States with sopranos Clara Louise Kellogg and Emma Thursby in 1884–1885, and later he toured Canada with Belgian violinist Ovide Musin. He returned to Europe to study with composer, organist, and pianist Camille Saint-Saëns in Paris from 1887–1890, during which time he gave concerts in France and England. Beginning in 1894, Godowsky made his home in the United States, first in Philadelphia, where he directed the piano department at the Broad Street Conservatory, and later in Chicago where he was head of piano studies at the Chicago Conservatory.

He returned to Europe again in 1900, settling in Berlin until 1909, and afterwards in Vienna where he taught advanced piano technique for three years at the Klaviermeisterschule of the Akademie der Tonkunst [Piano Master School at the Academy of Music]. In 1912, Godowsky returned to the United States for a series of concert tours that extended through 1914, and at the outbreak of the First World War, he settled in America, first in New York, then Los Angeles, Seattle, and again in New York. In 1920 Godowsky published *Triakontameron*, a series of thirty moods and dramatic scenes composed in triple meter. No. 4 of the series, "Rendezvous," was used with lyrics by Sidney Mitchell, and as dance music in the hat shop sequence of *Snapshots of 1921* at the Selwyn Theatre (2 June 1921).[702] Example 87, displaying the first eight measures of "Rendezvous" exhibits a "Claire de Lune [Moonlight]" atmosphere that anticipates the "Clara Da Loon" sketch in the program four scenes later. Given the contributions of more familiar musical theatre composers George Gershwin, Con Conrad, Harry Ruby, and James Monaco among the creative staff of *Snapshots*, the presence of Godowsky's composition in the revue attests to his continued drawing power in New York (and throughout the world) as a composer, pianist, and musical celebrity.

Although Godowsky's musical career continued to reach new heights through the 1920s, his personal life endured disappointment and loss into the early 1930s. On 11 February 1928, Godowsky's twenty-two-year-old

Example 87. "Rendezvous" from *Snapshots of 1921*

son, Gordon, a Harvard student, secretly married "Follies" girl Yvonne Evelyn Hughes,[703] much to Godowsky's dismay since the marriage caused Gordon to relinquish his plans to continue his studies at Oxford.[704] Two years later, while recording Chopin, Godowsky suffered a stroke that left him partially paralyzed and on 27 December 1932, Gordon Godowsky despondent over the collapse of his marriage and lack of financial security, committed suicide by inhaling gas in his rooming house on West 72nd Street in Manhattan.[705] Leopold Godowsky's mourning period extended through the following December when Frieda, his wife (since 1891) and childhood sweetheart, succumbed to a heart attack in her apartment at the Ansonia Hotel.[706] Six years later, following an operation for an intestinal ailment, Godowsky died at Lenox Hill Hospital on 21 November 1938, survived by his daughters Vanita and Dagmar, and his son Leopold, Jr.[707]

GOETZL, Anselm

Composer and musical director Anselm Goetzl was born in Karolinenthal, Bohemia on 20 August 1878. He studied with composers Alexander Winkler, Zdeněk Fibich, and Antonín Dvořák in Prague and with conductor Franz Schalk and music theorist Guido Adler in Vienna, completing his Ph.D. in 1899 with the dissertation "Beitrag zur Instrumentation der Beethovenschen Symphonien [Contribution to the Instrumentation of Beethoven's Symphonies]." After graduation, Dr. Goetzl established himself as a musical director of opera and operetta in the German-speaking theatre and composed two original musical theatre works, the one-act opera *Zierpuppen* [*Ornamental Dolls*] based on Molière's *Les Précieuses Ridicules* [*The Ridiculous Affected Ladies*] produced in Prague on 15 November 1905[708] and the operetta *Madame Flirt* (1909) based on the play *Divorçons* [*Let's Get a Divorce*] by Victorien Sardou.[709] Late in 1913 Goetzl came to America as the principal musical director of the [Andreas] Dippel Opera Comique Company with the production of Charles Cuvillier's operetta *The Lilac Domino* which opened at the Forty-Fourth Street Theatre on 28 October 1914[710] and remained there until 30 January 1915. In spring 1915, Goetzl moved to Madison Square Garden where he conducted a symphony orchestra creating incidental and entr'acte music for daily motion picture shows, and in the summer, he composed the music for Sylvester Schaeffer's "fantastic revue," *Ein Ritterspiel* [*A Tournament*] that played a four-week engagement at the German Theatre in New York City in the fall. A year later, Goetzl conducted the *Till Eulenspiegel* portion of the Ballet Russe performances at the Manhattan Opera House (21 October 1916) and composed incidental music for Maurice V. Samuels's play *The Wanderer*, based on the parable of the Prodigal Son, that opened on 1 February 1917 with the ageing James O'Neill in the cast. In spring 1917, Goetzl was engaged by producer Oliver Morosco to compose the score for his musical version of Avery Hopwood's farce, *Sadie Love*, entitled *A Full Honeymoon* (libretto by Morosco), and at the end of June, Goetzl left New York for Los Angeles where the musical was scheduled for a trial run late in the summer.[711] After the Morosco project expired on the West Coast, Goetzl returned to New York to continue work on *Cherry Blossoms*, an operetta he had composed with librettists Stephen Ivor Szinnyey and William Cary Duncan, that had recently been optioned for production under the title *The King's Double* by [George M.] Cohan and [Sam H.] Harris. After substantial revisions and the addition of music and lyrics by Cohan, Harry Tierney, Joseph McCarthy, William S. Gilbert, and Arthur Sullivan, the "Cohanized opera comique," newly titled *The Royal Vagabond*, opened at the Cohan and Harris Theatre in New York on 17 February 1919 and remained there until 3 January 1920.[712] If *The New York Times* reviewer was cautious in his praise for the piece admitting nonetheless that "Last night's audience received [the entertainment] with unstinted enthusiasm," the *New York Clipper* claimed that "all in all it is one of the best musical show entertainments the local stage has had in several years."[713] Following the success of *The Royal Vagabond*, Goetzl became a naturalized citizen of the United States (on 9 September 1919). In addition, with Henri Février, he composed incidental and dance music for the spectacle play *Aphrodite* (24 November 1919) at the Century Theatre in New York[714] and served as musical director for ballet and concert programs at the Metropolitan Opera House.[715] In April 1920, dissatisfied with the way his work had been treated by theatrical producers, Goetzl established his own producing company called "The Goetzl Theatrical Enterprises" to mount his new compositions, the first of which was to be *The Unknown Flower* (libretto by William Gary Duncan).[716] Retitled *The Rose Girl*, Goetzl's new musical opened in Harrisburg, Pennsylvania, on 2 September 1920 before moving to Atlantic City where tepid reviews forced it to close for a complete overhaul before attempting a run in New York City.[717] When the revamped musical reappeared in Atlantic City on 20 January 1921, reviewers were demonstrably pleased:

> *The Rose Girl* returned to the Globe last night practically a finished product. The cast was more sprightly and more capable of putting the comedy over than its predecessor, but while the piece entails plenty of laughs, its strong bid for recognition lies in its music.
>
> Anselm Goetzl has composed a score which has a most enjoyable rhythm and orchestration, and which may be most favorably compared with the best pieces heard this year. The lyrics and book of William Cary Duncan are also pleasing. The settings are effective, especially that of the Rose Garden in the final act.[718]

When the show opened in New York City, however, the critics were less effusive and the musical was gone in three months, and so, evidently, was Goetzl's producing company. He secured a job at the Hippodrome conducting the ballet music in the hit vaudeville revue *Get Together* (3 September 1921) which kept him employed through the following spring when he married Berlin-born Charlotte Oelschlagel, one of the skaters in the Ice Carnival portion of the revue. The couple honeymooned in Mexico and Cuba and left for Europe at the end of the year to introduce one another to their families. During a stopover in Barcelona, Spain, Goetzl fell ill and was taken to the hospital where he died on 9 January 1923 following an emergency operation. He was survived by his wife and twenty-year-old son, Robert, also a musician.

GOODMAN, Alfred

Composer, pianist, and musical director Alfred ("Al") Goodman was born in Nikopol, Russia (now the Ukraine), on 12 August 1890, the son of Tobias Goodman, a cantor at a local synagogue. From his father, Goodman learned the rudiments of music and by the time he was six, he could read music fluently. The following year, to escape one of the recurring pogroms the Russian government levelled against the Jewish population, the Goodmans, disguised as farmers, escaped to Rumania and eventually found their way to America, settling in Baltimore, Maryland. There Goodman received a public school education and sang in a synagogue with his father before matriculating at Baltimore City College and the Peabody Conservatory of Music where his studies included piano, organ, musical composition, and singing. After graduation, Goodman's first job was as a pianist at the Pickwick Theatre, a movie house in Baltimore,[719] and following a brief stint as a chorus boy in the touring Milton Aborn Opera Company, he became a song plugger. It was in that capacity that he drew the attention of musical theatre composer, director, and producer Earl Carroll[720] who hired him as rehearsal and show pianist for his musical farce *So Long Letty* (23 October 1916) and as musical director for the tour and Broadway run of his next show *Canary Cottage* (5 February 1917). With *Linger Longer Letty* (20November 1919),[721] Goodman became composer and dance arranger in addition to musical director on Broadway,[722] beginning a long list of shows that introduced his songs, dance music, and/or incidental music, including: *Cinderella on Broadway* (24 June 1920),[723] incidental music; *The Passing Show* (29 December 1920),[724] incidental and ballet music; *The Midnight Rounders of 1921* (7 February 1921), ballet music; *The Last Waltz* (10 May 1921),[725] additional music ("A Baby in Love," "The Next Dance with You," "The Charming Ladies"); *The Whirl of New York* (13 June 1921),[726] co-composer of songs with Gustave Kerker and Lew Pollock, also incidental and dance music; *The Mimic World of 1921* (17 August 1921), dance music;[727] *The Passing Show of 1922* (20 September 1922),[728] songs, incidental and dance music; *The Lady in Ermine* (2 October 1922),[729] co-composer of songs with Jean Gilbert; *The Dancing Girl* (24 January 1923), additional music ("I've Been Wanting You"); *Caroline* (31 January1923), additional music ("Argentine," "Land of Enchantment (Land of Romance)," "Rainbow Gold," "Till Dreams Come True," and "Way Down South"); *Dew Drop Inn* (17 May 1923), songs, and dance music; *Artists and Models* (20 August 1923), additional music ("Music of Love"), also dance music; *Topics of 1923* (20 November 1923), co-composer with Jean Schwartz, also dance music; *Artists and Models (1924)* (18 October 1924), dance music; and *Countess Maritza* (18 September 1926), additional music ("Call of Love"). Called the "Music Doctor" by composers and producers, Goodman was the musician typically called for when a show was in trouble, or needed a new song, or dance music.

Beginning in 1920 Goodman became the general musical director for the Shubert Brothers and all but a handful of the 150 Broadway musicals he conducted were produced by them. The list included *Sinbad* (the Canadian tour, summer 1920),[730] *Florodora* (replacement conductor, August 1920), *Bombo* (6 October 1921), *The Passing Show of 1922* (20 September 1922), *Blossom Time* (replacement conductor, November 1922), *Big Boy* (musical direction and Al Jolson's orchestrations, 7 January 1925), *Princess Flavia* (2 November 1905), *No Foolin'* (24 June 1928), *Cherry Blossoms* (28 March 1927), *Good News* (6 September 1927), *The New Moon* (18 September 1928), *Follow Thru* (9 January 1929), *The New Yorkers* (8 December 1930), *America's Sweetheart* (10 February 1931), *The Band Wagon* (3 June 1931), *George White's Scandals (1931)* (14 September 1931), *The Cat and the Fiddle* (15 October 1931), *Strike Me Pink* (4 March 1933), *Life Begins at 8:40* (27 August 1934), *Yokel Boy* (6 July 1939), *Higher and Higher* (4 April 1940) and *Hold on to Your Hats* (11 September 1940).[731] Beginning in 1926, Goodman began working as a musical director for films, including *The Plantation Act* (7 October 1926), *The Talk of Hollywood* (9 December 1929), and *Queen High* (29 August 1930); and he even appeared as himself in *The Talk of Hollywood* and *Soup for Nuts* (27 June 1934). In 1932 he began providing musical direction for radio shows such as *The Ziegfeld Follies of the Air* (3 April–26 June 1932), *Palmolive Beauty Box Theater* (1935–6 October 1937), *Your Hit Parade* (1936–1938), and *The Fred Allen Show* (2 October 1940–26 June 1949). Goodman moved to television in 1949 serving as musical director and/or composer for *Fireball Fun-For-All* (1949), *The Colgate Comedy Hour* (1950–1954), *The All Star Revue* (1952–1953), *The Abbott and Costello Show* (1953), *The Life of Riley* (1954–1955), and *The NBC Comedy Hour* (1956).

Despite Goodman's prolific output and unquestioned abilities, friends and colleagues seemed to agree that there is little about him that suggested a musician. "He has the build of a fullback and is a sartorial study with his sharply pressed gabardine slacks, brown sports jacket, shirt to match and a tie that is a blaze of color," said Irving Spiegel in *The New York Times*. "This Goodman has one obsession," he continued, "music and every phase of it. He conducts without benefit of a score. His musical chores have an inimitable vitality. His band has a versatility that could adjust itself at all times to the spirit of the program: Maestro Goodman's orchestra runs the gauntlet from a Bach suite—and with keen regard for its architectural design—to a blasting swing session."[732] His incidental and dance music exhibits the same versatility as his orchestra and displays great stylistic variety, ranging from adaptations of classical music ("Blue Danube Ballet," "Gypsy Dance adapted from *Carmen*," "Themes from Schubert's *Unfinished Symphony*") to atmospheric or contemporary dance idioms ("Button Waltz Blues," "Oriental Dance," "Movie Hop," "[Dorothy] Malone Mambo Dance," "Street Rock and Roll," "Square Dance") and novelty incidental numbers ("Dog Idyll," "Drug Store Scherzo," "[Art]

Linkletter Scherzo," "Western Jump"). On 10 January 1972, at the age of 81, Al Goodman died in New York City, survived by his daughter Rita, two grandchildren and two great-grandchildren.

GOTTSCHALK, Louis F[erdinand]

Pianist, composer, and musical director Louis F. Gottschalk was born on 7 October 1869[733] in St. Louis, Missouri. His father, Louis John Gottschalk, was a local judge who became the American Consul to Stuttgart, Germany, where Louis Ferdinand studied music.[734] Louis F. Gottschalk launched his musical theatre career on Broadway with the music and lyrics for "Laugh, and the World Laughs with You," a song interpolated into the score of Charles Hoyt and Richard Stahl's *A Black Sheep, And How It Came Out in the Wash* (6 January 1896). He provided the musical direction for Victor Herbert's *The Ameer* (4 December 1899), followed by Ivan Caryl and Lionel Monckton's *The Messenger Boy* (16 September 1901), for which he supplied musical direction and adaptations of the original dance music; and later that same month, Gottschalk provided additional music—"(The Song of a) Yankee Tar," and "In Florida"—to Aimé Lachaume's *The Liberty Belles* (30 September 1901). Subsequent musical direction assignments included *The Toreador* (6 January 1902), *Red Feather* (9 November 1903), *The Cingalee* (24 October 1904), *The Gingerbread Man* (25 December 1905), *The Rich Mr. Hoggenheimer* (22 October 1906), and *Dream City and The Magic Knight* (24 December 1906).[735] In the midst of his responsibilities as musical director, Gottschalk had the time to compose the music for *Cinderella and the Prince, or the Castle of Heart's Desire* (libretto by Robert Barnet), the 1904 musical presented by First Corps of Cadets at the Tremont Theatre in Boston on 1 February.[736] In addition to composing the music for most of the songs, Gottschalk also composed dance music and an extended Christmas ballet that functioned as the musical's third act finale. Beginning with an acapella arrangement of "God Rest You Merry, Gentlemen," the ballet included a fairy gavotte, a stately mazurka, a syncopated ragtime dance (example 88a) with a comical schottische interlude, a shimmering corps de ballet waltz, a vivacious reel, and a vigorous tarantella (example 88b) marked "allegro furioso" that dissolved into a recapitulation of the waltz theme of the show's "Katy Didn't" number (which also ended the second act) as the curtain fell. Although invested with popular ragtime syncopations, the ballet music was highly reminiscent of classical ballets such as *Coppélia*, *Sylvia*, *The Nutcracker*, and *Swan Lake*. The hodge-podge of musical styles was certainly appropriate for a musical extravaganza that combined the stories of Goldilocks and the Three Bears, Santa Claus, Robinson Crusoe, and Cinderella.

On 21 October 1907, Gottschalk gained a certain celebrity as the musical director for the first American production of Franz Lehár's global sensation *The Merry Widow*[737] after which he conducted the New York productions and tours of Victor Herbert's *Old Dutch* (22 November 1909), Robert Hood Bowers's *The Red Rose* (22 June 1911), Franz Lehár's *Gypsy Love* (17 October 1911),[738] and Jean Gilbert's *Modest Suzanne* (1 January 1912). Late in 1912 Gottschalk composed the music for L. Frank Baum's *The Tik-Tok Man of Oz*, a musical extravaganza loosely based on his book

Example 88a. Ragtime in "Ballet Music and Finale" from *Cinderella and the Prince*

Example 88b. Tarantella in "Ballet Music and Finale" from *Cinderella and the Prince*

Ozma of Oz, which opened in Los Angeles on 31 March 1913 before going on tour.[739] Gottschalk and Baum were members of the Lofty and Exalted Order of Uplifters, a society that, beginning in 1914, held annual outings with shows written by Baum, often with music by Gottschalk. The first show produced on 14 January 1914 by Baum and Gottschalk was called *Stagecraft, or The Adventure of a Strictly Moral Man*; the second they produced (on 23 October 1915) was *The Uplift of Lucifer, or, Raising Hell*; and a third was called *The Orpheus Road Show* (1917).[740] Gottschalk was also the vice president of the Oz Film Manufacturing Company, a film studio with exclusive rights to Baum's Oz books. Baum, who was the president of the organization, was to adapt his books to the screen and Gottschalk was to compose original music which would be sent along with the fims to be performed by the orchestras in movie theatres.[741] The silent films for which he composed music included *The Patchwork Girl of Oz* (28 September 1914), *The Magic Cloak of Oz* (28 September 1914), *His Majesty, the Scarecrow of Oz* (7 December 1914), and *The Last Egyptian* (12 December 1914). After the company shut down in the summer of 1915[742] Gottschalk composed the music for the films *The Despoiler* (15 December 1915) and *Honor's Altar* (13 February 1916) before returning to Broadway as musical director for Victor Herbert's *The Century Girl* (6 November 1916). After the Broadway production closed on 28 April 1917, Gottschalk returned to composing and arranging exclusively for films, including *The Curse of Eve* (October 1917), *Old Wives for New* (16 June 1918), *The Fall of Babylon* (21 July 1919),[743] *The Mother and the Law* (17 August 1919),[744] *Broken Blossoms* (20 October 1919),[745] *The Four Horsemen of the Apocalypse* (1921), *The Three Musketeers* (1921), *Little Lord Fauntleroy* (13 November 1921), *Orphans in the Storm* (1921),[746] *Shadows* (10 November 1922), *Hearts Aflame* (1 January 1923),[747] *Romola* (30 August 1925), *The Rainbow Man* (18 May 1929), and the re-edited *The Birth of a Nation* (1933).[748] On 15 July 1934, Gottschalk died of a stroke at his home in Los Angeles, survived by his wife, Marie Millard Gottschalk, his son [Ernest] Victor, and his daughter Gloria.[749]

GOULA [I SOLEY], Juan

Composer, performer, musical director, and educator, Juan Goula was born in Sant Feliu de Guixols, Catalonia, Spain, on 29 March 1843. In Barcelona he studied with Nicolau Manent before going off to work at the Théâtre des Champs-Élysées in Paris and the Gran Teatro del Liceo in Barcelona. In 1866 he began his career as musical director in Palma de Mallorca where he created l'Orfeó Mallorqui, a choir he directed until 1870, when he accepted the position of musical director at the Imperial Theatre in Moscow. In addition, with Lazar M. Puig and Melchior Vidal, Goula created an important Spanish school of singing that produced many fine students, including tenor Angelo Angioletti, baritone Ramon Blanchart, bass Francisco Mateu y Nicolau ("Uetam"), and soprano Dionisia Fité, who became his wife in 1868. He also served as musical director of the Italian Opera in St. Petersburg for three seasons, and, beginning in 1873, he conducted concerts and operas in the Grand Duchy of Baden, and Hamburg, Germany, and concert performances of the *Requiem* by

Giuseppe Verdi in Barcelona. In addition, Goula is credited with initiating the first performances of Richard Wagner's operas in Barcelona. Following musical direction assignments in St. Petersburg, Berlin, Dresden, Stuttgart, Leipzig, Munich, and other German cities, Goula moved to Argentina where he created a Spanish opera series at the Teatro Colon in Buenos Aires and established the Conservatory of Music there. Between 1881 and 1884, Goula was musical director at the Teatro Real in Madrid where he conducted Georges Bizet's *La jolie fille de Perth* [*The Fair Maid of Perth*], *Carmen*, Giuseppe Verdi's *Aida*, and his own opera, *Los Amantes de Teruel* [*The Lovers of Teruel*].

As a composer, Goula created the music for operettas *A orillas del mar* [*At the Seaside*], *Cuento de amor* [*Love Story*], and *El testament de un brujo* [*The Testament of a Sorcerer*] and the ballet spectacle *Triomf de Venus i Clio* [*Triumph of Venus and Clio*]. In New York, Goula's incidental and ballet music was heard in *Castles in Spain, or Castles in the Air*, a spectacle imported from the Teatro Principal, Barcelona, at Niblo's Garden on 9 May 1881.[750] The *New York Times* review was less than kind and concluded that "*Castles in Spain* is built upon a feeble story, it lacks the elements of striking novelty and beauty, its scenery is passable, its music is badly sung, its ballets are barely tolerable, and the whole thing is tiresome trash."[751] The review in the *New York Clipper* was mixed, admitting that "there is much in this spectacle that is worthy of high commendation and in the forefront must be placed the music and the scenery." The reviewer concluded that the "spectacle may become a favorite one with metropolitans after the rough edges are worn down to their allotted grooves; but it may be regarded as almost a certainty that there is no one or nothing in Spain that can edify New Yorkers in the matter of show-pieces."[752] On 10 July 1917, Juan Goula died in Buenos Aires, after a long illness. He was survived by his second wife, Elizabeth.

GRANGER, Frederick

Born in Prussia in 1760, composer, clarinetist, violinist, and musical director Frederick Granger came to Boston with his family at an early age.[753] There he married Jane Hughes on 1 December 1785 and established himself as a music teacher, arranger, clarinetist with the Philharmonic Society of Boston, and violinist-leader of the Federal Street Theatre Orchestra. In addition to musical direction, his theatre responsibilities typically included the composition of additional music, the arrangement or adaptation of dance music, the arrangement of orchestral parts for musical theatre works, and the adaptation or rearrangement of orchestral parts for pieces originally produced in London. The productions on which he labored included *Adelmorn, the Outlaw* (25 February 1802), *Raymond and Agnes, or, The Bleeding Nun* (7 May 1802), *La Perouse, or, The Desolate Island* (10 May 1803), *The Wife of Two Husbands* (4 April 1804), *The Paragraph, or, A Recipe for the Nervous* (23 November 1804), *Lodoiska, or, The Rescue of the Princess of Poland* (3 March 1806), *Feudal Times, or, The Banquet Gallery* (20 March 1809), and *The Exiles, or The Russian Daughters* (27 April 1810). During the 1819–1820 season Granger suffered a "stroke of palsy" and was given a benefit concert by the Philharmonic Society (featuring Haydn's "Surprise" Symphony and Pleyel's "La Chasse" Symphony) to raise money for Granger's medical expenses.[754] *The Euterpeiad, or Musical Intelligencer* wrote of the event: "A benefit, lovingly tendered Mr. Granger Sr. was recommended as worthy recompense for one who, having outlived his abilities, is now descending the vale, and may be denominated a *decayed musician*."[755] Granger remained musical director of the Federal Street Theatre until 1828 when the position passed to his son, Thomas. Two years later, Granger died in Boston on 7 February 1830, survived by his second wife, Charlotte Pierpont Granger, two daughters and two sons.

Granger's published compositions included "A Soldier to His Own Fireside," sung at the Federal Street Theatre in *The Wife of Two Husbands* (1806); "Massachusetts March" (1807–1810); "The Star of Bethlehem," a sacred song performed at concerts of the Handel and Haydn Society (1821); "Lafayette's Waltz," arranged by Granger; "Wreaths for the Chieftain," arranged by Granger from "Hail to the Chief" composed by James Sanderson for *The Lady of the Lake* (1815); and "The Waterloo March" composed by Joseph Dale, arranged by Granger with accompaniments for the violin and flute (1816).

GRANT, John B[everidge]

Born in Newburgh, New York on 25 November 1850, John B. Grant was an organist, ornithologist, composer, and dance arranger. After graduating from Columbia University he explored avocations: songwriting, which would result in the publication of "My Gentle Fisher-Maiden" in 1875, and birth-watching, which would peak with the publication of his seminal book, *Our Common Birds and How to Know Them*, in 1891. Between these two events, Grant composed the score for *The Mystic Isle*, or, *The Laws of Average*, a comic opera with book and lyrics by the well-known wordsmith Sydney Rosenfeld,[756] first performed at the Temple Theatre in Philadelphia on 2 October 1886.[757] Critics lauded the libretto for its "bright snappy bits" and "very clever taking songs" but found Grant's music "fluent, but conventional and rather serious. As to whether *The Mystic Isle will* be a 'go' or not, the general opinion of the best judges is that its music is not quite 'catchy' enough. The score shows strong signs of imitation of *The Pirates of Penzance*. The libretto is much superior to the music. I hear that … infectious music and taking airs are to be interpolated into the score."[758] On 11 October 1886, *The Mystic Isle* began the second week of its run with new "rollicking airs" added by Grant and the music as a whole appeared to be catching on.[759] Two of the favorite numbers in the comic opera involved dancing. "Country Board," an advertisement for the benefits of bucolic living sung by an original inhabitant of Mystic Island and his son, introduced an animated hornpipe with simple tonic-dominant-subdominant harmony and a melody comprised of steady (and relentless) sixteenth notes. The runaway hit of the musical, however, "The Hindoo was a Hoodoo," was a topical song composed in schottische style with dotted notes and triplets, followed by an eight-measure dance break written in the same fashion (example 89). Melodic interest is created by the tonal variations of the opening four notes (the triplet plus the following eighth note): measures 1–2 and 5–6 are exactly the same, but measures 3, 4, and 7 begin with the same rhythmic pattern (a triplet followed by an eighth note) but the pitches are different. Note also that measures 3–4 vary the rhythmic pattern of the other measures by placing quarter notes on beats 3 and 4, in an attempt, perhaps, to support and accent the rhythms of the stage choreography (or, at the very least, to provide the choreographer with rhythmically varied dance music).

A third number from the score that employs a "Turkey in the Straw" accompaniment, "Hen Chorus" is also noteworthy, if only because it anticipates the "Pickalittle (Talkalittle)" routine in *The Music Man* by seventy years.

Following *The Mystic Isle*, Grant returned to his ornithological pursuits, published his book, and became the musical director of the Alumni Glee Club of the Columbia College Musical Society and the Flushing Choral Club. In 1895, he succeeded James W. Treadwell as organist of the Flushing Congregational Church, and in 1902 he was engaged as musical director and organist at the First Presbyterian Church of New Rochelle, New York. His religious compositions included "Guide Me, O Thou Great Jehovah,"

Example 89. Dance in "The Hindoo Was a Hoodoo" from *The Mystic Isle*

"How Firm a Foundation," "Jesus! Name of Wondrous Love," "The Day of Resurrection," and "Sing, O Heavens." In addition, Grant composed several works for children, such as "Pussy Willow and other Nature Songs for Little Folk" (1911) and "Fourteen Cameos: Series 1" (1912), piano music for beginners. On 24 April 1912, Grant died at the New Rochelle home of his sister and was buried at Evergreen Cemetery in Morristown, New Jersey.

GRAUPNER, [Johann Christian] Gottlieb

Virtuoso oboist, pianist, and double bassist, Gottlieb Graupner was born in Verden an der Aller in Lower Saxony on 6 October 1767 into a musical family. Like his father, Gottlieb earned a position in the Hanoverian band as a teenager and received an honorable discharge from the unit when he was twenty-one years old. By 1791 Graupner had moved to London where he had been accepted into the orchestra conducted by Franz Josef Haydn for the introduction of the "Salomon" Symphonies in the 1791–1792 season.[760] Although his musical temperament lent itself to performing serious music in symphonic orchestras, in London, Graupner found more regular employment playing light operatic music in theatrical orchestras where his expertise on several instruments was an advantage. In 1795 Graupner immigrated to America, landing first at Prince Edward Island, from which he immediately set sail for Charleston, South Carolina. There he quickly became leader of the thirteen-piece orchestra at the City Theatre[761] where his first recorded solo appearance in America occurred on 21 March 1795 with his performance of one of Johann Christian Fischer's concertos for oboe. During the 1795–1796 season Graupner met a new member of the City Theatre Company, actress Catherine Comerford Hillier, and married her on 6 April 1796 before taking her and the rest of the company on tour to Norfolk and Portsmouth, Virginia. Late in 1796, the Graupners moved north to Boston and joined the company at the Federal Street Theatre, both making their debut (she on stage, he in the orchestra) in the production of André Grétry's *Richard Coeur de Lion* on 23 January 1797.[762] In 1800 Graupner became leader of the orchestra at the Federal Street Theatre and maintained his association with the theatre as musical director, dance arranger, and/or musician until 1832.[763]

On 24 November 1800, the *Boston Gazette* announced plans for the establishment of the first music conservatory in Boston, the American Conservatorio of Boston, headed by the triumvirate of Gottleib Graupner, François Delochaire Mallet, and Filippo Trajetta.[764] In conjunction with the conservatory, Graupner established a music publishing business through which he published his own compositions as well as those of popular local and foreign composers. Publications of Graupner's works included "The Attic Bower" (1802–1803) and "Governor Brook's Grand March" (1820), as well as important instructional books, *New Instructor for the Clarinet*, and *Rudiments of the Art of Playing on the Piano Forte* (1806). Graupner was also instrumental in the foundation and development of the Boston Philharmonic Society, which achieved its greatest celebrity between the years 1817–1822,[765] and in the establishment of the Handel and Haydn Society, an oratorio association, on 24 March 1815.[766] Although Graupner was reported to have "done more to improve the musical taste of [Boston], than any other person of his profession,"[767] it is difficult to assess his contributions to the theatre in general and to dance music in particular. More has been written about whether he conducted from the piano or from the contrabass than about his alteration and arrangement of the scores under his leadership. There is no controversy over Graupner's superlative musicianship; nor is there any question about the duties he would have had to fulfill as a theatrical musical director. The compositions already noted demonstrate the work of a highly proficient, if imitative composer, and it is a misfortune that his theatrical oeuvre apparently died with him on 16 April 1836.

GRESS, Louis [George]

Musical director, pianist, and dance arranger, Louis Gress was born in New York City on 20 January 1893 to German immigrants, George and Barbara Lanbreis Gress. When Louis was a teenager, the family moved to Philadelphia where he found employment as a musician in theatre orchestras at the age of seventeen. By his early twenties Gress was living in New York and playing in the orchestra of the New Amsterdam Theatre,[768] where he developed a friendship with Eddie Cantor[769] who was appearing in Ziegfeld's *Midnight Frolic* and the *Ziegfeld Follies of 1917*. Three years later, he became musical director for the Eddie Cantor revue at the Winter Garden Theatre, *Broadway Brevities of 1920* (29 September 1920), responsible for musical continuity, dance music, and vocal arrangements, in addition to conducting the orchestra. Gress performed the same function for Cantor's next Winter Garden show, *Make It Snappy* (13 April 1922), but this time he was given program credit for selecting and arranging the music for "Princess Beautiful," a ballet choreographed by Cleveland Bronner.[770] The next year, Gress and Cantor again joined forces with the production of *Kid Boots* (31 December 1923) which remained on Broadway for nearly 500 performances,[771] after which Gress became musical director of the *Ziegfeld Follies of 1925* (6 July 1925), back at the New Amsterdam Theatre,[772] and of other musical shows that included *Piggy* (11 January 1927), *Lady Do* (18 April 1927), *Talk about Girls* (14 June 1927), *Cross My Heart* (17 September 1928), and *You Said It* (19 January 1931). After *You Said It* closed on 4 July 1931, Gress traveled to Los Angeles to serve as musical director for Eddie Cantor's radio program, a position he held until early 1937 when he returned to New York to provide musical direction and continuity for *Orchids Preferred* (11May 1937), a musical that remained on Broadway for only a week. Following the failure of his latest project, Gress returned to Philadelphia where, at the age of fifty, he died of general peritonitis on 18 April 1943. Three days later a funeral mass for Louis Gress was celebrated at Saint Henry Catholic Church followed by his interment at Holy Sepulcher Cemetery in Philadelphia.

HADLEY, Henry K[imball]

Composer and conductor, Henry K. Hadley was born in Sommerville, Massachusetts, on 20 December 1871. As a boy he received instruction on the violin and piano from his father, a public school music teacher, and as a teenager he studied harmony and composition with Stephen Emery and George Whitefield Chadwick at the New England Conservatory of Music. After graduation he was engaged as orchestra leader of the Mapleson and Whitney Opera Comique Company for its 1893–1894 tour (beginning in Montreal on 11 September), and at the end of the season he travelled to Vienna where he studied counterpoint with Romanian musicologist and composer Eusebius Mandyczewski. In the fall 1895, Hadley became the director of music at St. Paul's School in Garden City, Long Island, and on 24 October 1895, his orchestral *Ballet Suite* was premiered by the Manuscript Society at Chickering Hall in New York City to highly enthusiastic reviews.[773] Two years later, when Hadley's *Symphony No. 1* was performed at Chickering Hall, the music critic of *The New York Times* wrote: "Mr. Hadley's symphony was the only [work] deserving serious consideration, and it deserves a good deal, not only because it achieves something, but also because it promises a good deal more.... Mr. Hadley is not yet master of the larger forms of music, and it is to this that some uncertainty of expression and occasional open joints in his structure must be attributed. But he has written a remarkably strong work for so young a man, and his independence promises well for his future."[774] In 1901, the composer demonstrated that the critic's belief in his potential was warranted when his *Symphony No. 2: The Four Seasons* won the Paderewski Prize for superior achievement in the field of orchestral music. The following year, Hadley ventured into the realm of theatre music and composed a well-reviewed incidental score for Harriet Ford and E.F. Boddington's play, *Audrey*, opening at the Academy of Music, Richmond, Virginia (17 November 1902) prior to a New York run at Hoyt's Madison Square Theatre (24 November 1902).[775] In advance of the production, Hadley's score was described as "written in ambitious strain, his entr'actes forming a suite and the dramatic moments heightened by accompaniments based on the musical expression of the emotions expressed on the stage."[776]

Encouraged by his success as a composer of incidental music, Hadley composed the score for *Nancy Brown* (book and lyrics by George H. Broadhurst and Frederic Rankin), a vehicle for comedienne Marie Cahill that opened at the Lyceum Theatre, New London, Connecticut, on 10 February 1903 before moving to Broadway a week later. Although critics were generally positive about the music, only about half of the score was actually composed by Hadley; the best reviewed numbers, "The Katydid, the Cricket and the Frog," "The Glowworm and the Moth" and "On the

Example 90. Dance in "Strange, Odd, Queer" from *Nancy Brown*

Congo" were interpolations by other composers.[777] One number Hadley did compose, "Strange, Odd, Queer," a patter quartet outlining the ironies of modern life, ended with a charming schottische dance (example 90), well within the musical fabric of theatrical soft-shoe numbers, although here and there—an unusual melodic turn, a striking change of harmony—the presence of a more "serious" composer was in evidence.

Hadley appeared to have a fondness for the schottische style in his light musical theatre dance music and used it frequently, often repeating melodic and harmonic motifs from one show to another. The dance from "Dancing Dinah" (example 91) in his 1917 operetta *The Fire-Prince* (libretto by David Stevens) displays many structural similarities to the previous example, the most obvious of which is the melodic rhythm of the phrase in measures 3 and 11 of example 90 that is repeated as the melodic rhythm of measures 1–2, 5–6 of example 91. In addition, the use of secondary dominants and harmonic inversions (the bass note is not always the tonic of the chord) is also common to both compositions. As a serious composer Hadley was not comfortable with ragtime or popular dance music; as a result the schottische formula afforded him the opportunity to work within a popular idiom with relative comfort.

After his foray into the realm of the Broadway musical, Hadley went to Europe to conduct, compose, and study with one of the leading opera composers of the "Munich School," Ludwig Thuille. On 27 December 1907 Hadley conducted the Berlin Philharmonic Orchestra in the premiere of his *Symphony No. 3* before moving to the Stadttheater of Mainz where he was engaged as associate conductor, and where he conducted the initial performance of his first opera *Safie, the Persian* on 4 April 1909.[778] After returning to the United States, his conducting assignments included the Seattle Symphony Orchestra (1909–1911), and the San Francisco Symphony Orchestra (1911–1916). On 10 August 1912, Hanley conducted his music drama *The Atonement of Pan* (libretto by Joseph D. Redding) produced by members of the Bohemian Club at their Grove in Sonoma County, California. Following his return to the East Coast, Hadley composed and conducted the music for an open-air pageant reenacting the history of Newark, New Jersey, performed at Weequahic Park in the spring of 1916 by a cast of 4,000 actors accompanied by a 92-member orchestra.[779] His opera *Azora* (libretto by David Stevens) was presented for the first time by the Chicago Grand Opera Company on 26 December 1917 and performed in New York City at the end of January 1918. While the critic from *The New York Times* found the opera lacking

Example 91. Dance in "Dancing Dinah" from *The Fire-Prince*

"somewhat the routine of the theatre, and still more the dramatic note," various musical passages were acclaimed, notably "a fine barbaric dance in the first act,"[780] a selection of which is given in example 92. The stage directions at the beginning of the dance suggest its context: "The Festal Procession appears. At its head are musicians. A company of Soldiers follow; then CANER, in the ceremonial robes of his office; Slaves, bearing censers; finally MONTEZUMA, PAPAN and others. Dancing Girls enter. Girls dance." Example 92 begins on the ninth measure of the Girls' dance and displays the tonal and Romantic musical idiom with which Hadley seemed most comfortable. Note how the dance music is divisible into two-measure phrases, each containing eight beats. Even though the ballet music of *Azora* appears far removed from the music of the typical Broadway dance break it is structured in a similar binary way.

In October 1918, Hadley's opera, *Bianca* (libretto by Grant Stewart, based on Goldoni's play *The Mistress of the Inn*), was given its first performance by the Society of American Singers at the Park Theatre in New York City,[781] and on 15 December 1919, Hadley conducted the orchestra and chorus of three thousand voices in his music for *The Wayfarer*, a spectacle production sponsored by the Inter-Church World Movement at Madison

Example 92. "Girls' Dance" from *Azora*

Square Garden.[782] While Hadley was working on *The Wayfarer*, his opera *Cleopatra's Night* (libretto by Alice Leal Pollock) was in preparation for a 31 January 1920 premiere at the Metropolitan Opera.[783] Later in 1920 Hadley accepted the position of associate conductor of the New York Philharmonic Orchestra, a position he held until 1927 and in 1929 he was instrumental in the creation of the Manhattan Symphony Orchestra, organized to promote the instrumental compositions of American composers. By the time of his death from cancer in New York City on 6 September 1937, Hadley's Romantic style of composition had grown out of fashion, and his extensive body of work, which had won prizes in an earlier generation, was found to be little more than conventional and superficial.[784]

HAIG, Alexander

Born on 26 March 1841 in Glasgow, Scotland, composer, dance arranger, and musical director Alexander Haig immigrated to the United States with his mother Margaret in 1850, settling in Cincinnati, Ohio, where the nine-year-old Scot studied music in the public school system. In his early twenties Haig supported his mother by working as a violin instructor and general music teacher in the Cincinnati school system and later, by giving private lessons and working at the iron fence factory in Covington, Kentucky. By the mid-1880s, Haig appeared in theatrical records as the leader of the orchestra at the Grand Opera House in Cincinnati. Subsequently, in the fall of 1887, Haig became the musical director of the touring W.T. Carleton English Opera Company, a position he held for several seasons before joining Russell's Comedians as musical director, composer, and dance arranger. In 1892 he co-composed (with W.S. Mullaly) the songs and dances for *The City Directory*, a Russell's Comedians tour that played the Grand Opera House (27 August) and the Fourteenth Street Theatre (12 September) in New York City; and at the end of the year he co-arranged (with Gustave Kerker) the music for *A Society Fad*, another Comedians farce that opened at New York's Bijou Theatre on 5 December. In the subsequent season, Haig selected and arranged the music (and provided musical direction) for *About Town*, an adaptation of Adolph Philips's German play, *Corner Grocer of Avenue A*, produced by Russell's Comedians at the Chicago Opera House on 24 December 1893, and at the Casino Theatre in New York on 26 February 1894. The two productions merited very different responses from the critics. The Chicago reviewer published in *The New York Times* determined that "the play gives opportunity for the introduction of specialties, and these were new and pleasing, and caught the public. A number of pretty girls tastefully costumed made success more certain.... A large and enthusiastic audience was present and a successful season for these dull times is assured."[785] The usually effusive critic from the *New York Clipper*, however, was not amused by the New York City production:

> It was a wearisome performance, which even the efforts of some very clever people failed to enliven.... Just why it was necessary to purchase the right to produce an English speaking version of Mr. Philips's play, and then bring forth such a weakling as this, is certainly not apparent. It is scarcely extravagant to state that anyone familiar with stage business could produce a better play without any severe mental tax.... There is a chorus of pretty girls, several of whom have good voices, but the voices do not blend, and in each concerted number there is a total lack of harmony, the soprano voices being overweighted by the altos. The solos, both humorous and sentimental, are introduced at inappropriate times, and the best musical number of the evening... was ruined, when repeated in response to an encore, by two members of the company, who indulged in a piece of clown business that was musty with age, but which nevertheless provoked laughter from people in front who would giggle at a box of monkeys.... Mr. Russell will have to give us something better than he has offered here upon his two visits this season if he wishes to retain metropolitan favor.[786]

Haig remained with Russell's Comedians through the 1890s after which he became the musical director of a summer season of light opera at Duquesne Garden in Pittsburgh, Pennsylvania, beginning 3 June 1901. Subsequent to his position in Pittsburgh, Haig disappeared from theatrical records. He continued to retain a residence in New York through 1920 when he died in the apartment he shared with church organist Edward Grimm and his family. He was buried beside his mother in Linden Grove Cemetery, Covington, Kentucky.

HAMMERSTEIN, Oscar

Theatrical producer, opera impresario, theatre builder, inventor, and composer Oscar Hammerstein was born in Szczecin, Prussia, on 8 May 1848,[787] to a middle-class German-speaking Jewish family. He expressed an interest in music at an early age and studied the violin, flute, and piano, much to the delight of his mother who fostered his musical aspirations but to the displeasure of his father who wanted him to engage in more useful (and lucrative) endeavors. Following the death of his mother when he was fifteen years old, and to escape his often brutal and controlling father, Hammerstein sold his violin for $35 to acquire the money necessary for passage to America and landed in New York City in 1864. He found employment as an apprentice at a Pearl Street cigar shop for $2.00 per week and subsequently invented and patented several practical devices for the manufacture of cigars which earned him a fortune. In addition to creating and editing the *United States Tobacco Journal*, Hammerstein authored three short plays, *Selo Sechsig [Sixty Selo]*, *Antonio*, and *Our Poor Relations*, that were produced at the Thalia Theatre in 1868,[788] and in 1870 he became the manager of the Stadt Theatre in the Bowery and later co-manager (with Adolf Neuendorff) of the Germania Theatre. In the late 1880s, Hammerstein began building his own theatres, beginning with the Harlem Opera House (1889), and including the Columbus Theatre (1890); the first Manhattan Opera House (1892), afterwards Koster and Bial's Music Hall (1893); the Olympia(1895); the Victoria (1899); the Republic (1900); the second Manhattan Opera House (1906); the Philadelphia Opera House (1908); the London Opera House (1911); and the Lexington Avenue Opera House (1913).

Known primarily as the opera impresario whose productions rivaled those of the Metropolitan Opera and who ultimately was paid $1,200,000 by the Metropolitan Opera Company to stop producing operas in New York and other major cities, Hammerstein was also a composer and dance arranger of great ability who created both words and music and supervised the production of several musical theatre works of interest. *The Koh-i-noor*, an operetta about the theft of a valuable diamond, which opened at Koster and Bial's Music Hall on 30 October 1893, was said to have been written and composed in forty-two hours, under the conditions of a bet.[789] In spite of its hasty genesis, the operetta earned positive reviews, with the *New York Clipper* proclaiming that "The *Koh-i-noor* proved itself to be a gem of considerable value, even if it contained some flaws to mar its sparkle. There are several good choruses in it, and much of the music is of the jingle order, an element conducive to comic opera success. There is no dialogue to speak of, and the verse will compare favorably with many more pretentious works."[790]

Hammerstein's next original effort, the spectacular comic opera and ballet *Marguerite*, based on the Faust legend, was produced at the Olympia Music Hall on 10 February 1896. In Hammerstein's version, Marguerite was married to Faust, an artist whose sole ambition was to paint a nude that was beyond reproach. Mephisto, a models' agent, offered to provide the perfect subject for the work if Faust would sign a contract to appear in Hades for an unlimited engagement. To prove his supernatural powers, Mephisto waved a dragon-headed staff, which he claimed would conjure up the most beautiful women in the world, unless, of course, the staff should fall into the hands of a person of pure spirit, in which case his powers would be destroyed. Faust signed the document and witnessed the conjuring of a bevy of beautiful women in dances and *poses plastiques*. The first group danced a minuet in the style of Louis XV, followed by Oriental dancers, Circus performers, the "March of the Hussars," French dancers performing the cancan, and a wedding procession before pure-spirited Marguerite managed to take possession of the staff. Mephisto and the women disappeared and in their place materialized a Gothic cathedral accompanied by the voices of an invisible choir. Reviewers praised the imagination and composition of the spectacle but devoted most of their approbation to the dances which they found the most appealing part of the production.[791]

Santa Maria, Hammerstein's opera about a king who sent a soldier to find a long-lost son but found a long-lost daughter instead, inaugurated the Olympia Theatre season on 24 September 1896.[792] Although critics found the libretto naïve, they praised the production and found the music "singable" "pleasing" and "decidedly catchy" if somewhat reminiscent.[793] Especially notable in the score was the "Santa Maria March," the "trio" of which is excerpted in example 93a. Following a lengthy fanfare, the deceptive cadence in measures 12–13 is particularly effective since measures 8–12 prepare the ear for a resolution in the key of A, not its upper mediant C. The result, however, is smooth since the E7 chord resolves to its upper mediant G creating a gentle surprise rather than a striking tonal shift. Also noteworthy is the use of melodic non-chordal tones on the downbeat of measures 13, 15, 17, 19, 21, and 23, creating forward motion toward resolution which enhances the energy of the march.

Hammerstein's subsequent musical theatre compositions included *Mrs. Radley Barton's Ball, or, In Great New York* (22 March 1897);[794] *War*

Example 93a. "Santa Maria March" from *Santa Maria*

Bubbles (16 May 1898), for which Hammerstein composed the crowd-pleasing "Dewey March" for the hero of the Battle of Manila Bay in the Spanish-American War;[795] *Sweet Marie* (10 October 1901), a spectacular musical comedy about the effect of the provisions of a will on the marriages of two sisters;[796] *Punch, Judy and Company* (1 June 1903), a "tuneful" extravaganza;[797] and *Parsifalia* (6 June 1904), a burlesque of the true story of Metropolitan Opera manager Heinrich Conried's production of Richard Wagner's *Parsifal* against the wishes of Wagner's widow,[798] for which Hammerstein composed an effective and jaunty "Firemen's March" (example 93b).

Example 93b. "Firemen's March" from *Parsifalia*

After 1906 when he began producing opera at the Manhattan Opera House, Hammerstein produced no more original musical theatre compositions, focusing instead on the artistic and financial problems of maintaining a solvent opera company. If the years when he was producing opera were the happiest of his life, those following the Metropolitan buy-out in 1910 were among the saddest, filled with litigations, bankruptcies, a divorce, and the deaths of three of his four sons in 1914. For some time he had suffered with diabetes and in late July 1919 he was taken to the Lenox Hill Hospital due to complications from the disease. Three days later he lapsed into a coma and died on 1 August, survived by his third wife, Mary Emma Swift,[799] his son Arthur, and his daughters, Rose and Stella. At the end of his obituary in *The New York Times*, Hammerstein was quoted, giving a summary of his life:

> "I've had the ideas," he once said in talking of his career, "but I've worked harder just getting them than most men do in the course of a whole lifetime, to say nothing of put-

ting them into execution. I have guarded my health zealously. I live a life of incredible simplicity—I never drink and I smoke only twenty-five cigars a day. Don't think in telling you this that I'm boasting of my qualifications for a proscenium-box seat up above, for I have no immediate desire to leave my life of usefulness here to go to heaven, where there is sure to be a chorus which I have not selected, like as not with wings, too."[800]

HAND, Edward Carl

Pianist, composer, and musical director Edward Carl Hand (often cited simply as Carl Hand) first appeared in theatrical notices in June 1899 as the musical director for the summer season of the Kennedy Players, following which he joined the Elroy Stock Company at Elizabeth, New Jersey on 14 August.[801] He was the leader of Lindell's Concert Orchestra, at Bar Harbor, Maine, during the summer 1900 and engaged as the musical director for the Jerre McAuliffe Stock Company selecting and arranging incidental music for *The Electrician*, *Under Sealed Orders*, and *The Man-o'-War's Man* during the 1900–1901 season.[802] Before the end of the season, however, Hand left the McAuliffe organization to become the musical director for Rider's touring *Night Owls* Company and J.J. Flynn's *My Aunt's Nephew* Company, prior to signing on as composer and musical director for Heath's *Peck's Bad Boy* Company opening the 1901–1902 season on 21 September 1901 at Marlboro, Massachusetts.[803] During the tour of *Peck's Bad Boy*, Hand composed the music for a comic opera called *Sweet Annie Moore*,[804] with a libretto by John Varden. Hand attached himself briefly to the *High Rollers* Company in Louisville, Kentucky, before rejoining *Peck's Bad Boy* for its summer tour of Maine, New Hampshire, and Vermont starting on 7 June 1902. He was engaged for the 1902–1903 season as the musical director for the Bryne Brothers production of *Le Voyage en Suisse*, after which he conducted the summer tour of J.J. Flynn's *The Trolley Party*, and joined the Rose Hill English Folly Company for the next three seasons. He toured with *The New Errand Boy* Company during the 1906–1907 season and provided the score and musical direction for *Patsy in Politics* (book by Joe Doe, lyrics by Seymour Furth), produced at the Fourteenth Street Theatre (2 September 1907) and on tour by the P.H. Sullivan Amusement Company.[805] In subsequent years Hand became musical director for orchestras on the Orpheum (vaudeville) Circuit. The last mention of his name appeared during the summer 1916 in Boston, when he conducted his orchestra on a vaudeville bill at Loew's Orpheum Theatre:

> Keystone comedy, "The Two O'Clock Train," was on No. 4 and got the usual laughs. The picture was helped along a great deal by Carl Hand's Orchestra, which, by the way, can hold their own with any here in the East.[806]

HARRISON, E[dward]

Composer and "trick" violinist E. Harrison was first associated with Shorey, Carle, Duprez, and Green's New Orleans Metropolitan Opera Troupe and Brass Band, a minstrel company that toured throughout the United States in the 1859–1860 season. He joined Wood's Minstrels in June 1860 and toured with them for several seasons before accepting a position with Sullivan's Hibernian Bards or Irish Minstrels for the 1865–1866 season[807] at the conclusion of which he advertised:

> MR. E. HARRISON,
> Leader, Plays Violin, Harp and Piano, can be engaged to travel, or for any Watering Place during the Summer, by applying to
> >Frank Rivers and Company
> >Dramatic Agents
> >25 West Houston Street, New York.[808]

Harrison was engaged as leader of the orchestra at the Opera House in Rochester, New York, for the 1866–1867 season, after which he toured as orchestra leader with J. Holmes Grover, the celebrated Irish comedian. However, by the summer of 1869, he was again advertising for work, this time adding "composer" to his list of abilities.[809] Following a stint with the Gilbert Sisters' Company in the early 1870s, Harrison was engaged by producer Augustin Daly to compose the score for *Around the World in Eighty Days*, a dramatization by James H. Connelly and Charles M. Pillet of Jules Verne's novel scheduled to open at the Grand Opera House on 16 August 1875. For the spectacular production, Harrison composed an appropriately spectacular score featuring an Amazonian March, as well as a variety of exotic dances, and incidental music to accompany a railroad disaster, an Indian massacre, a Chinese festival, and the sinking of a ship. In spite of positive reviews,[810] the production lasted only two weeks in New York City and was prevented from going on tour by an injunction procured by producers Imre and Bolossy Kiralfy who claimed that they alone owned the American rights to the property and that Connelly and Pillet had infringed upon those rights.[811] Three years later, Harrison was dead, having drowned in Providence, Rhode Island.[812]

HEARTZ, Harry L[awson]

Harry L. Heartz (also cited as H.L. Heartz) was born in Charlestown, Massachusetts, a community north of Boston, on 21 January 1869. Belonging to a family of musicians, he was educated in music from an early age in preparation for a musical career. At Columbia University he studied the piano and music theory with composer Edward MacDowell, but after only two years of college he left to assume the post of organist and choir director at All Souls' Unitarian Church in Roxbury, Massachusetts. His first theatrical venture occurred in 1896 when he was engaged to create the piano score and serve as accompanist for the First Corps of Cadets' amateur production of Robert Barnet's *The Strange Adventures of Jack in the Beanstalk* at the Tremont Theatre, Boston, 10–15 February 1896. He continued his association with both Barnet and the Cadets at the Tremont Theatre until 1902 composing songs and dance music for *Queen of the Ballet* (7–12 February 1898), *Miladi and the Musketeer* (5–10 February 1900), and *The Cap of Fortune and the Show Girl* (3–8 February 1902).[813] For the ballet in *Miladi and the Musketeer*, Heartz composed a sparkling and robust mazurka (example 94), exhibiting an adroit command of the musical style as well as a gifted facility for creating melodic and harmonic variety.

In addition to his work for First Corps of Cadets, Heartz composed the score for *Miss Simplicity*, a Barnet comedy commissioned by the Bank Officers' Association of Boston for amateur production at the Tremont Theatre in February 1901. Heartz's early association with amateurs proved to be a golden opportunity in the long run, for each of the shows he had composed was given a professional production on Broadway. *Queen of the Ballet*, for which Heartz had originally composed a brief ballet sequence and a charming schottische dance, appeared at the Fifth Avenue Theatre on 25 December 1899, with a new title, *Three Little Lambs*; *Miladi and the Musketeer*, for which Heartz composed the majority of the songs and half

Example 94. "Mazurka" from Miladi and the *Musketeer*

the ballet music, appeared at Hammerstein's Victoria Theatre on 11 February1901 as *My Lady*;[814] *Miss Simplicity*, for which Heartz composed the lion's share of the songs and dance music, appeared at the Casino Theatre under its original title on 10 February 1901;[815]and *The Cap of Fortune and the Show Girl*, for which Heartz composed dance music and about half of the songs, moved to Wallacks Theatre as *The Show Girl, or, The Cap of Fortune* on 5 may 1902.[816] The positive notices that Heartz received for his efforts did not go unnoticed by performer, composer, librettist Richard Carle who invited Heartz to compose the music for his new musical comedy vehicle *The Tenderfoot* which opened at the Dearborn Theatre in Chicago on 12 April 1903 and moved to the New York Theatre on 22 February 1904 after an extended tryout tour. Reviews for Heartz's music were especially positive: "Mr. Hertz [sic] has contributed very good music in the main, and several of his numbers were decidedly meritorious. His tendency toward the noisy kind of music, which was so noticeable in his other works shown here, has been subdued to some extent, although it comes to the surface at intervals in *The Tenderfoot*."[817] One of the hits of the production was an eccentric dance (performed by William Rock, as Hop Lee, a Chinese servant, and Ethel Johnson, as a waif), published in the vocal score as "Dance: Two-Step" and separately as "Hop Lee: Chi-

Example 95. "Hop Lee: Chinese Dance" from *The Tenderfoot*

nese Dance." The syncopated ragtime time dance in the vocal score was amplified by a fifty-measure introduction of pseudo "Chinese" music employing a hexachordal melody accompanied by relentless pounding eighth notes in parallel fifths. The ragtime dance that followed (of which example 95 is a segment) is notable for its stop-time (measures 3–4, 7–8) and for the *glissandi* indicated in measures 19–20 and 23–24. The stop-time measures were found in both published versions of the dance music, but the *glissandi* were only published in "Hop Lee" indicating that Heartz subtly revised the dance music to fit the choreography and stage business.

Following *The Tenderfoot*, Heartz and Carle produced *The Hurdy Gurdy Girl*, which opened at the Tremont Theatre in Boston on 3 June 1907 before moving to Wallack's Theatre in New York on 23 September. The Boston reviews were very complimentary to Heartz's music, particularly that in the *Boston Daily Globe*:

> Musically *The Hurdy Gurdy Girl* is enjoyable. The score was written by H.L. Heartz who has done much excellent work here in the past. His music is brightly tuneful and reasonably original. "The Hurdy Gurdy Girl" song is a charming melody, and the theme is cleverly woven through the entire score. It is also played on a real hurdy gurdy, and furnishes a touch of realism to several of the scenes that is thoroughly appreciated by the audience.
>
> There are three or four dainty melodies that are sure to become popular with the whistling fraternity. Several of the concerted numbers are of real musical value. Particularly charming is the tea party quartet in the second act, and the finale of the first act is another exceptionally good number. The instrumental setting is excellent and is efficiently interpreted by a large orchestra.[818]

Particularly interesting was the dance and incidental music Heartz composed for the opening number, in which members of various employments in New York City were introduced in song and dance. The first to appear were the cab drivers who sang and danced a bright galop; next to arrive were the French wine merchants who sang and danced a sophisticated Viennese waltz. The milkmen entered to a schottische tune, followed by the postmen, newsboys, and street cleaners, all of whom sang in schottische fashion and danced a duple time schottische dance. A "paraphrase of Irish melodies" introduced a group of chauvinistic workingmen who requested that a German band play Irish tunes (accompanied by the sound of a German band) and aggressively sang and danced a robust march about "Strike! Strike! Strike!"

Heartz's final association with Richard Carle, *The Boy and the Girl*, was commissioned by the Bank Officers Association of Boston for a Tremont Theatre production in February 1908 and produced at the roof garden atop the New Amsterdam Theatre on 31 May 1909.[819] Another production, *Mary's Lamb* at the New York Theatre (25 May 1908), was an adaptation by Carle (who also composed the music) of a French farce that interpolated Heartz's music for "Love Is Elusive" from the score of *The Tenderfoot*. Following *The Boy and the Girl*, Heartz retired from the musical theatre and devoted his time and efforts to his position as Church organist and music editor for a Boston music publishing firm. In 1907 he edited *A Catechism of Music* by J. Jousse, and in 1911 he assembled and published *The Church Festival Organist: A Collection of Thirty-Two Standard Organ Selections for the Church Festivals throughout the Year*. A later work, *The Two-Part Choir* was published in 1937, and Heartz remained active well into the 1940s, after which he disappeared from public accounts.

HEIN, Silvio

The son of a Viennese immigrant, composer, dance arranger, and musical director Silvio Hein was born in New York City on 15 March 1879. He received a musical education in Trieste, Italy, and Vienna, Austria, and had composed an opera when he was still a teenager.[820] After he returned to New York, he began his theatrical career by contributing the music for a song, "I Could Be Happy with Either One," added to the score of *Nancy Brown* (16 February 1903). Hein provided musical direction and composed the entire score of his next musical theatre work, *Moonshine* (libretto by Edwin Milton Royle and George V. Hobart) (30 October 1905),[821] a feat he repeated in *Marrying Mary* (book by Edwin Milton Royle, lyrics by Benjamin Hapgood Burt) (27 August 1906).[822] Hein's subsequent theatre compositions included the song "Moonshine" (lyrics by George V. Hobart and Edward Montagu) for the May Irwin vehicle, *Mrs. Wilson, That's All* (5 November 1906); the song "I Want to be a Drummer Boy" (lyrics by Matt Woodward) in the *Follies of 1907* (8 July 1907); the score and musical direction for *The Boys and Betty* (libretto by George V. Hobart) (2 November 1908); the song "The Laugh with a Tear in It" (with Chauncey Olcott) for *Ragged Robin* (24 January 1910); the score for *The Yankee Girl* (libretto by George V. Hobart) (10 February 1910);[823] and the score for *A Matinée Idol* (libretto by Armand and Barnard, based on Molière's play, *A Doctor in Spite of Himself*) (28 April 1910).[824] Hein composed the music for several dance routines in *A Matinée Idol* including a dainty schottische dance appended to "Nonsense," a jovial song about the silly things people say; a jaunty ragtime dance (example 96a) based on the melody of "The Rag-Time Barn Dance," a number suggesting that syncopated ragtime music is the way to win a woman's heart; and the "Hypnotic Dance" (example 96b), an infectious and mesmerizing waltz through which a self-proclaimed hypnotist demonstrates his powers.

Example 96a. Dance in "The Rag-Time Barn Dance" from *A Matinée Idol*

Example 96b. "Hypnotic Dance" from *A Matinée Idol*

Hein's subsequent musical theatre compositions included *Judy Forgot* (libretto by Avery Hopwood) (6 October 1910);[825] the song "Deedle-Dee-Dum (The Deedle-Dum-Dee)" (lyrics by Benjamin Hapgood Burt) in *The Wall Street Girl* (15 April 1912);[826] and *When Dreams Come True* (libretto by Philip Bartholomae) (18 August 1913), for which he composed the music for "The Santley Tango" (example 97), a sensuous tango flirting with the juxtaposition of major and minor modes, effectively performed in the production by Joseph Santley.[827]

With Philip Bartholomae, Hein composed *Gloriana* (Chicago, 12 October 1913);[828] *The Model Maid* (Providence, Rhode Island 17 August 1914);[829] *Miss Daisy* (a revision of *The Model Maid*) (New York 9 September 1914);[830] *At the Ball* (book by Bartholomae and Alice Gerstenberg) (Chicago, 25 December 1914);[831] and the vaudeville sketches at the Palace Theatre, *One of the Boys* and *Woman Proposes* (17 May 1915).[832] With Benjamin Hapgood Burt, Hein composed two songs ("[When You're] All Dressed Up and No Place to Go" and 'Twas in September") for *The Beauty Shop* (13 April 1914); the song, "Some Little Bug Will Find You Some

Example 97. "The Santley Tango" from *When Dreams Come True*

Day" (lyrics also by Roy Atwell) interpolated into Franz Lehár's score for *Alone at Last* (19 October 1915);[833] and the song "Eyes Have a Language" used in *Betty* (3 October 1916). "Some Little Bug Will Find You Some Day" had already been used in Hein's score for *All Over Town*, Joseph Santley and Harry B. Smith's musical variation on the Faust legend that opened in New Haven of 26 April 1915.[834]

Critics found the dances to be the most entertaining elements of the production of which the "Eccentric Dance" (example 98), the "Pierrette Dances" (example 99), and "The Parisian Trot" (example 100) are perhaps the most interesting musically. The "Eccentric Dance" occurred immediately after the opening number with an audience assembling to

Example 97 (continued). "The Santley Tango" from *When Dreams Come True*

view an opera at the Metropolitan Opera House. A Hat Boy appeared and proceeded to make a nuisance of himself, checking hats and coats to the syncopated music of the dance.

The hero of the piece, Reggie Faust, fell asleep during the opera (a production of Gounod's *Faust*) and dreamed that he was an old man who had made a bargain with the Devil's emissary Howitt Burns to seduce the man's wife in order to regain his youth. The "Pierrette Dances" occurred in act two of the dream, when young Reggie Faust was in the process of learning how to seduce women. During the dance, Reggie (played by Joseph Santley) practiced the art of seduction with Doris, the fiancée of his girlfriend's brother.

"The Parisian Trot," the final dance number in the dream, was performed by Reggie Faust and a character named Gloria Gay as one last hurrah before Reggie, having failed to seduce Burns's wife, turns back into an old man. Note that the music for the dance is in two parts: a common time fox trot in a moderate tempo using the schottische devices of dotted notes and triplets, followed by a faster and highly syncopated ragtime dance in 2/4.

Prior to *All Over Town*, Hein had composed songs and cabaret music for *Experience* (27 October 1914) and subsequent projects included the scores for *The Bare Idea*,[835] the film *Charity* (October 1916), the musicals *The Bride Shop* (1917),[836] *The Red Clock* (30 September 1917),[837] *Furs and Frills* (9 October 1917),[838] *Flo-Flo* (20 December 1917),[839] *The Golden Goose* (29 November 1917),[840] *He Didn't Want to Do It* (20 August

Example 98. "Eccentric Dance" from *All Over Town*

1918),[841] *Miss Blue Eyes* (3 October 1918),[842] *Suite 16*,[843] *Lady Kitty, Inc.*,[844] *Look Who's Here* (2 March 1920), *The New Dictator* (8 March 1920),[845] *The Girl From Home* (3 May 1920),[846] *The Old Home Town*,[847] and *Some Party* (15 April 1922).[848]

As a producer and theatre manager, Hein mounted Shakespeare's *The Merry Wives of Windsor*, opening in Albany, New York on 16 October 1916 prior to a New York City run at the Park Theatre (8 January 1917).[849] The production earned good reviews: "As a production it can be classed with the best," announced the critic from the *New York Clipper*, "and speaks well for Manager Hein's first attempt as a producer."[850] Hein's

Example 99. "Pierrette Dances" from *All Over Town*

first experience as a producer was also his last for as soon as *The Merry Wives of Windsor* had closed, he returned to his career as musical director for *His Little Widows* (AKA *The Six Winning Widows*) (30 April 1917),[851] *Hurrah for the Girls* (16 December 1918),[852] and *The Elusive Lady* (25 September 1922). [853]

In spring 1924 Hein was among the delegation of songwriters sent to Washington by the American Society of Composers, Authors, and Publishers (ASCAP) to try to discourage Congress from passing legislation that would exempt radio broadcasters from having to pay for the use of copyrighted music. Because of the efforts of the delegation, songwriters

Example 100. "The Parisian Trot" from All Over Town

were granted royalties for the radio transmission of their compositions.[854] Not long after the trip to Washington, Hein suffered a serious mental and physical breakdown, and he was sent to the North Woods Sanitarium at Saranac Lake, New York, where he spent the last four years of his life. He died on 19 December 1928 at Saranac Lake in the company of his wife and mother. At his funeral Rabbi Nathan D. Krass of Temple Emanu-El delivered the eulogy, which read in part:

> Silvio Hein was an artist who wove out of the strands of melody, beautiful, glorious and stirring songs that brought cheer and delight to thousands of his fellow men,

Example 100 (continued). "The Parisian Trot" from *All Over Town*

who were uplifted and diverted from their tragedies and sorrows on the wings of song. He was admired because he was noted in his chosen field of activity and among his artistic friends he loomed large, ranking in the foreground.

He was a fine composer of melody, but he composed even more; he composed troubled human hearts, lifting them out of their pain, lessening their grief and minimizing their sorrow. In the northern region of the State [Saranac Lake] they call him "the angel of mercy" among the underprivileged, heartbroken, suffering derelicts of mankind.[855]

HEINDL, [Robert] Anton [Antoine]

Born in Boston on 13 September 1878, Anton Heindl was the son of cellist and music educator Alexander Heindl who played principal cello in the Boston Symphony Orchestra.[856] Musically trained by his father, Heindl became the musical director of the *Gay Parisians* Company, touring throughout the 1895–1896 season, during which time it was reported that he was also composing a comic opera.[857] During the summer of the following year he was the musical director of the open-air amphitheatre at Madison Square Garden where he assisted composer Noah Brandt in the production of his musical *Captain Cook*.[858] Heindl later toured as musical director for *In At-*

lantic City beginning in September 1897. In 1902, he composed "A Song of Yesterday" (lyrics by Rida Johnson Young) for the tour of *The Sultan of Sulu*, and in 1903 he was engaged by Alfred E. Aarons as musical director for *The Knickerbocker Girl* and rehired as musical director for Aarons's *A China Doll* in 1904.[859] Subsequent musical direction assignments included John Philip Sousa's *The Free Lance* (16 April 1906), Reginald De Koven's *The Golden Butterfly* (12 October 1908),[860] Leo Fall's *The Girl on the Train* (3 October 1910), Franz Lehár's *The Count of Luxembourg* (16 September 1912), and Rudolf Friml's *The Little Whopper* (13 October 1919), *The Vagabond King* (21 September 1925), and *White Eagle* (26 December 1927).

In addition to his duties as musical director, Heindl also (uncredited, of course) arranged and adapted dance music for productions that included *Hip! Hip! Hooray* (10 October 1907), *The Little Café* (10 November 1913), and *Up She Goes* (6 November 1922). Of particular interest is his composition, "The Gobble Glide" (example 101), advertised on the cover as "Song Hits from the Comic Opera Success *The Beauty Spot*" and as "Staged by Joseph C. Smith." Since neither the song nor the choreographer appeared in the New York City program for De Koven's *The Beauty Spot* (10 April 1909), theatre scholar Donald J. Stubblebine argued for the existence of a failed *Beauty Spot* production in 1906, composed by Samuel Lehman and Anton Heindl.[861] However, since "The Gobble Glide" was published in 1911, it is difficult to believe that its cover would have advertised an association with a failed production five years earlier. A more feasible explanation might be that Heindl's number was an interpolation either late in the run, or inserted for the national tour of *The Beauty Spot* which extended through 1911 and beyond. In any case, example 101 presents the "B" section of the dance, a highly syncopated, danceable, and entertaining ragtime composition.

On 29 May 1911, Heindl conducted the revival of *The Country Girl* at the Herald Square Theatre,[862] and in August he was engaged as general musical director for the new producing firm of Dreyfus and Fellner.[863] A year later he became the favored musical director for the [Marc] Klaw and [A.L] Erlanger organization. In 1916, he served as musical director for Herbert Beerbohm Tree's production of *King Henry VIII* at the New Amsterdam Theatre, and in February 1917, Heindl succeeded Max Hoffman as musical director of Cocoanut Grove, the theatre on the roof of the Century Theatre.[864] He served as musical director for the New Haven premiere of Silvio Hein's *The Golden Goose* (3 December 1917), and subsequent assignments included the second season of *The Night Boat* at the Liberty Theatre[865] and *Lola in Love* at the Grand Theatre in Wilkes-Barre, Pennsylvania.[866] After conducting

Example 101. "The Gobble Glide" from *The Beauty Spot*

Friml's *White Eagle* during the 1927–1928 season, Anton Heindl retired to his home in Nassau County New York, with this wife Ana whom he married in Hoboken, New Jersey, in 1912. He died at home on 28 January 1932.

HEINRICH, Anthony [Anton] Philip [Philipp]

Born in Schönbüchel, Bohemia, on 11 March 1781, composer Anthony Philip Heinrich was the adopted son of a wealthy uncle from whom he inherited land, buildings, and a thriving business. As a boy he was given lessons on the violin and piano, and soon after he taught himself the rudiments of music theory, harmony, and counterpoint and began composing by instinct.[867] He came to the United States in 1805[868] and again in 1810, in the hope of extending his business affairs across the Atlantic, but the Napoleonic Wars (1803–1815) and the financial collapse in Austria (1811) gradually managed to destroy his prospects in Europe as well as in America.[869] It was reported that, in a kind of ironic prescience, Heinrich was acting as musical director of the Southwark Theatre in Philadelphia during the 1816–1817 season when he received the news that he was bankrupt.[870] Not long after, he set out for Pittsburgh, crossing the Allegheny Mountains on foot, and eventually he set up shop in a log cabin in Bardstown, Kentucky, where he began a solitary existence in the wilderness, composing music based on his observations of the natural universe. During this time Heinrich wrote a series of compositions under the umbrella title of *The Western Minstrel* (1820), one of which, "Gipsey [sic] Dance" (example 102) provides an interesting insight into his rough and improvisatory compositional style. The excerpt exhibits a wildly exciting contrapuntal dance filled with clashing suspensions and dramatic retardations that disguise a traditional tonic-subdominant-dominant harmonic structure. The viscerally exhilarating and ruggedly original first sixteen measures of the dance resolve to a highly imitative cadence (measures 17–22) evocative of late eighteenth-century Western European music.

According to Richard J. Wolfe, Heinrich traveled to London in 1827 to study music and returned to America in the early 1830s, serving as a church organist in Boston. From about 1833, he returned to London where he performed in the orchestras of Drury Lane, Covent Garden, and Vauxhall Gardens with his prized Cremona violin, which he had acquired during a visit to the island of Malta, until the instrument was accidently destroyed by a careless musician in the Drury Lane orchestra.[871] Following brief stays in Grätz, Austria, in 1836, and Bordeaux, near the eastern border of France, in 1837, Heinrich settled in New York City where he was considered America's first professional composer and dubbed "the Beethoven of America" by critics. As David Barron suggested:

> Although eccentric, occasionally rough, and unusually complex and elaborate, [Heinrich's] works are truly expressive and never without interest. The sources of his musical style are found in Haydn and to some extent Beethoven, but they have the greater ornateness of Italian opera and often a freer use of chromaticism both melodically and

Example 102. "Gypsey Dance" from *The Western Minstrel*

harmonically. Heinrich's melodic style is strongly influenced by classical dance music, and melodic quotation plays an important role in his compositional technique, particularly self-quotation and the quotation of popular, patriotic tunes.... The forms Heinrich favored most are those of the dance and the theme with variations.[872]

Heinrich's hundreds of compositions included "An Allemande," "Fair Haidée's Waltz," "A German Hopsassa Dance" and "Yankee Doodle Waltz," in *The Dawning of Music in Kentucky* (1820); "The Minstrel's March, or, Road to Kentucky" and "Philadelphia Waltz," in *The Western Minstrel*

(1920); an undated melodrama, *The Child of the Mountain*; the oratorios *Des Christen Tod* [*The Christian's Death*] (1836) and *The Wild Woods' Spirits Chant* (1845); the lost opera, *The Minstrel* (1835); and the lost oratorios, *The Ornithological Combat of Kings* (1837) and the undated *The Maiden Queen*.[873] Heinrich's compositions were known and respected on both sides of the Atlantic Ocean and in 1857 his works were performed in three concerts in Prague (some sources even suggest performances in Paris and Vienna), one of which was devoted entirely to Heinrich's orchestral music.[874] In spite of his earlier fame, however, Heinrich spent his final years in poverty and obscurity and died after a lingering illness at his boarding house in New York City on 3 May 1861.

HERBERT, Victor [Augustus]

Composer, dance arranger, and musical director Victor Herbert was born in Dublin on 1 February 1859, the son of artist Edward Herbert and Fanny Lover, daughter of the celebrated composer, artist, and writer Samuel Lover. Herbert's father died when his son was three years old and his mother later married a German doctor named Carl Schmid whom she had met when she and Victor traveled to Germany in order to further his education.[875] When Herbert was an adolescent, the family moved to Stuttgart where he received his secondary-school education at the Gymnasium and studied the cello with Bernhard Cossmann. In 1881 Herbert joined the cello section of the Royal Court Orchestra in Stuttgart and began several years of study with Max Seiffritz, the orchestra conductor, who taught Herbert harmony, counterpoint, and orchestration.[876] During this period Herbert composed his *Suite for Cello and Orchestra* (1883), his *Cello Concerto No. 1 in D Major* (1884), and two pieces for cello and piano (*Berceuse* and *Scherzino*). In 1885 he joined the faculty of the Neue Stuttgarter Musikschule but remained there for only a year, for on 14 August 1886, Herbert married soprano Therese Foerster in Vienna and soon after, the couple sailed for New York City where both had been engaged by the Metropolitan Opera, she as a principal soloist, and he as cellist in the orchestra.[877] Not long after his arrival in New York, Herbert became a professor at the National Conservatory of Music (whose director was composer Antonin Dvořák) and in 1889 he was hired as pianist, soloist, and assistant conductor for The Worcester [Massachusetts] Festival, a position he held for three seasons, and where, in the 1891 season, Herbert premiered his cantata, *The Captive*, to mostly negative reviews.[878]

Late in 1892, Herbert began composing for the theatre, first collaborating with Steele MacKaye on *Columbus*, a huge spectacle designed for the Columbian Exposition in Chicago (1893) that ultimately fell through, and next with Francis Neilson on *La Vivandiere*, his first completed operetta that was never produced.[879] The first of Herbert's 46 produced operettas was *Prince Ananias* (libretto by Francis Neilson) (20 November 1994) but his first successful musical theatre work was *The Wizard of the Nile* (libretto by Harry B. Smith) (4 November 1895). Herbert composed delightfully descriptive incidental music for Kibosh, the ersatz wizard, be-

Example 103. "Kibosh pursued by Alligator" from *The Wizard of the Nile*

ing chased by an alligator. Example 103 displays the first nine measures of the piece during which the pursuit occurs, after which Kibosh climbs up a palm tree, and the alligator "disappears slowly in disgust."

Most of Herbert's subsequent operettas were rich in incidental and dance music. Set in Madrid, *The Serenade* (libretto by Harry B. Smith) (16 March 1897) contains a lively comic march, dramatic incidental music, and characteristic Spanish dances. Set in Hungary, *The Fortune Teller* (Harry B. Smith) (26 September 1898) abounds in czardas-like Hungarian dances, mazurkas, polkas, and a Farandole (with stage choreography marked in the score). Set in Austria, *The Singing Girl* (Harry B. Smith and Stanislaus Stange) (23 October 1899) presents a ländler, a galop, a schottische hiccup dance (with stage business indicated in the score), a mazurka, a schottische, and a wedding march. *The Ameer* (libretto by Frederick Ranken and Kirk La Shelle) (4 December 1899) is set in Afghanistan and includes a military march and several dance breaks in a number entitled "Continuous Performances," satirizing vaudeville and society's need to be constantly entertained. The first series of dances are in schottische rhythm to represent the "tripping triplets from the town of Tipperary" in the lyrics; the second is a jig (example 104) to correspond to the Irish-isms in the lyrics: "Arrah Dinnis O'Grady your conduct's quite shady,/Shure that's not the way to be treatin' a lady, A-straddle a saddle an' dancin' a jig." Note how the accompaniment relentlessly pounds every beat of the dance, and note also the repetitions in the jigging melody: measures 1–2 are the same; measure 3 is different only by the addition of an eighth note at the beginning of the measure; measures 5–8 are exactly the same as measures 1–4; measures 9–10 are the same, measures 11–12 are the same; and measures 13–14 are a repetition of measures 9–10. The insistent attack on Denis O'Grady in the lyrics is replicated through the pounding beat and repetitions of the melodic phrases in the dance music.

Herbert's celebrated *Babes in Toyland* (Glen MacDonough) (13 October 1903) is perhaps most famous for its title song and the "March of the Toys," but that is only a fragment of the dance music that permeates the score. An extended "Country Dance" opened the show with a stately, if rustic, mazurka. "Floretta" was followed by a lively Hungarian dance, stylistically borrowed from the Hungarian dances of Brahms and rhapsodies of Liszt; and the first act ended in a ballet, "The Birth of the Butterfly," for which the music portrayed a gossamer-spun cocoon, the tension created by the larva seeking its release, and finally the materialization of the butterfly. Measures 9–22 of the ballet are displayed in

Example 104. Jig in "Continuous Performances" from *The Ameer*

example 105. Note the constant movement of scale-wise intervals first in the accompaniment ("e-d-e-d-e-d-e-d" in measure 1, for example) and then in the inner voices of the treble staff ("e-f-e-f-e" in measure 6; "f-g-f-g-f" in measure 8), and then finally in the melodic line beginning with measure 9. The ascent of that motif from the lower voices to those higher anticipated the incarnation of the butterfly as it emerged from its cocoon.

In the second act, the "March of the Toys" was followed by "The Military Ball" which incorporated toy instruments in a suite of dances that included a waltz and a galop; and an extended gavotte ended the act. The third act opened with "In the Toymaker's workshop," a minuet that incor-

"The Birth of the Butterfly" from *Babes in Toyland*

porated toy sounds, such as the crow of a rooster, a doll crying "Mamma," the barking of a dog, the "Moo" of a cow, and the quacking of a duck. The integration of toy instruments and sounds was obviously a special feature of Herbert's dance and incidental music for the show.

Wonderland (Glen MacDonough) (24 October 1905), which had been *Alice in Wonderland* until the show was revamped in Chicago, also displayed Herbert's characteristic instrumental score: descriptive incidental music; a schottische dance ("The Ossified Man"); a Highland fling and galop labelled "Kankakee Indian" in the score ("The Voice for It"); a minuet and Indian dance ("Ball Room Scene"); and a Bowery waltz

("Hallowe'en"). In *The Red Mill* (Henry Blossom) (24 September 1906) Herbert used a bourée ("Whistle It"); extended underscoring ("Finale Act One"); a Spanish Jota and a ragtime encore ("Good-a-bye, John!"); and a Bowery waltz ("The Streets of New York") . For *Little Nemo* (20 October 1908, Herbert composed a schottische dance following "The Happy Land of Once Upon a Time"; a polka in "There's Nothing the Matter with You"; a "Central Park Ballet" during which "various characters pass along illustrating various musical themes": the policeman, nurses rocking baby carriages, the lovers, the birds, "tramp steals baby from carriage and policeman kisses the nurse," a small child enters and picks a dandelion in the grass, "policeman arrests child and leads him off"; ballet music entitled "Valentines"; "March of the Valentines"; "Melodramatic Music"; descriptive incidental music, "The Cannibal Island"; an Indian dance following "Will-o-the-Wisp"; a bourée in "I Guess I Talk Too Much"; "Nemo's Dream of Fourth July," incidental music; and a sleepy waltz finale to "Won't You Be My Valentine?"

The Lady of the Slipper (libretto by James O'Dea, Anne Caldwell, and Lawrence McCarty) (28 October 1912), a Cinderella story, was especially balletic with a minor mode "Witches Ballet," and a galop ("The Ride to the Castle") " in the first act; in act two, a schottische dance ("Them Was Our Childhood Days"); an entire "Ballet Suite" that included an impassioned *pas de deux*, a "Pizzicato (Polka)" (example 106), "Valse lente," and a galop "Finale"; an eccentric dance with a silent final beat in most measures ("Punch Bowl Glide"); and in act three, a polka and galop ("Harlequinade"). The pizzicato element in the ballet was characteristic of many classical ballets, such as Léo Delibes's *Sylvia* (1876), and rarely had Herbert employed it so obviously in his dance music. Herbert's use of the idiom in concert with the *pas de deux*, slow waltz, and galop, all standard ballet fare, provided a self-conscious (perhaps even tongue-in-cheek) sense of importance, or legitimacy to the ballet.

In 1917, Herbert composed *Eileen* (AKA *Hearts of Erin*) (Henry Blossom), an operetta that permitted him to create an entirely Irish-flavored score, including dance music that recalled the finest drones and melodies of Irish jigs and reels. Two years later, he produced *The Velvet Lady* (Blossom) (3 February 1919), an unsuccessful effort, except for Herbert's attempt to adapt his compositional style to include contemporary dance music. He had been including touches of folk, ethnic, and ragtime music in his earlier operettas, so a movement into the area of the foxtrot would seem to be a natural progression. Herbert's inci-

Example 106. "Pizzicato (Polka)" in the "Ballet Suite" from *The Lady of the Slipper*

dental and dance music was true to form. There was dialogue underscore; the obligatory schottische dance ("Tonight's the Night"); polka ("Scandal"); Indian dance ("Little Girl and Boy"); march ("I've Danced to Beat the Band"), one of the rare times that Herbert indicates "repeat for dance" instead of writing separate dance music; bourée ("Merry Wedding Bells"); a Flamenco-inspired Spanish dance after which Herbert provided a foxtrot ("Throwing the Bull"). Example 107, beginning with measure 10 of the dance, displays the main theme of the foxtrot. Note the employment of schottische rhythms, an emphasis on the final beat in measures 1, 3, 9, 11, the syncopation in measure 14, and the silent beats in measures 5–6. Also noteworthy is the rigid on-the-beat regularity of the composition that appears to verify Edward N. Waters's conclusion that "[Herbert] was never comfortable in writing a typical popular song; and in a work made up of nothing else he was very much at a disadvantage."[880]

In addition to composing dance and ballet music for his own shows, Herbert contributed "The Birth of the Century Girl," "The Ballet Loose," "Under the Sea," "The Toy Soldiers," and "Jumping Jacks" to *The Century Girl* (6 November 1916); "The Mosquitos Frolic" and "Falling Leaves" to *Miss 1917* (5 November 1917); "The Circus Ballet" to the *Ziegfeld Follies of 1919* (16 June 1919); "The Birthday of the Dauphin" to the *Ziegfeld Follies of 1921* (21 June 1921); "Farljandio" and "Lace Ballet" ("Weaving My

Example 107. Foxtrot in "Throwing the Bull" from *The Velvet Lady*

Dreams") to the *Ziegfeld Follies of 1922* (5 June 1922); and "Webbing" and "Legend of the Drums" to the *Ziegfeld Follies of 1923* (20 October 1923). In all Herbert contributed music to nine editions of the *Follies* (1917, 1919–1925) but arguably his most famous ballet composed for a show that was not his own was "The Butterfly Ballet" designed for Marilyn Miller in the third act of Jerome Kern's *Sally* (21 December 1920). Following a majestic and musically ornate introduction (example 108), butterflies entered to a lilting waltz, after which moths appeared and danced to a limpid schottische before the music changed to an appoggiatura-filled waltz for a *pas de deux* entitled "The Moth and the Flame." A bright galop-like movement marked "Allegro brillante" completed the ballet which segued immediately into an instrumental version of "Wild Rose," Marilyn Miller's second-act dance number, a sung reprise of "Sally," and an instrumental version of "Look for the Silver Lining," Miller's big first-act number.

In addition to his activities as a composer and dance arranger, Herbert was the leader of the 22nd Regiment Band of the New York National Guard (1893–1898), the musical director of the Pittsburgh Symphony

Example 108. Introduction in "The Butterfly Ballet" from *Sally*

Orchestra from 1898–1904, and creator and conductor of the Victor Herbert Orchestra, 1904–1924. He composed the music for two operas: *Natoma*, which had its world premiere at the Philadelphia Metropolitan Opera House (25 February 1911) and *Madeleine*, which opened at the Metropolitan Opera House in New York (24 January 1914). Both works were critical failures.[881] He also composed incidental music for Charles H. Hoyt's play *A Midnight Bell* (9 April 1896) as well as a symphonic score for Thomas Dixon Jr.'s silent film *The Fall of a Nation* (6 June 1916). Moreover he was among the founders of the American Society of Composers, Authors and Publishers (ASCAP). On 26 May 1924, Victor Her-

Example 108 (continued). Introduction in "The Butterfly Ballet" from *Sally*

bert died of a heart attack climbing up the stairs to visit his doctor.[882] His last composition was said to have been "Romeo, Juliet, Johnny and Jane" (lyrics by Dorothy Parker), performed in the revue *Round the Town* (21 May 1924).

HEWITT, James

Violinist, cellist, composer, and musical director James Hewitt was born in Dartmoor, England, on 4 June 1770, the son of Captain John Hewitt of the Royal Navy. He displayed a prodigious musical ability from an early age and by the time he had reached his early twenties, he had become orchestra leader at the court of King George III, performed in Handel concerts at Westminster Abbey, and played in the orchestra at the Theatre Royal, Drury Lane.[883] He was nominated for membership in the Royal Society of Musicians in November 1791 but his subsequent marriage to a Miss Lamb voided the nomination. After his wife and infant child died in 1792, Hewitt left England on 28 June 1792 and arrived New York City on 5 September [884] where, on 20 September, he advertised a subscription concert for the following day to be presented by himself and other musicians "from the Opera House, Hanover Square, and professional concerts, under the direction of Hadyn, Pleyel, etc., London."[885] Although the advertised credentials have been questioned by historians, Hewitt's concert was a success and during his residence in New York, between 1792 and 1811, he established himself as an important and influential figure in the musical culture of that city. He served as musical director at the John Street Theatre and subsequently at the Park Theatre, where his duties included arranging, adapting, and composing songs, incidental, and dance music, for the musical theatre works in the repertoire. In addition, Hewitt played the organ and directed the choir at Trinity Church, conducted military bands, and organized concerts featuring his own music as well as that of European classical composers.[886] In 1794 he composed the songs and dance music for the opera *Tammany, or, The Indian Chief* (libretto by Anne Julia Hatton) produced on 3 March at the John Street Theatre, and on 24 February 1806, his ballad opera, *The Tars from Tripoli, or a Tribute of Respect to the Mediterranean Heroes*, adapted from Thomas Dibdin's *Naval Pillar*, was performed at the Park.[887] For the production, Hewitt provided three brief dance compositions under the umbrella title "Dance of Sailors": "Fife Hunt," composed in common time, "Danced by Miss Graham," in 6/8, and "Music While Columbia Descends," in 2/4.[888] Other musical theatre works and plays in New York for which Hewitt composed or arranged music included *Harlequin's Vagaries* (14 May 1794); *The Patriot, or Liberty Asserted* (5 June 1794); *Nootka Sound, or, The Adventures of Captain Douglas* (5 June 1794); *Tyranny Suppressed, or, Freedom Triumphant* (23 June 1795); *The Comet, or, He Would Be a Philosopher* (1 February 1797); *The Old Soldier* (9 December 1797); *Douglas* (28 March 1798); *Columbus* (15 May 1799); *The Mysterious Marriage, or The Heirship of Roselva* (5 June 1799); *The Wild Goose Chase, or, Mad Cap of Age Tomorrow* (24 January 1800); *Pizarro in Peru, or, The Death of Rolla* (26 March 1800); *Medea and Jason, or, The Golden Fleece* (17 September 1800); *Knight of Guadalquiver, or Spanish Castle* (5 December 1800); *A Tale of Mystery, or, The Dumb Man of Arpenay* (16 March 1803); *Black Beard* (4 July 1804); *Hunter of the Alps* (22 May 1805); *The Honey Moon* (29 May 1805); *Coronation of Napoleon Bonaparte, Emperor of the Gauls* (31 May 1805); *Lady of the Rock* (17 June 1805); *The Finger Post, or, Five Miles Off* (26 November 1806); *Adrian and Orrila, or, A Mother's Vengeance* (2 September 1807);[889] *Who Wins? or, the Widow's Choice* (12 March 1810); and *Timour the Tartar* (12 September 1912).

On 10 December 1795, Hewitt married Eliza King, daughter of Sir John King of the Royal British Army, who had been educated in Paris and a friend of Napoleon when he first came into prominence.[890] In 1811, the Hewitt family moved to Boston where James became musical director of the Federal Street Theatre and organist at Boston's Trinity Episcopal Church, but in 1816 Hewitt returned to New York with his two eldest sons, and between 1820 and 1825 Hewitt traveled between Boston and New York and also to the southern cities of Charleston, South Carolina, where his friends the Graupners had been involved with the theatre, and Augusta, Georgia, where he conducted a grand oratorio in 1821.[891] In 1825 Hewitt developed facial cancer, an affliction that caused him to resign his position as musical director of the Park Theatre in New York in 1826.[892] Late in 1826, an operation performed in New York was unsuccessful in removing the tumor and Hewitt returned to Boston where he died on 1 August 1827.[893] A letter written to his son, James, on 26 January 1827, offers a glimpse into Hewitt's final days:

> ... my present sufferings are from some part of the jaw being left which was injured at the finishing of the operation before he closed the wound (he had been cutting away part of my nose). I heard him say to his assistant that there appeared some small part yet but he thought it would be of no consequence and did not wish to continue my sufferings—therefore had the wounds closed. ...
> My sufferings are great and my death slow, but certain. I hope my dear James you will be here to receive my last

breath. I feel the want of home—tho every kind attention is paid me here—yet my heart longs once more to behold my family.⁸⁹⁴

In addition to his activities as composer and musical director, Hewitt was also a music publisher who published more than 639 compositions during his lifetime, of which 160 were his own. The other composers whose works he published included William Shield, James Hood, Michael Kelly, as well as Handel, Haydn, and Mozart.⁸⁹⁵ Hewitt's own compositions included hundreds of secular and sacred songs and choral works; orchestral overtures, thirty-nine marches, eleven waltzes and other dance music; five solo instrumental sonatas, four themes and variations, three rondos, and two program (battle) pieces.⁸⁹⁶

HEWITT, John Hill

Composer, playwright, musical director, poet, essayist, educator, flautist, pianist, and organist John Hill Hewitt was born on 11 July 1801 in New York City, the eldest son of composer James Hewitt who did not encourage his first-born's interest in a musical career. Instead, John was apprenticed to a variety of tradesmen, in the hope that he would aspire to a mercantile career. When the seventeen-year-old apprentice announced that he wanted to be a soldier, he was sent to the Military Academy at West Point where he received something of a formal music education from Richard S. Willis, the band master at the Academy, who encouraged the teenager's musical interests.⁸⁹⁷ The other professors, however, failed to make an impression upon him, and when Hewitt was told that he could not graduate with the rest of his class because of his grades, and that he would have to repeat his senior year, he accused the commandant of undermining his graduation and challenged him to a duel (which did not actually take place). He subsequently resigned from West Point and went to work for his father who invited him to participate in a theatrical venture in Augusta, Georgia, as musician, composer, and arranger for the troupe of actors he had assembled. Although the theatre was old and dilapidated, "situated on the banks of the river, and approached by dark and muddy streets,"⁸⁹⁸ the positive spirit of the company prevailed, and from 10 January 1823, when the season opened with an olio of songs and dances followed by a melodrama called *The Snow Storm*, until April when the wooden theatre burned down, John received a first-hand education in show business. After the fire, the elder Hewitt returned to New York, but John who had been charmed by southern gentility remained in the South. In 1824 he moved to Greenville, South Carolina, where he taught music at the Baptist Female Academy,[899] edited a literary journal, and composed his first hit song, "The Minstrel's Return'd from the War." In his book *Yesterdays: Popular Song in America*, Charles Hamm quotes Hewitt's comments on his autograph copy of the song in the Library of Congress:

> This song, as crude as it is, was one of my first musical efforts. It was composed in 1825 in the village of Greenville, S.C., now a city of 20,000 souls. When I returned to the North, I took this book with me to Boston. My brother James was a musical publisher. I gave him a copy to publish—he did it very reluctantly—did not think it worthy of a copyright. It was eagerly taken up by the public, and established my reputation as a ballad composer. It was sold all over the world—and my brother, not securing the right, told me that he missed making at least $10,000.[900]

Subsequent employments took Hewitt to Boston and Baltimore where he experienced a stormy relationship with Edgar Allen Poe and where he produced his first plays at the Front Street Theatre, *Washington* (1832) and *Rip Van Winkle* (1833). In Baltimore he composed his first musical theatre works for his students and amateur performance groups: the juvenile pastoral oratorio, *Flora's Festival* (1834); the cantata, *The Fairy Bridal* (1844); and the temperance oratorio, *The Revellers* (1847).[901] In addition, Hewitt's oratorio, *Jeptha*, was produced in New York City on 26 January 1846 by the New York Sacred Music Society to great acclaim.[902] In 1860, Hewitt moved from Baltimore to Richmond, Virginia, where his operatic version of *Rip Van Winkle*, described by William Craig Winden as his "most ambitious piece for the musical stage" was performed at the Academy of Music.[903] The opera was particularly interesting in its dramatic use of incidental and dance music to create atmosphere, delineate character, and support action. In its theatrical effect, it anticipated the finest examples of silent film music at the turn of the century.[904]

Hewitt assumed the management of the Richmond Broad Street Theatre in 1861where he produced his Civil War play, *The Scouts, or, The Plains of Manassas*, celebrating the first major victory of the Confederacy, [905] and after the theatre burned to the ground in 1862, he moved to Augusta, Georgia, where he functioned as theatre director for the Queen Sisters Company at the Augusta Concert Hall. There he adapted known theatrical pieces and composed new musical theatre compositions specifically designed to capitalize on the strengths of the troupe. The works he produced at the Concert Hall included an adaptation of Balfe's opera, *The Bohemian Girl* (1862); the operetta, *The Vivandiere* (1862), based on the story of Gaetano Donizetti's comic opera, *La fille du régiment*, transposed to Louisiana during the Civil War;[906] the ballad opera, *Lingomar the Seminole* (1863), for which Hewitt created new lyrics for existing popular tunes; the musical burletta, *King Linkum 1st* (1863), also employing popular music; and the operetta, *The Artist's Wife* (1863), with music composed by Frederick Königsberg, director of the Palmetto Band that provided the musical accompaniment to all of the Augusta Concert Hall productions.[907] While Hewitt was composing theatre works, he continued to publish individual songs that became hugely popular during the Civil War and after, including "Rock Me to Sleep Mother," "Somebody's Darling," and "All Quiet Along the Potomac Tonight," arguably the best song to come out of the war.[908]

Following the Confederacy's defeat and the subsequent economic devastation in the South, Hewitt returned to Baltimore in search of gainful employment. He composed a parlor operetta, *The Musical Enthusiast* (1872), "suitable for Schools, Singing Societies, or the Home Circle," employing both original and borrowed music, and full of Victorian sentimental moralizing. In 1878, he opened the East Baltimore Academy of Music, and in 1879, Hewitt produced his final musical theatre work, *Taken In* (libretto by Fanny Stewart), his only composition for which he did not write the words. With a plot freely adapted from David Garrick's play *The Clandestine Marriage*, *Taken In* was likely written for an amateur opera troupe Hewitt had intended to inaugurate in Baltimore, though there is no evidence that the work was ever performed.[909] In the years following the Civil War Hewitt also wrote a number of plays, including the comedy, *Heart Struggles* (1866); the historical drama, *The Polish Martyr* (1866); the tragic drama, *Temora* (1867); the dramatic Temperance sketch, *The Broken Pledge* (1873); the melodrama, *The Lone Star of Cuba* (1873); the society drama, *The Female Lobbyist* (1874); the melodrama, *The Avengers* (1876); *The Female Volunteer* (1877), and the parlor comedy, *Mother and Daughter* (1878).[910] After a life of good health, filled with exercise and creative activity, in February 1888, Hewitt fell down the stairs at his home in Baltimore and broke his hip, an injury that forced him to remain housebound until he died on 7 October 1890. John Hill Hewitt was married twice: first to Estelle Mangin in 1827, with whom he had seven children. After the death of his first wife in 1860, Hewitt married Mary Alithea Smith in 1863, with whom he produced four more children.[911] In his autobiography, *Shadows on the Wall* (1877), Hewitt offered an honest and profound reflection of his life and work:

> Music has always been, and still is, my frailty. Since my earliest youth I have sought its gentle influence; and though in early days I prepared myself for another and quite a different pursuit, yet the fondness of it clung to me, and it finally became my profession, though my parents were solicitous that I should adopt any other honorable calling but that. I studied it as an art and as a science; but only for the sake of the accomplishment, never thinking that I should use it as the means of support. I was educated at West Point, and prepared for the army, but never went into active service, for I resigned at the end of my fourth year, and commenced the study of law in South Carolina, thinking the law is a less dangerous way of achieving honors than the sword. Whenever I failed in any enterprise I fell back on music; it was my sheet-anchor.[912]

HILL, J[ohn] Leubrie

The birth of actor and composer J. Leubrie Hill is something of a mystery with varying sources in disagreement about when and where the performer was born. Eileen Southern suggests the year and place as circa 1869 in New Orleans, Louisiana, while the Internet Movie Database gives the year as 1873 and the birthplace as Memphis, Tennessee. Hill's biography in the Library of Congress gives the date as circa 1869 but does not supply a location, and Thomas L. Riis splits the difference by suggesting circa 1870, while census and death records in New York City complicate the matter further by suggesting the dates of circa 1875 and 1877.[913] It is appropriate to suggest, then, that J. Leubrie Hill was born at some point between 1869 and 1877 in the southern United States where he received a musical education in the Memphis public school system.[914] He worked as a newsboy for the *Times-Star* in Cincinnati, Ohio, before finding employment as a performer with a touring minstrel troupe in the 1890s where he met and formed a song-writing collaboration with actor- songwriter Alex Rogers. In the early years of the twentieth century, both were associated as cast members and writers with the [Bert] Williams and [George] Walker production of *In Dahomey* which previewed in Stamford, Connecticut (8 September 1902) prior to a Boston premiere (12 September 1902). [915] Hill performed the role of con-man Dr. Straight and composed the music for "My Dahomian Queen" (lyrics by Frank Williams) and "That's How the Cake Walk's Done" (lyrics by J. Leubrie Hill) as well as a syncopated dance composition entitled "Rag-time Drummer." He subsequently appeared in Ernest Hogan's *Rufus Rastas* (29 January 1906) as Dr. Fo-Jo, dealer in lucky charms; and in *Bandanna Land* (3 February 1908) he played the role of Sandy Turner, chairman of the Blackville Corporation meeting, and composed the music for two numbers (lyrics by Mord Allen), "When I Was Sweet Sixteen" and "The Sheath Gown in Darktown." In 1909 he was a featured performer in *Mr. Load of Coal* (1 November) for which he composed "Mum's the Word, Mr. Moon" (lyrics by Alex Rogers). The following year he toured with his production of *A Blackville Corporation* (an adaptation of *Bandanna Land)*; in 1910–1911, Hill toured with the two-act musical *My Friend from Dixie* (for which he composed both music and libretto), performing at the Amphion Theatre in Brooklyn and the Howard Theatre in Washington, D.C.;[916] and in summer 1911, he wrote the lyrics for *Hello, Paris* (music by J. Rosamond Johnson), a white-oriented "musical revuette" that played the Folies Bergère Theatre in August and September.[917] In 1912 Hill continued to tour with *My Friend from Dixie*, playing the Olympic Theatre in Cincinnati (24 March) where he paid special attention to the *Times-Star* newsboys who attended his performances en masse. By October 1913, when it opened at the Lafayette Theatre in Harlem, *My Friend from Dixie* had been expanded to three acts (with assistance from Alex Rogers) and retitled *My Friend from Kentucky*. With songs, such as the romantic ballad, "Rock Me in the Cradle of Love," and dance numbers such as "At the Ball, That's All," "Tango One-Step," and "Three Styles of Dancing," *My Friend from Kentucky* ran until February 1914 in Harlem and attracted the attention of white downtown theatregoers, the New York press, and Florenz Ziegfeld who included "Rock Me in the Cradle of Love" and At the Ball, That's All" in the *Ziegfeld Follies of 1914* (1 June 1914).[918] After the Harlem run, *My Friend from Kentucky* was reduced to a forty-minute sketch and combined with *Here and There*, another short musical sketch with libretto by Alex Rogers and music by Hill. Under the title *The Darktown Follies*, the shows moved downtown and performed at various Broadway theatres before going on tour.[919] In 1915, J. Leubrie Hill was one of three composers credited with the songs for *The Passing Show of 1915* (29 May), the others were Leo Edwards and William F. Peters.[920] His "My Trombone Man" (lyrics by Harold Atteridge), sang and danced by Marilyn Miller and chorus was one of the hits of the production. Later in the year, Hill contributed the song and dance "Syncopation" and "Rosey Posey" (lyrics by Harold Atteridge) to Sigmund Romberg's *A World of Pleasure* (14 October 1915) at the Winter Garden.[921] In addition to those already mentioned, Hill's popular compositions included "Daffy-Down-Dilly" (1907), "Chief Bunga Boo" (1909), "When the Sun Goes Down" (1910), "The Gay Manhattan Rag" (1911), and "Every Little Motion" (1914). J. Leubrie Hill died in New York City on 30 August 1916.

HINDLEY, Thomas W.

Composer, violinist, and musical director Thomas Hindley was born in 1854 in Hulme, Lancashire, England. He immigrated to the United States in 1870 and became bandmaster for P.T. Barnum's Circus,[922] before accepting the position of orchestra leader at Ward's Opera House in Portland, Maine.[923] On 18 January 1875, Hindley left Portland to lead the orchestra at the Theatre Comique in Providence, Rhode Island[924] and remained there until the end of the 1875–1876 season when he moved to Saratoga, New York. On 16 October 1876, Hindley and his five-man orchestra began an engagement at Ward's Opera House in Newark, New Jersey.[925] The ensemble so impressed theatre manager Frederick Waldmann that he hired Hindley as his musical director and the musicians as the house orchestra of his Newark Opera House. The stability of a steady income enabled Hindley to think seriously about starting a family, and on 19 November, he married actress Mary Mills Whittingham at the Church of the Assumption in New York City. In 1880, Hindley composed the songs and dance music for Frank Rogers's touring burletta, *Mosquitoes*, produced on 28 June at Waldmann's Mulberry Street Theatre in Newark, and in 1882, he composed the music for *Venus* (5 June 1882), a fairy extravaganza based on a burlesque by W.S. Gilbert and Gilbert a'Beckett, produced at Tony Pastor's New Fourteenth Street Theatre in New York City. On 16 February 1889, after a dozen years as leader of the orchestra at Waldmann's Opera House in Newark, Hindley retired from his position[926] and became musical director at Miner's Peoples' Theatre in the Bowery and later at the Fifth Avenue Theatre.[927] In 1896, he composed incidental and dance music for *The Sunshine of Paradise Alley* (11 May), a city melodrama at the Fourteenth Street Theatre, which was generally disliked by the critics, though the reviewer from the *New York Clipper* admitted that "although it possesses but little inherent interest, [the play] is likely to be popular because of its music and its scenic embellishment."[928] By October 1899, Hindley had become leader at the London Theatre in New York, where he conducted musical skits and provided incidental and dance music for variety acts such as "The Naughty Soubrettes."[929] In addition to his theatrical activities, Hindley was an active member of the Musical Mutual Protective Union, which, in December 1901, elected him vice-president, an office he held for eight years.[930] Hindley subsequently became the musical director at the Knickerbocker Theatre where he provided incidental music for plays, such *The New Henrietta*, by Winchell Smith and Victor Mapes (22 December 1913),[931] and at the Empire Theatre, where he led the orchestra for Zoe Akins's play *Declassee* starring Ethel Barrymore (7 October 1919).[932] On 21 January 1920, Hindley died at his home in the Bronx, following a sudden attack of acute gastritis that overcame him during a performance of *Declassee*.[933]

Hindley's compositions displayed the musical patterns and harmonic structures prevalent in the popular music of his day. He was as comfortable writing ragtime as he was composing a pathetic ballad and the result was always clever and eminently theatrical. His published compositions include the motto song, "Be Sure, Hit the Nail on the Head" (1884), a piano rag, "Patrol Comique" (1886), a song and dance, "There Is a Charming Creature, Oh So Winning" (1895), and a descriptive song, "Loved Ones" (1895).

HIRSCH, Louis A[chille]

Composer and pianist Louis A. Hirsch was born in New York City on 28 November 1881. Following his graduation from the College of the City of New York, he studied piano with Rafael Joseffy in New York and Ernst Jedliczka at the Stern Conservatory in Berlin, along with classes in music theory and composition with Max Spicker in New York and Robert Klein in Berlin.[934] Hirsch's aim was to become a concert pianist, and in Berlin he performed in recitals under the auspices of the Stern Conservatory; but when he returned to the United States in 1902, he felt unready to thrust himself into the concert arena. His skill as a performer of popular songs and musical theatre music encouraged him to pursue a career as a pianist and arranger in Tin Pan Alley, first with Gus Edwards's music publishing house in 1905, and subsequently with that of Shapiro-Bernstein.[935] Two years later, Hirsch produced his first song, "(Love's) Merry-Go-Round," sung by Blanche Ring in *The Gay White Way* (7 October 1907), and he began supplying Lew Dockstader with tunes for his various minstrel shows. Hirsch continued to compose songs that were interpolated into Broadway shows, including "That Wasn't All," in *The Soul Kiss* (28 January 1908); "I'm So Particular" and "Mary! My Heather Belle," in *Nearly a Hero* (24 February 1908); "My Post Card Girl," in *Miss Innocence* (30 November 1908); "La Belle Parisienne" and "Military Mary Ann," in *The Girl and the Wizard* (27 September 1909); and "When Sist' Tetrazin' Met Cousin Carus," in *Up and Down Broadway* (18 July 1910). He was credited as co-composer with Jerome Kern and Melville Gideon for *The Golden Widow* at the Belasco Theatre in Washington, D.C. (26 October 1909);[936] and with Ben M. Jerome, Hirsch co-composed the score for *He Came from Milwaukee* at the Casino Theatre in New York (21 September 1910). In 1911, Hirsch joined the staff of the Shubert organization and composed music as needed for *The Kiss Waltz* ("Elevation") (18 September 1911); *The Revue of Revues* ("The Board Walk Crawl") (27 September 1911); *Vera Violetta* ("Come Dance with Me," "The Gaby Glide") (20 November 1911); *Whirl of Society* ("My Sumurun Girl") (5 March 1912); *Two Little Brides* ("Some Time, Some Place, Some Girl") (23 April 1912); and *The Passing Show of 1912* ("The Wedding Glide," "The Bacchanal Rag," "My Reuben Girlie") (22 July 1912). Hirsch parted ways with the Shuberts after the *Passing Show*, moved to London (having been invited by Albert de Courville, the director of theatrical revues), and became an overnight success with his score for *Hullo, Ragtime!* at the London Hippodrome (23 December 1912), one of the first scores to "emphasize the 'new' American dance rhythms" in England.[937] In January 1913, Hirsch composed new dance music for Ethel Levey at the Hippodrome called the "London Lurch," which combined the glide and the waltz, with a ragtime inflection;[938] and in March 1913, it was formally announced that Hirsch and Nat D. Ayer had composed the music for *A Ragtime Revel*, a revue scheduled for the London Opera House.[939] Hirsch's other London projects included *Dora's Doze* (6 July 1914); *The Magic Touch*, co-composed with Leon Bassett and Maxwell Brunell (18 January 1915); and *Go to Jericho*, co-composed with Fred Godfrey (22 February 1915).[940]

When he returned to the United States Hirsch continued composing revue material for shows that included the *Ziegfeld Follies of 1915* ("My Radium Girl," "I'll Be a Santa Claus to You," "A Girl for Each Month of the

Year") (21 June 1915); *Around the Map* ("Let Us Stay Where the Crowd Is," "Billy the Bubbler") (1 November 1915); the *Ziegfeld Follies of 1916* ("I Left Her on the Beach at Honolulu") (12 June 1916); the *Ziegfeld Follies of 1918* ("When I Hear a Syncopated Tune" sung and danced by Marilyn Miller) (18 June 1918); the *Ziegfeld Follies of 1922* ("Blunderland," "Rambler Rose" [with Dave Stamper], "South Sea Moon" and "South Sea Dance" [with Stamper], "I Don't Want to Be in Dixie," "Sunny South") (5 June 1922); *The Greenwich Village Follies* (1922) ("You Are My Rain-Beau," "Antes de la Corrida Del Toro" ["Before the Bullfight"], a dance) (12 September 1922); and *The Greenwich Village Follies* (1923) ("Kama's Garden," and "The Birthday of the Infanta") (20 September 1923).

In addition, Hirsch composed the music for a number of musical comedies, including *Molly and I* (libretto by Frank R. Adams) (Chicago, 31 August 1915),[941] which closed out of town; *My Home Town Girl* (libretto by Frank M. Stammers) (Syracuse, New York, 15 November 1915),[942] which also closed out of town but which included a brief (sixteen measure) original ragtime dance used as an introduction to the chorus of "Dance, Dance, Dance"; *The Grass Widow* (libretto by Channing Pollock and Rennold Wolf) (3 December 1917); and *Going Up* (libretto by Otto Harbach), Hirsch's first hit musical comedy (25 December 1917)[943] for which he provided songs and dance music. Typical of Hirsch's musical comedy scores, his incidental and dance music in *Going Up* relied heavily on the melodies in the show with original material relegated to introductory or transitional functions. The incidental music for the flying effect in act three, for example, was based on the number "Here's to the Two of You," sung earlier in the act to the two aviators about to ascend in their airplanes, while the dance following "I Want a Boy" simply replicated the instrumental accompaniment to the chorus of the number, following an original eight-measure introduction in dotted rhythms that suggested "The Tickle Toe" performed later in the show. Surprisingly, there was no written dance music for "The Tickle Toe," the most obvious dance number in the production.

Hirsch's subsequent musical comedies included *The Rainbow Girl* (libretto by Rennold Wolf) (1 April 1918),[944] that introduced, along with dance music based on melodies in the score, original ballet music for a "Minuet" and "Fox Trot" in "We Fear You Will Not Do, Lady Wetherell," the ensemble number that ended the first act; *Back Again* (libretto by George V. Hobart and Frank Stammers) (22 April 1918);[945] *Ask Dad* (libretto by Guy Bolton and P.G. Wodehouse) (5 November 1918);[946] *Oh, My Dear!* (*Ask Dad* retitled) (27 November 1918); *See-Saw* (libretto by Earl Derr Biggers)

(23 September 1919);⁹⁴⁷ *The House That Jack Built* (libretto by Otto Harbach and Frank Mandel) (29 March 1920);⁹⁴⁸ and *Mary* (a retitled and revised *The House That Jack Built*) (18 October 1920),⁹⁴⁹ with interesting dance music that went beyond the simple repetition of sung melodies. For example, the dance following the number "Money! Money! Money!" began with the tune played in counterpoint with an original adaptation of the "Sailor's Hornpipe" before becoming a fox-trot variation of the original melody. The dance after "Every Time I Meet a Lady" cleverly outlined the tune in a masterfully constructed schottische that created a kind of perpetual motion of triplets and dotted notes. The dance music in *Mary* demonstrated a significant advance in Hirsch's compositions for stage choreography and suggested the possible influence of his musical director Charles J. Gebest.

On 15 January 1921 Hirsch was advertised as the composer of *The Koko of Kong* (book by Harry M. Vernon, lyrics by Clifford Gray) featuring the African-American team of Harry Scott and Eddie Whaley, and scheduled for a London engagement during the 1921–1922 season.⁹⁵⁰ Hirsch's final musical comedies were *The O'Brien Girl* (libretto by Otto Harbach and Frank Mandel) (25 April 1921), another collaboration with musical director Charles J. Gebest, with a significant amount of dance music;⁹⁵¹ *Naughty Diana* (libretto by Otto Harbach) (1923),⁹⁵² never produced; and *Betty Lee* (co-composed with Con Conrad; book by Otto Harbach, lyrics by Irving Caesar and Harbach) (25 December 1924).⁹⁵³ Hirsch did not live to see the production of *Betty Lee*. He died of pneumonia at the Knickerbocker Hospital on 13 May 1924, survived by his wife, the actress Genevieve Hall.

HOFFMAN, A[ugust] W[illiam]

Composer and musical director of German extraction, A.W. Hoffman first appeared in New York theatrical notices in the late 1870s as the musical director of the Grand Opera House where he conducted and/or arranged incidental and entr'acte entertainment for productions that included *Kerry Gow* (13 August 1877);⁹⁵⁴ *Evangeline, or, The Belle of Acadia* (18 March 1878); *The Danites* (26 August 1878);⁹⁵⁵ and *Fritz in Ireland* (23 August 1880).⁹⁵⁶ Hoffman became musical director at Niblo's Garden in 1881 where he conducted and composed additional music for the Kiralfy Brothers' revival of *The Black Crook* (7 March 1881) and satisfied the musical needs of productions that included: *Youth* (21 August 1882);⁹⁵⁷ the Kiralfy troupe's production of Luigi Manzotti and Romualdo Marenco's ballet *Excelsior* (21 August 1883);⁹⁵⁸ the drama, pantomime, opera, and ballet, *The Seven Ravens* (18 August 1884) based on a German play by Emil Pohl, with music by C. Lehnhardt and Ludwig Englander;[959] the Kiralfy Brothers production of *The Ratcatcher, or, The Pied Piper of Hamelin* (30 November 1885) with music by Selli Simonson;[960] a revival of the Kiralfy Brothers' production of *The Black Crook* (29 March 1886); Imre Kiralfy's production of *Lagardère, or, The Hunchback of Paris* (17 August 1887), for which Hoffman arranged ballet music for "Gypsy Revels" and "The Seven Ages"; Bolossy Kiralfy's production of *Mathias Sandorf* (18 August 1888), for which Hoffman arranged music for an "Automaton Dance," the "Grand Oriental Ballet, The Fête of the Storks," and "America," the "National and Military Ballet" that included an Indian dance, a cowboy dance, and a plantation dance;[961] and a revised version of the Miller Brothers' spectacular play *Kajanka* (16 August 1890) with music by Sidney H. Horner.[962] In November 1891, Hoffman was advertised as the musical director at the Academy of Music for the pantomime extravaganza *Cinderella*, written and produced by Henry John Leslie.[963] Three years later, Hoffman reappeared as the composer of the comic opera, *The Red Fez* (libretto by Robert Holmes Hazard) that gave its premiere performance at Uhrig's Cave in St. Louis on 23 June 1896. According to the St. Louis dispatch to the *New York Clipper*, "It is a bright opera, abounding in good music and comedy situations. The composer, A.W. Hoffman, belonging to the Mystic Shrine, his fellow Shriners turned out en masse to do him honor. The weather being bad the attendance was light. However, the full strength of the Cave Company made the production a pleasing one."[964] The opera was set in Turkey where, in a game of chess, the Sultan lost most of his possessions to a Captain of the United States Navy, including the red fez of the title, which was invested with the supernatural power of making the wearer invisible. The Captain set out to sea with the red fez, and the action of the opera centered on the Sultan's attempts to repossess it.[965] Hoffman's other compositions included *Der Zither Verein* [*The Zither Club*], composed and arranged for piano (1884); *The Patrol of the Continentals*, composed and arranged for orchestra (1884); and *Hermosa: Pizzicato* for piano (1890).

HOFFMANN, Max

Composer and musical director Max Hoffmann (also Hoffman) was born in Birnbaum, German Empire, on 8 December 1873 and immigrated with his family to St. Paul, Minnesota, in August 1878.[966] He first appeared in theatrical notices as musical director for *A Bowery Girl*, opening at Sioux City, Iowa, on 17 August 1895 followed by a run in Omaha, Nebraska,[967] and by the turn of the century, Hoffmann was sufficiently well known as an arranger and band leader (of the Musical Merry Makers) to be a featured selling point in advertising for music publishers, Hill, Horwitz, and Bowers.[968] In 1901, Hoffmann provided music (including incidental and dance music) and musical direction for *The Night of the Fourth* (lyrics by Sherrie Mathews) at Hammerstein's Victoria Theatre (21 January); he toured with the *Champagne Charley* Company during the 1901–1902 season, and played seaside engagements with his Musical Merry Makers during the summer 1902. The following summer, he provided musical direction and additional music for *George W. Lederer's Mid-Summer Night Fancies* (22 June 1903) opening the Crystal Gardens on the roof of the New York Theatre, and beginning with the fall 1903, Hoffmann began a long relationship with comedians Gus and Max Rogers, co-composing the score (with Melville Ellis) and providing musical direction for *The Rogers Brothers in London* (7 September). A week later, he composed the music and lyrics, as well as the dance music, for a number performed by his wife, Gertrude, and her dancing girls in *The Jersey Lily* (14 September 1903) before leaving with the Rogers Brothers' tour. The next installment of the Brothers' shenanigans for which Hoffmann supplied music and musical direction, *The Rogers Brothers in Paris*, opened in Buffalo (29 August 1904) before moving to New York on 5 September, and while he was on tour with the show, he composed the songs and dance music for *Me, Him and I* (31 December 1904), a musical

Example 109a. Irish Set Dance in "Killarney" from *The Rogers Brothers in Ireland*

Example 109b. Irish Reel in "Killarney" from *The Rogers Brothers in Ireland*

farce, choreographed by his wife. The next Rogers Brothers' hit, *The Rogers Brothers in Ireland* (4 September 1905) gave Hoffmann the opportunity to create an Irish-flavored score with dance music that accompanied traditional folk dances, including a jaunty set dance (example 109a), and a lusty reel (example 109b).

True to his fashion, while Hoffmann was leading the Rogers Brothers' show, he also composed the score for a one-act musical farce, *Friday, the 13th*, featured on the vaudeville bill at Proctor's Twenty-third Street Theatre (2 October 1905).[969] The next year, Hoffmann took a break from the Rogers Brothers to provide songs, dance music, and musical direction for Florenz Ziegfeld's vehicle for Anna Held, *A Parisian Model* (27 November

1906). In May, before the end of the New York run, Ziegfeld abruptly fired Hoffmann because of a disagreement over the "advisability of certain stage business" and at the end of his two weeks' notice, Hoffmann left the theatre, taking all of the music with him. He was arraigned on a charge of theft, but the charge was quickly dismissed when the theatre musicians demonstrated that they could perform the music from memory.[970] Almost immediately Hoffmann was back to work with Ziegfeld, providing the musical direction (and the music for a single number, "Cigarette,") for the *Follies of 1907* (8 July 1907). After the *Follies* closed Hoffmann provided songs and dance music for *The Rogers Brothers in Panama* (2 September 1907) but did not travel with the show as its musical director. Instead he toured the vaudeville circuit with his wife who and danced and performed caricatures of leading theatre performers (her imitation of Anna Held was particularly successful).[971] Hoffmann returned to composing for Broadway with *The Young Turk* (31 January 1910), a Max Rogers vehicle,[972] and his subsequent musical shows included *(From) Broadway to Paris* (20 November 1912) for which he provided songs, dance music, and musical direction;[973] *The Century Girl* (6 November 1916), for which he provided musical direction and incidental dance music (along with Louis Gottschalk); *Dance and Grow Thin* (18 January 1917), for which he provided musical direction and incidental dance arrangements; *The Tavern* (27 September 1920), musical direction and incidental music;[974] the *Ziegfeld Midnight Frolic* (28 November 1920), musical direction and additional music;[975] *A Night in Spain* (3 May 1927), musical direction; and *Shady Lady* (5 July 1933), musical direction. When he was not working on a Broadway show, Hoffmann was on tour with his wife's act, providing musical direction as well as a variety of dance compositions (a "bathing number," an "Up in the Air" number, a "Hawaiian" number) to suit her company of eighteen female and five male dancers.[976] Max and Gertrude Hoffmann and company performed in vaudeville houses and supper clubs throughout the United States before settling on the West Coast, where the couple retired in Encino, California. Max Hoffman died there on 21 May1963, six months shy of his ninetieth birthday.

HOFFMASTER, William

Violinist and composer William Hoffmaster was a little person of German birth who worked as a musician in New York City between 1785 and 1807, and likely a member of the orchestra at the John Street The-

Example 110. "Durang's Horn-Pipe"

atre, the home of the Old American Company of actors.[977] According to dancer John Durang who studied the violin with him, Hoffmaster was "a man about three foot, large head, hands and feet; his wife of the same statue. A good musician."[978] Expressly for Durang, Hoffmaster composed "Durang's Horn-Pipe" which became a popular dance composition during the early days of the American theatre, and as Durang has written, "well known in America, for I have since heard it play'd the other side of the Blue Mountains as well as in the cities."[979] The infectious simplicity of the tune made it easy to remember, and even easier to copy, and as a result, a number of different version of the original tune were developed over time. Example 110 offers an early piano arrangement of the dance music, published in Boston in 1823.

Lynn Matluck Brooks suggests that the performance of "Durang's Horn-Pipe" occurred in the spring of 1786,[980] and, writing in *Chronicles of the American Dance*, Lillian Moore cites Charles Durang's description of his father's dance, which he labelled "A Sailor Hornpipe—Old Style."

1. Glissade round (first part of tune).
2. Double shuffle down, do.
3. Heel and toe back, finish with back shuffle.
4. Cut the buckle down, finish the shuffle.
5. Side shuffle right and left, finishing with beats.
6. Pigeon wing going round.
7. Heel and toe haul in back.
8. Steady toes down.
9. Changes back, finish with back shuffle and beats.
10. Wave step down.
11. Heel and toe shuffle obliquely back.
12. Whirligig, with beats down.
13. Sissone and entrechats back.
14. Running forward on the heels.
15. Double Scotch step, with a heel Brand in Plase. [sic]
16. Single Scotch step back.
17. Parried toes round, or feet *in* and *out*.
18. The Cooper shuffle right and left back.
19. Grasshopper step down.
20. Terré-à-terré [sic] or beating on toes back.
21. Jockey crotch down.
22. Traverse round with hornpipe glissade.
   Bow and Finish

Each step takes up one strain of the tune. There are a variety of other shuffles, but the above are the principal, with their original names.[981]

Lynn Matluck Brooks also suggests that Hoffmaster may have been involved in the creation of another of Durang's early choreographic experiments, a "Dwarf Dance," suggested by Lewis Hallam, Jr., the manager of the Old American Company, and possibly triggered by Hoffmaster's presence in the orchestra.[982] John Durang described the dance which was first advertised for performance on 13 July 1786:

> Mr. Hallam gave me some idea of the "Dwarf Dance," which by a little study I soon brought to perfection as I thought and introduced it to admiration, but I was convinced to the contrary when I repeated the dance in Philadelphia a year after. The body and head of the Dwarf

were tied above my hip, and the upper part of my body and head were covered by a colored petticoat gathered with my hands at the top of my head. In this concealed manner I would make my entrance. Dancing in one night I was deluded by the stage lights, which I took for the wing lights, my situation being almost blindfold. I made my exit over the spikes of the stage and orchestra. Three spikes entered my left thigh and calf, where I hung till Mr. Gibbon, our assistant tailor, extricated my leg from the spikes. I was in a swoon the whole time. I was set on my feet in the pit passage. I recovered from the swoon and did not feel my wounds but run round the theatre into the dressing room, when I only discovered I was hurt. I was laid up two months. This mischance convinced my error, which made me make the addition to change from the man Dwarf to a woman before I quit the stage; this improvement made the dance complete. The metamorphosis was from a man of 3 foot to a woman of 6 foot.[983]

Whether or not Hoffmaster was instrumental in the creation of the dance, it is clear that he left a lasting impression on John Durang. If Hoffmaster was, indeed, a member of the Old American Company orchestra at the John Street Theatre, it is likely that he moved with the orchestra to the new Park Theatre when it opened in January 1798. Little is known about Hoffmaster after 1807 when the interior of the theatre was remodeled, though he may have remained with the orchestra until 1820 when the theatre burned down.

HORN, Charles E[dward]

Composer, singer, cellist, pianist, organist, musical director, and music publisher Charles E. Horn was born on 21 June 1786 in St. Martin's-in-the-Fields, London, the son of Karl Friedrich Horn, a German musician who immigrated to London in 1782 and became music master in ordinary to Queen Charlotte.[984] Charles received his initial education in music from his father and later studied harmony and composition with the German theorist Karl Friedrich Baumgarten and singing with the Italian composer and castrato Venanzio Rauzzini.[985] Horn began his performance career as violoncellist at Covent Garden in 1802; in 1806 he accompanied singer

Charles Incledon on the piano at the Lower Assembly Rooms Cheltenham;[986] and on 26 June 1809, he made his debut as a singer in M.P. King's opera *Up All Night* at the Lyceum Theatre.[987] Beginning in 1810, Horn composed a number of musical theatre works that included the comic opera, *Tricks upon Travelers* (9 July 1810); the romantic melodrama, *The Magic Bride* (26 December 1810); the musical farce, *The Bee-Hive* (19 January 1811); the operatic romance, *The Devil's Bridge* (6 May 1912), his most popular work; the seriocomic opera, *Narensky, or, The Road to Yaroslaf* (11 January 1814); the melodramatic romance, *The Woodman's Hut* (12 April 1814); the musical romance, *The Ninth Statue, or, The Irishman in Bagdad* (29 November 1814); the popular opera, *Lalla Rookh, or, The Cashmerian Minstrel* (1818); the all-sung serious recitative drama, *Dirce, or The Fatal Urn* (2 June 1821); and the spectacular romantic drama, *Faustus* (16 May 1825).[988] Originally produced at the Theatre Royal, Drury Lane, *Faustus* was performed at the Park Theatre in New York City on 11 October 1827, a week before Horn made his debut there on 17 October, singing the role of Seraskier in Stephen Storace's opera *The Siege of Belgrade*.[989] About Horn's performance, the *Albion* (20 October 1827) was enthusiastic:

> His voice is not remarkable for compass, power, or clearness of tone, but the extreme purity of his taste, and the resources of his science, enable him to overcome these defects with the greatest success. We have heard it objected to Mr. Horn, that there is a want of originality and variety in his *cadenzas* and other ornaments; as to their originality, they are certainly original here; and as to their variety, it is to be answered that they are natural, graceful and beautiful, and therefore worthy of admiration.... No English stage-singer in this country, *since* its discovery by Columbus has ever equaled Mr. Horn in knowledge of his art, or in delicacy and taste of execution.... He is superior in these points to [Charles] Incledon, [T.] Phillips or Pearman, though he may want the obstreperousness of one of these, and the dashing flourishes of the others.[990]

On 8 November 1827 Horn performed his most successful role, Caspar, in Carl Maria von Weber's opera *Der Freischütz* and again the critics were impressed. The *New York Mirror* (17 November 1827) even praised Horn's acting: "with the exception of Macready, we know of no one who would have played the character so well. In the musical department he was admirable."[991] Horn performed a variety of other roles during the 1827–1828 season with varying degrees of success and even his opera *The Devil's Bridge*, which had been performed in New York as early as 4 July 1815, and repeated regularly through the 1820s, was given again (on 18 December 1827) during Horn's debut season at the Park Theatre. On 21 January 1828, the Park Theatre produced Horn's adaptation of Mozart's *The Marriage of Figaro*, followed on 9 April by *Dido*, Horn's pasticcio of Rossini; *Isidore de Merida, or, the Devil's Creek*, Horn's version of Storace's *The Pirates* on 9 June; and *Oberon*, Horn's adaptation of Weber's opera on 9 October.

During his phenomenally successful debut season, Horn found the time to tour the United States with a company of singers, stopping in Philadelphia on 7 May 1828 to sing the role of Artabanes in Thomas Arne's *Artaxerses* at the Chestnut Street Theatre, followed by performances of *The Marriage of Figaro*, *Der Freischütz*, and *The Barber of Seville*. In December 1828, Horn returned to the Park Theatre with an original incidental score for Shakespeare's *The Tempest* (8 December 1828) with music for all of Ariel's songs in addition to shipwreck music, incidental music for the banquet scene, contrapuntal choruses of spirits, glees for demons, quartets for sea nymphs, operatic ensemble numbers, and songs for Stephano, Caliban, and Ferdinand, concluding with a hornpipe sung by "sailors and women."

Horn and his opera company returned to the Chestnut Street Theatre on 5 May 1829 to perform *Il Trionfo Della Musica*, Horn's adaptation of an opera by Johann Simon Mayr,[992] which had been produced successfully at the Bowery Theatre during the month of April (along with Horn's opera *The Quartetto, or, Interrupted Harmony* on 27 April). As the first Italian opera acted and sung in Philadelphia, *Il Trionfo Della Musica* met with great interest and enthusiasm, but even the nightly ticket sales of $400 were insufficient to defray the costs of the production.[993] The opera company disbanded and Horn returned to London where he premiered another musical theatre piece, *Honest Frauds* (29 July 1830) and accepted the position of musical director at the Olympic Theatre. He returned to New York in 1832 and became musical director at the Park Theatre where he continued to compose and adapt operas, including *Cinderella* (20 December 1832) based on the opera by Rossini; *Nadir and Zuleika* (27 December 1832), an original work; and *The Magic Flute* (17 April 1833) based on the singspiel by Mozart.

342 | *Incidental and Dance Music in the American Theatre from 1786 to 1923*

In 1835 Horn lost his voice but continued to compose, producing *The Remission of Sin*, credited as the first oratorio composed in the United States, and performed by the New York Sacred Music Society on 7 May 1835.[994] Horn became a music publisher in 1837, first with a partner, flautist W.J. Davis, and later alone, and when the business began to flounder, he created a series of six "Soireés Musicales" between 14 February 1839 and 24 April 1839 to earn money and advertise his publications. In 1840 Horn was engaged as musical director at the new National Theatre where the season opened with the production of Horn's grand opera *Ahmed al Kamel, the Pilgrim of Love* (12 October 1840). Although the complete score of the work is lost, "The Fairy Dance" (example 110a) published by

Example 110a. "The Fairy Dance" from *Ahmed al Kamel, the Pilgrim of Love*

Horn from the opera (and adapted for the piano by Henry C. Watson) offers a fine illustration of his classically-oriented compositional style and displays Horn's particular affinity for Mozart. The intentionally child-like nature of the piece creates a fairy ambiance, even if the piano reduction is a bit heavy in the bass, and the drone-like quality of the accompaniment is designed to generate a hypnotic effect. The melody is as simple as a folk tune, a significant characteristic of Horn's music: "He had a gift for incorporating and imitating elements of folksong (or, as it was termed in his day, 'national song'), and it was this that gave many of his songs their appeal."[995]

In 1842, Horn was instrumental in the creation of the New York Philharmonic Society,[996] and in the same year, his last opera, *The Maid of Saxony*, was produced at the Park Theatre (23 May).[997] In 1843 he returned to England where his American oratorio *The Remission of Sin* was performed under the new (and more provocative) title *Satan* on 18 March 1845, the same year that he became musical director at the Princess' Theatre. During his tenure at the theatre, Horn composed one final sacred work, *Daniel's Prediction, or, The Vision of Belshazzar*, produced in London on 19 May 1847. He returned to America and settled in Boston where he became conductor of the Handel and Haydn Society in July 1847, a position he held until his death on 21 October 1849. Horn was survived by his second wife, the actress Mary Ann Horton, and his son, Charles Horn, Jr.

HORNER, Sidney H[erbert]

Composer, violinist, and musical director Sidney H. Horner was born in England in August 1858. Interested in music from an early age, he studied the violin privately and performed in the British secondary school orchestras and ensembles before joining the orchestras of provincial theatrical troupes. He married actress Pauline Ferris in 1883, and moved to London where he became involved with the production of Christmas pantomimes at Covent Garden and Drury Lane. In June 1889, with his wife and young daughter by his side, he moved to Columbus, Ohio, at the invitation of the Miller Brothers, who engaged him to compose the music and provide the musical direction for an original spectacular pantomime based on Hindu mythology, entitled *Kajanka*. With a libretto by professional clown George D. Melville, the production began rehearsals in July and opened at the Grand Opera House in Columbus on 15 September

1889.[998] For the spectacle, Horner composed ballet music for the "Triumphant March of Kajanka," the "Fairy Papillon Dancers," the "Grand Floral March," and "Transformation Dances," as well as incidental music for the harlequinade, and five transformation sequences. While *Kajanka* was a hit in Columbus, it did not fare quite so well in Chicago (6 October 1889) where the correspondent for *The New York Times* ranted: "Lavish and unscrupulous advertising has foisted upon playgoers and upon the Columbia Theatre a provincial spectacle called *Kajanka*. Tawdry scenery and costumes and a worthless company conspired to make *Kajanka* one of the worst atrocities seen here in years. It opened to an enormous house, but business is said to have declined steadily all the week."[999] The reviews in New York City, where *Kajanka* opened at Niblo's Garden on 2 December 1889, were more of the same, though the *Times* critic did admit that the "audience filled every part of the big theatre, and the applause was so frequent and earnest that it suggested a prosperous New-York engagement."[1000] The tour of *Kajanka* kept Horner employed through the spring of 1893, after which he became the musical director of the People's Theatre, where he provided incidental music for popular melodramas such as Milton Nobles's *The Phoenix* (12 August 1893) and Charles Dickens's *Bleak House* (11 August 1894). Horner continued to compose and conduct for costume melodramas into the twentieth century, first at the Star Theatre, with Charles W. Chase's dramatization of *Quo Vadis* (11 August 1900), and later at the American Theatre, with Owen Davis's *The Gambler of the West* (28 July 1906). Horner, who had become an American citizen in 1899, sustained his career as a musical director through the first two decades of the twentieth century. He retired from that profession around 1920 when, on the United States Federal Census, he listed his occupation as "Importer: Strings Musical." By 1940, he was an eighty-year-old widower living with his daughter Violet, her dentist husband, Adolph Wagner, and a hospital attendant, ignored and forgotten by the musical theatre profession.

HOSCHNA, Karl [Ludwig]

Composer, arranger, and oboist Karl Hoschna was born in Kuschwarda, Bohemia on 16 August 1876.[1001] He received his musical education at the Vienna Conservatory where his principal instrument was the oboe. He was an oboist in the Austrian Army Band until 1896 when he moved to America where he found employment as a musician, most notably as featured oboist in Victory Herbert's orchestra. Believing that the embouchure and breath control required for playing the oboe was somehow harmful to his brain, Hoschna secured a position with Isidore Witmark, the music publisher—as a copyist and arranger of piano reductions of show music—where he could enjoy a career in music without damaging himself by playing the oboe. An early collaboration with advertising copywriter Otto Harbach (then spelling his surname as Hauerbach), entitled *Back Again*, failed to reach the stage, but in 1905 his *Belle of the West* (libretto by Harry B. Smith) opened at the Weller Theatre in Zanesville, Ohio, on 1 September, and after a two-and-a-half-month pre-Broadway tour, the show played a week at the Grand Opera House in Manhattan before moving to the Majestic Theatre in Brooklyn. Although the show failed to impress the critics, who only grudgingly revealed that several songs were encored,[1002] it was an important musical document because it produced the first example of Hoschna's dance music, the "Indian Dance" (example 110b). Following a thirty-two measure introduction in 3/4 with a single-note pentatonic melody over a drone accompaniment, the "Indian Dance" moves to a 2/4 march structure (A–B–A–C–A) with a minor mode "A" section, parallel major "B" section, and ragtime "C" or "trio" section in the key of the subdominant. Example 110b presents the final eight measures of the "A" section and the first twenty measures of the trio. Note the iconic "Indian" motif in measures 9–12 and the contrasting ragtime syncopations in measures 15–20 and 23–27 that anticipate later Native American dances in musicals such as *Annie Get Your Gun*, *Whoop-Up*, and *Peter Pan*.

Hoschna's next Broadway effort, *The Girl from Broadway* (book by Herbert Hall Winslow; lyrics by Charles Noel Douglas[1003]) fared better with the critics but still managed only a week's run at the Fourteenth Street Theatre (14 January 1907).[1004] His next work, however, *Three Twins* (with book by Charles Dickson; lyrics by Otto Hauerbach) (15 June 1908) was both a popular and critical success[1005] with the songs "Cuddle Up a Little Closer," and "The Yama-Yama Man," as well as the waltzing dance number, "The Hypnotic Kiss" singled out as hits. In addition, Hoschna created an effective schottische dance arrangement for "BooHoo! Tee Hee! (Crying and Laughing Song)," and composed a mazurka and Spanish-flavored dance music for the opening of act two.

Hoschna's subsequent musicals included *Prince Humbug* (libretto by Mark Swan) (7 September 1908) at the Park Theatre in Boston (closed on the road);[1006] *The Silver Star* (1 November 1909), for which he composed

Example 110b. "Indian Dance" from *The Belle of the West*

one number, "To Bring Up a Girl" (lyrics by Harry B. Smith); *Bright Eyes* (book by Charles Dickson; lyrics by Otto Hauerbach), New Haven (25 November 1909,[1007] New York 28 February 1910); *The Photo Shop* (book by Edward Clark; lyrics by Otto Hauerbach), touring vaudeville musical (1910); *The Echo* (17 August 1910) for which Hoschna composed "I Don't Want to Be a Soldier Boy" (lyrics by George V. Hobart); *Madame Sherry* (libretto by Otto Hauerbach) based on the German hit composed by Hugo Felix, producing another hit for Hoschna, "Every Little Movement" (30 August 1910);[1008] *Beau Broadway* (AKA *The Lady's Man*) (libretto by

Otto Hauerbach)[1009] unproduced; *Get-Rich-Quick Wallingford* (19 September 1910), a Cohan show borrowing songs from *Madame Sherry*; *Katie Did* (libretto by W.C. Duncan and Frank Smithson), Chicago (13 February 1911), closed out of town;[1010] *Jumping Jupiter* (libretto by Richard Carle and Sydney Rosenfeld) (6 March 1911); *Dr. De Luxe* (libretto by Otto Hauerbach) (17 April 1911);[1011] and *The Girl of My Dreams* (book by Wilbur D. Nesbit and Otto Hauerbach; lyrics by Hauerbach) (7 August 1911).[1012] Although Hoschna had been advertised as the composer of *The Fascinating Widow* (libretto by Otto Hauerbach), and a great deal of published sheet music for the show was composed by him, when the musical opened in Atlantic City on 28 August 1911, Kerry [Frederick W.] Mills was the credited composer.[1013]

On 30 September 1911, Hoschna, actress Blanche Ring, and the entire company of Hoschna's next musical, *A Wall Street Girl* (book by Margaret Mayo and Edgar Selwyn; lyrics by Benjamin Hapgood Burt), left New York City on a special train to Wilkes Barre, Pennsylvania where the pre-Broadway tour was scheduled to begin. While on the road, Hoschna caught a cold that gradually developed into a more serious condition and he was forced to return to New York to recuperate. He died "due to a complication of diseases" on 23 December 1911, survived by his widow, Hettie, three daughters, and a musical that would open on Broadway on 15 April 1912.[1014] The composer of two very successful musicals, several hit songs, and a large quantity of published music, Hoschna left a net estate of $6,424. The composer's widow revealed that her husband never kept account books and that she never knew what his income was at any given time because he cashed all of his royalty checks and never made a bank deposit.[1015]

HOWSON, Frank A[lfred] [Giralomo]

Born in London on 28 March 1841, toddler Frank A. Howson moved with his parents to Australia, where, in Hobart, Tasmania, his father produced Daniel Auber's *Fra Diavolo*, believed to have been the first grand opera performed in Australia.[1016] In 1844, three-year-old Frank played Cupid to his father's Silenus in a mythological ballet at Mrs. Clark's Royal Victoria Theatre,[1017] and in 1860, nineteen-year-old Frank conducted Verdi's *Il Trovatore* in Sydney.[1018] In July 1866, after a stop in Tahiti to perform for the islanders, the Howson family arrived in San Francisco where, calling themselves the Howson Opera Troupe, they produced several seasons of grand opera.[1019] Making a tour toward the East Coast, with performances in Truckee, California, Carson City, Nevada, and Denver, Colorado, the company stopped in Omaha, Nebraska, where Howson's father (and company manager) died on 16 September 1869.[1020] The company disbanded and the surviving members of the Howson family continued on to New York City where Howson's brother John and sister Clelia found employment at Wood's Museum, and his sister Emma became a member of Caroline Richings Bernard's English Opera Company. Frank became musical director for Mrs. James Oates Comic Opera and Burlesque Company which opened the 1872–1873 season on 16 September at the Academy of Music in Cleveland, Ohio, with *Fortunio and His Gifted Servants* (for which Howson composed incidental music), followed by *The King's Secret* and *Alarming Sacrifice* on 18 September, *The Flower Girl of Paris* on 19 September, and Offenbach's *Prima Donna of a Night* and the pasticco *The Fair One with the Blonde Wig* on 20 September.[1021] When the company performed at the Park Theatre in Brooklyn in March 1873, *Les Bavards*, an adaptation of Offenbach's comic opera, for which Howson "arranged the music very cleverly," was added to the repertoire.[1022] On 21 June, Howson sailed for England with his sister Emma, who would remain there to study and perform in London for a number of years. Howson, however, was back in America in time to begin the 1873–1874 season with the Oates Comic Opera Company, opening at the Olympic Theatre in New York on 29 September with an English production of Charles Lecocq's *La Fille de Madame Angot*, called *Mme. Angot's Child*, followed by performances of Offenbach's *The Grand Duchess* and *Monsieur Choufleuri*. Early in 1874, Howson joined Miss Kellogg's English Opera Company at the Park Theatre in Brooklyn where he conducted English versions of Donizetti's *Lucia di Lammermoor*, Flotow's *Martha*, Mozart's *The Marriage of Figaro*, Gounod's *Faust*, and Auber's *Fra Diavolo*, in addition to Balfe's *The Bohemian Girl*, and Wallace's *Maritana*.[1023] By the end of June 1874, the company was performing at the Victoria Skating Rink in Montreal, with Verdi's *Il Trovatore* added to the repertoire.[1024]

After touring Canada and various cities and the United States with the English Opera Company, Howson was engaged as musical director for the Wilbur Opera Company, for whom he conducted Audran's *The Mascot* at the Bijou Theatre (5 May 1881) in New York City. Soon after, he became musical director at the Madison Square Theatre where he selected and composed incidental music for a great number of plays, including *The Rajah* (6 June 1883); *May Blossom* (12 April 1884); *Broken Hearts* (12 February 1885*), Saints and Sinners* (7 November 1885); *Held by the Enemy*

(16 August 1886); *Jim, the Penman* (1 November 1886); *Doctor Jekyll and Mister Hyde* (12 September 1887); *The Martyr* (10 November 1887); *Heart of Hearts* (16 January 1888); *Partners* (14 November 1888); *Captain Swift* (29 April 1889); *Bootles Baby* (8 August 1889); *Aunt Jack* (21 April 1890); and *Jane* (28 September 1891). During this time, Howson also composed the music for two operettas, *Too Soon*, and *The Dreamland Tree*, both with librettos by Charles Barnard;[1025] a musical comedy, *The Baron* (libretto by H.M. Pitt) produced at the Grand Opera House in Brooklyn on 7 June 1886; as well as incidental music for *Uncle Tom's Cabin* at the Hollis Street Theatre in Boston (18 August 1888), *The Kaffir Diamond* at the Broadway Theatre (15 September 1888), and *The Still Alarm* (3 December 1888) at the Fourteenth Street Theatre. In the 1890s, Howson became musical director at the Lyceum Theatre under the management of Daniel Frohman. There he composed incidental music for many productions, including *The Prisoner of Zenda* (4 September 1895); *An Enemy to the King* (1 September 1896); *The Mayflower* (8 March 1897); and *Trelawny of the Wells* (22 November 1898). During the first decade of the twentieth century, Howson moved to the Garden Theatre where he scored music for *Hamlet* (17 September 1900); *Richard Lovelace* (9 September 1901); and *If I Were King* (7 January 1902). He later became musical director at Daly's Theatre, and Garrick's Theatre before he retired in 1918.

The "March and Two-Step" from the incidental music Howson composed for *The King's Musketeer* at the Knickerbocker Theatre (13 March 1899) provides a fine illustration of his compositional style, based firmly in the musical vocabulary of nineteenth-century European opera. Example 111 presents the "B" section of the piece (measures 1–24) and the recapitulation of the main theme (measures 25–40). The chromatic tonicizations in the "B" section create excitement and anticipation for the resolution to the tonic that occurs with the recapitulation. Note the use of augmented sixth chords and their resolutions (measures 17–22) that descend chromatically to the dominant (measure 22), adding more urgency for the imminent resolution to the majestic principal theme that is plainly diatonic with few chromatic interruptions (measures 27, 35, 37). The piece is sophisticated musically and well crafted, even if it evokes strains of Carl Maria von Weber, Giacomo Meyerbeer, Daniel Auber, and Giuseppe Verdi. As has been often said, familiarity is not necessarily a fault in incidental and dance music since it swiftly enables the listener to experience the locale, atmosphere, mood, or emotion that the sound must convey to be effective dramatically.

Example 111. "March and Two-Step" from *The King's Musketeer*

In December 1899 when Howson led the orchestra at Daly's Theatre, for intermission music, he created a medley of his incidental compositions at the Lyceum Theatre called "Lyceum Memories,"[1026] and in 1905, he composed an overture called "Saint Valentine" to be performed by a string orchestra under his direction at the premiere American production of *Mrs. Temple's Telegram* (1 February).[1027] Following his retirement in 1918, Howson continued composing at his home in Hollis, Long Island. In 1925, when he was eighty-four, he composed musical settings for Rudyard Kipling's poems, "Rolling Down in Rio," and "The Gypsy Trail."[1028] He died on 29 June 1926 after only a few days' illness and was

Example 111 (continued). "March and Two-Step" from *The King's Musketeer*

interred in Maple Grove Cemetery, Kew Gardens, New York. Howson was survived by his sisters Clelia and Emma, and his children, Ethel, Frank, and Albert.

HUBBELL, [John] Raymond

Pianist, composer, dance arranger, and musical director Raymond Hubbell was born on 1 June 1879, in Urbana, Ohio, where he studied piano as a youth. He moved to Chicago to continue his musical studies and, upon graduation, he became the arranger and leader of a dance band, an experience that enabled him to find employment as staff arranger and pianist for music publisher Charles K. Harris. In 1902, Hubbell composed his first musical theatre score for *Chow Chow* (libretto by Addison Burkhardt), the Chicago extravaganza that inaugurated the Orpheon Music Hall on 4 October and managed to run for 127 consecutive performances before closing in December.[1029] *Chow Chow* was revised for a Broadway production retitled *The Runaways* (11 May 1903) that earned positive reviews and an even longer run, partially because of the character called The Giant Rooster, whose barnyard strut was applauded by the critics, and achieved for Hubbell, his first commercial instrumental success, "The Rooster Dance."[1030] After an introduction in common time that was marked "Rooster's crow" in the score, the meter changed to 2/4 and the dance (example 112a) began with a musical suggestion of hens cackling in a minor mode (measures 1–6). By the time the Rooster started the cakewalk (measure 13) the mode changed to major by way of sixteenth-note phrases that evoked the style of old fiddle tunes, such as "Turkey in the Straw." With the music of the cakewalk came a series of syncopations that were repeated at regular intervals between measures 13 and 28. The syncopated rhythm of measure 13, for example, was repeated in measures 15, 17, 21, 23, and 25, while the rhythm of measure 14 was repeated in measures 16, 18, 19, 22, and 24. Repetitions of rhythmic phrases (isorhythms) were characteristic of ragtime and "The Rooster Dance" was a fine (if slightly overdone) example of the technique. Following the excerpt presented in the example, the Rooster was challenged to a cakewalk contest accompanied by music

Example 112a. "The Rooster Dance" from *The Runaways*

in the minor mode. The battle became fierce, but he ultimately prevailed and the music of measures 13–28 was repeated in a grander arrangement as the Rooster kicked and strutted in celebration.

Hubbell followed *The Runaways* with *Fantana* (book by Sam S. Shubert and Robert B. Smith; lyrics by Smith), a Japanese-American musical at the Garrick Theatre in Chicago (2 October 1904) prior to the New York production, opening 14 January 1905. Hubbell interspersed a melodious score with dance music that included an original minuet, a schottische (which by 1900 appeared to have been a requirement on Broadway), a can-can, and a cakewalk. Critics and audience were sufficiently impressed to dub the show a hit.[1031] Hubbell's subsequent musical theatre scores included *The Babes and the Baron* (25 December 1905), for which he composed one song, "Knock Wood"; *Mexicana* (book and lyrics by Clara Driscoll and Robert B. Smith), opening in New York on 29 January 1906 to one reviewer's headline: "Book Stupid; Music Dull And the Much-Advertised American Beauties Cannot Be Discovered with a Field Glass";[1032] *About Town* (30 August 1906), for which Hubbell composed four numbers ("The Gibson Girl," "Gossip," "The Great White Way," and "A French Tonic");[1033] *Mamselle Sallie* (libretto by Robert B. Smith), which opened at the New Montauk Theatre in Brooklyn (19 November 1906) prior to a three week run in Manhattan;[1034] *A Knight for a Day* (libretto by Smith), a complete revision of *Mamselle Sallie* that had a moderately successful run in New York (16 December 1907);[1035] *Spirit Land* (8 February 1909), a vaudeville act;[1036] *The Midnight Sons* (libretto by Glen MacDonough) for which Hubbell also composed dance music for the Pony Ballet, "The Harlequin Hoops," and a "Parasol Dance" (22 May 1909); *The Girl of the States* (libretto by Glen MacDonough), composed with A. Baldwin Sloane for actress Lulu Glaser, opening in Albany, New York (9 October 1909);[1037] *The Silver Star* (1 November 1909), a vehicle for ballerina Adeline Genée, for which Hubbell composed only the dance number "Dancing the Cotillion"; *The Air King* (libretto by Harry B. Smith), a success in Buffalo (22 November 1909) but closed in Chicago;[1038] *The Jolly Bachelors* (libretto by MacDonough) (6 January 1910); and *The Bachelor Belles* (libretto by Harry B. Smith), for which Hubbell composed the dances, "Song of the Fashions" and "Roses and Butterflies." Another vehicle for Genée, *The Bachelor Belles* opened in Philadelphia on 4 October 1910 prior to a month's run in New York (7 November 1910).[1039]

In 1911 Hubbell joined the staff of Ziegfeld's *Follies* as composer of eight editions of the revue (1911–1914, 1917, 1923–1925)[1040] for which he provided songs and dance music.[1041] For the *Ziegfeld Follies of 1911*,

Hubbell composed a heavily syncopated ragtime "Cake Walk" (example 112b) with a familiar sixteenth note–eighth note–sixteenth note pattern that repeats throughout the opening section of the piece.

After the *Follies*, Hubbell's musical theatre works included *The Never Homes* (libretto by Glen MacDonough), although A. Baldwin Sloane is credited as composer in the New York program (5 October 1911);[1042] *The Three Romeos* (libretto by R.H. Burnside) (13 November 1911);[1043] *The Man from Cook's* (libretto by Henry Blossom), premiered in Baltimore (12 February 1912) prior to the New York run (25 March 1912);[1044] *A Winsome Widow* (libretto adapted from Charles Hoyt), which inaugurated Ziegfeld's Moulin Rouge (formerly the New York Theatre) on 11 April

Example 112b. "Cake Walk" from the *Ziegfeld Follies of 1911*

1912;[1045] *The Money Burners* (libretto by Glen MacDonough) scheduled for production in December 1912;[1046] *The Model Girl* (AKA *The Model Maid*[1047]) (libretto by Anne Caldwell), opened in Atlantic City on 26 January 1915 and closed out of town;[1048] and *Fads and Fancies* (libretto by MacDonough), a poorly- received revue that opened in New York on 8 March 1915.

In August 1915 producer Charles Dillingham engaged Hubbell as the official composer for the New York Hippodrome, where he provided the music for *Hip-Hip Hooray* (30 September 1915);[1049] *The Big Show* (31 August 1916)[1050] which included Hubbell's most famous song, "Poor Butterfly";[1051] *Cheer Up* (23 August 1917);[1052] *Everything* (22 August1918);[1053] *Happy Days* (23 August 1919); *Good Times* (9 August 1920);[1054] and *Better Times* (2 September 1922).[1055] In January 1916, it was announced that Hubbell had been chosen to compose the overture and incidental music for a play, *The Heart o' th' Heather*, opening in Boston on 28 February 1916,[1056] and near the end of the year he contributed the title song to John Golden's musical *Go To It* (24 October 1916).

Hubble's ensuing projects included *The Kiss Burglar* (libretto by MacDonough), which opened in Baltimore to fine reviews (22 April 1918)[1057] and moved on to a three month run in New York; *Among the Girls* (libretto by Roy Cooper Megrue, Henry Blossom, R.H. Burnside, and Glen MacDonough), which, in spite of a successful premiere in New Haven (9 May 1919),[1058] closed on the road; *Miss Millions* (libretto by R.H. Burnside), which played just over a month in New York (beginning 9 December 1919), even with a review that boasted: "A well written libretto, with jokes that are mature but vigorous, set off by the most tuneful of music, to say nothing of a well-chosen cast, who sing, dance and act in a most admirable manner, make *Miss Millions*, which squeezed its way into the Punch and Judy Theatre last week one of the brightest spots in the current theatrical season";[1059] *Yumping Yimmy Yohnson* (libretto by Stanley Murphy), not produced;[1060] *Sonny* (libretto by George V. Hobart), which played to good reviews in Stamford, Connecticut, at the end of July 1921 but failed in New York (16 August 1921); *Sleepy Time* (lyrics by W. Lee Dickson), a play with music scheduled for a February 1922 opening in Los Angeles;[1061] *The Elusive Lady* (libretto by MacDonough), which was launched in Baltimore (2 October 1922)[1062] and closed on the road in mid-November; *Yours Truly*(book by Clyde North; lyrics by Anne Caldwell), which premiered in New York on 25 January 1927 to good reviews;[1063] and *Three Cheers* (libretto by Anne Caldwell and R.H. Burnside; lyrics by Caldwell), which opened in New York on 15 October 1928 to a positive notice from Brooks Atkinson who wrote: "Most of the music is unpretentiously melodious. Some of the song numbers are capital— "Pompanola," ... "Because You're Beautiful," ... "The Silver Tree,". . . "Let's All Sing the Lard Song," ... and "Happy Hoboes" .... *Three Cheers* seems to warrant the enthusiasm of its moniker."[1064]

In addition to all of his contributions to the musical theatre stage, Raymond Hubbell was one of the founders of the American Society of Composers, Authors and Publishers in 1914. In the late 1930s, Hubbell and his wife Estelle retired to Miami, Florida, where he suffered a minor stroke in March 1947 but from which he appeared to have gradually recovered. Seven years later, on 28 November, Hubbell suffered another stroke; on this occasion, he did not respond to treatment and died two weeks later on 13 December 1954.

HUGO, John Adam

Composer, pianist, and music educator John Adam Hugo was born in Bridgeport, Connecticut, on 5 January 1873, the son of German immigrants. He was musically trained in Europe as a concert pianist but poor health forced him to give up the concert stage in favor of private teaching and composing, first in Baltimore, Maryland, as adjunct to the Peabody Conservatory, and after 1910, in Bridgeport. He was the piano accompanist at various concerts organized by the New Assembly Salon at the Plaza Hotel in New York City, and he took second place in a song competition sponsored by the New Assembly on 6 March 1914.[1065] In September 1918, Giulio Gatti-Gasazza, the impresario at the Metropolitan Opera announced that Hugo's opera *The Temple Dancer* (libretto by Jutta Bell-Ranske) was chosen as one of three American operas to be produced at the Metropolitan Opera House late in the 1918–1919 season.[1066] As the title suggested, the story of the opera involved the principal dancer in the temple of Mahadeo, who plotted to steal the god's jewels in order to help her impoverished lover. For a time, she was blocked in this endeavor by the temple guard whom she subsequently seduced, then poisoned; but in the end, she managed to grasp the jewels, only to be struck dead by a lightning bolt. Such a frenzied and melodramatic story required frenzied and melodramatic music and John Adam Hugo was up to the task. In addition, because the temple dancer communicated more through movement than song, there was a fair amount of dance music in the opera: a sinewy "Snake Dance" through which she sanctified herself; an impassioned "Dance of Temptation" (of which example 113 is an excerpt) through which she seduced and poisoned the guard; and the final incidental music that accompanied the dancer's sacrilegious theft and her subsequent punishment. The use of descending chromatic diminished chords in the "Dance of Temptation" was certainly evocative of nineteenth-century German Romanticism and which, by 1918, was the sound moviegoers might have heard accompanying scenes of passion and conflict in silent films. Hugo, however, managed to create interest through the composition of an ascending melody in the bass as counterpoint to the descending

Example 113. "Dance of Temptation" from *The Temple Dancer*

Example 113 (continued). "Dance of Temptation" from *The Temple Dancer*

diminished chords in the treble clef (measures 2–7), musically portraying the onstage conflict between dancer and guard, until measure eight where the chords begin to ascend as well and treble and bass move in the same direction (measures 8–11) as the dramatic tension finds resolution in the guard's seduction.

When the opera premiered on 12 March 1919, on a triple bill with *The Legend*, a new opera by Joseph Breil (libretto by Jacques Byrne), and *Shanewis*, a familiar Indian operetta by Charles Cadman (libretto by Nelle Richmond Eberhart), music critics were miserly with their praise. The critic from *The New York Times* had this to say:

> It is not necessary to dwell at length upon the merits of the new music. The Breil score is melodious and commonplace. It ambles along and chokes the action whenever it can.... *The Temple Dancer* sounded more like the real thing—in Mr. Hugo's case, Richard Wagner. The glow of the mock sun saves the operetta from palling like the Breil score. At least there is orchestral color, rhythmic variety, part writing, and freer tonal modulations. From the sandy soil of the tonic and dominant we are rescued, even though the hands are those of Mr. Hugo and the voice that of Richard of Bayreuth. Neither Mr. Breil nor Mr. Hugo writes "gratefully" for the singers.[1067]

Undaunted by a less-than-mixed review in the *Times*, in 1921 Hugo began searching for a libretto for a new opera, and by spring 1922, he had finally settled on *The Sun God*, about Pizarro's conquest of the Incas, written by Reverend Bartlett B. James, Professor of History and Political Science at Western Maryland College. The two commenced a fruitful collaboration that led to the announcement of a production on the Isthmus of Panama in 1924, at the tenth-anniversary celebration of the opening of the Panama Canal (comparisons to Verdi's *Aida* and the opening of the Suez Canal, notwithstanding).[1068] Additionally, Hugo was commissioned in 1925 by the New York radio station WRNY to compose an opera specifically for radio broadcast, in an attempt to break from the tradition of broadcasting only works composed for another medium. In his *Our American Music*, John Tasker Howard verified that Hugo had, indeed, composed three operas but made no mention of performances beyond those of *The Temple Dancer*. As a result, it is unknown if or when the radio piece was broadcasted. Howard did, however, note that, in addition to the operas, Hugo composed a symphony, two piano concertos, a piano trio, and several songs and instrumental works before his death in 1945.[1069] He was survived by his second wife, Aimee, and his son, Roland.

HUMPHREY, Fred[erick] W[illiam]

The single association of British composer and arranger Fred W. Humphrey with the American musical theatre was George Wood's production of the Covent Garden burlesque pantomime *Robinson Crusoe* (8 May 1869)[1070] for which Humphrey had composed, selected, and arranged all the music, including dance music for "The Frolic of the Fairies Ballet," the "Grand Procession of the Tribes" the "Grand Characteristic Polka," and an "Irish Jig." In addition he provided dance music for various songs throughout the program (including a Dutch wooden shoe dance) and created incidental music for the harlequinade. Reviewers found the "Fairies Ballet" underwhelming, explaining that "Mr. Wood has been so unfortunate in the selecting of his *corps de ballet* at this house as to completely embarrass Miss [Julia] Feder. No *danseuse*, under the circumstances could have appeared to advantage."[1071] While incidental dances were found to be amusing and entertaining, it was the "Grand Procession of the Tribes" that drew the greatest praise:

> In this scene is witnessed one of the best processions ever seen on the American stage. First come twenty-four girls as Amazon Warriors, with shields and armors, followed by six Negro minstrels, who sing "De King Am Coming," accompanying themselves first on the banjo, then the bones, and do a wooden shoe dance. Six more savages appear as ostriches, followed by six Negro guards, six female savages, six with bells and fans, six native warriors and twenty-four female cymbal dancers, who dance and keep good time with their cymbals. The king brings up the rear in his alligator chariot, attended by six Negro guards. This scene lasts thirty minutes, and is not only the most attractive of the whole piece, but is one of the best we have ever seen.[1072]

Though the harlequinade that followed disappointed the audience, the pantomime was somewhat redeemed by the addition of twenty-four snare-drumming girls who marched well and maintained a well-rehearsed drum cadence as they marched. The greatest source of dissatisfaction in the performance, however, was the transformation scene that occurred at 11:30, two and a half hours after *Robinson Crusoe* began. It had been advertised as involving ten changes, and so complicated that it would eclipse anything ever before seen in America.[1073] As a result, expectations were high when the curtain rose to reveal an empty stage, in the middle of which a pedestal arose from a trap in the floor displaying a woman standing in the center, surrounded by eight reclining ladies. As the pedestal ascended, the mechanical apparatus, on which the eight ladies were lounging, began to spread out and the "red fire" fireworks display was ignited and the curtain descended. The intense discontent of the audience who had spent two and half hours in anticipation of the promised spectacular event was echoed in the press:

> We had been told that this transformation scene was in ten changes and was so complicated that it would eclipse anything ever before seen in this country. If the scene that was shown on the first night was really the transformation scene, then we are sorry for the management, for it is without exception the weakest affair yet seen. We do hope that something prevented its full development on

the first night, and that something worthy of the name of a transformation scene will be given. Taken on the whole, we cannot call *Robinson Crusoe* a success, either in its burlesque or pantomime dress, for the first has no fun and the last is as dull and as stupid as was the pantomime introduced here in the *Black Crook* by … pantomimists of England, who met with a disastrous failure.[1074]

After the production closed at the end of the season, Wood sold "all the magnificent scenery, gorgeous costumes, extensive and elaborate properties and appointments" connected with *Robinson Crusoe*, indicating that his theatre would never be touring or reviving the burlesque.[1075]

HYDES, Watty G.

Composer, dance arranger, and musical director Watty Hydes was born in Australia in May 1863, the son of the well-known theatre manager John P. Hydes and actress-singer-pianist Harriet Gordon, from whom Watty received his earliest musical education. Hydes first appeared in American theatrical notices as the musical director of *A Bunch of Keys, or, The Hotel*, a play with music by Charles H. Hoyt and Willie Edouin, produced by the "Sparks" Company of the San Francisco Minstrels at the San Francisco Opera House in New York City on 26 March 1883. After touring with *A Bunch of Keys*, Hydes joined the Thompson Opera Company as musical director for its 1885 season, beginning with Gilbert and Sullivan's *Iolanthe* on 26 April at the Standard Theatre in St. Louis. Subsequent touring musical direction assignments included *Aunt Bridget's Baby* for the Monroe's Celebrities Company;[1076] *A Jolly Surprise* for the Fanny Rice Opera Company;[1077] and the revival of *Hendrick Hudson, or, The Discovery of Columbus* for the [Jennie] Kimball Opera-Comique Company, for which, with Fred Perkins, Hydes arranged and compiled the music.[1078] For the summer season 1894, Hydes and his wife, Lillian, moved to St. Louis, where he accepted the position of musical director at the Terrace Garden, opening on 3 June with a production of Alfred Cellier's *Dorothy*, followed by Franz von Suppé's *Clover* two weeks later. On 23 July, Hydes abruptly quit in the middle of a performance due to a quarrel between his wife and the stage manager, Frank David, and the couple returned to New York.[1079] From September 1894 through January 1897, Hydes toured as musical director with the Pauline Hall Opera Company and composed a drinking song and dance music (a minuet) for the production of the pasticcio opera *Dorcas* (libretto by Harry and Edward Paulton) which premiered at the Lyceum Theatre in Elizabeth, New Jersey on 24 September 1894 and opened at Hammerstein's Olympia Theatre in New York City on 28 December 1896.[1080] In April 1897, Hydes was musical director for *Jim the Penman* at the Grand Opera House in Washington, D.C.,[1081] and the following year, he joined May Irwin as musical director for her touring production of *Kate Kip, Buyer*, for which he also composed incidental music.[1082] Hydes remained May Irwin's musical director for the next two seasons providing songs and incidental music for *Sister Mary* (15 September 1899),[1083] *The Belle of Bridgeport* (21 September 1900),[1084] and *Madge Smith, Attorney* (6 December 1900).[1085] *The New York Times* reviewer for *Sister Mary* in New Haven noted that Hydes's song and dance "The 'Possum Chase" (lyrics by May Irwin) "was liked better than any "coon song" she has sung. It was applauded so long that Miss Irwin had to refuse to sing any more verses. "[1086] Example 114 presents a segment of the dance music that followed the number, during which May Irwin entertained with fancy footwork and a series of character impersonations. Both the

Example 114. Dance in "The 'Possum Chase" from *Sister Mary*

melody and harmony of the dance music were simple and consonant, but the use of syncopations throughout helped sustain the momentum of the "possum chase" and create an even greater sense of commotion.

Following the tour of *Madge Smith, Attorney*, Watty Hydes became the musical director of the Frank Daniels Opera Company with the production of *The Office Boy* at the Star Theatre in Buffalo, New York (14 September 1903),[1087] and remained with Daniels through the end of the *Sergeant Brue* tour early in 1907[1088] when he became musical director for *Noah's Ark*, opening at the New National Theatre in Washington, D.C. on 29 April 1907.[1089] Hydes's subsequent musical directorships included *Lola from Berlin* opening 22 August 1907 in Rochester, New York;[1090] the revival of *A Parisian Model* with the Anna Held Company, touring from October 1907 through May 1908;[1091] *The Arcadians*, premiering in America at the Forrest Theatre in Philadelphia on 27 December 1909 prior to the New York run (17 January 1910) and a national tour; and the return engagement of *The Pink Lady* at the New Amsterdam Theatre, opening 26 August 1912. He is also credited as musical director for many of producer Henry W. Savage's productions.[1092] Watty Hydes died a widower on 8 December 1934 at the Home for Incurables in New York City, where he had been a patient for six weeks.

I

ITZEL, Adam, Jr.

Composer, musical director, and educator Adam Itzel was born on 30 November 1864 in Baltimore, Maryland, the son of Adam and Barbara Itzel, parents of German extraction. As a child he exhibited precocity for music and, through the public school system, he learned how to play virtually every instrument in the orchestra. With the violin as his primary instrument, Itzel graduated from the Peabody Conservatory of Music in 1882 with a "diploma of distinction," one of the first graduates to earn that honor.[1093] The following year, Itzel was engaged as the musical director, orchestrator, dance arranger, and composer at Harris's Academy of Music in Baltimore where *Jack Sheppard*, his first comic opera, with a libretto by Baltimore journalist A.K. Futon, premiered on 23 November 1885. The opera, set in 18th-century London, was positively received with the *New York Clipper* reviewer observing that "the libretto is bright and entertaining, and quite up to Major Fulton's usual high standard, while the music, though at times rather pretentious for a light opera, is very pleasing, notably so in the sentimental numbers. A drinking song by Jack and a bright waltz song by Bess were received with great favor, and the entire opera went remarkably well for a first performance."[1094] The "March" published from the score in 1890 offers a fine example of Itzel's contrapuntal style of composition with a trio (example 115) that anticipated the piccolo obbligato in John Philip Sousa's *Stars and Stripes Forever* (1896). Note that the accompaniment of the march does not rely solely on the traditional alternating tonic-to-dominant bass notes, but rather employs chordal inversions and countermelodies to add variety and texture to the composition, especially in measures 4–8, where the bass line is more interesting than the treble. Note also the obbligato beginning on measure 17 that creates an effective counterpoint to the melody written below it.

By 1888, Itzel had become the musical director at Albaugh's Lyceum Theatre in Baltimore and two years later he was admitted to the faculty of the Peabody Conservatory where he offered classed in music

"March" from *Jack Sheppard*

theory, harmony, and orchestration and established and conducted a student orchestra.[1095] Early in 1891, Itzel collaborated with librettist Harry B. Smith on a new comic opera about a shipwrecked sailor in Morocco who exchanges places with a world-weary Sultan. Called *The Tar and the Tartar*, the opera was produced by the McCaull Opera Company at the Chicago Opera House on 13 April 1891, with Itzel acting as musical director, orchestrator, and dance arranger. Although the Chicago critics were unkind, calling the music and libretto "mummified" and claiming that the opera had absolutely no chance of success,[1096] *The New York Times* wrote that "the opera made a decided hit. The music is catchy and the orchestration very fine. Many of the lines are bright."[1097] Harry B. Smith recalled:

> [Adam Itzel, Jr.] was an ingenuous youth. On the morning after the first performance—in Chicago—he came to rehearsal looking as if he was contemplating suicide, "It's a failure," he said. "I've been walking the streets since seven o'clock and haven't heard anyone whistle any of the music." The piece was produced in New York [on 11] May 1891. Itzel conducted on the opening night and thereby added to the comedy. One critic said, "The composer threw his whole soul into its interpretation and seemed to try hard to throw his body into it too. From his frantic gestures one might have fancied he was conducting all the dramas of the Niebelungen Tetralogy at once."[1098]

In New York City, *The Tar and the Tartar* earned promising reviews. "Composer Itzel directed the inaugural performance with more vigor than discretion," wrote the critic from the *New York Clipper*. "He has written some smooth and enticing melodies and a number of cleverly devised concerted numbers, while the orchestration is decidedly above the average. Several of the solos were heartily encored, and the audience seemed to be pleased with the score, take it all in all. Mr. Smith's libretto is interesting, and at intervals witty."[1099] The *Dramatic Mirror* reviewer added:

> If Messrs. Itzel and Smith have not made a particularly valuable contribution to the current comic opera repertoire in *The Tar and the Tartar*, they can claim credit, at least, for composing and writing a merry, jingling, care-killing piece that in all likelihood will enjoy a larger measure of popular success than any operetta of native origin that has yet had a metropolitan hearing. The first night audience received it heartily and lengthened the representation nearly half-an-hour by demanding numerous encores.[1100]

On 29 June the *Dramatic Mirror*'s prediction was proven true when *The Tar and the Tartar* became the first comic opera written by American-born writers to reach fifty performances in New York City,[1101] and by the end of the run, that number had more than doubled.

Something of a musical celebrity following the success of *The Tar and the Tartar*, Itzel contributed a musical arrangement to the musical farce *Tuxedo* at New York's Park Theatre (5 October 1891), began a collaboration with Robert Barnet in Boston on a comic opera called *Prince Pro Tem*,[1102] and composed a number ("Our National Song") for Edward E. Rice's production of *1492, Up to Date or Very Near It* (September 1892),[1103] all the while performing his professorial duties at Peabody and playing first violin in professional symphony orchestra concerts in Baltimore.[1104] Late in 1892, however, Itzel began exhibiting the symptoms of tuberculous but shrugged them off, believing that he was simply the victim of a common cold. By the time he agreed to visit a physician, the disease had become fatal, and on 5 September 1893 at his home on North Calvert Street in Baltimore, Adam Itzel, Jr. died. "Considered the finest leader of light opera in the United States,"[1105] twenty-eight-year-old Itzel was buried two days later in Baltimore Cemetery.

J

JACOBI, Georges

Born in Berlin on 13 February 1840, Georges Jacobi studied the violin with Eduard and Leopold Ganz in Berlin, Charles Auguste de Bériot in Brussels, and Lambert Massart in Paris, in addition to composition and orchestration with composers François-Auguste Gevaert, Victor Chéri, and Napoléon-Henri Réber at the Paris Conservatory. After graduation Jacobi was hired as a violinist, and subsequently leader of the orchestra at the Paris Opéra and in 1869, Jacobi became the musical director of the Bouffes Parisiens in Paris. At the outbreak of the Franco-Prussian War in 1870, Jacobi fled to London where he became musical director at the Alhambra Theatre in 1871, a position he held until 1896 when he joined the faculty of the Royal Academy of Music. At the Alhambra, Jacobi composed over a hundred ballets and dance interludes, as well as operettas, pasticcio scores, songs, and incidental music for the spectacular entertainments for which the theatre was famous.[1106] In the United States Jacobi's ballet music was first heard in Philadelphia on 1 September 1887, with the performance of the "Dresdina Ballet" (originally produced at the Alhambra Theatre on 15 November 1886) in Bolossy Kiralfy's Parisian extravaganza, *Dolores*.[1107] Jacobi next composed and selected all the music for Kiralfy's spectacle *The Water Queen*, which opened in Chicago on 24 December 1888 and moved to Niblo's Garden on 11 February 1889. The score contained a "Grand Stalactite Ballet" with music specified for the corps de ballet, the entrance of the principal dancers, and the traditional adagio, pizzicato, and "Finale Brilliante"; a "Masked Ball" that included a minuet, a Hungarian dance, and a variety of eccentric and characteristic dances for soloists and chorines; and the obligatory final transformation sequence. Reviews were unkind[1108] and *The Water Queen* closed after three weeks on Broadway, but Kiralfy was back to Niblo's Garden in August with *Antiope*, a pantomime ballet composed by Jacobi, that he purchased from the Alhambra Theatre, to which he added dialogue, songs, and variety acts to explode the original work into a genuine spectacle.[1109] Critics complained about Kiralfy's additions to the ballet but were impressed by the spectacle:

> As a spectacle, however, Bolossy's *Antiope* is very good indeed. The scenery is pretty and the dresses are gorgeous. There are girls enough in the ballet to crowd the stage, and their evolutions are pretty and well executed. The finale of Act I, the drill and departure to battle of the Amazons in Act II, and the concluding ballet are as good in their way as anyone could ask. The incidental divertissements include an exhibition by a couple of Italian gymnasts, a man and a woman, which is excellent of its kind, and a curious dance by Senorita Carmencita, an agile, graceful, mercurial woman, with flashing eyes and mobile features. Her dance is odd and attractive, and it is worthwhile to go to Niblo's to see that alone.[1110]

Jacobi was again heard on Broadway in 1893 when his ballet, "The Birth of the Rainbow" was inserted into the second act of *The Black Crook* at the Academy of Music (14 August). As in his previous work heard in New York, the ballet consisted of various movements including an adagio, several variations, a waltz, galop, and finale. Two years later, as "Georgio Jacobi," he composed the ballet music for the extravaganza, *Aladdin, Jr.* (8 April 1895); and, on 30 October 1899, Jacobi's incidental music for *Robespierre* (written by Victorien Sardou, translated by Laurence Irving) was rendered at the Knickerbocker Theatre in a production imported from the Lyceum Theatre in London, starring the eminent performers Henry Irving and Ellen Terry. Jacobi's incidental score included and overture and entr'actes; a song in act three; and music for the "fête scene" in which motifs from the "Marseillaise" and Étienne Méhul's "Partant pour la Syrie" were interwoven.[1111] Jacobi's contribution to the production was appreciated by critics and audience alike and marked the last time his music was heard in New York during his lifetime. Georges Jacobi died in London on 13 September 1906.

JACOBI, Victor

Victor Jacobi was born in Budapest on 22 October 1883 and studied at the Academy of Music there in the company of Hungarian composers

Emmerich Kálmán and Albert Szirmai.[1112] He enjoyed his first success as a musical theatre composer, *The Proud Princess* (libretto by Jenő Heltai) (17 December 1904) while he was still a student in Budapest, and many hits followed, including *The Brave Hussar* (Ferenc Martos) (30 December 1905), *The Sea Fairy* (Heltai and Zoltán Thury) (1906), *The Rose and the Thorn* (Martos) (23 March 1907), *Yes or No* (Martos) (30 October 1908), and *Johnny* (Martos) (7 May 1909).[1113] Jacobi's first musical play to be performed in New York City was *The Marriage Market* (Martos and Miksa Bródy; lyrics by Arthur Anderson and Adrian Ross; American adaptation by Gladys Unger) (22 September 1913), which was set in Mendocino Bluff, California, in the present, a significant departure from the mythical, fairytale operettas he had composed earlier in his career. The critic at the *New York Clipper* proclaimed that "the music of *The Marriage Market* is the catchiest the town has heard in many a long day, and we bear in mind some recent musical successes as we pen this statement."[1114] *The New York Times* reviewer agreed and also commended the musical arrangements, orchestrations, and dance numbers, ignoring the fact that the titles that were mentioned had been interpolations composed by Jerome Kern.[1115] On 31 October 1914, a year after *The Marriage Market* opened in New York, Jacobi immigrated to the United States[1116] where his next musical to appear in America was *Sybil* (libretto by Miksa Bródy and Ferenc Martos; American version by Harry Graham and Harry B. Smith) (10 January 1916), set in and around the Grand Hotel in Bomsk, Russia. Jacobi's incidental and dance music for the original Hungarian production (27 February 1914) displayed a tendency to use an instrumental arrangement of the preceding sung chorus with varying degrees of ornamentation. With Jacobi's participation, the New York City production rearranged many of the vocal numbers and added additional dance and incidental music to what Jacobi originally composed.[1117] The program of dance music in New York included a pizzicato polka (following "At a Grand Hotel"), a gavotte (appended to "Good Advice"), descriptive incidental music under dialogue and stage business ("Finale Act One"), an extended foxtrot (following "The Way to Do It"), an extended waltz (after "Lift Your Eyes to Mine"), a grand march ("Following the Drum"), a two-step ("I Like the Boys"), a waltz incidental ("Finale Act Two"), a grand waltz ("Two Can Play at That Game"), a syncopated two-step ("Girls, You Are Such Wonderful Things"), and a polka with schottische rhythms ("When Cupid Calls"). Two dance numbers in the English score were not used in New York: a rhythmic polka ("With Money You Can't Go Wrong") and a mazurka ("Keep Cool").

In the spring of 1917, the Charles Frohman Company engaged Victor Jacobi and Harry B. Smith to adapt Michael Morton's 1911 comedy *The Runaway* as a musical play. Consequently the pair spent the summer hammering the well-worn love-triangle plot into shape for a 10 September 1917 opening at the Empire Theatre. The score displayed a fair amount of incidental and dance music, of which notable examples included the "Dance Pantomime" following "Just a Little Bit in Love," the dance appended to "One Look, One Word," and the dance interlude in "Come to Gypsy Land." In typical fashion, Jacobi repeated the sung melodies in the dance music, though the "Dance Pantomime" was prettily embellished by an interesting countermelody. Most appealing of all, however, was a "Pantomimic Scene" with music that, instead of simply reprising melodies, established mood and intensified the dramatic action (music cues marked with brackets):

> [Allegretto moderato] Rose outside, knocks at door. Knocks again. [Moderato e comodo ma con grazia] She enters and goes to center. Looks around. [Più mosso] Goes up stage.[poco agitato] Looks around. Lays down her grip. [Allegretto]Sees a sculptured bust; goes behind it. [Moderato] Peers at first statue. Peers at the second statue, and then at the third. Goes toward window. [Largo] Opens it. [Allegro giocoso] Goes to table. Picks up deck of cards. [*ad lib*. harp arpeggios] Shuffles them. Throws them up [harp *glissando*].... [Allegretto moderato] She goes to center door. Listens. Hesitates, but does not open the door. [Tempo di Marcia moderato] Sees Angèles picture on easel. Registers jealousy [*sforzando* accents]. Clock strikes [bell]. [Andante amoroso] She goes to fireplace, sees photograph of Gerald, takes it up, kisses it, then replaces it [*tranquillo*].[1118]

Although Jacobi's music was found to be "delightfully whimsical" and "light, pleasant and tuneful," it was also said to be "about as original as the plot and general characterization," and the hit of the evening went to "Poor Little Rich Girl's Dog," an interpolation composed by Irving Berlin.[1119]

In 1918 Jacobi contributed incidental music for "A Dream" in the *Ziegfeld Follies of 1918* (18 June 1918), and the following year, he and violinist Fritz Kreisler joined forces to create the score for *Apple Blos-*

soms (libretto by William Le Baron) (7 October 1919), which featured dancers Fred and Adele Astaire. Following a number entitled "On the Banks of the Bronx," Jacobi composed a "Dance-Pantomime" (example 115a) for the Astaires, in which he deviated significantly from his typical brand of dance music by composing an original piece rather than repeating instrumentally what came before. The jaunty polka begins with an ascending two-measure phrase that is repeated in measures 5–6 with the addition of a rest that creates a displacement of accents (in measure 1, the accents fall on the strong beats; in measure five, they fall on the weak beats). Measures 3–4 and 7–8 are also similar and display a vari-

Example 115a. "Dance-Pantomime" from *Apple Blossoms*

ety of musical timbres, ranging from the high, hornpipe-like tune, to a midrange chordal accompaniment that ends with a syncopated *sforzando* pedal tone. Note also the syncopation in measures 10–12 where the emphasis again falls on weak beats in the measures. The Astaires enjoyed working with syncopated accents and abrupt variations in volume and timbre as indicated by the very specific articulation and dynamic markings in the dance music.

Reviews for *Apple Blossoms* were positive and the show ran for over 250 performances, closing in the spring of 1920[1120] when Jacobi was busily at work on *The Half Moon* (libretto by Le Baron), scheduled to premiere in Wilmington, Delaware on 27 September. The score abounded in dance and incidental music, beginning with an atmospheric incidental at the opening of the curtain. The first three numbers of the show were succeeded by dance music in Jacobi's usual mode, and a double duet entitled "The Little Book" was followed by a lengthy stretch of dance music that made ample use of the duet's chorus. In the second act, a rollicking chorus, "Love Makes Us Gay" became a briefly boisterous dance; a sweet Viennese waltz was sung and dance to; and the title song became the melody for a foxtrot at the end of the act. More atmospheric incidental music opened act three, followed later in the act by an incidental entitled "Melodrama" using the tune of the previous number, "Days that Used to Be." Dances featuring a march and another Viennese waltz completed the score, which found favor with critics but was unable to keep a weak libretto afloat for more than five weeks. Jacobi's next effort, *The Love Letter* (Le Baron) was even less successful in spite of the presence of Fred and Adele Astaire and glowing reviews for the score that included "a bit of a dance in the first act that sets the feet tapping, and a waltz that takes hold in the second."[1121] *The Love Letter* opened on 4 October 1921 and was gone by the end of the month. Almost immediately after the closing of *The Love Letter*, Jacobi became ill and was taken to the Lenox Hill Hospital where he died on 10 December 1921 at the age of thirty-eight. In his obituary, *The New York Times* noted that "critics of Jacobi's music have remarked on his versatility, his refusal to descend to the tricks of composition and his abstention from jazz and syncopation"[1122] by which, I assume, was meant the "ragtime" variety of syncopation. It was perhaps those very qualities that, in the 1920s, rendered Jacobi's music out date.

JACQUET, H. Maurice [Henri Louis Fernand]

French composer, dance arranger, and musical director H. Maurice Jacquet was born in Saint-Mandé, an eastern suburb of Paris, on 18 March 1886, the son of photographer Alfred Jacquet and singing teacher Jeanne Noël. He studied the piano with composer and pianist Francis Thomé, composition with Émile Vessard at the Paris Conservatory, and conducting with Alexander Luigini, composer and musical director at the Opéra-Comique in Paris. Jacquet's early compositions include the co-composed (with André Mauprey) comic opera *Messaouda* (libretto by Davin de Champelos) at the Théâtre Moncey (9 March 1908); the lyric drama *Romanitza* (libretto by Maurice Magre) at the Théâtre Municipal de Calais (April 1913); the comic operetta *Le Poilu* [*The Infantryman*] (libretto by Maurice Hennequin and Pierre Veber) at the Palais-Royal in Paris (14 January 1916); the vaudeville operetta *La Petite Dactylo* [*The Little Typist*] (libretto by Maurice Hennequin and Georges Mitchell) at the Gymnase in Paris (21 October 1916); and co-composition (with André Mauprey) of the operetta *Son Altesse Papillon* [*Her Highness Butterfly*] (libretto by P. Cerval and André Mauprey), at the Théâtre Lyon (6 April 1920).

In the United States, Jacquet was credited with the composition of the incidental and dance music (based on folk music from the Spanish Province of Murcia), arranged for an orchestra of sixteen musicians to accompany *Spanish Love*, a play by Avery Hopwood and Mary Roberts Rinehart adapted from the French play, *Aux Jardins de Murcie* [*In Murcie's Gardens*] by Carlos De Battle and Antonin Lavergne. *Spanish Love* opened in Washington D.C. on 9 August 1920 and moved to New York on 17 August where it played over three hundred performances in spite of lackluster reviews that did, however, praise the music and dance as two of the more successful aspects of the production.[1123] In the early 1920s, with his wife, harpist Andrée Amalou-Jacquet, Jacquet toured Canada and Cuba, where he conducted the Cuban National Philharmonic Orchestra. In 1927, Jacquet composed the symphonic score (arranged for 110 musicians) for the Gloria Swanson film *The Love of Sunya* (11 March 1927); the following year he contributed music to the Metro-Goldwyn-Mayer shorts *The Spanking Age* (15 December 1928) and *The Holy Terror* (9 March 1929); and in 1929, Jacquet composed the songs and ballet music for *The Silver Swan* (book by William S. Brady and Alonzo Price; lyrics by Brady), which opened at the Martin Beck Theatre in New York on 27 November to poor reviews.[1124] Almost a year later to the day, a revised version of

The Silver Swan entitled *The Well of Romance* was produced at the Craig Theatre (7 November 1930). Jacquet provided new songs, dance music (including a "Mazourka" and a "German Country Dance"), and musical direction for the production, and a new libretto was written by Preston Sturges, the celebrated film director and scriptwriter. Although reviewers were kinder to Jacquet's music, calling it "considerably superior" to Sturges's libretto,[1125] the show ran for only a week, two weeks fewer than *The Silver Swan*. Jacquet returned to composing incidental scores for film in the early 1930s providing (uncredited) music for B movies, such as the Halperin Brothers' film, *White Zombie* (28 July 1932) starring Bela Lugosi as a Haitian voodoo master, and Broadway favorite, Joseph Cawthorn, as a missionary who helps save the day. In 1937, Jacquet established The American Opera Company in Trenton, New Jersey, but after only two performances, the company went bankrupt and closed. He continued to conduct in the mid-Atlantic region until his death in New York City on 29 June 1954.

JAKOBOWSKI, Edward

Composer Edward Jakobowski was born in the London district of Islington on 17 April 1856 to a Polish-born cigar salesman and his Viennese wife. When Edward was still a child, the family moved to Vienna where Jakobowski later studied music with composer Joseph Hellmesberger. After he returned to England in the early 1880s, Jakobowski composed the music for the one-act comic opera *The Three Beggars* (libretto by Sinclair Dunn), produced at the Royal Academy of Music on 28 July 1883. Two musical theatre works followed, the burlesque *Little Carmen* (7 February 1884), and the comic opera *Dick* (17 April 1884), before Jakobowski composed *Erminie* (libretto by Harry Paulton and Classon Bellamy) (Birmingham, 26 October 1885; London, 9 November 1885), one of the outstanding hits of its generation, and the most successful comic opera on the nineteenth-century American stage.[1126] *Erminie* opened at the Casino Theatre in New York on 10 May 1886 and played over 500 performances in its initial run, even after mixed reviews in *The New York Times* and *New York Clipper*.[1127] It was subsequently revived in New York City on 16 January 1888, 1 April 1889, 3 October 1893, 23 May 1897, 23 May 1898, 9 May 1899, 19 October 1903, and 3 January 1921. So popular was the score of *Erminie* that selections from it appeared in revivals of *Our Irish Visitors* (6 June 1887) and *Pat's New Wardrobe* (20 May 1889); and in addition to the vocal music in the comic opera Jakobowski arranged a variety of incidental and dance pieces that included entrance music, changes of scene music, and dance music, all of which were based on the sung themes of the opera.[1128]

On 26 August 1889, Jakobowski's *Paola, or, The First of the Vendettas* (libretto by Harry Paulton and his son Edward) was produced at the Fifth Avenue Theatre after having been "scornfully rejected by Philadelphia" at its premiere at the Grand Opera House in that city on 6 May. As was the case for *Erminie*, reviews for *Paola* were mixed: critics found Jakobowski's music "pleasing" but "seldom original" with the best numbers sounding like "rather labored imitations of [Arthur] Sullivan." On the other hand, Jakobowski's orchestrations were considered excellent and found to be deserving of "especial praise,"[1129] and once again, the composer provided incidental and dance arrangements for the comic opera. Five years later, Jakabowski's *The Devil's Deputy* (libretto by J. Cheever Godwin) appeared at Abbey's Theatre in New York on 10 September 1894. Even though the work was vehicle for popular actor Francis Wilson and featured the beloved soubrette Lulu Glaser, *The Devil's Deputy* was not a success.[1130] Neither was *The Queen of the Brilliants* (libretto by Brandon Thomas,[1131] revised by H.J.W. Dam for the American production), a vehicle for Lillian Russell that followed at Abbey's Theatre on 7 November 1894. Lillian Russell's biographer, Parker Morell, quoted the *Spirit of the Times* review, which described the opera as "all showy scenery, glittering costumes, graceful dancers, and bang, bang, bang in the orchestra, with no melody that one can remember nor a line in the dialogue worth remembering."[1132] Jakobowski's next comic opera, *Tarantella* (libretto by Alfred Murray) was produced by the Castle Square Opera Company at Studebaker Theatre in Chicago on 17 July 1899. Although the work received generally positive reviews,[1133] *Tarantella* closed out of town. By 1902, the composer of *Erminie* was bankrupt, financially and artistically. By the time his final American musical *Winsome Winnie* (libretto by Harry Paulton) premiered at the Academy of Music in Baltimore (28 September 1903), it had been rewritten by Frederic Ranken and recomposed by the musical director, Gustave Kerker. Of the twenty-odd numbers in the show, only six composed by Jakobowski remained: 4 songs ("The Englishman," "Cities I Love," "Jenny," and "Montenegrin Patrol"), a chorus ("Oh, the Paying Guests"), and an ensemble ("Miss Walker of Kalamazoo").[1134] Jakobowski lived another twenty-five years but produced no new comic operas in America. As Kurt Gänzl wrote, "the man who had been the toast of Broadway in the late 1880s vanished into professional oblivion."[1135] He died in London on 29 April 1929

JAMES, Harry

Bandleader, dance arranger, and composer Harry James first appeared in theatre notices as a member of the Globe Dramatic Company opening its 1876–1877 season in Winchester, Illinois, on 28 August.[1136] He moved to Barlow's Southern Comedy Company beginning a Midwestern tour in October 1881[1137] and in the summer of 1884 James was credited as musical director of Hunter's Circus, where he and his seven-member orchestra were among the members of the company accidentally poisoned in Augusta, Kansas, by drinking tainted coffee.[1138] Everyone involved managed a quick and full recovery and the circus tour continued without further incident. James, however, disappeared from theatrical records between the end of the tour in 1885 and the fall of 1895 when he reappeared as musical director of the vaudeville troupe the Partellos, touring with the Daisie Claxton Specialty Company in the Midwest.[1139] The following year he was engaged by producer Oliver Labadie to compose music for his touring productions of *Faust*, *Nobody's Child*, and *A Yankee*[1140] and appointed general musical director and composer for all of producer Charles E. Blaney's touring attractions. James's first effort for Blaney, *A Boy Wanted* (book and lyrics by Charles E. Blaney) opened on 17 August 1896 in Lockport, New York, and appeared for a limited run at the Star Theatre in New York City five months later on 18 January 1897. The show may have been short on plot but it was rich in songs and dances that included buck dancing, acrobatics, an "Oriental March," a "College Girls' Song and Dance," and incidental music for the entrances of Cupid and a dragon.[1141] *A Hired Girl*, James's next collaboration with Blaney, premiered on 30 August 1897 at the Stone Opera House in Binghamton, New York, and opened at the Star Theatre on 10 January 1898. Like its predecessor, the musical abounded in dances that included the obviously popular buck dancing, a ragtime dance, a can-can, and trick dancing, as well as specialty music for featured dancers.[1142]

After the turn of the century, James secured the rights to produce Weber and Fields's plays on the Pacific coast and in Australia. He moved to San Francisco, where he became musical director and company manager at Fischer's Theatre, and in May 1904, James and his San Francisco ensemble (including orchestra and chorus), calling themselves the American Travesty Stars, left for a tour of Australia. A year later, on 8 May 1905, James and company were back in San Francisco performing *The Merry Whirl* and other musicals by Weber and Fields for the 1905–1906 season at Fischer's Theatre. The company moved to Los Angeles for a twelve-week summer season of Weber and Fields at the Mason Opera house before returning to San Francisco with *Fiddle-De-Dee* (12 August 1906), *Whirl-I-Gig* (21 August 1906), *Pousse Café* (2 October 1906), and *Barbara Fidgety* (22 October 1906).[1143] James's American Travesty Company followed the San Francisco engagement with another tour before disbanding early in 1908. James remained in San Francisco as musical director at the Princess Theatre until 29 June 1908, when he retired from conducting and ceded his baton to Selli Simonson.[1144]

James's name appeared on Broadway in 1916 as the musical director for *So Long Letty* (book by Oliver Morosco and Elmer Harris; music and lyrics by Earl Carroll), and again in 1922 as musical director for *Letty Pepper* (book by Oliver Morosco and George V. Hobart; music by Werner Janssen; lyrics by Leo Wood and Irving Bibo). Since the Morosco family was intimately involved with the theatre scene in Los Angeles and San Francisco during James's years on the West coast, it is likely that he and Morosco knew one another, and perhaps the producer drew James out of retirement for these projects. A slightly earlier Morosco musical, *Pretty Mrs. Smith* (1914), advertised book by Oliver Morosco and Elmer Harris, lyrics by Earl Carroll, and music by Alfred Robyn and Henry James. Given the similarities between the authors and producers of *So Long Letty* and *Pretty Mrs. Smith*, it is tempting to suggest that Henry James and Harry James are one and the same, particularly since this is the only appearance of "Henry" James in contemporary theatrical documents in connection with music. However, since there was no compelling reason for Harry to alter his name at such a late point in his career, the association remains conjectural.

JANNOTTA, A[lfredo Antonio]

Italian composer A. Jannotta was born in Capua, Italy, on 20 December 1843. He studied composition with the eminent opera composer Severio Mercadante and at the Royal Conservatory in Naples. After his graduation in 1861, he moved to London where he became the musical director for the Italian Orchestral Association, a concert ensemble of eighty-five musicians. After two seasons with the orchestra in London, Jannotta moved to Boston, Massachusetts, in 1865 where he became vocal master at the New England Conservatory of music.[1145] When *The Black Crook* and Marietta Ravel came to the Continental Theatre in Boston in 1867, Jannotta composed the "Marietta Ravel Galop," which she performed in the production; and one year later he produced the "Fire Fly Galop" (example 116) for a presentation of the *White Fawn*. Note the simple harmonic vocabulary of the composition and the fluttering melodic phrases, beginning in measure 10, that musically portray the flight and light of the firefly.

Also in 1868, Jannotta moved to Cincinnati, Ohio, where he spent the next twelve years teaching and organizing the Cincinnati Choral Soci-

Example 116. "Fire Fly Galop" from *The White Fawn*

ety and the city's first symphony orchestra. In addition, in 1869, Jannotta won $1000 prize for his composition, "Peace Festival Grand March," the only new work performed at Patrick Gilmore's National Peace Jubilee in Boston.[1146] On 1 March 1880 he resigned the directorship of the Cincinnati Choral Society[1147] and returned to Boston briefly in 1881 to direct the South Boston Philharmonic Society (an orchestra) and the Elmwood Club of Roxbury (a choral society) before relocating to St. Paul, Minnesota in 1882, where he taught vocal technique privately, organized music festivals, directed the St. Paul Choral Society, and conducted concerts and operas, including his opera *Alidor* which was performed on 13 June 1887.[1148] The following year, Jannotta moved to Chicago, where he continued to conduct and teach, advertising himself as an instructor "in all branches of voice culture, especially the study of operas, oratorios, and church and concert music" at $60per hour.[1149] Additionally, when the Chicago Conservatory opened for its fifth season on 16 September 1889, Jannotta was listed among the faculty.[1150] In 1902, Jannotta opened the new Warrington Opera House in the Chicago suburb of Oak Park, Illinois, but by 1905, his declining health forced him to move again, this time to Los Angeles, where he died on 11 April1913, survived by his wife Stella, and three sons.[1151]

JEFFERSON, William [Winter]

William Jefferson, born in London on 25 August 1876, was the ninth and last child of actor Joseph Jefferson and Sarah Warren, niece of actor William Warren. Although he displayed an aptitude for music, while he was growing up, William and his brother Joseph Jefferson, Jr. traveled with their father, playing minor roles in a repertoire of plays that included *Rip Van Winkle* and *The Cricket on the Hearth*. In the summer 1897, William joined the Columbia Stock Company in Washington, D.C. where he performed in a repertory of plays that included *Lady Windermere's Fan, Esmeralda, Captain Swift, All the Comforts of Home,* and *Arabian Nights*.[1152] The following season, Jefferson was a member of the [Claude] Duval and [Edwin] Lawrence Company, taking roles in *Hamlet, Richard III, Othello, Romeo and Juliet, The Fool's Revenge, The Three Guardsmen,* and *Don Cesar de Bazan*.[1153] In November 1898, William and Joseph, Jr. took over their father's tour in Pittsburgh[1154] and continued through the following season,[1155] with Joseph, Jr. playing his father's role in *Rip Van Winkle* (Rip Van Winkle), and William doing the same in *The Rivals* (Bob

Acres). On 29 October 1900, William was represented on Broadway as composer of the music, lyrics, and (uncredited) dance arrangement (with Watty Hydes) for "Dance on Friday Night" inserted into the score of *The Belle of Bridgeport* (book by Glen MacDonough; music by J. Rosamond Johnson; lyrics by Bob Cole and James Weldon Johnson).[1156] William continued to tour with his brother until 1905 when he appeared in the Broadway musical comedy, *The Catch of the Season* (28 August 1905). He resumed touring with Joseph, Jr. in 1906 but returned to Broadway in 1910 with *Welcome to Our City* (12 September), *The Senator Keeps House* (27 November 1911), and *A Fool of Fortune* (12 January 1912). In 1913 William married the vivacious, blond, Broadway actress Vivian Martin;[1157] and in the same year, he began to appear in silent films, including *The Rivals* (1913); *Wanted by the Police* (1913); *Soldiers of Fortune* (1914); *The Wages of Sin* (1914); *Butterflies and Orange Blossoms* (1914); *A Scrap of Paper* (1914); *Marrying Money* (1915); *Camille* (1915); *The Habit of Happiness* (1916); *The Right Direction* (1916); *Her Own People* (1917); and *Out of the Wreck* (1917). In April 1917, Jefferson joined the scenario department of the "Fatty" Arbuckle Film Company[1158] and a year later he acted in a popular Broadway farce by Mark Swan entitled *She Walked in Her Sleep* (4 April 1918). In 1919 Jefferson performed in the silent film *Wild Oats*, after which he appeared in Henry S. Creamer and J. Turner Layton's Broadway musical *Three Showers* (5 April 1920).[1159] On 9 November 1928 William Jefferson retired to Honolulu, Hawaii, where he died on 11 February 1946.

JEROME, Ben M. [Benhardt Jerome Michaelis]

Performer, pianist, composer, and musical director Ben M. Jerome was born in New York City on 6 April 1876,[1160] the son of German immigrants. He began his theatrical career as an accompanist and vaudeville entertainer, composing music for his own acts as well as for other performers. Early specialty numbers composed by Jerome included "If I Were Only a Boy" (1899), "Just Tell Her I'm Her Daddy," (1899), "Here Comes the Band" (1900) and "Kiss Me Goodbye and Go, Jack" (1901). In 1900, Jerome also began contributing numbers to Broadway musicals that included *Mam'selle 'Awkins* (26 February 1900) "The Sousa Girl" (lyrics by Matt C. Woodward); *The Supper Club* (23 December 1901); *The Wild Rose* (5 May 1902) "Those Things Cannot Be Explained" (lyrics by Junie McCree); *The Chaperons* (5 June 1902) "Blooming Lize" (lyrics by

Matt C. Woodward); *Mr. Bluebeard* (21 January 1903) "In the Pale Moonlight" (lyrics by Matt C. Woodward); and *A Girl from Dixie* (14 December 1903) "Love in an Orchard." Jerome composed the entire score for the curtain-raiser at the New York Theatre Roof Garden, *Queen of Balleyhoo Bey* (4 August 1902) (libretto by Percy Greenbush);[1161] and when the roof garden was reopened the following year as the "Crystal Gardens," Jerome composed the music for *Darling of the Gallery Gods* (22 June 1903) (book by George V. Hobart, lyrics by Matt C. Woodward and John Gilroy), *The Dress Parade* (22 June 1903) (book by George V. Hobart, lyrics by Matt C. Woodward and John Gilroy), and *Lifting the Cup* (27 July 1903) (book by George V. Hobart, lyrics by Matt C. Woodward and Nicholas H. Biddle).[1162]

At the beginning of the 1903–1904 season, Jerome became associated with Chicago's La Salle Theatre, for which he co-composed (with Paul Schindler) the music for *The Isle of Spice* (12 September 1903) (libretto by Allen Lowe and George E. Stoddard),[1163] a production that enjoyed a healthy run in Chicago, on Broadway (23 August 1904), and on tour.[1164] Jerome subsequently composed the scores for *The Belle of Newport* (libretto by Charles F. Dennee) at the La Salle Theatre (21 December 1903),[1165] and *The Royal Chef* (libretto by George E. Stoddard and Charles S. Taylor) at the La Salle Theatre (1 April 1904). In addition, he served as musical director for *The Royal Chef* tour that included a production at the Lyric Theatre on Broadway (1 September 1904).[1166] Jerome's score for *The Royal Chef* contained a significant amount of dance music that included an original ragtime march following "Would You if You Were I," a song about taking advantage of fortuitous situations ; a two-step dance, based on the melody of "The Maiden and The Kissing Bug," a novelty song that employed insect buzzing like the "Duo de la Mouche" in Offenbach's *Orphée aux Enfers*; an original schottische (example 117a) that followed "We Are a Band of Gentlemen," a song about poisoning a potentate; and an amusing hornpipe (example 117b) that, in Gilbert-and-Sullivan fashion, completed a number entitled "An Admirable Admiral."

On 16 February 1905, Jerome's musical farce *Alphonse and Gaston* premiered in Decatur, Illinois;[1167] on 12 August 1905 the La Salle Theatre opened Jerome's new musical, *The Yankee Regent*, libretto by two Chicago newspapermen, Charles Edelman and I.L. Blumenstock;[1168] and late in 1905, Jerome contributed music to *The Press Agent* at Fields' Theatre in New York City (29 November). In September 1906, he had a private reading of *In Command* (libretto by Will M. Hough and Frederick Donaghey),

Example 117a. Schottische in "We Are a Band of Gentlemen" from *The Royal Chef*

scheduled to be the first production of the Ben M. Jerome Amusement Company. The description of the piece is of interest because the musical appeared to anticipate later developments in the American musical theatre:

> The piece is said to be different from anything with which the name of Mr. Jerome has previously been associated. While a comedy strain prevails throughout, the climaxes are all intensely dramatic, and *the musical numbers have a direct connection with the action* (italics mine). The story is one of love and hate in Panama, and has to do with the affairs of Hector Elwood, a civil engineer in the U.S. Government service.[1169]

In Command, retitled as *The Girl of the Gate*, would open in Flint, Michigan, on 22 August 1912, prior to a 1 September opening at the La Salle Theatre in Chicago.[1170]

Example 117b. Hornpipe in "An Admirable Admiral" from *The Royal Chef*

Jerome's subsequent musical theatre projects included the comic opera, *Thebe, or, Marry a Marionette* (August 1906); the vaudeville act, *The Lady Buccaneers* (September 1906); the musical revue, *The Mimic World* (co-composed with Seymour Furth; book by Edgar Smith; lyrics by Edward Madden and Addison Burkhardt) (9 July 1908); the Eddie Foy vehicle, *Mr. Hamlet of Broadway* (book by Edgar Smith; lyrics by Edward Madden) (Philadelphia, 1 October 1908; New York City, 23 December 1908);[1171] musical direction for Julian Edwards's *The Motor Girl* (15 June 1909); the Sam Bernard vehicle, *The Duke's Understudy* (AKA *He Came from Milwaukee*) (co-composed with Louis A. Hirsch; book by Mark Swain and Edgar Smith; lyrics by Edward Madden) (31 December 1910); the musical comedy, *Louisiana Lou* (libretto by Addison Burkhardt and Frederick Donaghey) at the La Salle Theatre (3 September 1911);[1172] an extravaganza based on George Randolph Chester's stories, *The Jingo* (October 1912); additional music for *The Sun Dodgers* (30 November 1912); and a musicalization of Charles H. Hoyt's farce, *A Texas Steer*, entitled *A Trip to Washington* (libretto by Henry Blossom) at the La Salle Theatre (24 August 1913).

Late in November 1913, Jerome was engaged as musical director for G.M. Anderson's Gaiety Theatre in San Francisco where he conducted the orchestra during the showing of silent films as well as the live productions of *The Girl at the Golden Gate* (13 December 1913) and *The Merry Gambol* (2 February 1914). He was back in Chicago at McVickers' Theatre, at the beginning of the 1914–1915 season, with a new twenty-one-minute vaudeville revue (28 September 1914) that was subsequently staged at the Harlem Opera House in January 1915. Composed and directed by Jerome, the revue opened with "Skinny Hoo Hoo," a trio dance; followed by "In My Soap Bubble Aeroplane" with kiddie costumes, soap bubbles, and another dance; "Mama's Angel Child," with more dancing; "Nutty Honey" preceded Ben Jerome's medley of songs that included "My Love Is Like the Red, Red Rose," "The World's All Wrong Again," and "Louisiana Lou." The finale, "Yankee Doodle Girl" involved the company, led by a drum major, marching into the audience with prop brass instruments.[1173] In addition to his vaudeville revue, Jerome composed additional numbers for the American version of the German operetta, *A Modern Eve* (3 May 1915), "When the Madame Goes Away," and "A Quiet Evening at Home" (both with lyrics by Benjamin Hapgood Burt). He provided the musical direction for *Oh, Boy!* at the Cort Theatre in San Francisco, composed the score for the Joseph Santley vehicle, *Naughty, Naughty*,[1174] and returned to Chicago's La Salle Theatre as musical director of the *Century Midnight Whirl*.[1175] In 1926, he composed "My Lady" (lyrics by Frank Crumit) interpolated into the score of *Queen High* (8 September), and the next year he provided dance music, musical direction, and the score (co-composed with Philip Charig) for *Yes, Yes, Yvette* (book by James Montgomery and William Cary Duncan; lyrics by Irving Caesar) (3 October 1927).[1176] After *Yes, Yes, Yvette*, Jerome retired to Huntington Station, Long Island, where he died after a brief illness on 27 March 1938. He was married twice, first to Florence Liebenheim and later to Elizabeth Belle Caufield. Both marriages ended in divorce.

JOHNS, Al[bert]

Al Johns was born in Washington D.C. on 4 June 1878 and educated in the District's public school system. He took piano lessons at an early age, and when he was a teenager, he began an association with James Reese Europe that would last and flourish for thirty years. Johns moved to New York City before the turn of the century to play in nightclubs and write songs.[1177] His association with the musical theatre began in 1903 when he composed the music for "On Broadway in Dahomey Bye and Bye" (lyrics by Alex Rogers) for Will Marion Cook (another Washington D.C. native) and Paul Laurence Dunbar's *Dahomey* (18 February 1903). The song remained in the production that reappeared the following year as *In Dahomey* (27 August 1904) while Johns had moved on to compose special material for comedienne May Irwin and serve as accompanist in her shows. He composed music for "Bible Stories" (lyrics by John Lee Clarke) and "Sadie" (lyrics by Al Johns) as well as the dance music in *Mrs. Black Is Back* (7 November 1904) and toured with the production until the summer of 1906. Johns composed and arranged the ballet "Ethiopia" in Will Marion Cook's *Bandanna Land* (libretto by J.A. Shipp and Alex Rogers) (3 February 1908);[1178] he subsequently appeared in Charles Richman's play *The Revellers* (7 September 1909) as himself, a nightclub pianist;[1179] and he contributed "In Far Off Mandalay" (lyrics by Alex Rogers) to J. Rosamond Johnson's *Mr. Load of Koal* (libretto by Shipp and Rogers) (1 November 1909). In May 1910, Johns became assistant director for James Reese Europe's Clef Club Orchestra of 100 musicians, singers and dancers, and he was instrumental in the preparation of the initial Clef Club Concert on 27 May at the Manhattan Casino in Harlem.[1180] Johns traveled with the orchestra on tour through 1913 and later joined Europe's Society Orchestra, which toured with Vernon and Irene Castle, and the "Hellfighters" which toured Europe during World War I. Johns was also present at the concert on 9 May 1919 when James Reese Europe was murdered. After the United States outlawed alcohol on 17 January 1920, Johns spent the rest of his life performing in clubs in London and Paris, where he died on 16 June 1928.

Johns's published music displayed his great versatility as a composer. Ranging from sentimental parlor ballads to syncopated ragtime dance music, his titles included "I Thought I Heard Some-body Calling Me" (1898); "I Guess That Will Be About All" (1899); "Matinee Girl's Parade: March and Two-Step" (1901); "Those Naughty Harem Eyes" (words by Alfred Bryan) (1901; "I Just Don't Feel Like Being Disturbed" (lyrics by Elmer Bowman) (1902); "At a Garden Party" (1902); "Ianthia: March and Two-Step" (1902); "Dance Rubenesque: March and Two-Step" (1902); "A Darktown Invasion: Characteristic March and Two-Step" (1903); "Mister Bluebeard March and Two Step" (1903); "Araby: Characteristic Intermezzo" (1903); "Ethiopia: An African Intermezzo" (1903); "Two Hearts (Deux Coeurs): Waltz" (1904); "'Scuse Me Boss" (lyrics by Charles H. Lynch) (1904); "Caprice" (1904); "In Far Off Mandalay" (lyrics by Alex Rogers) (1909); "Chantecler: French Waltzes (1910); and "In Buenos Aires" (1927).

JOHNSON, J[ohn] Rosamond

J. Rosamnd Johnson was born on 11 August in Jacksonville, Florida, the younger brother of lyricist, author, and civil rights leader James Weldon Johnson. At the age of four, J. Rosamond began playing the piano, under the tutelage of his mother, a piano teacher, and at seventeen he entered the New England Conservatory, where his principal professors included composer and author of *The International Library of Music for Home and Studio*, Charles Dennee, the popular composer of "My Blue Heaven," George Whiting, and operatic baritone, David Bispham.[1181] Following his studies in Boston, Johnson traveled to London to study privately with composer Samuel Coleridge-Taylor, a protégé of Sir Edward Elgar.[1182] When he returned to the United States in 1896, he was cast (as Edward Platt) in John W. Isham's *Oriental America, or, In the Isle of San Domingo*, produced in New York City on 16November 1896, after which he returned to Jacksonville where he taught music to children in the public schools. Around the turn of the century, Johnson composed "Lift Ev'ry Voice and Sing" (lyrics by James Weldon Johnson), and taught it to his students. The song became very popular, so popular in fact, that the NAACP dubbed it the "Negro National Anthem."[1183]

By 1899, Johnson was back in New York City collaborating with performer, lyricist Bob Cole on songs interpolated into the scores of other composers. They composed "Why Don't My Baby Write?" for the May Irwin vehicle *Sister Mary* (27 October 1899) and "Run, Brudder Possum, Run" (with additional lyrics by Rosamond's brother, James Weldon Johnson) for *The Rogers Brothers in Central Park* (17 September 1900). The trio produced "My Castle on the Nile" for the Williams and Walker comedy *Sons of Ham* (15 October 1900), and they were credited as principal songwriters for *The Belle of Bridgeport*, another May Irwin vehicle (29 October 1900). Subsequent interpolations by the Johnson brothers and Bob Cole included three songs imported from The *Belle of Bridgeport* ("Why Don't the Band Play," "I've Got Troubles of My Own," and "I Ain't Going to Work No More") for May Irwin's *Madge Smith, Attorney* (10 December 1900); and the big hit in *The Little Duchess* (14 October 1901), "The Maiden with the Dreamy Eyes" (J. Rosamond and Cole only).[1184] Johnson and Cole[1185] also inserted a number of songs ("I Don't Want to Be No Actor Man," "My Castle on the Nile," and "Nobody's Looking But de Owl an' de Moon") into the score for *Champagne Charlie* (book by Augustus Thomas), a touring show (1901).[1186] The pair (reunited with James Weldon Johnson) composed "Dinah" and "The Moon and the Owl" for the spectacular extravaganza, *The Sleeping Beauty and the Beast* (4 November 1901); and again without James, the pair produced "When the Band Plays Ragtime," "Don't Butt In," and "The Maiden with the Dreamy Eyes" (from *The Little Duchess*) for *The Supper Club* (23 December 1901). "The Maiden with the Dreamy Eyes" was also used in *The Hall of Fame* (5 February 1902) for which the Brothers Johnson also composed "Angemima Green";[1187] Johnson and Cole composed "The Animals' Convention" for *Huckleberry Finn* (11 November 1902), which closed out of town; and for *Sally in Our Alley* (24 November 1902), Johnson and Cole produced, arguably their greatest hit, "Under the Bamboo Tree," which was subsequently interpolated into the scores of *Alphonse and Gaston* (29 December 1902), *Zig-Zag Alley* (19 January 1903), and "The Land Where Good Songs Go" segment of *Miss 1917* (3 November 1917).

Johnson and Cole composed "When the Colored Band Comes Marching Down the Street" for *Mr. Bluebeard* (21 January 1903); the Johnson Brothers produced "The Katydid, the Cricket and the Frog" and "Two Eyes," while the brothers and Cole created the "Congo Love Song" and "Cupid's Ramble" for *Nancy Brown* (16 February 1903). "Congo Love Song" was later inserted into the "River Song Medley" in Jerome Kern's *The Night Boat* (libretto by Anne Caldwell) (2 February 1920), and "Cupid's Ramble" was followed by a clever schottische dance (example 118) arranged by J. Rosamond Johnson that wittily employed a quotation from Mendelssohn's "Wedding March" (measures 5–7) from his incidental score for *A Midsummer Night's Dream*.

Dance in "Cupid's Ramble" from *Nancy Brown*

Johnson and Cole provided "The Maid of Timbuctoo" for Weber and Fields's extravaganza *Whoop-Dee-Doo* (24 September 1903); they added "The Evolution of Ragtime" (with James Weldon Johnson) to the fairy-tale extravaganza *Mother Goose* (2 December 1903);[1188] Johnson and Cole alone produced "When the Moon Comes Peeping O'er the Hill" for *A Girl from Dixie* (14 December 1903); the duo added two numbers ("Big Indian Chief," and "Prepossessing Maid" to the score of *An English Daisy* (18 January 1904); for the vaudeville musical *A Little of Everything* (6 June 1904), the pair composed nearly half the score: "The Pretty Little Squaw from Utah," "Fishing," "There is Something About You That I Love, Love, Love," "Como le Gusta Me?" "Let Him Dream" and "The Evolution of Rag Time" borrowed from *Mother Goose*. The Johnson brothers and Cole were credited as principal composers of *Humpty Dumpty* (14 November 1904) and *In Newport* (26 December 1904), for which J. Rosamond also provided dance arrangements. Without Cole the Johnsons interpolated "I'll Keep a Warm Spot in My Heart for You" into Will Marion Cook's score for *Abyssinia* (20 February 1906); and the Johnson brothers and Cole produced "My Hottentot" for the Marie Cahill vehicle, *Marrying Mary* (27 August 1906).

J. Rosamond and James Weldon Johnson were credited as the principal songwriters (Rosamond also provided dance arrangements) for *The Shoo-Fly Regiment* (3 June 1907);[1189] they interpolated "Southland" (originally in *The Shoo-Fly Regiment*) into Will Marion Cook's score for *Bandanna Land* (3 February 1908); J. Rosamond Johnson and Cole inserted "I Have Lost My Little Brown Bear" into the score of the Anna Held vehicle *Miss Innocence* (30 November 1908); additionally, J. Rosamond composed the songs and dance music for *The Red Moon* (libretto by Bob Cole) and also performed the role of "Plunk Green" (3 May 1909).[1190] Johnson was credited as the principal composer for *Mr. Lode of Coal* (book and lyrics by J.A. Shipp and Alex Rogers) (1 November 1909); the Johnson Brothers inserted "If You'll Be My Eve I'll Build an Eden for You" and "Excuse Me, Mister Moon" into the score for *Little Miss Fix It* (3 April 1911); and J. Rosamond Johnson was billed as principal composer for *Hello, Paris* (book by William LeBaron; lyrics by J. Leubrie Hill) (19 August 1911), for which he also composed uncredited dance arrangements.[1191]

After the death of Bob Cole in 1911, Johnson joined forces with Charlie Hart to write songs and develop a vaudeville sketch called "The Entertainers," performed for the first time at Proctor's Fifth Avenue Theatre on 3 June 1912. The duo continued on the American vaudeville circuit until April 1913 when they joined the company of a new vaudeville revue in London, *Come Over Here* (book by Wilson Mizner and Max Pemberton; lyrics by Harry Williams and Frank Sturgess; music by J. Rosamond Johnson and Louis Hirsch) (19 April 1913).[1192] After Johnson returned to the United States following the run of *Come Over Here*, he was appointed director of the New York Music School Settlement for Colored People at 6 West 131st Street in Harlem, where African-American students could attend classes and lectures about African-American music and history, and perform in concerts and recitals of African-American music. In 1919 Johnson returned to vaudeville and by the summer 1919, he had developed an act with five young men who sang and danced, called the "Jazz Five."[1193] The two main features of the act were the medley of Johnson and Cole's hit compositions and a "hot jazz" finale that involved improvisational scatting by the singers. He toured with the Jazz Five through the beginning of 1923 when he changed the personnel of his backup group to include a female singer-dancer, Eloise Bennett, a male singer, a drummer (who also danced), a pianist, and a violinist.[1194] In 1924, Johnson toured as musical director for an unsuccessful tabloid musical comedy called *Honey* (book by Flournoy E. Miller and Aubrey Lyles; music and lyrics by Porter Grainer, Rob Ricketts, and Jo Trent),[1195] and the following year he served as musical director and dance arranger of the touring vaudeville revue *Harlem Rounders*.[1196]

In 1926, Johnson moved from vaudeville to the concert hall when he and Taylor Gordon began a series of recitals of Negro spirituals at Aeolian Hall in New York City (21 November).[1197] Subsequently, in 1928, Johnson returned to Broadway, contributing additional music and dance arrangements ("Rubber Heels") (lyrics by J.P. McEvoy) for *Americana* (30 October 1928); incidental music for *The Rugged Road* (play by E.J. Robinson) (September 1930); lyrics ("Betty Lou") (music by Joe Jordan) for *Brown Buddies* (7 October 1930); vocal arrangements for *Blackbirds of 1930* (22 October 1930); additional music (dance arrangements) for *Rhapsody in Black* (4 May 1931); additional music and lyrics ("So Lonesome") (with Joe Jordan) for *Fast and Furious* (15 September 1931); vocal arrangements for *Blackbirds of 1939* (11 February 1939); and music for the musical farce *That Night* (libretto by George Lessey) (announced on 4 February 1940). As a performer, Johnson appeared as Frazier in *Porgy and Bess* (10 October 1933 and 22 January 1942); Reverend Quintus Whaley in *Mamba's Daughters* (3 January 1939); and Brother Green (also choir director) in *Cabin in the Sky* (25 October 1940). On 11 November 1954, J. Rosamond

Johnson died in his sleep due to cardiac arrest. He was survived by his wife, Nora, and his children, Mildred and Donald.

JOHNSON, James P[rice]

James P. ("Jimmie") Johnson was born on 1 February 1894 in New Brunswick, New Jersey, the youngest of William and Josephine (Harrison) Johnson's five children (four boys and a girl).[1198] When Jimmie was four years old, his mother taught him to play "Little Brown Jug" on the piano, and by the time he was six, he was earning money, singing on street corners the popular songs of the day. During this time, Johnson had a special fascination with the "shout dances" he witnessed at his parents' parties and many of his future compositions would be influenced by the dance.[1199] When Johnson was eight years old, the family moved to Jersey City where he performed buck-dancing while singing and accompanying himself on the guitar outside the saloons. He became intrigued by the ragtime pianists, or "ticklers" as they were customarily known, inside the taverns and decided that a tickler was what he wanted to be.[1200] In the fall of 1912 instead of returning to school, Johnson found employment playing piano at a sporting house on 27th Street between 8th and 9th Avenues before playing movie piano at the Nickelette on 8th Avenue and 37th Street, and moving uptown to Jim Allan's cabaret and the Jungles Casino on 62nd Street where, one night a week, Johnson played two-steps, waltzes, schottisches, and the newest dance craze, "The Metropolitan Glide." Many of the dancers at the establishment were Southerners who had gone to New York. For them, Johnson developed a series of dance music named for the home town of the dancers, "Charlestons," one of which was the famous "Charleston" included in Johnson's score for *Runnin' Wild* (25 August 1923).[1201] In 1913 Johnson began formally studying music for four years with an Italian music teacher by the name of Bruno Giannini who educated him in harmony and counterpoint as well as piano technique.[1202] The following year, on his way to a job in Atlantic City, Johnson met Eubie Blake, who remembered the meeting vividly:

> And James P. Johnson! Black James we called him. I wrote "Troublesome Ivories" to have a number to cut everybody with. It was even hard for me to play. Black James, he was only sixteen years old, he came by where I was workin' in Atlantic City and he heard me play the piece twice and

he had it. Only sixteen! He was still drinkin' sarsaparilla then. Greatest piano player I ever heard. I let him sit in for me for twenty minutes while I took a break. I come back and he's playin' "Troublesome Ivories" without no mistakes. I make mistakes, but not him.[1203]

Johnson claimed that around this time he began working in the theatre, as a pianist for *The Darktown Follies* (book by J. Leubrie Hill and Alex C. Rogers; music by Hill and Will Vodery), a popular African-American revue that played the Lafayette Theatre in Harlem in October 1913 before going on tour in February 1914. When the show returned to New York City, it was performed at Hammerstein's Victoria Theatre Roof Garden (1 June 1914) and subsequently at the Bijou Theatre (15 June 1914) and the Olympic Theatre (29 June 1914).[1204]

Following *The Darktown Follies*, Johnson's work in the theatre included the composition of incidental music and musical direction for *What's Your Husband Doing* (play by George V. Hobart) (12 November 1917);[1205] playing piano for Whitney and Tutt's *Smarter Set* (Salem Tutt Whitney and J. Homer Tutt), a 1919 touring production;[1206] providing songs, dance music, and musical direction for *Plantation Days* (with unauthorized interpolations by Noble Sissle and Eubie Blake), a 1922 touring show with performances beginning 2 April 1923 at the Lafayette Theatre in Harlem;[1207] songs and dance music for *Raisin' Cain* (book by Frank Montgomery) (9 July 1923), at the Lafayette Theatre; songs and dance music for *Runnin' Wild* (book by Flournoy E. Miller and Aubrey Lyles; lyrics by Cecil Mack) (29 October 1923), the musical that introduced the "Charleston" to Broadway; co-composition (with Will Marion Cook) and musical direction for *Negro Nuances* (book by Miller, Lyles, and Abbie Mitchell; lyrics by Will Marion Cook) (1924), a touring production beginning in Harlem;[1208] songs, dance music, and musical direction for *Cotton Land* (1924), another touring production;[1209] songs and dance arrangements for *Moochin' Along* (book by Jesse A. Shipp; lyrics by Cecil Mack), a revision of *Sunshine Sammy* (by the same authors) (9 September 1925), at the Lafayette Theatre (7 December 1925;[1210] music and dance arrangements for *Geechie* (book and lyrics by Henry S. Creamer), copyrighted 1926;[1211] additional music ("Kangaroo," "Stepping Out with Lulu," and "Whiskers," lyrics by Creamer) for *A La Carte* (book by Paul Kelly; music and lyrics by Herman Hupfeld) (25 July 1927), Johnson's songs borrowed from the unproduced *Geechie*; musical direction, dance arrangements, and songs (with Fats Waller and Clarence

Todd) for *Keep Shufflin'* (book by Miller and Lyles; lyrics by Creamer and Andy Razaf) (27 February 1928); songs, dance arrangements, and musical direction for *Messin' Around* (conception by Louis Isquity; lyrics by Perry Bradford) (22 April 1929), included in the score were Johnson's piano symphony "Yamekraw," and his popular ballad, "Your Love Is All I Crave"; music and musical direction for *A Great Day in N'Orleans* (conception by Miller), at the Pearl Theatre in Philadelphia (30 December 1929), closed out of town; songs (with Fats Waller), dance music, and musical direction for *Fireworks of 1930*, at the Lafayette Theatre (28 June 1930); songs and dance music for the *Kitchen Mechanics Revue* (lyrics by Andy Razaf) (1930), featuring the dance number, "Sambo's Syncopated Russian Dance," at Small's Paradise in Harlem;[1212] songs (lyrics by Cecil Mack) and incidental music for *Savage Rhythm* (play by Harry Hamilton and Norman Foster) (31 December 1931);[1213] songs, dance arrangements, and musical direction for *Sugar Hill: An Epoch of Negro Life in Harlem* (book by Lyles and Charles Tazewell; lyrics by Jo Trent) (25 December 1931);[1214] music, and dance arrangements for *Harlem Hotcha* (conception by Connie Immerman; lyrics by Razaf) (1932), performed as a floorshow at Connie's Inn in Harlem, and later at the Lafayette Theatre; music, dance arrangements, and musical direction for the *Plantation Follies* (also produced by Johnson) (1933), a touring revue; songs, dance music, and musical direction for the *Policy Kings* (libretto by Michael Ashwood; musical arrangements by Ken Macomber) (30 December 1938), a three-performance flop;[1215] music and musical direction for *Class Struggle in Swing* (additional music and sketches by Aarons and Stratton and Lewis Allen), produced at the Theatre Arts Committee Cabaret (7 November 1939);[1216] music and musical direction for *The Organizer* (libretto by Langston Hughes), a blues opera in one act, performed at Madison Square Garden in connection with the International Ladies Garment Workers Union Convention, and at the World's Fair (2 September 1940);[1217] musical direction for *Pinkard's Fantasies* (written by Maceo Pinkard) (1941);[1218] music for *The Dreamy Kid* (libretto based on the play by Eugene O'Neill), never produced (1942);[1219] and music for the *Kitchen Opera* (lyrics by Flournoy E. Miller), pubished in 1947 but not produced. Johnson was also credited as the composer of two ballets: *Sefronia's Dream* and *Manhattan Street Scene*.[1220]

As a pianist Johnson developed the "stride piano" style and his "Carolina Shout" is considered the first recorded jazz piano solo; as a dance arranger he introduced the "Charleston" to Broadway; as a serious African-American composer he produced *Yamekraw: A Negro Rhapsody* (1927),

Harlem Symphony (1932), *Concerto Jazz A Mine* for piano and orchestra (1934), *Symphony in Brown* (1935), *Drums: a Symphonic Poem* (1942), *Victory Stride* (1944), a clarinet concerto, a string quarter, and various suites, tone poems, and piano sonatas. A significant influence on the careers of Fats Waller and Duke Ellington, James Price Johnson died on 17 November 1955 after suffering a massive stroke. He was survived by his wife, Lillie Mae, his son James P. Johnson, Jr., his daughters Arceola and Lillie Mae, Jr., and three grandchildren.

JOHNSTONE, Alexander

Composer and performer Alexander Johnstone was born in Washington, D.C. in 1879. At the age of twelve he spent the summer touring with a production of *Captain Karl* that played the Grand Opera House in New York City for a week at the end of August 1891. After the tour Johnstone returned to the life of a teenage schoolboy, anxious for the summers to come with the promise of further theatrical activity. Twenty years later, after undergoing an intensive musical education in Washington, New York, and Europe, Johnstone reappeared in theatrical documents as the composer of *Betsy* (book by H. Kellett Chambers; lyrics by Will B. Johnstone), a comedy operetta that premiered in Atlantic City, New Jersey on 25 October 1911, prior to a Broadway opening on 11 December.[1221] Johnstone's music charmed the critics, as did his older brother Will's lyrics, but the show's stay in Manhattan was brief.[1222] Encouraged by their good reviews, the brothers Johnstone collaborated with veteran librettist Frank Mandel on *Miss Princess*, about an engaged Austrian Princess who visits the United States and falls in love with an American army officer. The show opened in Allentown, Pennsylvania, on 1 November 1912, prior to its New York run (23 December 1912).[1223] Although the piece was described as "dull" and the music as "neither distinctive, distinguished, nor distinguishable" critics did make special note of Johnstone's dance music, notably the "Temperamental Dances" in the second act.[1224] Dance music and splendid choreography were unable to save the musical and it was gone in two weeks. Johnstone's next musical project, *The Red Canary* (13 April 1914), proved a departure from his earlier work. Composer Harold Orlob composed the score, Will B. Johnstone did the lyrics, and Alexander Johnstone collaborated with William Le Baron on the book. The hackneyed forced-marriage plot proved too bitter a pill for New Yorkers to swallow and the operetta expired after two weeks.

After several misses, Johnstone joined forces with veteran book and lyric writer William Cary Duncan and composed his most successful score for the romantic operetta *Fiddlers Three* about three violinists in Cremona, Italy, entering a performance competition. The opening night in Atlantic City (19 August 1918) was rapturously reviewed by the *New York Clipper* and predicted that "*Fiddlers Three* is destined for a long time on Broadway."[1225] The Broadway production (3 September 1918) was greeted by headlines that read: "Operetta Returns in *Fiddlers Three*. The Good Old-Fashioned Thing Crops Up in Darkest Wartime.... Book and Music in the Ripe Tradition of Years and Years Ago."[1226] In *Fiddlers Three* Johnstone and Duncan created a plot that was intrinsically musical and Johnstone used it to his best advantage. In act one, following "Don't You Think You'll Miss Me?" Johnstone composed a delightfully flirtatious original dance melody in 3/8; "All on Account of Nipper" led to a lively doted-rhythm galop; an extended "Shadow Dance" began with a tentative staccato movement that developed into a lyrical and steady foxtrot; and "One Hour, Sweetheart, With You" was luxuriously reprised in a "Melodrama," underscoring dialogue and stage business. Act two began with a merry and exuberant march, "Carnival Music," that was followed by an elegant gavotte in "Six Little Pages"; and the "Melodrama" of the first act was reprised prior to the march to the violin competition, "Virtuosos Great Are We." The second scene of act two began with a ballet that included a march, a Gypsy dance in 2/4 with a virtuoso violin line; a waltz, a tarantella, a reprise of the march, and a final galop, the "Dance Excentrique." A violin incidental using the melody of "My Love of a Day" was particularly interesting since it anticipated (rather than followed) the sung performance of the number.

The two-and-a-half-month run of *Fiddlers Three* surpassed the total number of performances of Johnstone's previous shows combined and gave Johnstone the confidence to create his own production company with Jed F. Shaw, one of the producers of *Fiddlers Three*.[1227] The company's first production was *Sunshine*, a musical comedy "set in Spain ... not burdened with any real plot to speak of,"[1228] written by William Carey Duncan and composed by Johnstone. The show opened in Trenton, New Jersey, on 11 April 1919, to promising reviews based mostly on the excellence of the music, but by the time it opened in Chicago a month later, the book had been improved and several dance numbers had been added. Moreover, the addition of popular musical theatre performer Richard Carle to the cast late in June gave the show the added lift it needed to keep running through the rest of the summer in Chicago where in closed in late August. Johnstone and Shaw's second production, *The Sympathetic Twin*, was a Richard Carle vehicle that opened in Washington, D.C. in May 1920 to mixed notices and closed two weeks later in Baltimore, Maryland, where the scenery and stage properties had been attached by one of Johnstone's creditors, forcing the show to close immediately. Actors' Equity Association subsequently sued Johnstone to recover the money for unpaid salaries due to the principals and chorus members: Richard Carle, for example claimed that Johnstone still owed him $500.00 from *Sunshine*, in addition to the $960.00 due him for *The Sympathetic Twin*. Consequently Johnstone's career as a producer came to an abrupt end and his name disappeared from theatre notices.

JONES, [James] Sidney

Born in Islington, London, on 17 June 1861, Sidney Jones was the son of military bandmaster Sidney Jones who was forced to move the family frequently to various military posts in England and Ireland, where young Jones studied with organist and composer Sir Robert Stewart, a lecturer at Trinity College. Eventually the family settled in Leeds where the elder Jones presided over the local military band, Leeds Rifles, as well as the orchestra at the Grand Theatre.[1229] Young Jones played clarinet in his father's orchestra and later became a musical director for a variety of producers and touring companies, the most important of which was producer George Edwardes and his Gaiety Theatre tour of America and Australia in 1891. When the burlesque *Cinder-Ellen-Up-too-Late* was produced in Australia, Jones contributed the music for a dance number to the original score composed by Meyer Lutz.[1230] Jones continued his association with producer George Edwardes upon his return to London, first as a musical director, and later as a composer of songs interpolated into the scores of London musicals, one of which, "Linger Longer, Loo," brought him fame after it was performed in the Gaiety Theatre burlesque *Don Juan* (28 October 1893).[1231] Before he became famous, however, he composed the score for the musical comedy *A Gaiety Girl* (libretto by Harry Greenbank and Owen Hall [Jimmy Davis]), produced at the Prince of Wales Theatre on 14 October 1893, and which virtually created the template for the music in the musical comedies of the era: hummable melodies evocative of the London Music Hall, but also reminiscent of Arthur Sullivan and Alfred Cellier; light chorus numbers and ensembles, again in the style of Arthur Sullivan; and dance music—polkas, waltzes, and jigs—based on sung melodies in addition to original ballet incidentals. On 18 September 1894, *A Gaiety Girl* was produced at Daly's Theatre in New York City to mixed reviews but the show managed a stay of ten weeks.[1232] Jones subsequently became musical director of Daly's Theatre in London where he composed a string of London hit musical comedies that included *An Artist's Model* (Libretto by Harry Greenbank and Owen Hall) (London on 2 February 1895, New York on 23 December 1895);[1233] *The Geisha* (Greenbank and Hall) (London on 25 April 1896, New York on 9 September 1896);[1234] *A Greek Slave* (Greenbank, Hall, and Adrian Ross) (London 6 June 1898, New York on 28 November 1899);[1235] and *San Toy* (Greenbank, Ross, and Edward Morton) (London 21 October 1899, New York 1 October 1900).[1236] The score of *San Toy* exhibited Jones's characteristic dance music based on the sung themes in the score. Of special note, however, was the "Pas Seul" in the second act, an original ballet incidental comprised of a schottische, a waltz, and a galop.

After composing a string of success at Daly's Theatre in London, as well as at Daly's and other theatres in New York, Jones moved on to other theatres in London and produced more hits and misses in his distinctive style. The list included *My Lady Molly* (Greenbank, C.H. Taylor, and George H. Jessop) (London on 14 March 1902, Boston on 30 November 1903, New York on 5 January 1904);[1237] *The Medal and the Maid* (Taylor and Hall) (London on 25 April 1903, New York on 11 January 1904), the show was generally regarded as a failure but it contained one of Jones's finest ballets, the "Shoeblack Dance," comprised of a "Polka," a "Graceful Dance" (schottische), "The Storm," and a recapitulation of "The Polka" as a final galop;[1238] *See See* (Ross, Greenbank, and C.H.E. Brookfield) (London on 20 June 1906), optioned but not produced in New York;[1239] *The King of Cadonia* (Ross and Frederick Lonsdale) (London on 3 September 1908, New Haven on 20 November 1909, New York on 10 January 1910), the piece ended with a tarantella followed by a majestic instrumental march rather than a sung ensemble number;[1240] *A Persian Princess* (Greenbank, Leedham Bantock, and P.J. Barrow) (London on 27 April 1909), optioned but not produced in New York;[1241] *The Girl From Utah* (composed with Paul Rubens; libretto by Ross, Greenbank, Rubens, and James Tanner) (London on 18 October 1913, New York on 24 August 1914), the hits in the New York production were interpolations by Herman Finck ("Gilbert the Filbert") and Jerome Kern ("They Didn't Believe Me") and the most notable dance music was composed by Chris Smith ("Ballin' the Jack");[1242]

and *The Happy Day* (composed with Rubens, libretto by Ross, Rubens, and Seymour Hicks) (London on 13 May), not produced in New York. However, notable dance music included a march, an extended mazurka, a schottische by Jones, and a foxtrot by Rubens.[1243]

In 1905, during the height of his musical theatre activity, Jones became the musical director for London's Empire Theatre, for which he composed ballet music that included *The Bugle Call* (1905) and *Cinderella* (1906).[1244] He continued composing dance music and musicals into the nineteen-teens in his characteristic musical style, virtually immune to the influence of ragtime and syncopation on theatre music and the prevailing musical tastes of the audience. Jones did, however, include the popular foxtrot in his later dance music and filled it with subtle but effective syncopations. It would certainly have been interesting to hear what Jones might have produced in the 1920s when jazz affected musical theatre music, but after 1916 he no longer composed. Instead, he retired to his home in Kew, Surrey, and died there on 29 January 1946.

JONES, Stephen [Oscar]

Composer and orchestrator Stephen Jones was born in New York City on 12 July 1880. Although known chiefly as a staff orchestrator of Broadway musicals for T.B. Harms Publishers, Stephen Jones (sometimes cited as Stephen O. Jones) began his theatrical career as a composer of songs interpolated into the scores of other songwriters. Among his earliest efforts was "I Thought My Troubles Were Over, But They'd Scarce Begun" (lyrics by Roger Gray), performed by Bert Williams in Will Marion Cook's *Abyssinia* (libretto by Jesse A. Shipp and Alex Rogers; additional music by Bert Williams and James J. Vaughn) (20 February 1906). His later musical interpolations included the music for "Under Any Old Tree at All" (lyrics by J.R. Freeman and W.J. Dunham) in *The Heartbreakers* (music by Harold Orlob and Melville Gideon; lyrics by Will M. Hough and Frank R. Adams), a heavy dance show that was a hit in Chicago during the summer of 1911; "June Days" (lyrics by Clifford Grey and Cyrus Wood) in the score of *June Days* (music by J. Fred Coots; book by Harry Wagstaff Gribble and Cyrus Wood; lyrics by Clifford Grey) (6 August 1925); "Talk about Girls" (lyrics by Irving Caesar) in *Talk about Girls* (music by Harold Orlob; book by William Cary Duncan and Daniel Kussell; lyrics by Irving Caesar) (14 June 1927); "How'd You Like To?" (lyrics by Irving Caesar) in *Yes, Yes, Yvette* (music by Phil Charig and Ben Jerome; book by

James Montgomery and William Cary Duncan; lyrics by Irving Caesar) (3 October 1927); and "'Twas a Kiss in the Moonlight" (lyrics by Henry Creamer) in *Keep Shufflin'* (music by James Price Johnson. Fats Waller, Will Vodery, Clarence Todd; libretto by Aubrey L. Lyles and Flournoy E. Miller) (27 February 1928).

In addition, Jones was a principal composer and dance arranger for several Broadway musicals that included *Poppy* (libretto by Dorothy Donnelly; additional music by Arthur Samuels) (3 September 1923);[1245] *Majorie* (libretto by Fred Thompson, Clifford Grey, and Harold Atteridge; music also by Sigmund Romberg, Herbert Stothart, and Philip Culkin) (11 August 1924);[1246] *Toni* (lyrics by Douglas Furber) (1924 unproduced); *Captain Jinks* (book by Frank Mandel and Laurence Schwab; lyrics by Buddy G. DeSylva; music also by Lewis E. Gensler) (8 September 1925);[1247] and *A Regular Guy* (book by William Cary Duncan; lyrics by Irving Caesar; additional music by Winthrop Cortalyou) (September 1926).

Jones's orchestrations for Broadway musicals included *Miss 1917* (5 November 1917); *Ziegfeld Follies of 1918* (18 June 1918); *Ziegfeld Follies of 1919* (16 June 1919);[1248] *Look Who's Here* (2 March 1920); *Broadway Brevities of 1920* (29 September 1920); *Two Little Girls in Blue* (3 May 1921); *Music Box Revue* (22 September 1921); *Good Morning, Dearie* (1 November 1921); *The Bunch and Judy* (28 November 1922); *Poppy* (3 September 1923); *Lady Be Good* (1 December 1924); *The Cocoanuts* (8 December 1925); *Sweetheart Time* (19 January 1926); *No Foolin'* (24 June 1926); *Hit the Deck* (26 April 1927); *Hello, Daddy* (26 December 1928); *Great Day* (17 October 1929); *Take a Chance* (26 November 1932); and *Hollywood Pinafore* (31 May 1945). Jones's published compositions included "A Bird in the Hand Is Worth Two in the Bush" (lyrics by Roger Gray), 1906; "Burglar Buck" (lyrics by Rose Stammer), 1909; "Bees: a Novelette," for orchestra, 1912; "The York 1913 Medley Overture," for orchestra, 1913; "Barcelona Tango," for piano, 1914; "We're Going to See It Through" (lyrics by D.D. Mullins), 1918; and "Sunday Mary," foxtrot, 1924.

Following the death of his wife Della in 1941, Stephen Jones retired to Interlaken, New Jersey, where, as an avid golfer, he surrounded himself with easy access to the links. After twenty-six years of relative anonymity, Jones died on 12 April 1967, at the age of 86, survived by his daughters Alice and Edith and sons Stephen and Edward.

JOPLIN, Scott

Ragtime composer and pianist Scott Joplin was born into a musical family on 24 November 1868[1249] in Linden, Texas. When he was still a child, the family moved to Texarkana where Scott was given a rudimentary musical education by his parents who played the violin and banjo, and at the age of seven he developed a serious interest in playing the piano. Julius Weiss, a German music teacher who had immigrated to the United States, took an interest in young Joplin's musical development and tutored him for five years in music theory, harmony, and composition, as well as the aesthetics and history of music. When he was sixteen years old, Joplin left Texarkana to become an itinerant musician and, after several years of playing in brothels and saloons throughout the Midwest, he settled in St. Louis.[1250] In 1891, he returned to Texarkana to perform with the Texarkana Minstrels, and in 1893, Joplin went to the World's Fair in Chicago where he came in contact with other African-American musicians and formed a brass ensemble, for which he arranged music and played the cornet. He left Chicago in 1894 and moved to Sedalia, Missouri, where he played second cornet in the Queen City Concert Band and studied music at the George R. Smith College.[1251] Joplin also gave private music lessons and toured with a vocal group he had created called the Texas Medley Quartet. In 1895 he published his first compositions, "Please Say You Will" and "A Picture of Her Face," and the following year he published the "Great Crush Collision March." In 1897, Joplin composed "Original Rags," his first published ragtime piece (1899), which was followed by the "Maple Leaf Rag" (1899), and a number of ragtime compositions that included "Peacherine Rag" (1901), "The Easy Winners," ragtime two step (1901), "Cleopha," march and two step (1902), "Elite Syncopations" (1902), "The Entertainer," ragtime two step (1902), and "The Ragtime Dance," a brief theatrical piece (1902). In 1903 Joplin composed his first opera, *A Guest of Honor*, and created the Scott Joplin Drama Company to tour it throughout the Midwest. The *Indianapolis Freeman* considered the work "the most complete and unique collection of words and music produced by any Negro writer" and gave the name of two of its prominent numbers, "Dude's Parade" and "Patriotic Patrol."[1252] On one of the tour stops, someone ran off with the box office receipts and, out of funds, the tour collapsed and the words and music to the opera were lost.

Undaunted, Joplin began work on a second opera, *Treemonisha*, in 1905 and completed it in 1907. He moved to New York to find a publisher and producer for the opera and supported himself by performing on the vaudeville circuit and making piano rolls of his ragtime compositions. Unable to find a publisher for *Treemonisha*, he published it himself in 1911 and received positive feedback from the *American Musician and Art Journal* that proclaimed the work "a thoroughly American opera."[1253] Productions of the opera in Atlantic City and at the Lafayette Theatre in Harlem failed to materialize[1254] so, in 1915, Joplin produced a bare-bones piano-vocal performance of *Treemonisha* in a rehearsal hall in Harlem for an invited audience of friends and potential producers. Again, no full productions materialized, except for the performance of the "Frolic of the Bears" at the eighth annual recital of the Martin-Smith School of Music on 5 May 1915. Example 119 presents the first sixteen measures of the waltz-time ballet, starting with an eight-measure introduction that accompanies the bears' entrance with ascending and descending chromatic scales and rolling neighbor tones that culminate in a B7 chord (measure 8), the dominant seventh of E minor, the key of the dance. Note that measures 1–7 are occupied entirely by eighth notes but measure 8 is filled with quarter notes and dotted half notes that retard the rhythm and create a heightened sense of anticipation for the resolution in measure 9. Note the subtle syncopations in the final eight measures that drive forward the pulse of the music and the sophisticated (though unpretentious) use of leading-tone diminished chords (measures 10, 12) and an augmented sixth chord (measure 15), each of which appear on the third beat of the measure to add color and a hint of tension before the release in the next measure. Note as well the ascending melodic line and the frolicking grace notes that appear regularly throughout the section to add a sense of playfulness to the dance music.

Following the *Treemonisha* experience, Joplin advertised in the *Indianapolis Freeman* the composition of a vaudeville sketch, "The Syncopated Jambouree" (18 September 1915) and in the *New York Age*, the completion of a musical comedy called *If* (7 September 1916). In the same issue of the *New York Age*, Joplin announced the composition of his *Symphony No. 1*, a work, which like "The Syncopated Jambouree" and *If*, is now lost. Four months later, having experienced the dementia that accompanies tertiary syphilis, Joplin was admitted to Manhattan State Hospital on Wards Island, where he died on 1 April 1917. Joplin was married three times: first to Belle Jones, whom he divorced; next to Freddie Alexander, who died ten weeks after the wedding; and finally to Lottie Stokes, who survived him. Joplin was buried in Saint Michael's Cemetery in East Elmhurst, Queens.

Example 119. "Frolic of the Bears" from *Treemonisha*

Additional ragtime dance compositions by Scott Joplin include "Swipesy Cakewalk," composed with Arthur Marshall (1900); "Sunflower Slow Drag," a ragtime two step composed with Scott Hayden (1901); Augustan Club Waltz" (1901), "A Breeze from Alabama," march and two step (1902); "Weeping Willow," ragtime two step (1903); "The Favorite," ragtime two step (1904); "The Rosebud March," two step (1905); "Searchlight Rag," syncopated march and two step (1907); "Sugar Cane," ragtime classic two step (1908); "Pleasant Moments," ragtime waltz (1909); and "Country Club," ragtime two step (1909).

JORDAN, Joe [Joseph Zachariah Taylor]

Pianist, composer, dance arranger, and musical director Joe Jordan was born in Cincinnati, Ohio, on 11 February 1882. He exhibited a prodigious musical talent at an early age and taught himself to play the piano by imitating his sister who was taking piano lessons.[1255] Not long after, his family moved to St. Louis, where Jordan learned to read music from

Tom Turpin, the first African-American to publish a rag, "Harlem Rag" (1897).[1256] The year before "Harlem Rag" was published Jordan entered the Lincoln Institute at Jefferson City, Missouri, where he learned to play the drums, cornet, trombone, and double bass, and took classes in music theory, harmony, and composition. After two years at the Institute, Jordan left to become a musician with the Georgia-Up-to-Date Minstrels, followed by a stint with A.G. Allen's New Orleans Minstrels, for which Jordan served as musical director.[1257] Around the turn of the century, Jordan returned to St. Louis where he supported himself by playing piano, singing, and composing music. He performed in a four-piano combo with Turpin, Louis Chauvin, and Sam Patterson, and for a time, he played the violin and drums with the ten-piece Tamborian Band. In 1902, he toured briefly with the New Orleans Minstrels and produced his earliest-known published compositions, "The Century March" and "Double Fudge." In 1903, He joined Patterson and Chauvin in the creation of a musical called *The Dandy Coon* and served as musical and stage director of the production which opened in St. Louis before going on tour and closing abruptly in Des Moines, Iowa.[1258] In 1904 Jordan moved to Chicago where he played piano at the Pekin saloon, which later was rebuilt as the Pekin Theatre, for which Jordan served as composer, arranger, and musical director for the princely sum of $25.00 per week.

In 1905, during the reconstruction of the Pekin into a full-fledged theatre, Jordan traveled to New York City where he composed additional music for the touring and Broadway production of the Ernest Hogan vehicle, *Rufus Rastus* (29 January 1906). Two months after *Rufus Rastus* opened in New York, the Pekin Theatre opened in Chicago with *The Man from 'Bam* (31 March 1906), book by Flournoy E. Miller and Aubrey Lyles, music (including dance music) by Joe Jordan and Will H. Vodery. In the three years that followed, Jordan composed the songs and dance music for 15 musicals that included *The Husband* (libretto by Miller and Lyles; additional numbers by James T[im] Brymn, Bob Cole, and J. Rosamond Johnson) (22 April 1906);[1259] *The Mayor of Dixie* (Flournoy and Lyles) (27 August 1906); *Count of No-Account* (book by Alfred Anderson; lyrics by Will Dixon) (17 December 1906); *In Zululand* (libretto by J. Edward Green; additional music by Will Marion Cook and James T. Brymn) (7 January 1907);[1260] *The Grafters* (book by Green; additional music by Brymn) (4 March 1907); *The Bachelor* (libretto by Anderson and Will Dixon; additional music by Brymn) (13 May 1907); and *Captain Rufus* (libretto by Green and Anderson; additional music by Brymn and H.L.

Freeman) (1 July 1907). When he had free time from the Pekin Theatre, Jordan composed additional music for Broadway shows that included *The Shoo-Fly Regiment*(3 June 1907) "I Think an Awful Lot of You" (lyrics by Alfred Anderson); *Bandanna Land* (3 February 1908), dance music and orchestrations for "The Dancing of Salome";[1261] Ziegfeld's *Follies of 1910* (20 June 1910), "Lovey Joe" (lyrics attributed to Will Marion Cook), the song that made a star of Fanny Brice;[1262] *Maid in America* (18 February 1915), "At the Fox Trot Ball" music and lyrics and dance arrangement; and *Strut, Miss Lizzie* (19 June 1922), "Ebony Rag," "Bernice," dance arrangements and musical direction.

In the 1920s, Joe Jordan continued his work as musical and stage director for shows that included *The Streets of Cairo* (11 November 1922) and *Ginger and Spice* (December 1922), both in Chicago; and in 1923 he became the musical director of the 3,300-seat Loew's State Theatre in New York City's Times Square. By the summer of 1925, he had been hired by the Columbia Theatrical Circuit to produce the touring entertainment *Rarin' to Go*, which remained on the road until late 1926; and the following year, with Clarence Williams, he created the revue *Bottomland* that was produced at the Princess Theatre in New York on 27 June 1927. In 1928, Jordan was musical director for James Price Johnson's *Keep Shufflin'* (27 February) and the composer of *Deep Harlem* (book by Salem Tutt Whitney and J. Homer Tutt; lyrics by Tutt and Henry Creamer), a musical that told the story of African-Americans from their origins as kings and princes in Africa, through slavery, to life in Harlem in the 1920s. The show, which anticipated Duke Ellington's *Black, Brown, and Beige* (1943) and *My People* (1963) appeared on Broadway on 7 January 1929 for an unsuccessful run of 8 performances.[1263] Although rich in dance music and songs that explored a variety of musical styles, Jordan's score was unable to prevent the musical from sinking beneath the weight of its sodden and proselytizing libretto.

Jordan's subsequent musical theatre scores[1264] included *Brown Buddies* (libretto by Carl Rickman) (7 October 1930), co-composition with Millard Thomas, Porter Grainger, J.C. Johnson, J. Rosamond Johnson, and Shelton Brooks; *Ziegfeld Follies of 1931* (1 July 1931), orchestrations only; *Fast and Furious* (assembled by Forbes Randolph) (15 September 1931), musical direction and co-composition with J. Rosamond Johnson, Porter Grainger, Mack Gordon, Harry Revel, and others; *Smile at Me* (23 August 1935), orchestrations only ; *Sea Legs* (18 May 1937), orchestrations; *De Gospel Train* (book by J. Homer Tutt; lyrics by Henry Creamer)

(1940? unproduced), score and arrangements; and *Here'Tis* (libretto by Jesse James) (1941) musical direction only. During World War II Captain Joe Jordan was posted at Fort Huachuca in Arizona, where he composed and arranged musical shows to support the morale of the army's African-American soldiers. In 1944 he retired to Tacoma, Washington, where he continued to compose and teach privately until his death on 11 September 1971 at the age of eighty-nine.

Joe Jordan's published dance compositions included "Nappy Lee: A Slow Drag" (1903), "That Teasin' Rag" (1909), "That Raggedy Rag: A Ragtime Dance Song" (1910), "Play Dat Darkey Todalo: A Darkey Dance" (1910), "The Tango: Two Step" (1913), and "Sweetie Dear: Fox-Trot" (1914).

Endnotes

1. *The New York Times* 17 November 1936; Kurt Gänzl (1994) 1:1-2.
2. *New York Clipper* 16 March 1901.
3. Bernard L. Peterson, Jr. (1993) 146.
4. John Franceschina (2003B) 165–166. Instead of producing the musical, Aarons assumed the role of musical director.
5. *New York Clipper* 26 November 1904.
6. Peterson (1993) 69-70.
7. Eileen Southern (1982) 3-4.
8. *The New York Times* 27 April 1904.
9. http://africlassical.blogspot.com/2012/12/will-accooe-1874-1904-composed-black.html
10. *The New York Times* 4 September 1961.
11. *The New York Times* 31 January 1892.
12. Rudolph Aronson (1913) 28-29.
13. *The New York Times* 6 February 1919; Aronson (1913), 28-29.
14. *New York Clipper* 30 September 1893. The reviewer notes: "It is the first ambitious work of its composer, and does not even require such a statement to be made in an apologetic way. While its musical numbers are of uneven merit, the average result is quite satisfactory. The music is of a sufficiently high standard for comic opera, and is in the main tuneful and pleasing. It is, moreover, original and nowhere reminiscent, a rare charm, sufficient to condone for many shortcomings. In fact, the music is good enough to cause regret that there is not more of it, some of the solos, duets and choruses being sufficiently meritorious and pleasing to stimulate this desire."
15. Gänzl (1994) 1:63. Other sources give Ayer's birthdate as 5 August 1887.
16. Gänzl (1994) 1:63 and other sources give the date for *Miss Innocence* as 1908, the initial presentation of that show on Broadway. However, Ayer's song is not listed in the program for that production.

17. *The Times* 3 March 1913 and 11 April 1913.
18. *New York Clipper* 29 March 1913.
19. *New York Clipper* 19 July 1922.
20. *The New York Times* 9 August 1925.
21. *New York Clipper* 12 December 1863.
22. In Spitzer (2012), John Graziano reports that Baker's orchestra consisted of sixteen players: 1 flute/piccolo, 1 oboe, 2 clarinets, 2 cornets, 1 trombone, 1 percussion, 3 first violins, 2 second violins, 1 viola, 1 cello, 1 bass (113).
23. Henneke (1990) 167. See also *The New York Times* 23 September 1862 and 11 April 1863.
24. *New York Clipper* 18 June 1864.
25. *The New York Times* 8 November 1864.
26. *New York Clipper* 9 February 1867.
27. Quoted in Pisani (2014) 216.
28. In Spitzer (2012), John Graziano notes that the Niblo's Garden orchestra is similar to that of Laura Keene's Theatre: 1 flute/piccolo, 1 oboe, 1 clarinet, 2 horns, 2 trumpets/cornets, 1 trombone, 1 percussion, 2 first violins, 2 second violins, 1 viola, 1 cello, 1 bass (113). The two horns are important additions to the ensemble because they can function both as woodwind and brass instruments.
29. *The New York Times* 6 October 1878.
30. Barras (1866) 165.
31. *The New York Times* 6 October 1878.
32. *New York Clipper* 12 December 1863.
33. *The New York Times* 13 March 1939.
34. *The New York Times* 25 January 1926 and 26 April 1926.
35. *The New York Times* (2 July 1914) reported that the Barratts had been married in London in 1897 and subsequently moved to New York City. Claiming that Barratt deserted her in 1912 when she traveled to England to visit family, Lizzie May appealed to him to resume marital relations. When that option failed, she served him with divorce papers and obtained a final decree on 1 July 1914.
36. Barratt's obituary in *The New York Times* (15 April 1947) notes that he was survived by his second wife, Ethel, and a brother living in London.
37. In an interview in *The New York Times* (23 April 1894) Oscar Barrett explains that the British "pantomime" is not "wordless ac-

tion" as Americans define the term, but an extravaganza, "a mere vehicle for spectacular effects and variety business." He goes on to emphasize the importance of music in the creation of pantomimes, noting that in his *Cinderella*, at no time does an interval of more than six minutes pass without the presence of vocal or instrumental music. "The work is practically an opera, so far as music can make it one."

38. *New York Clipper* 14 January 1899.
39. *New York Clipper* 14 January 1882.
40. A year after it opened in Chicago, the American Extravaganza Company's production of *Sinbad* appeared at the Garden Theatre in New York City and enjoyed a successful run of 105 performances.
41. *Aladdin, Jr.* , which was a runaway hit in Chicago, moved to the Broadway Theatre on 8 April 1895 to begin an unremarkable run of forty-eight performances.
42. John Franceschina (2003B) 82–83.
43. Although Batchelor's association with the American Extravaganza Company began in 1890, in the first year, he was hired as a replacement musical director (for the departing Fred Eustis). His tenure as "permanent" musical director began in 1891.
44. Citing a production of Johann Strauss Jr.'s *The Bat*, the *New York Clipper* (4 June 1887) notes that "The orchestra, containing about fifteen musicians under the leadership of Adolph Bauer, was the feature of the entertainment."
45. In *Harlequin Jack, the Giant Killer* there were several ballets and specialty numbers, including "Queen of the Magical Islands" (a grand ballet and chorus), a grand transformation scene, a mazurka, and a grand fairy tableau.
46. Odell (1931) 7:569.
47. According to the *New York Clipper* (4 July 1863) the fixed scale of salaries was as follows: Operatic performances: first performance, $15 per head; every subsequent performance, $3 in Manhattan, $5 in Brooklyn. Salaries in Broadway theatres (including Barnum's Museum), $12 per week; in Bowery theatres and concert saloons, $10 per week, but if engaged on Sundays or matinees, $15 per week. Wedding parties, supper parties, political meetings with procession, $5 each. Balls at the Academy of Music, Irving Hall, City Assembly Rooms, or Niblo's Garden, $5.50 each; balls

in other places, $4.50. No ball to exceed eight hours. Serenades lasting one hour, $3; $1 extra for each subsequent hour. Society or political meetings without procession, $4; regimental parades, $5 each; regimental funerals, $5 if to the cemetery, and $4 if to the ferry. Small funerals, $1 less. Orchestra leaders to have four per cent from these salaries beyond their regular pay. See also the *New York Post* 11 March 1864.

48. The program for *The Elves* reveals a number of dances: a "Grand Pas des Elves," a clog dance, a pas de deux, and a double hornpipe.
49. *The New York Times* 7 December 1945.
50. *The New York Times* 18 September 1896.
51. *The New York Times* 21 January 1955. See also *The New York Times* 30 January 1910.
52. The *New York Clipper* (6 October 1883) gives Bendix's birthplace as Cleveland, Ohio and suggests that he is the son of "Prof. Bendix, formerly leader of the orchestra at the Opera-house."
53. *New York Clipper* 3 September 1881; Kurt Gänzl (2002B) 119.
54. Gänzl (2002B) 202.
55. *New York Clipper* 19 May 1888.
56. The *New York Clipper* (6 June 1891) reports that "Bendix was married in 1879, but since 1885 he has not lived with his wife, and she has resided with her parents at Philadelphia, with her two children, aged five and eight years.... Mr. Noonan counsel for Mrs. Bendix, claimed that her husband earned a salary of about $80 per week, and since Jan. 1 has not contributed anything to the support of his wife. Mr. Bendix stated that his salary was only $50 a week, and that he gave his wife $6 a week to support herself and children."
57. See *The New York Times* 4 December 1904 for a notice of *The Fortunes of the King*, one of Hackett's productions for which Bendix supplied incidental music.
58. *The New York Times* 5 October 1913 and 21 October 1913.
59. *The New York Times* (26 March 1919) reports that Sally Bendix insisted that her husband was supporting another woman who calls herself his wife. Bendix responded that he only paid board to the other woman. Evidently his arguments influenced the judge in the case since Sally was awarded only a fraction of what she requested in alimony.
60. *The New York Times* 23 July 1912.

61. Allen Woll (1989) 62, gives the date as 1883 based on Blake's statements about his birthdate. Official government records, however, show that he was, indeed, born in 1887. See Peter Hanley, "James Hubert Blake's WWI Draft Registration Card" (http://www.doctorjazz.co.uk/draftcards3.html#ragdcjhb).
62. Reid Badger (1995) 132.
63. Eileen Southern (1982) 36.
64. Woll (1989) 60, 69–70. *Shuffle Along* produced a great many hit songs including "Love Will Find a Way," "Bandanna Days," "I'm Craving for That Kind of Love," "In Honeysuckle Time," and the perennial "I'm Just Wild About Harry."
65. Southern (1982) 36. He was a frequent guest on the *Merv Griffin Show* and *The Tonight Show Starring Johnny Carson*.
66. Southern (1997) 326.
67. Southern (1997) 330.
68. *New York Clipper* 5 September 1891.
69. *New York Clipper* 15 September 1894, and 5 May 1895.
70. *New York Clipper* 6 May 1899.
71. *New York Clipper* 5 October 1901.
72. *New York Clipper* 10 May 1867.
73. Sonneck (1905) 178, and Porter (1991) 375–376, 380.
74. Alden (1955) 59. Porter (1991) also credits Mr. DeMarque a cellist and composer with the music for *The Miraculous Mill*.
75. *The New York Times* 2 May 1961. Donald J. Stubblebine (2010) notes that Bowers and Charles Horwitz wrote "No One but You" for *Fritz and Schnitz*, a touring act dated 1885. Bowers would have been ten years old at the time.
76. *New York Clipper* 6 June 1896.
77. *New York Clipper* 19 January 1901.
78. *The New York Times* 7 September 1902.
79. *New York Clipper* 25 December 1909.
80. *The New York Times* 31 December 1941.
81. *New York Clipper* 23 August 1873. The company was advertised as having a double quartet of male and female voices as well as a brass band of thirteen performers. In addition to the minstrel show entertainment, the company would present a burlesque opera "with all the music of the original," i.e., the opera being satirized.
82. *New York Clipper* 9 September 1882.

83. John Franceschina (2003A) 29.
84. Franceschina (2003A) 35.
85. John Franceschina (2003A) 26.
86. Franceschina (2003A) 120.
87. Franceschina (2003A) 158.
88. Franceschina (2003A) 173. When the musical opened in New York (11 May 1885), however, reviewers were mixed. *The Spirit of the Times* (16 May 1885), for example, wished that the show had expired in Philadelphia but the *New York Clipper* (16 May 1885) found the music melodious and catching if not entirely original, and the show filled with good humor winning the approval of the audience.
89. Franceschina (2003A) 200–202.
90. *New York Clipper* 19 September 1903. *Under Cover* originally opened in Boston on 31 August 1903 after a preview performance in Newport, Rhode Island.
91. Braham had begun his affiliation with Rice in the 1878–1879 season as musical director for the national tour of *Evangeline*.
92. Parker Morell (1940) 23.
93. *New York Clipper* 1 March 1884
94. *The New York Times* 7 May 1885. The New York Clipper 29 November 1884) rumored that Harry Braham was "shortly to be married" to Belle Jackson" of *A Rag Baby* Company. Evidently, Lillian was not the only one with a wandering eye. He did marry a second time, though not to Belle Jackson. The *New York Clipper* (2 March 1901) reports that on 20 February 1901 he was sued for divorce in Cincinnati by Mrs. Hannah Braham.
95. Morell (1940) 24.
96. Kurt Gänzl (2002) 243–244.
97. *The Brooklyn Daily Eagle* 28 October 1919.
98. *The New York Times* 15 February 1938.
99. The New York, New York, Death Index 1862–1948 gives Harry Braham's death date as 13 January 1938. However, the U.S. Find a Grave Index, 1600s–Current, gives the death date as 17 January 1938. In either case, Braham would have died prior to the article cited above in *The New York Times* regarding the Bohemian restaurant.
100. John's father, Joseph Braham, was musical director of the Tony Pastor Company when it played the Morris Brothers' Opera House in Boston. See John Franceschina (2003A) 26.

101. Franceschina (2003A) 50–51.
102. The *New York Clipper* review (5 January 1878) was not entirely complimentary: "The music is not wholly of that catching character which can be retained in the memory, ... though some of the airs are pleasing and tuneful, among which may be mentioned the short overture and opening chorus, the ballad of 'Hippomenes,' 'Cupid's Idyl,' 'Paidagogus's Narrative and Laughing Chorus,' the finale to the first act, Atalanta's song, 'No Wedded Life for Me,' the 'Sea Song,' the 'Good-night Chorus' ... these, in most cases, elicited repetition."
103. *New York Clipper* 21 June 1879.
104. *New York Clipper* 6 December 1890.
105. Among the acts in *Rice's Summer Nights* was an African-American novelty called *Clorindy*, written by Paul Laurence Dunbar and composed by Will Marion Cook. John Braham was so impressed with Cook's work that he turned his orchestra over to him for the performance of *Clorindy*. This was the first instance of an African-American conducting a Broadway orchestra.
106. For a perceptive review and description of the production, see *The New York Times* 7 November 1899.
107. See *The New York Times* 6 December 1914 and 8 December 1914.
108. *The New York Times* 16 March 1901.
109. *New York Clipper* 3 November 1900.
110. *New York Clipper* 18 October 1902 reports that Bratton secured the dramatic rights for the *Buster Brown* series in the year the comic strip was created.
111. For reviews see the *New York Clipper* 27 March 1909 and 24 July 1909.
112. *New York Clipper* 22 August 1917.
113. *The New York Times* 9 February 1947.
114. Reese D. James (1968) 9. Richard J. Wolfe ([1964] 1:128) gives the year as 1804, but Bray's name does not appear in Chestnut Street documents until the 1805–1806 season.
115. During his residence with the Philadelphia theatre company, Bray produced many musical theatre works for theatres in New York, Boston, and Richmond, Virginia. One of his published songs, for example, even credits him as "John Bray of the Richmond Theatre" (Wolfe [1964] I: 133).
116. *The Euterpeiad, or, Musical Intelligencer and Ladies' Gazette* (16 March 1822) II: 207.

117. James Nelson Barker (1808) 69–70.
118. Breil's father was a prominent Prussian lawyer who had immigrated to the United States and settled in Pittsburgh.
119. Breil graduated from Duquesne in 1888 and, in the same year, his first opera, *Orlando of Milan*, was given an amateur production in Pittsburgh. Until he went to the Leipzig Conservatory, Breil was largely self-taught as a composer and this piece of juvenilia was the result of his early efforts. Slavishly imitative in its plot and musical program, the opera follows the traditions of late nineteenth-century European opera with little that suggests originality on the part of the composer.
120. *The New York Times* 13 March 1919.
121. Joseph Carl Breil (1919) 48–55.
122. Breil (1922) 85.
123. An undated program exists for the Grand Theatre of London production of *Rollicking Robinson Crusoe, or, Harlequin Good Man Friday, Who Kept the House Tidy, and Pretty Polly of Wapping Old Stairs*, for which Brickworth composed an overture and incidental music. It is unknown where this burlesque fits in Brinkworth's career.
124. George C.D. Odell ([1937] 9: 594–595) reports that Henry Wannemacher served as the musical director for the 1874–1875 season. Brinkworth replaced him in the fall of 1875.
125. *New York Clipper* 18 September 1875. See also Odell (1938) 10: 88.
126. The song relates the plight of two freed slaves after the Civil War, using an African-American dialect that would be considered offensive today.
127. Bristow was an inveterate champion of American music and American themes. He is said to have refused to play with the New York Philharmonic Society in 1854 because of their Eurocentric programming. See *The New York Times* 10 October 1999.
128. *New York Clipper* 11 April 1891. Although Brode's name appears late in the 1876–1877 season, it is likely that he was musical director from October, when the season began. See also the *New York Clipper* 28 June 1879.
129. The *New York Clipper* (28 January 1882) provides this review of Brode's musical direction for *The Money-Spinner*: "It is due to the musical part of the entertainment at Wallack's, where the or-

chestra is now under the direction of Herman Brode, in place of the veteran Thomas Baker, to add that the selections have thus far been marked by good judgment, as well as by about the right quantity of Popp, without too much Waldteufel or Audran." Wilhelm Popp (1828–1903) was a German composer of light classical music. Emil Waldteufel was a German composer of dance music, whose waltzes and polkas were overused as entr'acte and incidental music in New York theatres. Edmund Audran (1840–1901) was a French composer of light operas that had taken the New York stage by storm (*Olivette* in 1880, *The Mascot* in 1881).

130. See the *New York Clipper* 10 May 1890. The Actors' Fund Benefit was performed at Palmer's Theatre, with Herman Brode conducting the theatre orchestra along with musical director Frank Howson conducting the orchestra from the Madison Square Theatre.
131. *New York Clipper* 28 May 1904.
132. *The New York Times* 12 October 1890, and 19 October 1890.
133. *New York Clipper* 1 November 1890. The reviewer goes on to note that the lions "did not quite realize all that [had] been promised in their behalf."
134. *The New York Times* 9 November 1890.
135. *New York Clipper* 1 November 1890. Evidently the burning of Rome was not considered an elaborate spectacle by the reviewer.
136. *New York Clipper* 5 July 1884.
137. *New York Clipper* 2 January 1886.
138. *New York Clipper* 17 May 1902.
139. *New York Clipper* 13 January 1906.
140. *New York Clipper* 26 October 1907. The musical had its premiere performance on 26 August at the New Royal Alexandria Theatre in Toronto.
141. *New York Clipper* 26 October 1907. See also *The New York Times* 20 October 1907.
142. Anne Caldwell's Broadway musical theatre credits include: *The Lady of the Slipper* (28 October 1912), *Chin Chin*, (20 October 1914), *Pom-Pom* (28 February 1916), *She's a Good Fellow* (5 May 1919), *The Night Boat* (2 February 1920), *The Sweetheart Shop* (31 August 1920), *Hitchy-Koo* (19 October 1920), *Good Morning Dearie* (1 November 1921), *The Bunch and Judy* (28 November 1922), *Stepping Stones* (6 November 1923), *The City Chap* (26 October

1925), *Criss Cross* (22 October 1926), *Take the Air* (22 November 1927), and *Three Cheers* (15 October 1928).

143. For *Dixiana*, Caldwell wrote lyrics for "Here's to the Old Days," "My One Ambition is You," "A Lady Loved a Soldier," "Guiding Star," "A Tear, a Kiss, a Smile," and "Mr. and Mrs. Sippi." For *Half Shot at Sunrise*, she composed lyrics for "Whistling the Blues Away" and "Nothing but Love."

144. *Variety* 28 October 1936. See also *The New York Times* 24 October 1936.

145. Oscar George Theodore Sonneck (1905) 178–179; Richard J. Wolfe (1964) 1:152; Stanley Sadie (1995) 3:822. Carr's father, mother, and brother, Thomas, followed him to the United States in 1794 and established a music publishing firm in Baltimore. In 1897, Benjamin Carr sold the New York publishing firm to James Hewitt and settled in Philadelphia, then the nation's capital.

146. Sonneck (1905) 179.

147. See Susan L. Porter (1991) 425–500 for a comprehensive list of the musical theatre creations of Benjamin Carr and other composers of the period.

148. John Tasker Howard (1946) 97–98. Howard writes that in December 1794, Carr made his debut with the Old American Company's production of Thomas A. Arne's comic opera, *Love in a Village*. He also quotes the reviewer from the *New York Magazine* who had this to say about Carr's performance:

> Mr. Carr made on this occasion his first appearance on our stage; and we confess, to us a very prepossessing first appearance. Good sense and modesty, united to a perfect knowledge of his profession as a musician, and a pleasing and comprehensive voice are not the only qualifications which this young gentleman possesses for the stage; he speaks with propriety, and we doubt not but practice will make him a good actor, in addition to his being an excellent singer.
>
> Howard goes on to say that Carr's name frequently appeared as vocalist on concert programs in Philadelphia and that, in 1797, he was a principal singer at Mrs. Grattan's "Ladies' Concerts.

149. Sonneck (1905) 179.
150. Howard (1946) 98.
151. Howard (1946) 99.
152. Sadie (1995) 6: 157. Often the term, "sentimentality" is used in connection with *empfindsamer Stil*.
153. Howard (1946) 101.
154. Kurt Gänzl (1994) 1: 229. Gänzl notes that the authors of *Faddimir* used pseudonyms when the work was produced. Adrian Ross was credited as "Ropes" and Carr as "Oscar Neville." Having already achieved several university degrees and on his way toward earning a Ph.D. in music at Oxford, Carr was, perhaps, reticent to expose himself in a burlesque entertainment.
155. Gänzl (1994) 1: 229–230. Gänzl provides the following titles and places of performance: *Billy* (11 April 1898), Newcastle; *The Celestials* (1 August 1898), Blackpool; *The Southern Belle* (7 March 1901), Southend-on-Sea; *The Rose of the Riviera* (25 May 1903), Brighton; *Miss Mischief* (30 October 1904), West London; *The Scottish Bluebells* (31 March 1907), Edinburgh.
156. Ivo Guest (1958) 82. Guest recalls that the scenario for the ballet was produced by Adrian Ross and that Carr, utilizing a number of old English folk tunes, created a "most appropriate and delightful score." The role of the female ingénue (Lady Dolly) was danced by the internationally celebrated ballerina, Adeline Genée.
157. *New York Clipper* 16 April 1892.
158. Kurt Gänzl (1994) 1:233. According to "A Chat with Mr. Ivan Caryll," (1897) 756, Caryll had given the score to Camille Saint-Saëns, a composer he met in Paris, in the hope that he would use his influence to have the opera staged at the famous home of comic opera in Paris, the Bouffes Parisiens. Melnotte secured the English rights to the piece.
159. Throughout Caryll's tenure at the Gaiety, composer Lionel Monckton provided additional songs (or was credited as "co-composer") for Caryll's shows. Since, quite often, Monckton composed the "hit songs" of the productions, there arose a professional rivalry between the composers,
160. Caryll arrived in New York on 2 July 1910 on business concerning the upcoming production of *Marriage à la Carte* at the Casino Theatre. See the *New York Clipper* 9 July 1910. He departed for Europe a week later and returned in October to oversee rehearsals

of *Marriage à la Carte*. See "American Chorus Girls Better than English Ones" in *The New York Times* 10 July 1910.
161. Gänzl (1994) 1:235.
162. Harry B. Smith (1931) 263–264. See also John Franceschina (2003B) 234.
163. *New York Clipper* 24 May 1922. See also *New York Clipper* 4 July 1923.
164. Ivan Caryll (1898) 144–150.
165. Caryll (1903) 52–54.
166. Caryll (1911) 154–158.
167. Caryll (1914) 110–119.
168. *New York Clipper* 19 May 1860.
169. *New York Clipper* 26 September 1863.
170. *New York Clipper* 31 May 1879.
171. *New York Clipper* 19 January 1884.
172. *New York Clipper* 26 October 1889.
173. *Boston Daily Globe* 28 May 1926. The *Boston Daily Globe* 23 March 1916 agrees that the date was 1911, but the *Boston Daily Globe* 24 April 1921 suggests that Catlin's retirement occurred in 1906. An article in the *Boston Daily Globe* 29 December 1906, reporting the theft of Catlin's violin in the restaurant below his Boston apartment, affirms that he was still the musical director at the Tremont Theatre as of the 1906–1907 season.
174. *New York Clipper* 12 August 1871.
175. Mark Knowles (2002) 174. Knowles suggests that the *schühplattler* was developed from "a distinctive group of folk dances called 'shoe clapping' dances.
176. *Boston Daily Globe* 24 April 1921.
177. *Boston Daily Globe* 5 November 1899.
178. Kurt Gänzl (1994) 1:245 notes that during this time, Cellier was also busy composing music for Covent Garden pantomimes, as well as incidental music for plays, including George Lash Gordon's *Millions in It* (1877) and Ross Neil's *Elfinella* (1878). Later, in 1885, Cellier would compose a score for William and Madge Kendals' production of *As You Like It* at the St. James Theatre in London.
179. In New York City, under the auspices of Richard D'Oyly Carte, Cellier conducted 120 performances of Edward Solomon's *Billee Taylor* (opening 19 February 1881), 27 performances of Offen-

bach's *Mme. Favart* (opening 19 September 1881), 39 performances of *Olivette* (beginning 10 October 1881), 9 performances of Lecocq's *Manola!, or, Blonde and Brunette* (starting on 6 February 1882), 36 performances of Bucalossi's *Les Manteaux Noirs* (opening 26 September 1882), 28 performances of Planquette's *Rip Van Winkle* (opening 28 October 1882), and 105 performances of *Iolanthe, or, The Peer and the Peri* (commencing on 25 November 1882). *Mme. Favart*, *Olivette*, and *Manola* were produced by the [W.J.] Conley-[James] Barton Opera Company, by arrangement with Richard D'Oyly Carte.

180. *Dorothy* ran for 931 performances in England, breaking all records as the longest running musical theatre work to date. In New York, it did not fare quite so well, running only slightly over forty performances.

181. *The Mountebanks* had previously opened at the Lyric Theatre in London on 4 January 1892. Between *Dorothy* and *The Mounterbanks*, Cellier had composed three musicals: *The Carp* (13 February 1886), described as a one-act "whimsicality," an operetta, *Mrs. Jarramie's Genie* (14 February 1888), and a three-act comic opera, *Doris* (20 April 1889). None of these was produced in New York.

182. See Gänzl (1994) 1:245. See also Stanley Sadie (1995) 4: 51.

183. See *The New York Times* 5 April 1931, and 12 April 1931.

184. Because he had dropped out of high school, Chadwick could not attend the conservatory as a regular college student. Biographies tend to differ in their interpretation of Chadwick's reasons for not finishing high school. The Library of Congress biography (http://memory.loc.gov/diglib/ihas/loc.natlib.ihas.200153248/default.html), for example, argues that he left high school to devote more time to the study of music. *The New Grove Dictionary of Music and Musicians* (Stanley Sadie [1995] 4: 105), on the other hand presents a more negative spin on Chadwick's lack of a high school diploma, noting that he was born of "rural stock," and lived as a "vagabond scholar."

185. Sadie (1995) 4: 105,

186. *New York Clipper* 14 October 1893. The contract also stipulated that the Boston Cadets (an amateur performance group for whom Barnet had previously written *Injured Innocents* and *1492*) would be allowed to appear in the work for a week in May 1894 at the Tremont Theatre, Boston.

187. *New York Clipper* 19 May 1894. *The New York Times* found much to attack in Chadwick's music, however, in an article dated 20 May 1894.
188. For an account of the initial production of *Judith* at the Worcester Festival, see *The New York Times* 1 October 1902.
189. For a review of Chadwick's *Judith* at Boston's Symphony Hall, see the *Boston Daily Globe* 27 January 1902.
190. *The New York Times* 28 February 1911; *New York Clipper* 4 March 1911.
191. *The New York Times* 11 October 1910.
192. *New York Clipper* 4 March 1911.
193. *The New York Times* 21 May 1922.
194. In a statement given to *The New York Times* (1 June 1908), Oscar Hammerstein, the impresario who built and managed the Manhattan Opera House, announced:

> I will introduce an entire novelty, which has never been tried anywhere. It is my firm belief in the appreciation of so artistic and opera-going and music-loving people as the Americans that tempts me to try the experiment. In the repertoire there are many operas which barely fill out an evening: in Europe great, but usually very tiresome, ballets are interpolated on such occasions. Instead of such ballets I will add to these operas what I may term "grand opera pantomimes."
>
> I have discovered a French composer and an author, Albert Chantrier and Georges Wague, whose pantomimes have heretofore been only seen and heard in obscure environments. I consider them worthy of presentation on a large scale. The names of their works, for which I have obtained the exclusive American rights are *La Chair*, *L'Hallall*, and *L'Age d'or*.... The great orchestras of both my houses... will doubtless enter into the proper spirit for the musical presentation of these novelties.

195. *The New York Times* 5 December 1908.
196. *Encyclopédie multimedia de la comédie musicale théâtrale en France*. Website: http://194.254.96.55/cm/?for=lis&compalp=c.
197. See Kurt Gänzl (1994) 1: 253–254 for a complete list of Chassaigne's one-act comic operas and musical sketches .

198. The descriptive text reads (in my translation): "During the first part of the dance, Pichenette dances alone; at the place [in the score] marked 'A' Balandard kneels down and puts on airs while Pichenette dances around him. At the spot marked 'B' Pichenette exchanges places with Balandard who dances around her, ludicrously imitating her. At 'C' both come downstage and dance together. Balandard allows himself to fall into the arms of Pichenette who lets him drop with a thud; they finish with a funny pose" (Chassaigne [1876] 53).

199. *The New York Times* review of the original production (15 April 1884) noted that Falka "lacks wholly the gracefulness and rhythmic charm of the Strauss and Millöcker dance music, and it has none of those dashing, piquant galop and polka movements which sparkle through the works of the German comic opera composers. Here and there it has a bit of catchy writing, but not enough to hold a lasting place in the popular ear." *The New York Times* review (13 July 1886) of the first revival in 1886, however, had this to say: "The well-known melodies of Chassaigne which were whistled on the streets when *Falka* was running at the Casino two years ago were all heard again with demonstrations of pleasure, and they deserved to be, for they are not only better than anything in the German operettas, but they were sung with so much spirit and dash by Miss Bertha Ricci and her associates as to enhance their real value."

200. *The New York Times* (15 April 1884). See note 3 above.

201. The plot of *Nadjy* involved the attempt of the Austrian Emperor to force a marriage between the kidnapped Princess of Hungary and the nephew of the high-ranking Margrave of Bobrumkorff, who happens to be in love with Nadjy, a première danseuse. Evidently Hungarian motifs abounded in the design of the production, but less so in the music. See *The New York Times* 13 May 1888, and 15 May 1888.

202. Rudolph Aronson (1913) 177–178.

203. *The New York Times* 3 January 1933.

204. Chilvers had already been a published composer. His complex and sophisticated "Detroit Light Infantry Grand March" was published in 1884when he was twelve.

205. *The New York Times* 27 December 1898. *The Little Host* opened at the Herald Square Theatre in New York on 26 December 1898.

206. *New York Clipper* 1 June 1901.
207. *Boston Daily Globe* 9 April 1899.
208. *Boston Daily Globe* 11 April 1900.
209. *Boston Daily Globe* 10 January 1904, and 2 February 1904. See also Anne Alison Barnet (2004) 142–143.
210. *Boston Daily Globe* 10 April 1904.
211. *Boston Daily Globe* 6 February 1906.
212. *New York Clipper* 20 September 1890.
213. *New York Clipper* 17 October 1891.
214. *New York Clipper* 8 November 1918.
215. *New York Clipper* 18 June 1919.
216. *New York Clipper* 4 July 1874 and 19 September 1874.
217. *New York Clipper* 10 February 1883
218. *The New York Times* 6 February 1883.
219. *The New York Times* 2 October 1885.
220. Chubb arranged a piano accompaniment for "I'd Marry Him To-morrow" (Chubb [1836] 1–4), which was sung by Mrs. Keely during her debut at the Park.
221. *New York Clipper* 20 November 1875.
222. Chubb (1844) 2–7.
223. Chubb (1846) 3–4.
224. Ivor Guest (1938) 63, 80, 84, 155.
225. Guest (1938) 90–93.
226. Clarke's sizeable catalog of musical monologues includes, "'is Pipe" (1905), "A False Alarm" (1907), "The Plumber" (1916), "The Shooting of Dan McGrew" (1917), "Work" (1920), "The Street Waif" (1929), and "The Cockney Girl at the Cinema" (1935). The following is a small sample of titles from Clarke's oeuvre of songs and dances: "Ship Ahoy! Military Two-Step" (1911), "S'wot I'm Used To!" (1922), "Belinda and the Curate: Character Song" (1923), "What a Mokel" (1924), "And the Rain Came Pouring Down" (1928).
227. Frank J. Metcalf (1923) 268.
228. Martha Furman Schleifer (1990) xxiii.
229. Schleifer (1990) xxiv.
230. Richard J. Wolfe (1964) 192.
231. Schleifer (1990) gives the date as 25 May, but Reese D. James (1968) suggests that the premiere was two days later, on 27 May. Susan L. Porter (1991) suggests that Clifton composed additional

music for a production of Thomas Moore's *M.P., or, The Bluestocking* (467–458). Wolfe (1964) adds that "When Charles was deceived," the number Clifton added to *M.P.*, dates from 1823. He also suggests that the composer interpolated at least one number ("Hurrah! Hurrah!") into the score of *Sweedish* [sic] *Patriotism* (1823) and composed the "Dance Champêtre" performed by Miss Durang in *Henri Quatre* (1824–1827). In addition, Wolfe notes that Clifton provided a number of songs that were regularly performed at the theatres in Baltimore and Philadelphia (195–200).

232. Schleifer (1990) xxiv. Citing the authority of Frank J. Metcalf, Schleifer suggests that Clifton neglected to divorce his first wife before marrying again.
233. Schleifer (1990) xxvi.
234. Quoted in Metcalf (1923) 270.
235. See Anne Alison Barnet (2004) 35–44. See also *The New York Times* 16 May 1893 and 21 May 1893; *New York Clipper* 20 May 1893.
236. *New York Clipper* 15 February 1902. The play featured Joseph Kline Emmet in his famous role of Fritz Von Niedlandt.
237. *New York Clipper* 19 April 1902.
238. *New York Clipper* 17 September 1904. *The Street Singer* featured Florence Bindley in the title role. Colwell's wife, Maud Bergrath (whom he had married on 6 November 1900), was also in the cast, playing the role of Effie Pearl.
239. *New York Clipper* 17 September 1904.
240. *New York Clipper* 11 August 1877. George C.D. Odell (1928) quotes an early review of Comer's performance from the *Albion* (15 September 1827): "Mr. Comer's second appearance in the part of a Yorkshire servant justifies the opinion that his talents will augment considerably the strength of the company" (3: 327).
241. *New York Clipper* 11 October 1862. All reports state that Comer died at the Bromfield House, an inn located at 34 Bromfield Street, Boston, not far from the Howard Athenaeum.
242. Michael V. Pisani (2014) 158–159. Pisani notes that Comer's orchestral score contains twenty-nine numbered cues, of which, three are dances, seven are establishing cues (opening an act or setting the scene), and a variety of internal and closing (end of act or scene) cues.
243. For a review of the production, see *The New York Times* 1 October 1868.

244. With *The Forty Thieves*, Connelly moved with the Lydia Thompson Company to Niblo's Garden.
245. With *Lurline*, Connelly and company returned to Wood's Museum.
246. With *Bluebeard*, the company moved to Wallack's Theatre.
247. *New York Clipper* 9 August 1873.
248. For a lengthy review of the production see *New York Clipper* 22 August 1874.
249. Kurt Gänzl (2002) 174.
250. Gänzl (2002) 188.
251. *New York Clipper* 2 September 1911.
252. Thomas L. Riis reports that both John Hartwell Cook and Belle Lewis, Will's father and mother, both graduated from Oberlin College (Riis [1989] 40). The Library of Congress biography of Will Marion Cook notes that John Cook was in the first class of students at the Howard University Law School but makes no mention of his undergraduate work at Oberlin (http//memory.loc.gov/diglib/ihas/loc.natlib.ihas.200038839/default.html). Both sources agree that John Cook had been the first dean of the Howard University Law School. Eileen Southern (1982), who provides a detailed account of Cook's career, does not comment on his parents (81-82).
253. Riis (1989) explains that Cook actually entered Oberlin College around 1886 when he was seventeen. He suggests that at the age of fifteen, he attended an Oberlin preparatory school (41).
254. *Clorindy* was the first all African-American show to be performed in a mainstream theatre, and Cook served as his own musical director for the piece. John Braham, the musical director for *Rice's Summer Nights*, was so impressed with Cook's compositions and arrangements that, every night, when it was time for *Clorindy* to be performed, he handed Cook the baton, respectfully enabling him to conduct his own work. This marked the first time that an African-American would conduct an orchestra in a mainstream theatre.
255. *New York Clipper* 30 September 1899.
256. *New York Clipper* 10 October 1901. Bernard L. Peterson, Jr. (1993) reports that *The Cannibal King* was a reworking of material from *Jes Lak White Fo'ks*, and that it was produced at a New York theatre in August 1901 for a short run. He also indicates that the tour

in November 1901 opened in Hartford and played Indianapolis (69–70).

257. *In Dahomey* originally previewed in Stamford, Connecticut on 8 September 1902 before opening in Boston on 12 September. Following a five month tour, the show opened on Broadway in February 1903, played two weeks in Philadelphia, then went to London where it opened at the Shaftsbury Theatre on 16 May 1903 and closed there, two hundred performances later, on 13 February 1904. After a tour of the British Isles, *In Dahomey* returned to the United States for a ten-month cross-country tour before closing in June 1905. A second *In Dahomey* company went back to Europe in August 1904 and returned the following year. See Peterson (1993) 187–188.

258. Although not integrated in the way *Show Boat* would be twenty years later, *The Southerners* was among the earliest attempts to present an integrated cast on the Broadway stage. White actors played all the speaking roles while African-American performers appeared in specialty acts, and a singing and dancing chorus, with Ida Forsyne as featured solo dancer, and Abbie Mitchell Cook, a featured vocal soloist. *The New York Times* (24 May 1904) reported that patrons "trembled in their seats" when a real African-American chorus appeared to dance the cakewalk. See John Franceschina (2003) 160.

259. See Southern (1982) 82.

260. Internet sources cite the title *Ghost Ship* (1907) as the work of Will Marion Cook. See https://en.wikipedia.org/wiki/Will_Marion_Cook

261. Southern (1982) gives the title as *In Darkeydom* (82). The original title of the show was *Way Down South*. See Reid Badger (1995) 128–131; and Peterson (1993) 103. The show featured the comedy team Flournoy Miller and Aubrey Lyles as hobos on a train.

262. For a review of the concert, see the *New York Clipper* 12 March 1919.

263. The Clef Club was an organization of African Americans organized by James Reese Europe. Will Marion Cook had become a member in 1910 and became choral master in 1912 of a 150-voice chorus that performed at Carnegie Hall (2 May 1912). See the Library of Congress biography of Will Marion Cook (http//memory.loc.gov/diglib/ihas/loc.natlib.ihas.200038839/default.html)

and Badger (1995) 112. For a review of one of the performances by the Clef Club Orchestra see the *New York Clipper* 2 May 1923. In May 1923, members of the Clef Club Orchestra issued a complaint against Cook for back salary allegedly due them, and in June 1923, the Clef Club sued Will Marion Cook for $591.89, alleging that it loaned Cook the money between 25 February and 1 April and had yet to be repaid. See the *New York Clipper* 16 May 1823 and 27 June 1923.
264. Peterson (1993) 205.
265. Southern (1982) 82.
266. Quoted in Franceschina (2001) 203 n.3.
267. *The New York Times* 6 October 1878.
268. George C.D. Odell (1931) 6: 206.
269. *New York Clipper* 15 February 1890.
270. Odell (1931) 7: 120–126.
271. *New York Clipper* 24 June 1865. According to the Clipper article, "Mr. John Cooke led the orchestra; there was a decided improvement in the music over that we have been used to at this house the past season." During the summer season he arranged the music for "Pat Malloy" a song performed in the Irish melodrama *Arrah-Na-Pogue, or, The Wicklow Wedding* (12 July 1865).
272. *The New York Times* 6 October 1878.
273. *New York Clipper* 26 May 1900, 14 September 1901, and 2 August 1902.
274. *The New York Times* 16 June 1908. During the musical's engagement at the Boston Theatre, one of the performers, Ada Gordon secretly married Lieutenant Carlos Stolbrand of the Army Engineer Corps. Coolman learned of the wedding from one of the "Yama Yama" girls, and when the actress made her final entrance in the last act, she was pelted with rice, while the orchestra played Mendelssohn's "Wedding March" from his incidental score for *A Midsummer Night's Dream*. See the *Boston Daily Globe* 13 November 1909 and *The New York Times* 13 November, 1909.
275. See the *New York Clipper* 2 April 1910. The musical opened at the Globe Theatre in New York on 17 August 1910. See the *New York Clipper* 27 August 1910.
276. *New York Clipper* 20 January 1912.
277. *New York Clipper* 30 November 1912.

278. See the *New York Clipper* 4 October 1913. *The Red Canary* opened at the Lyric Theatre in New York on 13 April 1914. See the *New York Clipper* 18 April 1914.
279. *New York Clipper* 19 December 1914.
280. *The New York Times* 21 May 1915; *New York Clipper* 29 May 1915.
281. *Boston Daily Globe* 26 January 1902. Edward's father, William Corliss, was an inventor of national repute, and his uncle, George Henry Corliss, was the internationally famous inventor of the Corliss Steam Engine.
282. *New York Clipper* 23 December 1899. See also *New York Clipper* 30 December 1899 and 6 January 1900.
283. *The New York Times* 1 October 1901. *Miss Simplicity* opened at Ford's Opera House in Baltimore and toured before appearing at the Casino Theatre in New York on 10 February 1902. See also *The New York Times* 11 February 1902.
284. See the *Boston Daily Globe* 26 January 1902 and 23 March 1902. See also *The New York Times* 6 May 1902 and 6 July 1902.
285. *The New York Times* 12 August 1908. See the *New York Clipper* 19 September 1908. According to the *Clipper* account, Corliss's music was especially praised. In *the New York Clipper* 3 October 1908, Hopper is quoted as saying that *And What Happened Then* will be the success of his life.
286. *Boston Daily Globe* 26 January 1902.
287. *The New York Times* 4 June 1920. See also Kurt Gänzl (1994) 1:314.
288. *Boston Daily Globe* 3 June 1920; *The New York Times* 4 June 1920 and 6 June 1920.
289. *New York Clipper* 21 December 1889.
290. The *New York Clipper* (10 September 1892) reports that "Dox" Cruger provided the orchestration for Thatcher's production of *Tuxedo* at the Hollis Street Theatre in Boston, beginning 5 September 1892.
291. *New York Clipper* 3 June 1893 and 17 June 1893. The story of *Africa* involves Maurice Merrill, a college graduate who decides to explore Africa from where Sir Henry M. Stanley left off. Unable to persuade his son to abandon such a preposterous project, Merrill senior takes him and all of his friends to an island sugar plantation that he has outfitted to look like Africa. Everyone but Maurice is in on the ruse and his friends combine their efforts to make the bogus Africa un-

bearable for him. For a time, Merrill bravely defies their tortures, but in the end, he returns to his senses and gives up his quest.
292. *Boston Daily Globe* 22 August 1893.
293. *New York Clipper* 30 December 1893.
294. *The New York Times* 5 April 1952.
295. *New York Clipper* 6 May 1905 and 20 May 1905. The critic for the *New York Clipper* called the show a "decided hit."
296. *New York Clipper* 9 September 1905.
297. *The New York Times* 21 October 1906.
298. *Variety* 8:5 (31 August 1907).
299. *Variety* 16:11 (20 November 1909).
300. Bill Edwards. Ford Dabney at http://ragpiano.com/comps/fdabney.shtml.
301. Eileen Southern (1982) 91.
302. Edwards. Ford Dabney at http://ragpiano.com/comps/fdabney.shtml.
303. *Washington Times* 31 December 1903.
304. Edwards. Ford Dabney at http://ragpiano.com/comps/fdabney.shtml.
305. Southern (1982) 92.
306. Southern (1982) 91.
307. The *New York Clipper* (26 May 1920) gives a complete list of the summer attractions at the park, including Everett's Monkey Music Hall; a Chinese illusion act, "China's Fairy Fountains"; Dolores Vallecita's Leopards; Madame Jean Berzac's Pony Circus, from the Coliseum, London; the Hellkvists, "Fire Divers"; "Ouija Land"; "The Dragon's Gorge"; and "The Whip," a novelty ride.
308. Edwards. Ford Dabney at http://ragpiano.com/comps/fdabney.shtml.
309. Before New York, *Hands Up* appeared in previews at New Haven, Connecticut on 3 June 1915. For his first Broadway show, Daly was certainly in good company. It starred Lew Fields and his co-composers were E. Ray Goetz and Cole Porter. See the *New York Clipper* 29 May 1915. By the time the show got to Broadway, however, Cole Porter was replaced by Sigmund Romberg, and Daly's material was jettisoned.
310. Howard Pollack (2006) 252–253.
311. See the *New York Clipper* 1 February 1922, 15 February 1922, and 8 March 1922.

312. See *The New York Times* 5 December 1922 and the *New York Clipper* 13 December 1922.
313. Pollack (2006) 191.
314. See *The New York Times* 29 January 1927 and 30 January 1930.
315. Quoted in Pollack (2006) 191.
316. *The New York Times* 5 December 1936.
317. *The Brooklyn Daily Eagle* 30 August 1896.
318. See *The New York Times* 11 July 1930, 29 September 1933, and 3 October 1934.
319. In 1850, Darley composed a ballad, "The Last Leaf," and in 1851, he composed a "Grand March" dedicated to the Diligent Fire Engine Company. These are the first published works of the teenage composer.
320. *New York Clipper* 25 December 1875.
321. *New York Clipper* 13 May 1882.
322. *New York Clipper* 9 July 1881.
323. *The New York Times* 24 April 1883. The reviewer goes on to note that "the exuberance of individual members of the orchestra should be restrained so that they may have some regard for essential conditions of concerted playing." Evidently there was something amateurish about the production, if only in the orchestra pit.
324. Darley (1883) 124.
325. Darley (1883) 129.
326. Planché (1986) 143.
327. *New York Clipper* 28 January 1889.
328. *New York Clipper* 8 July 1899.
329. *New York Clipper* 2 June 1900.
330. Before he left the Savage Company, Darling conducted a production of *The Prince of Pilsen* at the Academy of Music in Manhattan for a month beginning 6 May 1907.
331. *The New York Times* 10 May 1910. It was also noted that Darling would be in charge of a thirty-two-piece orchestra.
332. *The New York Times* 10 November 1935.
333. John Franceschina (2003B) 23-24. The name of the Chicago publication was *The Rambler: A Journal of Men, Manners and Things*, first appearing on 29 March 1884.
334. See the *New York Mirror* (19 November 1887); *The New York Times* (22 November 1887); the *Spirit of the Times* (26 November 1887); and the *New York Mirror* (26 November 1887).

335. For an in-depth study of De Koven's works, see Orly Leah Krasner (1995).
336. *Red Feather, Happyland,* and *The Girls of Holland* were De Koven's only comic operas that were produced at the Lyric Theatre. His American School of Opera was not a success and was discontinued even before construction of the theatre had been completed.
337. *The New York Times* 17 January 1920.
338. *The New York Times* 21 January 1920 and 28 January 1920.
339. Deane played in the orchestras of the City of London, Standard, and Pavilion theatres among others. See *The New York Times* 6 October 1878.
340. *The New York Times* 6 October 1878. The theatre is referred to as the National Theatre in the *New York Clipper* 12 April 1879. In his *Annals of the New York Stage,* George C.D. Odell refers to the Chatham as the "late National Theatre" (Odell [1931] 7: 250).
341. *New York Clipper* 4 May 1867.
342. In the autumn of 1853, Deane joined Louis-Antoine Julien's Orchestra, which was making an American tour, and he participated in the "Monster" orchestral concerts at Castle Garden. In the late 1850s and early 1860s, Deane was also the principal tenor in the choir at Trinity Church and Trinity Chapel in New York City. In 1862, Deane married the widow of W.G. Jones, an actress and singer at the New Bowery Theatre.
343. *The String of Pearls,* based on the Victorian penny dreadful; of the same name, was an early version of *Sweeney Todd the Demon Barber of Fleet Street.*
344. *The New York Times* (9 October 1868) noted the presence of three ballet specialties: a "Demon Dance," a "Fish Ballet," and a "Can-Can." Quoted in Odell (1936) 8: 465.
345. The *New York Clipper* obituary (12 April 1879) calls Deane "one of the few really good orchestra-leaders of whom the metropolis could boast during the past dozen years or so, and he and Tom Baker were about the last of the old-timers to remain in harness." His funeral took place at the Church of St. Chrysostom on 6 April. Deane was a member of the Masonic Lodge, No. 330, and the Musical Fund and Protective Union.
346. *Baker's Biographical Dictionary of Musicians* (1919), 195–196.
347. http://bnf.fr/documents-by-rdt/14831649/220/page1
348. Jules Verne (2012) 69–71, 90, 91, and 146.

349. Jules Verne (2012) 69–71.
350. *Boston Daily Globe* 27 October 1880 and 14 November 1880.
351. *New York Clipper* 26 March 1881.
352. In his *A Bibliography of Early Secular American Music*, Oscar Sonneck ([1905]180) suggests that Demarque was "probably one of the musicians who fled from Cape François to the U.S." presumably after the beginning of the Haitian Revolution in 1791. If the date of his first musical theatre contribution is correct, Demarque was working in New York four years earlier than Sonneck imagined.
353. Susan L. Porter (1991) 445.
354. Sonneck (1905) 138.
355. Sonneck (1905) 180.
356. Ludwig Englander (1900A) 100.
357. *The New York Times* 28 April 1911; *New York Clipper* 29 April 1911 and 8 May 1911. *Temptations* was the second offering on the program. The first was a "profane burlesque" entitled *Hell*, and the third was a "satirical revuette" called *Gaby*. A cabaret completed the evening, which typically released patrons at around 1:30 in the morning.
358. In Greek Mythology it was prophesied that the son of Danaë would murder his grandfather. As a result, Danaë's father, King Acrisius, imprisoned her in an extremely tall tower without door or windows, but with a small hole in the roof to allow in light and air. In the form of a golden rain, Zeus impregnated Danaë resulting in the birth of Perseus.
359. The *Brooklyn Daily Eagle* (26 January 1891) notes that Harvey Dodworth played the piccolo in the orchestra of the Park Theatre in New York when he was ten years old.
360. Rosetta O'Neill (1948), 91.
361. See *The New York Times* 24 February 1863.
362. See *The New York Times* 3 June 1863 and *the New York Clipper* 1 August 1863.
363. A set of manuscript orchestral parts exists at the Folger Shakespeare Library in Washington, D.C.. Parts for cornets, saxhorns and trombones include music for both an untitled piece in act 1 and a "slow march" in act 5. Parts for flute and clarinets consist of the slow march only. Parts are in the composer hand and signed "H.B. Dodworth, 5th Ave. Theatre.

364. *New York Clipper* 6 August 1864.
365. Deane L. Root (1981) 81, 89–90.
366. *The New York Times* 24 November 1873.
367. *New York Clipper* 20 November 1875.
368. *New York Clipper* 25 December 1875.
369. *The New York Times* 17 July 1876.
370. Dodworth gave an interview to *The New York Times* published 29 June 1879. In it he makes clear his intentions: "I have led several seasons in Niblo's, for both dramatic and operatic business; in Daly's for a long time; in Booth's, and for an infinite number of symphony concerts, oratorios, and operas. But in doing so I have neglected my band business, which has consequently suffered, and hereafter I propose to devote myself to that exclusively."
371. *The New York Times* 25 March 1879 and 31 May 1879.
372. It should be noted that in the early 1850s, Dodworth published his compositions in collaboration with William Hall and Son. Commencing in 1853, Dodworth published under his own imprint: H.B. Dodworth and Co. The preponderance of dance music in Dodworth's catalog attests to the interest of the Dodworth family in the performance and instruction of ballroom dancing. See Rosetta O'Neill (1948) for an in-depth study of Harvey Dodworth's brother Allen, who published in 1885 a seminal book on social dancing entitled *Dancing and Its Relation to Education and Social Life, with a New Method of Instruction, Including a Complete Guide to the Cotillion (German) with 250 Figures*.
373. For a review of the production, see the *New York Clipper* 16 October 1915. The musical play was original titled *The Missing Link* (see the *New York Clipper* 4 September 1915).
374. *New York Clipper* 17 February 1912. For other examples of Dyring's responsibilities, see the *New York Clipper* 22 August 1874, 10 October 1875, 4 August 1877, 13 October 1877, and 26 October 1878.
375. *New York Clipper* 2 November 1878.
376. See Kurt Gänzl (1994) 1: 400–401.
377. *The New York Times* 10 June 1881.
378. John Franceschina (2003B) 64. See also *The New York Times* 15 April 1892, 3 May 1892, 29 May 1892, and 26 December 1892.
379. *The New York Times* 13 December 1899.
380. *The New York Times* 28 May 1901.

381. *The New York Times* 17 December 1902.
382. *New York Clipper* 21 July 1906, 28 July 1906, and 11 August 1906.
383. Gänzl (1994) 1: 400–401. The *New York Clipper* (17 September 1910) mentions an additional sacred cantata, *Mary Magdalen* (undated).
384. *The New York Times* 24 November 1908. *The Patriot* was performed at the seventh annual Newport Music Festival in 1975 and received the following critique in *The New York Times* (26 July 1975): "Edwards was an experienced composer. He did not have original ideas, so [he] went to *Tosca*, Gilbert and Sullivan, Tchaikovsky, even Richard Strauss. All that plus vintage American theater music.… There was something curiously appealing about this vapid but innocent and even charming piece. And nowhere but at the Newport Music Festival does this kind of music ever get played."
385. *New York Clipper* 17 September 1910. See also *The New York Times* 25 October 1910 and 28 October 1910.
386. *New York Clipper* 30 July 1904.
387. *New York Clipper* 16 September 1905.
388. *New York Clipper* 15 September 1906.
389. It is not unusual for the composer of a show's tunes to arrange dance breaks based on the melody of the number that preceded the dance. In fact, in the first quarter of the twentieth century, dance music was often simply a repetition of a number without the vocal part. Song manuscripts are often noted "repeat for dance" and incidental orchestral figures are penciled in to accent the movement on stage. Edwards goes beyond a simple repetition; he actually transforms the original melody to create dance music of a distinctive character.
390. *New York Clipper* 4 March 1916.
391. Edwards also composed an act for Natalie Alt which he accompanied on the piano and conducted a twelve-piece orchestra (*New York Clipper* 14 October 1916). Edwards and librettist Blanche Merrill contrived a vehicle for Fay, Two Cooleys, and Fay in which the performers appear as forest birds (*New York Clipper* 31 January 1918); with director-choreographer Ned Wayburn, Edwards composed a twenty-minute musical entitled *The Moth and the Flame* (*New York Clipper* 12 January 1921). In 1923 Edwards created an act for himself (on the piano) and vocalist Harry Preston, formerly of the team of "Preston and Morton" (*New York Clipper* 4 July 1923).

392. *New York Clipper* 29 October 1919.
393. *New York Clipper* 18 September 1918. See also the *New York Clipper* 14 April 1920. Near the end of the following year, Joe Mittenthal, Inc. was announced as "distributors for all Leo Edwards music publications" (*New York Clipper* 23 November 1921). In 1922, Fred Fisher, Inc. sued Leo Edwards for $300 due on a demand note he signed and delivered to the publisher on 10 January 1922. When payment was due, Edwards allegedly refused to pay. See the *New York Clipper* 19 July 1922. In May 1923, Edwards filed suit against Joseph Alexander, father of the "Alexander Girls" for whom he had composed, arranged, and staged a vaudeville act. Edwards contractually was due ten percent of the girls' earnings, but when he asked for his commission, Mr. Alexander refused to pay. See the *New York Clipper* (30 May 1923).
394. *New York Clipper* 14 July 1920. The revue makes special note of Edwards's spectacular dance number, "The Story of the Waltz," which included themes from "The Blue Danube," "My Hero," from *The Chocolate Soldier*, "The Merry Widow Waltz," and "My Beautiful Lady," from *The Pink Lady*.
395. See *The New York Times* 14 June 1921.
396. See *The New York Times* 9 February 1949.
397. *The New York Times* 14 February 1916.
398. *New York Clipper* 18 March 1921.
399. *The New York Times* 13 July 1978.
400. Deane L. Root (1981) 136.
401. *The New York Times* 20 January 1893.
402. Gerald Bordman (1986) 20.
403. Alcantara is a city in western Spain near the border of Portugal.
404. According to the Boston Museum advertisement for the production, Eichberg's orchestra was scheduled to perform an overture entitled "Midnight Angel" (Eichberg), "Selections from *Rigoletto*" (Verdi), "St. Patrick's Quadrille" (D'Albert), and "Col. Chickering's Battle March" (Eichberg).
405. Root (1981) 140.
406. For a complete list of Einödshofer's musical theatre works, see Kurt Gänzl (1994) 1:402.
407. The reviews of the ballet were glowing. *The New York Dramatic Mirror* (6 October 1915) called it "one of the prettiest ballets that has ever come out of Europe," while *The New York Times* (1 Octo-

ber 1915) added, "Quite the handsomest scene as well as the gayest novelty is the ice ballet which winds up the entertainment.... On the pretty rink a skating ballet from Germany disports itself with lovely grace and striking skill."

408. For description and reviews of the program see the *New York Clipper* 28 August 1916 and *The New York Times* 9 September 1916.
409. Gänzl (1994) 1:402.
410. U.S. Census documents suggest birthdates ranging from 1876 to 1879, but the year 1875 is given in the "Melville Morris Ellis" entry of the *California, Biographical Index Cards, 1781-1990*. *The New York Times* obituary (5 April 1917) reports that Ellis was born in Phoenix, Arizona, in 1879.
411. *New York Clipper* 1 July 1899.
412. *New York Clipper* 30 September 1899. *Sister Mary* opened in New York on 27 October 1899. For a review of the production, see *The New York Times* 28 October 1899. Shortly after the opening in New York, Ellis took ill and had to leave the production. See *The New York Times* 18 November 1899.
413. Ellis played the role of Augustus Triall, a thankless role for which he labored conscientiously according to the *New York Clipper* 11 January 1902.
414. The *New York Clipper* (18 April 1908) reported:

> A strikingly effective dancing and singing number in *Nearly a Hero* was arranged by that clever young Californian, Melville Ellis. It is carried out by eight young women of handsome face and figure. They appear in long white cloth capes, lined with poppy red satin. The flesh colored tights of the girls are covered, and paradoxically thereby disclosed, by long robes of thin figured lace through which is seen every movement of the limbs beneath. At the finish of the dance the girls join their outstretched hands and gracefully disappear in a line, one by one, at the entrance. The brilliant effect is gained at the joining of their hands, which lifts the big flame-lined capes, and against this lurid background the lace covered limbs of this line of beauties are fascinatingly apparent.

415. The dance was so popular that Hoffmann toured with it on the vaudeville circuit. See *The New York Times* 25 July 1908.
416. According to *The New York Times* (10 September 1908) Melville Ellis was scheduled to compose the score for *The Mimic World* of 1909, and President Theodore Roosevelt's African hunting trip was advertised as the setting for the revue. Perhaps because the *Ziegfeld Follies of 1909* (14 June 1909) anticipated the Shuberts' concept by satirizing Roosevelt's hunting trip with the popular "Moving Day in Jungle Town," plans for *The Mimic World* in 1909 were scrapped.
417. For a description and review of the production, see the *New York Clipper* 1 October 1910.
418. For a description and review, see the *New York Clipper* 7 October 1911. Prior to his work on *The Revue of Revues*, Ellis spent the summer touring with Marguerite Keeler's Company on the Orpheum vaudeville circuit. In June and July, they were performing at the Orpheum Theatre in San Francisco. See the *New York Clipper* 1 July 1911.
419. For a description and review of the production, see the *New York Clipper* 18 November 1911 and *The New York Times* 21 November 1911.
420. The list includes *All for the Ladies* (30 December 1912), costumes; *The Man with Three Wives* (23 January 1913), costumes; *The Honeymoon Express* (6 February 1913), costumes, and the supervision of dance arrangements; *The Beggar Student* (22 March 1913), costumes; *The Geisha* (27 March 1913), costumes; *H.M.S. Pinafore* (5 May 1913), costumes; *Iolanthe* (12 May 1913), costumes; *All Aboard* (5 June 1913), costumes, and the supervision of dance arrangements; *The Passing Show of 1913* (24 July 1913), costumes, and the supervision of ballet and dance arrangements; *Lieber Augustin* (3 September 1913), costumes; *A Glimpse of the Great White Way/The Modiste Shop* (27 October 1913), costumes; *Oh, I Say!* (30 October 1913), costumes, and the supervision of incidental and dance music; *The Darling of Paris* (15 December 1913), dance music arrangements; *The Whirl of the World* (10 January 1914), costumes; *The Midnight Girl* (23 February 1914), costumes; and *The Belle of Bond Street* (30 March 1914), costumes.
421. For a description of the show and a review of Ellis's costumes, see the *New York Clipper* 20 June 1914.

422. See the *New York Clipper* 10 October 1914 and *The New York Times* 11 October 1914.
423. For a review of Ellis's costumes, see the *New York Clipper* 27 February 1915.
424. See the *New York Clipper* 16 October 1915.
425. *New York Clipper* 8 January 1916 and 15 January 1916.
426. For a description and reviews of the act, see the *New York Clipper* 27 May 1916, 15 November 1916, and 31 January 1916.
427. hatchingcatnyc.com/tag/j-k-emmet/.
428. *New York Clipper* 20 June 1891.
429. *New York Clipper* 20 June 1891.
430. For a firsthand account of Emmet's start in Cincinnati, see the *New York Clipper* 27 June 1891.
431. George C.D. Odell (1936) 8: 352.
432. hatchingcatnyc.com/tag/j-k-emmet/.
433. Odell (1936) 8: 565. For the production Emmet composed and sang a "Lullaby" that also became a perennial favorite.
434. *The New York Times* 31 August 1878.
435. *New York Clipper* 4 November 1876, 25 November 1876, and 20 June 1891.
436. hatchingcatnyc.com/tag/j-k-emmet/.
437. hatchingcatnyc.com/tag/j-k-emmet/. See also alcue.wordpress.com/2014/02/26/joseph-k-fritz-emmet-and-the-building-of-wolferts-roost/ and frenchhatchingcat.files.wordpress.com/2014/07/fritzvilla.jpg.
438. For an incident occurring in September 1880 when a drunken Emmet purchased a gun, alarming a nearby policeman, who thought the actor was going to shoot himself, see *The New York Times* 4 September 1880. For a report of one of Emmet's performances while intoxicated, see the *New York Clipper* 7 March 1885. In the mid-1870s, Emmet entered the Fort Hamilton Inebriate Asylum in an attempt to conquer his addiction to alcohol. Sobriety was difficult for him to maintain, however, when he was on tour and, in 1881, when his intoxication forced him to cancel an engagement in Liverpool, he was taken to the Workhouse Hospital and placed in the lunatic ward. See the *New York Clipper* 20 June 1891.
439. *The New York Times* 16 June 1891.
440. Emmet's wife was Eleanor ("Libbie") Webber, daughter of a music publisher in St. Louis. The couple married in 1864, contrary to

the wishes of the bride's parents who aggressively opposed the union, and produced one child, Joseph Kline Emmet, Jr., an actor who took over the *Fritz* franchise after his father's death. Eleanor Emmet was granted a divorce on 29 May 1890, at which time Emmet gave her the estate near Albany and $100,000 in government bonds (*New York Clipper* 20 June 1891).

441. *The New York Times* 14 September 1914.
442. Kurt Gänzl (1994) 1: 411.
443. For *The Passing Show*, Englander composed a "Wooden Shoe Ballet," a "Hungarian Czardas Dance," as well as individual songs and dances and the arrangements of operatic music in the production number, "Round the Operas in Twenty Minutes." See the *New York Clipper* 19 May 1894.
444. All original scores by Englander except where noted.
445. *New York Clipper* 12 January 1895.
446. The reviewer from the *New York Clipper* (12 September 1896) had this to say about Englander's score:

> The music is fortunately much better than the book and not only does it possess this comparative merit, but much of it is thoroughly enjoyable. It is well written according to the school of which its composer is a votary, a school, however, in which novelty in form and color [is] not greatly encouraged. In justice to Mr. Englander, however, it must be admitted that his score does not lack variety; that all of his choruses are good and his finales quite stirring, one especially, in march tempo, being highly commendable.

447. Englander's score earned the following review: "Mr. Englander's music ranges from indifferent to good, some compositions being full of vigor and possessing great merit, although none are sufficiently catchy to become popular." See the *New York Clipper* 22 September 1900.
448. *New York Clipper* 12 October 1901.
449. This time out, Englander's score was judged "bright, tuneful and pleasing. Many of the numbers are the catchy kind that are whistled by the gallery gods, and this in itself would make the work popular" (*New York Clipper* 10 May 1902).
450. *New York Clipper* 20 January 1906.

451. See the *New York Clipper* 30 May 1914.
452. Gerald Boardman (1986) 119.
453. Gänzl (1994) 1: 411.
454. Eileen Southern (1982) 128.
455. Reid Badger (1995) 28-29.
456. *New York Clipper* 20 May 1905.
457. J. Rosamond Johnson composed the music and his brother James Weldon Johnson wrote the lyrics.
458. Badger (1995) 34-35. Badger also quotes Sylvester Russell, the critic from the *Freeman*, who was especially appreciative of Europe's efforts: "[James Reese Europe] is leader of the orchestra and a very good one. His music gives evidence that he possesses more ability as a composer than he has hitherto been given a chance to exhibit" (35). See also Bernard L. Peterson, Jr. (1993) 46.
459. Quoted in Badger (1995) 37. Badger notes that in addition to James Reese Europe, the founding members of the club included Bert Williams, George Walker, Bob Cole, J. Rosamond Johnson, Jesse Shipp, R.C. McPherson, Sam Corker, Alex Rogers, Tom Brown, and Lester Walton.
460. See Badger (1995) 39. For the second season of *The Red Moon*, Europe composed the music for three additional numbers: "Pickaninny Days," "Pliney, Come Out in the Moonlight," and "Red Moon."
461. See Badger (1995) 85-86; see also Peterson (1993) 137.
462. See http://memory.loc.gov/diglib/ihas/loc.natlib.ihas.200038842/default.html. See also Badger (1995) 114-118.
463. Published in New York by Joseph W. Stern. See http://imslp.org/wiki/The_Castle_(Europe,_James_Reese) . Badger (1995) notes other examples of Europe's dance music published by Stern but not the "Doggy Fox Trot" which he attributes to the publisher G. Ricordi in 1915 (233).
464. Badger (1995) 114.
465. Southern (1982) 128. Southern (1997) notes that Europe's eleven-piece orchestra consisted of violins, cornets, clarinets, mandolins, piano, and drums (347).
466. Peterson (1993) 103.
467. Southern (1982) 129.
468. Badger (1995) 219.
469. *Boston Daily Globe* 21 September 1877.

470. A representative list of the speakers and entertainers handled by the agency established by James Redpath included Mark Twain, Ralph Waldo Emerson, Frederick Douglass, Edward Everett Hale, Susan B. Anthony, Julia Ward Howe, and the chamber ensemble, Mendelssohn Quintette Club.
471. *Boston Daily Globe* 1 May 1878.
472. The correspondent for the *New York Clipper* (28 June 1879) provided this report:

> It is but justice to say that the managers labored under many disadvantages in producing the work, and consequently the rendition on the opening night was a very uneven one, and not calculated to give this latest home production a satisfactory send-off, as, with but few exceptions, the company were decidedly amateurish and unable and unfit to cope with any work. The piece is in three acts, and, with the overture, contains thirty odd musical numbers, the most of which are highly reminiscent, the principal hit being made by Sadie Martinot in the introduced song-and-dance "Pretty as a Picture," After cutting out the parts of the Duke and Lady Blanche, and judiciously pruning the piece, it went off much better at later performances; but it is doubtful if it ever proves a success.

473. *New York Clipper* 25 June 1881. The *New York Clipper* (20 August 1881) reports that the combination company was scheduled to perform *Evangeline* at the Windsor Theatre in New York City on 22 August 1881.
474. *New York Clipper* 11 August 1883. See also the *Boston Daily Globe* 12 August 1883.
475. Kurt Gänzl (2002B) 181–183. See also the *New York Clipper* 23 May 1885.
476. The *New York Clipper* (19 September 1885) also notes interpolations in the score from opera composers Rossini, Verdi, and Arditi.
477. *New York Clipper* 11 December 1886.
478. *New York Clipper* 1 January 1887.
479. *The New York Times* 13 January 1887.
480. *The New York Times* 13 January 1887. Evidently Fred Eustis was the possessive and jealous type of husband. The 18 December

1886 edition of the *New York Clipper* reported that he intended to sue Henry E. Dixey, the star of *Adonis*, for alienating the affections of his wife. Dixey denied the allegation and insisted that Eustis was trying to blackmail him.

481. *Boston Daily Globe* 13 November 1887.
482. *New York Clipper* 3 December 1887. Ida Bell had filed for divorce prior to the Philadelphia incident, though it had been pending at that time. According to the *New York Clipper* (25 June 1887), the divorce was granted while Eustis was in London.
483. *New York Clipper* 14 January 1893.
484. New York Clipper 7 July 1894, 11 August 1894, and 22 September 1894.
485. *Los Angeles Herald* 9 August 1908.
486. *The New York Times* 12 June 1911; *New York Clipper* 17 June 1911.
487. *New York Clipper* 15 July 1911.
488. *Boston Daily Globe* 24 March 1912.
489. Kurt Gänzl (1994) 1: 424.
490. *New York Clipper* 17 July 1879.
491. *New York Clipper* 8 October 1881. The *Clipper* review goes on to say: "The play possesses but little strength, being one of the weakest efforts of its author, and whatever success it has achieved is undoubtedly due to the excellent and humorous impersonation of the title role by Mr. Fehrmann, who is compelled to carry the entire weight of a poor play and a far worse company."
492. See the *New York Clipper* 14 February 1891, 16 May 1891, 29 August 1891, and 12 September 1891.
493. See the *New York Clipper* 11 October 1890; see also *The New York Times* 6 October 1890 and 25 November 1890.
494. *The New York Times* 13 November 1931.
495. *New York Clipper* 17 November 1906.
496. Kurt Gänzl ([1994] 1:445) notes that the interpolation was originally made for the London production of *The Quaker Girl* (5 November 1910).
497. *New York Clipper* 10 August 1912. See also the *New York Clipper* 27 May 1911 and 27 July 1912. The latter edition reports that when producer A.H. Woods approached Felix for a copy of the score for *Tantalizing Tommy*, he refused to send it out of fear that someone might steal some of the music. Felix agreed to come to New York and bring the music with him. In addition, he stipu-

lated that he would conduct the musical rehearsals personally and that no one other than members of the cast would be permitted in the rehearsal room.

498. *New York Clipper* 7 September 1912 and 12 October 1912.
499. *The New York Times* 3 October 1912.
500. *Boston Daily Globe* 1 February 1916.
501. *New York Clipper* 5 August 1916.
502. See the *New York Clipper* 24 December 1919, 28 January 1920, 4 February 1920, 17 March 1920, 28 April 1920, and 20 October 1920.
503. See the *New York Clipper* 1 October 1919, 17 December 1919, 4 February 1920, 18 February 1920, 3 March 1920, 31 March 1920, 15 September 1920,
504. See the *New York Clipper* 5 October 1921, 9 November 1921, 7 December 1921, 28 December 1921, 28 December 1921, and 1 February 1922.
505. See the *Boston Daily Globe* 18 November 1923 and 20 January 1924.
506. See the *Boston Daily Globe* 26 September 1926 and 17 October 1926.
507. *The New York Times* 18 November 1928. See also the *Boston Daily Globe* 17 February 1929.
508. Gänzl (1994) 1:445. Gänzl gives Hugo Felix's date of death as 25 August; other sources give 24 August. The *Los Angeles Times* (27 August 1934) announced burial services on 27 August at 1:00 P.M. from the Pierce Brothers funeral home.
509. James M. Glover (1912) 72.
510. *The New York Times* 22 April 1939. See also Glover (1912) 72.
511. Kurt Gänzl (1994) 1: 462.
512. The review of *Around the Map* in the *New York Clipper* (13 November 1915) reports that "Mr. Finck, who stands in the very front rank of composers of light music, has given to *Around the Map* some of the prettiest tunes heard in the theatre in a long time, and long before this review reaches the *Clipper*'s readers, it will enjoy the distinction of being whistled all over town."
513. For a complete list, see Gänzl (1994) 1: 463.
514. *The New York Times* 22 April 1939.
515. *New York Clipper* 13 October 1920.
516. *The New York Times* 13 July 1902 suggests a date closer to 1867 but genealogical sources give his birth as 1861 in Mobile, Alabama.

517. *New York Clipper* 20 June 1885.
518. *New York Clipper* 10 May 1890 and 28 June 1890. A new operetta composed by W.T. Francis was also promised in newspaper notices
519. During the tour, *The Idea* also played the Fourteenth Street Theatre in New York on 24 October 1892 and 25 September 1893. Audience and critics' reactions were positive at both engagements.
520. *New York Clipper* 26 September 1896.
521. *New York Clipper* 1 May 1897.
522. *The New York Times* 27 December 1898.
523. *The New York Times* 23 December 1900 and 25 December 1900.
524. *The New York Times* 11 July 1902.
525. *The New York Times* 13 July 1902 and 7 September 1902.
526. *New York Clipper* 27 December 1902. See also *The New York Times* 22 February 1903 and *New York Clipper* 7 March 1903.
527. *The New York Times* 13 September 1903 and the *New York Clipper* 3 October 1903. See also Armond Fields (1993) 190–191.
528. *New York Clipper* 30 July 1904.
529. For a positive review of Francis's music see the *New York Clipper* 6 May 1905.
530. *New York Clipper* 16 April 1910.
531. *The Wife Hunters* was produced by Lew Fields and the Shubert Brothers. For a detailed account of the production, see Armond Fields (1993) 294–296.
532. *The New York Times* 25 May 1913. Armond Fields (1993) 326–327.The *New York Clipper* (7 June 1913) found the score "bright and catchy, being written along the popular melody lines."
533. *New York Clipper* 23 January 1915. Andreas Dippel's Opera Company had produced *The Lilac Domino* on Broadway. *Queen of the Roses* was an American adaptation of *La reginetta delle rose* (24 June 1912) by Italian opera composer Ruggiero Leoncavallo.
534. *New York Clipper* 3 November 1920.
535. *The New York Times* 3 May 1904.
536. *New York Clipper* 9 July 1904.
537. See *The New York Times* 26 June 1906, the *New York Clipper* 30 June 1926, and *The New York Times* 11 May 1954.
538. *New York Clipper* 30 June 1906.
539. See the *New York Clipper* 7 February 1914.
540. *The New York Times* 10 August 1924.

541. *The New York Times* 11 May 1954.
542. http://www.imdb.com/name/nm0294577/?ref_=fn_al_nm_1
543. *The New York Times* 14 February 1952.
544. *The New York Times* 27 August 1911. The article gives no name for the original musical.
545. *New York Clipper* 21 May 1914, 11 July 1914, and 17 October 1914.
546. *New York Clipper* 12 March 1919 and 14 May 1919.
547. Friedland's Passport Application and WWI Draft Registration Card record his birthdate as 21 March 1884. Other sources, such as the U.S. Find a Grave Index, 1660s–Current, give the year as 1881. In the New York, State Census, 1925, the birth year is given as 1886.
548. According to the passenger manifest, Friedland arrived in New York City on 25 August 1903. His age was given as nineteen, reinforcing the claim for a birthdate in 1884.
549. *The New York Times* 11 May 1926.
550. See *The New York Times* 8 August 1932.
551. William Everett (2008) 3–4.
552. Various members of the German audience, protesting the ill-treatment of Germans by Bohemians, made every attempt to stop the concert while other patrons, wanting to hear the music, tried to quell the commotion. Both sides were adamant in their positions and fights broke out when the protesters struggled to storm the stage injuring many of the audience members in their path. See *The New York Times* 16 March 1904.
553. For example, the reviewer from *The New York Times* (18 November 1904) wrote:

> As a composer [Friml] has little to offer. His concerto in B flat [sic], which he played first, is a thing of shreds and patches, of short phrases dressed up in passages, work of a highly "pianistic" but otherwise insignificant character. The chromatic scale has served Mr. Friml well in this work, and his orchestral effects are sonorously reinforced by the bass drum and bass tuba.
>
> See also Everett (2008) 10–11. At the end of the concert Friml improvised a composition based on a theme written by a member of the audience. He felt that his abil-

ity to improvise was his greatest strength and he continued to delight audiences (if not critics) with his improvisations well into his eighties.

554. *Los Angeles Times* 27 May 1909.
555. Hammerstein's first choice of a composer, Victor Herbert, refused to work with Trentini; he was subsequently persuaded by music publisher Max Dreyfus to hire Friml. See *The New York Times* 22 June 1912. See also Everett (2008) 17–20. Otto Hauerbach later shortened the spelling of his last name to Harbach.
556. For reviews of the production see *The New York Times* 3 December 1912; the *Dramatic Mirror* 4 December 1912; the *New York Clipper* 7 December 1912.
557. For reviews see *The New York Times* 11 December 1913; the *Dramatic Mirror* 17 December 1913; the *New York Clipper* 22 December 1913.
558. *The New York Times* 3 March 1915; *Dramatic Mirror* 10 March 1915; *New York Clipper* 13 March 1915.
559. *The New York Times* 7 May 1915. According to *The New York Times* (25 July 1915) the divorce was granted and a settlement agreed upon in July.
560. Friml's unproduced musicals included *John Paul Jones* (1935), *The Singing Girl* (1936), *Tina* (1937), *Ramona* (1945), *Frontier Americans* (1946), *The Indian Legend* (1948), and *Our Dear Children* (1951).
561. *The New York Times* 10 June 1926.
562. *The New York Times* 9 August 1936.
563. *The New York Times* (15 September 1963) reported that Friml "is not the romantic that his music indicates. 'Women took advantage of me,' he said. 'They could not understand that I cared much more for my music than for them. Women gave me inspiration, but they often interfered with my work.'"
564. *Time* 13 November 1939; *The New York Times* 17 December 1939.
565. From a conversation between Miles Kreuger, the president and founder of the Institute of the American Musical, and the author.
566. *The New York Times* 14 November 1972.
567. *The New York Times* 15 September 1963.
568. *The New York Times* 14 November 1972.
569. *The New York Times* 8 December 1969.

570. *The Sun* 12 July 1917.
571. For a review of the production see *The Sun* 26 August 1879.
572. *New York Clipper* 9 July 1881.
573. Many sources cite Bartlay Campbell's play *My Geraldine* as an early "operetta" composition (dated 1880) by Furst. The play was produced at Ford's Opera House on 24 January 1881 with incidental music by Furst. See *The Sun* 25 January 1881. In 1883 Furst was musical director for the (Nate) Salsbury's Troubadors' production of *Green-Room Fun* which played the Standard Theatre in New York City. See *The New York Times* 11 April 1883.
574. *New York Clipper* 21 September 1889. See also *The New York Times* 12 July 1917.
575. See the *New York Clipper* 9 July 1887 and 13 August 1887.
576. While he was in New York, Furst conducted a concert at Steinway Hall on 18 December 1887. See the *New York Clipper* 24 December 1887.
577. *The New York Times* 1 November 1891. Furst had met Belasco in San Francisco when Belasco was working as stage director at the Baldwin Theatre. See the *New York Clipper* 18 July 1917.
578. *New York Clipper* 3 December 1892 and 10 December 1892; *The New York Times* 6 December 1892.
579. *The New York Times* 25 January 1893. Furst would remain the musical director at the Empire until October 1902.
580. *The New York Times* 26 August 1894 and 31 August 1894.
581. *The New York Times* 25 September 1894.
582. *New York Clipper* 18 September 1897 and 26 September 1897.
583. *New York Clipper* 15 January 1898.
584. *The New York Times* 22 February 1898.
585. *New York Clipper* 29 October 1898.
586. *New York Clipper* 31 December 1898.
587. Furst's incidental score for *David Harum* included an especially spirited march, published as the "David Harum March" by Howley, Haviland, and Dresser in 1900.
588. *The New York Times* 30 November 1902.
589. The "War March" carries the inscription: "Zinkuan Yoken Shinsi (A true Samurai, who set an example to all, and who used his sword where it was required)."
590. For an extensive analysis of Furst's incidental score for *The Darling of the Gods*, see Michael Pisani (2014) 298–308.

591. For an account of a dress rehearsal of *Sweet Kitty Bellairs* see *The New York Times* 13 December 1903.

592. See *The New York Times* 19 June 1907, 11 July 1907, 10 November 1907; see also *The Sun* 20 October 1907; and the *New York Clipper* 26 October 1907.

593. *The New York Times* 24 September 1915. An earlier edition of *The New York Times* (12 September 1915) provided a colorful account of Furst's return from the West Coast carrying orchestrations incidental to the films scheduled to be shown at the Knickerbocker Theatre:

> "The bundle was heavy," said Mr. Furst, "but the music is light. I can guarantee that it won't put the audience to sleep at the Knickerbocker. I spent twelve days divided among the studios of [D.W.] Griffith, [Mack] Sennett, and [Thomas H.] Ince. In a week I met more old friends than I am likely to meet in a month of Sundays in New York.
>
> "The writing of music for motion pictures is now in its infancy. The music should be treated symphonically as in *The Birth of a Nation*. I hope to have thematic music for all of the Triangle [Motion Picture Company] plays, and it is certainly a large order, as more than one hundred will be produced in the course of a season."

594. *The New York Times* 20 December 1892; *New York Clipper* 24 December 1892.

595. *New York Clipper* 3 June 1893.

596. *New York Clipper* 5 August 1893.

597. *The New York Times* 5 May 1898; *New York Clipper* 28 May 1898.

598. *New York Clipper* 4 June 1898; *The New York Times* 5 June 1898.

599. *The New York Times* 20 September 1898; *New York Clipper* 24 September 1898.

600. *The New York Times* 27 October 1898; *New York Clipper* 29 October 1898.

601. *New York Clipper* 11 August 1906.

602. *The New York Times* 3 August 1902.

603. *The New York Times* 10 August 1902.

604. Kurt Gänzl (1994) 1: 512.

605. *The New York Times* 21 September 1910.

606. *The New York Times* 6 May 1923.
607. *New York Clipper* 29 March 1884. Intropidi (1852–1908) was also a member of the Manhattan Chess Club and one of the best players of the St. George's Men's Club. See http://www.chessgames.com/perl/chessplayer?pid=99710
608. *New York Clipper* 14 March 1885.
609. *New York Clipper* 12 February 1887.
610. *A Midnight Bell* had originally opened at the Alcazar Theatre in San Francisco on 4 April 1888 and on the East Coast it premiered at the Star Theatre in Buffalo on 18 February 1889. See the *New York Clipper* 16 March 1889.
611. *The New York Times* 15 November 1891; *New York Clipper* 21 November 1891;*The New York Times* 10 February 1893 and 11 February 1894.
612. *The New York Times* 7 October 1894.
613. *The New York Times* 27 May 1896.
614. *Boston Daily Globe* 5 September 1896.
615. Throughout his life, Charles J. Gebest gave Zanesville, Ohio, as his birthplace.
616. *New York Clipper* 26 June 1897.
617. *New York Clipper* 9 February 1901.
618. *Little Johnny Jones* was also Cohan's first collaboration with producer Sam H. Harris.
619. *The Talk of New York* opened in Chicago on 8 September 1907. See the *New York Clipper* 21 September 1907. With this show Harris and Cohan began co-producing.
620. *New York Clipper* 22 May 1909.
621. *The New York Times* 14 June 1910; *New York Clipper* 18 June 1910.
622. *New York Clipper* 3June 1911; *The New York Times* 7 November 1911.
623. *New York Clipper* 18 November 1911 and 2 December 1911.
624. *The New York Times* 7 September 1913; *New York Clipper* 25 October 1913 and 1 November 1913; *The New York Times* 14 April 1914. In 1919, producer Harry A. March acquired the rights to *The Beauty Shop* and condensed it for vaudeville, reducing the cast to twenty. See the *New York Clipper* 15 January 1919.
625. *New York Clipper* 29 January 1919. $5,000 in 1919 dollars would be worth in excess of $71,500 in 2016.
626. *The New York Times* 29 January 1928.

627. The review of the production in the *New York Clipper* (10 June 1911) reported that Gideon's song "Antidotes" was one of the hits of the show. See also the *New York Clipper* 22 July 1911.
628. *The New York Times* 23 February 1913.
629. *The New York Times* 31 December 1913. *The New York Times* (7 March 1914) reported that Gideon had less than $3.00 cash on hand.
630. *New York Clipper* 6 June 1914.
631. *The New York Times* 10 July 1914. Gideon was required to make a cash payment of $3,750 as a condition of receiving his discharge. In April 1923, Gideon was back in bankruptcy court claiming liabilities of $21, 320 and assets of $4,000, and attributing his present failure to gambling, extravagance, and high interest on borrowed money. See the *New York Clipper* 11 April 1923.
632. *New York Clipper* 13 February 1915.
633. *New York Clipper* 11 December 1915 and 1 January 1916.
634. *New York Clipper* 20 November 1918.
635. *Buddies* received its premiere in Newport, Rhode Island, on 8 August 1919. See the *New York Clipper* 13 August 1919.
636. The *New York Clipper* 2 July 1919 and 27 August 1919. Gideon's song, "We'll Settle Down in Washington Square," was cut from *Buddies* in the New York City production (27 October 1919) and reappeared as "In Chelsea Somewhere" in *The Eclipse*, produced 12 November 1919. The song resurfaced as "Washington Square" in *As You Were*, the American version of Cochran's London revue, produced on 27 January 1920 in New York City.
637. See the *New York Clipper* 23 March 1921, 9 November 1921, and 30 November 1921.
638. *The New York Times* 29 January 1928.
639. See the *New York Clipper* 11 January 1922, 7 June 1922, and 18 October 1922; see also *The New York Times* 29 January 1928.
640. *The New York Times* 31 January 1928.
641. Kurt Gänzl (1994) 1: 538.
642. Oscar Sonneck (1905) 181.
643. George C.D. Odell (1927) 1: 327. Odell makes special mention that Mr. Gilfert was Charles Gilfert's father. Susan L. Porter (1991) 373 reveals that George Gilfert was a viola player in the John Street Theatre orchestra.
644. Odell (1927) 2: 93.

645. Richard J. Wolfe (1964) 1: 305. Charles Hamm (1979) suggests that Gilfert had moved to Charleston as early as 1805 (100).
646. Odell (1927) 2: 413.
647. A French gentleman residing in Albany shares his recollections of lending money to Gilfert in *The New York Times* 20 October 1872.
648. Odell (1928) 3: 407.
649. Odell (1928) 3: 414.
650. Hamm (1979) 100.
651. See George C.D. Odell (1936) 8: 339.
652. *Medea* was the only production for which Gilles was advertised as writing new music. For a review of the production, see the *New York Clipper* 30 November 1867.
653. Odell (1936) 8: 440.
654. Odell (1936) 8: 312–313.
655. *New York Clipper* 14 August 1880 and 21 August 1880. The newspaper gives the date of death as 9 August but the death certificate is dated the following day.
656. There is a baptismal record dated 11 December 1768, so Gillingham was probably born the week before.
657. Philip H. Highfill (1978) 6: 212.
658. See John Tasker Howard (1946) 78. See also Susan L. Porter (1991) 385–386.
659. Howard (1946) 92–93, 97.
660. Philip H. Highfill (1978) 6: 212.
661. Howard (1946) 85 cites a note dated 1826 but George C.D. Odell (1928) 3: 9 indicates that Gillingham was leader when the new theatre opened in 1821.
662. Quoted in Odell (1928) 3: 9.
663. *The Euterpeiad, or, Musical Intelligencer* 2, no.22 (19 January 1822), 170. Quoted in Porter (1991) 385.
664. *The Theatrical Censor* 2 (12 December 1805) 13. Quoted in Potter (1991) 386.
665. Giorza's year of birth appears to be a matter of contention. The *Australian Town and Country Journal* 6 March 1880 gives the year as 1837; "*The Etude*" *Music Magazine* June 1914 gives the year as 1838; John Carmody in the supplementary volume of the *Australian Dictionary of Biography* gives the year as 1832; and Stanley Sadie (1980) 7: 398 gives the year as 1832. The year 1837 is better suited to the documents surrounding Giorza's admittance to the

Milan Conservatory and the Revolution of 1848. If he had been born five years earlier, the revolution would have had no impact on his attending the conservatory.
666. The first opera he saw at La Scala was Rossini's *Mose in Egitto*.
667. The name of Giorza's first ballet differs in various sources. The *Australian Town and Country Journal* 6 March 1880 gives the title as *Il Farnaretto*, while John Carmody in the supplementary volume of the *Australian Dictionary of Biography* gives the title as *Il Giucatore*. The issue is complicated further by the existence of a five act "azione mimica," *Cleopatra*, composed by Giorza, choreographed by G. Rota, and published in 1852, a year earlier than his "earliest" ballet.
668. See Sadie (1980) 7:398.
669. See Sadie (1980) 7:398.
670. George C.D. Odell (1936) 8: 295.
671. *New York Clipper* 18 December 1869.
672. *New York Clipper* 17 August 1901.
673. *New York Clipper* 11 June 1904.
674. Sadie (1980) 7:398.
675. Ivor Guest (1958) 77.
676. Guest (1958) 80.
677. *New York Clipper* 23 October 1909.
678. Quoted in Guest (1958) 114.
679. Guest (1958) 114; *New York Clipper* 23 October 1909; *The New York Times* 2 November 1909.
680. Guest (1958) 114; *New York Clipper* 23 October 1909; *The New York Times* 2 November 1909.
681. Details of Glover's early life and London career are taken from Sir Leslie Stephen (1890) 22: 9, and Stanley Sadie (1980), 7: 454.
682. See *The New York Times* 12 April 1868, and the *New York Clipper* 18 April 1868 and 13 October 1888.
683. *New York Clipper* 20 November 1875.
684. George C.D. Odell (1936) gives Fred W. Zaulig as musical director for the Waverley in 1869 (8: 499). Since the Holt Burlesque Company had a repertory of several burlesques, it is likely that Zaulig and Glover shared musical directorial duties.
685. *The New York Times* 4 December 1870.
686. *New York Clipper* 28 February 1874; *The New York Times* 13 March 1874.

687. Glover published the work with New York music publisher J.L. Peters.
688. *New York Clipper* 5 June 1875.
689. James M. Glover (1911) 19.
690. *New York Clipper* 11 February 1882.
691. *New York Clipper* 2 May 1885. The work was described as not possessing a redeemable feature.
692. In his memoir (1911) Glover described the event as follows:

> ...conducted it, later on leading the unseen choruses of the opera in the first act, then in an emergency dressed in a Venetian gown, doing a dance in the second act, what time I chanted these words:—
> Oh, we are the Council of Ten,
> All truly remarkable men,
> And he is the doge—a deuce of a doge—
> And we are the Council of Ten.
> The second act finished, I put on evening dress and conducted the entire ballets of the third act. (69–70)

693. *New York Clipper* 9 January 1886 and 30 January 1886. When *Jack-in-the-Box* was produced at the Union Square Theatre in New York (8 February 1886), W.C. Levey was credited as composer.
694. *The New York Times* 27 March 1892. The *Times* article does not give a date for the production. In his memoir (1911), Glover assigns the production of the ballet to the Palace Theatre in London where he claimed to have been musical director from 1891.
695. *New York Clipper* 20 June 1896. When *The Telephone Girl* was produced in New York (27 December 1897), the score was recomposed by Gustave Kerker.
696. *New York Clipper* 16 November 1901. See also *The New York Times* 5 November 1901.
697. *The New York Times* 9 August 1903; *New York Clipper* 10 October 1903.
698. *New York Clipper* 19 November 1904.
699. *New York Clipper* 6 December 1913.
700. *New York Clipper* 7 June 1913.

701. Writing an article about "Dull Music" for *The London Telegraph*, Glover wrote about American composer and bandleader John Philip Sousa:

> It is worthy of note that Mr. Sousa, in his repertory, although occasionally descending to cheap theatrical effects, makes a general rule that anything approaching to dullness or tiresome iteration should be tabooed, and again Sousa made the movements so quickly consecutive that dull periods were absent. Sousa even went so far as to change his men's uniforms in the interval of every concert, so he must have had some experience of the beneficial effects of variety.
> Quoted in the *New York Clipper* 19 November 1910.

702. See Armond Fields (1993), 398–399; 406–407. For reviews of the production, see *The New York Times* 3 June 1921 and the *New York Clipper* 8 June 1921.
703. *The New York Times* 16 February 1928.
704. *The New York Times* 28 December 1932.
705. *The New York Times* 28 December 1932.
706. *The New York Times* 6 December 1933.
707. *Daily Boston Globe* 22 November 1938. See also *The New York Times* 22 November 1938.
708. *New York Clipper* (17 January 1923) reports that the work was also performed at the Royal Opera House in Dresden in 1907 and won for Goetzl the cross of the Legion of Honor. *Zierpuppen* was Goetzl's most successful musical theatre work and held the stage in German theatres for thirty years.
709. See *The New York Times* 4 June 1922.
710. See the *New York Clipper* 30 May 1914 and 10 October 1914. For a review of the production, see the *New York Clipper* 7 November 1915.
711. *New York Clipper* 13 June 1917 and 4 July 1917.
712. For details of Cohan's revisions during the out-of-town run of the operetta, see the *New York Clipper* 15 January 1919, 22 January 1919, and 5 February 1919. See also *The New York Times* 5 January 1919 and 9 February 1919.
713. *The New York Times* 18 February 1919; *New York Clipper* 26 February 1919.

714. *The New York Times* 2 December 1919.
715. *The New York Times* 18 February 1920 and 28 April 1920.
716. *New York Clipper* 28 April 1920; *The New York Times* 2 May 1920.
717. The *New York Clipper* (29 September 1920) reported that the show was credited with a fine musical score but a weak and unfunny book. After having the book revamped (by veteran librettist Otto Harbach) and spending more money on new scenery, Goetzl planned to reopen the show in Baltimore on 17 January 1921, with some changes in the casting, and the addition of ten more chorus girls.
718. *New York Clipper* 26 January 1921.
719. *The New York Times* 10 May 1925.
720. *The New York Times* 15 October 1944.
721. *The New York Times* 21 November 1919.
722. Goodman had previously composed the music for *Merry Mary Brown*, a show that opened at the Court Square Theatre in Springfield, Massachusetts early in November 1919 but closed out of town. *Linger Longer Letty* was the first show Goodman composed that played a Broadway theatre. See the *New York Clipper* 19 November 1919.
723. *New York Clipper* 9 June 1920 and 30 June 1920.
724. *New York Clipper* 5 January 1921.
725. *New York Clipper* 16 May 1921 and 22 June 1921.
726. *New York Clipper* 22 June 1921.
727. The *New York Clipper* (18 January 1922 and 25 January 1922) advertised that Goodman would compose several songs to be interpolated into the score of *The Rose of Stamboul* (7 March 1922) but I have found no evidence of this. However, since Goodman was the musical director of the show, it is not unlikely that he had a hand in shaping the original score by Leo Fall and Sigmund Romberg.
728. *New York Clipper* 1 November 1922.
729. *New York Clipper* 11 October 1922.
730. Goodman was Al Jolson's preferred musical director. After *Sinbad*, Goodman was involved with every Jolson show except for *The Wonder Bar* (17 March 1931) because, at the time, he was conducting the Rodgers and Hart musical *America's Sweetheart* (10 February 1931). However, since Jolson relied heavily on Goodman's musical direction, Goodman might well have provid-

ed Jolson with uncredited (and probably unpaid) musical advice for *The Wonder Bar*.
731. *The New York Times* 21 July 1940 and 20 October 1940.
732. *The New York Times* 15 October 1944.
733. Gottschalk's year of birth appears to be questionable. California Biographical Index Cards. 1781–1990 gives the year as 1869, a date substantiated by the 1910 United States Federal Census, which gives the birth year as "around 1870." Gottschalk's obituary notice in *The New York Times* (17 July 1934), however, reports his age as 70, causing many other sources to give the birth year as 1863 or 1864.
734. *The New York Times* 17 July 1934.
735. *The New York Times* 23 December 1906.
736. *Boston Daily Globe* 3 January 1904, 10 January 1904, and 2 February 1904. See also Anne Alison Barnet (2004) 141–144.
737. *The New York Times* 22 October 1907. Gottschalk also conducted the operetta's debut in Chicago. See *The New York Times* 26 November 1907.
738. *The New York Times* 18 October 1911.
739. Katherine M. Rogers (2002) 202. See also Mark Evan Swartz (2000) 157.
740. Rogers (2002) 182–183.
741. Rogers (2002) 202–203.
742. Rogers (2002) 205.
743. *The New York Times* 20 July 1919.
744. *The New York Times* 17 August 1919.
745. *Boston Daily Globe* 29 May 1919.
746. *The New York Times* 23 August 1997.
747. The *Boston Daily Globe* (14 January 1923) wrote that Gottschalk "has prepared a special score for this production. It is said to be a rich musical interpretation of the story. He sought in his work to demonstrate his theory that there is no word or emotion which cannot be expressed in music. Entering into the mood of the picture, Mr. Gottschalk decided that he ought to compose a score without any minors entering into the underlying theme in order to create a proper psychological background. There are strains of stirring music, but they are used only in the final climaxes."
748. *The New York Times* 10 March 1985.

749. Gottschalk's obituary in *The New York Times* (17 July 1934) gives his date of death as 16 July based on the AP Los Angeles account. The California Death Index, however, records the date as 15 July.
750. *New York Clipper* 2 April 1881 and 21 May 1881.
751. *The New York Times* 11 May 1881. Eight days later *The New York Times* (19 May 1881) reveled in reporting the unpaid salaries due to performers, scene-shifters, carpenters, and stage hands, all of whom refused to work until their accounts were settled.
752. *New York Clipper* 14 May 1881.
753. It has been conjectured that Granger was among the Hessians who came to America to fight in the Revolution and remained after the hostilities ceased. See Richard J. Wolfe (1964) 1:322, and H. Earle Johnson (1967) 170.
754. Johnson (1967) 147.
755. Quoted in Johnson (1967) 251. See also Susan L. Porter (1991) 384.
756. Sydney Rosenfeld had made a name for himself in the musical theatre as an adaptor of foreign comic operas and operettas and wanted to try his hand at writing an original libretto. The advertisements for *The Mystic Isle* announced both author and composer as if New Yorkers would be familiar with their work.
757. *The New York Times* 3 October 1886; *New York Clipper* 21 August 1886 and 9 October 1886.
758. *New York Clipper* 9 October 1886.
759. *New York Clipper* 16 October 1886.
760. H. Earle Johnson (1967) 167.
761. Susan L. Porter (1991) 377.
762. Johnson (1967) 172.
763. Porter (1991) 211.
764. Teresa F. Mazzulli (2011) http://www.classIcal-scene,com/2011/09/30/boston%E2%80%99s-%E2%80%9Cconservatorio%E2%80%9D-%E2%80%94-the-first/.
765. Johnson (1967) 126. It is difficult to determine the exact date on which the Philharmonic Society was founded. Since an early notification of a rehearsal is dated 4 October 1809, the society must have been up and running by then.
766. Johnson (1967) 191.
767. *Boston Gazette* 26 April 1810. Quoted in Porter (1991) 211.
768. On his WWI draft registration, dated 1 June 1917, Gress cites his occupation as musical director, working for Henry Clifton at the

New Amsterdam Theatre. Presumably Clifton was music contractor for the theatre and Gress served as assistant musical director, as did most orchestra pianists at the time.
769. For Eddie Cantor's views on Louis Gress, see Cantor (2000) 2: 239, 269–270.
770. See *The New York Times* 14 April 1922; *New York Clipper* 19 April 1922.
771. See *The New York Times* 1 January 1924.
772. For the marriage of *Follies* dancer Linda Basquette to film producer Samuel L. Warner (of Warner Brothers), Gress composed a song performed by the bride at the wedding reception held at the Biltmore Cascades in Coral Gables, Florida. See *The New York Times* 5 July 1925. Later in July, after obtaining a divorce from his first wife, Alice Humphries, whom he married on 27 November 1918, Gress married his second wife, Avonne Taylor, a chorine in *Kid Boots* (*The New York Times* 25 July 1925).
773. *The New York Times* 25 October 1895.
774. *The New York Times* 16 December 1897.
775. *The New York Times* 16 November 1902. See also the *New York Clipper* 29 November 1902.
776. *The New York Times* 23 November 1902.
777. *The New York Times* 17 February 1903; *New York Clipper* 21 February 1903.
778. *The New York Times* 14 March 1909.
779. *The New York Times* 31 May 1916.
780. *The New York Times* 28 January 1918. See also *The New York Times* 30 December 1917 and the *New York Clipper* 2 January 1918.
781. *The New York Times* 10 October 1918 and 13 October 1918.
782. *New York Clipper* 29 October 1919; *The New York Times* 16 December 1919.
783. For a review of the opera see *The New York Times* 1 February 1920. Again critics found much to admire in Hadley's music, even if it was somewhat reminiscent of Richard Strauss and Richard Wagner, and again critics made special mention of Hadley's dance music.
784. Stanley Sadie (1980) 8: 18.
785. *The New York Times* 25 December 1893.
786. *New York Clipper* 3 March 1894.
787. The obituaries in both *The New York Times* (2 August 1919) and *New York Clipper* (6 August 1919) give Hammerstein's birth year

as 1847 and other sources suggest the year 1846. However, Hammerstein's tombstone at Woodlawn Cemetery gives the year as 1848 as does his family tree.
788. *The New York Times* 18 November 1906.
789. *The New York Times* 29 October 1893.
790. *New York Clipper* 4 November 1893.
791. *The New York Times* 9 February 1896, 11 February 1896, 13 September 1896; *New York Clipper* 15 February 1896. *The New York Times* reviewer (11 February 1896) noted that Hammerstein employed some of the music he had written for *Koh-i-noor* in the score as well as an occasional measure from one or another popular comic opera. Instead of viewing the borrowings as a fault, the reviewer concluded that they "hindered not in the least the triumph of the composer. On the contrary, it showed his good judgment."
792. *The New York Times* 20 September 1896.
793. *The New York Times* 25 September 1896; *New York Clipper* 3 October 1896.
794. *The New York Times* 24 March 1897, 26 March 1897, and 30 March 1897; *New York Clipper* 27 March 1897. The usually positive *Clipper* reviewer found little to enjoy in the production, claiming that "a more amateurish and inane attempt at playwriting has seldom, if ever, found its way to the metropolitan stage, and surely no greater offences against public decency have ever been tolerated for any length of time, which leads one to the belief and hope that the life of this extraordinary production will be mercifully short." Hammerstein made note of the poor reviews and wrought many changes in the piece causing later evaluations to be more positive. On 30 March, for example, the critic from *The New York Times* called the production "bright and amusing."
795. *New York Clipper* 21 May 1898.
796. *The New York Times* 6 October 1901.
797. *The New York Times* 31 May 1903 and 28 June 1903.
798. *The New York Times* 1 June 1904, 5 June 1904, 7 June 1904, and 7 August 1904; *New-York Tribune* 26 June 1904.
799. Hammerstein married Swift in 1915. His first wife was Rose Blau whom he married in 1868 and his second wife was Malvina Jacobi whom he married in 1880. Both marriages ended in divorce.
800. *The New York Times* 2 August 1919.

801. *New York Clipper* 24 June 1899 and 22 July 1899.
802. *New York Clipper* 11 August 1900 and 13 October 1900.
803. *New York Clipper* 3 August 1901 and 28 September 1901.
804. There is no record of a production of *Sweet Annie Moore*.
805. The *New York Clipper* (22 June 1907) reported that *The Mollie Coddle*, a musical comedy with libretto by Charles Baswitz, and music by Carl Hand, was scheduled to have its initial performance in August 1907. There is no record of a production of *The Mollie Coddle*. It is likely that, in *Patsy in Politics*, Hand employed some of the music he had composed for *Sweet Annie Moore* and *The Mollie Coddle*.
806. *New York Clipper* 1 July 1916.
807. *New York Clipper* 16 June 1860, 22 September 1860, and 25 November 1865.
808. *New York Clipper* 26 May 1866.
809. *New York Clipper* 5 June 1869.
810. *The New York Times* 17 August 1875; *New York Clipper* 28 August 1875.
811. See *The New York Times* 14 September 1875, 18 September 1875, and 7 November 1875; see also the *New York Clipper* 18 September 1875.
812. *New York Clipper* 15 March 1879.
813. See Anne Alison Barnet (2004). See also the *Boston Daily Globe* 26 January 1902.
814. See the *Boston Daily Globe* 23 December 1900; *New York Clipper* 29 December 1900; and *The New York Times* 12 February 1901.
815. See *The New York Times* 9 February 1902 and 11 February 1902; see also the *New York Clipper* 15 February 1902.
816. See the *New York Clipper* 5 April 1902 and 10 May 1902; *The New York Times* 4 May 1902, 6 May 1902, and 6 July 1902 (with the announcement that *The Show Girl* was to appear at Manhattan Beach on the following day).
817. *New York Clipper* 27 February 1904. See also *The New York Times* 23 February 1904; and *Boston Daily Globe* 1 January 1905.
818. *Boston Daily Globe* 4 June 1907. Regarding the New York production, the *New York Clipper* (28 September 1907) found the music "tuneful and catchy," but *The New York Times* (24 September 1907) ignored the music entirely and found the show "utterly inconsequent, most of it is desperately silly, and a deal of it in the worst possible taste."

819. *The New York Times* 28 July 1907; *Boston Daily Globe* 15 January 1908; *New York Clipper* 4 July 1908, 3 April 1909, and 5 June 1909.
820. *The New York Times* 20 December 1928.
821. *New York Clipper* 4 November 1905.
822. *Marrying Mary* is rather unique in that it opens with an extended waltz, anticipating the "Carousel Waltz" by some forty years. In the chorus of *Moonshine* and *Marrying Mary* was a chorus girl named Anna V. Mooney who captured the attention of the young composer and conductor. The couple married on 17 June 1908.
823. *The New York Times* 11 February 1910; *New York Clipper* 19 February 1910. The *Times* found Hein's music "really charming" while the *Clipper* found it "not up to other recent efforts by this author."
824. *A Matinée Idol* opened in Norristown, Pennsylvania, on 16 September 1909. See *The New York Times* 17 September 1909 and 18 May 1910. See also the *New York Clipper* 7 May 1910.
825. *The New York Times* 15 September 1910; *New York Clipper* 15 October 1910.
826. Between *Judy Forgot* and *The Wall Street Girl*, Hein served as musical director for *The Paradise of Mahomet* (17 January 1911); *H.M.S. Pinafore* (29 May 1911) including a juvenile production on 28 June 1911 (see *The New York Times* 12 June 1911 and *New York Clipper* 24 June 1911); *Peggy* (7 December 1911); and *The Pearl Maiden* (22 January 1912). Silvio Hein also filed for bankruptcy in October 1911, claiming liabilities of $18, 924 and assets of less than $1.00. See *The New York Times* 19 October 1911.
827. *New York Clipper* 12 April 1913 and 30 August 1913; *The New York Times* 14 July 1913. In the 23 August 1913 edition of the *New York Clipper*, Silvio Hein tells an amusing story regarding his career as a musical director on tour:

> I was directing the orchestra rehearsal in a one-nighter in Iowa, and, as usual, the members of the small town orchestra knew less about music than anything. "I want the tempo about twice as fast," I announced, especially directing my remark to the cornet player. "Twice as fast. Now please try it again." But that cornet player was impossible. "Look here," I shouted, thoroughly peeved, "can't you get some speed into that blankety-blank instrument of yours?" The man with the cornet jumped to his feet. "No,

gol darn you," he yelled. "That's as fast as I can play it, that's as fast as you're going to get it, and if you don't like it take your darned troupe and get out. I'm the manager here, and what I say goes."

828. *New York Clipper* 18 October 1913 and 25 October 1913.
829. *New York Clipper* 29 August 1914 and 8 September 1914.
830. *New York Clipper* 19 September 1914.
831. *New York Clipper* 26 December 1914.
832. *The New York Times* 18 May 1915; *New York Clipper* 22 May 1915.
833. *New York Clipper* 30 October 1915.
834. John Franceschina (2003B) 240. See also the *New York Clipper* 29 May 1915.
835. *The New York Times* 26 October 1915.
836. *New York Clipper* 5 September 1917.
837. *New York Clipper* 3 October 1917.
838. Hein replaced Rudolf Friml on *Furs and Frills*. See the *New York Clipper* 25 July 1917 and 17 October 1917; see also *The New York Times* 10 October 1917.
839. *The New York Times* 21 December 1917; *New York Clipper* 26 December 1917.
840. *The Golden Goose* was a revision of *The Red Clock*. See *New York Clipper* 28 November 1917, 5 December 1917, and 19 December 1917.
841. *New York Clipper* 28 August 1918.
842. *New York Clipper* 26 June 1918 and 9 October 1918.
843. *New York Clipper* 23 July 1919. *Suite 16* was to be a musical adaptation of Marie Dressler's comedy *The Mix-Up*.
844. *Lady Kitty, Inc.* was to be a vehicle for Kitty Gordon, written by Edward Paulton, and composed by Silvio Hein. See *New York Clipper* 16 December 1919.
845. *New York Clipper* 10 March 1920.
846. *The Girl from Home* was a revised version of *The Dictator*. See *The New York Times* 4 May 1920; see also the *New York Clipper* 12 May 1920.
847. *The Old Home Town*, written by J. Young and composed by Hein was put into rehearsal in August 1921 and halted five weeks later when the producer ran out of money. See the *New York Clipper* 28 September 1921. Two months later Silvio Hein was in the Bridge-

port [Connecticut] Hospital suffering from an ailment in his digestive tract. See the *New York Clipper* 30 November 1921.
848. During the production week of *Some Party*, Hein underwent an operation for a tumor on his spine at Lenox Hills Hospital. See *New York Clipper* 19 April 1922.
849. *New York Clipper* 23 September 1916, 18 October 1916, 13 December 1916; *The New York Times* 7 January 1917.
850. *New York Clipper* 10 January 1917.
851. *New York Clipper* 28 March 1917 and 16 May 1917; *The New York Times* 29 April 1917.
852. *The New York Times* 17 December 1918.
853. *New York Clipper* 30 August 1922 and 27 September 1922.
854. Franceschina (2003B) 264.
855. *The New York Times* 22 December 1928.
856. Alexander Heindl is credited as the first professional cellist to do solo recordings.
857. *New York Clipper* 29 February 1896.
858. *New York Clipper* 10 July 1897.
859. *New York Clipper* 8 October 1904. Theatre programs list Alfred E. Aarons as musical director. Evidently Heindl functioned as his assistant.
860. *The New York Times* 13 October 1908.
861. Donald J. Stubblebine (2002) 18.
862. *The New York Times* 28 May 1911.
863. *New York Clipper* 2 September 1911.
864. *New York Clipper* 21 February 1917.
865. *New York Clipper* 22 September 1920.
866. *New York Clipper* 3 January 1923.
867. Richard J. Wolfe (1964) 1: 361.
868. *New York Clipper* 11 May 1861.
869. Stanley Sadie (1980) 8: 441.
870. *New York Clipper* 11 May 1861.
871. Wolfe (1864) 1: 361. See also the *New York Clipper* 11 May 1861 and Sadie (1980) 8:441.
872. Sadie (1980) 8:441.
873. For a complete list of Heinrich's compositions, see Sadie (1980) 8: 442–443.
874. Sadie (1980) 8: 441 gives only Prague; *New York Clipper* (11 May 1861) gives Paris and Vienna.

875. Neil Gould (2008) 8.
876. Gould (2008) 10; Edward N. Waters (1955) 14–15.
877. Waters (1955) 22–25; Stanley Sadie (1980) 8:500.
878. Gould (2008) 59–61.
879. Gould (2008) 256–257; Waters (1955) 72–73; Kurt Gänzl (1994) 1: 644.
880. Waters (1955) 514.
881. Gould notes that *New York Herald* critic Edward Krehbiel savaged Herbert's *Madeleine*, calling it "futile, far-fetched, frivolous, fuliginous [referring to odors emitted by bodily orifices], fumid [murky], fustian in the score and inept, ill devised in the text." Quoted in Gould (2008) 453.
882. *The New York Times* 27 May 1924. See also *The New York Times* 28 May 1924 and 29 May 1924.
883. Philip H. Highfill, Jr., Kalman A. Burnim, and Edward A. Langhans (1982) 7: 281. In *Our American Music* (1946), John Tasker Howard reports that Hewitt was a good friend of the Prince of Wales who presented him with an Amati violoncello, valued at $500 (84).
884. Stanley Sadie (1980) 8: 542.
885. Oscar Sonneck (1905) 183.
886. Highfill (1982) 7: 282. John Tasker Howard (1946) adds that Hewitt conducted the orchestras at outdoor summer resorts including Delacroix's Vaux Hall, Columbia and Mount Vernon Gardens, and that from 1805 to 1809, he was director of all the military bands in New York City and commanded the Third Company of artillery (85).
887. George C.D. Odell (1927) 2: 256.
888. John Waldorf Wagner (1969) 286–288.
889. List prepared from Susan L. Porter (1991) and George C.D. Odell (1927) 2.
890. Howard (1946) 85.
891. Sadie (1980) 8: 542; Howard (1946) 85–86. Howard notes that for some time, Hewitt had been estranged from his wife. She remained in Boston while he lived in New York.
892. Howard (1946) 85. Hewitt was succeeded as musical director by violinist George Gillingham.
893. James Hewitt (1980) vii. In his discussion of James Hewitt in Sadie ([1980] 8: 542), John W. Wagner gives the date of Hewitt's death as 2 August 1827.

894. Quoted in Howard (1946) 86.
895. Sadie (1980) 8: 542.
896. Hewitt (1980) viii.
897. John Hill Hewitt (1994) xiv–xv.
898. Hewitt (1994) xv.
899. E. Lawrence Abel (2003) . http://www.historynet.com/john-hill-hewitt-dixies-original-one-man-band.htm.
900. Charles Hamm (1979) 103.
901. William Craig Winden (1972) 137.
902. George C.D. Odell (1931) 236.
903. Winden (1972) 78.
904. See Winden (1972) 83–85.
905. Hewitt (1994) xvi–xvii; Abel (2003).
906. Hewitt (1994) xix.
907. Winden (1972) 97. Königsberg's authorship, however, is challenged in Hewitt (1994) xx–xxi.
908. Hamm (1979) 245.
909. Winden (1972) 124.
910. See Winden (1972) 139. See also Coy Elliot Huggins (1964) 170.
911. See Hewitt (1994) xvi; see also Abel (2003).
912. Quoted in Huggins (1964) 66.
913. Eileen Southern (1982) 181; http://www.imdb.com/name/nm4672277/?ref_=fn_al_nm_1; https://www.loc.gov/item/ihas.200038843/; Thomas L. Riis (1996) xxii; 1910 Federal Census; New York, New York Death Index, 1862–1948.
914. Southern (1982) 181. The fact of his studying in Memphis at an early age may have led the IMDB to conclude that he was, in fact, born there, and not in New Orleans.
915. Bernard L. Peterson, Jr. (1993) 187.
916. See Thomas L. Riis (1989) 174; see also Peterson (1993) 99.
917. Peterson (1993) 168.
918. Peterson (1993) 99–100; Riis (1989) 179.
919. Peterson (1993) 100.
920. *New York Clipper* 5 June 1915.
921. Peterson (1993) credits Hill with the music for "Rosey Posey" as published by G. Schirmer in 1915. Other sources, however, credit the music to Sigmund Romberg. See Ken Bloom (1996) 2: 1220; see also Donald J. Stubblebine (2002) 268–269.
922. *The New York Times* 23 January 1920.

923. *New York Clipper* 19 September 1874.
924. *New York Clipper* 30 January 1875.
925. *New York Clipper* 28 October 1876.
926. New York Clipper 16 February 1889. Frederick Waldmann, manager of the Opera House in Newark had died in November 1888 and Hindley did not find the new management to his liking.
927. *New York Clipper* 10 January 1891.
928. *New York Clipper* 16 May 1896. See also *The New York Times* 10 May 1896.
929. New York Clipper 21 October 1899.
930. *The New York Times* 12 December 1901. See also *The New York Times* 14 November 1901 and 23 January 1920.
931. *The New York Times* 23 December 1913; *New York Clipper* 3 January 1914.
932. *New York Clipper* 15 October 1919.
933. *The New York Times* 23 January 1920; *New York Clipper* 28 January 1920.
934. *The New York Times* 6 January 1918.
935. Kurt Gänzl (1994) 1:658.
936. *New York Clipper* 6 November 1909.
937. Gänzl (1994) 1:658. The score was basically a compilation of songs that Hirsch had previously composed for shows in New York.
938. *New York Clipper* 11 January 1913.
939. *New York Clipper* 29 March 1913. See also *Variety* 21 February 1913.
940. Gänzl (1994) 1:658.
941. *New York Clipper* 4 September 1915.
942. *New York Clipper* 13 November 1915.
943. *The New York Times* 26 December 1917.
944. *The New York Times* 2 April 1918; *New York Clipper* 3 April 1918. See also the *New York Clipper* 20 March 1918.
945. *The New York Times* 23 April 1918; *New York Clipper* 24 April 1918. See also *New York Clipper* 28 May 1919. *Back Again* closed in Philadelphia after a month's run at the Chestnut Street Opera House at a loss of $25,000.
946. *New York Clipper* 6 November 1918. *Ask Dad* opened in Toronto and played in New York as *Oh, My Dear!*
947. *The New York Times* 24 September 1919. The *Times* reviewer, Alexander Woollcott, enjoyed the "sprightly and uncommonly en-

tertaining" show and wrote the following about Hirsch's music:

> The score is a happy one. Mr. Hirsch knows how to write the music that hath charms to soothe the Savage breast. Several of the numbers are likely to be whistled till we are all sick of them. It is noted that one of the numbers promised in the program was omitted last night. As it was entitled: "When You Come Near Me, I Feel All of a Ooh?" the great-hearted first-nighters bore up splendidly. It is also noted that one number, called "You'll Have to Find Out," is so startling like a Kern number in the not-quite-forgotten *Oh Boy* that something ought to be said about it. So something has been.

948. New York Clipper 10 March 1920. *The House That Jack Built* opened at the National Theatre in Washington and appeared in New York as *Mary*.
949. *The New York Times* 19 October 1920. Again the *Times* reviewer praised Hirsch's score, with particular emphasis on "The Love Nest," which became the hit of the show.
950. *New York Clipper* 19 January 1921.
951. *New York Clipper* 27 April 1921; *The New York Times* 1 May 1921. *The O'Brien Girl* opened at the Apollo Theatre in Atlantic City where all of the reviewers complained about the quality of Hirsch's music. Even when the show moved to Broadway on 3 October 1921, critics continued to find fault with Hirsch's music (see *The New York Times* 4 October 1921). The one song that was considered tuneful, "Learn to Smile" became the subject of a plagiarism suit suggesting that Hirsch's melody was little more than a fox-trot arrangement of Emmerich Kalman's waltz, "Love Has Wings." See the *New York Clipper* 22 June 1921.
952. *New York Clipper* 18 April 1923.
953. *The New York Times* 26 December 1924.
954. *New York Clipper* 18 August 1877.
955. *New York Clipper* 7 September 1878.
956. *New York Clipper* 21 August 1880.
957. *New York Clipper* 19 August 1882.
958. For a detailed review, see the *New York Clipper* 1 September 1883. See also the *Spirit of the Times* 5 January 1884.

959. *The New York Times* 19 August 1884.
960. *New York Clipper* 5 December 1885; *Spirit of the Times* 19 December 1885.
961. Bolossy Kiralfy (1988) 245. See *The New York Times* 19 August 1888; see also the *Dramatic Mirror* 25 August 1888.
962. Programs for *Kajanka* list Horner as musical director. Since Hoffman was still credited as the musical director of Niblo's Garden, he may have simply conducted the performances after opening night. It was not unusual for the composer to conduct the first night's performance. For a detailed review of the production see the *New York Clipper* 23 August 1890.
963. *New York Clipper* 5 December 1891.
964. *New York Clipper* 27 June 1896.
965. *New York Clipper* 11 July 1896.
966. Birth and immigration dates are taken from Hoffmann's 1921 U.S. passport application. The California Death Index and other sources give his year of birth as 1874.
967. *New York Clipper* 31 August 1895.
968. *New York Clipper* 20 January 1900. Hoffmann was advertised as the orchestrator for all of Hill, Horwitz and Bowers's publications.
969. *New York Clipper* 7 October 1905.
970. *The New York Times* 14 May 1907. See also *The New York Times* 16 May 1907.
971. *New York Clipper* 5 October 1907. *The New York Times* (11 July 1909) provided a revealing account of Gertrude Hoffmann's performance and the vaudeville acts surrounding her:

> Gertrude Hoffman begins her annual engagement at Hammerstein's Roof Garden and Victoria Theatre of Varieties tomorrow. For the first two weeks of her season an elaborate revival of "A Vision of Salome" and Mendelssohn's "Spring Song" will be used. An orchestra of thirty musicians under the direction of Max Hoffman will furnish the music. Annette Kellermann will share equal prominence with Miss Hoffman in her swimming and diving feats. Others on the bill are the Seldoms in classic and marble poses, Maude Rochez's, "A Night in a Monkey Music Hall;" the Quartette; Martinette and Sylvester, ec-

centric acrobats; the Three Musical Johnsons, xylophone experts; Ryan and Walker, wooden shoe dancers, and the Dalys in comedy and trick roller skating.

972. *New York Clipper* 5 February 1910.
973. *New York Clipper* 22 June 1912.
974. *New York Clipper* 24 November 1920.
975. *New York Clipper* 1 December 1920.
976. See the *New York Clipper* 11 December 1918 and 2 May 1923.
977. Lynn Matluck Brooks (2011) 34–35.
978. John Durang (1966) 22.
979. John Durang (1966) 22.
980. Brooks (2011) 258.
981. Paul Magriel (1978) 21.
982. Brooks (2011) 35.
983. Durang (1966) 23–24, with spelling regularized.
984. John Tasker Howard (1946) 156.
985. The Horn Family. http://freepages.genealogy.rootsweb.ancestry.com/~hartsman/Horn/HornPage2/horn%20family%20page2.html#charlesedwardhorn.
986. The Horn Family.
987. Stanley Sadie (1980) 8: 712.
988. For a complete list of Horn's musical theatre compositions see Sadie (1980) 8: 713–714. It is perhaps significant to note that in 1823, Horn mentored the young William Balfe, composer of many great English operas, notably *The Bohemian Girl* (1843). See Eric Walter White (1983) 263.
989. *The New York Times* 24 November 1872; George C.D. Odell (1928) 3: 304; Sadie (1980) 8: 712 incorrectly gives the date as 20 July.
990. Quoted in Odell (1928) 3: 304–305.
991. Quoted in Odell (1928) 3: 305. See also *The New York Times* 24 November 1872.
992. The Horn Family.
993. *New York Clipper* 13 November 1875.
994. Odell (1928) 4: 45.
995. Sadie (1980) 8: 713.
996. *The New York Times* 11 April 1916.
997. Odell (1928) 4: 545. Odell notes that "This piece, like others of Horn's, was a failure, despite lengthy cast and fine scenery."

998. *New York Clipper* 21 September 1889. For a detailed synopsis see the *New York Clipper* 7 September 1889. There is confusion about the actual premiere date in Columbus, Ohio. The *Clipper* (7 September 1889) gives the premiere on 2 September (and provides a comprehensive summary of the production) while the *Clipper* (21 September 1889) tells us that "for the first time on any stage" was played on 15 September. The earlier performances were evidently previews.
999. *The New York Times* 7 October 1889 and 15 October 1889.
1000. *The New York Times* 3 December 1889. See also *The New York Times* 25 November 1889.
1001. Kurt Gänzl (1994) 1: 678. Gänzl gives the birth year as 1877 but all other sources including New York City death records give 1876.
1002. John Franceschina (2003B) 170–171.
1003. In 1906, Hoschna and Douglas published a musical folio for juvenile audiences called *Crest Action and Dialog Songs: with Dances*. Selections included "The Barnyard Frolic," "Jolly Sailor Boys," "Little Housekeepers," "The Lilliputian Police," "Tidyville," and "Upside-Downy-Land." Advertisements indicated that the work was designed for sixteen boys under the age of twelve and one "larger boy" as captain. Also included were instructions for costumes and the arrangement of the performers. In 1907, Hoschna and Douglas published a more ambitious work called *Across the Continent in the Stationary Express*, advertised as "a unique operatic novelty in one act."
1004. *New York Clipper* 19 January 1907. The *Clipper* reviewer reported that the show, which was initially produced on 11 August 1906 at New Rochelle, New York, "scored a decided success" in Manhattan. "It is replete with bright, catchy musical numbers, and at the conclusion of the performance many departed whistling a number after the title of the play. The entire company is a capable one and includes a chorus of pretty girls who are all surprisingly good singers."
1005. *The New York Times* 16 June 1908; *New York Clipper* 20 June 1908.
1006. *New York Clipper* 1 August 1908 and 29 August 1908.
1007. *New York Clipper* 4 December 1909.
1008. *New York Clipper* 10 September 1910.
1009. *The New York Times* 26 September 1910; *New York Clipper* 15 October 1910.

1010. *New York Clipper* 3 December 1910 and 18 February 1911. A date of 18 February 1910 is given by both Gänzl (1994) 1: 678 and Ken Bloom (1996) 1: 584.

1011. *New York Clipper* 25 February 1911; *The New York Times* 16 April 1911.

1012. *New York Clipper* 9 July 1910 and 5 August 1911; *The New York Times* 6 August 1911.

1013. *New York Clipper* 3 December 1910; *The New York Times* 29 August 1911. See also Bloom (1996) 1: 308–309, and Gänzl (1994) 1: 678.

1014. *The New York Times* 24 December 1911; *New York Clipper* 30 December 1911.

1015. *The New York Times* 28 February 1913.

1016. *The New York Times* 30 June 1926.

1017. Kurt Gänzl (1994) 1:683.

1018. On 24 July 1862, the Howson family produced William Balfe's opera *The Rose of Castile* and John Maddison Morton's farce *Box and Cox* at the Exhibition Opera House in Sydney. See the *New York Clipper* 9 January 1875.

1019. *New York Clipper* 28 July 1866. The *Clipper* reported that the troupe consisted of Howson's father, Frank, the conductor and company manager; his sister, Emma, the prima donna soprano; his sister Clelia [given as Celia in some programs] Howson, prima donna contralto; Frank A. Howson, baritone; his brother, John Howson; and hired singers, H. Herberti, tenor; Mr. Fraszee and a lady; and E.S. Gould. The *Clipper* notice designated Emma Howson as "Mrs. Emma Howson," Frank A. Howson's mother. In earlier programs, however, the prima donna soprano role was typically given to "Miss Emma Howson," Frank's sister. With father and son named Frank and mother and daughter named Emma, who actually performed a specific role was often confusing. See also Gänzl (1994) 1: 682–683.

1020. *New York Clipper* 2 October 1869. The citizens of Omaha supported a grand testimonial benefit for the Howson family on 2 October 1869 at the Academy of Music. Performances included the first act of Offenbach's *La Grande-Duchesse* with Emma Howson as the Duchess; the third act of Wallace's *Maritana*, again with Emma Howson in the title role; von Suppé's Overture to the *Poet and Peasant*, with cello obligato performed by Frank A. Howson;

and the concluding farce, Landseer's *The Pretty Horsebreaker*" with Celia Howson in the leading role. See the *New York Clipper* 16 October 1869.
1021. *New York Clipper* 28 September 1872. John Howson was also a member of the company. During the previous summer, the same program was played at the Union Square Theatre in New York, and on 3 July, at the same theatre, Howson conducted his sister Emma and brother John in Offenbach's *La Grande-Duchesse*. See George C.D. Odell (1937) 9: 203.
1022. *New York Clipper* 22 March 1873.
1023. *New York Clipper* 21 February 1874.
1024. *New York Clipper* 27 June 1874. The *New York Clipper* (11 July 1874) noted that the production of *Il Trovatore* "was almost perfection… and what with a strong chorus and an excellent orchestra under the able leadership of Frank Howson, the troupe is all that could be desired."
1025. See the *New York Clipper* 16 August 1884 and 11 July 1885.
1026. *New York Clipper* 30 December 1899.
1027. *New York Clipper* 11 February 1905.
1028. *The New York Times* 30 June 1926.
1029. *New York Clipper* 11 October 1902 and 27 December 1902.
1030. *The New York Times* 12 May 1903; *New York Clipper* 16 May 1903 and 24 October 1903. Hubbell also inserted another dance composition, "The Rose Ballet," into the second act during the run of the show. See Richard C. Norton (2002) 1: 739.
1031. *The New York Times* 15 January 1905; *New York Clipper* 21 January 1905.
1032. *The New York Times* 30 January 1906.
1033. *The New York Times* 31 August 1906.
1034. *New York Clipper* 24 November 1906; *The New York Times* 27 November 1906.
1035. *New York Clipper* 21 December 1907.
1036. *New York Clipper* 13 February 1909.
1037. *New York Clipper* 11 September 1909 and 16 October 1909.
1038. John Franceschina (2003B) 200–201.
1039. *New York Clipper* 15 October 1910 and 12 November 1910. The 17 December 1910 issue of the *Clipper* announced that for *The Bachelor Belles*, "Mr. Hubbell has written the best music of his career."

1040. *The New York Times* 14 December 1954.
1041. *New York Clipper* 1 July 1911.
1042. Kurt Gänzl (1994) 1: 686; Ken Bloom (1996) 1: 790.
1043. *New York Clipper* 18 November 1911.
1044. *New York Clipper* 24 February 1912. The *Clipper* (30 March 1912), however, proclaims "for the first time on any stage, at the Apollo Theatre, Atlantic City, N.J., on March 18, a new musical comedy called *The Man from Cook's*."
1045. *New York Clipper* 13 April 1912.
1046. *New York Clipper* 29 June 1912 and 24 August 1912.
1047. *New York Clipper* (29 August 1914) reports the production of a show called *The Model Maid* at the Majestic Theatre in Boston, with music composed by Silvio Hein.
1048. *New York Clipper* 23 January 1915.
1049. *New York Clipper* 2 October 1915.
1050. *New York Clipper* 26 August 1916. For a detailed review of the production, see the *New York Clipper* 9 September 1916.
1051. By January 1918, "Poor Butterfly" was said to have earned $90,000 in royalties. See the *New York Clipper* 23 January 1918.
1052. *New York Clipper* 29 August 1917.
1053. *New York Clipper* 28 August 1918.
1054. *New York Clipper* 18 August 1920.
1055. *New York Clipper* 6 September 1922.
1056. *New York Clipper* 22 January 1916 and 4 March 1916.
1057. *New York Clipper* 24 April 1918.
1058. *New York Clipper* 14 May 1919.
1059. *New York Clipper* 17 December 1919.
1060. *New York Clipper* 18 August 1920.
1061. *New York Clipper* 21 December 1921.
1062. Gänzl (1994) 1: 686.
1063. *The New York Times* 9 January 1927 and 26 January 1927.
1064. *The New York Times* 16 October 1928.
1065. *The New York Times* 7 March 1914.
1066. *The New York Times* 8 September 1918.
1067. *The New York Times* 13 March 1919. *The New York Times* (8 May 1923) noted the possibility that *The Temple Dancer* would be produced in the summer 1923 at Ravinia Park in Chicago along with Wagner's *Tristan und Isolde*, Giordani's *Andrea Chenier*, and Massenet's *Sappho*

1068. *The New York Times* 8 April 1923.
1069. John Tasker Howard (1946) 400.
1070. In April 1869, George Wood announced that he had acquired from Mercer H. Simpson, a manager of an English provincial theatre, the rights to the pantomime, *Robinson Crusoe*, which had been successfully produced at Coven Garden Theatre at Christmas 1868. Fred W. Humphrey had provided the music for the original British production, and Simpson supervised the New York production. See the *New York Clipper* 10 April 1869.
1071. *New York Clipper* 15 May 1869. See also *The New York Times* 9 May 1869.
1072. *New York Clipper* 15 May 1869.
1073. See the *New York Clipper* 24 April 1869.
1074. *New York Clipper* 15 May 1869.
1075. *New York Clipper* 3 July 1869.
1076. *Aunt Bridget's Baby* was performed at the Bijou Theatre in New York beginning 18 May 1891.
1077. *A Jolly Surprise* also played the Bijou Theatre, opening on 18 April 1892.
1078. *Hendrick Hudson* opened at the Fourteenth Street Theatre in New York on 19 March 1894.
1079. The *New York Clipper* (4 August 1894) reported that "Watty Hydes, musical director of the orchestra at Terrance Garden, threw down his baton at the close of the first act, 23 [July], on account of some misunderstanding his wife had with Stage Manager David. Otto Knaeble took his place temporarily, and the opera was carried through successfully. John Land took the position 24 [July] and will keep it till the close of the season."
1080. *New York Clipper* 27 October 1894 and 2 January 1897.
1081. *New York Clipper* 24 April 1897.
1082. See the *New York Clipper* 21 May 1898. The production opened at the Bijou Theatre in New York on 31 October 1898. See *The New York Times* 8 November 1898.
1083. *Sister Mary* opened in New Haven, Connecticut. The New York City run at the Bijou Theatre began on 27 October 1899.
1084. *The Belle of Bridgeport* premiered in New Haven. The New York production opened at the Bijou Theatre on 29 October 1900. See *The New York Times* 22 September 1900 and 30 October 1900.

1085. May Irwin gave a preview performance of *Madge Smith, Attorney* at the Bijou Theatre on 6 December, about which *The New York Times* published a mixed review the follow day.
1086. *The New York Times* 16 September 1899.
1087. John Franceschina (2003B) 153. The New York production opened on 2 November 1903 at the Victoria Theatre. On 29 November *The New York Times* ran an interesting human interest story that provided a brief behind-the-scenes observation of Hydes's interaction with his co-workers:

> Frank Daniels, Watty Hydes, his director of music, and A.M. Holbrook, his stage manager, took a recess from rehearsal the other day and went to a restaurant for luncheon. Hydes and Holbrook found consolation "splitting" a big steak, but Daniels saw something on the menu with a big French name, spiked it with his index finger, and told the waiter to "bring some of that."
> When it came it looked, good, smelled good, tasted good.
> "Great!" said Daniels, with his mouth full. "Taste it."
> Hydes and Holbrook sampled the mess and confirmed Daniels's judgment. "Wonder what it is?" they asked in concert.
> "Don't know," said Daniels, "but I'll find out mighty quick. Hey, waiter, what is this dish, anyway?"
> "Sixty cents," said the waiter.
> And then Daniels asked: "Is my face red?"

1088. *Sergeant Brue* began its New York run on 24 April 1905 at the Knickerbocker Theatre.
1089. *The Washington Post* 28 April 1907. Noah's Ark was an early work composed by Clare Kummer.
1090. *New York Clipper* 17 August 1907. The Broadway run of *Lola from Berlin* began on 16 September 1907.
1091. *A Parisian Model* opened at the Broadway Theatre in New York City on 6 January 1908.
1092. *The New York Times* 9 December 1934.
1093. *The New York Times* 6 September 1893.
1094. *New York Clipper* 24 November 1885.

1095. *The New York Times* 6 September 1893.
1096. John Franceschina (2003B) 58–59.
1097. *The New York Times* 16 April 1891.
1098. Harry B. Smith (1931) 156.
1099. *New York Clipper* 16 May 1891.
1100. *Dramatic Mirror* 16 May 1891. Quoted in Franceschina (2003B) 59.
1101. *The New York Times* 14 June 1891.
1102. *The New York Times* 22 November 1892. See also Anne Alison Barnet (2004) 55–57. The composer of record for *Prince Pro Tem* was Harvard graduate Lewis S. Thompson. Itzel's responsibilities at Peabody, coupled with his illness, ultimately rendered the collaboration with Barnet unfeasible. It is unknown if he completed any music for the show.
1103. Barnet (2004) 45.
1104. *The New York Times* 27 March 1892.
1105. *The New York Times* 6 September 1893.
1106. Kurt Gänzl (1994) 1: 712.
1107. Bolossy Kiralfy (1988) 131, 133, 266.
1108. *The New York Times* 12 February 1889. See also Kiralfy (1988) 246–247.
1109. Kiralfy (1988) 248.
1110. *The New York Times* 18 August 1889.
1111. *The New York Times* 29 October 1899 and 31 October 1899; *New York Clipper* 4 November 1899.
1112. Kurt Gänzl (1994) 1:713.
1113. *The New York Times* 11 December 1921. See also Gänzl (1994) 1:714.
1114. *New York Clipper* 27 September 1913.
1115. *The New York Times* 23 September 1913.
1116. Harry B. Smith, who had many tales to tell about Jacobi whom he found extremely talented but overly sensitive, erroneously wrote that he came to America with the production of *The Marriage Market*. See Smith (1931) 237.
1117. Rather than being absent from the production (like he was for *The Marriage Market*), Jacobi was on hand to supervise the music for *Sybil*. Unlike the reviews for *The Marriage Market*, notices for *Sybil* were mixed. The *New York Clipper* continued to praise Jacobi announcing that "his music in *Sybil* places him in the very front rank of composers" (15 January 1916) while *The New York*

Times was less impressed, suggesting that "the book as it stands really invited rather more distinctive, colorful, and melodious music than composer Jacobi has been inspired to provide.... The score of *Sybil* is nothing to get excited about, but it is nothing to get mad about either" (11 January 1916).

1118. Victor Jacobi (1917) 101–104.
1119. John Franceschina (2003B) 248–249; *The New York Times* 11 September 1917; *New York Clipper* 26 September 1917; *New York Dramatic Mirror* 22 September 1917.
1120. *The New York Times* 8 October 1919 and 12 October 1919; *New York Clipper* 15 October 1919.
1121. *The New York Times* 5 October 1921. See also the *New York Clipper* 12 October 1921.
1122. *The New York Times* 11 December 1921.
1123. *The New York Times* 18 August 1920; *New York Clipper* 25 August 1920. See also the *New York Clipper* 18 May 1921. The successful runs of *Spanish Love* in New York and Chicago barely broke even due to the high cost of producing the show, and tours to cities, such as Philadelphia and Boston, failed to do well. In fact, one Philadelphia critic was credited with saying: "It impresses one as a dreary play enacted by a mediocre company and scarcely a ripple of applause was heard at any stage of the performance." See the *New York Clipper* 14 September 1921.
1124. *The New York Times* (28 November 1929) was especially critical of Jacquet's score, calling it "so far from being memorable that it is, instead, merely adequate.... attractive without suggesting melodic originality, and rhythmic without any strong hint of versatile orchestration."
1125. *The New York Times* (8 November 1930) continued: "Mr. Jacquet's reminiscent score lacks character, but does all that can be reasonably expected of it. It is melodious when melody is called for, lilting when lilt is demanded, and full-throated on such occasions as when the 'Continental male chorus' sings a sort of football cheer song 'Hail the King.'"
1126. Kurt Gänzl (1994) 1: 717.
1127. The critic from *The New York Times* (11 May 1886) wrote:

> If the composer—a certain Mr. Jakobowski—is possessed of any originality or felicity in invention, he has careful-

ly concealed it, and his music, although bright, fluent, and pleasantly rhythmical, cannot be compared with the second-rate efforts, even of Strauss or Millöcker. On the other hand, the solo numbers and concerted pieces in *Erminie* appeal to the ear with all the eloquence needed in a work of this sort. The semi-sentimental parts of the score, such as the cradle song in the second act, are its least happy measures, while the march movements, the choruses, and most of the airs for female voices are quite taking, if not sufficiently novel to stamp themselves upon the memory and haunt the spectator after he leaves the theatre. The chief merit of *Erminie*, however, is the combination it offers of pleasing and enlivening strains with an exceptionally good libretto. If the second and third acts of the operetta were as full of incident and as cleverly managed as the first, the story of *Erminie* would in truth be one of the best that a musician could be equipped with.

It is interesting to note that the cradle song the *Times* critic disliked became the popular American hit of the comic opera. The *New York Clipper* reviewer uncharacteristically agreed with the *Times* review: "The opera was beautifully staged, generally well sung and briskly acted, and promises to gain a popular success. Its melodies are bright and pleasing, without possessing actual merit of originality, and its libretto is not without interest, despite the resemblance of the story to the tale of *Macaire and Strop*, or to *Robert and Bertram*" (15 May 1886).

1128. See Edward Jakobowski (1886) 57, 60, 126, 136.
1129. *The New York Times* 27 August 1889; *New York Clipper* 7 September 1889.
1130. According to the *New York Clipper* (22 September 1894), the failure of the work was due to the libretto and poor casting. Jakobowski's score was praised as enjoyable and always musicianly. "Every single number is melodious, the choruses and ensemble numbers command and repay the closest attention, and the orchestration is rich, sonorous and fluent without being in the least florid or bizarre," *The New York Times* (11 September 1894) found

fewer faults with the casting and performances and found that "most of the music is pretty and some of it is extremely attractive.... The ensembles and finales are so good that they must have been written by Jakobowski."

1131. *Queen of the Brilliants* was originally produced as *Die Brillanten-Königin* (libretto by Theodore Taube and Isidore Fuchs) at the Carltheater in Vienna on 25 March 1894. The English version (libretto by Brandon Thomas) was produced at the Lyceum Theatre in London on 8 September 1894. Lillian Russell appeared in the title role in London and New York.

1132. Parker Morell (1940) 156. *The New York Times* (8 November 1894) reiterated the view of the *Spirit of the Times* and added that Jakobowski's music "is the veriest trash. It is cheap, reminiscent of his former works, and by no means catchy. The audience last night showed plainly a lack of approval for it, for the only genuine encores were those which were personal compliments from the friends of Miss Russell." In agreement with the other reviews, the *New York Clipper* (17 November 1894) concluded that "it does not seem possible to secure for the production sufficient public favor to warrant its retention upon the stage."

1133. *The New York Times* 18 July 1899; *New York Clipper* 22 July 1899 and 5 August 1899.

1134. Richard C. Norton (2002) 1: 754.

1135. Gänzl (1994) 1: 717.

1136. *New York Clipper* 9 September 1876. See also the *New York Clipper* 28 July 1877.

1137. *New York Clipper* 15 October 1881.

1138. *New York Clipper* 14 June 1884.

1139. New York Clipper 14 December 1895.

1140. *New York Clipper* 28 March 1896. A performer named Harry James appeared on the roster at the People's Theatre in New York City for the 1885–1886 season. It is not known if the actor and the musical director are the same Harry James.

1141. For a descriptive review of the production see the *New York Clipper* 23 January 1897. By the end of April 1897, *A Boy Wanted* had subsequently performed in New York City at the Murray Hill Theatre, the People's Theatre, the Columbus Theatre, and Proctor's Pleasure Palace. See also *The New York Times* 25 April 1897.

1142. For the plot of *A Hired Girl*, see the *New York Clipper* 11 September 1897. For a descriptive review of the New York City production see the *New York Clipper* 15 January 1898.
1143. *New York Clipper* 20 May 1905; 26 June 1906; 11 August 1906; 18 August 1906; 25 August 1906; 6 October 1906; 27 October 1906.
1144. *New York Clipper* 4 July 1908. James's final production in San Francisco was Victor Herbert's *It Happened in Nordland*.
1145. Jannotta Family Papers 1809–1972.
1146. *New York Clipper* (4 December 1869) reports that Jannotta was forced to close his concert series in Cincinnati on 23 November 1869 because of lack of patronage.
1147. *New York Clipper* 13 March 1880.
1148. *New York Clipper* 11 June 1887. *Alidor* had also been performed in Cincinnati in 1874 probably by the same amateur company that produced Flotow's opera *Martha* on 8 April 1875. See the *New York Clipper* 3 April 1875.
1149. Jannotta Family Papers 1809–1972.
1150. *New York Clipper* 21 September 1889.
1151. *Chicago Daily Tribune* 17 April 1913. See also Jannotta Famila Papers 1809–1972.
1152. *New York Clipper* 8 May 1897.
1153. *New York Clipper* 15 May 1897.
1154. *New York Clipper* 19 November 1898. See also the *New York Clipper* 26 August 1899.
1155. *The New York Times* 19 August 1899.
1156. *The New York Times* 22 September 1900 and 30 October 1900; *New York Clipper* 27 October 1900 and 10 November 1900. Jefferson's participation in subsequent Broadway musicals as a performer suggests that this one-time musical contribution was more than simply a fluke.
1157. Vivian Martin was Jefferson's second wife. He had previously married operatic soprano Christie MacDonald in May 1901 but the marriage ended in divorce.
1158. *New York Clipper* 11 April 1917.
1159. *The New York Times* 6 April 1920; *New York Dramatic Mirror* 10 April 1920; *New York Clipper* 14 April 1920;
1160. Jerome gives the date 6 April 1876 on his WWI Draft Registration Card but gives the year as 1875 on his 1896 Passport Application. His obituary in *The New York Times* (29 March 1938), however,

gives his age as 56, which suggests a birth year of 1872. To further complicate the matter, entries for Jerome in the New York Public Library, give the year as 1881.

1161. *The New York Times* 3 August 1902.
1162. *New York Clipper* 20 June 1903 and 27 June 1903; *The New York Times* 23 June 1903.
1163. *New York Clipper* 26 September 1903.
1164 .*The New York Times* 21 August 1904; *New York Clipper* 3 September 1904. See also Kurt Gänzl (1994) 1: 723.
1165. *New York Clipper* 5 December 1903.
1166. *The New York Times* 28 August 1904; *New York Clipper* 10 September 1904.
1167. *The Daily Review* 16 February 1905.
1168. *New York Clipper* 19 August 1905.
1169. *New York Clipper* 15 September 1906.
1170. *New York Clipper* 24 August 1912 and 14 September 1912.
1171. *The New York Times* 2 October 1908; *New York Clipper* 10 October 1908 and 2 January 1909.
1172. *New York Clipper* 16 September 1911 and 6 April 1912. *Louisiana Lou*, featuring Sophie Tucker marked its three-hundredth performance late in March 1912. It began a tour of California in July 1912 that continued through Canada, Minneapolis/St. Paul, Detroit, Philadelphia, and Boston.
1173. *New York Clipper* 16 January 1915.
1174. *New York Clipper* 1 May 1918.
1175. *New York Clipper* 23 June 1920.
1176. *The New York Times* 4 October 1927.
1177. *New York Clipper* 27 October 1900. There is also a Manhattan marriage record dated 17 July 1900 for Al Johns and Rosie Stahl.
1178. *New York Clipper* 8 February 1908.
1179. *New York Clipper* 18 September 1909.
1180. Reid Badger (1995) 56–57.
1181. Eileen Southern (1982) 210.
1182. John Rosamond Johnson. http://memory.loc.gov/diglib/ihas/loc.natlib.ihas.200038845 /default.html.
1183. Southern (1982) 211. See also http://www.blackpast.org/aah/johnson-j-rosamond-1873-1954.
1184. Johnson and Cole also composed "Strolling Along the Beach" and "Sweet Salome" for *The Little Duchess*.

1185. The usual billing was Cole and Johnson, but since this book focuses on the composer rather than the lyricist, the composer is always placed first in the discussion.
1186. Bernard L. Peterson, Jr. (1993) 76.
1187. Peterson (1993), 160.
1188. "The Evolution of Ragtime" was a complex number that consisted of six separate movements: "a Zulu dance, called "Voice of the Savage," a plantation song, "Echoes of the Day," African-American dance music, "Essence of the Jug," a minstrel song, "Darkies Delight," a folk song, "The Spirit of the Banjo," and a ragtime dance, "Sounds of the Times." See Peterson (1993) 243.
1189. *The New York Times* 7 August 1907; *New York Clipper* 26 October 1907. J. Rosamond Johnson also performed in *The Shoo-Fly Regiment* as Edward Jackson, a graduate of Tuskegee, and received good notices from the critics.
1190. *The New York Times* 4 May 1900; *New York Clipper* 8 May 1909. The show was generally panned by the critics and, although the music was considered only "fair," it was found to be the saving grace of the production. Cole's performance in the musical was roundly appreciated; Johnson's, however, was not.
1191. *The New York Times* 16 August 1911; *New York Clipper* 2 September 1911. It should be noted that Johnson's longtime collaborator, Bob Cole, committed suicide on 2 August 1911, at Catskill, New York, where his mother was spending the summer. He waded into the water of Catskill Creek late in the afternoon and drowned.
1192. On 2 July 1913, during the run of the London revue, Johnson married Nora Ethel Floyd, a musician (and one of Johnson's former students) from Jacksonville, Florida, who sailed to London with her mother, the week before. See *The New York Times* 2 July 1913.
1193. The Jazz Five was comprised of Earl Burford, Eddie Ranson, Pete Zabriski, Taylor Gordon, and William Butler. See the *New York Clipper* 17 December 1919.
1194. *New York Clipper* 14 February 1923.
1195. Peterson (1993) 173.
1196. Peterson (1993) 164.
1197. *The New York Times* (22 November 1926) wrote: "Neither of the singers has a voice that would attract attention in the usual concert program, but in the field of spirituals they have made a place

for themselves. Their earnestness, their single-mindedness, the semi-religious character of their offering draw upon the sympathies on an audience which is not looking so much for art as emotion. The spirituals stand as a perpetual memorial of the tribulations of a race and are a contribution to the genuine folk-songs of America."

1198. Scott E. Brown (1986) 10–12.
1199. Johnson revealed that "A lot of my music is based on set, cotillion and other southern dance steps and rhythms, I think the 'Carolina Balmoral' was the most spirited dance in the South. I find I have a strong feeling for these dances that goes away back—and I haven't found anyone else with it yet." Quoted in Brown (1986) 22.
1200. Brown cites the story of Johnson's first tickling experience when he was eight years old. He had been approached by a woman who asked if he'd like to earn a quarter ($.25). She took him to her parlor, sat him at the piano, and told him to play, forbidding him to turn around. Evidently the woman's parlor was a bordello and, facing only the piano, Johnson would not have been able to witness the comings and goings of the establishment. See Brown (1986) 25–26.
1201. Brown (1986) 51–56.
1202. Eileen Southern (1982) 209. See also Brown (1986) 70.
1203. Quoted in Brown (1986) 74–75. Brown notes that Johnson was older than sixteen at the time. He would have been twenty, still a young man, but definitely not a teenager.
1204. See Brown (1986) 265. See also Bernard L. Peterson, Jr. (1993) 99–101.
1205. Peterson (1993) 376. Uncredited, Johnson led a five-piece band during one scene of the play.
1206. *New York Clipper* 18 April 1917; Peterson (1993) 322–323. Originally titled *Smart Set*, the name of the show was changed in April 1917. Following the tour of *Smarter Set*, Johnson composed the music for another touring production called *Me and You* (1922).
1207. Peterson (1993) 270–271. Following the Harlem production, the company sailed to London where *Plantation Days* was reduced to a twelve-minute segment of George Gershwin's *The Rainbow* at the Empire Theatre.
1208. Peterson (1993) 249.
1209. Brown (1986) 267.
1210. Peterson (1993) 241–242.

1211. Peterson (1993) 141. In the same year, Creamer copyrighted *Chicago Loop*, another unproduced musical comedy with music by Johnson.
1212. Also in 1930, two of Johnson's songs ("My Idea of Love" and "Never Mind") were included in the proposed Shubert production of *Three Little Maids* (1930) that never materialized.
1213. Peterson (1993) 304.
1214. See Allen Woll (1989) 152. *Sugar Hill* was later produced as *Meet Miss Jones* by the Negro Musical Comedy Experimental Theatre at the American Negro Theatre in Harlem (November 1947) and subsequently mounted as *Sugar Hill: Meet Miss Jones* at the Las Palmas Theatre in Hollywood, California (June 1949). See Peterson (1993) 335–337.
1215. *The New York Times* 31 December 1938 and 8 January 1939; the *New York Herald Tribune* 31 December 1938; *Variety* 11 January 1939.
1216. *New York Herald Tribune* 6 October 1939.
1217. *The New York Times* 2 September 1940; see also *The New York Times* 16 June 1940 and 27 October 1940.
1218. Peterson (1993) 270.
1219. Brown (1986) 274–275.
1220. Brown (1986) 277.
1221. *New York Clipper* 14 October 1911.
1222. *The New York Times* 12 December 1911; *New York Clipper* 23 December 1911.
1223. *The New York Times* 2 November 1912.
1224. *The New York Times* 24 December 1912; *New York Clipper* 4 January 1913.
1225. *New York Clipper* 21 August 1918.
1226. *The New York Times* 4 September 1918.
1227. *New York Clipper* 5 March 1919.
1228. *New York Clipper* 16 April 1919.
1229. Kurt Gänzl (1994) 1: 734. See also Stanley Sadie (1980) 9: 704.
1230. Gänzl (1994) 1: 734.
1231. Sadie (1980) 9: 704. See also W. Macqueen-Pope (1949) 313. Jones had previously composed scores for musicals at provincial theatres: the pantomime *Aladdin II* at Leeds (1889) and *Our Family Legend* at Brighton (1992). "Linger Longer, Loo" was his first West-End success.

1232. *The New York Times* (19 September 1894) called the show "bright, and charming in spite of the dull passages mentioned; it is a feast of color to the eye, and if some of the music of Sidney Jones sounded but poorly last night, there was, at least, 'Tommy Atkins,' which is stirring in a way, though it does not touch our own national pride; the Pierrot song, and two sentimental ballads that are satisfying—and who expects fine music in a piece of this sort? It would be wasted." The *New York Clipper* (29 September 1894) found the dancing and acting of the company far superior to the singing and lodged a complaint against the vulgar and coarse language in the libretto: "England has recently furnished us with many plays of questionable character, and now to further prove the decay of healthy moral sentiment within her boarders, she sends us a sample of the vulgar stuff to which she has given countenance and financial support for the greater part of a year. In many respects *A Gaiety Girl* is entertaining; in this later respect it is disgusting."

1233. *The New York Times* 24 December 1895; *New York Clipper* 28 December 1895.

1234. *The New York Times* 10 September 1896; *New York Clipper* 19 September 1896.

1235. *The New York Times* 22 May 1898 and 29 November 1899; *New York Clipper* 9December 1899.

1236. *The New York Times* 30 September 1900 and 2 October 1900; *New York Clipper* 8 October 1900.

1237. *New York Clipper* 4 April 1903; *The New York Times* 1 December 1903.

1238. *New York Clipper* 16 May 1903 and 16 January 1904; *The New York Times* 10 January 1904, 12 January 1904, and 17 January 1904.

1239. *New York Clipper* 12 August 1905 and 7 September 1907.

1240. *New York Clipper* 5 September 1908, 27 November 1909, and 15 January 1910; *The New York Times* 14 December 1909 and 11 January 1910.

1241. *The New York Times* 13 May 1909; *New York Clipper* 22 May 1909.

1242. *The New York Times* 19 October 1913 and 25 August 1914; *New York Clipper* 25 July 1914.

1243. *The New York Times* 4 June 1916.

1244. *The New York Times* 30 January 1946.

1245. *The New York Times* 4 September 1923; *New York Clipper* 7 September 1923.

1246. *The New York Times* 12 August 1924.

1247. *The New York Times* 9 September 1925.

1248. Jones also orchestrated the *Follies* of 1920, 1921, 1924, and 1925.

1249. The exact date of Joplin's birth is disputed. Some sources give the date as June 1867, while others suggest "early in 1868." Find a Grave Index gives the birthdate as 24 November 1868 and that date has been accepted by some biographers. See http://www.lsjunction.com/people/ joplin.htm.

1250. Eileen Southern (1982) 220,

1251. Southern (1982) 221.

1252. *Indianapolis Freeman* 12 September 1903. Quoted in Southern (1982) 221.

1253. *American Musician and Art Journal* 14 June 1911. Quoted in Southern (1982) 221.

1254. Barrymore Laurence Scherer's article "Opera 'Treemonisha' as It Was Intended To Be" in the *Wall Street Journal* (6 December 2011) argues that the opera was, indeed, performed in 1913 before a paying audience in Bayonne, New Jersey. http://www.wsj.com/articles/SB10001424052970203833104577070683505219416

1255. Rick Benjamin. "From Barrelhouse to Broadway: The Musical Odyssey of Joe Jordan." See also Eileen Southern (1982) 222.

1256. Southern (1982) 378.

1257. Bill Edwards. http://ragpiano.com/comps/jjordan.shtml.

1258. Rick Benjamin. See also Edwards. http://ragpiano.com/comps/jjordan.shtml. Jordan is credited by Bernard L. Peterson, Jr. ([1993] 324) as having contributed material to the production of *The Sons of Ham* (1900–1902) but there is no published material to support the claim. However, Jordan may well have contributed musical arrangements or unpublished dance music.

1259. *The Husband* also appeared at the Harlem Music Hall for eight performances beginning on 19 August 1907.

1260. Rick Benjamin. Peterson (1993) gives the date as 29 June 1907.

1261. Peterson ([1993] 288) suggested that Jordan was also co-composer (with J. Rosamond Johnson, Bob Cole, and James Reese Europe) of *The Red Moon* (3 May 1909) but supplied no song titles to verify Jordan's association with the project. Given his experience with the Pekin Theatre, it is possible that Jordan composed or co-composed some or most of the dance music for the show.

1262. In the summer 1910, Joe Jordan began a vaudeville tour of England and Europe that lasted nearly eighteen months, and after his return to Chicago in 1912 he opened a cabaret called The Mecca Buffet that featured high class entertainment. In spring 1913, he created, with Alvin Joyner, a theatrical sketch, *The Composer and the Moving Van*, that toured the vaudeville circuit, and the following year, he was one of the conductors at the National Negro Orchestra's concert of African-American Music (8 April 1914). See Edwards. http://ragpiano.com/comps/jjordan.shtml.

1263. Peterson (1993) 104.

1264. The published copy of Joe Jordan's "Love for a Day" (1929) (co-composed with Porter Grainger) indicates that the song was "featured in *The Siren of the Tropics*, the 1927 silent film starring Josephine Baker. With Grainger, Shelton Brooks, and Edgar Dorwell, Jordan is also credited with the composition of "special music" for the film *Harlem Is Heaven* (27 May 1932) staring Eubie Blake, Noble Sissle, and Bill Robinson.

Bibliography

Musical Scores

Aarons, Alfred E., Harry B. Smith, and Robert B. Smith. *A China Doll*. New York: M. Witmark, 1904.

Aronson, Rudolph. "Marche Triomphale." New York: C.H. Ditson, 1875.

——— ———. "Mazurka Melodique." New York: C.H. Ditson, 1874.

Aronson, Rudolph, and Sydney Rosenfeld. *The Rainmakers of Syria*. Comic Opera in Two Acts. New York: T.B. Harms, 1893.

Baker, Thomas. "The Emperor's March." Performed at Barnum's Museum, in the Grand Spectacle, *The Christian Martyrs*. New York: William A. Pond, 1867.

——— ———. *Gems from* The Black Crook. New York: William A. Pond, 1866.

——— ———. "The Laura Keene Schottisch." New York: Firth, Pond, 1856.

——— ———. "The Rachel Schottisch." New York: Horace Waters, 1855.

——— ———. "The Seven Sons Galop." New York: Horace Waters, 1861.

——— ———. *Thomas Baker's Operatic Quadrilles composed on themes selected from the most Celebrated Operas, Performed at the Academy of Music*. New York: Horace Waters, 1855.

——— ———. "Transformation Polka." From *The Black Crook*. New York: William A. Pond, 1867.

Baker, Thomas, arr. *Overture to Auber's Opera* The Syren, *as performed at Niblo's Garden*. Arranged for the pianoforte. New York: Horace Waters, 1854.

Barratt, W. Augustus. *The Death of Cuthullin*. London: Paterson and Sons, [1897].

——— ———. *Little Simplicity: Selections*. New York: Shapiro, Bernstein, 1918.

Barratt, W. Augustus, Howard Talbot, and Adrian Ross. *Kitty Grey*. Adapted from *Les Fêtards* by J.S. Pigott. With additional numbers by Lionel Monckton, Paul Rubens, and Bernard Rolt. London: E. Ascherberg, 1901.

Batchelor, W.H. "March of the Forty Thieves." Cincinnati: John Church, 1892.

Batchelor, W.H., and Harry B. Smith. *Selections from the Operatic Extravaganza* Sinbad. Cincinnati: John Church, 1891.

Batchelor, W.H., Willard Thompson, and H.T. Vynne. *Musical Selections from "Ali Baba," or, Morgiana and the Forty Thieves.* Cincinnati: John Church, 1892.

Bendix, Theo. *The Commuters*: "A Suburban Scramble." New York: Leo Feist, 1910.

———. *The Great Name* "Waltzes." New York: Leo Feist, 1911.

———. "Nat-u-ritch. An Indian Idyll." Intermezzo from *The Squaw Man*. New York: Jos. W. Stern, 1906.

———. *Seven Days* "Waltzes." New York: Leo Feist, 1910.

Bendix, Theo, and George H. Jessop. "I Am So Shy." As sung by Miss Minnie Palmer, With great success in the Musical Comedy *My Sweetheart*. New York: C.H. Ditson, 1882.

Berlin, Irving, and Harry B. Smith. *Watch Your Step*. New York: Irving Berlin, 1914.

Blake, Eubie, Noble Sissle, Flournoy Miller, and Aubrey Lyle. *Shuffle Along*. New York: M. Witmark, 1921.

Böteführ, W.D.C. "Pas de Demons." As performed at the Varieties Theatre in The Black Crook. St. Louis: R.J. Compton, 1867.

Bowers, Robert Hood. "Cute an' Cunnin'." Slow Fox Trot. From *A Lonely Romeo*. New York: Jerome H. Remick, 1919.

———. "Galop." From *The Vanderbilt Cup*. New York: Jerome H. Remick, 1906.

———. "Melodrama." From *The Spring Maid*. New York: Joseph W. Stern, 1911.

Bowers, Robert Hood, and Richard Carle. *The Maid and the Mummy*. New York: M. Witmark, 1904.

Bowers, Robert Hood, Harry B. Smith, and Robert B. Smith. *The Red Rose*. New York: Jerome H. Remick, 1911.

Braham, David, and Edward Harrigan. *Collected Songs*. Edited with an introduction by Jon W. Finson. Recent Researches in American Music, vol. 27. Music of the United States of America, vol. 7. Madison, WI: A-R Editions, 1997.

Braham, George. *Selection from Ed. Harrigan's Musical Play "Under Cover."* Arr. By Karl L. Hoschna. New York: M. Witmark, 1903.

Braham, John, and Edward Harrigan. "Steady Company." Boston: White and Goullaud, 1872.

Braham, John, and Edward Righton. "Young Village Beauty." Boston: White, Smith and Perry, 1869.
Braham, John, and J. Cheever Goodwin. "A Long Time Ago." Song (Mock Sentimental). Boston: Miles and Thompson, 1891.
Braham, John, and J. Cohan. "Rowing on the Lake." Song and Dance. Boston: White and Goullaud, 1870.
Braham, John, and William Cavanah. "Kaloolah," Song and Dance. Boston: John P. Perry, 1875.
Bratton, John W., and Paul West. *The Man from China*. New York: M. Witmark, 1904.
——. *The Pearl and the Pumpkin*. New York: M. Witmark, 1905.
Bray, John, and James Nelson Barker. *The Indian Princess*. Earlier American Music, vol. 11. New introduction by H. Wiley Hitchcock. New York: Da Capo Press, 1972.
Breil, Joseph, and Jacques Byrne. *The Legend*. London: Chappell, 1919.
Brinkworth, W.H., and James Barnes. "Happy Little Flip-Flaps." Double Song and Dance. New York: William A. Pond, 1875.
Bristow, George F. *Rip Van Winkle*. Earlier American Music, vol. 25. Edited with a new introduction by Steven Ledbetter. New York: Da Capo Press, 1991.
Brode, Herman. "March." In *Choice Selections from* The Silver King. Played Nightly at Wallack's Theatre. New York: Williams, 1883.
Carr, Benjamin. *Musical Miscellany in Occasional Numbers*. Earlier American Music, vol. 21. Compiled and with a new introduction by Eve R. Meyer. New York: Da Capo Press, 1982.
——. *Selected Secular and Sacred Songs*. Recent Researches in American Music, vol. 15. Edited by Eve R. Meyer. Madison, WI: A-R Editions, 1986.
Carr, F. Osmond, and W.S. Gilbert. *His Excellency*. London: Joseph Williams, 1894.
Caryll, Ivan, and C.M.S. McLellan. *The Little Café*. New York: Chappell, 1913.
——. *The Pink Lady*. New York: Chappell, 1911.
Caryll, Ivan, and Harry B. Smith. *Papa's Darling*. Based on *Le Fils Surnaturel* by Grenet D'Ancourt and Maurice Vaucaire. New York: Chappell, 1904.
Caryll, Ivan, and Henry Hamilton. *The Duchess of Dantzic*. London: Chappell, 1903.

Caryll, Ivan, and H.J.W. Dam. *The Shop Girl*. Additional numbers by Adrian Ross and Lionel Monckton. London: Hopwood and Crew, n.d.

Caryll, Ivan, Cecil Cook, Owen Hall, Adrian Ross, and Claude Aveling. *The Girl from Kay's*. London: Chappell, 1903.

Caryll, Ivan, George Grossman, Jr., Adrian Ross, Percy Greenbank, and Lionel Monckton. *The Spring Chicken*. London: Chappell, 1905.

Caryll, Ivan, Owen Hall, and Adrian Ross. *The Little Cherub*. London: Chappell, 1906.

Caryll, Ivan, Seymour Hicks, and Percy Greenbank. *The Earl and the Girl*. London: Chappell, 1904.

Caryll, Ivan, Seymour Hicks, Harry Nicholls, Aubrey Hopwood, Harry Greenbank, and Lionel Monckton. *A Runaway Girl*. London: Chappell, 1898.

Catlin, E[dward] N[oble], and Edward Harrigan. "Sweet Louisa." From *The Little Frauds*. Boston: White and Goullaud, 1871.

Cellier, Alfred, and Albert Jarret. *The Sultan of Mocha*. London: Enoch, [1874].

Cellier, Alfred, and B.C. Stephenson. *Doris*. Arranged from the full score by Ivan Caryll. London: Chappell, [1889].

——— ———. *Dorothy*. London: Chappell, [1886].

Cellier, Alfred, and James Albery. *The Spectre Knight*. London: Metzler, [1878].

Cellier, Alfred, and W.S. Gilbert. *The Mountebanks*. London: Chappell, 1892.

Chadwick, George W., and R.A. Barnet. *Tabasco*. Boston: B.F. Wood, 1894.

Chadwick, George W., and Robert Grant. *The Peer and the Pauper*. Ms., 1884.

Chadwick, George W., and William Chauncy Langdon. *Judith*. New York: G. Schirmer, 1901.

Chassaigne, Francis, and A. de Leuven. *Actéon et le centaure Chiron*. Paris: Ph. Feuchot, 1878.

Chassaigne, Francis, Eugène Leterrier, and Albert Vanloo. *Falka*. English version by H.B. Farnie. Boston: White-Smith, 1884.

Chassaigne, Francis, Louis Péricaud, and Lucien Delormel. *Deux Mauvaises Bonnes*. Paris: Ph. Feuchot, 1876.

——— ———. *Les Enfants de la balle*. Paris: Ph. Feuchot, 1877.

Chilvers, Thomas H. "Beautiful Ivy Leaf." *The Ivy Leaf*. Arranged by J.C. Mayseder. Boston: Oliver Ditson, 1891.

———. "Detroit Light Infantry Grand March." Detroit: C.J. Whitney, 1884.

———. "I ove You All." *The Head Waiters*. Detroit: Whitney Warner, 1901.

Chilvers, Thomas H., and Edgar Smith. "If This Were the Age of Romance." *The Little Host*. New York: Edward Schuberth, 1898.

———. "I'm a Shy Little Innocent Thing." The Little Host. New York: Edward Schuberth, 1898.

Chilvers, Thomas H., and William J. Dawson. "Maureen Mavourneen." *The Ivy Leaf*. Detroit: C.J. Whitney, 1885.

Chipman, J.S. "Three Bears." Song. In *Cinderella and the Prince, or, Castle of Heart's Desire*. Book by R.A. Barnet. Lyrics by D.K. Stevens and R.A. Barnet. Music by Louis F. Gottschalk and Edward W. Corliss. Boston: White-Smith, 1904.

Chubb, T. Youres. "Fifth Washington Greys." Grand March. New York: Firth and Hall, 1846.

———. "I'd Marry Him Tomorrow." From *A Loan of a Lover*. With an Arrangement for the Piano Forte, Arranged by T. Youres Chubb. New York: Gier and Walker, 1836.

———. "The Music of Balfe's Celebrated Opera *The Bohemian Girl*." New York: Atwill, 1844.

Clifton, Arthur, and Colonel W.H. Hamilton. *The Enterprise*. Baltimore: Arthur Clifton, [1823].

Comer, Thomas, and S.S. Steele. *Favourite Melodies from the Grand Chinese Spectacle of Aladdin or the Wonderful Lamp*. Boston: Prentiss and Clark, 1847.

Connelly, Michael. "Galop." In *The Forty Thieves*. New York: William A. Pond, 1869.

Cook, Will Marion, J.A. Shipp, Alex Rogers, and Bert A. Williams. *Bandana Land*. New York: Gotham-Attucks, 1908.

Corliss, Edward W. and R.A. Barnet. *Queen of the Ballet*. With additional numbers by Alfred Norman, George Lowell Tracy, Henry Lawson Heartz, Walter Gould, and Hastings Weblyn. Lyrical assistance by Frederic W. Arnold, Jr. Boston: White-Smith, 1893.

Darley, Francis T.S., and James Robinson Planché. *Fortunio and His Seven Gifted Servants*. Philadelphia: J.M. Stoddart, 1883.

Debillemont, Jean-Jacques. *Le Tour du Monde* de Dennery et Jules Verne. Transcrits pour Piano par Jean-Jacques Debillemont. Paris: Léon Grus, [1875].

Debillemont, Jean-Jacques, and H. Boisseaux. *Astaroth*. Paris: E. Girod, [1861].
De Koven, Reginald. *Ballet Music*. "Fireflies, Ballet." "Japanese Ballet." As Performed in *From Broadway to Tokio*. New York: G. Schirmer, 1900.
———. *Ballet Music from The Man in the Moon*. Cincinnati: John Church, 1899.
———. "Pantomime Dance." From *The Little Duchess*. New York: Edward Schuberth, 1901.
DeKoven, Reginald, and Frederic Ranken. *Happyland, or, The King of Elysia*. New York: Jos. W. Stern, 1905.
De Koven, Reginald, and Harry B. Smith. *Foxy Quiller*. New York: Edward Schuberth, 1900.
———. *The Highwayman*. New York: T.B. Harms, 1898.
———. *Maid Marian*. New York: Edward Schuberth, 1901.
———. *Robin Hood*. New York: G. Schirmer, 1891.
———. *Rob Roy*. New York: G. Schirmer, 1894.
De Koven, Reginald, and Joseph W. Herbert. *The Beauty Spot*. New York: Jos. W. Stern, 1909.
De Koven, Reginald, Charles Klein, and Charles Emerson Cook. *Red Feather*. New York: Jos. W. Stern, 1903.
DeKoven, Reginald, Fred DeGresac, and Harry B. Smith. *The Wedding Trip*. New York: Jerome H. Remick, 1911.
De Koven, Reginald, Frederic Ranken, and Stanislaus Stange. *The Student King*. New York: Jos. W. Stern, 1906.
Devin, William. "Ballet." In *The Casino Girl*. Book by Harry B. Smith. Music by Ludwig Englander. Interpolated numbers by Harry T. MacConnell and Arthur Nevin. New York: E. Schuberth, 1900.
Diet, Edmund, and A. Curti. *Temptations*. Paris: Edmund Diet, 1911.
Drigo, Richard (Riccardo). *Les Millions d'Arlequin*. Ballet en 2 actes de Marius Petipa. Leipzig: Zimmermann, 1901.
Dumont, Frank. *Africanus Blue Beard*. Music arranged for the piano by Alfred B. Sedgwick. New York: De Witt, 1876.
———. *Gambrinus, King of Lager Beer*. Music arranged for the piano by Alfred B. Sedgwick. New York: De Witt, 1876.
Edwards, Julian, and Harry B. Smith. *Jupiter, or, The Cobbler and the King*. Cincinnati: John Church, 1893.
Edwards, Julian, and Stanislaus Stangé. *Brian Boru*. Cincinnati, OH: John Church, 1896.

———— ————. *Dolly Varden*. New York: M. Witmark, 1901.
———— ————. *The Jolly Musketeer*. New York: M. Witmark, 1898.
———— ————. *Love's Lottery*. New York: M. Witmark, 1904.
———— ————. *When Johnny Comes Marching Home*. New York: M. Witmark, 1902.
Edwards, Leo, and Harold Atteridge. *The Passing Show of 1915*. Additional numbers by William F. Peters and J. Leubrie Hill. New York: G. Schirmer, 1915.
Eichberg, Julius, and Benjamin E. Woolf. *The Doctor of Alcantara*. New enlarged and revised edition. Boston: Oliver Ditson, 1879.
Einödshofer, Julius. "Flirt Waltz." From the ballet, *Flirting in St. Moritz*. Berlin: C.M. Roehr, 1913; New York: Jerome H. Remick, 1913.
Ellis, Melville. "Malena." Intermezzo from *The Road to Yesterday*. New York: M. Witmark, 1907.
———— ————. "School-Boy and Girl: Dance." New York: M. Witmark, 1905.
———— ————. "The Tango Dance." From *The Merry Countess*. New York: M. Witmark, 1912.
Emmet, J. K. "Emmet's Baby Song." As sung in *Fritz in Bohemia*. Cincinnati: John Church, 1884.
_____. "Emmet's Swell Song." From *Fritz in Ireland*. Cincinnati: John Church, 1881.
_____. "I Know What Love Is." As sung in *Fritz in Ireland*. Cincinnati: John Church. 1879.
Englander, Ludwig. *Selections from the Romantic Comic Opera* 1776. New York: Wm. A. Pond, 1884.
Englander, Ludwig, and Harry B. Smith. *The Casino Girl*. Interpolated numbers by Harry T. MacConnell and Arthur Nevin. New York: E. Schuberth, 1900A.
———— ————. *The Little Corporal*. New York: Breitkopf and Härtel, 1898.
———— ————. *A Madcap Princess*. New York: Jos. W. Stern, 1904.
———— ————. *The Office Boy*. New York: Jos. W. Stern, 1903.
———— ————. *The Rounders*. New York: Edward Schuberth, 1899.
———— ————. *The Strollers*. New York: Edward Schuberth, 1901.
Englander, Ludwig, and J. Cheever Goodwin. *The Monks of Malabar*. New York: Edward Schuberth, 1900B.
Englander, Ludwig, and Stanislaus Stange. *The Two Roses*. New York: Jos. W. Stern, 1904.
Englander, Ludwig, Frederic Ranken, and Harry B. Smith. *The Jewel of Asia*. New York: Jos. W. Stern, 1903.

Europe, James Reese. "The Castle Doggy Fox Trot." New York: Joseph W. Stern, [1913].

Eysler, Edmund, and Leo Stein. *Vera Violetta*. Leipzig: Josef Weinberger, 1908.

Eysler, Edmund, Leo Stein, and Carl Lindau. *The Love-Cure*. English version and adaptation for the American stage by Oliver Herford. New York: G. Schirmer, 1909.

Eysler, Edmund, Sigmund Romberg, Edgar Smith, and Herbert Reynolds. *The Blue Paradise*. Based on the original libretto by Leo Stein and Bela Jenbasch. New York: G. Schirmer, 1915.

Fall, Leo, A.M. Willner, and F. Grünbaum. *The Dollar Princess*. American version by George Grossmith, Jr. New York: T.B. Harms and Francis, Day and Hunter, 1909.

Felix, Hugo, and Anne Caldwell. *Pom-Pom*. New York: T.B. Harms, 1916.

Felix, Hugo, and Victorien Sardou. *The Merveilleuses*. Adapted for the English stage by Basil Hood. Lyrics by Adrian Ross. London: Chappell, 1906.

Felix, Hugo, Basil Hood, and Howard Talbot. *The Pearl Girl*. London: Chappell, 1913.

Felix, Hugo, C.E. Hands, and Adrian Ross. *Madame Sherry*. London: Chappell, 1904.

Felix, Hugo, Michael Morton, Paul Gavault, and Adrian Ross. *Tantalizing Tommy*. London: Chappell, 1912.

Fletcher, Percy, and Oscar Asche. *Cairo, a Mosaic in Music and Mime*. London: Ascherberg, Hopwood and Crew, 1920.

Francis, W.T. "Dance of the Angeles." New Orleans: Junius Hart, 1885.

_____. "La Media Noche." Arranged for Piano by W.T. Francis. Played at the World's Exposition at New Orleans, by the Celebrated Mexican Military Band. New Orleans: Junius Hart, 1885.

_____. "Les Petites Blondes. Gavotte." New Orleans: Louis Grunewald, 1885.

_____. "Priscilla: Dance Characteristique." New York: M. Witmark, 1902.

Francis, W.T., and Edgar Smith. "Golf-Song. In *The Little Host*. New York: Edward Schuberth, 1898.

Francis, W.T., and Sydney Rosenfeld. *The Rollicking Girl*. New York: M. Witmark, 1905.

Franklin, Malvin. *Modern Dances: Society's Latest Dance Folio*. New York: Knickerbocker Music, 1914.

Franklin, Malvin M., Robert Hood Bowers, Harry B. Smith, Lew Fields, and Robert B. Smith. *A Lonely Romeo*. Chicago: Jerome H. Remick, 1919.

Freeborn, Cass. "The Stop-Trot Rag." New York: M. Witmark, 1914.

Friml, Rudolf. "A Garden Matinee: Entr'Acte." Chicago: Lyon and Healy, 1906.

——. "Three Dances for Piano." From the Japanese Ballet, *O Mitake San*. New York: G. Schirmer, 1911.

Friml, Rudolf, and Otto Hauerbach (Harbach). *Katinka*. New York: G. Schirmer, 1916.

Friml, Rudolf, and Rida Johnson Young. *Some Time*. New York: G. Schirmer, 1919.

Friml, Rudolf, Leo Dietrichstein, and Otto Hauerbach (Harbach). *High Jinks*. New York: G. Schirmer, 1913.

Furst, William. *Selections from* The Darling of the Gods. Chicago: Howley, Haviland, and Dresser, 1903.

——. *David Harum*: "March." Chicago: Howley, Haviland, and Dresser, 1900.

Gabriel, Max. *In Gotham*: "Waltzes." New York: M. Witmark, 1898.

Gabriel, Max, and Georg Okonkowski. *Stolze Thea*. Berlin: Kollo-Verlag, 1917.

Ganne, Louis, and Maurice Ordonneau. *Les Saltimbanques*. Partition Chant et Piano. Paris: Choudens, 1900.

Ganne, Louis, Maurice Vaucaire, and Georges Mitchell. *Hans, Le Joueur de Flûte*. Partition Complète pour Chant et Piano. Paris: G. Ricordi, 1906.

Gaunt, Percy. *Songs from Hoyt's* A Trip to Chinatown. New York: T.B. Harms, 1892.

Gebest, Charles J. *The American Idea*: "March." New York: Cohan and Harris, 1908.

Gebest, Charles J., Channing Pollock, and Rennold Wolf. *The Red Widow*. New York: M. Witmark, 1911.

Giorza, Paolo. "Skirt Dance." London: Hopwood and Crew, 1896.

Glaser, C.J.M. *The Silver Star: Ballet Music*. New York: C.J.M. Glaser, 1910.

Glover, Howard. *Palomita; or, the Veiled Songstress*. New York: J.L. Peters, 1875.

Glover, Howard, and Robert Burns. *Tam O'Shanter*. London: Chappell, [1855].

Gottschalk, Louis F., Edward W. Corliss, R.A. Barnet, and D.K. Stevens. *Cinderella and the Prince, or, Castle of Heart's Desire*. Additional musical numbers by D.J. Sullivan and J.S. Chipman. New York: White-Smith, 1904.

Grant, John B., and Sydney Rosenfeld. *The Mystic Isle*. Philadelphia: Lee and Walker, 1886.

Graziano, John, ed. *Italian Opera in English*. Nineteenth-Century American Musical Theater, vol. 3. New York: Garland, 1994.

Hadley, Henry K., and David Stevens. *Azora, the Daughter of Montezuma*. New York: G. Schirmer, 1917.

Hadley, Henry K., and Frederic Ranken. *Nancy Brown*. New York: Jos. W. Stern, 1903.

Heartz, Harry Lawson "Hop Lee." Chinese Dance from *The Tenderfoot*. New York: M. Witmark, 1903.

Heartz, Harry Lawson, and R.A. Barnet. *Miladi and the Musketeer*. Boston: White-Smith, 1900.

——— ———. *Miss Simplicity*. With additional numbers by Edward W. Corliss and Clifton Crawford. Lyrical assistance by Edward A. Church and D.K. Stevens. Boston: White-Smith, 1901.

Heartz, Harry Lawson, and Richard Carle. *The Hurdy Gurdy Girl*. Boston: White-Smith, 1907.

——— ———. *The Tenderfoot*. New York: M. Witmark, 1903.

Hein, Silvio. *When Dreams Come True*: "The Santley Tango." New York: T.B. Harms and Francis, Day and Hunter, 1913.

Hein, Silvio, and George V. Hobart. *The Boys and Betty*. New York: Marie Cahill, 1908.

——— ———. *The Yankee Girl*. New York: Blanche Ring, 1909.

Hein, Silvio, Armand Barnard, E. Ray Goetz, and Seymour Brown. *A Matinée Idol*. New York: Shapiro, 1909.

Hein, Silvio, Edwin Milton Royle, and Benjamin Hapgood Burt. *Marrying Mary*. New York: Jos. W. Stern, 1906.

Hein, Silvio, Joseph Santley, and Harry B. Smith. *All Over Town*. New York: T.B. Harms and Francis, Day, and Hunter, 1915.

Herbert, Victor, and Harry B. Smith. *Babette*. New York: M. Witmark, 1903.

——— ———. *The Idol's Eye*. New York: Edward Schuberth, 1897.

——— ———. *Little Nemo*. Based on Winsor McCay's cartoons. New York: Cohan and Harris, 1908.

——— ———. *The Wizard of the Nile*. New York: Edward Schuberth, 1895.

Herbert, Victor, and Henry Blossom. *Eileen*. New York: M. Witmark, 1917.
—— ——. *Mlle. Modiste*. New York: M. Witmark, 1905.
—— ——. *The Prima Donna*. New York: M. Witmark, 1908.
—— ——. *The Princess Pat*. New York: M. Witmark, 1915.
—— ——. *The Velvet Lady*. New York: M. Witmark, 1919.
Herbert, Victor, and Rida Johnson Young. *Naughty Marietta*. New York: M. Witmark, 1910.
Herbert, Victor, Anna Caldwell, Laurence McCarty, and James O'Dea. *The Lady of the Slipper*. New York: M. Witmark, 1912.
Herbert, Victor, David Stevens, and Justin Huntly McCarthy. *The Madcap Duchess*. New York: G. Schirmer, 1913.
Herbert, Victor, and Glen MacDonough. *Algeria*. Chicago: Chas. K. Harris, 1908.
Herbert, Victor, Harry B. Smith, and A.N.C. Fowler. *The Tattooed Man*. New York: M. Witmark, 1907.
Herbert, Victor, Harry B. Smith, and Robert B. Smith. *The Débutante*. New York: G. Schirmer, 1914.
Herbert, Victor, Harry B. Smith, Fred De Grésac, and Robert B. Smith. *Sweethearts*. New York: G. Schirmer, 1913.
Hewitt, James. *Selected Compositions*. Recent Researches in American Music, vol 7. Edited by John W. Wagner. Madison, WI: A-R Editions, 1980.
Hewitt, John Hill. *The Collected Works of John Hill Hewitt*. Edited by N. Lee Orr and Lynn Wood Bertrand. Nineteenth-Century American Musical Theater vol. 6. New York: Garland, 1994.
Hill, J. Leubrie. "Rag-time Drummer." London: Keith, Prowse, 1903.
Hirsch, Louis A., and Rennold Wolf. *The Rainbow Girl*. New York: M. Witmark, 1917.
Hirsch, Louis A., Ben M. Jerome, Mark Swan, Edgar Smith, and Edward Madden. *He Came from Milwaukee*. New York: Chas. K. Harris, 1910.
Hirsch, Louis A., Otto Harbach, and Frank Mandel. *Mary*. New York: Victoria, 1921.
Hirsch, Louis A., Otto Harbach, and James Montgomery. *Going Up*. New York: M. Witmark, 1918.
Hoffmann, Max. *Broadway to Paris*. New York: T.B. Harms and Francis, Day and Hunter, 1912.
—— ——. *The Rogers Bros. in Ireland*: "Killarney." New York: Rogers Bros. Music, 1905.

Hoffmann, Max, Edward Madden, Sylvester Maguire, and Aaron Hoffman. *The Rogers Bros in Panama*. New York:Rogers Bros, 1907.

Hoffmaster, William. "Durang's Horn-Pipe." Boston: Oliver Ditson, 1823.

Howson, Frank A. "Fireman's Song and Chorus." New York: Frank A. Howson, 1887.

——— ———. *The King's Musketeer*: "March and Two Step." New York: Jos. W. Stern, 1899.

Hubbell, Raymond. "The Rooster Dance." From *The Runaways*. New York: Chas. K. Harris, 1903.

Hubbell, Raymond, and Addison Burkhardt. *The Runaways*. New York: Chas. K. Harris, 1903.

Hubbell, Raymond, Robert B. Smith, and Clara Driscoll. *Mexicana*. New York: Chas. K. Harris, 1906.

Hubbell, Raymond, Robert B. Smith, and Sam S. Shubert. *Fantana*. New York: M. Wimark, 1904.

Jacobi, Victor, and Harry B. Smith. *Rambler Rose*. New York: T.B. Harms and Francis, Day and Hunter, 1917.

Jacobi, Victor, and William Le Baron. *The Half Moon*. New York: T.B. Harms and Francis, Day and Hunter, 1920.

Jacobi, Victor, M[iksa] Bródy, and F[erenc] Martos. *The Marriage Market*. Adapted for the English stage by Gladys Unger. Lyrics by Arthur Anderson and Adrian Ross. Arranged by H.M. Higgs. London: Chappell, 1913.

——— ———. *Sybill*. Leipzig: W. Karczag, 1919.

Jacobi, Victor, M[iksa] Bródy, and F[erenc] Martos. *Sybil*. English version and lyrics by Harry Graham. Additional lyrics by Harry B. Smith. London: Chappell, 1915 and 1916.

Jakobowski, Edward, Claxton Bellamy, and Harry Paulton. *Erminie*. Boston: White-Smith, [1886].

Jerome, Ben M., George E. Stoddard, and Charles S. Taylor. *The Royal Chef*. New York: F.B. Haviland, 1904.

Johnstone, Alexander, and William Cary Duncan. *Fiddlers Three*. New York: M. Witmark, 1918.

Jones, Sidney, Edward Morton, Harry Greenbank, and Adrian Ross. *San Toy, or, The Emperor's Own*. London: Keith, Prowse, 1899.

Jones, Sidney, Owen Hall, and C.H. Taylor. *The Medal and the Maid*. London: Keith, Prowse, 1903.

Jones, Sidney, Owen Hall, and Harry Greenbank. *An Artist's Model*. London: Hopwood and Crew, 1895.

———— ———— . *A Gaiety Girl*. London: Hopwood and Crew, n.d.
———— ———— . *The Geisha*. London: Hopwood and Crew, 1896.
Joplin, Scott. *Treemonisha*. New York: Scott Joplin, 1911.
Kelley, Edgar Stillman. *Aladdin*. New York: G. Schirmer, 1915.
———— ———— . *Ben-Hur*. Edited by Charles Feleky. New York: Towers and Curran, 1902.
Kelly, Michael, and George Coleman the Younger. *The Grand Dramatic Romance of Blue-Beard, or Female Curiosity*. London: Longman and Broderip, 1798.
Kerker, Gustave, and Frederic Ranken. *Winsome Winnie*. New York: Jos. W. Stern, 1903.
Kerker, Gustave, and Hugh Morton. *The Belle of New York*. New York: T.B. Harms, 1897-8.
Kerker, Gustave, and Joseph Herbert. *The Social Whirl*. New York: T.B. Harms, 1906.
Kerker, Gustave, and R.H. Burnside. *Burning to Sing, or Singing to Burn*. New York: T.B. Harms, 1904.
———— ———— . *The Tourists*. New York: T.B. Harms, 1906.
Kern, Jerome, and Anne Caldwell. *Good Morning, Dearie*. New York: T.B. Harms, 1921.
Kern, Jerome, Guy Bolton, and Clifford Grey. *Sally*. New York: T.B. Harms, 1921.
Kern, Jerome, Guy Bolton, and P.G. Wodehouse. *Have a Heart*. New York: T.B. Harms, 1917.
———— ———— . *Oh, Lady! Lady!!* New York: T.B. Harms, 1918.
Kern, Jerome, Philip Bartholmae, Guy Bolton, Schuyler Greene, and Herbert Reynolds. *Very Good Eddie*. New York: T.B. Harms, 1916.
Kiefert, Carl, James T. Tanner, and Adrian Ross. *The Ballet Girl*. London: Enoch and Sons, 1897.
Klein, Manuel. *The International Cup*: "Seaside Frolics: Skipping Rope Dance." New York: M. Witmark, 1910.
———— ———— . *Neptune's Daughter: Selection*. New York: M. Witmark, 1907.
———— ———— . *The Proud Prince*: "Triumphal March." New York: M. Witmark, 1903.
———— ———— . *A Society Circus*: "March of the Flowers." New York: M. Witmark, 1906.
Klein, Manuel, and R.H. Burnside. *Ballet. Music by Manuel Klein. New York Hippodrome, Season 1910-1911*. Copyist's MS. NYPL, *MSP.

Klein, Manuel, Anna Caldwell, Mark E. Swan, and James O'Dea. *The Top o' the World.* New York: M. Witmark, 1907.

Klein, Manuel, John Kendrick Bangs, and Vincent Bryan. *The Man from Now.* New York: M. Witmark, 1906.

Klein, Manuel, R.H. Burnside, and Austin Strong. *The Pied Piper.* New York: M. Witmark, 1909.

Koppitz, Charles. *Incidental Music to Shakespeare's* Henry VIII. MS parts [c. 1872]. Library of Congress M1510/.K83H4/Case.

Kreisler, Fritz, Victor Jacobi, and William Le Baron. *Apple Blossoms.* New York: T.B. Harms and Francis, Day and Hunter, 1919.

Levi, Maurice, and Harry B. Smith. *The Soul Kiss.* New York: M. Witmark, 1908.

Levi, Maurice, Grant Stewart, and John J. McNally. *The Rogers Bros.: A Reign of Error.* New York: Howley, Haviland, 1899.

Lingard, William Horace. "The Grecian Bend." New York: Wm. A. Pond, 1898.

Linné, Hans S. "Rose Waltz." From *Mama's Baby Boy.* New York: M. Witmark, 1903.

Linné, Hans S., and Junie McCree. *Mama's Baby Boy.* New York: M. Witmark, 1911.

Loraine, William. "Franco-American Dance." From *Peggy from Paris.* New York: M. Witmark, 1903.

Loraine, William, and George Ade. *Peggy from Paris.* New York: M. Witmark, 1903.

Loraine, William, and John P. Wilson. *The Filibuster.* New York: M. Witmark, 1905.

Luders, Gustav, and Frank Pixley. *The Burgomaster.* New York: M. Witmark, 1900.

——. *The Grand Mogul.* New York: M. Witmark, 1906.

——. Marcelle. New York: M. Witmark, 1908.

——. *The Prince of Pilsen.* New York: M. Witmark, 1902.

——. *Woodland.* New York: M. Witmark, 1904.

Luders, Gustav, and George Ade. *The Fair Co-Ed.* New York: M. Witmark, 1908.

——. *The Sho-Gun.* New York: M. Witmark, 1904.

Lutz, W. Meyer, A.C. Torr, and Horace Mills. *Miss Esmeralda.* With incidental songs by Robert Martin. London: C. Jefferys, n.d.

Lutz, W. Meyer, George R. Sims, and Henry Pettitt. *Faust Up To Date.* Edited by Howard Paul. Pianoforte accompaniment arranged by

Martyn Van Lennep. New York: William A. Pond, 1889.
Maeder, J. Gaspard, and S.J. Burr. *The Peri, or, the Enchanted Fountain*. New York: William Hall, 1852.
Mallet, Francis D. *Mons. Labasses's Quadrilles*. Boston: G. Graupner, n.d.
Mann, Nat D. *The Second Fiddle*: "Waltzes." New York: M. Witmark, 1904.
Marenco, Romualdo, and Luigi Manzotti. *Excelsior*. Milan: Ricordi, [1881].
Mazzinghi, Joseph, and William Reeve. *Paul and Virginia*. London: Goulding, Phipps and D'Almaine, [1800].
[Mollenhauer, Edward]. "Marche d'Aika Amazonian." New York: Dodworth, 1868.
Mollenhauer, Edward, and Charles Barnard. *The Wager, or, the Masked Ball*. Vocal selections. New York: Edward Schuberth, 1879.
Monckton, Lionel, Howard Talbot, Mark Ambient, A.M. Thompson, and Arthur Wimperis. *The Arcadians*. London: Chappell, 1909.
Morse, Woolson, and J. Cheever Goodwin. *Songs from the Comic Opera* Panjandrum. New York: T.B. Harms, 1893.
———. *Vocal Gems from* Lost, Strayed or Stolen. New York: T.B. Harms, 1896.
———. *Vocal Gems from* Wang. New York: T.B. Harms, 1891.
Neuendorff, Adolf, and H. Italiener. *The Rat-Charmer of Hamelin*. New York: Edward Schuberth, 1881.
Nevin, Arthur, and Randolph Hartley. *A Daughter of the Forest*. Cincinnati: John Church, 1912.
———. *Poia*. Founded on legends collected by Walter McClintock. Berlin: Adolph Fürstner, 1909.
Norton, Frederic, and Oscar Ashe. *Chu Chin Chow*. New York: Edward B. Marks, 1916.
Operti, Giuseppe. *Aladdin*. Boston: G.D. Russell, 1874.
———. *Selections from* The Black Crook. New York: J.L. Peters, 1871.
Operti, Giuseppe, and Philip Lawrence. *Selections from* The Blacksmith's Treasure. Cincinnati: Geo. D. Newhall, 1879.
Operti, Giuseppe, and David Belasco. *The Stranglers of Paris: Music Selected and Composed by G. Operti*. MS orchestra parts. American Music Collection. NYPL, JPB 83–138.
Orlob, Harold, Harry B. Smith, Thomas J. Gray, and Robert B. Smith. *Ned Wayburn's Town Topics*. New York: G. Schirmer, 1915.
Pelissier, Victor. *Pelissier's Columbian Melodies*. Recent Researches in American Music, vols. 13 and 14. Edited by Karl Kroeger. Madison, WI: A-R Editions, 1984.

Peters, William Frederick, and Richard Carle. *The Mayor of Tokyo*. New York: M. Witmark, 1905.

Peters, William, Frederick, Heinrich Reinhardt, Fred de Gressac, and William Cary Duncan. *The Purple Road*. New York: T.B. Harms, 1903.

Pflueger, Carl, and R.A. Barnet. *1492*. Boston: White-Smith, 1892.

Planquette, Robert, and Henri Blondeau. *Le Paradis de Mahomet*. Completée par Louis Ganne. Partition Chant et Piano. Paris: Choudens, 1906.

Porter, Susan L., ed. *British Opera in America*. Nineteenth-Century American Musical Theater, vol. 1. New York: Garland, 1994.

Puerner, Charles. *The Diamond Arrow*. Holograph MS. American Music Collection. NYPL, JPG 78–45.

——— ———. *Mary of Magdala*: "Egyptian Dance." New York: M. Witmark, 1903.

Reinagle, Alexander, and Alexander Martin. *The Music in the Historical Play of* Columbus. Philadelphia: A. Reinagle, [1797].

Reinagle, Alexander. *The Philadelphia Sonatas*. Recent Researches in American Music, vol. 5. Edited by Robert Hopkins. Madison, WI: A-R Editions, 1978.

Rice, Edward E., and J. Cheever Goodwin. *Evangeline*. Boston: Louis P. Goullaud, 1877.

Riis, Thomas L., ed. *The Music and Scripts of* In Dahomey. Music of the United States of America. Vol. 5. Madison, WI: A-R Editions, 1996.

Ringleben, Justus. "Jovial Joe: Slow Drag and Two Step (March)." New York: Ring Music, 1904.

Robyn, Alfred G., and Edward Paulton. *Princess Beggar*. New York: M. Witmark, 1906.

Robyn, Alfred G., and Henry M. Blossom, Jr. *The Yankee Consul*. New York: M. Witmark, 1903.

Romberg, Sigmund, Jean Schwartz, and Harold Atteridge. "Jazzamarimba Dance." New York: Jerome H. Remick, 1919.

——— ———. *Monte Cristo Jr*. New York: Jerome H. Remick, 1919.

Romberg, Sigmund, Rida Johnson Young, and Cyrus Wood. *Maytime*. New York: G. Schirmer, 1917.

Rooke, W.M., and I.T. Haines. *Amilie, or, The Love Test*. London: Duff and Hodgson, n.d.

Root, George F. *The Haymakers*. Recent Researches in American Music, vols. 9 and 10. Edited by Dennis R. Martin. Madison, WI: A-R Editions, 1984.

Rubens, Paul A. *Three Little Maids*. Additional numbers by Percy Greenbank and Howard Talbot. London: Chappell, 1902.
Schindler, Paul, Ben M. Jerome, Allen Lowe, and George E. Stoddard. *The Isle of Spice, or, His Majesty of Nicobar!* New York: Jos. W. Stern, 1903.
Schleiffarth, George, and Harry B. Smith. *Rosita, or, Cupid and Cupidity*. Chicago: Geo. Schleiffarth, 1885.
Schwartz, Jean. "Pony Galop: Skipping Rope Dance." New York: Francis, Day and Hunter, 1906.
Schwartz, Jean, Stanislaus Stange, and William Jerome. *Piff! Paff! Pouf!* New York: Shapiro, Remick, 1904.
Sedgwick, Alfred B. *The Collected Works of Alfred B. Sedgwick*. Edited by Michael Meckna. Nineteenth-Century American Musical Theater, vol. 7. New York: Garland, 1994.
Shook, Benjamin L. "Dat Gal of Mine." Cleveland, OH: H.N. White, 1902.
Skelly, Joseph P. *The Charge of the Hash Brigade*. Music arranged for the pianoforte by Alfred B. Sedgwick. New York: De Witt, 1876.
Slaughter, Walter, and Basil Hood. *The French Maid*. London: E. Ascherberg, 1896.
Sloane, A. Baldwin, and R.A. Barnet. *The Strange Adventures of Jack and the Bean-stalk*. Boston: White-Smith, 1896.
Sloane, A. Baldwin, and Sydney Rosenfeld. *The Mocking Bird*. New York: Jos. W. Stern, 1902.
Solomon, Edward, and H.P. Stephens. *The Red Hussar*. London: Metzler, 1889.
Solomon, Frederic. *Polly of the Circus*: "March." New York: Maurice Shapiro, 1908.
Sousa, John Philip, and Charles Klein. *El Capitan*. New York: G. Schirmer, n.d.
Spenser, Willard. *The Little Tycoon*. New York: Willard Spenser, 1882.
Spink, George, and Silvio Hein. "Melody" from *The Pride of Race*. New York: T.B. Harms, 1916.
Stahl, Richard. "Hot Stuff: March." New York: Carl Fisher, 1895.
——— . *Shing Ching* "Potpourri." Cincinnati: John Church, 1894.
Stanford, Charles Villiers, and George H. Jessop. *Shamus O'Brien*. Based on the poem by Joseph Sheridan Le Fanu. Pianoforte arrangement by Myles B. Foster. London: Boosey, 1896.
Stöpel, R[obert], arr. *The Corsican Brothers*: "The Ghost Melody." London: Chappell, n.d.

Stothart, Herbert P., and George B. Hill. *The Orphan and the Octopus*. Madison, WI: University of Wisconsin, 1913.

Stromberg, John, W.T. Francis, Edgar Smith, and Robert B. Smith. *Twirly Whirly*. New York: M. Witmark, 1902.

Stuart, Leslie, Charles H.E. Brookfield, and Cosmo Hamilton. *The Belle of Mayfair*. London: Francis, Day, and Hunter, 1906.

Stuart, Leslie, Owen Hall, and W.H. Risque. *The Silver Slipper*. New York: T.B. Harms, 1901.

Sullivan, Dan J., R.A. Barnet, and R.M. Baker. *Miss Pocahontas: An Indian War-Whoop in Two Whoops*. Boston: White-Smith, 1906.

Talbot, Howard, and George Dance. *A Chinese Honeymoon*. London: Hopwood and Crew, 1901.

Talbot, Howard, Fred Thompson, C.H. Bovill, and Ralph Roberts. *Mr. Manhattan*. Additional numbers by Silvio Hein and Philip Braham. New York: Leo Feist, 1916.

Taylor, Raynor, and William Diamond. *The Ethiop*. Philadelphia: G.E. Blake, n.d.

Tierney, Harry, James Montgomery, and Joseph McCarthy. *Irene*. New York: Leo Feist, 1920.

Tietjens, Paul. "Dance of the Beauties." New York: G. Schirmer, 1917.

Tietjens, Paul, and L. Frank Baum. *The Wizard of Oz*. New York: M. Witmark, 1902.

Trajetta, Phil. *Six Sacred Hymns, with an Accompaniment for the Organ, to which are added an Overture and Five Ricercarios, making a Cantata entitled The Day of Rest*. Philadelphia: Phil. Trajetta, 1845.

Vaughan, James. "Happy Jim." London: Keith, Prowse, 1903.

Venanzi, Angelo, and Imre Kiralfy. *America: Grand Spectacle*. Copyist's MS, 3–18 December 1893. American Music Collection. NYPL, JPB 84–353.

Vodery, Will H., Henry Creamer, Ben Harris, and Eddie Hunter. *How Come?* New York: Goodman and Rose, 1923.

Von Tilzer, Harry. "Chocolate Drops." New York: Harry Von Tilzer Music, 1902.

Ware, William. *A Selection of the most Admired Airs in the New Pantomime of* Harlequin and Mother Goose. London: W. Hodsoll, n.d.

———. *The much admired Overture to the New Pantomime call'd* Harlequin and Mother Goose. London: W. Hodsoll, n.d.

Wathall, Alfred G. *Pasquita: A Romance of the Philippines*. Cincinnati: Fillmore Music, 1910. Reprint, Delhi: Facsimile, 2015.

———. *Singbad the Sailor*. Cincinnati, OH: Fillmore Music, 1911.
Wathall, Alfred G., and George Ade. *The Sultan of Sulu*. New York: M. Witmark, 1902.
Williams, Bert. "Jig." London: Keith, Prowse, 1903.
Witmark, Isidore. "Schottische (Barn Dance)" from *The Chaperons*. New York: M. Witmark, 1901.
———. "The Witmark Minstrel Overture." New York: M. Witmark, 1909.
Witmark, Isidore, and Frederic Ranken. *The Chaperons*. New York: M. Witmark, 1901.
Witt, Max S. *Henry V*: "Danse Antique." New York: Jos. W. Stern, 1900.

Books, Dissertations, and Articles

Able, E. Lawrence. "John Hill Hewitt: Dixie's Original One-Man Band." *Civil War Times* October 2003. http://www.historynet.com/john-hill-hewitt-dixies-original-one-man-band.htm.
Alden, John. "A Season in Federal Street: J.B. Williamson and the Boston Theatre 1796–1797." *Proceedings of the American Antiquarian Society* 65no.1 (1955): 9–74.
Anderson, Gillian R. "'The Temple of Minerva' and Francis Hopkinson: A Reappraisal of America's First Poet-Composer." *Proceedings of the American Philosophical Society* 120 no. 3 (June 1976): 166–177.
Appletons' Annual Cyclopaedia and Register of Important Events of the Year 1891. New series, vol. 16. New York: D. Appleton, 1892.
Aronson, Rudolph. *Theatrical and Musical Memoirs*. New York: McBride, Nast and Co., 1913.
Badger, Reid. *A Life in Ragtime*. New York: Oxford University Press, 1995.
Baker's Biographical Dictionary of Musicians. 3rd ed. Revised and enlarged by Alfred Remy, M.A. New York: G. Schirmer, 1919.
Banfield, Stephen. *Jerome Kern*. Yale Broadway Masters series, with a foreword by Geoffrey Block, general editor. New Haven: Yale University Press, 2006.
Barker, James Nelson. *The Indian Princess, or, La Belle Sauvage*. Philadelphia: T. and G. Palmer, 1808.
Barnard, Charles, and Frank A. Howson. *The Dreamland Tree*. New York: Charles Barnard, 1883.

Barnet, Anne Alison. *Extravaganza King: Robert Barnet and Boston Musical Theater*. Boston: Northeastern University Press, 2004.

Barras, Charles M. *The Black Crook*. Harvard University, Houghton Library, 1866. MS Thr 271 (2).

Benjamin, Rick. "From Barrelhouse to Broadway: The Musical Odyssey of Joe Jordan." http://www.dramonline.org/albums/from-barrelhouse-to-broadway-the-musical-odyssey-of-joe-jordan/notes.

Bennett, Robert Russell. *The Broadway Sound: The Autobiography and selected Essays of Robert Russell Bennett*. Edited by George J. Ferencz. Rochester, NY: University of Rochester Press, 1999.

Bierley, Paul E. *John Philip Sousa: A Descriptive Catalog of His Works*. Music in American Life series. Urbana: University of Illinois Press, 1973.

Bordman, Gerald. *American Musical Theatre: A Chronicle*. Expanded edition. New York: Oxford University Press, 1986.

———. *Jerome Kern: His Life and Music*. New York: Oxford University Press, 1980.

Boucicault, Dion. *Plays by Dion Boucicault*. British and American Playwrights series. Edited with an introduction and notes by Peter Thomson. Cambridge: Cambridge University Press, 1984.

Breil, Joseph Carl. "Making the Musical Adaptation." *Opportunities in the Motion Picture Industry—and How to Qualify for Positions in its Many Branches* 2 (1922): 85–87.

Brooks, Lynn Matluck. *John Durang*. Amherst, NY: Cambria Press, 2011.

Brown, Scott E. *James P. Johnson*. With a James P.Johnson Discography 1917–1950 by Robert Hilbert. Metuchen, NJ: Scarecrow Press, 1986.

Cantor, Eddie. *My Life Is in Your Hands and Take My Life: The Autobiographies of Eddie Cantor*. Foreword by Will Rogers. New introduction by Leonard Maltin. New preface and addendum by Brian Gari. New York: Cooper Square Press, 2000.

Charters, Ann. *Nobody: The Story of Bert Williams*. London: Macmillan, 1970.

"A Chat with Mr. Ivan Caryll." *Musical Opinion and Music Trade Review* 21 no. 251 (August 1897): 756.

Durang, John. *The Memoir of John Durang*. Edited by Alan S. Downer. Pittsburgh: Historical Society of York County, 1966.

Edwards, Bill. "Ford Dabney." http://ragpiano.com/comps/fdabney.shtml.

———. "Joseph Zachariah Taylor Jordan." http://ragpiano.com/comps/jjordan.shtml.
Encyclopédie multimedia de la comédie musicale théâtrale en France. Website: http://194.254.96.55/cm/?for=lis&compalp=0&init=o
The Euterpeiad, or, Musical Intelligencer and Ladies' Gazette. Vol. 2. Boston: Thomas Badger Jr., 1822. Reprint, New York: DaCapo, 1977.
Everett, William. *Rudolf Friml.* American Composers series. Urbana: University of Illinois Press, 2008.
Ewen, David. *Great Men of American Popular Song.* Englewood Cliffs, N.J.: Prentice-Hall, 1970.
Fiske, Harrison Grey. *The New York Mirror Annual and Directory of the Theatrical Profession for 1888.* New York: New York Mirror, 1888.
Fiske, Roger. *English Theatre Music in the Eighteenth Century.* London: Oxford University Press, 1973.
Franceschina, John. *David Braham: The American Offenbach.* New York: Routledge, 2003A.
———. *Duke Ellington's Music for the Theatre.* Jefferson, NC: McFarland, 2001.
———. *Harry B. Smith: Dean of American Librettists.* New York: Routledge, 2003B.
———. *Music Theory through Musical Theatre: Putting It Together.* New York: Oxford University Press, 2015.
Furst, William, George C. Hazelton, and [Joseph Henry] Benrimo. *The Yellow Jacket.* New York: Samuel French, 1912–1913.
Furst, William, William B. Hazelton, and Edward Spencer. *Electric Light.* Baltimore: Sun, 1879.
Gänzl, Kurt. *The Encyclopedia of The Musical Theatre.* 2 vols. New York: Schirmer, 1994.
———. *Lydia Thompson: Queen of Burlesque.* New York: Routledge, 2002A.
———. *William B. Gill: From the Goldfields to Broadway.* New York: Routledge, 2002B.
Glover, James M. *Jimmy Glover His Book.* London: Methuen, 1911.
Gold, Sylviane. "Tailoring the music: choreographers' secret collaborators: dance arrangers." *Dance Magazine* 1 January 2010.
Gould, Neil. *Victor Herbert.* New York: Fordham University Press, 2008.
Guest, Ivor. *Adeline Genée.* London: Adam and Charles Black, 1958
Hamm, Charles. Yesterdays: Popular Song in America. New York: W.W. Norton, 1979.

Hanley, Peter. "James Hubert Blake's WWI Draft Registration Card" http://www.doctorjazz.co.uk/draftcards3.html#ragdcjhb.

Highfill, Philip H., Jr., Kalman A. Burnim, and Edward A. Langhans. *A Biographical Dictionary of Actors, Actresses, Musicians, Dancers, Managers, and Other Stage Personnel in London 1660–1800.* Vol. 6. Carbondale, Illinois: Southern Illinois University Press, 1978.

Henneke, Ben Graf. *Laura Keene.* Tulsa, OK: Council Oak Books, 1990.

The Horn Family. http://freepages.genealogy.rootsweb.ancestry.com/~hartsman/ Horn/HornPage2/horn%20family%20page2.html#charlesedwardhorn.

Howard, Joe. *Gay Nineties Troubadour.* Miami Beach: Joe Howard Music, 1956.

Howard, John Tasker. *Our American Music: Three Hundred Years of It.* 3rd ed. New York: Thomas Y. Crowell, 1946.

Huggins, Coy Elliott. "John Hill Hewitt: Bard of the Confederacy." Ph.D. diss., Florida State University, 1964.

Ives, E., Jr., ed. *The Musical Review and Record of Musical Science, Literature, and Intelligence.* New York: William Osborn, 1839.

James, Reese D. *Old Drury of Philadelphia: A History of the Philadelphia Stage 1800–1835.* New York: Greenwood Press, 1968.

Jannotta Family Papers, 1809–1972. Abraham Lincoln Presidential Library and Museum, Springfield, IL.

John Rosamond Johnson. http://memory.loc.gov/diglib/ihas/loc.natlib.ihas.200038845 /default.html.

Johnson, H, Earle. *Musical Interludes in Boston 1795–1830.* New York: Columbia University Press, 1943. Reprint, New York: AMS Press, 1967.

Kattwinkel, Susan. *Tony Pastor Presents: Afterpieces from the Vaudeville Stage.* Westport, CT: Greenwood Press, 1998.

Kimball, Robert, ed. *Cole.* With a biographical essay by Brendan Gill. New York: Holt, Rinehart and Winston, 1971.

Kiralfy, Bolossy. *Bolossy Kiralfy, Creator of Great Musical Spectacles: An Autobiography.* Barbara M. Barker, ed. Ann Arbor: UMI Research Press, 1988.

Kirstein, Lincoln. *Dance: A Short History of Classical Theatrical Dancing.* With an appreciation by Nancy Reynolds. Anniversary edition. Princeton: Princeton Book Company, 1987.

Knowles, Mark. *Tap Roots: The Early History of Tap Dancing.* Jefferson, NC: McFarland, 2002.

Krasner, Orly Leah. "Reginald De Koven (1859–1920) and American Comic Opera at the Turn of the Century." Ph.D. diss., CUNY, 1995.

Loney, Glenn, ed. *Musical Theatre in America*. Westport, CT: Greenwood, 1984.

Lowens, Irving. *Music and Musicians in Early America*. New York: W.W. Norton, 1964.

Magriel, Paul, ed. *Chronicles of the American Dance: From the Shakers to Martha Graham*. New York: Dance Index, 1948. Reprint, New York: Da Capo Paperback, 1978.

Mandell, Jonathan. "What Is a Dance Arranger?" *TDF Stages: A Theatre Magazine*, Ju;y 2011. http://wp.tdf.org/index.php/2011/07/what-is-a-dance-arranger/

Maretzek, Max. *Revelations of an Opera Manager in 19th Century America*. With a new introduction by Charles Haywood. New York: Dover, 1968.

———. *Further Revelations of an Opera Manager in 19th Century America*. Edited and annotated by Ruth Henderson. Sterling Heights, MI: Harmonie Park Press, 2006.

Marrocco, W. Thomas, and Harold Gleason. *Music in America: An Anthology from the Landing of the Pilgrims to the Close of the Civil War, 1620–1865*. New York: W.W. Norton, 1964.

Mates, Julian. *The American Musical Stage before 1800*. New Brunswick, NJ: Rutgers University Press, 1962.

Mazzulli, Teresa F. "Boston's 'Conservatorio'—The First." *The Boston Musical Intelligencer*, 30 September 2011. http://www.classical-scene.com/2011/09/30/boston%E2%80%99s-%E2%80%9Cconservatorio%E2%80%9D-%E2%80%94-the-first/.

McCabe, John. *George M. Cohan: The Man Who Owned Broadway*. Garden City, NY: Doubleday, 1973.

Metcalf, Frank J. "Philip Anthony Corri and Arthur Clifton." *Journal of the Presbyterian Historical Society (1901-1930)*, vol. 11 no. 7 (April 1923): 268–272. Retrieved from http://www.jstor.org/stable/23323600

Morell, Parker. *Lillian Russell: The Era of Plush*. New York: Random House, 1940.

"Musical Items." *The Etude* 15:6 (June, 1897), 145.

Nathan, Hans. *Dan Emmett and the Rise of Early Negro Minstrelsy*. Norman: University of Oklahoma Press, 1962.

Nettl, Paul. *The Story of Dance Music*. New York: Philosophical Library, 1947.

Norton, Richard C. *A Chronology of American Musical Theater*. 3 vols. New York: Oxford University Press, 2002.

Odell, George C.D. *Annals of the New York Stage*. 15 vols. New York: Columbia University Press, 1927–1949.

O'Neill, Rosetta. "The Dodworth Family and Ballroom Dancing in New York." In . *Chronicles of the American Dance: From the Shakers to Martha Graham*. Paul Magriel, ed. New York: Dance Index, 1948. Reprint, New York: Da Capo Paperback, 1978.

Paterek, Josephine D. "A Survey of Costuming on the New York Commercial Stage: 1914–1934." 2 vols. Ph.D. diss., University of Minnesota, 1961.

Peterson, Bernard L., Jr. *A Century of Musicals in Black and White*. Westport, CT: Greenwood Press, 1993.

Pflueger, Carl, and R.A. Barnet. *Injured Innocents*. Boston: White-Smith, 1890.

Pincus-Roth, Zachary. "The Dance Arranger." *Ask Playbill.Com* 8 May 2008.

Pisani, Michael V. *Music for the Melodramatic Theatre in Nineteenth-Century London and New York*. Iowa City: University of Iowa Press, 2014.

Planché, James Robinson. *Plays by James Robinson Planché*. British and American Playwrights series. Edited with an introduction and notes by Donald Roy. Cambridge: Cambridge University Press, 1986.

Porter, Cole. *The Complete Lyrics of Cole Porter*. Edited by Robert Kimball. With a foreword by John Updike. New York: Alfred A. Knopf, 1983.

Porter, Susan L. *With an Air Debonair: Musical Theatre in America: 1785–1815*. Washington, D.C.: Smithsonian Institution Press, 1991.

Reiff, Anthony, Jr. *Anthony Reiff Papers*. Special Collections Research Center, Swem Library, College of William and Mary.

Riis, Thomas L. *Just Before Jazz: Black Musical Theater in New York, 1890 to 1915*. Washington, DC: Smithsonian Institution Press, 1989.

Rogers, Katharine M. *L. Frank Baum, Creator of Oz*. New York: St. Martin's Press, 2002; New York: Da Capo Press, 2003.

Root, Deane L. *American Popular Stage Music 1860–1880*. Ann Arbor: UMI Research Press, 1981.

Sadie, Stanley, ed. *The New Grove Dictionary of Music and Musicians.* 20 vols. London: Macmillan, 1980; reprint, New York: Grove, 1995.

Sanjek, Russell. *American Popular Music and its Business: The First Four Hundred Years.* Volume 2: From 1790 to 1909. New York: Oxford University Press, 1988.

Scherer, Barrymore Laurence. "Opera 'Treemonisha' as It Was Intended To Be." *Wall Street Journal* (6 December 2011). http://www.wsj.com/articles/SB10001424052970203833104577070683505219416.

Schleifer, Martha Furman. *American Opera and Music for the Stage Eighteenth and Nineteenth Centuries. Three Centuries of American Music: A Collection of American Sacred and Secular Music.* Vol. 5. N.p.: G.K. Hall, 1990.

Sciannameo, Franco. *Phil Trajetta (1777–1854), Patriot, Musician, Immigrant.* Hillsdale, NY: Pendragon Press, 2010.

Smith, Harry B. *First Nights and First Editions.* Boston: Little, Brown, and Company, 1931.

Sonneck, Oscar George Theodore. *A Bibliography of Early Secular American Music.* Washington, D.C.: H.L. McQueen, 1905. Reprint, Lexington, KY: Ulan Press, 2014.

———. *Early Opera in America.* New York: G. Schirmer, 1915.

Southern, Eileen. *Biographical Dictionary of Afro-American and African Musicians.* Westport, CT: Greenwood, 1982.

———. *The Music of Black Americans: A History.* Third edition. New York: W.W. Norton, 1997.

Spitzer, John, ed. *American Orchestras in the Nineteenth Century.* Chicago: University of Chicago Press, 2012.

Stephen, Sir Leslie, ed. *Dictionary of National Biography.* Vol. 22. New York: Macmillan, 1890.

Stubblebine, Donald J. *Early Broadway Sheet Music.* Jefferson, NC: McFarland, 2010.

Suskin, Steven. *The Sound of Broadway Music: A Book of Orchestrators and Orchestrations.* New York: Oxford University Press, 2009

Swartz, Mark Evan. *Before the Rainbow.* Baltimore: Johns Hopkins University Press, 2000.

The Theatrical Censor. Philadelphia, 1805–1806.

Thompson, Brian C. "Henri Drayton, English Opera and Anglo-American Relations, 1850–72." *Journal of the Royal Musical Association* 136:2, 247–303.

———. "Journeys of an Immigrant Violinist: Jacques Oliveira in Civil War-Era New York and New Orleans." *Journal of the Society for American Music* 6:1 (2012), 51–82.

Verne, Jules and Adolphe d'Ennery. *Around the World in 80 Days: The 1874 Play*. Contributors: Philippe Burgaud, Jean-Louis Trudel, Jean-Michel Margot, and Brian Taves. Edited by Brian Taves for the North American Jules Verne Society. The Palik Series. Albany, GA: BearManor Fiction, 2012.

Wagner, John Waldorf. "James Hewitt: His Life and Works." Ph.D. diss., Indiana University, 1969.

Waters, Edward N. *Victor Herbert*. New York: Macmillan, 1955.

Weinert-Kendt, Rob. "A Tailor of Music, Skilled in Alterations: The Arranger Glen Kelly Knows the Broadway Score." *The New York Times* 26 June 2014.

Westover, Jonas. "A Study and Reconstruction of *The Passing Show of 1914*: The American Musical Revue and Its Development in the Early Twentieth Century." 2 vols. Ph.D. diss., CUNY, 2010.

White, Eric Walter. *A History of English Opera*. London: Faber and Faber, 1983.

Whitton, Joseph. *"The Naked Truth!" An Inside History of* The Black Crook. Philadelphia: H.W. Shaw, 1897.

Will Accooe. http://africlassical.blogspot.com/2012/12/will-accooe-1874-1904-composed-black.html

Winden, William Craig. "The Life and Music Theater Works of John Hill Hewitt." D. Mus. A. diss., University of Illinois at Urbana-Champaign, 1972.

Wolfe, Richard J. *Secular Music in America 1801–1825*. 3 vols. New York: New York Public Library, 1964.

Woll, Allen. *Black Musical Theatre*. Baton Rouge: Louisiana State University Press, 1989. Reprint, New York: Da Capo, n.d.

Index

A

Aarons, Alfred E., 3–7, 41, 167, 307, 394, 407n4, 462n859
Abbey's Theatre, 25, 135, 377
About Town, 175, 286–287, 353
Abyssinia, 118, 390, 399
Academy of Music (Baltimore), 329, 365, 377
Academy of Music (Brooklyn), 259
Academy of Music (Cleveland), 348
Academy of Music (New York), 333, 370, 409n47, 429n330
Academy of Music (Omaha), 470n1020
Academy of Music (Richmond), 281, 324
Accooe, Will, 7–8, 407n9
An Adamless Eden, 54
"An Admirable Admiral," 383, 385
"Adolphus Morning-Glory," 47
Adonis, 190, 440n480
Africa, 125
Ahmed al Kamel, the Pilgrim of Love, 342
Aladdin, Jr., 26, 370, 409n41
Aladdin, or, the Wonderful Lamp, 17, 110, 111, 112
"Aladdin Quick Step," 111–112
Aladdin the Second, 47
Aladdin, The Wonderful Scamp, 244
Alcazar Theatre (San Francisco), 31, 50, 448n610
Ali Baba, 26, 27, 28
Alidor, 381, 479n1148
All Aboard, 121, 210, 436n420

All Over Town, 301, 302, 303, 304, 305, 306
All Quiet on the Western Front (film), 213
The Amber Empress, 30, 218
The Ameer, 192, 270, 313, 314
American Conservatorio of Boston, 278
American Extravaganza Company, 25, 26, 27, 409n40, n43
The American Idea, 234, 235
The American in London, 78
American Society of Composers, Authors and Publishers, 169, 212, 220, 304, 319, 356
Aminta, the Coquette, 257
L'Amour de l'Artist, 41–42
Les amours de la reine Elizabeth (film), 66
Annina, 219
Antiope, 369–370
An Arabian Girl and Forty Thieves, 27, 55, 208
Anderson, Hilding, 8–9,
And What Happened Then, 123, 427n285
"Apache Dance Parody," 199, 200
Aphrodite, 201, 266
Apple Blossoms, 372, 373, 374
Aquilo, 28
Arcadia, 54
The Archers, 78–79
Are You Insured?, 50
"Argentine Dance," 218

Arnold, Richard, 9–10
Aronson, Rudolph, 10–12, 96, 97, 407n12, n13, 421n202
Around the Map, 202, 331, 442n512
Around the World in 80 Days (Deane), 141
Around the World in 80 Days (Debillemont), 141, 142, 143
Around the World in 80 Days (Harrison) 293–294
Artists and Models, 268
An Artist's Model, 398
Astaire, Adele, 129, 373, 374
Astaire, Fred, 129, 373, 374
As You Like It, 31, 119, 225, 418n178
The Atonement of Pan, 283
Audrey, 281
Auf Japan, 215
Au Japon (ballet), 229, 230
Ayer, Nat, 13–14, 58, 330, 407n15, n16
Azora, 283, 285

B

The Babes in the Wood, 68, 89, 261
Babes in Toyland, 313–315
"Bacchanale" (*Mecca*), 204, 205
The Bachelor Belles, 353, 471n1039
Bad Dickey, 10
Baker, Thomas, 15–21, 408n22, 414–415n129, 430n345
"Ballet Divertissement: Will O' the Wisp," 84, 85
Ballet of 1830, 34–35
"Ballet of the Illuminated City of Valparaiso," 143–144
"Ballet of Hussars," 81
"Ballet Music and Finale," 270, 271, 272
Ballet Suite (Hadley), 281
"Ballet" (*The Casino Girl*), 145
"Ballin' the Jack," 398
Bandanna Land, 118, , 327, 387, 390, 405
Baravelle, Victor, 21–22
Barnard, Charles, 349
The Baron, 349

Barratt, (Walter) Augustus, 22–24, 129, 408n35, n36
Barrett, Oscar, 24–25, 408–409n37
Batchelor, W.H., 25–28, 409n43
Bauer, Adolph, 28–29, 409n44
Baum, L. Frank, 200, 271, 272
The Beauty Spot, 135, 137, 138, 211, 238, 307, 308
The Begum, 134, 135
"Behold the Governor," 233, 234
Beisenherz, Henry, 29
Belasco, David, 51, 222, 223, 224, 226, 446n577
Belasco Theatre (Mew York), 225, 226
Belasco Theatre (Washington D.C.), 135, 238, 330
The Belle of Bridgeport, 7, 362, 382, 388
The Belle of New York, 27, 30
Belle of the West, 345, 346
Bell, Ida, 190, 191, 441n482
Bendix, Max, 29–30
Bendix, Theodore, 30–34
Ben Hur, 31
Berlin, Irving, 42, 129, 372
Bernard, George P., 34
Better Times, 355
Betty, 128, 301
Betty Lee, 332
Bianca, 285
The Big Show, 173, 355
Bijou Theatre (Boston), 52, 54
Bijou Theatre (New York), 10, 46, 54, 81, 88, 118, 286, 348, 393, 473n1076, n1077, n1082, n1083, n1084, 474n1085
Bing, George, 34–35
The Birth of a Nation (film), 66, 273, 447n593
"The Birth of the Butterfly," 313, 315
"The Birth of the Rainbow," 370
The Black Crook, 19, 20, 21, 37, 38, 39, 101, 114, 156, 171, 332, 333, 361, 370, 380
Black Patti Troubadours, 118
The Black Politician, 186
A Black Sheep, 270

The Black Venus, 101–102
Blake, Eubie, 35–36, 392, 393, 411n61, 486n1264
Blake, Louis, 36–37
Blaney, Charles E., 126, 378
Blossom, Henry, 316, 354, 355, 385
Bluebeard, Jr., 54, 191, 192
The Blue Paradise, 169, 196
Bone Squash Diavolo, or Il Nicceret, 1
Booth's Theatre, 101, 114, 143, 156
Boston Museum, 53, 55, 86, 110, 112, 113, 171, 434n404
Böteführ, W.D.C., 37–38
Bottom's Dream, 54
"The Boulevard Glide," 238
Boullay, Louis, 38–39
Bourville Castle, 78
Bowers, Frederick V., 39–41, 334, 411n75, 467n968
Bowers, Robert Hood, 41–45, 210, 271
Bowery Theatre, 29, 86, 110, 140, 181, 243, 244, 341, 409n47, 430n342
Bowron, George, 45–46,
Bowron, William Lloyd, 45–46
The Boy and the Girl, 298
A Boy Wanted, 378, 478n1141
The Boys and Betty, 118, 238, 298
Braham, David, 46–49
Braham, George, 49–51
Braham, Harry, 51–53, 412n94, n99
Braham, John J., 53–58, 412n91, n100, 413n105, 424n254
Braham, Philip, 185
Braham's Park Garden, 53–54
Bratton, John W., 13, 58–62, 413n110
"Bravura Song," 39
Bray, John, 62–65, 413n114, n115
The Brazilian, 96, 97
Breil, Joseph Carl, 65–67, 358, 414n118, n119, n121, n122
The Bride of the Nile, 214
Brinkworth, W.H., 67–70, 414n123, n124
Bristow, George F., 70–71, 414n127
Broadhurst, George H., 211, 282
Broadway Brevities of 1920, 279, 400

Broadway Theatre, 55, 81, 92, 120, 135, 184, 210, 213, 222, 261, 349, 409n41, 474n1091
Brode, Herman, 71–73, 414n128, n129, 415n130
Broschi, Karl, 73
Brown, A. Seymour, 13, 14, 58, 214
Brymn, James T., 404
The Bugle Call, 399
The Bunch and Judy, 22, 400, 415n142
Burkhardt, Addison, 210, 351, 385
Burnside, R.H., 209, 354, 355
Burt, Benjamin Hapgood, 298, 300, 347, 386
Buster Brown, 58, 413n110
"The Butterfly Ballet," 318, 319–320
By the Sad Sea Waves, 233

C

Cabin in the Sky, 391
Cadman, Charles, 66, 358
Caesar, Irving, 212, 219, 332, 386, 399, 400
"Cake Walk" (Hubbell), 354
Caldwell, Anne, 75–77, 199, 200, 316, 355, 356, 389, 415n142, 416n143
The Caledonian Frolic, 77
California Theatre (San Francisco), 125, 248
The Caliph, 184, 185, 192
"Call Me Uncle," 215, 216
The Canary, 82, 83
The Cannibal King, 8, 117, 424n256
Cantor, Eddie, 279, 459n769
The Cap of Fortune and the Show Girl, 294, *see also* The Show Girl
The Captive (Bendix), 31
The Captive (Ganne), 230–231
The Captive (Herbert), 311
Carle, Richard, 3, 41, 133, 228, 295, 297, 298, 347, 396, 397
"Carnival Scene Ballet," 84
"Carolina Shout," 394
Carr, Benjamin, 77–80, 245, 416n145, n147
Carr, F. Osmond, 80–81

Caryll, Ivan, 77, 81–85, 89, 195, 213, 417n158, n159, n160, 418n164, n165, n166, n167
The Casino Girl, 7–8, 117, 135, 145, 184
Casino Theatre, 10, 28, 45, 55, 56, 96, 97, 115, 117, 135, 145, 172, 174, 184, 188, 207, 211, 214, 222, 286, 295, 330, 376, 417n160, 427n283
"The Castle Doggy Fox Trot," 187, 188
"Castle Innovation Tango," 128
"Castle Maxixe," 128
"Castle's Half and Half," 128
Castles in Spain, or Castles in the Air, 274
Castles in the Air, 30
Castle, Vernon and Irene, 128, 179–180, 187, 188, 387, 439n463
"The Castle Walk," 128
The Cat and the Fiddle, 22, 269
Catlin, E.N., 86–87, 418n173
A Celebrated Hard Case, 48
Cellier, Alfred, 88–89, 361, 397
The Century Girl, 273, 317, 336
Century Theatre, 203, 266, 307
A Certain Party, 42
Chadwick, George W., 89–93, 281, 419n184, 420n187, n189
La Chair, 94
"Charleston,' 392
"Champagne Dance," 250,
Chantrier, Albert, 94–95, 420n194
Charity Begins at Home, 88
"Charleston Rag," 35
Chassaigne, Francis, 28, 95–97, 420n197, 421n198, n199
Cheer Up, 355
Cherry Blossoms, 266, 269
Chestnut Street Theatre (Philadelphia), 62, 114, 144, 190, 261, 341
Chicago Opera House, 25, 26, 135, 191, 286, 366
The Children of Captain Grant, 142, 143
Childs, Nathaniel, 53, 54
Chilvers, Thomas H., 97–98, 207, 421n204
A China Doll, 4, 5, 6, 307

Chin-Chin, 82, 84
A Chinese Honeymoon, 31, 174
Chipman, J.S., 98–100
The Chocolate Dandies, 35
The Chocolate Soldier, 30, 434n394
Chow, Chow (Brinkworth), 68
Chow Chow (Hubbell), 351
Christiani, Emil, 100–101
The Christian Martyrs, 17, 18, 19
Christrup, Charles, 101–102
Chubb, T. Youres, 102, 422n220, n222, n223
Chu Chin Chow, 203
Cinderella, 15, 24, 25, 89, 261, 333, 341, 399, 408–409n37
Cinderella and the Prince, 98, 99, 123, 270, 271, 272
Cinderella, or, The Lover, the Lackey, and the Little Glass Slipper, 244
The City Chap, 22, 169, 415n142
The City Directory, 286
City Hotel (theatre), 242, 245
City Theatre (Charleston), 144, 278
City Theatre (New York), 246
Clarke, Cuthbert Edward, 102–103, 250, 422n226
Class Struggle in Swing, 394
Claudius Nero, 73
Clef Club, 118, 127, 187, 188, 387, 425–426n263
Cleopatra's Night, 286
Clifton, Arthur, 104–107, 422n231, 423n232
Clifton, Henry, 456–457n768
The Climax, 65
Clorindy, or, The Origin of the Cakewalk, 117
"The Coconut Dance," 137, 138
Cohan, George M., 51, 75, 158, 214, 233–234, 235, 237, 238, 266, 347, 448n618, n619, 453n712
Cole, Bob, 4, 7, 117, 186, 262, 382, 388, 389, 390, 391, 404, 439n459, 480n1184, 481n1190, n1191, 485n1261
Cole and Johnson, 7, 481n1185

Colon, Aberano, 108–109
Columbiana, or 1992, 192
Colwell, Victor, 109, 423n238
Come Over Here, 391
Comer, Thomas, 110–113, 423n240, n241, n242
Commencement Days, 40
The Commuters, 31, 32, 34
Coney Island, 54
Connelly, Michael, 113–116
Constantinople, 248
Cook, Will Marion, 8, 115–119, 127, 184, 186, 188, 387, 390, 393, 399, 404, 405, 413n105, 424n252, n253, n254, 425n260, n263
Cooke, J.P., 119–120, 420n271
Coolman, DeWitt C., 120–121
"The Co-Optimists," 239, 240
Cordelia's Aspirations, 48, 50
Corliss, Edward W., 121–123
The Corsair, 54
Cort, John, 40
Cotton Land, 393
Countess Coquette, 214
Cramer, François, 15
Crawford, Clifton, 123–124
Creamer, Henry S., 382, 393, 394, 400, 405, 483n1211
Criss Cross, 22, 416n142
Cruger, Randolph, 124–125, 427n290
The Cruise of the Summer Girl, 174
The Crystal Slipper, 26, 191
"Cuddle Up a Little Closer," 345
"Cupid's Dart," 130
"Cupid's Ramble," 389
"Cute an' Cunnin,'" 43, 44
Cutty, Thomas 125–126
"Czardas," 252, 256

D

Dabney, Ford, 127–128, 428n300, n302, n304, n308
Daly, Augustin, 156, 293,
Daly's Theatre, 55, 203, 349, 350, 398, 432n370
Daly, William, 428–430, 428n309

Dance and Grow Thin, 336
"Dance of Temptation, 357–358
"Dance of the Harem," 92, 93
"Dance of the Orchid," 213
"Dance on Friday Night," 382
"Dance-Pantomime" (Apple Blossoms), 373
Dancing Around, 178, 241
"Dancing Dinah," 283, 284
"The Dancing of Salome," 405
The Dandy Coon, 404
Daniels, Frank, 192, 363, 474n1087
Dannenberg, Louis, 130
Dan's Tribulations, 48, 50
The Darktown Follies, 393
Darkydom, 118, 188
Darley, Francis T.S., 130–133, 429n319, n324, n325
Darling, Frank N., 133–134, 429n330, n331
Darling of the Gallery Gods, 383
The Darling of the Gods, 224, 225, 226, 446n590
A Daughter of the Gods, 42
A Daughter of the Revolution, 184, 185
David Garrick, 86
The Deacon and the Lady, 7
The Death of Cuthullin, 22, 23, 24
Deane, Benjamin J., 19, 21, 120, 140–141, 430n339, n342, n345
De Angeles, Jefferson, 10, 209
Dearie, 211
Debillemont, Jean-Jacques, 141–144
Le début de Chichine, 94
Deep Harlem, 405
De Koven, Reginald, 134–140, 184, 211, 307, 430n335, n336
Delamater, A.G., 214
Delibes, Léo, 62, 93, 122, 134, 194, 250, 316
Demarque, Charles, 144
Demonio, 47
Deseret Deserted, 119
DeSylva, Buddy G., 218, 400
Deux Chasseurs et la Laitiere, 144
Deux mauvaises bonnes, 95, 421n198

The Devil in the Bowery, 29
The Devil's Bridge, 340, 341
The Devil's Deputy, 377
Devin, William, 145–146, 184
Dew Drop Inn, 218, 268
DeWolfe, Elsie, 179, 180
Dick Whittington, 24–25
Dick Whittington and His Cat, 68
Diet, Edmond-Marie, 146–154
Dillingham, Charles, 83, 120, 121, 355
Dinklespeil's Blunders, 158
"Dinner (Quintet)," 235, 236
Dockstader Minstrels, 40
Doctor of Alcantara, 170, 171
Dodworth Band, 155, 156
Dodworth, Harvey B., 19, 155–156, 431n359, n363, 432n370, n372
"Doll Song," 76–77
Dolly Varden, 165, 166
Dolores, 369
"Don't You Want to Be My Bow-wow-wow," 76
Dorothy, 82, 89, 361, 419n180, n181
"Down Ole Tampa Bay," 207
The Dreamland Tree, 349
Dreams, 52, 54, 231
"Dresdina Ballet," 369
The Dress Parade, 383
Drigo, Riccardo, 157–158
The Duchess of Dantzig, 82, 83, 84
The Duke's Motto, 155
Dunbar, Paul Laurence, 8, 117, 387, 413n105
Duncan, Isadora, 231
Duncan, William Carey, 396
"Durang's Horn-Pipe," 337–338
Dvořák, Antonin, 117, 215, 265, 311
"Dwarf Dance," 338–339
Dyring, H.T., 158–161, 432n374

E

Eagle Theatre, 48, 114
The Earl and the Girl, 82, 174, 175, 176
Earl Carrol's Vanities, 129
East Is West, 42
Easy Dawson, 53

"Eccentric Dance" (Hein), 301, 303
The Echo, 13, 120, 346
Edwards, George, 213
Edwards, Gus, 169, 330
Edwards, Julian, 6, 41, 163–167, 211, 385
Edwards, Leo, 59, 167–169, 328
Eichberg, Julius, 170–172, 434n404
Eileen, 316
Einödshofer, Julius, 172–174, 434n406
The Electrician, 292
The Electric Light, 221
Ellis, Melville, 174–180, 334, 435n410, n412, n413, n414, 436n416, n418, n421, 437n423
The Elopement, or, Harlequin's Tour through the Continent of North America, 144
The Elopers, 213
Elsie, 35
Elsie Janis and Her Gang, 202
The Elves, 15, 29, 410n48
The Emigrant Car, or, Go West, 159
Emmet, Joseph K., 181–183, 423n236, 437n426, n430, n433, n438, n439
"Emmet's Swell Song," 183
"The Emperor's March," 17, 18, 19
"Empire Dance," 103
Empire Theatre (London), 81, 103, 125, 202, 250, 260, 399
Empire Theatre (New York), 222, 223, 329, 372, 482n1207
The Enchanted Beauty, 113
The Enchanted Horse, 112
Les Enfants de la balle, 95
Engländer (Englander), Ludwig, 7, 134, 184–186, 333, 438n443, n444, n446, n447, n449
The Enterprise, 105, 106, 237
Erminie, 10, 45, 55, 82, 376, 377, 476–477n1127
"Ethiopia" (ballet), 387
Europe, James Reese, 35, 118, 127, 186–188, 386, 387, 425n263, 439n458, n459, n463, n465, 485n1261

Eustis, Fred J., 189–194, 409n43, 440n480, 441n482
Evangeline, 55, 189, 190, 225, 332, 412n91, 440n473
Everything, 129, 355
Everywoman, 93, 213
"The Evolution of Ragtime," 390, 481n1188
Excelsior, Jr., 55
Eysler, Edmund, 169, 195–196

F

1492, Up to Date or Very Near It, 108, 368,
Faddimir, 80, 417n154
"Fairy Dance" (Glaser), 250, 251
"The Fairy Dance" (Horn), 342–343
Falka, 96, 421n199
The Fall of a Nation (film), 319
Fancy Free, 23, 124
Fantana, 353
Farnie, H.B., 96
Faust and Marguerite, 155
Faustus, 340
"Feast Dance of the African Chiefs," 125
Federal Overture, 78
Federal Street Theatre (Boston), 39, 62, 274, 275, 278, 322
Fehrmann, Max, 197, 441n491
Felix, Hugo, 77, 198–201, 346, 441n497, 442n508
Février, Henri, 201, 266
Fiddlers Three, 396
The Field of the Cloth of Gold, 259
Fields, Lew, 55, 121, 210, 211, 428n309, 443n531
Fifth Avenue Theatre, 40, 45, 93, 123, 134, 156, 244, 294, 329, 377, 390
Fifty Million Frenchmen, 215
Finck, Herman, 201–203, 398, 442n512
The Finish of Mr. Fresh, 48, 55
The Firefly, 215, 216, 217
The Firefly (film), 219
"The Fire Fly Galop," 380
The Fire-Prince, 283, 284

First Corps of Cadets, 98, 108, 121, 270, 294
Fletcher, Percy E., 203–205
Flick Flock, 248
Flirt in St. Moritz (*Flirting at St. Moritz*), 172, 173
"Flirt-Waltz," 173
Fokine, Michel, 201, 203, 204
Follies of 1907, 298, 336
Follies of 1909, 13, 436n416
Follies of 1910, 127, 134, 168, 405
Ford Dabney's Ginger Girls, 127
Ford's Opera House (Baltimore), 221, 222, 427n283, 446n573
For Freedom Ho, 243, 244
For Goodness Sake, 129
The Fortune Teller, 313
Fortunio and his Seven Gifted Servants (Darley), 131, 132
Fortunio and His Gifted Servants (Howson), 348
The Forty Thieves, 113
Fourteenth Street Theatre, 30, 54, 126, 189, 286, 292, 329, 345, 349, 443n519, 473n1078
"Fox Trot," 129, 188, 302, 331, 332, 406, 466n951
Fra Diavolo, 29, 120, 227, 347, 348,
Fra Diavolo, or, The Beauty and the Brigands, 244
Francis, W.T., 206–210, 443n518
Franklin, Malvin M., 42, 210–211, 214
Freckles, 214
Freeborn, Cassius ("Cass"), 211–212
Frey, Hugo, 212–213
"Fricassée," 84
Friedland, Anatol(e), 180, 210, 213–215, 444n547, n548
Friml, Rudolf, 215–221, 307, 308, 444n553, 445n555, n560, n563, 461n838
Fritz among the Gypsies, 183
Fritz in Ireland, 182, 183
Fritz, Our Cousin German, 181, 182
The Frog Families, 118

Frohman, Charles, 209, 222, 223, 372
"Frolic of the Bears," 402, 403
(From)Broadway to Paris, 214, 336
From Broadway to Tokio, 135, 136, 137
A Full Honeymoon, 266
Furst, William W., 28, 29, 221–226, 446n573, n576, n577, n579, n587, n590, 447n593
Furth, Seymour, 292, 385

G

Gabriel Grub, 48
Gabriel, Max, 227–229
A Gaiety Girl, 397, 398
Gaiety Theatre (Boston), 189
Gaiety Theatre (London), 82, 83, 397
Gaiety Theatre (San Francisco), 386
Gallops, 51
"Galop," (*The Forty Thieves*), 115–116
"Galop" (*The Man in the Moon*), 138–139
"Galop" (*The Vanderbilt Cup*), 42–43
Ganne, Louis, 229–231
Gant, "Willie," 35
Garden Theatre, 37, 89, 135, 215, 279, 349, 409n40
Garrick Theatre (Chicago), 353
Garrick Theatre (New York), 206, 223
Garrick Theatre(Philadelphia), 225
Gaunt, Percy, 231–232
Gayest Manhattan, 27
The Gay White Way, 185
Gebest, Charles J., 232–238, 332, 448n615
Geechie, 393
The Geisha, 398, 436n420
Genée, Adeline, 41, 103, 250, 251, 253, 254, 353, 417n156
Genée, Richard, 134, 227
Gershwin, George, 129, 130, 264, 482n1207
Get-Rich-Quick Wallingford, 346
Get Together, 267
Gideon, Melville, 238–240, 330, 399, 449n627, n629, n631, n636

Gilbert and Sullivan, 5, 28, 42, 48, 52, 53, 54, 55, 71, 86, 88, 90, 161, 193, 206, 234, 361, 383, 433n384
Gilbert, Jean, 241–242, 268, 271
Gilbert, L. Wolfe, 210, 214, 215
Gilfert, Charles, 242–244, 449n643
Gill, William, 30, 52, 55
Gilles, Napoleon, 244–245
Gillingham, George, 245–246, 450n656, n661, 463n892
Gillingham, Louisa, 242
Giorza, Paolo, 246–250, 450n665, 450n666, n667
"Gipsey Dance," 309, 310
The Girl and the Wizard, 167, 177, 211, 238, 330
The Girl behind the Gun, 82, 83
The Girl from Broadway, 345
A (The) Girl from Dixie, 4, 117, 184, 383, 390
The Girl From Utah, 202, 398
The Girl I Left behind Me, 222
The Girl of the Gate, 384
The Girl Question, 8
Giroflé-Girofla, 30, 48, 101
Il Giucatore [The Player], 247
Glaser, C.J.M., 250–256
Glaser, Lulu, 353, 377
Globe Theatre (Boston), 30, 53,
Globe Theatre (New York), 68, 121, 426n275
Glover, Howard, 257–260
Glover, James ("Jimmy"), 260–263
"The Gobble Glide," 307, 308
Godowsky, Leopold, 263–265
Goetz, E. Ray, 210, 238, 428n309
Goetzl, Anselm, 201, 265–267, 453n708, 454n717
Going Up, 237, 331
The Golden Butterfly, 67, 135, 307
"Golf-Song," 206, 208
The Gondoliers, 55
Goodman, Alfred ("Al"), 241, 267–270, 454n722, n727, n730
Good Morning Dearie, 22, 400, 415n142

Good Times, 355
Goodwin, J. Cheever, 26, 53, 54, 55, 125, 222
Gottschalk Louis F. Louis F., 270–273
Goula, Juan, 273–274
The Governor's Son, 233, 234
Grainger, Porter, 391, 405, 486n1264
Grand Opera House (Brooklyn), 349
Grand Opera House (Cincinnati), 286
Grand Opera House (Columbus), 343
Grand Opera House (New York), 34, 52, 72, 98, 293, 332, 345, 395
Grand Opera House (Philadelphia), 40, 249, 377
Grand Opera House (St. Louis), 75
Grand Opera House (Washington, D.C.), 362
Granger, Frederick, 274–275, 456n753
Grant, John B., 275–277
Graupner, Gottlieb, 277–278, 322
Gray, Thomas J., 210
Great Day, 118, 400
The Great Name, 31
The Great Ruby, 30, 261
Greek Slave, 398
Greenbank, Harry, 222, 397, 398
Greenwich Street Theatre, 245
Gress, Louis, 279, 457n769
The Grim Goblin, 25
A Guest of Honor, 401

H

Hadley, Henry K., 281–286, 457n783
Haig, Alexander, 286–287
Half a King, 27, 184
The Half Moon, 374
The Ham Tree, 40
Hammerstein, Arthur, 215, 445n555
Hammerstein, Oscar, 3, 55, 182, 219, 288–292, 420n194, 457–458n787, 458n791, n794, n799
Hammerstein, Oscar II, 25
Hammerstein's Olympia Theatre, 55, 362
Hammerstein's Victoria Theatre, 3, 118, 124, 228, 295, 334, 393, 467n971

Hand, Edward Carl, 292–293
Hands Up, 128, 428n309
Hans the Flute Player, 229–230
The Happy Day, 399
Happy Days, 355
"Happy Little Flip-Flaps," 69
Harbach, Otto, 218, 219, 331, 332, 345, 445n555, 454n717, *see also* Hauerbach, Otto
Harlem Hotcha, 394
Harlem Opera House, 81, 126, 182, 192, 288, 386
"Harlem Rag," 404
Harlequin Jack, the Giant Killer, 29, 409n45
Harlequin Shipwrecked, or The Power of Enchantment, 144
Harlequin's Invasion, 245
Harrigan and Hart, 53, 86, 87
Harrigan, Edward, 48, 49, 50, 51, 53, 57, 86, 87
Harrison, E., 293–294
Hauerbach, Otto, 215, 217, 218, 345, 346, 347, 445n555, *see also* Harbach, Otto
The Head Waiters, 98
The Heart Breakers, 9
The Heartbreakers, 239, 399
The Heart of Maryland, 222
The Heart o' th' Heather, 355
Heartz, Harry L., 294–298
He Came from Milwaukee, 178, 330, 385
Hein, Silvio, 118, 213, 298–306, 307, 460n826, n827, 461n844, n847, 472n1047
Heindl, Anton, 306–308
Heinrich, Anthony Philip, 308–311, 462n873
Held, Anna, 30, 134, 335, 336, 363, 390
Hell, a Profane Burlesque, 42
Hendrick Hudson, 361, 473n1078
The Hen-Pecks, 202
Henry VIII (burlesque), 52
Herald Square Theatre, 55, 93, 117, 120, 135, 166, 172, 208, 214, 222, 223, 307, 421n205

Herbert, Victor, 42, 77, 137, 193, 219, 270, 271, 273, 311–320, 445n555, 479n1144
Heroes of the Street (film), 169
Her Little Highness, 30, 135
Hewitt, James, 245, 321–323, 416n145, 463n883, n886, 891, n892, n893
Hewitt, John Hill, 107, 323–326, 464n897, n899
Hiawatha, 54
Hiawatha (film), 55
High Jinks (Clarke), 103
High Jinks (Friml), 217
The Highwayman, 135, 139
Hill, J. Leubrie, 118, 326–328, 390, 393
Hindley, Thomas, 328–329
"The Hindoo was a Hoodoo," 276, 277
Hip! Hip! Hooray, 307
Hip-Hip Hooray, 173, 355
A Hired Girl, 378, 479n1142
Hirsch, Louis A., 196, 238, 239, 329–332, 385, 391, 465n937, 465–466n947, 466n949, n951
His Excellency, 81
His Honor, the Barber, 127
His Honor the Mayor (farce), 223
His Honor the Mayor (musical), 6, 7, 167
H.M.S. Pinafore, 51, 52, 53, 86, 88, 140, 193, 436n420, 460n826
Hobart, George V., 211, 239, 298, 299, 331, 346, 355, 379, 383, 393
Hodge, Podge and Co., 58
Hoffman, A.W., 332–333, 467n962
Hoffmann, Gertrude, 177, 334, 335, 336, 467n971
Hoffman(n), Max, 333–336, 436n415, 467n966, n968, n971
Hoffmaster, William, 336–339
Hollis Street Theatre (Boston), 54, 349, 427n290
"Hop Lee: Chinese Dance, 296–297
Hop o' My Thumb, 262
Horn, Charles E., 339–343, 468n985, n988, n997

Horner, Sydney H., 333, 343–344
The Horn of a Dilemma, 113
"Hornpipe" (*The Highwayman*), 139–140
"Hornpipe" (*The Silver Star*), 250, 252
Horwitz, Charles, 40, 334, 411n75, 467n968
Hoschna, Karl. 198, 344–347, 469n1003
The Hotel Clerk, 7
The Hottest Coon in Dixie, 8
Howard Athenaeum, 53, 86, 111, 423n241
Howard, Joseph E., 8, 210
Howson, Frank A., 190, 347–351, 415n130, 471n1024
Howson Opera Troupe, 470n1018, n1019, n1020, 471n1021
The Hoyden, 41
Hoyt, Charles H., 46, 52, 231, 232, 270, 281, 319, 354, 361, 385
Hubbell, Raymond, 77, 129, 173, 175, 351–356, 471n1030, n1039
Hughes, Langston, 394
Hugo, John Adam, 66, 356–359
Hullo America, 202
Humphrey, Fred W., 359–361, 473n1070
Humpty Dumpty (Cole and Johnson), 390
Humpty-Dumpty (Dyring), 161
Humpty Dumpty Junior, 68
Humpty Dumpty Up to Date, 227
The Hurdy Gurdy Girl, 41, 297–298
Hydes, Watty, 361–363, 382, 473n1079, 474n1087
"Hypnotic Dance," 299, 300

I

"I Am So Shy," 31–32
"If They Must Tear Me from Thy Heart," 193–194
"I'm a Shy Little Innocent Thing," 97
"Incidental Music" (Friml), 217
In Dahomey, 117, 327, 387, 425n257
"Indian Dance," 345, 346

The Indian Princess, 62, 63, 64
In Gotham, 3, 228
"In My Soap Bubble Aeroplane," 386
In the Jungles, 118
In the Land of the Head Hunters (film), 55–56
"In the Shadows," 202
Intolerance (film), 65
The Invisible Prince, 29
In Zululand, 118
Iolanthe, 42, 52, 54, 361, 418–419n179, 436n420
Isham, John W., 7, 388
The Isle of Champagne, 221
The Isle of Spice, 383
Itzel, Adam, 365–368
The Ivy Leaf, 97
Ixion, 47, 68, 113, 140

J

Jack and Jill, 23, 129
Jack-in-the-Box, 261, 452n693
Jack Sheppard, 365, 366
Jack the Giant Killer, 68
Jacobi, Georges, 369–370
Jacobi, Victor, 370–374, 475n1116, n1117
Jacquet, H. Maurice, 375–376, 476n1124, n1125
Jakobowski, Edward, 45, 55, 82, 376–378, 476n1127, 477n1130, 478n1132
James, Harry, 378–379, 478n1140, 479n1144
Jannotta, A., 379–381, 479n1146, n1148
"Japanese Ballet," 136, 137
Jefferson, William, 381–382, 479n1156, n1157
Jerome, Ben M., 330, 382–386, 479n1160
The Jersey Lily, 135, 334
Jes Lak White Fo'ks, 8, 117, 424n256
Jessie Brown, 119
The Jewel of Asia, 124, 184, 185
Johns, Al, 386–387

Johnson, James Price, 35, 392–395, 400, 405, 482n1199, n1200, n1203, n1205, n1207, 483n1211, n1212, n1214
Johnson, James Weldon, 4, 186, 382, 388, 389, 390
Johnson, J. Rosamond, 4, 8, 118, 186, 188, 261, 327, 382, 387, 388–392, 404, 405, 481n1189, n1190, n1191, n1192
Johnson, Billy, 7
Johnstone, Alexander, 395–397
Johnstone, Will B., 395
John Street Theatre, 78, 242, 321, 336–337, 339, 449n643
The Jolly Tar, 209
Jones, Sidney, 222, 397–399, 483n1231, 484n1232
Jones, Stephen, 399–400, 485n1248
Joplin, Scott, 401–403, 485n1289
Jordan, Joe, 391, 403–406, 485n1258, n1259, n1261, 486n1262, n1264
Judith, 93, 420n188, n189
Jullien, Louis Antoine, 15
Jupiter, or, The King and the Cobbler, 163, 164

K

The Kaffir Diamond, 349
Kafoozleum, 54
Kajanka, 343, 344, 469n998
Kate Kip, Buyer, 362
Katinka, 218
Keene, Laura, 15, 16, 17, 408n28
Keep Shufflin', 394, 400, 405
Kelly and Leon, 244,
Kern, Jerome, 23, 42, 77, 130, 158, 185, 238, 241, 318, 330, 371, 389, 398, 465–466n947
The Khedive, 36, 37
Kid Boots, 279, 457n772
"Killarney," 334, 335
King Charming, 119
King Henry VIII, 307
King Highball, 40
King John, 102

The King's Musketeer, 349, 350, 351
The King's Quest, 127
King René's Daughter, 164
Kiralfy, Bolossy, 101, 142, 248, 294, 333, 369, 370, 467n961
Kiralfy Brothers, 71, 332, 333
Kiralfy, Imre, 40, 192, 249, 333
Kitty MacKay, 31, 200
Klaw and Erlanger, 6, 83
The Koh-i-noor, 288
Koster and Bial's Music Hall, 3, 55, 228, 288
Kreisler, Fritz, 372
Kubelík, Jan, 215

L

The Ladies' Lion, 209
The Lady from Chicago, 174
The Lady of the Slipper, 316, 317, 415n142
Lafayette Theatre (Harlem), 118, 188, 327, 393, 394, 402
Lalla Rookh,, 120, 340
"Lancashire Songs and Dances," 49
La Salle Theatre (Chicago), 210, 383, 384, 385, 386
The Leather Patch, 48
Le Baron, William, 373, 374, 395
The Legend, 66–67, 358
Leo and Lotos, 114
Let George Do It, 13
The Liberty Belles, 8, 124, 270
The Life and Death of Natty Bumpo, 68
"Life Is Too Short to Be Wasting Your Time," 59, 60
Life on the Streets, 140
"Lift Ev'ry Voice and Sing," 388
Lifting the Cup, 383
Lights o' London, 52, 114
The Lilac Domino, 210, 265, 443n533
Linger Longer Letty, 268, 454n722
Listen In, 42
The Little Café, 82, 307
Little Christopher Columbus, 82
The Little Frauds, 53, 57, 86, 87

The Little Host, 97, 98, 206, 208, 421n205
"Little Lord Fauntleroy," 194
Little Jack Sheppard, 88
Little Miss Raffles, 83, 84
Little Nemo, 316
A Little of Everything, 186, 390
Little Red Riding Hood, 68, 192
Little Robinson Crusoe, 26
Little Simplicity, 23
The Little Trooper, 28, 29, 222
The Little Whopper, 218, 307
The Little Yankee Sailor, 245
A Loan for a Lover, 102
"London Lurch," 330
A Lonely Romeo, 42, 43, 44, 210–211
Louisiana Lou, 385, 480n1172
The Louisiana Purchase, 40, 249
The Love Cure, 23, 195, 196
Love Laughs at Locksmiths, 65
The Love Leash, 31
The Love Letter, 374
The Love of Sunya (film), 375
Love's Sacrifice, 93
Luders, Gustav, 26, 233
Luna, 68
"The Lucknow Quadrilles," 113
Lurline, 68, 114, 424n245
Lyceum Theatre (Baltimore), 365
Lyceum Theatre (Elizabeth, New Jersey), 362
Lyceum Theatre (London), 257, 340, 370, 478n1131
Lyceum Theatre (New London, Connecticut), 282
Lyceum Theatre (New York), 25, 349, 350

M

Madame Sherry, 198, 346, 347
Macbeth, 77, 114
MacDonough, Glen, 313, 315, 353, 354, 355, 382
The Madcap Duchess, 42
Madeleine (Edwards), 164
Madeleine (Engländer), 184

Madeleine (Herbert), 319, 463n881
Madge Smith, Attorney, 362, 363, 388, 474n1085
Madison Square Theatre, 58, 281, 348, 415n130
The Magic Bell, 131
The Maid and the Mummy, 41
"The Maiden with the Dreamy Eyes," 388, 389
The Major and the Judge, 40
Make It Snappy, 279
"Malena," 176–177
Mamba's Daughters, 391
Mam'selle 'Awkins, 3, 228
Mam'zelle Champagne, 211
Mandel, Frank, 332, 395, 400
The Man from 'Bam, 404
The Man from China, 58, 59, 60
The Man from Wicklow, 212
Manhattan Opera House, 3, 22, 30, 94, 212, 222, 229, 266, 288, 291, 420n194
Manhattan Street Scene (ballet), 394
The Man in the Moon, 135, 138, 139, 184, 185
The Man-o'-War's Man, 292
Marbury, Elisabeth, 179, 180
"March and Two-Step" (Howson), 349, 350–351
"The March of the Amazons," 101
"March of the Pasha's Guard," 91, 93
Marenco, Romualdo, 55, 332
Marguerite (ballet), 289
Marie Antoinette, 248
The Marriage Market, 371, 475n1116, n1117
Marrying Mary, 298, 390, 460n822
Mary, 332
"Matapa March," 131, 133
Mathias Sandorf, 333
A Matinée Idol, 299, 300, 460n824
McSorley's Inflation, 48, 49
Mecca, 203–205
Medea (burlesque), 29, 244, 450n652
The Medal and the Maid, 398
Me, Him and I, 334–335

The Melting of Molly, 22
The Merchant of Venice, 119, 244
The Merry Countess, 178, 179
The Merry Doll, 173
The Merry-Go-Round, 58
Merry Mary, 9, 454n722
The Merry Widow, 23, 153, 173, 271, 434n394
The Merry Widow and the Devil, 213
The Merry Widow (burlesque), 213
The Merry Wives of Windsor, 52, 225, 303, 304
The Messenger Boy, 82, 270
Messin' Around, 394
"The Metropolitan Glide," 392
Metropolitan Opera Company, 37, 66, 93, 135, 286, 288, 290, 311, 356
Metropolitan Opera House, 22, 30, 167, 231, 266, 302, 319, 356
Mexicana, 353
A Midnight Bell, 231, 319, 448n610
The Midnight Rounders, 169
The Midnight Rounders of 1921, 268
The Midnight Sons, 177, 213, 238, 353
The Mikado, 5, 54, 178, 206
Miladi and the Musketeer, 123, 124, 294, 295
The Military Maid (Aarons), 3
The Military Maid (Blake), 37
A Milk White Flag, 231, 232
"The Milk-White Flag March," 231, 232
Miller and Lyles, 35, 188, 391, 393, 394, 400, 404, 425n261
Les Millions d'Arlequin, 158
The Million, 13
The Mimic World of 1921, 268
"The Minstrel's Return'd from the War," 324
Miraculous Mill, or, The Old Ground Young, 38, 144, 411n74
Miss Information, 157, 158, 180, 202
Miss Innocence, 13, 134, 185, 238, 330, 390, 407n16
Miss Millions, 355
Miss 1917, 42, 317, 389, 400
Miss Pocahontas, 23, 99–100

Miss Princess, 30, 395
Miss Simplicity, 123, 124, 192, 294, 295, 427n283
Mister Roberts, 51
M'liss, Child of the Sierras, 34
Modern Dances: Society's Latest Dance Folio, 210
A Modern Eve, 241, 386
Modest Suzanne, 241, 242, 271
Mollenhauer, Edward, 258
"Money Ballet," 103
Monte Carlo, 248, 249
Moonshine, 298, 460n822
Mordecai Lyons, 48
Morosco, Oliver, 266, 379
Morosco Theatre, 31
Mosquitoes, 328
Mother Goose, 124, 186, 192, 262, 390
Moochin' Along, 393
The Mountebanks, 89, 419n181
"Moving Day in Jungle Town," 13
Mr. Load of Coal, 187, 327
Mrs. Black Is Back, 117–118, 58, 387
Mrs. Radley Barton's Ball, or In Great New York, 289
Mrs. Temple's Telegram, 350
The Muddy Day, 48, 49
The Mulligan Guard, 48
The Mulligan Guard Ball, 48, 49
The Mulligan Guard's Chowder, 48
The Mulligan Guards' Nominee, 48, 49
The Mulligan Guards' Surprise, 48
The Mulligans' Silver Wedding, 48
Murray Hill Theatre, 50, 478n1141
"Musical Clock," 498, 499
Musical Fund Society, 78, 80
Musical Mutual Protective Association, 29, 329
Music in the Air, 22
Musicland, 214
My Best Girl, 23, 124
My Cinderella Girl, 41
My Fair Lady, 220
My Friend from Kentucky, 327
My Lady Dragon Fly (ballet), 202
My Lady Molly, 398

The Mystic Isle, 275, 276, 277, 456n756
My Sweetheart, 30, 31, 32
My Tom-boy Girl, 126

N

Nadjy, 28, 96, 421n201
Nancy Brown, 282, 298, 389
National Theatre (Rochester, New York), 109, 168
National Theatre (New York), 342, 430n340
National Theatre (Washington, D.C.), 28, 192, 214, 224, 363, 466n948
Natoma, 319
"Nat-u-ritch, an Indian Idyll," 33, 34
Neptune's Daughter, 42
New Amsterdam Theatre, 6, 121, 127, 128, 180, 198, 209, 235, 250, 262, 279, 298, 307, 363, 456–457n768
The Newlyweds and Their Baby, 13, 58, 59
New Theatre (Broadway), 242, 450n661
New Theatre (Philadelphia), 144, 245, *see also* Chestnut Street Theatre
The New Yorkers, 117, 184, 269
London Hippodrome, 202, 330
New York Hippodrome, 129, 172, 173, 267, 355
Niblo's Garden, 15, 19, 37, 46, 54, 55, 70, 73, 89, 100, 101, 114, 120, 155, 192, 222, 257, 274, 332, 344, 369, 408n28, 409n47, 424n244, 467n962
The Night Boat, 22, 307, 389, 415n142
The Night of the Fourth, 334
"The Night Revels of the Automata," 101
Nobody Home, 127, 188
No, No, Nanette, 41

O

Octoroons, 7
O'Dea, James J., 76, 316
Oedipus Rex, 91
Offenbach, Jacques, 68, 70, 172, 184, 199, 206, 227, 348, 383, 470n1020, 471n1021

The Office Boy, 58, 184, 363
Off the Earth, 81, 192
Oh, Ernest!, 42
Oh! Oh! Delphine, 82
"Oh! That Yankiana Rag," 238
"Oh, You Beautiful Doll," 14
The Old Homestead, 52
Old Lavender, 48
Ollemus, 17
Olympic Theatre, 17, 48, 70, 260, 327, 341, 348, 393
O Mitake San (ballet), 215
Once too Often, 257, 258
"The One Girl," 77
The Only Girl, 42
"On the Gay Luneta," 186
On the Track!, 86, 140
The Optimists, 240
The Orchid, 176, 213
The Organizer, 394
Oriental America, 388
"The Original Bogie Man," 27
Orlob, Harold, 239, 395, 399
Orphée aux Enfers, 70, 227, 383
Oscar the Half-Blood, 244
The Outpost, 109
Over the Garden Wall, 30, 89
Over the River, 120
"Overture to *The Archers*," 79–80
Oxygen, 54, 114

P

"Pack up Your Troubles in Your Old Kit Bag," 124
Paderewski, Ignace Jan, 128, 281
The Padrone, 93
Palace Theatre (Cincinnati), 181
Palace Theatre (London), 202, 240, 452n694
Palace Theatre (Manchester), 103
Palace Theatre (New York), 39–40, 180, 214, 300
Palomita, or, The Veiled Songstress, 259
"Pantomime and Dance" (*Queen of the Ballet*), 121, 122
"Pantomimic Scene" (*The Runaway*), 372

Paola, or, The First of the Vendettas, 163, 377
Papa Gou Gou, 222, 223
Papa's Darling, 82, 83
The Paradise of Mahomet, 230, 460n826
A Parisian Model, 335–336, 363, 474n1091
"The Parisian Trot," 301, 302, 305–306
"The Parisian Two Step," 84, 85
Paris, or, The Judgment, 259
Park Theatre (Boston), 54, 55, 86, 345
Park Theatre (Brooklyn), 348
Park Theatre (New York), 101, 102, 206, 242, 244, 245, 285, 303, 321, 322, 339, 340, 341, 343, 367, 431n359
Parsifalia, 290, 291
"Pas de Demons," 37–39
The Passing Show, 184, 185, 438n443
The Passing Show of 1915, 124, 168, 328
The Passing Show of 1917, 124
The Passing Show of 1920, 268
The Passing Show of 1922, 268
Pastor, Tony, 53, 158, 159, 160, 161, 328, 412n100
Patience, 54, 71, 178
Patria, 42
The Patriot, 77
Patsy in Politics, 292, 459n805
Paulton, Edward, 362, 377, 461n844
Paulton, Harry, 362, 376, 377
The Pearl and the Pumpkin, 58, 61
The Peasant Girl, 124, 178, 218
Peck's Bad Boy, 292
The Peer and the Pauper, 90
Pekin Theatre (Chicago), 118, 404, 405, 485n1261
Penny-Ante, 189, 190,
Le Petit Corsair, 53
The Phantom of the Opera (film), 66
Piccadilly to Broadway, 129
The Pie-Rats of Penn-Yann, 161
"Pierrette Dances," 301, 302, 304
The Pink Hussars, 6, 41
The Pink Lady, 82, 84, 363, 434n394

Pippins, 53, 55
The Pirates of Penzance, 28, 88, 161, 276
Pixley, Annie, 34
Plantation Days, 393
Pluto, 47
Policy Kings, 394
Policy Players, 117
Poet and Peasant, 37, 470n1020
Pollock, Channing, 235, 237, 331
Pollock, Emma, 50
Pollock, Lew, 268
Pom-Pom, 30, 199, 200, 415n142
"Poor Butterfly," 355, 472n1051
Poor Jack, 78
Poppy, 400
Porgy and Bess, 391
Porter, Cole, 180, 215, 428n309
Porte-Saint-Martin Theatre, 141,
"The 'Possum Chase," 362–363
Prince Ananias, 312
Princess Ida, 54
"Priscilla," 207, 208
Punch, Judy and Company, 290

Q

Queen of Balleyhoo Bey, 383
The Queen of Hearts, 9
Queen of the Ballet, 121, 122, 123, 294
The Queen of the Brilliants, 377
Queen of the Roses, 210, 443n533
A Quiet Lodging, 91

R

A Rag Baby, 52, 412n94
Ragged Robin, 299
"The Rag-Time Barn Dance," 299
"Rag-time Drummer," 327
"Ragtime Land," 238
The Rainbow Girl, 331
The Rainmaker of Syria, 11, 12
Raisin' Cain, 393
Rang Tang, 127
Razaf, Andy, 394
The Red Canary, 395
The Red Fez, 333
The Red Mill, 316

The Red Moon, 186–187, 390, 439n460, 485n1261
The Red Rose, 13, 42, 271
The Red Widow, 235, 236, 237
The Regatta Girl, 55, 192
Reilly and the Four Hundred, 48, 49, 50
"Return from the Hunt," 103
The Revue of Revues, 94, 178, 230, 239, 330, 436n418
Rice, Edward E., 51, 52, 53, 54, 55, 91, 108, 117, 189, 190, 191, 368, 412n91, 413n105, 424n254
Rice's Summer Nights, 55, 117, 413n105, 424n254
Rip Van Winkle (Baker), 17
Rip Van Winkle (Brinkworth), 68
Rip Van Winkle (Bristow), 70
Rip Van Winkle (concert overture), 90
Rip Van Winkle (De Koven), 135, 136
Rip Van Winkle (John Hill Hewitt), 324
Rip Van Winkle (Planquette), 418–419n179
Rip Van Winkle (play), 381
Ein Ritterspiel [*A Tournament*], 265
The Road to Yesterday, 175, 177
Roberta, 22
Robespierre, 370
Robin Hood, 114, 135
Robinson Crusoe, 359–361
"Rock Me in the Cradle of Love," 327
Rogers, Alex, 118, 327, 387, 390, 399, 439n459
Rogers Brothers in Ireland, 334, 335
The Rogers Brothers in London, 174, 334
The Rogers Brothers in Panama, 336
The Rogers Brothers in Paris, 334
The Rollicking Girl, 58, 195, 209
Roly Poly, 121
"Romeo, Juliet, Johnny and Jane," 320
"The Rooster Dance," 351, 352
The Rose Girl, 266, 267
The Rose of Tyrol, 171
The Rose Maid, 42
Rosenfeld, Sydney, 86, 276, 347, 456n756

The Rose of Panama, 31, 202
Ross, Adrian, 80, 81, 371, 398, 399, 417n154, n156
The Rounders, 184, 185
'Round New York in Eighty Minutes, 55
Round of Pleasure, 184, 185
"Rowing on the Lake," 56, 57
The Royal Chef, 383, 384, 385
A Royal Joke, 37
The Royal Vagabond, 266
Rubens, Paul, 398, 399
Ruddigore, 55
The Runaway, 372
A Runaway Colt, 52
A Runaway Girl, 82, 84
The Runaways, 351, 352, 353
Rufus Rastus, 404
Runnin' Wild, 392
Russell, Lillian, 10, 51, 52, 89, 184, 192, 377, 478n1131
Ruy Blas, 257

S

Safie, the Persian, 283
Sally, 318, 319, 320
Salsbury's Troubadours, 30
Les Saltimbanques, 229, 230
"Saltarello," 71
"Sambo's Syncopated Russian Dance," 394
Sancho Pedro, 189
"The San Francisco Fair" (dance music), 127, 188
Santa Maria, 289, 290
"The Santley Tango," 300, 301–302
San Toy, 398
Sari, 30
Scaramouche, 31
Scenes from the Opera of Uncle Tom's Cabin, 116
"School Boy and Girl Dance," 174, 175, 176
School for Greybeards, 78
The School Girl, 58, 209, 211
The Sea of Ice, 120
See America First, 180

Sefronia's Dream (ballet), 394
Senegambian Carnival, 117
"Serenade" (Drigo), 157, 158
The Serenade (Herbert), 313
Sergeant Brue, 58, 76, 363, 474n1088
The Seven Ages, 55
"The Seven Ages" (ballet), 333
The Seven Dwarfs, 140
The Seven Sons!, 16
The Seventh Chord, 66
Shadows on the Wall, 107, 326
Shameen Dhu, 212
Shanewis, 66, 358
She, 222
"Shoeblack Dance" (ballet), 398
The Shoo-Fly Regiment, 186, 390, 405, 481n1189
The Shop Girl, 82
Show Boat, 22, 203, 425n258
The Show Girl, or, The Cap of Fortune, 123, 208, 294, 295, 459n816
Shuffle Along, 35, 36, 127, 411n64
Sieba and the Seven Ravens, 71
The Silver King, 72, 114
The Silver Star, 41, 210, 250–256, 345, 353
The Silver Swan, 23, 375, 376, 476n1124
Simple Simon Simple, 31
Sinbad, 26, 27, 268, 409n40, 454n730
Sindbad the Sailor, 113
The Singing Girl (Friml), 445n560
The Singing Girl (Herbert), 313
Sir Roger de Coverly (ballet), 81
Sissle, Noble, 35, 393, 486n1264
Sister Mary, 174, 362, 388, 435n412, 473n1083
"The Six Musical Cuttys," 125
"Skirt Dance," 248, 249
A Skylark, 31
The Sleeping Beauty and the Beast, 261, 289
Smith, Chris, 398
Smith, Edgar, 96, 218, 385
Smith, Harry B., 4, 25–26, 27, 83, 230, 301, 312, 313, 345, 346, 353, 366, 367, 371, 372

Smith, John P., 45
Smith, Joseph C., 307
Smith, Robert B., 230, 353
Smith, "Willie-the Lion," 35
Snapshots of 1921, 211, 264
"Solemn March of the Rajahs," 142–143
Solomon, Edward, 52, 163, 185, 418n179
Solomon, Frederic(k), 261, 262
Some Time, 218
"The Song of a Soul," 65
Sons of Ham, 7, 117, 388, 485n1258
The Sorcerer, 88
The Soul Kiss, 103, 330
Sousa, John Philip, 3, 11, 40, 93, 123, 126, 129, 207, 307, 365, 382
The Southerners, 117, 425n258
Souvenir d'Australia, 248
"Spanish Dance," 108–109
Spanish Love, 375, 476n1123
The Spanish Patriots, 243, 244
The Spectre Knight, 88, 89
"Spilling the Beans" (fox trot), 129
The Spring Chicken, 41, 82
The Spring Maid, 30, 42
Squatter Sovereignty, 48
The Squaw Man, 31, 33, 34
Standard Theatre (New York), 3, 31, 54, 55, 446n573
Standard Theatre (St. Louis), 361
Stange, Stanislaus, 163, 165, 313
Star and Garter, 40, 58
Star Theatre, 52, 55, 71, 75, 125, 191, 192, 222, 344, 363, 378, 448n610
"Steady Company," 57
Stepping Stones, 22, 415n142
Stevens, David, 93, 283
St. Louis 'ooman, 119
Stop! Look! Listen!, 42
"The Stop-Trot Rag," 212
The Story of Vernon and Irene Castle, 22
The Strange Adventures of Jack in the Beanstalk, 294
"Strange, Odd, Queer," 282, 283
The Street Singer, 109, 423n238
"Stride piano," 394

The String of Pearls, or, the Barber Assassin and the Pie Woman of Bell Yard, 140
The Striped Petticoat, 37
The Strollers, 184, 185
"A Suburban Scramble," 32, 34
Sugar Hill: An Epoch of Negro Life in Harlem, 394, 483n1214
Sullivan's Christmas, 48
The Sultan of Mocha, 88
"The Sunny Riviera Bay," 210
Sunshine, 396
The Sunshine of Paradise Alley, 329
Superba, 197
Sweet Annie Moore, 292, 459n804, n805
"Sweet Louisa," 87
Sweet Marie, 290
Sybil, 371, 475n1117
The Sympathetic Twin, 397

T

Tabasco, 91–93
"Taiko Hon Rei (Thunder Drummer)," 224
Talbot, Howard, 22, 202, 248
Tammany, 321
Tam o' Shanter, 257, 258
"The Tango Dance," 178
Tantalizing Tommy, 198, 199, 441n497
The Tar and the Tartar, 75, 163, 366, 367
"Tarantella," 251, 255
Tarantella, 377
The Tars from Tripoli, 321
Tchaikovsky, Pyotr Ilyich, 62, 122, 157, 230, 250, 433n384
"The Teddy Bears Picnic," 59
"Temperamental Dances," 395
The Tempest, 341
The Temple Dancer, 66, 356–358, 359, 472n1067
Temptations (ballet-pantomime), 146–154, 431n357
The Tenderfoot, 192, 295–296, 297, 298
Thalia Theater, 172, 184, 241
Thaw, Henry K., 211

Theatre Comique (New York), 47, 49, 140, 244
Theatre Comique (Providence), 328
Thebe, or, Marry a Marionette, 385
"They Didn't Believe Me," 398
Those Bells, 86
"Three Bears," 98–99
Three Cheers, 355–356
Three Little Lambs, 93, 123, 294
"Three Little Lambs," 121, 122
The Three Mus-Ke-Teers (burlesque), 68
The Three Musketeers (Friml), 219
The Three Sisters!, 29
Three Twins, 120, 124, 345
The Ticket of Leave Man, 120
"The Tickle Toe" 331
Tierney, Harry, 129, 169, 266
The Tik-Tok Man of Oz, 271
Tivoli Opera House (San Francisco), 28, 222
"Tomorrow's America," 169
Tom-Tom, the Piper's Son Stole a Pig and Way he Run, 140
Too Many Wives, 40
Too Soon, 349
The Top o' th' World, 76
(T.P.S.) Canal Boat Pinafore, 160
"Transformation Music" (*Fortunio*), 133
Treemonisha, 401–402, 403
Tremont Theatre (Boston), 86, 108, 110, 112, 270, 294, 297, 298, 418n173, 419n186
A Trip to Chinatown, 231
A Trip to Coontown, 7
A Trip to Niagara, 243
"Turkey-Trot," 188
Tutt, J. Homer, 393, 405
Twirly-Whirly, 207, 208
The Two Cadis, 171

U

Uhrig's Cave (St. Louis), 28, 37, 221, 333
Uncle Eph's Christmas, 117
Uncle Tom's Cabin, 113, 349

Under Cover, 50, 412n90
"Under the Bamboo Tree," 389
Under Sealed Orders, 292
Union Square Theatre, 30, 54, 88, 452n693, 471n1021
Up and Down Broadway, 178, 239, 330
Utopia, Limited, 55

V

The Vagabond King, 219, 307
The Vanderbilt Cup, 41, 42, 43
Vaughn, James J., 8, 118, 187, 399
The Velvet Lady, 316–317, 318
Virgin of the Sun, 243, 244
Vodery, Will H., 118, 393, 400, 404
Von Suppé, Franz, 37, 93, 133, 134, 361, 470n1020

W

"Waiting for the Robert E. Lee," 210
Wallack's Theatre, 18, 25, 31, 48, 53, 55, 71, 72, 114, 115, 118, 119, 181, 184, 259, 297, 424n246
Waller, Fats, 393, 394, 395, 400
The (A) Wall Street Girl, 13, 300, 347, 460n826
"Waltz Ballet," 211
The Wanderer, 266
War Brides, 42
War Bubbles, 289–290
Warriors of the Sun, 47
The Water Queen, 369
Wayburn, Ned, 212, 433n391
The Wayfarer, 285
"We Are a Band of Gentlemen," 383, 384
Weber and Fields, 121, 208, 209, 210, 378, 379, 390
Weber and Fields Theatre, 121, 207
The Well of Romance, 376, 476n1125
"We Must Have a Ballet," 202
The Western Minstrel, 309, 310
West, Paul, 13, 58
Westward Ho!, 55
We, Us and Company at Mud Springs, 189, 190

What a Widow (film), 201
"What Do You Think," 194
What's in a Name?, 23
When Dreams Come True, 300, 301, 302
When Johnny Comes Marching Home, 166, 167
"When Sist' Tetrazin' Met Cousin Carus,'" 238–239, 330
"When Sousa Leads the Band," 40
The Whirl of New York, 169, 268
The White Eagle, 219
The White Fawn, 257, 380
White, Stanford, 211
White Zombie (film), 376
Whitney, Salem Tutt, , 393, 405
The Widow Jones, 10
The Wife Hunters, 210, 214, 443n531
The Wife of Two Husbands, 78, 275
The Wife Tamers, 42
The Wild Rose, 117, 124, 174, 184, 219, 382
Williams and Walker, 7, 8, 118, 388
Williams, Bert, 118, 187, 327, 399, 439n459
Williams, Harry, 13, 391
Wilson, John P., 211
Winsome Winnie, 377
Winter Garden Theatre, 35, 94, 214, 279
Witmark, Isidore, 345
Witmark, M. and Sons, 31, 41, 168
The Wizard of the Nile, 312
Wolf, Rennold, 235, 237, 331
Wonderland, 315–316
Wood's Museum, 67, 68, 69, 113, 259, 348, 424n245
Woodward, Matt C., 298, 382, 383
Woolf, Benjamin E., 54, 55
Woolf, Edgar Allan, 211, 214
A World of Pleasure, 124, 328

Y

"Yamekraw," 394
"Yankee Doodle Girl," 386
The Yankee Girl, 299
Yeast Lynn!, 158–159
The Yeomen of the Guard, 55
Yes, Yes, Yvette, 386, 399
Youmans, Vincent, 77, 118, 129, 130, 201
Young, Rida Johnson, 175, 212, 218, 307
"You're Getting Better Looking Every Day," 210

Z

Zara!, 34
Der Zauberlehrling, 100, 101
Ziegfeld Follies of 1911, 353, 354
Ziegfeld Follies of 1913, 130, 168
Ziegfeld Follies of 1916, 14, 169, 331
Ziegfeld Follies of 1920, 169
Ziegfeld Follies of 1921, 169, 218, 317
Ziegfeld Follies of 1923, 169, 219, 318
Ziegfeld's Midnight Frolic(s), 128, 180, 279
Die Zwergenhochzeit, 100, 101

www.ingramcontent.com/pod-product-compliance
Lightning Source LLC
Chambersburg PA
CBHW060311230426
43663CB00009B/1664